Our Heavenly Father Has No Equals

Our Heavenly Father Has No Equals

Historical Arguments Against the Doctrine of the Trinity

D. R. Snedeker

SOTERION PRESS

Soterion Press
An imprint of Spirit & Truth Fellowship International
10 S Main Street #1737
Martinsville, IN 46151
stfi.org

Printed in the United States of America

CATALOGING-IN-PUBLICATION DATA
Names: Snedeker, D. R., 1961—author.
Title: Our Heavenly Father Has No Equals: Historical Arguments Against the Doctrine of the Trinity / D. R. Snedeker
Description: Martinsville: Soterion Press, an imprint Spirit & Truth Fellowship International [2026] | Includes index.
Identifiers: LCCN 2026904518 | ISBN 978-1-970908-04-6 (paperback) | ISBN 978-1-970908-05-3 (hardback) | ISBN 978-1-970908-08-4 (ebook)
Subjects: LCSH: Bible.—Theology. | Church History.—Primitive and early church, ca. 30-600. | Theology, Doctrinal.—History.—Early church, ca. 30-600. | Unitarianism.—History.—Biblical teaching.
Classification: DDC 231.044/2—dc23/eng/20260224
LC record available at: https://lccn.loc.gov/2026904518

The views expressed are those of the author and the author alone and do not necessarily reflect the official policy or position of the publisher. Any references to real persons are used with permission or are drawn from publicly available sources. But where necessary, certain names or identifying details have been altered or changed to protect privacy and anonymity.

Cover design by Ihar Matsiunou
Interior design by Nurdiansyah and Ihar Matsinuou

For information, permissions, and all other inquiries, please contact: drs.author@gmail.com

Table of Contents

FOREWORD

Our Heavenly Father Has No Equals is a significant milestone in the ongoing dialogue between Unitarian and Trinitarian systems of thought. Within these pages, Don Snedeker provides an immense body of research predicated on the internal consistency of the biblical canon, common sense, and the historical record of the early Christian church. The work does not merely aim to champion a theological cause but seeks to organize a vast collection of scholarship and Christian literature into a cohesive, accessible reference for the modern seeker. In doing so, it offers a profound theological and historical contribution to one of the most enduring debates in Christian history.

The theological value of this work lies in its defense of what Snedeker terms, "true monotheism." He posits that the foundational teaching of the Torah, and subsequently Christianity, is that God is a single, independent, and undivided being. The core of the Unitarian system presented here is the unrivaled majesty of God, the heavenly Father — a theme that Snedeker argues is consistently maintained by the writers of both the Hebrew and Greek texts.

One of the major theological contributions of the book is its systematic critique of the Trinitarian system as one based on self-contradictory and incomprehensible dogmas. Snedeker argues that Trinitarianism removes theology from the realm of reasonableness, demanding that believers accept the nature of God as a "mystery" that cannot be logically understood by the human mind. In light of that, Snedeker challenges the idea that the Christian faith can be divorced from sound thinking and logic, suggesting instead that "reasonableness is requisite to understanding." By contrasting the bewilderment engendered by the complexity and theoretical philosophy of the Trinitarian system with the "inexhaustible simplicity" of the Father's supremacy, Snedeker's work empowers the individual to use their own mind to form a rational opinion about what the Bible says.

Furthermore, the book offers a rigorous examination of Christology, specifically the doctrine of the double nature of Christ. Snedeker tackles the theory of Jesus being simultaneously fully God and fully man and unmasks it as mere *ad hoc* argumentation designed to reconcile the biblical portrayal of Jesus as a genuine human being with post-biblical claims of his deity. The theological value here is found in reclaiming the human Jesus — the mediator who relied entirely on the Father for his power, wisdom, and very existence.

The historical value of this work is found in its meticulous tracing of the historical and traditional development of Trinitarianism. Snedeker lays out a strong case that the doctrine of the Trinity is not a biblical revelation but a post-biblical invention that took several centuries to arrive in its current (and still) amorphous state. By providing a detailed account of how Christianity, born into a polytheistic world, gradually became spoiled through the intermixture of Greek philosophy, particularly Platonism, Snedeker traces the pagan influences and cultural contamination that led to the corruption of the biblical view of true monotheism.

By examining the early church Fathers, such as Justin Martyr, Origen, and Tertullian, Snedeker aptly demonstrates that the first three centuries of the church were characterized by a Unitarian faith that recognized the Father alone as the supreme God. The shift toward Trinitarianism is shown to be a product of the councils of the fourth century, specifically Nicea (325 A.D.) and Constantinople (381 A.D.).

Moreover, the political climate of the fourth century with its imperial pressures exerted by Emperor Constantine, who sought a unified creed to maintain the tranquility of his empire rather than to establish theological truth, Snedeker illuminates the historical narrative of coercion and duress that accompanied the establishment of these creeds, including the exile of dissenters like Arius and his followers. This historical context is vital for modern readers to understand that was it deemed Christian "orthodoxy" was not reached through unanimous consent but was often forced on the faith of the church by state-sponsored authority.

Perhaps the most significant contribution of Snedeker's work to the Unitarian-Trinitarian debate is its focus on the methodology of interpretation. Snedeker challenges the inferential nature of Trinitarian argumentation and "proofs," noting that the doctrine of the Trinity must be ransacked and reassembled from scattered verses because it lacks a single, plain declaration in Scripture. Certain primary "proof-texts" of Trinitarianism — such as Matthew 28:19, 2 Corinthians 13:14, and the prologue of John — are systematically addressed and alternative interpretations provided based on biblical context, linguistics, Hebraisms, the principle of agency, and other established data of exegesis.

Even with the robust critique of the doctrine of the Trinity and the robust historical and biblical analysis for true monotheism, Snedeker humbly appeals to the explicit fact that the Bible never makes belief in a triune nature of God a requirement for salvation. Instead, the requirement is consistently stated as faith/trust in Jesus as the Christ, the Son of God. This provides a theological reprieve for those who find Trinitarian dogma incomprehensible but fear that rejecting it may jeopardize their entrance into God's kingdom and everlasting life.

Finally, the revised edition of this book contributes to the question of whether the Heavenly Father alone is the one Supreme Being by modeling a more genial approach. Snedeker acknowledges that in his earlier years he was more contentious and ardent, but he now values kindness and a willingness to allow for genuine exploration for understanding God. While Snedeker remains resolute in his position toward the book's primary conclusion about the Heavenly Father having no equals, he recognizes that it is just as important to see unity as staying in it with one another, not in achieving uniformity of all opinions.

By presenting the works of past scholars with clarity and eloquence, Snedeker has created an accessible reference work that does not demand agreement but invites the reader on a quest. He encourages the reader to use their God-given mind to inquire into matters like these and to find as much information as possible in order to form an opinion without the fear of divine judgment if they get a detail wrong in their theological understanding.

Without doubt, *Our Heavenly Father Has No Equals* is a vital resource for anyone seeking to understand the biblical and historical roots of the Unitarian-Trinitarian controversy. Its theological depth, historical rigor, and commitment to the use of reason provide a powerful challenge to tradition Christian dogma. It serves as a bulwark against intellectual servitude and a guide toward a clearer, consistent, and more biblical understanding of our Creator and His Son.

Jeremiah J. E. Wierwille
May 2026

PREFACE

Due to numerous requests since this book went out of print a few years after its publication, and due to the advent of digital publication in the intervening twenty years, I decided to republish it, and with a few adjustments—some necessary, some stylistic. Some were due to a change in my theological disposition, in which I am no longer as contentious as I had been in my earlier years, which dismays some folks who would like to see me champion one theological cause or another. I write what makes sense to me, not because I belong to any particular group, and I am now more amenable to various theological (and non-theological) opinions—if they make more sense than what I currently believe I have no problem jettisoning my beliefs in favor of other, better ideas, no matter whose they are. This tends to be the process of aging, but is also more in line with my natural disposition, prior authorial evidence notwithstanding. But the work in this book may be of benefit to those who wish to pursue the subject, and hopefully whatever the reader concludes from this work, either pro or con, those views will be held with kindness toward all people, with the idea that any belief one holds may be in need of minor or major adjustments. Such is the nature of being human.

I take no issue with those who hold their beliefs with kindness, even if their opinions are diametrically opposed to mine. As I've aged I've learned to be as skeptical of my own beliefs as I am of others'—an opinion is an opinion, regardless of who holds it, and though my views may be dear to me, they are of value only if they lead me to kindness, thoughtfulness, and generosity toward others. Religious, political, social, and other realms of thought may all be held with decorum in the recognition that we're all in this game of humanity together. *I may be wrong* is a helpful, even rational, stance to hold, and helps us get along with one another—it keeps us from becoming overly fond of our own ideas and causes us to seek the ideas of others. Unity is staying in it with one another, not in uniformity of opinions.

When I first wrote this book I was more contentious, and that approach created some problems more than I would have preferred. I know many people who do not share my theological opinions who are far more considerate of me than some who hold a similar theology. I value kindness and a willingness to explore more highly than agreement, which I felt must be said before republishing this work. People can stand in their opinions without becoming prideful or defensive—consideration of one another is more valuable than theological agreement. Take time to listen, take time to think, take time to explore one's own premises and expose oneself to various lines of argumentation, and one's own opinions may change over time. They typically do.

As a body of research predicated on the Bible being the word of God, or, as some prefer, words directly from Him, the canonized texts of the Bible, common sense and human experience make the case that God is one person—one independent, un-split being—is completely rational to me. An argument is only as good as the premises it is based upon, and if the writings of the Hebrew Bible (the Old Testament) and the Greek Bible (the New Testament) are considered to have been dictated by God, then the work contained herein seems reasonable to me. I have had Trinitarians become very upset with me for not believing in the supreme divinity of Jesus and the triune nature of God, just as I have had Unitarians remove themselves from my life for questioning the validity of the notion that the writings of our contemporary Bibles were dictated by God. Such is the nature of people who prefer agreement, even if forced, over self-driven thoughtfulness and stamina. Sometimes I reached conclusions that were inconvenient for me, since they occasionally were diametrically opposed to what I believed at the time. Those were uncomfortable moments, but that's what it is to be human—use our minds, find as much information as we can, then form an opinion if one can reasonably be formed, and don't fear that a malicious God is waiting to pounce if we get something wrong.

I deliberated whether I would leave the book as it was originally published in 1998, and perhaps simply add this new introduction. The other option was to rewrite many parts to reflect my newly acquired realizations and doubts about certain aspects of my formerly held beliefs, as well as a more convivial approach. My decision was to modify some of the stronger statements I made in the original work, but leave the sense of the arguments intact. Most of the works from which I quoted extensively have been in the public domain for a long time, and in some cases I allowed the authors to speak for themselves at length when it seemed good to their positions. They said things in ways that caused me to marvel and occasionally demanded more of a reader than the shorter sentences that are *de rigueur* in today's writing styles.

No matter your theological opinions, I hope you accept others with compassion. It isn't easy being human, and part of the unfortunate package we are handed is that, regardless of our beliefs regarding what happens when we die, we still have to die to find out if we were right. That puts us all in the same boat, and worthy of kindness and patience.

D. R. Snedeker
May 2026

INTRODUCTION

In my years of Bible study, as in life generally, I've seen good arguments that seem to have equally good counter-arguments. When trying to determine which of two or more arguments makes the most sense, if any, it is common to employ what we call reason to determine if premises and connections are made properly, or well enough to be confident that there might be something to the argument. Occasionally more than one position has merit, even when those positions are diametrically opposed, so I settle on the stance that, because both arguments make sense, I should refrain from drawing a hard and fast conclusion. More information is needed, which is a normal thing on life's journey. In such cases I do not pass judgment on either position or on those who embrace either one. If it yields fruit in their lives and seems to assist them in being kinder, more thoughtful people, then I say that, whatever the differences, the differences are due to human limitations and that we will therefore not all arrive at the same conclusions.

And since, as is commonly professed, Christianity is founded upon Judaism, which itself is predicated upon a fundamental teaching in the Torah, that there is one God and that there is not a strange conception of the word *one*, but that God is truly one being, Christians thus have a confession of true monotheism as a foundation. With this foundation, and with the advent of Christianity and the well-read and circulated writings of the New Testament, the conception of God being one to God being three-in-one eventually took off, resulting in debates and sometimes worse, including death and the threat of death and imprisonment, in various places and at various times since councils of the fourth century gave expression to Trinitarian ideologies. This book is a collection of many writings and arguments in favor of and in opposition to the notion that there are three persons in God, and that there is a dual nature in Jesus, which are two separate claims, each with arguments meant to support them. The Unitarian position is similar to the original Hebrew conception, which is that there is truly only one God, the Father, and that all other being are subordinate to Him.

In Christian theology, the primary system of arguments against the Father's supremacy is Trinitarianism, which, as I hope to show, is a system of self-contradictory and incomprehensible dogmas that got its start in a polytheistic world and slowly formed and adopted by early church councils, then gradually taking shape over hundreds of years. Its advocates expend considerable energy in constructing arguments to make it acceptable to remove it from the realm of what constitutes sound thinking and sound theology—reasonableness.

Few efforts have been made to make the doctrine of the Trinity comprehensible. Since few have ever claimed to understand this doctrine, its advocates implore us to accept it as a mystery. So the doctrine does not rest in reasonableness, but in mysteriousness, which is a good reason to question it as a foundational belief. Eminent Trinitarians have admitted it is not a doctrine that can be found in the Bible, and arguments to elucidate its meaning of the doctrine still have a long way to go to clarify its meaning. If it had a semblance of soundness it might stand on equal footing with other doctrines that warrant serious consideration. If greater understanding resulted from Trinitarian dogma, it would be worth investing our time into exploring it. But little or nothing in this system yields understanding—the Trinitarian system simply engenders bewilderment because it was developed outside the realm of reasonableness, and reasonableness is requisite to understanding.

In contrast stands the Unitarian system, which is comprehensible and requires little elaboration, and is based upon reasonable standards of biblical interpretation. The core of the Unitarian system is the unrivaled majesty of our heavenly Father, which is a constant theme of the writers of the Hebrew and Greek texts.

The doctrine of the Trinity has many parts, which will be explored in the ensuing pages, but in its basic form is a system that attempts to make one God have three persons within his being (the triune nature), attempts to make Jesus be both fully God and fully man (his so-called double nature), and demands we stop inquiring into how this could be since no mind can rest upon such abstruse and contradictory propositions as those entailed in Trinitarian thought.

Arguments are constructed that segue Christians into a state where faith is no longer expected to make sense. We were initially introduced to beliefs that made sense, then, once friends were made and lives were somewhat rearranged around being with others of a similar faith, we were essentially told we must not question Trinitarian doctrines regardless of how patently absurd they appeared to be or how many problems receiving them might cause us. We are told what conclusions we must reach, but are not given adequate reasons for accepting them. We are simply told that the doctrine is true, and must accept it "on faith." For those who accept this, a mechanism is in place that trivializes the benefits of reason, thus removing the primary means of distinguishing between what is sound and what is not—logic, otherwise known as reason and/or common sense. Many have accepted the dogmas of those ostensibly more knowledgeable than themselves, and though we each take our own path through this life and make choices about our own faith, the problem, as I see it historically and have experienced it personally, are the verbal, personal, and sometimes egregious attacks on those who aren't satsified with doctrines that make no sense.

Regarding the doctrine of the Trinity, *It's a mystery!* is the common defense. If it is, then it follows that it is something not understood, and if not understood then it hardly seems right to make one's perceived status as a Christian (or heretic) dependent upon believing it. If Christians were diligent in the first place to follow a course that expected the basic tenets of the faith to be understood, there would be a corresponding confidence in the doctrines espoused, and all this talk of mystery would fade away.

Along my journey in this life, I have found that too few are willing to scrutinize ideas based upon independent inquiry and thought. Many follow a group-think mentality, fearing to challenge doctrines they admit they cannot make sense of. Maybe this is part and parcel of the human condition, but it is unnecessary once we are made aware of it. Independent thought is more challenging, but results in an awareness of, and confidence in, what one believes, as well as a comfortable acceptance of our own limitations. The doctrine of the Trinity is a mystery that cannot be understood, due to, as the argument goes, the inadequacy of our minds to comprehend it. How, then, can its truth be so strongly asserted when it is not comprehended? This is one of the simple but perplexing issues confronting Trinitarians when defending this system of beliefs. Unitarians encounter no such difficulties in defending the idea that God is one, and that he is supreme.

I am not the first to reject Trinitarian dogma and certainly will not be the last. A modern historian recently wrote, "Although this doctrine has had a venerable history, it has always been difficult to understand. In our own time an increasing number of Christians have come to consider it so much excess theological baggage and have urged its retirement.[1] For those willing to challenge tradition, many of the popular beliefs will be seen as theological baggage worthy of being discarded and a more complete theological search will continue. In summarizing the Unitarian-Trinitarian debate in Poland in the sixteenth century, Stanislas Kot observed:

> The scope of the activity may be measured by the output of printed texts: the works printed by the Polish Brethren [Unitarians] during their one hundred years' stay in Poland and their thirty years of exile total nearly five hundred in bibliographies, while the polemical works directed against them from Germany, Switzerland, Holland, France, and England would fill the shelves of a considerable library.[2]

Challenging traditional beliefs in any realm is rarely easy. Most people do not like being told their opinions are wrong, regardless of subject matter. Few teachers of wrong doctrine can endure this since it means acknowledging they have done damage to those whom they were supposed to be benefiting. When pressed to explain or make an account of nonsensical doctrines that people have been teaching and defending for many years, unpleasantries commonly arise, as a nineteenth-century Unitarian observed:

> I have given one reason why it is little to my taste to discuss this doctrine of the Trinity. Whoever treats of the subject is liable to be confounded with a class of writers with whom an

---

[1] Linwood Urban, *A Short History of Christian Thought* (New York: Oxford University Press, 1995), 45.

[2] Stanislas Kot, *Socinianism In Poland* (Warsaw: 1932; translated into English in 1957 by Earl Wilbur and published in Boston by Starr King Press).

intelligent Christian would not willingly be thought to have anything in common. By many who look with indifference on the whole discussion, he who contends for the truth will be placed on a level with those who defend error. Others will think that he is agitating questions which might better be left at rest; and those who hold the traditionary belief will regard him as a disturber of the Christian community... The feeling, however, naturally arising from the causes I have mentioned, might prevent one from engaging in this controversy, were it not for the deep sense which a sincere Christian must have of the value of true Christianity, and of the necessity of redeeming it from the imputations to which it has been exposed.

But there are other causes which make this an unpleasant subject. It presents human nature in the most humiliating aspect. The absurdities that have been maintained are so gross, the zeal in maintaining them has been so ferocious, there is such an absence of any redeeming quality in the spectacle presented, that it spreads a temporary gloom over our whole view of the character and destiny of man. We seem ourselves to sink in the scale of being, and it demands an effort to recollect the glorious powers with which God has endued our race. While inquiring concerning the truths of religion, we appear to have descended to some obscure region where folly and prejudice are the sole rulers.... And is this all that mankind have to hope? Must this dreary prospect for ever lie before us? We trust not. Still, in the confutation of such doctrines as have been taught, the triumph, if it may be so called, is humbling. It is a triumph over our common nature reduced to imbecility. We discover not how strong human reason is, but how weak.[3]

This circumstance would change if we used common sense as our guide, then stand for where it leads. The following quote is from a writer who formerly had embraced the doctrine of the Trinity, but at some point realized that she should be willing to look into it. She

---

[3] Andrews Norton, *A Statement of Reasons for Not Believing the Doctrines of Trinitarians* (Boston: American Unitarian Association, 10th ed., 1877), 31-34.

came to the conclusion that it was not worth keeping a belief she could not make sense of and that disagreed with so many clear verses in the Bible. Here is her first announcement of this in a letter to her parents:

January 19th, 1845

MY KIND AND VENERATED PARENTS:

IT has become my solemn duty to make you an announcement, which, I fear, will fill your hearts with sorrow. Would to God, that I could save you from the pain, which, from my knowledge of your views and feelings, I am sure awaits you; but I believe, as God is my Judge, that *truth* is dearer to me than life itself, and I dare no longer disavow the sentiments, which, after thorough, and *honest*, and prayerful deliberation, I have at length adopted.

I will keep you no longer in suspense, but will proceed to declare, that I do not now believe that my blessed Lord and Saviour Jesus Christ is the Supreme God. I believe that there is but one God, the Father, of whom are all things, and one Lord Jesus Christ, by whom are all things. I believe that "all power" was given unto him in Heaven and on earth; that he was the Messiah predicted by the Old Testament writers, who, in the fullness of time, came into the world with a commission from God, and full power and authority to do the work which God had given him to do. In other words, after long and earnest deliberation, much diligent study of the Holy Scriptures, and fervent prayer to God for the assistance of his spirit, I conscientiously and firmly reject the doctrine of the Trinity.

This doctrine was part of my education. I received it, as many others do, without thorough investigation, though, I must confess, it has often perplexed me beyond measure. Still I held it, as it seems to me all must do, as a strange mystery, which I must not attempt to comprehend; not considering, that a mystery does not necessarily suppose an incomprehensibility; and losing sight of the danger of admitting, what now appears to me to be an impossibility. It is impossible for me, and I now perceive that it has always been impossible to make one of three, or three of one,—one perfect and infinite being equal to three perfect and infinite beings. There may be gifted minds capable of comprehending this doctrine, but such is not mine. It is plain to me now, that I have all my life been worshipping three distinct beings; never having been able, with the most strenuous efforts, to combine the three in my own mind so as to form a simple idea. But now I bow to the divine authority, when I hear Jehovah saying, "Hear, O Israel, the Lord the God is one Lord."

But to return. So anxious have I been for clearer views on this point, that I have eagerly read everything upon the Trinitarian side of the question which came my way; yet always without the satisfaction so desirable to an honest and inquisitive mind, and always with the same melancholy feeling, that it was a *strange mystery*; though still I felt bound to receive it.

And now I will relate to you the process through which my mind has passed. For many years, I have not been able to believe, that faith in the Trinity was *necessary* to salvation, because I saw a great many exemplary Christians who did not hold the doctrine, but who nevertheless believed that Jesus was "the Christ," and "the Son of God;" and because the Apostle John has said, that whosoever believeth that Jesus is the Christ is born of God, and that whosoever shall confess that Jesus is the Son of God, God dwelleth in him, and he in God. I have often been startled, by hearing passages of Scripture wrested from what appeared to me to be their legitimate meaning, and forced to an agreement with some favorite hypothesis. Not long ago, in a bible class which I attended, the first part of the gospel by John was examined, and then many doubts found their way into my mind, but not with so much force, or in so tangible a form, as they have recently assumed. But, had I ever been disposed to give the subject a thorough examination, I have never had access to the arguments in favor of Unitarianism, nor have I ever in my life before read upon that side of the question.

Not very long ago, while conversing with a much loved friend, (you will know to whom I allude,) I found that my impressions with regard to Unitarians and to their system were extremely erroneous; and I expressed a wish to know a little more about their faith and practice. Was this desire wrong? Was it not in accordance with that Christian charity, which "hopeth all things," and "thinketh no evil?"

And here let me exonerate from blame the two individuals from whom, entirely at my own request, I have procured the information which I wanted. In both instances, they expressed a hesitation in complying with my request, fearing to be considered obtrusive, if not by myself, at least by my friends. I cannot but believe, that this feeling arose from a confidence in the strength of their position, and a foresight of the consequences which have actually ensued.

Now what was I to do? Shut my eyes resolutely, and *blindly* cherish the faith in which I had been educated, or sift the matter for myself? What kind of faith is that, which fears to stand the test of impartial inquiry? Would not an ingenuous mind lose all confidence in itself, and its received opinions, while there remained a consciousness of this fear and dread of investigation? Was it not my sacred duty to "prove all things," and "hold fast" only to that which I have found to be good?[4]

Dana illustrates a point that cannot be overstated. We all, as individuals, must decide what we believe only after scrutinizing the ideas and arguments that are presented to us. But once a person becomes part of a group or denomination, there is a greater tendency to agree with the group's system of beliefs without continuing the personal investigation that brought one to the faith in the first place.

Regarding Christology and for the sake of this discussion, there are essentially two classes of Christians: Unitarians and Trinitarians. We may compare the two divergent systems of beliefs in order to see which makes sense, keeping in mind that Arianism is a form of Unitarianism:

The various opinions which have been entertained respecting the nature and person of our Lord Jesus Christ, by those who have professed to be his disciples, may now be considered

---

4 Mary Dana, *Letters Addressed To Relatives and Friends* (Boston: James Munroe and Co., 1845), 1-3.

as divided into three distinct classes. The first maintain that Christ has existed from eternity, and is the second person of the Trinity, *co-equal* and *co-eternal* with God; the second, that he is a subordinate spirit, or intelligent being, employed by God in creating and governing the world, and who upon his miraculous conception and birth, animated his body, and supplied the place of a human soul. The third class, maintain that Jesus Christ was in body and mind, truly a human being, who had no existence before his conception, but was distinguished from all other human beings and prophets of the most High God, by being appointed or chosen of the Father, to be the Saviour of men. The first of these doctrines is called the *Trinitarian*, the second the *Arian*, and the third the *Unitarian*.[5]

The second class, the Arian, will not be separately addressed since it is a form of Unitarianism. Arians believe that Jesus pre-existed his birth and is subordinate to the Father. At the onset it must be understood that the debate is not whether or not Jesus is an ordinary man. He is not. It is whether or not a reasonable case has been made by Trinitarians throughout the centuries that he is both man and God, living his life as part of a three-fold deity:

> The question is not whether the Scriptures do or do not assign to Jesus Christ an exalted and mysterious nature and range of being, which lift him above the sphere of mere humanity. The question is not whether from what is revealed of the Saviour we can fashion a full and satisfactory theory, which will make him to us a perfectly intelligible and well-defined being, holding a fixed place on the scale between man and God. But the question is this: Do all the offices and functions and honors assigned to Jesus Christ exhibit him as indistinguishable from God in time and essence and underived existence, and in self-centered, inherent qualities?[6]

---

5 T. F. Thomas, *Familiar Lectures on the Doctrine of the Trinity, and Other Subjects* (Ipswich: R. Root, 1838), 19.

6 George Ellis, *A Half-Century of the Unitarian Controversy* (Boston: Crosby, Nichols, and Co., 1857), 130-131.

This is the central issue—is God, our heavenly Father, indistinguishable from Jesus, or are there real differences? Whether Jesus pre-existed his life on earth is not of primary relevance to this discussion (though it could settle the issue, it is not necessary to settle it). The whole issue rests on the answer to this question: Is Jesus represented in the Bible as the one true God, co-eternal and co-equal with the Father, and with the holy spirit?

In response to this question, Unitarians believe the Father is the one true God, that Jesus could not therefore be Him, and that the Trinitarian system of three-part co-equality is a system of loosely patched assertions. There are differences among Unitarians regarding Jesus and holy spirit, but the prevailing position is that our heavenly Father has no equals:

> Some Unitarians are of opinion, that Christ was, in his entire nature, a man, raised up by the Almighty, and endowed with an inspiration far surpassing that of any other Heaven-taught Prophet; others, that, before his appearance on the earth, he had existed in heaven as a created, superhuman, if not superangelic, being. Some have thought the Holy Ghost, the Holy Spirit, or the Spirit of God, particularly as shown by Jesus and the apostles, had also a personal though derived existence; while others, the majority, have considered the divine spirit, flowing throughout the Sacred Records, to be either God himself, or his gifts, agency, and influence, whether physical, moral, or spiritual—whether natural or supernatural. They all, however, believe in the strict or simple Unity and the unrivaled perfections of Him who is God and Father, and in the derivation of Christ's nature, power, and glory, and of the existence and attributes of all other persons or beings, from the one Creator, the one Parent, the One God.[7]

It should also be acknowledged that we, not God, would be the primary beneficiaries of truth. He will always be God. If we worship other gods by abandoning logic, confusion and uncertainty will arise in our minds. Some verses suggest that we will also offend God, and

---

[7] John Wilson, *Unitarian Principles Confirmed by Trinitarian Testimonies* Boston: American Unitarian Association, 8th ed., 1872), 1-2.

the simple truth is that this is entirely avoidable. All doctrines must be proven on reasonable grounds, and if found to be questionable or, even worse, erroneous, they should be discarded:

> The Unitarian belief is, that there is one God, the Father Almighty, maker of heaven and earth. The Trinitarian believes that there is one God, Father, Son, and Spirit; that the Father is God, that the Son is God, and that the Spirit is God, yet that there are not three Gods, but one God. Which of these is the true doctrine? You see the exact point of difference, and I cannot help here saying that we have this advantage: we can express our whole belief in unaltered Bible language. We believe in one God the Father; and the Apostle Paul speaks with us when he says, "To us there is but one God, the Father, of whom are all things, and one Lord Jesus Christ, by whom are all things, and we by him." (1 Cor. viii. 6.) And again, when he says, "There is one God and Father of all, who is above all and through all and in you all." (Eph. iv. 6.) We say the Father alone is the supreme God; and herein we have the testimony of Christ himself in the words of our text, "that we may know thee, the only true God, and Jesus Christ whom thou hast sent." It is very important, in the defence of what we believe, to say that no similar statement of the Trinitarian belief, concerning God, can be made in unaltered Scripture language. It seems to me almost fatal to that belief, because, being confessedly obscure and difficult, its plain statement is by so much more desirable, and, if it were true, might be confidently expected from those who "declared the whole counsel of God." It is a very strong argument against such a doctrine, that it cannot be expressed or explained without a departure from Scripture language.[8]

Eliot illustrates a focal point of the debate: Trinitarian dogma cannot be expressed in biblical language. When we listen to the words employed by those defending Trinitarian doctrines we have entered a realm in which common words and their meanings are discarded,

---

8 William G. Eliot, *Discourses on the Doctrines of Christianity* (Boston: American Unitarian Association, 1877), 11-12.

and not only this, they are discarded without being replaced with other intelligible words and meanings. Since we cannot understand them, they are of no practical use to us and thus become extraneous thoughts taking up space in our minds—they are theological baggage.

In Matthew 16:13-20, and the corresponding record in Luke 9:18-20, there is an account of Jesus talking with Peter and the other disciples. Jesus inquired of them as to who the people were saying he was. Once it was established that the general populace was ignorant of his identity, Jesus asked Peter, "Whom say ye that I am?" Peter's responded, "Thou art the Christ, the Son of the living God." To which Jesus responded, "Blessed art thou, Simon Barjona...." In considering the issue of Jesus's identity, we would expect Peter's response to have been different if Jesus were God. Peter's response was so simple that nobody could misunderstand it. Jesus is the *son of* the living God. For these words to mean anything other than what their obvious meanings imply requires enormous effort and intricacy, which ardent Trinitarians have been putting forth for seventeen hundred years, but still cannot be understood.

It has been asked, "What difference does it make whether I consider Jesus to be my Lord or my God?" A short answer is that any wrong understanding that arises between people necessarily results in confusion in the relationship. For example, if I insist on calling the mayor of my town "Mr. President," our relationship suffers in some way. If I refer to the President of the United States as "Mr. Mayor," confusion will arise here, too. It is the same in our relationship with God and Jesus:

> In order to secure distinctness and clearness of thought upon Scripture doctrine, we must subordinate the Son to the Father, and having done this to take our first step in Christian faith, we cannot complete our progress in that faith by confounding the Son with the Father. We must distinguish between that being who appeared in Judaea as a messenger from God, and the God whose messenger he was.[9]

We must be careful not to confuse people, places or things in our biblical studies. This is not only true in biblical pursuits, but in

---

[9] Ellis, 131-132.

all areas of our lives. It helps us keep things straight. If one were to confuse his brother with his father, or his sister with his mother, or endeavor through some extrapolation to prove that his mother actually is his sister, nobody would pay heed to the conclusions reached or the proofs intended to convince others that his case was sound. It is nothing short of amazing that most Christians have been so willing to accept a system of doctrines that is no different in its effects than mistaking who our dearest family members are. Insight into the question, "What difference does it make whether I consider Jesus to be my Lord or my God?" can be gained the next time you see your sister and say "Hi, Mom," or your brother and say "Hi, Dad," or the mayor of your town and say "Good morning, Mr. President." Do it repeatedly, or try to convince others to do it, and it will not be long before you see the parallel importance of getting God's and Jesus's identities correct. This is not just a doctrinal distinction, it is a relational distinction with corresponding implications.

There are plenty of verses that implore us to use reason, and clarity of thought is required in order for us to stand firm on what we believe. There are many who have been taught to believe the doctrine of the Trinity, but it has not been proven, nor could it be due to its self-contradictoriness:

> The more earnestly we seek to explain this apparent contradiction, that there are three and yet only one, three persons but one being, the greater the difficulty becomes; until we must end, as most persons do end, with saying that it is an unfathomable mystery, in which we must believe without questioning. Now we distinctly say, that, if the Scripture is so, we will try to believe it. We do not set up our reason against Scripture, which is the acknowledged revelation of God; but we must use our reason to search the Scripture before we can admit a doctrine so obscure and so difficult. We have a right to expect plain proof before we can be required to believe it.[10]

The use of the word *admit* in the above statement is appropriate to this discussion, not only in the sense that we agree with a doctrine, but in the sense that we allow it into our system of faith. When

---

[10] Eliot, 11.

an unknown person knocks on the door of our home, we ordinarily do not just allow him in. We ascertain his reason for being there and scrutinize his behavior. In contrast, Christians have not been so guarded as to what we will allow to take up residence in our minds.

It is not the purpose of this work to divide people, it is simply my desire that God and Jesus not be so misrepresented. Presently and historically, creeds and opinions of others, including, but not limited to, pastors, preachers, televangelists, popular theologians and reformers, have been relied upon so heavily that beliefs are rarely generated from independent inquiry and judgment. The result is a society of people not only unaccustomed to forming independent opinions, but seemingly unwilling to formulate them. Christians have voluntarily incapacitated themselves from making the type of judgments that are obtained by implementing reasonable methodologies, and what has resulted is a mass of incongruous beliefs and self-contradictory dogmas, and a zeal to maintain these as though they were, without question, delivered directly by God to mankind, without a sense that there might be something wrong with them.

The pointing out of error to a body of Christians operating in this way has generally been unwelcome. Suggestions that are contrary to the prevailing system of beliefs have been squashed and ridiculed. Many Christians, as individuals, have not only become passive in their own searches for truth, but, somewhat inexplicably, are actively defend something they admittedly don't understand—Trinitarianism, and how it developed.

Unitarians, as I use the term in this book, believe that God, our heavenly Father, is strictly one being. There is no divisibility within Him, there is no possibility that He is three-in-one. As we will observe later in this work, the role the recorded words of Jesus said played in confirming this view of God is easily seen when common sense is applied in our reading of the texts. A contemporary author, in a study that has broad-ranging applications, writes:

> Logical thinking empowers the mind in a way that no other kind of thinking can. It frees the highly educated from the habit of presuming every claim to be true until proven false. It enables average Americans to stand up against the forces of political correctness, see through the chicanery, and make

independent decisions for themselves. And it is the bulwark against intellectual servitude for the underprivileged.[11]

A common argument Trinitarians make against the use of reason is that, since God is above our complete comprehension, reason will not lead us to a knowledge of Him. We are "only human" and cannot figure it all out, let alone trying to know who God fully is. It is sometimes said that only an arrogant person expects God to make sense. So when ardent Trinitarians are pressed to explain who God is, the realization that Trinitarian dogma makes no sense necessarily forces them behind the claim that God is a "mystery," and that He is therefore unknowable. Among the many problems with this line of thinking is that it renders Trinitarian doctrine impervious to challenge. It also produces a state of mind in which the notion of making sense of things becomes more and more distant. If we are seeking mystery, then that which makes sense will not satisfy us and common sense will become so trivialized that there will cease to be a standard against which to judge our beliefs. Only the conclusion becomes important, not how we arrived at it.

Unitarians have been accused of making too little of Jesus because we do not believe he is God almighty. This sort of all-or-nothing thinking is a misrepresentation of how the Bible develops the way we are to formulate our thoughts in order to see things more clearly. Much will be said on this later, but for now it is enough to point out that Trinitarians have placed themselves in a theological camp of their own making. This camp is a place where emphasis is not placed on the reasonability of beliefs, so doctrines that are not understood or are patently absurd may still be acceptable. The underpinning of this reasoning is that God is not completely knowable so we cannot expect to understand Him, so when claims are made that are absurd, they may still be, or are, true. As we shall see, this way of thinking has given many carte blanche to make the most absurd and contradictory statements about God as long as somewhere in these statements is the proposition that He is three-in-one. It has been one of the biggest tasks of Trinitarian theologians throughout the ages to construct

---

[11] Marilyn Vos Savant, *The Power of Logical Thinking* (New York: St. Martin's Press, 1996), xix.

arguments that make it acceptable to remove biblical pursuits from the realm of human understanding. Once Christians cease expecting beliefs to make sense, the clergy's job becomes easier, and doctrines, regardless of how little they contribute to our understanding, are accepted without much of a challenge.

I regret that it was necessary for me throughout this work to refer to those who ardently defend the doctrine of the Trinity as "Trinitarians." The fact that I employ such a term may be construed as derogatory or separatist. The term as I use it carries none of these senses. I had no other, non-cumbersome way of developing my thoughts when I spoke of those who embrace Trinitarian doctrines. It is also relevant that many Christians are nominal Trinitarians. They may call themselves Trinitarians, but really abide by the supremacy of the Father in mind and worship, and do not understand what the doctrine of the Trinity is. When asked whether they believe that Jesus is God himself or is His only begotten Son, nominal Trinitarians answer the latter. Orthodox Trinitarians answer both. There is therefore a distinction to be made between orthodox Trinitarianism and nominal Trinitarianism. Nominal Trinitarianism is the belief in the Father, Son and holy spirit, but that the Father is supreme. In this sense it may be considered Unitarian. Orthodox Trinitarianism is the belief in the Father, Son and Holy Spirit, and that these three are co-equal and co-eternal with each other, that each is God and that there is still only one God. When I refer to Trinitarians in this work I am referring to those who defend orthodox Trinitarianism.

I have quoted other authors liberally in this work. I discovered their works years after I had come to the conclusion that the Father is the one true God, and they so eloquently gave expression to my thoughts and sentiments. The clarity and eloquence with which they wrote should be seen by all who care to read upon this subject. Most of their works are long out of print, and in order to preserve as much of the context and give the reader the benefit of these works, I have taken the liberty of quoting them at length, permitting the authors to speak for themselves. My task was organizing their thoughts into a cohesive, fluid whole, and though it took years to complete, it is now an accessible reference work.

The debates about God's and Jesus's identities engendered by the councils of the fourth century have, in many ways, contributed to the historical and contemporary polarization within the Christian community. For most Trinitarians, acceptance of Jesus as the Messiah is no longer enough for one to be considered a Christian. One must now go beyond this and believe that Jesus is God and man, *and* that there are three persons in the Godhead. Unfortunately, some who embrace the supremacy of the Father have argued so frequently that Jesus is subordinate to the Father that they have been sidetracked from the Bible representing Jesus as more than a mere man. The conflicting views of Jesus have sent Christians into opposing corners and thinking disparaging thoughts about each other. That this trend is reversed one can only hope:

> One exalts Christ to the very supreme God; the other humbles Him to the rank of mere man; and between the two the Christian world oscillates. Men swing from one extreme to the other. If one comes to the conclusion that Christ is not God, he is very likely to conclude that He is only a man. If he rejects the Trinitarian view, he is quite likely to swing over to the humanitarian. On the other hand, if he cannot bring himself to believe that Christ is a man, and nothing more, he is very likely to take the opposite extreme, and affirm His absolute Deity.
>
> The negative style of argument prevails on either side. Prove that Christ is not God, and we are supposed to have proved that He is a man and nothing more. Prove that He is not a mere man, and you are supposed to have proved that He is God. It does not seem to occur to people that between God and man there is a long way; that between the finite and the infinite there is a vast distance; and that Christ may be something unique, neither absolutely God nor absolutely man, but *sui generis*,—a being after his own order, a "mediator between God and man." Surely there is room enough for such a being.[12]

---

12 Rev. Stephen Crane, *Jesus the Christ,* (Boston: Universalit Publishing House, 1889), 24-25.

CHAPTER 1

UNITARIANISM

The foundational tenet of Unitarianism is that our heavenly Father, whose name the Bible states is a form of the word *Yahweh*, is the one true God, and that every other being, including the Messiah, is subordinate to Him.[1] God is to be worshipped in the highe st sense of the word *worship*, and has no equals. He promised a messiah to Israel via prophecy, and in due time sent him to redeem mankind from sin. Once the Messiah, Jesus, lived a sinless life, was crucified and raised from the dead, a comforter was promised to those who accepted him as Lord in their lives and acted accordingly. This comforter is referred to in Scripture as the "holy spirit" or the "holy ghost," and represents or describes the divine influences in the lives of Christians. At times the term "Holy Spirit" may refer to the Father Himself and is typically capitalized when such references are made.[2]

Unitarianism maintains the strict unity of God. In this sense it is synonymous with monotheism, since both constitute a belief in only one God in the simple sense of the word "one":

> When we speak of the Unity of God, we take the word in its common meaning; we mean simple, absolute, undivided unity. We mean that God is one being, one person, one infinite and almighty Jehovah, the creator and upholder of all things. We do not pretend to understand the nature of God perfectly. Both in his being and in his attributes he is far above our com-

---

[1] Unitarianism is not to be confused with contemporary Unitarian-Universalism; the latter is a much less biblically oriented religion(s), whereas the former relies upon biblical interpretation.

[2] An argument has been advanced that the phrase "Holy Spirit" refers to the Father only, as a personification of his spirit (or some part of his being), and is therefore not a reference to Him personally.

prehension. But we find no sufficient authority in the Scripture for increasing the difficulty, by dividing the unity of his being into a Trinity of persons; a distinction which is beyond our clear conception, and which seems to lead to hopeless contradiction.[3]

Unitarianism's primary tenet is stated explicitly in the Bible, both the Hebrew Bible and the texts of the New Testament. No departure from biblical language or common sense is required to make sense of this system of beliefs, and even though there will always be texts that give difficulty to the most astute Bible student—such is the nature of literary interpretation of ancient texts—a few basic rules of interpretation make it easier to arrive at sensible notions of God and Jesus. These typically lead the unprejudiced theology student to see that our heavenly Father has no equals. Unitarianism's precepts are readily grasped by the simplest seeker, and the idea that the Father is the one true God is easily understood.[4] These principles are beautifully simple yet inexhaustible. They do not contain the contradictions and difficulties in their terminologies that the Trinitarian system does. And lest it be assumed that Unitarians consider Jesus to be a mere man, it needs to be made clear at the onset that he is not:

> "What think ye of Christ?" We believe that Jesus of Nazareth is the Christ that should come into the world, the glorious person foretold by Moses and the Prophets. We believe that Jesus Christ is the Son of God, and not God himself, the Saviour and the Mediator between God and man. That He did no sin, that never man spake like him—that *God* gave not the spirit by measure to him—that the Father sanctified and sent him into the world—that he anointed him with the holy spirit and with power, and that Jesus went about

---

3 Eliot, 10.

4 The phrase "easily understood" must here be qualified. It would take an individual an entire lifetime of reflection to grasp the impact of this sentence, and the understanding would still be incomplete. "Easily understood" is thus not the equivalent of "immediately understood," but that the statement poses no difficulty as a starting point for reflecting on what has been done to accomplish the redemption of mankind. There are no inherent difficulties, such as contradictions or departures from common sense, contained in statements that are easily understood. Trinitarian dogma, on the other hand, has few or no statements of this sort.

doing good. We believe that God was with Christ in all his labours, instructions and sufferings—that Christ was holy, harmless, undefiled, and separate from sin,—that the doctrines he taught were true—that his precepts are pure and just—that his miracles are proofs of his divine mission—that his prophecies have been and will be fulfilled—that he always did those things which pleased the Father—that he had such a knowledge of the Father, such communications from the Father, such communion with God, as to justify him in saying, "I and my Father are one, he that hath seen me, hath seen the Father." Unitarians believe that Jesus Christ is, except the Father, the most glorious being mankind have ever known—worthy to be honoured, loved, trusted, and obeyed, but not to be worshipped as God supreme. We believe he is the way, the truth, the resurrection and the life; the light of the world, and the glory of God: that *He* has the words of eternal life, that *He* was betrayed, condemned, scourged, crucified, dead, and buried—that He rose again from the dead, by the power of God—that He ascended to Heaven, and now sitteth on the right hand of God. We believe that all our prayers should be offered to the Father, *in the name of Jesus Christ*—that we should possess the mind and spirit of Christ, and imitate his holy example—that Christ came into the world, because he was sent by the Father, to redeem mankind from the tyranny of base passions—from evil enticements, from sinful lusts, and thus to save sinners to God, to teach mankind to love God, to obey him, to urge upon mankind the necessity of offering themselves as living sacrifices to God, and to look to God for pardon and eternal life and joy. This, my friends, is what Unitarians think of Christ.

Why then should other Christians speak falsely of us, and say we deny Christ,—that we do not believe in him, and that we trust to a *mere man* for salvation, when *they know* as well as ourselves, that we believe Christ to be the Son of God, but not God himself: when they know that we teach, that we must, in this life, conform ourselves to his holy and spotless life, ere we can be rendered meet for the society of the saints in light. All Unitarians believe that Christ shall come a second time on the earth, and call all men to a righteous judgment; and then shall come the end, when he, *i.e.* Christ shall have delivered up the kingdom to God even the Father, when he shall have put down all rule and authority and power. For Christ must reign till he hath put all enemies under his feet—the last enemy that shall be destroyed is death, for he hath put all things under his feet; but when he shall have put all things under him, it is manifest that he is excepted, *i.e.* God who did put all things under him. And when all things shall be subdued unto him, then shall the Son also himself be subject unto him, *i.e. God*, that put all things under him, that *God* may be all in all. We heed not the misrepresentations of men, nor the harsh antichristian denunciations of the bigot; we know in whom we trust, and our religious views lead us to cherish the animating hope, that if we transform ourselves into the image of our blessed Saviour, when he shall appear, then shall we also appear with him in glory.[5]

Recognizing Jesus as he is does not diminish him by bestowing the highest exaltation upon the Father. When the Father is known as the fountain of life for all beings, the wellspring of theological and intellectual inquiry can begin with a rational basis.

The following verses from the Hebrew Bible make it clear that our heavenly Father is the one true God. These also make it necessary for those endeavoring to prove a plurality of persons in God, which is a most enigmatic concept, to find *clearer* evidence for it in both the Hebrew and Christian texts. This has not been done, simply because those verse are not presented to us in the texts:

- Deut. 6:4—"Hear, O Israel, The Lord our God is one Lord."
- Exod. 20:3—"Thou shalt have no other Gods before me."
- Deut. 32:39—"See now that I, even I am He, and there is no God with me."
- Isaiah 40:25—"To whom then will ye liken me, or shall I be equal? saith the holy One."
- Isaiah 44:6—"I am the first, and I am the last, and besides me

---

5 Thomas, 37-39.

there is no God."
- Isaiah 44:8—"Is there a God besides me? yea, there is no God: I know not any."
- Isaiah 45:21—"There is no God else beside me; a just God, and a saviour: there is none beside me."
- Isaiah 46:9—"For I am God, and there is none else: I am God, and there is none like me."
- Psalm 83:18—"That men may know that thou, whose name alone is Jehovah, art the most high over all the earth."
- Psalm 86:10—"For thou art great, and doest wondrous things: thou art God alone."

It is apparent from these texts that God is represented in the Hebrew Bible as one "person" or "being" in the simple sense of the word "one." Accordingly, Unitarians maintain that altering the sense of these clear verses by making God appear to be a multiple being is offensive to Him:

> Serious and thinking men cannot help being persuaded, that the holding any being whatsoever, in any possible sense, to be equal to the Father is, not withstanding any qualifications that may be offered, a dangerous, palpable, and direct attack on His Supremacy; Whom, the Bible proclaims to be the one God and Father of all; Who is above all; Lord of Heaven and Earth. And further, that the doctrines contained in what is called the Creeds of Saint Athanasius, have conveyed down to us, through a more entangled medium, the very polytheism of the heathen Platonists; and, of course, have helped (however unintentionally) to contaminate the First Principle of true Religion, and to lessen, though they cannot destroy, the effects of the gracious and directive light which was communicated to man *at the beginning*, and uniformly strengthened by every subsequent dispensation.[6]

The doctrine that the Father is supreme and is therefore the one true God is continued in the following New Testament texts:

---

6 James Gifford, *An Elucidation of the Unity of God, Deduced from Scripture and Reason* (London: 5th ed., 1815), 82-83.

- Acts 2:36—"Therefore let the house of Israel know assuredly, that God hath made that same Jesus, whom ye have crucified, both Lord and Christ."
- John 14:1—"Let not your heart be troubled: ye believe in God, believe also in me."
- 1 Cor. 8:6—"But to us there is but one God, the Father, of whom are all things, and we in him; and one Lord Jesus Christ, by whom are all things, and we by him."
- 1 Tim. 2:5—"For there is one God, and one mediator between God and men, the man Christ Jesus..."

Despite the obvious meaning of these verses, Trinitarians have argued that, since Unitarians do not believe the Father has equals, they do not "make enough" of Jesus. This assessment is improper. One need not consider anyone, including the Messiah, to be the supreme God in order to honor him appropriately, just as one need not consider gold to be diamonds in order to recognize its true value. The charge that Unitarians make too little of Jesus is simply false:

> First of all, you will observe, and I call your attention particularly to it, that those who accuse us of believing that Christ is a mere man, are in error. They are prejudiced or misinformed. If by a mere man they mean one like ourselves, or like the prophets of the olden time, Moses, or Isaiah, or Ezekiel, or John the Baptist, the charge is entirely untrue....I feel satisfied, from observation which has been very extended, that there is no denomination in which Christ is more heartily received than in our own. A vulgar prejudice has been sometimes excited against us, by calling Unitarianism the half-way house to infidelity; but I believe that it has been the means of saving more persons from infidelity than any other form of belief. It addresses itself to thinking men and encourages them to think independently, but it does not make shipwreck of faith. It receives Christ as the divine master and guide, but at the same time proves his doctrines to be consistent with enlightened reason.
>
> Unitarians, as a body of believers, everywhere, agree in the belief that Christ is the special messenger of God; that his mission was divine; that his character was sinless; that his

authority was so directly from God, that whatever he taught is the teaching of the Father. "For he spake not of himself, but as the Father gave him commandment, so he taught." He was divine, therefore, in his mission, in his character, and in his authority. This is not the description of a mere man. Consider only the distinction of absolute freedom from sin, to say nothing of his superhuman wisdom and power; how completely does that distinction alone place him by himself! What nearness to God does it give him! We can but imperfectly conceive it. Our own sinfulness is so great, it is so inherent in our nature, so inseparable from the development of our thoughts and affections, that we but imperfectly understand its debasing influence. I believe that, if we could this day be absolutely freed from sin, we should be lost in amazement at the height to which we would rise, and the comparative degradation in which we now stand. To be absolutely freed from sin, is to be indeed the Son of God; it is the highest moral exaltation; and when we add thereto such authority and power as belonged to Jesus, we see how very far he is from all our ideas of a mere man.[7]

MY BELOVED FRIEND:

I HAVE received, perused, and reperused your affectionate letters, and thank you for them. They were dictated, I know, by the most ardent love for me, and zeal for the honor and glory of the dear Redeemer. But they are altogether an appeal to my feelings, and are founded, I think, upon incorrect premises. And I will tell you why I say so. You write thus: "Crushed and almost heart-broken, my beloved friend, I have just risen from my knees, where, if ever my soul was poured out in prayer, it has been now for you, that God would, in his great mercy, for his dear Son's sake, and especially for your own soul's sake, even now arrest your hand before it tears the crown from the head of our glorious and exalted Saviour. O, how my heart clings to him when I see him thus sorely wounded in the house of his friends." My dear friend, the

---

7 Eliot, 41-42.

strength of your feelings has misled you. What an expression! *"Tears the crown!"* I speak the truth, and I weep while I write it, when I declare that I would sooner die than rob the blessed Saviour—my once crucified, but now risen and glorified Lord, my Advocate, my Intercessor with the Father—of one particle of the honor and glory which is his due. Every word that the Bible speaks concerning him I believe to be true. I believe that "God hath highly exalted him, and given him a name which is above every name, that at the name of JESUS every knee should bow, and every tongue confess that He is Lord, to the glory of God the Father." I *love* my Lord and Master in sincerity and in truth—"whom having not seen, I *love*; in whom, though now I see him not, yet *believing*, I *rejoice with joy unspeakable, and full of glory.*" I go to the Father only through him, because I believe that He is "the way, and the truth, and the life," and that "other foundation can no man lay." And when I arrive at Heaven, which I shall certainly do if I heartily strive to do the will of my Father which is in Heaven, I expect to unite with my dear sainted husband and son, and with "many angels round about the throne, and the beasts and the elders—ten thousand times ten thousand, and thousands of thousands—saying with a loud voice, Worthy is *the Lamb that was slain* to receive power, and riches, and wisdom, and strength, and honor, and glory, and blessing!" We read in 2 Pet. i. 17, that he "received from God the Father honor and glory, when there came such a voice from the *excellent* glory, (there is, we know, a glory that *excelleth*,) this is my beloved Son, in whom I am well pleased." Why may we not say to that Son of God, "Thou art worthy to receive, &c.?"

It is hard, my dear friend, to accuse me of tearing the crown from my glorious Redeemer's head; and yet I know that the expression is dictated by your love to that Redeemer, and so I freely forgive it. Aye, more; I rejoice that you love him so well; but do not take it for granted that I do not love him, because I cannot render him the *supreme* homage which I *honestly* think belongs to God alone. *The crown is still upon his head;* he is at the head of the mediatorial kingdom, and will be there until that hour when "cometh the end, when he shall have delivered up the kingdom to God, even the Father, when he shall have put down all rule, and all authority, and power. For he must reign till he hath put all his enemies under his feet. The last enemy that shall be destroyed is death. For he hath put all things under his feet. And when he saith, all things are put under him, it is *manifest* that He is excepted, which did put all things under him. And when all things shall be subdued unto him, then shall the Son also himself be subject unto him that put all things under him, that GOD may be *all in all*." It must take *a very explicit statement* of the doctrine that there are three equal persons in one God, to set aside a text so full, so *unqualified*, so clear as this; given, as it seems to me, in consideration of our weakness and want of knowledge.[8]

Some Christians, including Unitarians, have fallen into the trap of regarding Jesus primarily as an example to be followed. It is a mistake to merely view him from afar, which is the consequence of making him just an example, as though the primary purpose of his mission were simply to show us how we should act:

> We are not to regard him as our example in any stiff, formal, perfunctory way. He is not to be thought of as "busying himself," while on earth, "in setting an example." We are not to think of Him as·some superior being, living among men merely to show them how they ought to live. He was not "acting a part" in the great drama of life. Far from it. He lived out spontaneously the life that was in Him. What He appeared to be, He was. His deeds were but the outflow of His spirit. In Him the ideal and the real were one. He realized in Himself the ideal life of a man, not in a formal, unnatural way, but in a perfectly natural, real way. He was not another order of being, acting in human dress for man's enlightenment, but He was a man, living a manly life among men, and so showing them the life they ought to live.[9]

---

8 Dana, 81-83.

9 Crane, 73-74.

Loving, honoring and respecting our heavenly Father as the one true God is the case the Bible makes clear, and corresponds directly to worshipping Him in spirit and in truth. Unitarians believe in the supremacy of the Father because the idea is clearly laid out in the Bible and involves no contradiction. What is left to discover is whether Trinitarianism is preferable to Unitarianism after studying Scripture and employing common sense.

CHAPTER 2

TRINITARIANISM

Generally speaking, there are three types of Trinitarianism, each with its own peculiarities and ways of being described or categorized. Due to the language employed and subtleties involved in Trinitarian theology, it can be difficult to distinguish between the three, but there are some differences, even if only theoretical.

The first type is modalism, which is the belief that God acts in three different capacities, or modes. At any given time He might be in the character or capacity of the Father, at times He might represent Himself as the Son, and at others as the Holy Spirit. The doctrine is that these are simply manifestations of the same person whom we call God. There are not, however, three distinct persons that make up this "godhead." This type of Trinitarianism is rejected by most Trinitarians because it fails to represent God as three individual persons united into one. In explaining modalism, Miethe says it is:

> A heresy stressing the radical unity of God. Modalism teaches that the three parts of the Trinity—Father, Son, and Holy Spirit—are merely different modes, or manifestations, of God, rather than three distinct persons who are at the same time one in substance.[1]

Some Christians embrace Trinitarianism, perhaps unwittingly, from a modalist perspective, which is derived from a fairly common analogy given in defense of God being three-in-one. The analogy is that a man may be a father, a son, and a husband; he is therefore three things but only one person. The problem with this, according to most

---

[1] Terry Miethe, *The Compact Dictionary of Doctrinal Words* (Minneapolis: Bethany House Publishers, 1988), "Modalism."

Trinitarians, is that this analogy, when applied to God, would fail to represent him as three *separate* persons, which is the crux of Trinitarianism. Another problem with the analogy is that a man may be a father, a son, and a husband, and he may also be an uncle, a nephew, a grandfather, a grandson, a teacher, an athlete, etc. Apply this analogy to God and He becomes more than three! But since modalism is not a widely-held form of Trinitarianism, there is little need to examine it at length here.

Unlike modalism, the second type of Trinitarianism lacks a formal name. It is the belief that there are three persons in the godhead, but the word *persons* is not used in the usual sense of the word. In this form of Trinitarianism, the term *person* has never been clearly defined or explained, it is simply a statement positing three persons in the godhead, each of whom is fully God. To this it is added that there are not three Gods, but that there is only one God. Here the difficulty begins for advocates of this form of Trinitarianism. This is as conceptually elusive as any other form of Trinitarianism because it makes there to be three Gods and at the same time only one which, as has been admitted by some of the doctrine's proponents, is a difficulty for which an adequate explanation has yet to be found. The common argument for its acceptance is simply not to question its veracity and "take it on faith" as a mystery—it is true whether anyone understands it or not. This type of Trinitarianism is probably the most widely-held of the three types.

The third type of Trinitarianism also lacks a name. It is the belief that there are three persons, each of whom is fully God, and the term *persons* is used in its usual sense. This is the belief in three separate Gods: God the Father, God the Son, and God the Holy Spirit. Most Trinitarians adhering to this theology make little or no attempt to undergo the philosophical rigors of making these three subjects appear as only one, it is a straightforward declaration that there are three Gods. The problem with this is that it proposes a belief in more than one God, which is at variance with many Bible verses that establish the existence of only one supreme God. Few Trinitarians admit to embracing this form of Trinitarianism—most embrace the second type, which involves some of the most subtle and absurd philosophical notions in theology.

Much of the problem for defenders of the second type of Trinitarianism is in the attempt to make three persons appear as one. It is an attempt to make an apparent polytheism fit into some concept of monotheism, since monotheism is a constant theme of the Bible. Over and over God represents Himself as one, so having three Gods must be accompanied by explanations as to how they are compatible with the idea that there is only one God. Despite the effort to accomplish this over the past seventeen hundred years, it hasn't yet produced a cogent nexus between the premises and the conclusion. No intelligible explanation has emerged from the thousands of publications and millions of verbal arguments put forward to reconcile the notion that three Gods are, in any sense, the same as one God. This lack of intelligibility accounts for the disparity of thought between Trinitarians regarding how to explain the doctrine of the Trinity:

> "The three persons are God understanding himself, God understood by himself, and God loving Himself."—Richard Baxter
>
> "My admiring thoughts of God are of one single essence, yet Three in subsistence; of Three, that One cannot be the others, yet all three are One, that are really distinct, yet really are the same."—Doolittle
>
> "There is One, infinite, eternal Mind, and three somethings that are not distinct minds."—Robert South
>
> "The Father, Son, and Holy Ghost, are as really distinct persons as Peter, James, and John—each of which is God. We must allow each person to be a God."—Bishop Sherlock
>
> "The three persons are only three *external* relations of God to his creatures, as Creator, Redeemer, and Sanctifier."—Dr. Wallis
>
> "The three Person are *internal* relations of the Deity to itself."—Dr. South[2]

These examples demonstrate how little consensus there has been among ardent Trinitarians regarding what is said to be the most fundamental element of their faith.

When it is said that there are three persons in the godhead, in the

---

2 Dr. Frederick Farley, *Unitarianism Defined: The Scripture Doctrine of the Father, Son, and Holy Ghost* (Boston: American Unitarian Association, 1873), 18-19.

absence of an explanation as to what the word *person* means, we are left to assign our common understanding to it. In other words, we are forced to conclude exactly what Bishop Sherlock admitted—there really are three Gods. But most Trinitarians take another step and deny this, and to have this denial sound credible, as well as to have a sense of monotheism preserved, strange and undefined senses to the word *person* are then assigned:

> The proper modern doctrine of the Trinity, as it appears in the creeds of latter times, is, that there are three persons in the Divinity, who equally possess all divine attributes; and the doctrine is connected with the statement that there is but one God. Now, this doctrine is to be rejected, because, taken in connection with that of the unity of God, it is essentially incredible; one which no man, who has compared the two doctrines together with right conceptions of both, ever did or ever could believe. Three persons, each equally possessing divine attributes, are three Gods. A person is a being. No one who has any correct notion of the meaning of words will deny this. And the being who possesses divine attributes must be God or a God. The doctrine of Trinity, then, affirms that there are three Gods. It is affirmed at the same time, that there is but one God. But no one can believe that there are three Gods, and that there is but one God.[3]

In studying Trinitarian theology, one realizes early on that words are used that have no identifiable meanings. The word *person* is not used in its ordinary sense, yet the new sense is never defined. We are told there are *three* Gods and yet only *one*. A truth seeker is forced to wonder from the outset, How can this be? Since numbers are assigned meaning (i.e. defined), what could possibly be meant by the statement that there are three Gods and simultaneously one? A reasonable person would recognize, or at least suspect, that this cannot be true. There are either three or one, but not both. In the example above, Bishop Sherlock made it clear he worshipped three, which serves to assist anyone considering his ideas whether or not to accept them. But the statement that there are three and one is disingenuous

---

3 Norton, 40-41.

and is employed as a subterfuge to prevent Trinitarian dogma from being evaluated according to the same principles by which we judge all other things. Trinitarian dogma is hidden behind a veil of twisted language and sloppy development of thought. Take, for, example, the following account of the Trinity by a more modern author:

> In Jesus's disclosure of the divine Family the theme that runs through his discourses is the generosity of the social God. The manner of Jesus's speech indicates his conviction that the persons of the divine Community inwardly enjoy one another's love, hospitality, generosity, and interpersonal communion, so much so that they are one God, and being one God, express such love to one another.[4]

The development of thought in the above quote is astounding. It is said that there is a divine "Family." A family is constituted of individuals, and if each is an individual, and each is God, are there not three separate gods? But the argument proceeds that since the individual members of the "divine Community" enjoy each other's love, hospitality, generosity, and interpersonal communion, they somehow, fantasy-like, cease to be individuals! We are told, without any development of thought regarding how love and generosity, when expressed, diminishes individuals as individuals, and causes them to merge into those whom they love, in ambiguous and flowery language that masks the deception, that the three are really one God. In spite of the many arguments put forth in support of it, this sort of Trinitarian expression is unintelligible even to those making such claims. This is due to the application of words and concepts that are commonly used which, when cast in a Trinitarian sense, are allegedly no longer used according to their common meaning. But we are never told what the new meanings are, so it is fair to assume those employing such words and concepts did not know what they were talking about. The words they use are crucial to the development of Trinitarian dogma, yet nobody knows what they mean! The words and their ostensible new meanings are heartily and frequently used, as though there were no doubt as to their meanings, yet when pressed for an explanation

---

4 Royce Gordon Gruenler, *The Trinity in the Doctrine of John* (Grand Rapids, MI: Baker Book House, 1986), 121.

of what, for example, the word *person* means, nothing other than the common meaning has been given.

The peculiar usage of words in Trinitarian thought requires an allowance which Trinitarians grant themselves in response to challenges made against Trinitarian dogma. There is little hesitancy in reconceptualizing common terminologies to suit traditional hypotheses. Words such as *three, one, person, being,* and *nature* are used in new ways, but when asked for new and reasonable definitions of these words, none are produced. What is expected is that we simply accept these (now) strange words according to their peculiar senses, even though we have no idea as to what we would be saying if we were to use them in a Trinitarian sense. And though it is true that, since language is not static, and words and phrases may take on new senses over time, these new senses are capable of definition and/or explanation. Changes in connotation and denotation are identifiable. In Trinitarian theology, new meanings are purportedly assigned to common words, but these new connotations are not defined in such a way that we could apply them according to some rule or application of language:

> The whole controversy turns upon the use of words. It turns upon the distinction between a Person and a Being. The common idea conveyed by the word Person, is a separate, intelligent Being. When you say, that there are three Persons in God, you mean three Beings, or you must define the word Person. If by Person you mean Being, you assert that there are three Gods, which is impossible; if Person is used in any other sense, you must explain that sense. If you cannot do this, then it evidently has no meaning in your mind. You use words without ideas. You make a proposition which has no signification. In other words, you make an affirmation which affirms nothing. The matter then is reduced to this, the proposition that there are three Persons in God, in the only sense in which it is intelligible is false, and if unintelligible cannot be perceived to be true. It is impossible then, that it should be asserted from conviction, and as impossible that it should be assented to from a perception of its truth....
>
> A man demands my assent to the proposition, there are

three Persons in God. I ask him, what he means by person? I ask him, if he means a separate independent intelligent Being? He answers, he does not. He does not use the word in the common sense, but in a sense peculiar to this case. I ask him what that sense is? He cannot tell. You demand of me then, I answer, to assent to a proposition which conveys to my mind no intelligible idea, and, it appears to be equally unintelligible to you. We both, in reality, in assenting to it, assent to nothing but words, and if they convey to us no intelligible meaning, to us they are nothing, and we assent to nothing. Were these words in the Bible, then I might say that I believed they expressed truth, though I could not understand it. But not being in the Bible, or any words of the same import, I consider them the mere invention of fallible men. I cannot believe on their authority. So far from supposing them to be true, as I cannot understand them myself, I think it fair to conclude that those who framed them had no clear ideas.[5]

If the doctrine of the Trinity could be found in the Bible, it would seem that those who have sought to explain it would have had enough clear ideas that others could comprehend it more readily. A review of just a few of the three-in-one explanations shows that mankind's imagination has been stretched in every attempt to explain it. Had the doctrine been biblical, it would be able to be explained and understood without resorting to such claims as "It's a mystery!" Accounting for the absence of the doctrine from Scripture has been, and still is, a Herculean task for Trinitarians. In the past few centuries, though, with the rise of Protestantism, there has been increased confidence in the claim that the doctrine may be found in the Bible. This relatively recent and excessive confidence in the biblical origins of the doctrine is misguided:

The opinion that the Trinity is plainly taught in the Scriptures, has not generally prevailed till of late. So far were Trinitarians from holding such an opinion in former times, that in nothing did they exercise their ingenuity more than in

---

[5] George Burnap, *Lectures on the Doctrines of Christianity* (Boston and Cambridge: James Munroe and Co., 1848), 20-22.

devising reasons why this doctrine should be only obscurely shadowed forth by the Saviour and the Apostles, and why it should be kept concealed from the Jews.[6]

The doctrine of the Trinity, since it is not strictly biblical, must be a post-biblical invention. Commenting on the post-biblical origination of the doctrine, the *Oxford Companion to the Bible* says:

> Because the doctrine of the Trinity is such an important part of later Christian doctrine, it is striking that the term does not appear in the New Testament. Likewise, the developed concept of three coequal partners in the Godhead found in later creedal formulations cannot be clearly detected within the confines of the canon...
>
> While the New Testament writers say a great deal about God, Jesus, and the Spirit of each, no New Testament writer expounds on the relationship among the three in the detail that *later Christian* writers do.[7] (emphasis mine)

The Catholic clergy have been fairly consistent throughout the centuries in maintaining that the doctrine is not biblical, but is traditional, and they are well aware of the doctrine's origins, since the Catholic Church was responsible for the development and establishment of the doctrine as official Church dogma. Petavius, an early church figure, said:

> Concerning the three persons of the divinity, and their essence, nothing was fully written or known, before the council of Nice [325 A.D.], because this mystery *was not revealed and confirmed, till after the conflict between the Arians and Catholics.*[8]

An inference to be drawn from the above statement is that the doctrine is not of biblical origins, since the last of the gospels was written about the year 80, and the Arian dispute did not occur until about 320. And though Petavius makes the comment that the doc-

---

6 Jared Sparks, quoted in Dana, 171.

7 *The Oxford Companion to the Bible,* Bruce Metzger and Michael Coogan, editors (New York: Oxford University Press, 1993), "Trinity," 782.

8 Petavius, quoted in Dana, 181.

trine of the Trinity was not revealed until the council of Nice, the question is, was it revealed by God or by man? If we contend that it was revealed by God, we must explain how we arrived at that contention—it isn't enough to make the claim that God's hand was in something if it wasn't. If man's stamp is on something, that changes the discussion as to what influences were present and does whatever those men came up with make sense. The argument typically comes back to whether it is in the Bible, and, being admitted to be absent from the Bible, it is easy to trace the doctrine's origins to the imagination of man, not the mind of God. Trinitarians have admitted the doctrine's absence from Scripture in every century the issue has been debated. In the twentieth century, Arthur Wainwright, whose work is regarded highly among Trinitarian scholars, writes:

> (My) book has been written in the conviction that the problem of the Trinity was being raised and answered in New Testament times, and had its roots in the worship, experience, and thought of first-century Christianity. The word "problem" has been preferred to the word "doctrine," because there is no formal statement of the doctrine of the Trinity in the New Testament....There is no formal statement of Trinitarian doctrine in the New Testament as there is in the Athanasian Creed or in Augustine's *De Trinitate*. It will be argued that the problem of the Trinity was in the minds of certain New Testament writers, and that they made an attempt to answer it. None of their writings, however, was written specifically to deal with it, and most of the signs that a writer had tackled the problem are incidental. There was no elaborate or systematic answer to the problem. For this reason the word "problem" has been preferred to the word "doctrine." But it must be understood that the New Testament writers did not entirely neglect to answer the problem, although other matters occupied most of their attention. In so far as a doctrine is an answer, however fragmentary, to a problem, there is a doctrine of the Trinity in the New Testament. Insofar as it is a formal statement of a position, there is no doctrine of the

Trinity in the New Testament.[9]

Shirley Guthrie, whose work is also highly regarded among many Trinitarians, writes:

> The Bible does not teach the doctrine of the Trinity. Neither the word "Trinity" itself, nor such language as "one-in-three," three-in-one," one "essence" or "substance," or three "persons" is biblical language. The language of the doctrine is the language of the ancient church, taken not from the Bible but from classical Greek philosophy. But the church did not simply invent this doctrine. It used the language and concepts available to it to interpret what the Bible itself says about God and his dealings with men in the world. (We shall have to ask later whether this language is adequate, or whether we ought to try to find new ways to say it.) While we cannot find the doctrine itself spelled out in Scripture, we can find there the *roots* of the doctrine, some affirmations which forced the church to ask questions which led it to formulate the doctrine.[10]

Similar admissions were made in the 19th century:

> Our belief in the Trinity, the co-eternity of the Son of God with his Father, the proceeding of the Spirit from the Father and the Son,... these, with such other principal points, ... are in Scripture nowhere to be found by express literal mention; only deduced they are out of Scripture by collection—Richard Hooker: *Ecclesiastical Polity*, book i. chap. xiv. 2; in *Works*, vol. i. 187.
>
> It must be owned, that the doctrine of the Trinity, as it is proposed in our Articles, our Liturgy, our Creeds, is not in so many words taught us in the Holy Scriptures. What we profess in our prayers we nowhere read in Scripture,—that the one God, the one Lord, is not one only person, but three persons in one substance. There is no such text in the Scriptures

---

[9] Arthur Wainwright, *The Trinity in the New Testament,* London: S.P.C.K., 1962), vii, 4.

[10] Shirley Guthrie, *Christian Doctrine: Teachings of the Christian Church* (Atlanta: John Knox Press, 1968), 92-93.

as this, that "the Unity in Trinity, and the Trinity in Unity, is to be worshipped."—Bishop Smallridge: *Sixty Sermons*; No. XXXIII. 348.[11]

People seeking meaning from the Bible have a legitimate basis for expecting fundamental elements of their faith to be clearly found in its texts. Fundamental doctrines are there, the Trinity is not, from which we may conclude that the doctrine of the Trinity to have emanated from man. This wouldn't in and of itself make something wrong, but it changes how the discussion proceeds and the way in which we consider the so-called evidence for its establishment. If we have little confidence that God somehow told us about it, then we shouldn't fear rejecting it.

THE DOCTRINE OF THE TRINITY IS ABSENT FROM SCRIPTURE

Since there is no direct mention of the doctrine of the Trinity in Scripture, its advocates have inferred it from scattered (and reassembled) verses throughout the Bible. Shirley Guthrie's admission of its absence is not as rare as one might expect: there are others who are forthright about its absence. In contrast to this are the many who claim to find the doctrine clearly laid out in the Bible. This not only typifies the range of opinions regarding the doctrine, it explains why there are so many contrary explanations given for it.

In accordance with the admissions of those who admit the Trinity is not found in the Bible, there are admissions that there are large sections of the Bible that are silent regarding it:

> Not only have many learned, judicious, and candid writers in the orthodox body been unable to discern satisfactory proof for the doctrines of a Triune God, and the personal Deity of Christ and the Holy Ghost, in those texts, singly and separately considered, which have been deemed by others as perfectly demonstrative: not a few have conceded that there are whole classes of passages and entire books of the Bible which afford no evidence whatever of Trinitarianism. Thus it

---

[11] Richard Hooker and Bishop Smallridge, quoted in Wilson, 347.

has been acknowledged not only by Roman Catholic but by Protestant divines, of whom the number is increasing every day with the increase of knowledge as to the true modes of investigating the sense of Scripture, that the Old Testament affords nought but the faintest glimmerings of the dogma of a Triune God; by others that it is altogether silent on the subject of a plurality in the divine nature; by others, again, that the great Teacher himself, the Founder and Perfecter of our Faith, taught not these and other related tenets of Orthodoxy; and that the apostles, even after they were furnished with the fullest supplies of inspiration, when they obtained such ideas of the nature of Christ's kingdom as they had been incapable of comprehending from the lips of their Master, did not, in their oral discourses, deliver those doctrines concerning God, Christ, and the Spirit, which have been commonly regarded by "evangelical" writers as saving truths of the gospel.[12]

In contrast to those who proclaim that the doctrine may be adduced with ease from Scripture, other of its advocates candidly acknowledge its absence but who nonetheless believe it. I have no objection against whatever someone believes, whether Trinitarian, Unitarian, agnostic or atheist. My primary objection is against those who make proclamations and scathing indictments against those who aren't satisfied with the arguments given in support of a triune God. For those who believe in a triune God but acknowledge its absence from the Bible, accounts are made for the doctrine's absence, but these accounts turn out to be damaging to other elements of Trinitarian theology. For example, in explaining why the Old Testament does not contain the doctrine, some have argued that the doctrine of a triune God was not revealed until after the day of Pentecost. But this argument contradicts the arguments of those who find support for it from the Old Testament, whose accounts took place prior to Pentecost. This contradiction is emblematic of the struggle Trinitarians face in finding proof in the Bible to justify such an enigmatic concept of God:

I WILL now adduce the evidence which is brought by Profes-

---

[12] Wilson, 11-12.

sor Sparks from early ecclesiastical writers. He says: "Let us see, in the next place, how this result (at the conclusion of the last letter) agrees with some of the early fathers. We shall here find almost a universal opinion that the deity of Christ was not plainly taught in the Scriptures; and as for a Trinity of persons, nothing is heard of it, till the deity of the Holy Spirit was decreed by the council of Constantinople, near the close of the fourth century. A few passages shall be here introduced, merely to substantiate the fact, that in their opinion the Trinity was not explicitly taught, either in the Old Testament or the New."

"Athanasius allows, that Christ did not make known his deity to the Jews, and endeavors to account for it, by intimating, that the world could not yet bear such a doctrine. And he adds, 'I venture to affirm, that even the blessed disciples themselves had not a clear knowledge of his deity till the Holy Spirit came on them at the day of Pentecost.' This passage has a comprehensive import, and proves most clearly, that, in the opinion of Athanasius, the deity of Christ was not known even to the Apostles till after his death. Theodoret speaks to the same purpose. 'Before his death and sufferings, the Lord Christ, did not appear as God either to the Jews generally or to his Apostles.' Chrysostom often intimates, that Christ made but an imperfect indication of his deity to his disciples. On one occasion he observes, 'Christ did not immediately reveal his deity; at first he was thought to be a prophet, Christ, simply a man, but at last from his works and sayings, it appeared what he was.' Chrysostom further says, that Mary, the mother of Jesus, did not herself know the secret of his being the Supreme God."

"The Fathers, also, acknowledged, that after the death of Christ the Apostles did not teach this doctrine openly; as we learn from the hypothesis framed by them to account for the fact. They profess to consider it a mark of prudence and caution in the Apostles to avoid promulgating so unpopular a tenet. It would shock the prejudices of the Jews, on the one hand, who thought the unity of God a vital doctrine; and on the other hand, it would encourage the heathens in their polytheism and idolatry; and thus serious obstacles would be thrown in the way of their converting either the Jews or Gentiles to Christianity. It was deemed wise, therefore, to conceal for a time a doctrine of such dangerous tendency.

"Let the Fathers speak on this point. Chrysostom acquaints us, that our Saviour confined himself to instructions concerning his human powers, by reason of the 'weakness of his hearers, and the inability of those who saw and heard him for the first time, to receive more sublime discourses.' He makes the same remark in commenting on the introductory words of the Epistle to the Hebrews. Ecumenius says, in remarking on the text, *There is one God, the Father, and one Lord Jesus Christ,* that 'the Apostle speaks cautiously of the Father and the Son, calling the Father one God, lest they should think there were two Gods, and the Son one Lord, lest they should think there were two Lords.' In commenting on another text, we have the following remark of Theophylact; 'Because polytheism then prevailed, the Apostle did not speak plainly of the deity of Christ, lest he should be thought to introduce many Gods.' Again, 'As others had *made no mention* of the existence of the Logos before the ages, John taught this doctrine, lest the Logos of God should be thought to be a mere man.' "

"From these sentiments of the Fathers, it may justly be inferred, that, in their opinion, no such doctrine as the Trinity, nor even the deity of Christ, is plainly set forth in the Scriptures. They all agree that our Saviour did not thus teach, and Athanasius represents the Apostles as ignorant of his deity, till the day of Pentecost, which was some time after his death. And when instructed in this sublime truth, they are described as *studiously avoiding to divulge it,* lest offense might be given to weak minds, and to the unconverted. We must remember that these were the opinions of men, who for the most part believed in the divinity of Christ in some sense, and were solicitous to find a reason *why the Scriptures were so silent upon the subject.* The circumstance of their forming an hypothesis makes it evident, that they did not see the Trinity in the writings of the Apostles. Theophylact, it is true, and some others, believed John to have been more bold, and to have spoken more to the point in regard to this doctrine; but this is no other than saying, that it is not taught anywhere else, for John was the last of the sacred writers.

"Dr. Horsley thought to weaken the force of the above conclusion, by supposing that it was the *unbelieving Jews* only, towards whom the caution, or, as he prefers to call it, the 'sagacity' of the Apostles was exercised. To persons of the description the plainer parts of the Christian faith were preached, and when they had become partially initiated, the deeper mysteries of the Trinity were brought to their knowledge. A conjecture so forced hardly deserved the notice which Dr. Priestly condescended to give it. Where do we hear of the Apostles preaching in private? They preached openly to Jews and Gentiles, converted and unconverted. *Were not their writings intended for the instruction of the whole Christian world?* And is it to be admitted, that the most essential parts of the true faith were left out to accommodate the unbelieving Jews of that day?"

"From the Fathers we may descend to the later writers in the Catholic church, who were ardent defenders of the Trinity, but have not considered it a Scripture doctrine. On this subject Chillingworth says to a Catholic, 'As for Scripture, your men deny very plainly and frequently, that this doctrine can be proved by it.' But the dogma of the Trinity was in the creeds, and therefore must be defended. Tradition was invoked with success. but without any appeal to the authority of Scripture. Wolzogenius has collected the sentiments of several writers of the Romish Church, a few specimens of which shall be here adduced.

"Petavius, in his celebrated work on the Trinity, speaks as follows: 'Concerning the three persons of the divinity, and their essence, nothing was fully written or known, before the council of Nice, because this mystery *was not revealed and confirmed, till after the conflict between the Arians and Catholics.'* Sacroboscus tells us, also, that as the Arians appealed to the Scriptures in support of their opinions, they were not condemned by the Scriptures, but by tradition. The Jesuit Scarga writes, that the 'Apostles were at first accustomed to conceal the dogma of the Trinity on account of its difficulty;' and that Paul did not preach the deity of Christ to the Athenians, lest they should think he meant to introduce a multitude of Gods. According to Bellarmine, 'since the Arians could not be convinced out of the Scriptures, because they interpreted them differently from the Catholics, they were condemned by the unwritten word of God, piously understood.' In commenting on the text, in which Christ tells his disciples, that he has many things to say to them, which they cannot hear, Salmeron says he refers to the three persons in one God, and the two natures in Christ. Remundus warns the Lutherans and Calvinists, that if they rely on the Scriptures alone, they will be obliged to yield to modern Arians, not less than were the Fathers to the Arians of old, and he admonishes them to take refuge in tradition, and the consent of the church.

"From these sentiments of Trinitarian writers, it is obvious, that, whatever may have been their zeal for a Trinity, it was a common opinion in the Catholic Church, that this doctrine was not to be supported from the Scriptures. Let all due allowance be made for their love of tradition, it will hardly be urged, that this fondness would make them contented with resting so important a dogma on tradition alone, if they felt secure in having a just claim to the additional and irresistible weight of the revealed word of God. And least of all, as Wolzogenius observes, would they have used this argument to those, who put no confidence in any tradition not sanctioned by the plain language of the Bible. All parties held up the Scriptures as their standard, and if the Catholic doctors had believed them to contain the Trinity, it would seem the part of wisdom and policy, if nothing else, first to entrench themselves with this authority, and then to build up the outworks of tradition.

"Many distinguished Trinitarian writers among the early Lutherans, were of opinion, that their doctrine could not be found in the Old Testament. Wolzogenius mentions particularly the learned Calixtus, professor of theology at Helmstadt, and also Dreger, Leterman, Behm, and some others." [13]

Many accepting Trinitarian dogma find it difficult to accept that this system is not biblical, despite contrary admissions of some of their co-believers in it:

> There are men who seem unable to comprehend the possibility that the doctrines of their sect may make no part of the Christian revelation. What pretence, then, is there for asserting that the doctrines in question are taught in the Scriptures? Certainly they are nowhere expressly taught. It cannot even be pretended that they are. There is not a passage from one end of the Bible to the other on which one can by any violence force such a meaning as to make it affirm the proposition, "that there are three persons in the Godhead, the Father, Son, and the Holy Ghost; and these three are one God, the same in substance, equal in power and glory;" or the proposition that Christ "was and continues to be God and man in two distinct natures and one person forever." [14]

The best explanation for the doctrine of the Trinity, then, is that it is a complicated invention of mankind, which in any of the various forms it takes stands in contrast to the simplicity of most biblical concepts:

> The passages in Scripture which *seem* to cloud the *divine Unity*, and to favour the received opinions of the *distinct* deity of the holy Spirit, and also the equal Godhead of our Saviour, are *comparatively*, remarkably *few*: and even of these several are highly *figurative*, and require much explication; some are improperly translated, and others are at length found to be *Interpolations*. At any rate, it surely appears to be extremely dangerous and presumptuous to allow those few obscure and indeterminate passages, to outweigh the plain *general* testimony of the sacred Writings, which, in so many instances, proclaim the *absolute Unity* of the ALMIGHTY, in the most distinct and positive terms; making it the very basis of our Religion; and referring us directly to HIM as the Holy Object

---

[13] Dana, 176-182 (excluding footnotes from those quotes).

[14] Norton, 62-63.

of our reverential fear, and the exhaustless source of every permanent Blessing.

It may be premised, that as the Christian Religion was certainly not intended for the learned and penetrating only, but, happily, for all ranks and conditions of men; it, therefore, doth not appear at all probable, that a Doctrine, of such magnitude and consequence of the Trinity is made to be, should be involved in deep obscurity by those who were sent to give us light; scattered (as some think they perceive) by piecemeal, as it were, in their records; and left to be discovered, explained, and reconciled by the weak and discordant faculties of men; while the doctrine of one God, even *the Father*, is enforced throughout, by a testimony equally *clear* and *uniform*.

Our Saviour marks it as one of the peculiar blessings of the Gospel, that it was *preached to the Poor* (Matt. xi. 5); who would, however, have been little benefited by it, if its principal saving doctrines had really been (not such as *wayfaring men, though simple, should not err therein*, but) such as the most skillful Science or Literature have never been able to understand.[15]

When we consider the number of verses that comprise the Bible, there are relatively few brought forth in support of the doctrine of the Trinity. Entire sections of Scripture are never even advanced to support it due to the lack of a Trinitarian sense that could be assigned to the words in those sections. Even if the doctrine of a triune God were true, it is not as important as some have urged. In order for there to be equilibrium between tenets of the Bible and the importance placed upon the doctrine of the Trinity by some of its advocates, evidence for it would have to appear on virtually every page of Scripture. Scripture does not seem to keep pace with the importance that some have placed upon the doctrine of God existing in three persons:

Let us next look into the Epistles. The state of the case with respect to them is as follows. In the Epistles addressed to the Thessalonians and the Galatians, and in those of Philemon,

---

[15] Gifford, xxvii-xxviii, 17-18.

James, and 2d Timothy, it is not pretended that there is a single passage that supports the orthodox opinions. And in the rest it is not contended that there are more than a few incidental scattered passages that countenance those doctrines. An obscure inference favours them in one Epistle, and a text or two are claimed for them in another, but nothing more. Among those Epistles, I of course include those addressed to the Romans and the Hebrews. The former is the only one that contains a methodical and systematic account of the principles of the Christian faith; and in it how many texts are there that have been adduced as favourable to Trinitarianism? Merely two, and these wholly of an incidental occurrence. It is much the same in the Epistle to the Hebrews, though there, as the value and importance of Christ's death are dwelt on, we should naturally have expected that account of the economy of redemption in which, according to the current theology, the Deity of Christ enters as an essential article, and from which the value of his death is absurdly conceived to arise.[16]

Verses from the gospel of John are frequently cited in support of the doctrine of the Trinity. In considering John's style of writing and the development of ideas in his discourses, it is far-fetched to suppose that the doctrine of the Trinity or the double nature of Christ was intended. The supremacy of the Father was stressed, as was the messianic character of Jesus. With this understanding, the gospel of John makes sense. Without it, it yields utter confusion:

I have a few remarks to make in regard to the Gospel of John. It is generally supposed that the apostle John wrote his Gospel to supply what had been omitted by the other evangelists. He could not have written it to prove the human nature of our Lord; that was a self-evident truth. Nor could he have written it to prove his divine nature, for the drift and tenor of the book evidently implies an inferiority of some kind to the Father. If his main object were to prove that he had *two natures*, it is strange that he pays so little attention to it. If that were his object, would he not, as a man of common sense,

---

16 J.S. Hyndman, *Lectures on the Principles of Unitarianism* (Alnwick: 1824), 48.

much more as a man inspired by God, have so announced it, that, at least, the proposition could be stated in his own words—not by taking detached portions of the book, laying them together, and inferring what his object was—but by the clear, explicit, *unquestionable* statement of the doctrine which he was writing a book to establish. It appears plain to me, that his object was to prove the *divinity of the mission* of his beloved master; that he came from God with full power and authority to establish a new dispensation—to create all things new. And this view throws a flood of light upon the whole book, especially upon the fourteen first verses, which can thus be explained in several ways without a resort to the perplexing and impossible ideas of three perfect beings equal to one perfect being; or of two incompatible natures, with different perceptions, existing in one of those beings. For it is only on this hypothesis that the declaration of Christ respecting the day and the hour which no man knew, neither the Son—and several other declarations—can be explained without impeaching the veracity of our blessed Lord, in whom was no sin, neither was guile found in his mouth. But if the divine and human will of our Saviour were one and the same, and the will of the three persons in the Trinity—of whom he was one—was one and the same, Christ virtually said, I seek not mine own will, but the will of myself, &c. In fact, just try to read the New Testament, with this idea, which grows naturally out of Trinitarianism, in the mind, and you will see what sad confusion it makes.[17]

The inferential nature of the doctrine of the Trinity makes it fertile ground for yielding misinterpretations of Scripture. It is fair to ask, why is this doctrine, which is alleged to be monumentally important to the life of a Christian, so obscurely set forth in the Bible and impossible to be understood? If God is triune and if the Bible was dictated by God (which is another topic in and of itself), it seems that God would have plainly revealed this about Himself if it were necessary to be believed. The gospel of John is so frequently cited as

---

[17] Dana, 36-38.

containing proof of the doctrine, yet John did not write about anything approaching a three-in-one God:

> If St. John intended to teach that his Master was God, the Absolute, the Supreme God, would he not have said so plainly? Why use a circumlocution? Why all this ado about the Logos? Why not have continued to call him God throughout his Gospel, throughout his Epistles and Apocalypse, which he has never done? Why, on the contrary, write him always as "the Son"—"the Son of God"—"the Son of Man"—"the Christ?" Nay, reverting again to the close of his Gospel, why did he not there when summing up his labors, declare explicitly—"These are written that ye might believe that Jesus is God"—instead of, as he does—"These are written, that ye might believe that Jesus is the CHRIST, the SON of GOD; and that, believing," (believing that, believing so,) "ye might have life through his name?" [18]

Scattered verses from the writings of Paul are frequently used to support Trinitarian dogma. Contradicting this approach, R. S. Franks, a twentieth century Trinitarian, in commenting on the absence of a doctrinal development of the Trinity in the New Testament, especially in the writings of Paul, says:

> Neither here nor elsewhere in the New Testament is there any explanation of the mode of the Incarnation, any more than there is any explicit doctrine of the Trinity. All that was to follow from reflection upon the primitive charismatic expression of Christianity... But the problems were there all the same, and the subsequent history of Christian theology has largely been occupied in dealing with them. Paul did not say that Christ was God, but he did say that He was originally in the form of God (Phil. ii. 5).[19]

As mentioned earlier, one explanation sometimes given for the doctrine's absence from the Bible is that it was not revealed until

---

[18] Farley, 115.

[19] Dr. R. S. Franks, *The Doctrine of the Trinity* (London: Gerald Duckworth and Co. Ltd., 1953), 30, 38.

after the day of Pentecost. We are told that God chose to reveal the doctrine after this time because, among other things, the apostles themselves would not have understood it. This same argument has been applied to Moses and to Solomon, as well as to all of the Jews of the Old Testament era—they simply were not ready for it. If some explanation, some differentiating factor were offered as to why we can understand it today but they could not, we might be able to extend some credibility to the argument. But no qualifications are made. The statement is simply made and not supported, from which it is fair to conclude that such arguments are hopeful attempts meant to sustain the doctrine:

> What if it were so? What if they did not know that their Master was God, till they had shared the special illumination of Pentecost, or that which immediately followed? They assuredly, according to all critical authority, did not write their Gospels till long after this. The earliest date assigned to either of the Greek Gospels is A.D. 60. Is the marvel of the absence of the least hint or trace of any such doctrine, or of their singular reserve upon it, throughout the four, materially lessened by the supposition referred to? They knew it all the while. To them it must have been, whenever communicated, most amazing, that he with whom they represent themselves to have made so free—conversing unembarrassed with him, catechising him, contradicting him, rebuking him, and finally deserting and denying him when arrested, put through a mock trial, condemned, and crucified, was, nevertheless, their GOD! Yes, all the while they were writing their memoirs of him, they knew this, and yet, without one word of comment, record his words: "I can of mine own self do nothing"—"My Father is greater than I"—"I came not to do mine own will, but the will of Him that sent me"! On far less important points they thought it worth while to throw in a word of explanation (e.g. John 12:33; 21:19); but on this, not one. Is it credible, with their minds possessed of this grand, yet overwhelming idea of their Master, nay, knowing verily, beyond question, by direct revelation, that he was God, they could thus calmly, with no emotions of awe which we can discover, write out

their several accounts of him in such a way, that had these Gospels perished, and no other books been written by his followers, the world would have been in the dark to this hour on this momentous subject? Nay, more; take the case of John the Beloved, the last of the Evangelists, who wrote his Gospel in his old age. Is it credible that he, near the close of that Gospel, knowing at that moment as is generally understood, all that the other three Gospels contained or omitted, and having brought his own narrative down to the Resurrection of his Master—knowing at the same time that that Master was God, very and Supreme God—should nevertheless have thus summed up, and declared the great and special purpose of his work? "These are written, that ye might believe that Jesus is"—what, or who, I ask? God? No—nothing like it. A clear, broad line of separation is preserved, perfectly corresponding to all that he and the other Evangelists had before recorded, perfectly in accordance with the whole tenor and drift of the entire New Testament. "These are written, that ye might believe that Jesus is the CHRIST, the SON of GOD; and that, believing, ye might have Life through his name." [20]

Farley's comments allude to one of the damaging consequences of the Trinitarian method of biblical interpretation—it turns biblical inquiry into a sterile exercise, removing human components, such as the mindset and passions of each writer, and turns the biblical writings into emotionless statements of facts. If we are to gain a fuller sense of each writer, bearing in mind that each was a human being with his or her own mind and life experiences, we must always be mindful that each record was penned by a living, breathing human being, each with his or her own variety and intensity of passions. They did not simply take dictation from God and write the letters that would eventually be canonized as the Bible. They recorded events based on their own experiences. The Trinitarian scheme sanitizes the human element from the events the biblical writers described:

Suppose a Christian were writing an epistle to a heathen nation with the view of giving them a definite and comprehen-

---

20 Farley, 91-93.

sive view of the Christian religion, would he just incidentally allude to its grand and essential doctrines? Would he not, on the contrary, give a distinct, precise, and perspicuous account of the person of Christ as constituted both of God and man? Would he not dwell on the incarnation? Would he not make this the foundation stone of all his spiritual structure? Would he not place it in various lights? Would he not expatiate at large on the infinite condescension and glory of Immanuel, and endeavour by every possible means in his power to produce faith in the mysterious principles of his creed? That this is not the case in the New Testament Epistles, some of which are addressed to large bodies of Christians and dwell at great length on the doctrines Unitarians exclusively receive, which, if the orthodox system be correct, are of little importance compared with the others that are neglected, is to me a clear and indisputable proof that those doctrines were unknown to the Apostles.[21]

Those who wrote the various parts of the Bible were emotional and thoughtful people, cognizant that those who wanted to must be able to comprehend what they were writing. Romans 10:17 says, "Faith comes by hearing, and hearing by the Word of God." Those relying on the biblical texts obviously must interpret it in order to believe what is written there, and eminent Trinitarians have admitted the doctrine of a triune God is absent. Given such admissions, it is reasonable to conclude that the Bible is highly inefficient if it were meant to teach the doctrine of the Trinity:

> Surely an event that held so prominent and special a place in the divine intentions, and to which all the three dispensations preceding Christianity were only preparatory, had it been known, would have been the frequent theme and most rapturous topic of Moses and the prophets Is it at all consistent with the truth of the doctrine, that in all the prophetic strains confessedly almost nothing should be said on the incarnation of God Jehovah? Can we suppose it possible that this overwhelming wonder, Jehovah in human nature for the salvation

---

21 Hyndman, 48-49.

of the world, the grand, the only foundation of human hope for eternity, should not have inspired and even been the burden of their song, and that their faith in this inconceivably singular event should not have frequently burst forth in the effusions of wonder, love, and praise? Upon this we should have thought they would have with delight and ecstasy expatiated unceasingly—upon this expended all the language of loftiness and sublimity of which they were possessed. But no. On other subjects they do dwell in warm and animated strain, and upon the work and salvation of the Messiah they are not deficient in elevated and triumphant praise; but not once are their compositions inflamed with what, had they known of it, must have highly exalted them—the Deity of Jesus Christ. On this they are silent.

Go forward next to the New Testament, where all must be clear and effulgent. The Gospel of Matthew was for about thirty years after Christ the only one in existence. The writer must have intended it as an independent history of the doctrines of Jesus, and no other means of information on those subjects existed. And how many passages in it are thought to have any reference to the Deity of Christ? Only two, from which it is contended that it may be inferred, while it is directly opposed by the tenor of the whole. Now here is a Gospel professing to contain a record of the principles of Christian faith—professing to teach the doctrines of Christianity; the Deity of Jesus is supposed to be the soul and substance, the very foundation stone of the Christian religion; and yet what is the information we have on the subject? Suppose that a modern Trinitarian wrote a history of Christianity for the use of some brethren tribe who had no other means of knowing the truths of our religion, would he, think you, neglect stating the doctrines of the Trinity, the compound nature of Christ, and other points connected with them?

It is remarkable also that in the Gospel of Mark there is only one passage claimed by Trinitarians; and in that of Luke there are only two. Here, then, is a most singular case. Three of the Messiah's disciples write an account of the doctrines he taught respecting the terms of our acceptance with

God—belief in the supreme divinity of Christ is the condition of salvation, and these Gospels are ushered into the world for the purpose of teaching men all that is necessary to be believed, each independently professing to give all saving knowledge; and yet it seems they contain confessedly nothing on the grand points of Christian doctrine, except a few incidental detached passages, from which the details of orthodoxy can be deduced. Is this not a plain and decisive proof that the Deity of Jesus was a doctrine totally unknown to the writers, and consequently that Jesus never taught anything of the kind respecting himself? And since these Gospels were written under the divine inspiration, how much stronger does the argument become. How should God have allowed them to neglect that very part of the teaching of Jesus which was of the greatest importance to all generations, for whom the books were designed?

Even in the Gospel of John, which was probably written to supply the deficiencies of the other Gospels, there are not avowedly above a few passages that Trinitarians can bring into their service. The sun of the Gospel firmament does not shine even here, though John wrote his Gospel to supply the light which the others failed to communicate. I shall hereafter shew that the few passages adduced in support of orthodoxy from that Gospel are not only insufficient to prove it, but that they are all reconcilable with the general tenor of Scripture, as it relates to the sentiments maintained by us; that some of them may be brought with greater reason into the service of our cause, and are absolutely inconsistent with any other. I shall also shew not only that the general voice of Revelation supports Unitarianism, and that our doctrines are stated in the very terms; but also that in many different points of view the erroneousness of the current theology may be deduced, while in various classes of passages it is directly contradicted.

We next advert to the preaching of the Apostles, in which, if the Deity of Christ and the Trinity be doctrines of Christianity, we shall find them blazing forth in meridian splendour. Only examine, then, the sermon of Peter preaching on the day of Pentecost, and those of Paul on various occasions. See

Acts ii. 22—37. iii. 12—23. iv. 10. v. 29. x. 34—44. xiii. 32—42. xiv. 11—17. xvii. 22—32. xviii. 4—7. xxiv. 14—25. xxvi. 22—24. Now Peter and Paul must have known what Christianity was, and is there any thing in their discourses that has the smallest connexion with that popular faith which is now preached? Do the Trinitarian missionaries among the heathen preach in the manner Paul and Peter did? Are they content with stating simply that 'Jesus was a man sent to bless mankind by turning them from iniquity,' that he was raised from the dead as a pledge of our future life, and that he was appointed judge of the world? Do they not press upon the attention of their auditors the doctrine of Christ's Godhead, his wonderful incarnation and the grand purposes of it? Do they not make these topics the beginning and the end of their sermons? Do they not dwell upon them with the most solemn and pathetic emotions? Do they not earnestly beseech the heathen tribes to acquiesce in the plan of salvation accomplished by the second person in the Trinity, and threaten them with damnation if they reject their Trinitarian dogmas? All this is a decisive proof that they believe their system to be true; and so, by parity of reason, Paul, Peter, and Philip's not having preached a system similar to theirs, is an equal proof that they had no knowledge and no belief of such a system. The Apostles preached no God but the Father; and unless we suppose they were unfaithful to their trust, how can that be the Gospel which is commonly preached among us? This difficulty, no Trinitarian that I know of has ever attempted to solve, and I am confidently persuaded no one can.[22]

The absence of the doctrine from the Bible makes it comparable to other doctrines and practices that had been part of the Christian community for hundreds of years, but are now rejected by many Christians:

This tritheistic element, however, or anything really like it, is not to be found in the pages of the Scriptures,—any more than is the worship of the Virgin Mary. The one, in truth, we

---

[22] Hyndman, 44-48.

must say, has much the same foundation as the other; that is to say, it is equally founded, not in the teaching of the Bible, but on Church authority, and on the creeds which have come to us from comparatively ignorant and corrupt ages—ages too of subtle and daring speculation on divine things.[23]

There are two schools of thought among Trinitarians regarding the origin of the doctrine of the Trinity. The first is that the doctrine is not founded upon the Bible, but upon tradition. This will be discussed later in this work. The second is that the doctrine is clearly established in the Bible. In general those that rest upon tradition for the establishment of the doctrine are Catholic, while those that believe they find the doctrine in Scripture are Protestant. These divergent claims require separate consideration. In the former case one may study the history of the doctrine, including the councils and creeds, to get some perspective regarding the doctrine's development. In the latter case effort must be made in reviewing the specific claims about where it is supposedly found in the Bible in order to determine its veracity:

> I NOW come to consider the claims of the Trinity, or the grounds on which it is held as a doctrine of Revealed Religion, and especially of the Gospel. How often and how confidently has it been called preëminently the doctrine of the Bible—alleged to be written out, nay, standing out on its pages from Genesis to Revelation in such bold relief, that "he who runs may read"! And yet nothing is farther from the truth. Beginning with the Hebrew race, in all their generations, and for whose special instruction the Old Testament was compiled, they are a standing testimony that it teaches no such doctrine. With a firmness and clearness of statement which admit of neither tampering nor evasion, they hold, and always held, that their Sacred Books declare most emphatically the doctrine of the strict, simple Unity of God. Christian Trinitarian expositors, Catholic and Protestant, affirm the same; and confess, with Bishop Burnet, "that it would not

---

23 Dr. G. Vance, *The Bible and Popular Theology,* (London: Longmans, Green, Reader, and Dyer, 1871), 86.

be easy to prove the Trinity from the Old Testament." Finally, the Christian Fathers did not so much as pretend that the doctrine was plainly taught in the New Testament, or by Christ and his Apostles. On the contrary, they often use the utmost ingenuity to account for the obscurity in which it was kept by them, as well as for the total ignorance concerning it of the favored people. What Christ and his Apostles did not plainly teach, would not be likely to appear in what the latter wrote. Some of the Fathers, as Athanasius, assigned as a reason why Christ did not declare his Deity to the Jews, that the world could not yet bear the doctrine; and he affirmed that the disciples had no knowledge of it before Pentecost. Theodoret declares, that before his death, Jesus did not appear as God either to the Jews or the Apostles. And Chrysostom not only says, that Christ did not immediately reveal his Deity, but that Mary did not herself know the secret that he was God Supreme. (Serm. Maj. de fide, in Montf. Collect. Pat. vol. 2, 39.) All through the writings of these men, so far as they are preserved to us, we have their acknowledgments that even after the death of Christ his Apostles did not openly teach the doctrine; alleging the fact as a proof of their prudence and wisdom—on the one hand as regarded the Jews, who held so tenaciously to the Unity of Jehovah, and whose prejudices would be shocked; on the other, the Gentiles, who might thereby be confirmed in their polytheism. Chrysostom would have us believe that the Apostle begins his Epistle to the Hebrews by declaring that "it was God who spake by the prophets, and not that Christ himself had spoken by them, because their minds were weak, and they were not able to bear the doctrine concerning Christ." (Op. ii. 15. Ed. Hal.) Ecumenius, on the text in Paul's first Epistle to the Corinthians, eighth chapter and sixth verse—"There is one God the Father, and one Lord Jesus Christ"—says: "The Apostle speaks cautiously of the Father and Son, calling the Father One God, lest they should think there were two Gods; and the Son One Lord, lest they should think there were two Lords." (Op. iii. 289.) And Theophylact, on 1 Tim. 2:5—"For there is One God, and One Mediator between God and men, the man

Christ Jesus"—says: "Because polytheism then prevailed, the Apostle did not speak plainly of the Deity of Christ, lest he should be thought to introduce many Gods." None of these writers are later than A.D. 320. Of course, if Christ be not plainly taught by the Apostles to be God, no such Trinity as is alleged can have been.[24]

For those who contend that the doctrine was not revealed until after the day of Pentecost, those "proofs" given by their fellow Trinitarians based on verses from the Old Testament and the gospels must be received pessimistically, if not entirely rejected. If one finds the doctrine blazing forth in the whole Bible, and another finds it only in the records of events that occurred after the day of Pentecost, and others do not find it in the Bible at all, how can this doctrine be trusted?

Trinitarians of the Protestant Faith have confessed the obscurity of the Sacred Text upon this subject. The zealous French Reformer, Jurieu, though holding that, to deny the Trinity, was to be guilty of one of the deadliest heresies, allows, in his Pastoral Letters, that it was not known in its proper shape till the early part of the fourth century, at the Council of Nice—nay, till the Council of Constantinople—and even proves, *from the Fathers*, that during the first three centuries it was the universal opinion, that the Son was not equal to the Father, nor his existence of the same duration.

Bishop Smallridge, of the English Church, has this language: "It must be owned that the doctrine of the Trinity, as it is proposed in our Articles, our Liturgy, our Creeds, is not in so many words taught us in the Holy Scriptures. What we profess in our prayers we nowhere read in Scripture, that the One God, the One Lord, is not only one Person, but Three Persons in one substance. There is no such text in Scripture as this, that 'the Unity in Trinity, and the Trinity in Unity, is so to be worshipped.' No one of the inspired writers hath expressly affirmed that in the Trinity none is afore or after other, but the whole three persons are co-eternal together and co-equal."

---

[24] Farley, 32-24.

But the most striking acknowledgment upon this point from a learned Protestant, was made in a speech delivered to the Irish House of Lords by Dr. Clayton, Bishop of Clogher, on the second of February, 1756. He said: "The strongest abettors of the Nicene Creed do not so much as pretend that the doctrine of the consubstantiality of the Father and the Son is to be found in Scriptures, but only in the writings of some of the Primitive Fathers. And I beseech your Lordships to consider whether it is not absolutely contradictory to the fundamental principles on which the Reformation of the Religion from Popery is built, to have any doctrine established as a rule of faith which is founded barely on Tradition, and is not plainly and clearly revealed in the Scriptures?" I cannot refrain from adding what has a strong bearing on this entire discussion, that he said: "As to the ecclesiastical history of this and the following century, (the third and the fourth,) I must inform your Lordships that all those books which were published in opposition to the decrees of the Council of Nice have been destroyed—so that all our information comes from the other side. And of all those histories suffered to come down to our hands, I do not know of one, except Eusebius of Caesarea, (who says little on this subject,) but what is so filled with falsehood, vagaries or contradictions, that their veracity is not to be depended on." [25]

An unbiblical doctrine cannot be a fundamental article of Christian faith. I wish such statements were not necessary, but in a theology that is lacking reasonableness, occasions arise in which the most obvious statements must be articulated. Statements such as "three does not equal one," as basic as they may be, do not seem to be obviated by any principle within the realm of Trinitarian exegesis. The most obvious must be stated at times in order to refute the most absurd. So the doctrine of the Trinity, due, at least in part, to its unreasonableness, cannot be a fundamental article of Christian faith:

As a fundamental doctrine of our religion, it is one which they must have been constantly employed in teaching. If it

---

[25] Farley, 36-38.

were a doctrine of Christianity, the evidence for it would burst from every part of the New Testament in a blaze of light. Can any one think that we should be left to collect the proof of a fundamental article of our faith, and the evidence of incomparably the most astonishing fact that ever occurred upon our earth, from some expressions scattered here and there, the greater part of them being dropped incidentally; and that really one of the most plausible arguments for it would be found in the omission of the Greek article in four or five texts? [26]

If the doctrine were as true and necessary as some say, it stands to reason that the corresponding evidence for it would be everywhere in the Bible. The fact that the evidence for it is scattered piecemeal raises a strong presumption against the doctrine:

Though Christians have insisted upon the fundamental character of this doctrine, they find it utterly impossible to state it in the language of Scripture. A human formula is necessarily the vehicle for its expression. Though the Scriptures, as we often affirm, have a peculiar directness and simplicity of phrase, and excel all other forms of literature in the conciseness and vigor with which they express truths and precepts, they nevertheless fail to furnish one single sentence which can be used in a creed to announce the Trinity. Yes, this so-called primary and all-essential article of the Christian faith,—"the foundation of all our communion with God,"—cannot be uttered in any divine oracle, but must look to uninspired men for an expression. No announcement of it can be quoted from the lips of prophet or apostle, or from Him who spake as never man spake.[27]

One of the reasons for the unintelligibility of the doctrine of a triune God is that it is not possible to state it in the language of Scripture. It is one thing for someone who is careless not to state Christian precepts in biblical language, it is quite another to be unable to state

---

[26] Norton, 84.

[27] Ellis, 121.

them in biblical language. The former does not necessarily rule out the veracity of a doctrine. The latter does. The fact that the doctrine of the Trinity cannot be stated in biblical language negates any claim that it is a fundamental article of Christianity:

> Holy Scriptures, then, being our witness—and our appeal lies there—Holy Scriptures nowhere affirms the doctrine. I say this deliberately. The direct, positive, literal, express declarations of Scripture affirm the opposite. "There is One God; and there is none other but He." No creed in Christendom expresses the doctrine in Scripture language, for the simple reason that it is impossible. Its stoutest advocates, who most insist on calling it a plain doctrine of the Bible, who are most ready to demand faith in it as a Fundamental, have never defined, because they cannot define it, in the words of Scripture. In saying this, it is with full knowledge that our Trinitarian brethren profess to hold, nevertheless, the doctrine of the Divine Unity; nor would I cast the least doubt or imputation on their sincerity in that profession. But they hold it in such a way as seems to me virtually to deny, and practically do it away, by merging it in this great "mystery." I repeat that I do not object to the Trinity for its mere mysteriousness. As I have already said, I find mystery every where. But I do object to its unscripturalness, self-contradictoriness, absurdity, and polytheistic aspect. I can see it in no other light. I can think of nothing more absurd—nothing which savours more of polytheism. That many Trinitarians conscientiously and honestly, as well as devoutly, adore the Trinity as a Divine mystery, I gladly admit; but they make or find a mystery where I do not and cannot. In me, therefore, it would be plain polytheism to worship the Three Persons each as God; and all who do so worship, are solemnly bound to see it by their allegiance to the Truth—"the Truth as it is in Jesus"—that they have express Scripture warrant. Moreover, I say, nay, I insist, and on this am ready to join issue, that they have no right in this or in any case to set that up as a fundamental article of Faith, to make that a condition of holding the Christian name, or of Christian fellowship, which is not taught with the utmost di-

rectness, explicitness, and perspicuity, in the Christian Scriptures. And such is not the Trinity.

Again, the various and contradictory forms of stating and expounding the doctrine, the different senses in which it is accepted and held, raise a violent presumption against the doctrine as belonging to Christ's holy Gospel; suggest and furnish reasons for the weightiest doubts of its truth; and, at the very least, stamp it as unimportant, and refute all pretension to its being fundamental and essential. Any doctrine essentially belonging to Revealed Religion, would be clearly stated in the Records of that Revelation; it would be so clearly stated there, that nobody could mistake it; it would be one and uniform in all ages of the Church, and everywhere in Christendom.[28]

Most defenders of the doctrine of the Trinity do not stop at merely pronouncing it a fundamental article of faith. Just as Miethe (quoted earlier) does, there are many who declare that those who do not believe it are heretics and therefore not Christian. This has been, and still is, a common charge of Trinitarians against Unitarians:

My dear Sir, why should you seek to make my heart sad, when the Lord has not made it so? I thank God that such assertions cannot deprive me of that peace of conscience which I feel at this moment; but such allusions to my venerable parents as the one you have made above, do make me sad indeed. God knows how it has wrung my heart to give them pain; but He also knows that I could not conscientiously act otherwise than I have done. And what right have you to say that I have given up my allegiance to our common Lord? You require, before you will allow to me the title of Christian, far more than Christ or his apostles—the establishers of this religion— ever required. Now what right has any one to do this? In the New Testament I constantly find that men were commanded to believe that the Messiah was the Son of God; but in the present day a very different faith is required of us. Instead of saying, "I believe that thou art the Christ, the Son of the

---

[28] Farley, 39-41, 53.

living God," men are required to say, "I believe that thou art the living God himself." The former is the Unitarian faith, the latter the Trinitarian; which of them is the more scriptural belief, it appears to me is very plain.

You cannot produce one passage of Scripture in which the primitive teachers of Christianity required a belief in Jesus as the Supreme Being. They called upon men to believe and confess that Jesus was the Christ; that is, the Anointed; he who was to come; who was typified and promised throughout the Old Testament, as the great Mediator between God and man. He was to be received as the glorious Saviour of the world—anointed and sent of God for this purpose, and therefore clothed with the authority of God himself. A knowledge of his original nature was never made a requisite before men could receive the salvation he came to bring. It was enough that they recognized his divine authority, and joyfully submitted to it. And what right have modern divines to require more than their Master ever did? [29]

It must be at least a little disconcerting to Trinitarians that no verse says God is three. The number *three* is not assigned to God in any way except in one verse, 1 John 5:7, which is a known forgery:

No passage of Scripture asserts that God is three.

If it be asked what I intend to qualify by the numeral *three*, I answer, anything which the reader pleases. *There is no Scripture which asserts that God is three persons, three agents, three beings, three Gods, three spirits, three subsistences, three modes, three offices, three attributes, three divinities, three infinite minds, three somewhats, three opposites, or three in any sense whatever.*[30]

It is fairly clear to an unbiased person that the doctrine of the Trinity is unbiblical, which gives its defenders abundant difficulty in every attempt at explaining it.

---

[29] Dana, 99-100.

[30] Charles Morgridge, *The True Believers Defence Against Charges Preferred by Trinitarians* (Boston: Benjamin Greene, 1837), 32.

THE DOCTRINE OF THE TRINITY IS INEXPLICABLE

Because the doctrine of the Trinity cannot be explained reasonably to anybody seeking to understand it, it is referred to as a mystery. There are those who have mastered the terminologies employed in this branch of theology, but they are still faced with the reality that the doctrine cannot be explained well enough to be understood. It must ultimately be designated a mystery, which demonstrates its inexplicability and incomprehensibility. Nothing of substance is transferred in explanations of the doctrine of the Trinity. The following quote of Rev. Thomas Hill, an ardent defender of the doctrine of the Trinity, illustrates this point:

> The Sacred Three have perfect union with each other, inasmuch as they are three distinct coequal Persons, each of whom possesses the same undivided essence. The God-man Christ Jesus has perfect union with the Father and with the Holy Ghost, inasmuch as he is the same in person with the second coequal, coeternal, and coessential Person of the Godhead. The Father doeth the works of the God-man in him, not personally, but by the Holy Ghost. Neither is it the Father, essentially considered, who works the works of Christ by the Holy Ghost, but the Father considered in his covenant office, as the depositary of the will of the sacred and coequal three.[31]

Now what can this possibly convey to one seeking to know about God? It means nothing, and therefore cannot be applied in the life of a Christian. Its effect is to make God more distant from us. Some degree of comprehension is required before assent can be given, and Trinitarians are faced with the simple truth that cogent explanations of what it is for God to be triune cannot be given because its advocates do not understand what it is they believe. It is simply impossible to explain what one does not understand:

> We trust that as a body of Christians, it is, and ever will be our desire to avoid offending against the Unity of the Deity,

---

31 Rev. Thomas Hill, *The Doctrine of the Trinity Vindicated* (London: F.C. and J. Rivington, 1820), 13.

so explicitly revealed in Scripture, and to hold fast the belief of one God, in one being. The Trinitarian thinks he can believe a God in three persons, without destroying the Unity of the Deity—be it so. But as he cannot explain the conceptions of his own mind to the satisfaction of those who enquire into his doctrine—as he cannot express his own notions, without appearing to destroy the Unity of the Deity—let him learn to forbear with his Unitarian brother who clings to the more literal interpretation of Scripture, who is fearful of offending the Deity by representing him to be what he is not, especially since the Trinitarian cannot produce a single passage in the Bible, in which his doctrine is taught, in the language he employs in stating it.[32]

There are certain phrases in Trinitarian thought that may not arrest the attention of the hearer because they have been heard so frequently. When one gives an "advanced" description of God, such as Rev. Thomas Hill's above, it is obvious that the foundations of Trinitarian thought lead to more abstract conceptions of God. Trinitarians ride a slippery slope from the beginnings of a theology toward more nonsensical conceptions of God. The ultimate resting points are inanities predicated upon some notion of mystery. It is as if those who stop at the plea of mystery seem to recognize that if they were to continue to develop this theology it would require great invention, perhaps exceeding their own innovative abilities, or yield nothing that can be understood. Or both. The explanations given to support it are of no benefit because we will not be able to comprehend them and cannot truly assent to them. In the final analysis the doctrine is still not understood, so the explanations of the past sixteen hundred years have not made this doctrine any clearer than when it was first being developed.

It is an option for us to us to give up the reasoning ability and intuition with which the human race has been endowed, but we do so at great risk. "Prove all things" it says in 1 Thes. 5:21. How can this be accomplished if we are unwilling to rule out that which is unreasonable, contradictory and incomprehensible? According to the

---

[32] Thomas, 14.

Trinitarian scheme, the Bible becomes a puzzle, a maze that invites navigating one's way without sound reasoning and, perhaps worse, those involved in such practices encourage others to continue in the practice.

There are those who have developed their Trinitarian faith to such an extent that they accept its incomprehensibility. For some, the doctrine of the Trinity is believed to be true because they consider it to be a foregone conclusion. Reasons have thus been developed that make it acceptable to believe doctrines without subjecting them to any form of scrutiny. Bishop Beveridge, a Trinitarian, advanced the following reasoning:

> I ever did, and ever shall, look upon those apprehensions of God to be the truest, whereby we apprehend him to be the most incomprehensible, and that to be the most true of God, which seems most impossible to us. Upon this ground, therefore, it is that the mysteries of the Gospel, which I am less able to conceive, I think myself the more obliged to believe; especially this mystery of mysteries, the Trinity in Unity, and Unity in Trinity, which I am so far from being able to comprehend, or indeed to apprehend, that I cannot set myself seriously to think of it, or to screw up my thoughts a little concerning it, but I immediately lose myself as in a trance or ecstasy. That God the Father should be one perfect God of himself, God the Son one perfect God of himself, and God the Holy Ghost one perfect God of himself; and yet that these three should be but one perfect God of himself, so that one should be perfectly three, and three perfectly one; that the Father, Son, and Holy Ghost should be three, and yet but one; but one, and yet three,—oh heart-amazing, thought-devouring, unconceivable mystery! Who cannot believe it to be true of the glorious Deity?[33]

The appropriateness of the Bishop's passionate response depends upon whether his conception of God is true. If it is not, then his emotional, self-induced trance or ecstasy is misguided. If the Trinity is not a biblical doctrine, then his approach must be wrong. His first

---

[33] Bishop Beveridge, *Private Thoughts on Religion*, Art. III. 52-53; quoted in Wilson, 320.

principle, which is that he considers those things that are impossible to be the truest, is foolish. This principle opens one up to believing anything which would ordinarily be rejected. Among the things which the mind rightly rejects are contradictions and absurdities. In courses on logic, this is related to the most elemental principle or thought and language, which is known as the Law of Contradiction. This states that something cannot be true and not true because it contradicts itself, and breaks down all meaning of words and thoughts. If I say I ate an apple and you ask me how was it, and I respond that I don't know because I did not eat an apple, you would be correct in being bewildered because I will have contradicted myself. So if, according to some Trinitarian methodologies, it is true that those things that appear to us to be impossible or inconceivable are the truest, then it follows that those things that are the most obvious to us are the most false, and contradictions are in play. Whatever we conceive to be true has become false, and whatever we conceive to be impossible or inconceivable is what we must consider to be true! Where are we to stop with this? What could not be forced into one's mind on such grounds? Contrary to the Bishop's ideology, we are better equipped to recognize mistakes on more reasonable grounds than those the Bishop imposed on himself.

THE DOCTRINE OF THE TRINITY IS UNINTELLIGIBLE

Simply put, there is no way to make sense of the collection of contradictory propositions that comprise Trinitarian thought. For example, the proposition that Jesus is a man is intelligible. The proposition that Jesus is God is also intelligible. But they cannot both be true. When it is proposed that Jesus is both God and man, the mind recoils. When it is proposed that any being, whether God or otherwise, is three persons in one, the same reaction occurs. It is impossible to form manageable conceptions of what those propositions mean, and Trinitarian dogma is carried on this undercurrent of unintelligibility. Dr. Barrow, a learned Trinitarian, wrote:

> There is one divine nature or essence, common unto three Persons incomprehensibly united, and ineffably distinguished; united in essential attributes, distinguished by pe-

culiar idioms and relations; all equally infinite in every divine perfection, each different from the other in order and manner of subsistence; that there is a mutual inexistence of one in all, and all in one; a communication without deprivation or diminution in the communicant; an eternal generation, and an eternal procession, without precedence or succession, without proper causality or dependence; a Father imparting his own, and the Son receiving his Father's life, and a Spirit issuing from both, without any division or multiplication of essence.[34]

As accustomed as I am to parsing thoughts and extracting possible meaning from statements, and as many times as I've read Dr. Barrow's comments to elicit some meaning, they continue to appear to me as mere theological jargon. There is nothing in this but the advancement of nonsensical philosophies. This is an example of what the foundational principles of Trinitarian theology result in when carried to the extreme. If there is anything of practical benefit in his commentary it would be difficult to detect, as Morgridge writes:

> To one who seeks for ideas with words, what can all this signify? It is totally unintelligible. It is a mere jumble of words without sense or meaning. Professor Stewart, one of the most learned Trinitarians in the world, who stands at the head of his profession, speaking of the definitions of person, or distinction in the Godhead, says, "I do not, and cannot understand them. And to a definition I cannot consent, still less *defend* it; until I do understand what it signifies. I have no hesitation in saying, that my mind is absolutely unable to elicit any distinct and certain *ideas*, from any of the definitions of *person* in the Godhead, which I have ever examined." [35]

For Trinitarians to assert that they believe particular doctrines is one thing; to assert them to be true yet another; to claim that those who do not believe them will be deprived of eternal life is quite another and is what has contributed to the ugliness that has become

---

[34] Dr. Barrow, *Barrow's Works*, Vol. iv. 307, London, 1831: quoted in Morgridge, 17.

[35] Morgridge, 37.

part of the landscape of the Unitarian-Trinitarian debate. Holding one's views as part of the journey of life is not only normal, it is a valuable part of the contributions we make to one another's lives when we share ideas. But the harsh claims of some regarding the depravity of others sets an entirely different tone, and is unwarranted. But claims against the Unitarian view of God and Jesus are made, however, in the face of admissions that the doctrine cannot be understood. Time after time the doctrine of the Trinity is called a mystery because its advocates consider it to be unintelligible. Had the doctrine been intelligible, by definition it would be capable of comprehension. Since it is not, we must conclude that the doctrine lacks the desirable quality of being founded upon true ideas:

> And why cannot Trinitarians be understood? Is it not because the writers themselves had no ideas to express? St. Augustine being questioned on this subject, said, "Human learning is scanty, and affords not terms to express it; it is therefore answered, *three persons*, not as if that was to the purpose, but somewhat must be said, and we must not be silent."—*Aug. de Trin. L. 5, c. 9.*

> This is partly true and partly false. It is true that he who says, God is three persons, does not speak "to the purpose." But it is not true that the poverty of language, or the scantiness of learning, makes it impossible for Trinitarians to be understood. It is because "somewhat must be said," and they talk words without ideas. One who has "distinct and certain ideas," can express them. When I say God is a spiritual, self-existent, and eternal Being, I know what I mean, I have ideas. Others, too, can elicit ideas from my words. If Trinitarians had ideas of the doctrine of the Trinity, that is, if they meant *any thing* by it, they could certainly tell what they meant. Others, too, could understand them. They could "elicit ideas from their words."

> Bishop Tillotson, speaking of the "jargon and canting language" of the schoolmen, says, "I envy no man the understanding these phrases; but to me they seem to signify nothing but to have been words invented by idle and conceited men, which a great many ever since, lest they should

seem to be ignorant, would seem to understand; but I wonder most, that men, when they have amused and puzzled themselves and others with hard words, should call this *explaining things*."—*Tillotson's Works, Vol.* vi. 383.

"The language of Scripture is the language of common sense; the plain, artless language of nature. Why should writers adopt such language as renders their meaning obscure; and not only obscure, but unintelligible; and not only unintelligible, but utterly lost in the strangeness of their phraseology."—*Dr. Dwight.*

"Except ye utter by the tongue words easy to be understood, how shall it be known what is spoken? for ye shall speak into the air."—*St. Paul.*

But Trinitarians render the way to heaven obscure not only by a single definition, but by definitions essentially contradictory. As soon as it is admitted that the terms of salvation are not sufficiently defined in the Bible, and that men have a right to attempt an improvement of the Gospel, the church is liable to be perplexed and embarrassed with as many different editions of it as there are writers. One man has the same right to claim a hearing that another has. This right has not been overlooked by Trinitarians, who have furnished us with a great variety of contradictory hypotheses, each *professedly* the true one.

Mr. Baxter says, "Abundance of heretics have troubled the church with their self-devised opinions about the Trinity, and the person and nature of Christ. And I am loath to say how much many of the orthodox have troubled it also, with their self-conceited, misguided, and uncharitable zeal against those they judged heretics." [36]

There have always been defenders of orthodoxy who seek to label a group as heretical, and the search for heresy is always successful. In the search, though, what has been overlooked is that intelligibility is lacking in Trinitarian thought. We can see from the following quote that some Trinitarians consider intelligibility to be an enemy of truth:

---

[36] Morgridge, 17-19.

Methinks there be not impossibilities in religion enough for an active faith: the deepest mysteries ours contains have not only been illustrated, but maintained, by syllogism and the rule of reason. I love to lose myself in a mystery,—to pursue my reason to an *O altitudo!* 'Tis my solitary recreation to pose my apprehension with those involved enigmas and riddles of the Trinity, incarnation, and resurrection. I can answer all the objections of Satan and my rebellious reason with that odd resolution I learned of TERTULLIAN, *"Certum est quia impossibile est"* [It is certain because impossible]. I desire to exercise my faith in the difficultest point; for to credit ordinary and visible objects is not faith, but persuasion.... This, I think, is no vulgar part of faith, to believe a thing not only above, but contrary to, reason, and against the arguments of our proper senses.[37]

Sir Thomas Browne placed reason in the same destructive context as Satan. I can only surmise that he meant that both are obstacles to a constructive faith. But he himself used argumentation, which requires deliberate and constructed thoughts, to dethrone reason. This sort of argument is self-defeating, among other things.

It is a common belief that God and His communications to mankind are mysteries that we fallible humans cannot fully comprehend, and that there is such a large chasm between God and man that to assume we can fully understand Him would be the height of arrogance. I share in that belief. Nevertheless, for those endeavoring to adhere to the Bible in forming ideas about God, John 17:3 says: "And this is life eternal, that they might know thee, the only true God, and Jesus Christ whom thou hast sent." From this it seems possible to know God and Jesus and to possess an active knowledge of them. We need not—indeed, *cannot*—invent contradictory propositions and then assent to them in order to have faith.

On the Trinitarian scheme, faith is, at least in part, the means by which we come to accept those things that our "rebellious" reason would otherwise reject. This is a misguided conception of faith. Faith

---

37 Sir Thomas Browne, *Religio Medici*, sect. 9, 10; in *Works*, vol. ii. 332, 334-335; quoted in Wilson, 319-320.

is not something we conjure up or employ when our mind recoils at some proposition, essentially operating as a mechanism that serves to override what our minds tell us cannot be true. Faith is an exercise of the understanding. Faith is now used by some as a means of accepting absurdities and launch themselves into a realm where understanding is not coveted. This is the opposite of what faith is, which is to assent to (i.e. have faith in) what we understand. Proverbs 16:22 supports that contention: "Understanding is a wellspring of life to them that have it, but the instruction of fools is folly."

In the defense of Trinitarianism, the unintelligibility and self-contradictoriness of the various ideas about God are present. The following are some examples of these two common features of Trinitarian thought:

> Dr. Wallis, of the English Church, holds, that "The Father, Son, and Holy Ghost, are no more three distinct intelligent persons than the God of Abraham, of Isaac, and of Jacob, is three Gods; the three Persons are only three external relations of God to his creatures, as Creator, Redeemer, and Sanctifier." But Dr. South says: "The three Persons are internal relations of the Deity to itself." Dr. Hopkins warns us that "It must be carefully observed, that when the word Person is applied to the Father, Son, and Holy Ghost, as three distinct persons, it does not import the same distinction as when applied to men." While on the other hand, Bishop Waterland calls them "proper, distinct persons, entirely equal to, and independent of, each other; yet making up one and the same being." Archbishop Secker says: "Since there is not a plurality of Gods, and yet the Son and Spirit are each of them God not less than the Father, it plainly follows, that they are in a manner, by us inconceivable, so united to Him, that these Three are One; but still in a manner equally inconceivable, so distinguished from Him, that no one of them is the other." Bishop Burnet's statement is this: "If I say the Father, Son, and Holy Spirit be three, and every one distinctly God, it is true; but if I say, they be three, and every one a distinct God, it is false. I may say, the divine persons are distinct in the divine nature; but I cannot say, the divine nature is divided into the divine

persons. I may say, God the Father is one God—and the Son is God—and the Holy Ghost is God; but I cannot say, the Father is one God—the Son another God—and the Holy Ghost a third God. I may say, the Father begat another, who is God; yet I cannot say, he begat another God. And from the Father and the Son proceedeth another, who is God; yet I cannot say, from the Father and the Son proceedeth another God." Bishop Gastrell takes the ground that "The three names of God, the Father, Son, and Holy Ghost, must denote a threefold difference or distinction belonging to God, but such as is consistent with the unity and simplicity of the divine nature: for each of these includes the whole idea of God, and something more." Upon which it has been well remarked that, according to this view, "The Father includes the whole idea of God, and something more—the Son includes the whole idea of God, and something more—the Holy Ghost includes the whole idea of God, and something more; while altogether, the Father, Son, and Holy Ghost, make one entire God, and no more!" Bishop Burgess insists, that "the Father is a Person, but not a Being; the Son, a Person, but not a Being; the Holy Ghost, a Person, but not a Being. And these three non-entities (!) make one perfect Being." The celebrated Bishop Heber, one of the most brilliant members of the English hierarchy, discovered, that "The Father is the First person in the Trinity; the Archangel Michael, the Second; and the Angel Gabriel, the Third." The learned Barrow goes a trifle more into details, and says: "There is one divine nature or essence common to the three Persons, incomprehensibly united and ineffably distinguished; united in essential attributes—distinguished by peculiar relations; all equally infinite in every divine perfection; each different from the others in order and manner of subsistence. There is a mutual existence of one in all, and all in one; a communication, without any deprivation or domination in the communicant; an eternal generation and an eternal procession, without proper causality or dependence; a Father imparting his own—the Son receiving the Father's life—and a Spirit issuing from both, without any division or multiplication of essence. These are notions which may well puzzle our reason, in conceiving how they agree; but should not stagger our faith in asserting that they are true." And, to close my citations of statements and expositions by eminent men of this great dogma, let me place on record in these pages the words of Henry Ward Beecher: "My God? Christ Jesus is his name. All that there is of God to me is bound up in that name. A dim and shadowy effluence rises from Christ, and that I am taught to call the Father. A yet more tenuous and invisible film of thought arises, and that is the Holy Spirit. But neither are to me aught tangible, restful, accessible." While Dr. Nehemiah Adams, of Boston, says: " 'Do you worship three?' is often asked. Surely we do, nor do we strive to make them appear like one. They have specific offices; we have specific wants, which lead us appropriately to worship, now one, now another, now the third."

I stop not to analyze any of these various and utterly contradictory opinions. But I ask whether the various and contradictory ways in which the doctrine is stated and expounded do not raise a strong presumption at the outset against the doctrine itself? One thing must be granted—all of them cannot be true, for they make essentially different and inconsistent doctrines. And if so, surely it is possible that even admitting the Trinity to be a Scriptural doctrine, the true, the only true, the absolutely orthodox mode of receiving and holding the doctrine, remains to this hour unknown, since every one of all that have been ventured may be false.[38]

As we have seen, many learned Trinitarians have formed their own version of the doctrine of the Trinity, but there is no consensus as to what it is they collectively believe. It is as if it were acceptable to start with the premise that Jesus is God, then go anywhere from that point without regard to either common sense or the agreement of others who started with the same premise. But this is what results when a conclusion is assumed to be true, and afterwards evidence for it is sought from wherever the remotest hints of it are believed or hoped to exist.

---

[38] Farley, 19-22.

As with any argument, irrespective of subject matter, all of the premises may be evaluated regarding their individual content, and, as importantly, how well they relate to the other premises. Each premise, or statement, must convey something of substance in order to be part of an argument and, as previously stated, cannot contradict itself. In Trinitarian thought, the statement "Jesus is God" conveys intelligible meaning. I understand what is being said well enough to accept or reject it. If I don't understand what is meant, I may ask for further clarification, which is also common in trying to understand someone's argument. But when other Trinitarian statements are added to the idea that "Jesus is God," or that God exists as three-in-one, it becomes impossible to merge them into a larger, comprehensible idea because they contain so many contradictions:

> The proposition that God is a Spirit, meaning one pure and underived mind, is possible, is conceivable, is probable, is agreeable to the analogy, reason and nature of things. But that God is a Trinity of Persons, is supported by no analogy, is inconceivable, contradictory, and incredible. So that, besides the difficulties in words, arising from the fewness of the passages in which it is found only by inference, and its contradiction to a much greater number of texts, where the Unity is expressly, and in so many words declared, it encounters and involves insuperable difficulties in things, the very things which it asserts. To overcome such difficulties in the nature of the proposition which it sustains, the number of passages in which it is found ought to be greater, and their meaning more plain, than those which declare the opposite. Whereas they are incomparable fewer, and do not in so many words declare the doctrine at all.[39]

If the number of passages in Scripture supporting Trinitarian dogma were greater, there would most likely be fewer differing interpretations regarding God and Jesus. It would be a system rooted in the texts and therefore limited by them. The converse is also true; any doctrine not found in Scripture would have many explanations offered in support of it, and these would at times contradict each other.

---

[39] Burnap, 43-44.

The latter is what is observable in Trinitarian thought, and because it isn't securely grounded in the texts or reason, it is quite natural that the accounts would be as numerous and contradictory as they are. The same is not true, however, of Unitarianism, since there are so many verses that define it. Unitarians are voluntarily and necessarily limited in the scope of opinions about God, so Unitarian accounts of God are more agreeable with one another and with Scripture. Agreement among people doesn't make a belief right, whether Unitarian or Trinitarian, but a variety of opinions among those who believe a given thing is emblematic of a lack of a solid basis, whether textual, rational, or both.

Due to the common theme within the writings of the Old and New Testaments that there is only one God, most ardent Trinitarians assert that Trinitarianism is monotheistic, since they claim to believe in only one God. This cannot be true since Trinitarianism is a system that posits a belief in three Gods (as has been admitted by some), despite the claim that the three are somehow, inexplicably, one. The two views are simply incompatible, despite the myriad attempts to merge them:

> For we have to object once more, that the Scriptures bear a positive testimony against this doctrine of the Trinity, by insisting upon the absolute Unity of God. Trinitarians think that they recognize the force of these reiterated and emphatic assertions of Scripture by afterwards gathering up into one God those whom they have made three divine persons. But as the analysis was forced, the synthesis must be strained. As the ingenuity of the human mind could alone devise the triplicate distinction, the same ingenuity has to nullify its own work to construct the Unity. Trinitarians do indeed assure us there is no incongruity, nothing inconceivable, in the essential substance of their doctrinal statement. But we must be judges as to that matter, certainly so far as our own minds are concerned. Our minds assure us that violence must be done to the most explicit statements of every page of Scripture, before it can be made to yield to us the doctrine of the Trinity.[40]

---

40 Ellis, 128-129.

The various Trinitarian systems of belief required a great deal of ingenuity to construct. The terminology and the obfuscation of common language are constructs of the human mind rather than, as is alleged, a direct revelation from God. The mass of contradictions involved in the construction of the systems have rendered them unintelligible. For example, in Mark 1:12-13 we read that Jesus was tempted with evil, yet in James 1:13 we are told that God cannot be tempted with evil. John 1:18 says that no man has seen God at any time, yet it is historically understood that Jesus was seen by thousands. Due to the widespread acceptance of this doctrine there is work to be done, as Sir Isaac Newton writes:

> As the few and obscure prophecies concerning Christ's first coming were for setting up the Christian religion, which all nations have since corrupted; so the many and clear prophecies concerning the things to be done at Christ's second coming, are not only for predicting, but also for effecting, a recovery and re-establishment of the long-lost truth, and setting up a kingdom wherein dwells righteousness.[41]

The unintelligibility of the doctrine of the Trinity, at least to my mind, has possibly kept untold millions from pursuing Christianity, or at least from being able to make sense of it. Jews overwhelmingly reject the doctrine because, among other reasons, they cannot consider the Messiah as God. This would be a violation of the commands given to Moses and Israel. There are many Jews and Muslims, in addition to others, who reject Christianity partly because of the absurdities of Trinitarianism:

> In the Muslim states the Christians and the Jews were given a special place because they were 'people of the Book'; that is, they shared in the Old Testament. The Christians were often accused of tampering with it, making it mean what it could not mean; and, because they talked of God as a Trinity, of not really believing in one God.[42]

---

[41] Sir Isaac Newton, quoted by W.J. Fox in his *Course of Lectures on Subjects Connected With the Corruption, Revival, and Future Influence of Genuine Christianity* (London: G. Smallfield, Pub., 1819), front cover.

[42] Owen Chadwick, *A History of Christianity* (New York: St. Martin's Press, 1995), 128.

So most Christians are rightly accused of not believing in one God in spite of the exertion of energy in finding evidence to support this theological and masterful absurdity. Along with this ostensible evidence come brand new terminologies designed to describe God in ways that fit the desired conclusion, which is not argumentation but prejudice.

TERMINOLOGY PECULIAR TO THE DOCTRINE OF THE TRINITY

Trinitarian dogma requires a vernacular that is not found in the Bible or in any other realm of human experience. Given that many seek proof for its establishment in the biblical texts, the absence of concomitant language detracts from its appeal. It is well known, for example, that the word *Trinity* itself is not in the Bible. What is not widely known (or at least not widely published) is that the early church borrowed terminologies from the philosophers to express the doctrine:

> In order to articulate the dogma of the Trinity, the Church had to develop its own terminology with the help of certain notions of philosophical origin: "substance," "person" or "hypostasis," "relation," and so on. In doing this, she did not submit the faith to human wisdom, but gave a new and unprecedented meaning to these terms, which from then on would be used to signify an ineffable mystery, "infinitely beyond all that we can humanly understand." [43]

If, according to the Catholic Church's own admission, this doctrine is "infinitely beyond all that we can humanly understand," how can we be sure that this new terminology, which is founded upon "notions of philosophical origins," is accurate in its depiction of God? The doctrine of the supremacy of the Father carries with it none of this difficulty, and certainly requires no new language to explain or comprehend:

> Now, in direct opposition to this great, fundamental doctrine

---

[43] *The Catechism of the Catholic Church* (New York: Doubleday, 1995), § 251, 74.

of the simple Unity of God, the vast majority of the Christian Church accepts, and for long centuries has accepted, the mysterious, irrational, unscriptural dogma of a Trinity of Persons in the Godhead. But not only is the dogma unscriptural, which is our cardinal objection to it, the very term "Trinity" is not of Scriptural derivation; and, as all who are familiar with the Scriptures know, is not to be found there, nor any word or term corresponding to it.[44]

The fact that a new language needed to be invented in order to express the doctrine is part of the problem with this amorphous theology, as those employing this new language presume that biblical language is inadequate in its accounts of God and Jesus. This new language also throws the Bible student into bewilderment. Archbishop Tillotson, a Trinitarian, writes:

Great difficulty, I acknowledge, there is in the explication of it, in which the farther we go beyond what God has thought fit to reveal to us in Scripture concerning it, the more we are entangled; and that which men are pleased to call an explaining of it, does, in my apprehension, often make it more obscure, that is, less plain than it was before; which does not so very well agree with a pretence of explication.... It cannot be denied but that these speculative and very acute men [the schoolmen], who wrought a great part of their divinity out of their own brains, as spiders do cobwebs out of their own bowels, have started a thousand subtleties about this mystery, such as no Christian is bound to trouble his head withal; much less is it necessary for him to understand those niceties which we may reasonably presume that they who talk of them did themselves never thoroughly understand, and least of all is it necessary to believe them.... A man may be "a barbarian" that speaks to people in unknown phrases and metaphors, as well as "he that speaks in an unknown tongue;" and the very same reason that obligeth us to put the Scripture into a known language doth oblige men to explain the doctrines contained in it by such phrases and metaphors as are known and used in

---

[44] Farley, 15.

that language.... If men would but content themselves with those plain and simple descriptions which the Scripture gives us of faith, there could not be any great difference about it.[45]

Not only is the term *Trinity* not found in the Bible, none of the other words used to describe it are, either:

The words and phrases are not in the Bible, which are indispensably necessary to the doctrine of the Trinity, and without which no one ever attempts either to state or to defend the doctrine.

The phraseology which is peculiar to the doctrine of the Trinity is chiefly the following:—Trinity, Triune, Triad, God the Son, God the Spirit, God the Holy Ghost, Jehovah-Jesus, God-man, God-mediator, incarnate God, first person, second person, third person, three in one, one in three, three equal persons in the Godhead, three-one God, The Sacred Three, Eternal Three, two natures, double nature, human and divine nature, very God and very man, coequal, coeternal, coessential, eternally begotten, eternally proceeding, eternal Son of God.

Not one of these terms or phrases is in the Bible. But without the words necessary to teach the doctrine of the Trinity, how can it be taught? How can any doctrine be taught without the use of appropriate words?

The absence of the phrase "God the Son" from the Bible is strong evidence that there is no such person. For if there were, no reason can be assigned why he should not be mentioned as frequently as God the Father, or the Son of God. But as "God the Son" is not so much as *named* in the Bible, I must conclude he is not *known* there, but is the creature of human creeds.[46]

One can only assume that the absence of Trinitarian vernacular from the Bible is not perceived to be problematic, or at least compelling enough to cause ardent Trinitarians to question the veracity of

---

45 Archbishop Tillotson, *Sermon* 44, 28, in *Works*, vol. iii, 215, 288, and vol. xi., 259: quoted in Wilson, 324-325.

46 Morgridge, 34, 158.

the doctrine. As it is commonly said, the theology must be "taken on faith." This is the equivalent of urging that we believe it in spite of its unbiblical and irrational foundation. And what is to prevent proponents of other theologies from expecting assent to their doctrines on the same grounds? Can it be true that the doctrine of the Trinity should be received on such grounds to the exclusion of all others? We certainly do not read in Scripture that we are to believe anything "on faith" (i.e. without proving it) because *anything* could be established on these grounds. The Trinitarian believes in a three-in-one God, but I might even demand you assent to the proposition that God exists as four persons, adding to the three "members" of the so-called godhead that he also exists as the person of Wisdom. I might also assert that since "God is love," He therefore exists as five persons. Then I can demand you believe this also, exclaiming that you must take it on faith! What a mess man has made of our ability to reason things through. Reason is being used to dethrone reason, let the reader decide for himself or herself what that implies.

THE INFERENTIAL NATURE OF THE DOCTRINE OF THE TRINITY

The doctrine of the Trinity is inferred from a collection of verses scattered throughout the biblical texts, as there are no direct statements in the whole Bible that establishes that God is triune. That the doctrine is inferred is quite amazing, since the degree of certainty with which it is proclaimed is so great that we would think it appeared on every page of the Bible with unmatched clarity. The problem with inference is that there is too much room for the development and incorporation of error, and isn't ideal to have a system of beliefs founded upon a method so prone to the incorporation of mistakes. Fundamental biblical doctrines are not of an inferential nature, they are explicit:

> Trinitarians in all ages of the Christian Church have defended the Trinity, not on the ground of its being clearly taught, but solely as a doctrine of *tradition*, or of *inference*. Some have inclined to one, and some to the other, according to the period and country in which they lived. When tradition was more in vogue than at present, this was made to bear the burden of

proof; but when, in the progress of inquiry and knowledge, this refuge of the dark ages was stripped of its authority, a broader foundation was to be sought out for the Trinity. The Bible was now taken up in earnest; where the Trinity was once seen darkly, even by the keen eyes of wisdom and learning, it now came out in such bright and imposing colors as to be distinctly perceived by the shortest vision; it was discovered to be at the bottom of every religious truth; from the first verse of Genesis to the last chapter of Revelation, the whole Bible was full of the Trinity.

"It is worthy of special observation, however, that it has never been formally defended as a plain doctrine of Scripture; nor in Christendom is there a creed in which it is expressed in Scripture language; nor is it ever defined in this language by those who are loudest in proclaiming it a plain Scripture doctrine. It is deduced by *inference*, and inference only. When the matter is brought to the test, it is not pretended that Christ was ever called God, the same Being as the Father, or the Supreme Jehovah. All that is pretended comes to no more than this, that many things are said of Christ, which it is supposed could not be said of him if he were not God. This is called an argument, and then follows the *inference*, that he was God. So in regard to the Holy Spirit, to which certain characteristics are ascribed, that are supposed to be peculiar to the Supreme Being, and hence comes the *inference*, that the Holy Spirit is God. Hitherto we have three Gods, and the labor of *inferring* must be continued, or the unity will be destroyed. It must be *inferred*, that the Son is the same Being as the Father; and again it must be inferred, that the Holy Spirit is the same Being as the Father, and also the same Being as the Son. We are now arrived at what is called a Trinity in Unity, and the point has been gained by building up inference on inference with very little aid from the express words of Scripture." [47]

R. S. Franks, a Trinitarian scholar, agrees with the above assess-

---

[47] Atterbury, *Sermons and Discourses on Several Subjects and Occasions,* Vol. III. 266, 267 [c. 1840]: quoted in Dana, 186-187.

ment regarding the inferential nature of Trinitarian dogma:

> It has been said that the New Testament represents the matrix
> in which the doctrine of the Trinity begins to be formed. Pas-
> sages of a directly Trinitarian complexion are, however, few
> in number, and in no case amount to the definite statement
> of a doctrine. What we find is just the putting together in a
> suggestive way of the names of the Father, the Son and the
> Holy Spirit, notably in the benediction of II Cor. xiii. 14 and
> the baptismal formula of Mt. xxviii. 19. Longer passages of
> the same kind are I Cor. xii. 4-6, Eph. iv. 4-6, I Pet. i. 1-2 and
> Jude 20, 21. The verse I John v. 7 in the Authorized Version
> has no support in the best manuscripts, and has disappeared
> without leaving so much as a trace in the margin.
>
> The real evidence for the doctrine of the Trinity to be
> found in the New Testament is not in such texts as the above,
> but must be collected by a wider survey, which is above all
> directed to the developing Christology, but also looks to what
> is said of God and the Spirit in connection with it.[48]

The New Bible Dictionary explains it this way:

> Though it is not a biblical doctrine in the sense that any for-
> mulation of it can be found in the Bible, it can be seen to
> underlie the revelation of God, implicit in the OT and ex-
> plicit in the NT. By this we mean that though we cannot
> speak confidently of the revelation of the Trinity in the OT,
> yet once the substance of the doctrine had been revealed in
> the NT, we can read back many implications of it in the OT.[49]

As the above quote shows, Trinitarian exegetes are forced to account for there being no statement of the doctrine in the Bible. The
so-called proof for it is gathered piecemeal from the New Testament,
then the Old Testament is gone through to find hints that will agree
with this idea that was inferred from the New Testament. The inferential basis of Trinitarianism has been largely accepted since the
fourth century and continues to make Trinitarianism so prone to

---

[48] Franks, 4-5.

[49] *New Bible Dictionary*, (Illinois: Tyndale House Publishers, 2nd ed., 1982), "Trinity," 1221.

the development of error. For a doctrine to be foundational, some unequivocal statement of it must be made somewhere in the Bible. The absence of such explicit statements is responsible for the need to scour the Bible to find texts that can, in some way, either in context or out, be used to satisfy people that it is true.

The fact that the Bible does not teach the doctrine of the Trinity explicitly is reason to conclude it is not found in Scripture at all, since a doctrine of such importance would necessarily be plain:

> The most accurate consideration of the subject will lead us to acquiesce in the statement, as a general truth, that the doctrines in question have never been learned merely from Scripture; surely the sacred volume was never intended, and was not adapted, to teach our creed.[50]
>
> If, then, the Trinity be not a doctrine *expressly taught* in Scripture, it can be at the best but a matter of *inference*. And so accordingly it is often declared to be by Trinitarian Protestants. The Romanist takes it on tradition, but they on inference. Mr. Carlisle, in his "Jesus Christ the Great God our Saviour," admits that: "The doctrine of the Trinity is rather a doctrine of inference and of direct intimation, than a doctrine directly and explicitly declared." And still further: "That a doctrine of inference ought never to be placed on a footing of equality with a doctrine of direct and explicit revelation." The celebrated Oxford Tracts ask: "Where is this solemn and comfortable mystery (of the Trinity) formally stated in Scripture as we find it in the Creeds?" and proceed to declare it a thing of inference. The same Bishop Smallridge, from whom I just now quoted, goes on, in close connection, to say: "But although these truths are not read in Scripture, yet they may easily, regularly, and undeniably be inferred from Scripture." And well does he add: "If, indeed, it can be shown that these inferences are wrong, they may safely be rejected." Beyond all question they may; and this is the very thing I am trying to

---

50 Newman, *Arians of the Fourth Century,* 55, quoted in Wiseman's Lectures, 93: quoted in Eliot, 85.

show, and hope to make plain.[51]

The doctrine that God is one (monotheism) is clearly set forth in Scripture. The Trinitarian places a great deal of confidence in an ability to infer a trinity of persons in God, which is a most abstract proposition. In order to make the change from that which is biblical and comprehensible (e.g. God is one), to that which is abstract, unbiblical and incomprehensible (e.g. God is three-in-one), requires a reasonable basis to justify the change. Without this we would be prone to believing anything that came our way and would be defenseless against every idea. So we use common sense and explicit statements of the Bible when we are seeking to establish an idea based on the biblical texts. Trinitarians, since there is no explicit statement of their doctrine in the Bible, simply place too much confidence in their ability to develop their system through the process of inference:

> But you say, that there are some passages of Scripture which would lead you to think there were three Persons in the Divine nature, and that Christ was one of those Persons, and the Holy Spirit another. There are other passages which seem to teach that God subsists in one Person, and that one Person is the Father. Both of them cannot be true. There is a Trinity or a Unity in the Divine nature. Now which is to be believed? In making up your mind there are these two material considerations to guide you. The doctrine of the Trinity is not directly asserted in any of the passages which are brought to prove it. It is only inferred. It is drawn from them as an inference, which seems more or less certain to different individuals, and therefore may not be a true inference. The doctrine of the Father being the one and only true God, is expressly asserted in so many words. "To us there is but one God, the Father." Here the Unitarian doctrine is not inferred, but is in so many words asserted. The choice, therefore, is between inference, on the one side, and unequivocal assertion, on the other.
>
> The second consideration is, that there are but very few passages in the Bible, where the doctrine of the Trinity is pretended to be contained, even by implication; whereas the

---

[51] Farley, 38.

Unity and supremacy of God the Father is the common and prevailing doctrine of the Scriptures, and the passages in the New Testament in which he is emphatically called the one or only God, amount to seventeen.

There is not a passage in the Bible which unequivocally asserts the Trinity. There are many which unequivocally assert the Unity. In order to reconcile Scripture with itself, either the passages which are thought to teach the Trinity must be explained in consistency with the Unity, or those which declare the Unity must have a sense put on them which will not contradict the Trinity. Is it not more reasonable to suppose that the Trinity—which is an inference, merely, from a very few texts of Scripture—may be a mistaken inference, than to suppose there can be any mistake in the overwhelming majority of texts which unequivocally assert the Unity.[52]

Those who rely so heavily upon inference are at far greater risk of wandering off course. If teaching, we should be far more careful in what we demand others assent to. Jesus's brother James put it this way: "Not many of you should presume to be teachers, my brothers, because you know that we who teach will be judged more strictly."—James 3:1 (NIV). It is wiser to teach what is explicitly stated than to venture into the world of guesswork when taking on the responsibility of teaching about God.

It must be a little disconcerting after all the effort that has gone into formulating Trinitarian theories, that the doctrine must still be called a mystery. After all that effort designed to explain how God is three-in-one, we are no closer to understanding God than we were prior to the proffered explanations:

But the disadvantage of the doctrine of the Trinity does not stop here. There are difficulties in things, as well as words, involved in it. Taking the side that the Unity is true, then the only difficulties you have to encounter, are in the interpretation of a few words and sentences. In the thing itself there is no difficulty. That there should be one God in one Person, is all plain and reasonable, and intrinsically probable. It in-

---

[52] Burnap, 40-42.

volves no mystery, or contradiction.

But taking the doctrine of the Trinity as true, there are not only the difficulties in words which exist in those passages which assert that there is but one God, and the Father alone is that God, but there are difficulties in things. A doctrine is asserted which is, in itself, essentially incredible. It is strange, unreasonable and contradictory. A Being is presented to our faith, made up of elements entirely inconsistent with each other, one and yet three, three Persons, and yet one Being, a Trinity, the first Person of which, in the ideas of all, has some sort of preeminence over the other two, and yet either of the other two is of equal power and glory. One is Son to another, and yet is as ancient as his Father. The first Person is said to do things by the instrumentality of the other two, and yet they have equal and original agency in all things with the first.[53]

The difficulties involved in sustaining Trinitarian theology, when viewed in light of verses such as 1 Timothy 2:5,[54] show how inference has been used to overthrow the simple import of verses that establish the Father's supremacy. Trinitarian dogma is defended by a heavy reliance upon inference and tradition, and is, in this sense, self-perpetuating. New arguments must constantly be developed to keep the former ones from crumbling. These new arguments, in turn, suffer the same fate as the older ones, namely, they also begin to fall under the weight of simple challenges, so further additions to the older arguments are developed. It is a never-ending process. This is another reason why the doctrine of the Trinity must be "taken on faith" as "a mystery." It is this plea of mysteriousness that its adherents argue in order to immunize it from criticism.

Because the doctrine of the Trinity is a doctrine of inference, the burden of proof is upon the Trinitarian to show that his or her conclusions were developed reasonably. History has shown that this cannot be done:

I might begin with a well-known fact, that many theologians,

---

[53] Burnap, 42-43.

[54] 1 Tim. 2:5—For there is one God, and one mediator between God and men, the man Christ Jesus.

chiefly of the English Church, have acknowledged the insufficiency of the Scripture evidence, and so have insisted on the need of church authority to establish it. The doctrine itself they would not abandon. It was inherited from the Roman Church, which professes it not from Scripture but from tradition; and without the paramount authority of the Church, they thought, it must go to the ground. Accordingly, many of this class of theologians have embraced the Roman faith. But I do not insist upon this fact, because it might unfairly warp and prejudice your minds. I only refer to it to show that Unitarians are not alone in contending that the doctrine is not sufficiently sustained by Scripture,—though these, indeed, think it is corroborated and implied there, which we do not. But let this be borne in mind, that the burden of proof rests on that side. Our Orthodox friends offer to prove to us the Trinity out of Scripture. What is the amount and value of that proof?

By their own acknowledgment, the doctrine is one, not of direct revelation, but of inference; not explicitly taught in Scripture, but only alluded to, and made out from comparison of various parts. Few persons who have not given particular attention to it are aware how scanty is the Scripture proof.[55]

The doctrine of the supremacy of the Father involves no difficulties or contradictions—it has the advantage of being easily comprehended. People are familiar with the idea of one person having one mind, and that there is no divisibility within another person. So to make the assertion that God is three-in-one is to enter a realm in which attempts to elucidate any meaning will ultimately fail. Nothing in our collective human experience teaches us to break people into parts, and nothing in the Bible tells us we should do this to God. The Unitarian system is one that does not need to be explained the same way the Trinitarian system does. Trinitarian doctrines need to be continually explained and updated because they make no sense.

---

55 Joseph Allen, *Ten Discourses on Orthodoxy* (Boston: Wm. Crosby and H.P. Nichols, 1849), 51-52.

If they made sense there would be no need to spend so much time explaining what the tenets mean. All of Trinitarianism's extra-biblical explanations have not alleviated the problem—they have exacerbated it.

It is amazing that so many Christians are willing to accept a doctrine that makes no sense, even to themselves. The reason for this may be found in the traditional and historical development of the doctrine itself. It was decreed, as we shall see later, at councils of the Catholic Church in the fourth century and beyond. In the theocracies that followed, people were forced to abide by the creeds of the Catholic Church. If anyone opposed them, they were branded heretics and faced excommunication, imprisonment, exile or death. It became expedient for families to teach their children the prevailing church doctrine in order to protect them from such harsh treatment. After the threat of governmental sanctions against individuals in matters of religion ceased, the damage was already done. Generation after generation had been taught the same thing—the doctrines of the early councils. Since then, few have actively challenged the creeds they produced. This is primarily due to members of the Christian community bringing their own form of persecution upon perceived heretics:

> THE days of torture, fire, and the sword, have, happily, almost entirely passed away. He who changes his religious opinions has not now, in Protestant countries at least, to fear the strong arm of ecclesiastical power, nor the civil law; no Inquisition holds over our heads its rod of terror; no dungeons open to receive us; no "Form of Concord" is imposed upon us; no "Act of Uniformity" binds us to submit to certain rites and ceremonies. But is there not a kind of persecution still enacted, which, though less extreme and violent, is quite as onerous, and no less difficult to bear?
>
> The days of proscription, slander, insult, and neglect, have by no means passed away. Cold greetings, averted looks, long and intimate friendships sundered in a moment, tell a mournful tale in respect to the toleration *really* exercised, in this country, so proud of its civil and religious liberty, towards those who have conscientiously changed their opinions. Nor are these the only methods by which the spirit of unyielding

intolerance is developed. Injurious suspicions; direct charges which would almost break the heart of the sufferer, did he not feel himself above their reach; the imputation of any and every motive but the real one; all these must be experienced and endured by the one who feels it his duty to leave the ranks of the popular or orthodox theology, commonly so called, and candidly avow his honest opinions.

Many people do not seem to imagine, that one *can* honestly depart from the faith in which he has been educated. Independent thought in matters of religion seems to be regarded as an arrogant assumption, and to excite general indignation and surprise. It is evidently thought to be an innovation on the established order of things. It is a phenomenon for which people are not prepared. And when I look around me, and observe how the great majority of mankind are blindly following the lead of others, how few there are who think for themselves, how few are willing to test their religious opinions by comparing them with other systems of faith, by bringing them all to "the law and the testimony" of God's inspired word, clinging firmly to truth, following it wherever it might lead, and boldly rejecting error,—when these things meet my view, though I may be distressed at the exhibition of intolerance, I ought not, perhaps, to be *surprised* at the spirit which is manifested.[56]

There seems to be in Christians, as in mankind generally, a predisposition toward the status quo. The consequences of making a challenge to commonly accepted things can be severe, including threats, ostracization and isolation. The loss of eternal life for not believing Trinitarian dogma is frequently given as a reason for believing it. Without this pressure, more people would be comfortable questioning or rejecting the doctrine. Christians would be freed from the effects of so-called "Christian" tyranny. But the pressure from those working to preserve orthodoxy forces people into accepting things that they would otherwise judge in a more impartial manner. The doctrine of the Trinity must be abided by, we are told, otherwise our

---

[56] Dana, iii-iv.

salvation is at risk:

> It appears impossible, that any mind which had never been prejudiced in favour of creeds and catechisms, could deduce either the *Athanasian* or the *Nicene Creed* from the New Testament....There are about twenty-eight ascriptions of praise to God in the New Testament, but from none of them could an unprejudiced mind deduce the doctrine of the Trinity.[57]

It requires a powerful prejudicing to cause people to receive such a doctrine as the Trinity. What's worse, the doctrine of the Trinity is said to be the well-spring of all other doctrines! But anybody who had never heard of the doctrine would not find it in the Bible:

> Here remember, that no such words or phrases as the Trinity, the Triune God, the God-man, occur in Scripture. They savor certainly far more of the subtleties of the schoolmen than of the simplicity of Holy writ. But not only are no such words and phrases to be found there, where is the known case of any man for the first time taking these Scriptures into his hands, whether in the original or in translation, in any language, in any land, with no previous knowledge of the religion they teach, with no preconceptions of Christian doctrine of any kind, and of himself finding there the dogmas which those words and phrases are made to cover? Where, in the authentic records of any Christian missionary labors, throughout the world, Papal or Protestant, is there such an experience? I confidently believe, nowhere. No such case can be cited. No such experience is recorded or known. On the other hand we can produce two, each beyond challenge for simplicity and integrity, though very opposite in personal conditions and circumstances, of men who found in their own independent search of the Bible, the one in the original languages in which it was written, the other in a translation into his vernacular tongue, the doctrine of the strict simple Unity of God, the Father, and the subordination and inferiority therefore of our blessed Lord. I refer to the late Rajah Ram Mohun Roy, at Calcutta,

---

[57] Thomas, 6-7, 11.

and William Roberts, at Madras. The one, a high-caste Brahmin, accomplished in all the learning of the Orient; having every advantage of wealth, social position, and personal culture. The other, a native of the lowest caste, the servant of an English resident merchant, uneducated, obscure, and poor. The latter read the Bible in a translation into his own tongue, but could not find there the doctrine which the Liturgy of his master's Church, the Church of England, embodied, but only our own simple Unitarian faith. The former sought the Hebrew and Greek Scriptures, and studied them profoundly, with the same result.[58]

The common method of "proving" the doctrine of the Trinity is to take detached verses out of context, collect them and somehow show how they allude to or prove the doctrine. This is an unfair treatment of biblical texts. It is no different than the propaganda films the people of the former Soviet Union were shown in which America was depicted as a land of slums. The purpose of the films was to persuade the Soviet citizenry that America is a bad place because democracy had made it that way. A predictable consequence of the films was that it worked. America was taken out of context by showing just a small portion of American society. The worst-case scenario was presented without any other influencing factors, such as the beautiful landscapes and the lovely small-town communities. These would have allowed the Soviet viewers to make an impartial decision based upon a broader context. By the same means people come to accept the doctrine of the Trinity. Verses that are most favorable to the reception of the doctrine are used, without the benefit of context. And even though the mind recoils at such a proposition as God is three and one, the prejudicing is effective. People are saddled with an incomplete and erratic view of God, but it maintains the status quo. And all this has resulted from assumption and inference.

---

58 Farley, 51-52.

BELIEF IN THE DOCTRINE OF THE TRINITY NOT NECESSARY FOR SALVATION

Salvation is a big topic, with different notions about what is required to secure it from God. Some believe that the idea of hell is entirely discordant with a loving God, and others believe that everybody will be saved based on the same premise—if God is love, He would want everyone to be saved and enjoy a happy afterlife, wherever that might be and whatever it may look like. These sorts of considerations are outside the parameters of this book, but of relevance and what will be considered here are the claims that have been made that belief in a triune God is necessary for one to be saved.

The number of Christians who claimed that the doctrine of the Trinity is biblical increased dramatically with the rise of Protestantism. Protestants were encouraged to search the Bible to find their doctrines, which stood in contrast to Catholicism, in which its adherents have traditionally relied upon the church to interpret the Bible for them. But it was not always this way, as people had to rely upon the clergy and tradition for their doctrines. This was partly due to the unavailability of Bibles, since the printing press was not in widespread use until about the sixteenth century. Owen Chadwick, a modern historian, speaking about the effect which education and the availability of Bibles had on Christians, writes:

> First, the Church held up the Bible as the source of truth. But it taught various doctrines that no one could find in the Bible. This was possible only as long as not many people read the Bible; and not many people did, because few could read, fewer still could read Latin, and even fewer owned a copy. But with the coming of printed books in the 1450s, and a general growth in literacy, this was no longer possible. The contradictions stood clear; the Church must end them.[59]

Until the Reformation and the invention of the printing press, Christians had little recourse but to rely on tradition and the interpretations of the Bible given by those most prominent in the churches. Church services were given in Latin, a language which few even

---

59 Chadwick, 196.

spoke.[60] The clergy did not regard it as of paramount importance that their doctrines were understood—only accepted. Once encouraged to read their own Bibles, though, the masses did not divorce themselves from the teachings of the church. The doctrine of the Trinity had such a long history and was so entrenched that it was not going to be seriously questioned. But when some began asking questions about the idea of a triune God, explanations were given which were quite naturally subject to evaluation. Those who asked questions now had Bibles to compare these explanations to, and it became apparent to some that Trinitarian dogma was not true, and if not true then it could not be necessary to secure salvation:

> That it is not *explicitly* taught in the Scriptures appears to me so plain, that all attempts to prove the fact seem superfluous; yet when men insist upon it as a *fundamental* article of faith, and affirm a denial of it to be "a soul ruining error," the proof becomes important and even necessary. Professor Sparks proves that it is not thus taught. I have been glancing my eye over the pages of his work, and find every word that he says so important—so much to the point in my argument with you—and so much better said than anything I could say, that I shall probably lay the whole of it before you, trusting that I shall be excused by the author for giving myself such latitude.
>
> "In the first place, then," he says, "it will not be denied that the great design of the revelations, contained in the Old Testament, was to acquaint the Jews with *the true nature of God;* nor will it be denied, that from all these revelations, they had no conceptions of any other mode of existence, than that of *his simple unity.* It was perpetually enforced upon them, as a fundamental truth, that 'the Lord their God was *one.*' No history, either sacred or profane, acquaints us with a single fact, from which it can be inferred, that the Jews had any knowledge of a three-fold nature in the Deity. On the contrary, all history is against such an inference; and the demonstrable certainty, that these people, for whose light

---

60 The practice of giving Mass in a language other than Latin was not permitted until the 1960s.

and improvement the Old Testament was expressly designed, never had the remotest suspicion of such a doctrine being contained in their sacred books, is the clearest possible evidence, that it is not plainly taught there, whatever may now be deduced from types, and shadows, and dark sayings, and Hebrew idioms, and double meanings.

"This subject merits discussion," he [Prof. Sparks] says, "not because it affects the Scriptural evidence in regard to the truth or falsehood of the doctrine; but because it is intimately connected with the presumption *of making the Trinity a necessary article of faith,* which all persons must believe before they can be called Christians, or hope for salvation. If the primitive Christians knew nothing of this doctrine, it is absurd to clothe it with so much importance; nay, it is absolutely putting a false character upon the religion of Jesus, and deceiving the humble inquirer into a fatal reliance on things which can have no good tendency on his religious or moral conduct. In this light the subject is worth pursuing."

Professor Sparks then goes back to the time of the Saviour and of his Apostles; refers to the first believers in Christianity; to the early and later Fathers; to the Catholics after the Reformation; to some of the first reformers; to the Arminians of Holland; and to eminent English divines; and clearly shows "with how little discretion the Trinity is *now* affirmed to be plainly taught in the Scriptures; and with how little regard to consistency it is imposed as a necessary article of faith." [61]

It is commonly affirmed by ardent Trinitarians that in order to be saved one must believe that God exists in three persons and that Jesus Christ is God. In his defense of the doctrine of the Trinity, Robert Bowman writes without the mean-spiritedness that is commonly featured in such defenses, but nonetheless leaves the door open for the reader to conclude that one must believe the doctrine of the Trinity in order to be saved. Early in his work, he says:

Trinitarians do not believe that it is necessary to have a perfectly accurate understanding of the doctrine of the Trinity

---

[61] Dana, 172-173.

as elaborated in the creeds in order to be saved. The J[eho-vah's] W[itnesses] are right when they point out that in the Bible "common people" had faith in Jesus and knew the truth about God. Thus, if some people find the Trinity difficult to apprehend, they need not fear for their salvation.[62]

Near the end of his book, however, he is far more direct in stating that salvation is dependent upon receiving Trinitarian dogma:

> To be a Christian, it is not necessary to know or understand the formal expressions of Trinitarianism that were the result of centuries of reflection on the New Testament in the light of heretical distortions of that faith. However, to be a Christian, one must not reject the faith that the doctrine of the Trinity was designed to safeguard.
>
> Moreover, to be a responsible Christian—not merely in the sense of obtaining personal salvation, but in the sense of being a full partner with the rest of Christ's church in the fellowship and service of Christ—one must accept the doctrine of the Trinity.[63]

Mr. Bowman makes the same sort of argument that is common among Trinitarian apologists: one need not understand the doctrine but must still believe it in order to be considered a Christian and be saved. In Bob and Gretchen Passantino's book *Witch Hunt*, in which the authors oppose current trends in so-called cult awareness groups due to a lack of uniform standards in determining what constitutes a cult, the following criteria are given in the chapters titled, *What Christians Believe About God* and *What Christians Believe About Jesus Christ*:

> The Bible summarizes the minimum necessary for belief in the true God of Scripture. We believe in only one God (Isa. 43:10; 1 Tim. 2:5); in the doctrine of the Trinity, that is, that within the nature of the one true God there are three eternal, distinct persons, the Father, the Son, and the Holy Spirit.... We believe that Jesus Christ is truly God (John 1:1, Titus

---

62 Bowman, 17.

63 Bowman, 132.

2:13); truly man (Phil. 2:5-11); the second person of the Trinity…[64]

According to the Passantinos, if one believes that the Father is supreme then he or she is not Christian and, by extension, is not saved. The development of this way of thinking rests upon the authors' interpretation of Luke 3.22.[65] Their interpretation involves inference upon inference to conclude that it contains a statement remotely approaching that of a triune god. Still further, to claim that those who do not interpret this verse (and others of a similar inferential nature) in a Trinitarian sense are not Christians, is to create a circuitous, man-made route to salvation. This approach to salvation implies that the Bible is not direct in its teachings about arguably its most important feature. President Andrew Jackson comments:

> We ought, indeed, to expect occasional obscurity in such a book as the Bible, which was written for past and future ages, as well as for the present. But God's wisdom is a pledge, that whatever is necessary for *us*, and necessary for salvation, is revealed too plainly to be mistaken, and too consistently, to be questioned by sound and upright minds. It is not the mark of wisdom, to use an unintelligible phraseology, to communicate what is above our capacities, to confuse and unsettle the intellect, by appearances of contradiction. We honour our heavenly Teacher too much to ascribe to him such a revelation. A revelation is a gift of light. It cannot thicken our darkness and multiply our perplexities.[66]

Farley echoes the President's sentiments:

> Is it, then, to be believed that such a doctrine, known in reality only by its name, can be an essential, fundamental doctrine of Revelation? Would God, such a God as "the Father of our Lord Jesus Christ" is represented to be in the gospel, have left

---

[64] Bob and Gretchen Passantino, *Witch Hunt* (Nashville, TN: Thomas Nelson, Inc., 1990), 46, 47.

[65] Luke 3:22—And the Holy Ghost descended in a bodily shape like a dove upon him, and a voice from heaven, which said, Thou art my beloved Son; in thee I am well pleased.

[66] John Anthony Scott, *Living Documents in American History* (New York: Washington Square Press, 1963), 262.

a doctrine of that character—on the belief of which it used to be said, and is even now said in some quarters, that the salvation of the soul depends—so obscurely set forth in His revealed word?[67]

Trinitarians have admitted the obscure and inferential nature of the doctrine which they ardently defend. In his book on cults, which is regarded by some Christians as a standard work on the subject, Walter Martin describes how he came to believe in the notion of a triune God—not by express biblical statement, but by intimation:

> There is ample ground for this belief in the Scriptures, where plurality in the Godhead is very strongly *intimated*, if not expressly declared.[68] (emphasis mine)

A doctrine gained by intimation, then, most assuredly is not necessary to be believed in order to secure salvation. Given its importance, whatever is necessary to salvation would be laid out in such a way that nobody seeking for it could overlook it. Traces and hints and intimations are not an ideal way of communicating something as significant as how to procure everlasting life. The Trinitarian system makes discovering the requirements of salvation as difficult as possible:

> The case stands simply thus: There is not a shadow of pretence for calling it a plainly revealed doctrine of Scripture. It is, as evidently, a doctrine of inference, and inference merely. Christ is never in the Scripture styled God, identically, or, if you prefer, equally, the same being as the Father, the Infinite, the Supreme, the "Only True God." But, things are said of him, or by him, which it is supposed could have been spoken only of or by Jehovah, from which it is inferred that Christ is God. Many things are ascribed to the Holy Spirit which are supposed peculiar to Jehovah: therefore it is inferred that the Holy Spirit is God. Again: since this would look like having Three Gods, and yet God being undeniably and over and over

---

[67] Farley, 22.

[68] Walter Martin, *The Kingdom of the Cults* (Bethany house Publishers, Minneapolis, MN, 1985), 61.

again declared to be but ONE, it is further inferred that the Father, the Son, and the Holy Spirit, must all be that One God. And so, by heaping inference on inference, comes this Trinity in Unity. How unreasonable to call such a doctrine an essential, fundamental article of Christian Faith! The moment it is permitted to establish and require assent on one article on such grounds, where are we to stop? What might not be established in this way? By a little ingenuity, and false interpretation of Scripture language, we might infer the most absurd notions, and open a floodgate of scandal and reproach on the Truth. No; the very term *inferred*, negatives any allegation that the doctrine *inferred* is one *revealed* or *declared* to be true, and all claim to its being essential to be believed.[69]

It is interesting that defenders of the doctrine of the Trinity include themselves, by definition, within the fold of those who have obtained salvation, and exclude those, by the same definition, who disagree with the doctrine. Perhaps this is a commentary on human nature, as those on both sides of the debate have done this, and the point is worth making. Aside from the pomposity of judging another out of eternal life regardless of who does it, whether Unitarian or Trinitarian, Trinitarians have no biblical foundation for their special claims to it:

> But is it true that the definitions of doctrine, as given by Trinitarians, are better than those given by Christ? We think not. Promises of salvation are expressly made to all who embrace the gospel as it is defined by Christ and the Apostles. But no promise is made to the *Trinitarian as such*. There is no Scripture which asserts that whosoever believes in the Trinity, or in the two natures, or in the Son's equality with the Father, or in the divinity of Christ, shall be saved. Nor does any Scripture assert that whosoever believeth not these doctrines shall be damned. But if no promise is made to him who embraces the gospel *as it is defined by Trinitarians*, and no threatening against him who does not embrace it *as thus defined*, is not this sufficient evidence that their definitions are not correct?

---

[69] Farley, 38-39.

All who believe on Jesus Christ, *as the Son of God*, have an assurance from Christ himself, of everlasting life. All who do not believe Jesus to be the *Son of God*, are assured, by the same authority, that they shall not see life; but the wrath of God abideth on them. What, then, does the true believer gain by admitting the doctrine of the Trinity? If it does not secure to him a single promise, nor shield him from a single threatening, of what use can it possibly be to him? It cannot make one hair either white or black.[70]

The requirements some Trinitarians assert are necessary to secure salvation, which typically involves, in the final analysis, a reception of the doctrine "on faith" as a "mystery," have no basis in Scripture. These requirements are, like the doctrine of the Trinity itself, gained by inference and prejudice:

> When I consider what your professed belief upon this subject is, I really cannot wonder at your strong expressions; but I do wonder that you can believe there is a fatal difference between us. You surely cannot believe that the souls of some whom I could name, who have died in the Unitarian faith, are lost. *Show me* where either our Master or his apostles declared that a belief in him, *as the eternal God*, is *necessary* to salvation, and I will acknowledge that you have good reason for this item of your faith; but all I can see that they ever gave as a test of Christian faith was such a belief in Jesus, *as the Messiah*, as would cause men to yield *implicitly* to his authority.
>
> They never say it is necessary to our salvation to be certain whether that authority is entirely his own, or is derived from his Father; though, at the same time, they tell us plainly enough from whence it really comes. Yet that is never made a prominent and necessary article of belief. The main point of inquiry is, dost thou believe that Jesus is *the Christ*—that is, the anointed—he who was to come? If we believe that he came commissioned by God, we shall obey him, and thus be his followers; and, of course, entitled to the Christian name. When the belief of Unitarians leads them to *reject* the au-

---

[70] Morgridge, 14.

thority of Christ, it will be time to deny them the name of Christians; but when they recognize that authority as fully and joyfully as you do, how can you consistently assert that they are not Christians?

I repeat it, we are merely told in the Scriptures, that we must believe on the Lord Jesus Christ, and we shall be saved. And we must see to it that we have such a faith in Christ as will bring forth fruit unto holiness; for we are also informed that *without holiness* no man shall see the Lord. Now, this is *all* which the Scriptures declare to be necessary to salvation; namely, faith showing itself by works. If you can show me one passage in which it is declared that we must regard him who was sent by God as God himself—the same being by whom he was sent—the case will be radically altered, and I will allow that you are right when you insist that I am in a *fatal* error. But until you can show me some such passage—for I want no *inferences* in regard to *fundamental* doctrines—beware how you judge concerning my future prospects; beware how you add to the word of God.[71]

How plain and well defined are the terms of salvation in the Bible, may be seen by the following quotations.

"What must I do to be saved? ... Believe on the Lord Jesus Christ and thou shalt be saved."—*Acts* xvi. 30, 31.

"But whom say ye that I am? And Simon Peter answered and said, 'Thou art the Christ, the Son of the living God.' And Jesus answered and said unto him, 'Blessed art thou Simon Bar-Jona: for flesh and blood hath not revealed it unto thee, but my Father which is in heaven.' "—*Matt.* xvi. 15-17. "Who is he that overcometh the world, but he that believeth that Jesus is the Son of God?"—*I John* v. 5. "But these things are written, that ye might believe that Jesus is the Christ, the Son of God; and that believing ye might have life through his name."—*John* xx. 31.

So plain and easy of comprehension are the terms of sal-

---

[71] Dana, 250-251.

vation as defined by Jesus Christ and his Apostles.[72]

Nowhere in the Bible are we told that anyone must acknowledge Jesus to be God. Nothing in the Bible tells us we must believe, in order to be saved, that God exists in three persons. There is nothing that says we must believe anything about God's *nature* in order to secure eternal life. The Bible says that God is love, yet there is no requirement that we believe this as a condition of salvation. Regarding Jesus, even though things about his nature are discussed in the Bible, nowhere does it declare a requirement that one has to believe in him as co-equal with God, or fully God and fully man, or anything of the sort:

> Even Dr. J. Pye Smith says: "It is plain that the immediate object, in the writings of Matthew, Mark, and Luke, was to produce a conviction that Jesus of Nazareth was the Messiah announced and described in the prophetic writings." Yes, and the same was John's, as the passage just quoted from his Gospel shows. He had written all he had written there; all, including every text and passage ever since cited to prove either a Trinity of Persons in the Godhead or the Godhead of Christ*he had written it all to convince his readers, to make them "believe" just this one great, fundamental truth, namely, "that Jesus is the Christ," i.e. the Messiah, the two terms meaning precisely the same; the latter from the Hebrew, the former from the Greek: that he is "the *Son* of God" and not God Himself. Nay, more; to show that this was the essential thing to be believed, he adds: "And that believing, ye might have Life through his name." "Life" here includes all, in the highest sense, which our Lord promises to his faithful followers; and all the knowledge of his Master necessary to secure to us that, John has unfolded in his previous pages. It is, I repeat, "that Jesus is the Christ, the Son of God."[73]

Some Unitarians believe that good works and/or water baptism are necessary to secure salvation, some believe that belief in his resur-

---

72 Morgridge, 12.

73 Farley, 93-94.

rection is the sole requirement. Arguments have been made for both, but since this study concerns the supremacy of the Father and the elements of Trinitarianism, I will leave those for another time.

For the ardent Christian, some of verses in the New Testament that enunciate the requirements for salvation are:

- Romans 10:9—That if thou shalt confess with the mouth the Lord Jesus, and shalt believe in thine heart that God hath raised him from the dead, thou shalt be saved.
- John 3:16—For God so loved the world, that he gave his only begotten Son, that whosoever believeth in him should not perish, but have everlasting life.
- John 17:3—And this is life eternal, that they might know thee the only true God, and Jesus Christ, whom thou hast sent.
- John 20:31—But these are written, that ye might believe that Jesus is the Christ, the Son of God; and that believing ye might have life through his name.
- Acts 16:30-31—And brought them out, and said, Sirs, what must I do to be saved? And they said, Believe on the Lord Jesus Christ, and thou shalt be saved, and the house.
- 1 John 5:5—Who is he that overcometh the world, but he that believeth that Jesus is the Son of God?

These verses make it clear that no burden is placed upon the Christian to believe the various Trinitarian dogmas. No such belief as "God exists in three persons, Father, Son, and Holy Ghost, and these three are one," or "Jesus is very God and very man," or any statements of similar import, are necessary. By comparing the two models of salvation, the Trinitarian and the Unitarian, one can see which is correct and which is the most damaging to Christians vis-à-vis hope for eternal life:

> But it would be well for Christianity if the human fixtures which have been appended to it, were merely useless. But this is far from being the case. The new definitions which Trinitarians have given of the way to heaven, instead of making it more plain, have greatly obscured it. With their pretended improvements, it is no longer a HIGHWAY *cast up*. It has become private property, full of gates, and bars, and intricate

windings.

Previous to the crucifixion of our blessed Saviour, but one article of faith was made essential to the believer, viz. that *Jesus is the Christ, the Son of God.* Subsequently the doctrine of the resurrection was added. Hence St. Paul says, "that if thou shalt confess with the mouth the Lord Jesus, and shalt believe in the heart that God hath raised him from the dead, thou shalt be saved." These two articles were all which the apostles required as the terms of Christian character and eternal salvation. And they contain plain and simple propositions, which everybody can understand. But now, in some churches, there are not less than thirty or forty articles of faith, all purporting to be essential to salvation. And some of them involving such nice distinctions as scarcely to be comprehended by any created mind. Take, for example, the doctrine of the Trinity, as described by the learned, the pious, and the orthodox Bishop Beveridge.

"We are to consider the order of those persons in the Trinity described in the words before us, Matt. xxviii. 19. First, the Father, and then the Son, and then the Holy Ghost; every one of which is really and truly God. A mystery which we are all bound to believe, but yet must have a great care how we speak of it, it being both easy and dangerous to mistake in expressing so great a truth as this is. If we think of it, how hard it is to imagine one numerically divine *nature* in more than one and the same divine *person*? Or, three divine persons in no more than one and the same divine nature? If we speak of it, how hard it is to find out words to express it? If I say, the Father, Son, and Holy Ghost be three, and every one distinctly God, it is true; but if I say, they be three, and every one a distinct God, it is false. I may say, God the Father is one God, and the Son is one God, and the Holy Ghost is one God, but I cannot say, that the Father is one God, and the Son is another God, and the Holy Ghost is a third God. I may say, the Father begat another who is God; yet I cannot say that he begat another God. And from the Father and the Son proceedeth another who is God; yet I cannot say, from the Father and the Son proceedeth another God. For all this while, though their nature be the same their persons are distinct; and though their persons be distinct, yet still their nature is the same. So that, though the Father be the first person in the God-head, the Son the second, the Holy Ghost the third, yet the Father is not the first, the Son a second, and the Holy Ghost a third God. So hard a thing is it to word so great a mystery aright; or to fit so high a truth with expressions suitable and proper to it, without going one way or another from it."

The Bishop, a few pages farther on, adds,—"This is the principal, if not the only characteristical note whereby to distinguish a Christian from another man; yea, from a Turk; for this is the chief thing that the Turks both in their Koran and other writings upbraid Christians for, even because they believe a Trinity of persons in the divine nature. For which cause they frequently say, they are people that believe God hath companions; so that, take away this article of our Christian faith, and what depends upon it, and there would be but little difference between a Christian and a Turk."

If the Bishop is correct, I ask with the deepest concern, "*Who then can be saved?*" There is not probably one Trinitarian in a thousand that could define the doctrine correctly, without the Bishop's copy to write by. "So hard a thing is it to word so great a mystery aright." And yet we are assured it is as dangerous to get it wrong as it is difficult to get it right.[74]

By comparing the complex Trinitarian claims regarding salvation to the simple Unitarian statements of the Bible, it becomes apparent how far some have separated themselves from the writings of the apostles and gospels, as well as the Hebrew texts.

THE POLYTHEISTIC NATURE OF TRINITARIANISM

Since Trinitarianism is a system of beliefs that maintains that there are three persons, each of whom is *fully* God, it is fair to conclude that this establishes the worship of more than one God. The only thing that obscures it from being thus recognized is the constant claim that

---

[74] Morgridge, 14-17.

there is only one God being worshipped. It might even be said that it involves the worship of at least four gods, since each "person" of the Trinitarian godhead is considered to be God, making three gods, and a fourth one emerges when all three are worshipped as a trinity. It is quite a confusing mess which has yet to be sorted out.

Since Trinitarianism is a belief system that involves the worship of three persons, each classified as fully God, even with fanciful language it gives more than a strong appearance of tritheism. Trinitarians seemingly recognize this as contrary to many clear biblical statements about God being one, so add the disclaimer that there is only one God. Not only is this single disclaimer at the root of many the problems with Trinitarian theology and the cause of countless hours spent to remedy said problems, it results in other propositions that are equally impossible for even its advocates to make sense of. Dr. John Hey, a Trinitarian, writes:

> When it is proposed to me to affirm, that "in the unity of the Godhead there be three persons, of one substance, power, and eternity,—the Father, the Son, and the Holy Ghost,"—I have difficulty enough! My understanding is involved in perplexity, my conceptions bewildered in the thickest darkness. I pause, I hesitate; I ask what necessity there is for making such a declaration.... But does not this confound all our conceptions, and make us use words without meaning? I think it does. I profess and proclaim my confusion in the most unequivocal manner: I make it an essential part of my declaration. Did I pretend to understand what I say, I might be a Tritheist or an Infidel; but I could not both worship the one true God, and acknowledge Jesus Christ to be Lord of all.... It might tend to promote moderation, and, in the end, agreement, if we were industrious on all occasions to represent our doctrine as wholly unintelligible.[75]

Dr. Hey openly admitted his confusion about his own doctrine, and it should not be overlooked that this was an educated man giving an account of his own beliefs. He was saddled with the realization that if he understood what he was saying he would be a tritheist or an

---

75 Dr. John Hey, *Lectures in Divinity*, vol. ii, 249, 251, 253; quoted in Wilson, 322

infidel. What an option! Bishop Sherlock (quoted earlier) referred to the three persons in the Godhead as "really distinct persons as Peter, James, and John—each of which is God." It is no wonder it must be called a mystery and received on such grounds. James Hughes, a Catholic priest, writes:

> My belief in the Trinity is based on the authority of the church: no other authority is sufficient. I will now show from reason, that the Athanasian Creed and Scripture are opposed to one another. The doctrine of the Trinity is this: There is one God in three persons,—Father, Son, and Holy Ghost. The Father is God, the Son is God, and the Holy Ghost is God. Mind, the Father is one person, the Son is another person, and the Holy Ghost is another person. Now, according to every principle of mathematics, arithmetic, human wisdom, and policy, there must be three Gods; for no one could say that there are three persons and three Gods, and yet only one God.... The Athanasian Creed gives the universal opinion of the church, that the Father is uncreated, the Son uncreated, and the Holy Ghost uncreated; that they existed from all eternity. Now, the Son was born of the Father, and, if born, must have been created. The Holy Ghost must also have been created, as he came from the Father and the Son. And, if so, there must have been a time when they did not exist. If they did not exist, they must have been created; and therefore to assert that they are eternal is absurd, and bangs nonsense. Each has his distinct personality: each has his own essence. How, then, can they be one Eternal? How can they be all God? The Athanasian Creed says that they are three persons, and still only one God. Absurd; extravagant! This is rejected by Arians, Socinians, Presbyterians, and every man following human reason. The Creed further says that our Lord Jesus Christ is the Son of God and of man, "not by conversion of the Godhead into flesh, but by taking of the manhood into God." Now, I ask you, did the Divinity absorb the manhood? He could not be, at the same time, one person and two persons. I have now

proved the Trinity opposed to human reason.[76]

Everybody has difficulty understanding Trinitarian dogma. There are few who claim to understand it, while many accept it in spite of its unintelligibility. To be sure, the "orthodox" have developed a most enigmatic concept of God:

> What a confused object is the God of the Trinity, to use the words of a modern writer; the Trinitarian Deity is a heterogeneous being, who is, at the same moment, one and many—who, being viewed as one person, is at the same moment, the supreme God, and a mortal man; omniscient and ignorant, almighty and impotent; such a being is certainly the most puzzling and distracting object ever presented to human thought. In contemplating so changing a God, the mind finds nothing to rest upon; and instead of receiving distinct and harmonious impressions, is disturbed by shifting unsettled images.[77]

Divided worship among competing gods leads to the confusion Dr. Hey spoke of. The language used in Trinitarian dogma makes a strong case for believing that Trinitarianism is polytheism:

> Dr. Hopkins says, "The blessed Trinity, in the one God may be considered as a most exalted, happy, and glorious society or family, uniting in the plan of divine operations, especially in accomplishing the work of redemption. In this, each one has his part to perform, according to a most wise, mutual regulation or *agreement*, which may be called a *covenant*. In performing these several parts of this work, one acts as *superior*, another as *inferior*; or one acts *under another*, and by his authority, as appointed or sent by him. This, by divines, is called the economy of the work of redemption. According to this economy, the Son, the Redeemer, acts under the Father, and by his will and appointment, and in this respect takes an inferior part; and in this sense he is supposed to speak, when he says, *The Father is greater than I.*"

---

[76] James Hughes, *Bible Christology for January,* 1839: quoted in Wilson, 322-323.

[77] Thomas, 12-13.

Now what can we infer from such statements, but the doctrine of three Gods? A family of what? A society of what? A compact, a covenant, an agreement, between what? Not men, nor angels. If we pay any regard to the meaning of words, and the force of language, we must consider them a family of Gods, a society of Gods, a company, or co-partnership of Gods. If such descriptions of the Supreme Being were found in the writings of Voltaire, they would be regarded as an attempt to burlesque Christianity. And while they appear in creeds professedly founded on the Scriptures; while they are published in sermons, and proclaimed from the pulpit as essential to salvation, is it surprising that the gospel should have so little influence on the hearts and lives of men? What means could be devised more likely to make unbelievers and infidels? If the gospel is the basis of the moral virtues, and indispensable to the welfare of mankind, is it surprising that its progress is so slow, and its influence so inefficient in promoting human virtue and happiness? Is it strange that the chariot of salvation should be so tardy, while its wheels are thus encumbered?[78]

By definition it is impossible to have more than one *supreme* God. The effort exerted by Trinitarians to have more than one God, while at the same time endeavoring to avoid the charge of polytheism, is not small. In order for the doctrine to appear to agree with simple verses that declare there is only one God, the Trinitarian, if he is to have three objects of worship, has only one recourse, which is to develop an argument or mechanism that makes the three become one. It is a preposterous task to take on, but many have tried. Once it is recognized that this is a tactic designed to prevent a man-made doctrine from falling, the doctrine can be safely discarded:

There are others, who maintain, with those last mentioned, that, in the terms employed in stating the doctrine of the Trinity, the word *person* is not to be taken in its usual sense; but who differ from them, in maintaining that those terms ought to be understood as affirming a real three-fold distinc-

---

[78] Morgridge, 29-30.

tion in the Godhead. But this is nothing more than a mere evasion, introduced into the general statement of the doctrine for the purpose of rescuing it from the charge of absurdity, to which those who thus explain it allow that it would be liable, if the language in which it is usually expressed were to be understood in its common acceptation. They themselves, however, after giving this general statement, immediately relapse into the common belief. When they speak particularly of the Father, the Son, or the Spirit, they speak of each unequivocally as a person in the proper sense of the word. They ascribe to them *personal* attributes. They speak of each as sustaining *personal* relations peculiar to himself, and performing *personal* actions, distinct from those of either of the others. It was the Son who was sanctified and sent into the world; and the Father by whom he was sanctified and sent. It was the Son who became incarnate, and not the Father. It was the Son who made atonement for the sins of men, and the Father by whom the atonement was received. The Son was in the bosom of the Father, but the Father was not in the bosom of the Son. The Son was the Logos who was with God, but it would sound harsh to say that the Father was with God. The Son was the first-born of every creature, the image of the Invisible God, and did not desire to retain his equality with God. There is no one who would not be shocked at the thought of applying this language to the Father. Again, it was the Holy Spirit who was sent as the "Comforter" to our Lord's Apostles, after his ascension, and not the Father nor the Son. All this, those who assert the doctrine of three distinctions, but not of three persons, in the divine nature, must and do say and allow; and therefore they do in fact maintain, with other Trinitarians, that there are three divine persons, in the proper sense of the word, distinguished from each other.[79]

All this talk of "distinctions" and "persons" has been used to blur the differences between the so-called three persons of the Godhead.

---

[79] Norton, 48-49.

There are even more "advanced" concepts, such as perichoresis,[80] designed to blur the distinction even more. In practice, though, Trinitarians represent the three "subjects" in the godhead as distinct persons, each of whom is supposedly God. It therefore follows that three gods are being worshipped.

The confusion in a person's understanding of God will cause confusion in worshipping Him. For those embracing the supremacy of the Father there is no confusion; He is the supreme God and is worshipped as the supreme God. For those embracing the concept of a three-in-one God, however, there is confusion in worship that necessarily arises from such an ill-defined and unsettled understanding of God. Take, for example, the following account of instability in worship:

> There is, then, clearly enough, to be the presence of the Holy Spirit; the presence of Christ; the presence of the Father. And Jesus would have been the last to suggest the idea of three Gods; He taught one God. What Gregory of Nianza exclaimed many centuries ago remains eternally true, "I cannot think of the One but am immediately surrounded with the splendor of the Three; nor can I clearly discover the Three but I am suddenly carried back to the One." [81]

Due to such oscillations between the "one" and the "three," the mind cannot focus on one "object" of worship:

> We come now to an important topic, the object of worship. Worship strictly Trinitarian is impracticable. It is so, considered merely as a mental exercise. Three objects of worship in one object of worship, is an idea which cannot be formed in the mind, for it is a self-contradiction. While the mind thinks of the Unity, it must forget the Trinity, and while it thinks of the Trinity it must forget the Unity. So to address the Trinity in Unity, is equally an impossibility. A new language must be invented to correspond to it, a language which must discard

---

80 "Perichoresis" is a term that is defined as the "indwelling interpenetration" of the three members of the so-called Godhead, and is conceptually useless to the majority of people.

81 Dr. Gerrit Verkuyl, *Reclaim Those Unitarian Wastes* (Grand Rapids, MI: Zondervan Publishing House, 1935), 90.

from its parts of speech all distinction of number, or rather confound all distinction, and express at the same time, unity and plurality, and designate its objects, as at once, three and one. This idea of three-one, is so anomalous, that there is only one word in the whole compass of language which corresponds to it, and that word is Trinity. But this word, strange as it may seem, is not found in Scripture, nor was it invented till several ages after the New Testament was written. It was introduced with the doctrine it was intended to express. Unscriptural as it is, however, it has played a most important part in theology. It has bound together a mass of incongruous ideas, which but for this word, would have dissolved under their own mutual repulsion. The language of strictly Trinitarian devotion, could never wander beyond this single expression, Trinity. All other appellations of Deity must signify either one or many. If a singular form of address be employed, then only one Person is addressed, and the Trinity is lost sight of. If a plural form were used, and the three Persons addressed at once, the Unity is lost.[82]

To underscore the problems Trinitarians encounter vis-à-vis worship, Mary Dana's assessment of her difficulty as a former Trinitarian is to the point:

This doctrine was part of my education. I received it, as many others do, without thorough investigation, though, I must confess, it has often perplexed me beyond measure. Still I held it, as it seems to me all must do, as a strange mystery, which I must not attempt to comprehend; not considering, that a mystery does not necessarily suppose an incomprehensibility; and losing sight of the danger of admitting, what now appears to me to be an impossibility. It is impossible for me, and I now perceive that it has always been impossible to make one of three, or three of one,—one perfect and infinite being equal to three perfect and infinite beings. There may be gifted minds capable of comprehending this doctrine, but such is not mine. It is plain to me now, that I have all my life been

---

⁸² Burnap, 36-37.

worshipping three distinct beings; never having been able, with the most strenuous efforts, to combine the three in my own mind so as to form a simple idea. But now I bow to the divine authority, when I hear Jehovah saying, "Hear, O Israel, the Lord the God is *one* Lord." [83]

The argument is sometimes advanced that we ought to elevate Jesus to the status of God just to be "on the safe side." This presumes there is not enough written in the Bible to differentiate between God and Jesus. Yet without a doubt there is enough to draw a clear distinction between God and Jesus, and to say any more or less than this is to simply quit the pursuit of common-sensical research. To make "more" of anyone is to make a false representation of that person:

I dare not say less: for there is his own emphatic declaration: "Whosoever shall confess me before men, him will I confess before my Father who is in heaven. But whosoever shall deny me before men, him will I also deny before my Father who is in heaven." How confess him, if not in the very offices he claimed?—I dare not say more; assuredly, I dare not say aught which shall seem as far as words can to dethrone God, aught which shall seem to derogate from the essential, underived, unrivaled Supremacy of the Father. I know that I am required to "honor the Son, even as I honor the Father," but in this connection I also know that I can honor the Father rightly and justly, only by receiving and honoring the Son as His Minister and Representative, in precisely those Offices and Relations in which it has pleased God to place and reveal him. I should dishonor God, nay, I should dishonor the Son, by attempting any thing more. [84]

Biblical statements make it fairly clear that placing anybody or anything on a level of equality with God is an attack on His supremacy:

IN regard to the different senses in which the term God may be used, I have recently met with testimony, which, to

---

[83] Dana, 3-4.

[84] Farley, 123-124.

some persons, may be rather new and startling. I will introduce this testimony by a short extract from a published sermon recently preached by the Rev. Dr. Gilman in the Unitarian church of Charleston, S. C. It is entitled "Unitarian Christianity no Novel Device." "Nearly a hundred years ago," says he, "the Pastor of a Baptist Church in this city, with his congregation, adopted Arian sentiments, which he publicly defended in his discourses, and explained in a printed catechism still extant, and of which a copy may be seen in the library of your speaker." In an Appendix, he says: "The Baptist Catechism, referred to in this page, is a curious document, dated Charleston, and is dedicated to Mrs. Amarantha Farr, Mrs. Francis Elliott, Mrs. Elizabeth Elliott, and Mrs. Elizabeth Williamson, all descendants, by blood or marriage, of Mr. William Elliott. The following extracts will sufficiently illustrate the assertion made in the discourse:

Qu. Can we be guilty of Idolatry in worshipping Jesus Christ?

Ans. Yes, the Majority of Christians are guilty of it, by giving him the Worship proper to the Father alone. They exceed the Limit of God's Command in this Particular, whereby Jesus Christ, who came to abolish Idolatry is made the greatest Idol in the world.'" [85]

---

[85] Dana, Appendix A, 277.

THREE PRIMARY TRINITARIAN VERSES

Among the various nuances contained in verses thought to support Trinitrian ideology, three verses are most heaveily relied upon as statements in favor of a three-in-one God. As we shall see, there is nothing remotely approaching the notion of a triune god in them when the slightest bit of common sense is employed in considering their actual or probable meanings. The Trinitarian interpretations are so strained that they raise a strong presumption against the doctrine itself. It is important to note again that I have no problem with anything anyone believes, as I am not of the school that thinks God needs my protection so everyone understands who or what God is. My primary objection is the charges that are still leveled against those who don't embrace the interpretations and subsequent theologies sprouting out of an odd use of language and from strained logic.

The first verse is Matthew 28:19: "Go ye therefore, and teach all nations, baptizing them in the name of the Father, and of the Son, and of the Holy Ghost." This is sometimes referred to as the baptismal formula, since it is employed during water baptism by some who believe they are to confess, in conjunction with their immersion in water, that the subjects mentioned in this verse are each God. Since this verse says that Christians are to be *baptized into* each of these subjects, this is argued as proof of their co-equality with each other. This, however, is simply a prejudicial interpretation:

> The passage most commonly quoted to support the Trinity is the form of baptism, Matt. 28c. 19v. Now I ask, can the popular notions of the Trinity be fairly deduced from this passage! Does it assert that the Father, Son, and Holy Spirit, are three

persons united in the Godhead? No! Does it say they are all equal? No! Does it affirm that each of these is to be worshipped in Unity? No such thing; then where is the doctrine in question to found here?[1]

These are good questions. Can it be reasonably inferred from this verse that, by the mere mention of three subjects, they are equal with each other? Are we to infer that wherever more than one subject is mentioned in the same verse that co-equality is to be assumed, or, more absurdly, that they are the same person?

> The apostle says, that the Israelites "were baptized into Moses in the cloud and in the sea." Is Moses therefore God, or a person of the Trinity? In the Old Testament it is said "the people worshipped God and the king." Was the king therefore God, because he is thus associated with him? The Israelites were baptized into Moses, as the prophet of God; could they not be baptized into Christ, as the only Mediator between God and man?[2]

By comparing Matt. 28:19 to other verses that contain the expression *baptized into*, we see that the expression has a meaning that is more reasonable than what Trinitarians contend. And it should be noted that it is not necessary to know what the true meaning is in order to rule out an absurd interpretation. In the case of Matt. 28:19, we need only learn that the Israelites were *baptized into* Moses to see that this expression does not make make Moses God:

> In judging whether or not we have here, as alleged, a clear statement of the doctrine of the Trinity, it should be remembered that, throughout the whole Gospel of Matthew, there is no expression or word, in which that doctrine can be supposed to be alluded to, until we come to this, the last verse but one of the Gospel. So far, therefore, as this Gospel is concerned, it would appear that throughout all the ministry of Christ, in all his discourses, parables and sayings of various kinds here recorded, there is nothing to show that the trinity

---

[1] Thomas, 5.

[2] Burnap, 28.

of Persons was ever spoken of between our Lord and his disciples, until we come to the latest moments of his life on earth. And then (we are asked to believe), by using the words now under notice, he revealed the truth to the disciples and to the Christian world of future ages.

Is the supposition a probable one? Could such a doctrine have been withheld from the world in such a manner—left to be revealed to them only in this slight and accidental sort of way,—and that too, not directly, or as a doctrine of supreme importance offered to their faith, but, after all, only as something implied or deducible by way of inference from the words employed?

For, it will be observed, even this verse does not explicitly declare Three Persons and One God. It does not say that the three are each equally God, one as much as the other; it does not say that the Son is God, or the Holy Spirit, but simply "Go and baptize into the name" of the Three, whatever these may each severally be.

But what, then, is the meaning of the injunction? To be baptized into the name of any person (or into that person) does not presuppose that he is accepted as an object of worship, but as one of religious faith. Such baptism makes him the subject of recognition and belief, under some implied or imputed character, whatever that may be. St. Paul says of the fathers of his nation that they were "all baptized into Moses" (1 Cor. x. 1, 2). He does not mean that they had been taught to consider Moses as God, or to make him an object of their worship. He can only mean that they recognized and had faith in him as their leader, and adopted the religious system which he gave them....

Baptism "into the name of the Father," was baptism into the confession of the One God, the Heavenly Father:—no unimportant article of faith to a convert from heathenism, who had perhaps been a believer in many gods, or in none. Baptism into the name of the Son was the distinctively Christian part of the rite. It was baptism into the belief and reception of Jesus as Christ, the Messiah, or "Son of God." This was evidently an essential part of the new disciple's confession.

Neither Jew nor heathen could become a Christian without it. Baptism into the Holy Spirit was, to the convert of those days, baptism into the confession and participation of those gifts of the Spirit, which in the Book of Acts are stated to have been shed upon the disciples, and are often referred to in the course of that book.

We must not forget that in the early Christian times it was a disputed question whether the Messiah (the Son) had come or not. The Jewish nation did not receive Jesus of Nazareth in that character. They rejected and crucified him. Hence it was indispensable that converts should make a distinct confession of what was thus denied, and should be baptized into the name of the Son; that is to say, into the belief in Jesus, not as God, but as Christ. In regard to the Holy Spirit, it will be remembered that there is a passage in the Acts where the Christian disciples, imperfectly instructed, are said to know nothing of that object of faith. "We have not so much as heard whether there be any Holy Spirit" (Acts xix. 2). It is impossible to think that they could have been left in such ignorance, when they became Christians, had the term "Holy Spirit" really denoted the third co-equal member of a Divine Trinity, into the confession of which converts were received by baptism.[3]

Some have argued that the phrase *in the name of* proves that all three subjects mentioned in this verse are real persons, as the following quote illustrates:

> It may be admitted that one might speak of baptism into a doctrine or religion. However, the expression "baptizing them in the name of" removes all doubt that persons are meant.[4]

Mr. Bowman's inference is simple conjecture. Reliance on the phrase *in the name of,* in light of the fact that it is not commonly used in our culture today, is insufficient to prove that a plurality of

---

3 Smith, 88-91.

4 Robert Bowman, *Why You Should Believe In the Trinity* (Grand Rapids, MI: Baker Books, 1989), 125.

persons was implied by the writer. If this expression were meant to prove there are three persons, then it would say "in the *names* of," which is grammatically correct. All things considered, there are more reasonable explanations as to what the expression means:

> There are but two texts of any importance which are supposed to imply the doctrine of a Trinity. The first is the form of baptism: "Go ye and baptize all nations in the name of the Father, of the Son, and of the Holy Ghost." But this teaches no Trinity of persons, much less of equal persons in the Godhead. On the contrary, the use of the word Son implies inferiority. The words mean that we should be baptized into faith in God as our Father, in the Son as our Saviour, and in the Holy Spirit as the guiding influence which proceeds from God. This comprises the whole Christian faith.[5]

The more one considers this verse, the more it becomes apparent that the Trinitarian explanations are a matter of bias. Mr. Bowman, a little further on in his book, in developing a Trinitarian formula from this verse, in language not as certain as his earlier pronouncement, says:

> Moreover, we already know that the Father is God, so that coordination of the Son and the Spirit with the Father *tends to support* their being God also.[6] (Emphasis mine.)

This interpretation depends upon inference, with the result being that the "coordination of" (what an expression!) the Son and Spirit only "tends to" support the doctrine of the Trinity. Such imprecise language should not be taken seriously, but since the doctrine is considered to be a foregone conclusion by its advocates this sort of sloppiness is commonplace and overlooked.

Regarding the "baptismal formula," as it was eventually called, it is significant to note that it was never carried out in the New Testament. In the accounts of water baptism there is no record of anyone being baptized according to this so-called formula or blueprint. This is fairly convincing against it being prescribed as a ritualistic form, as

---

[5] Eliot, 22.

[6] Bowman, 125.

well as against it being support for the strange notion of three persons existing in one God:

> Here we beg leave to refer to the Acts of the Apostles, as confirmatory of this view of the passage. By this reference we see at once, that the direction which our Lord gave respecting baptism, was not intended as a baptismal form, *i.e.* as a set of words to be employed when even baptism was performed, much less was it intended to convey a particular notion of the divine nature, into which converts were to be baptized: we infer this from the fact that the Apostles never used the words contained in the above direction; when they baptized, we never find them baptizing into the *Father, Son, &c.,* but always simply into the name of Jesus. Now had our Lord intended his direction respecting baptism, to convey peculiar notions of the Deity—of his consisting of a union of three persons: for instance, had the Apostles viewed it, in this light, they certainly would never have baptized one convert without using the very expressions of our Lord—they would not merely have baptized into the *name of* Jesus, as they did, but into the Father, Son, and Holy Spirit.[7]

Many make the common mistake of accepting the most widely held belief in the absence of being able to personally explain a given verse. If, for example, somebody were unable to explain what it meant to be "baptized into," it is not uncommon that he would, in his zeal for an explanation, go along with the prevailing explanation for the verse. The availability of prevailing opinions makes it easier to have opinions about things, theological or otherwise, which is part of the dynamic of groupthink. But this is a dangerous habit to develop, since by adopting beliefs in this way one is not critiquing the texts for oneself and therefore not truly developing a faith of one's own. Nonetheless, there are much better explanations as to what it means to be "baptized into":

> Here, as in many other passages, the error and obscurity of the version have favored the imposition of a sense upon the

---

[7] Thomas, 7-8.

passage which the original does not suggest. "To baptize *in the name* of another" is to baptize by authority from him, as his representative. But this every scholar knows is not the sense of our Saviour's direction. The Greek word rendered "name" is in this passage, as often in the Scriptures, redundant. It is used pleonastically, by an idiom of the Hebraistic Greek, in which the Septuagint and New Testament are written. We have not the same turn of expression in our own language. In the original, it adds nothing to the sense of the passage. When literally rendered into another language in which the same idiom does not exist, it tends only to obscure the meaning. It should not therefore appear in a translation into English.

But even if the term "name" be retained, there is no ground for the rendering, "baptizing them in the name." The Greek preposition *eis* should here be rendered *to*. The whole passage may be thus translated:—

"Go ye, therefore, and make disciples of all nations; baptizing them to the Father, and to the Son, and to the holy spirit."

The meaning of which is, Go and make converts of men of all nations, dedicating them by baptism, through which they are to make a solemn public profession of their faith, to the worship of the Father, the only true God, to the religion which he has taught men by his Son, and to the enjoyment of those holy influences and spiritual blessings which accompany its reception.

One may easily understand how this passage has appeared to Trinitarians to convey so clear a notice of the Trinity, since they have adopted its terms as technical in their theology, and imposed upon them new and arbitrary senses, which have become strongly associated with the words, Father, Son, and Holy Ghost. But he who contends that any proof of the doctrine is to be derived from it, must proceed altogether upon assumptions obviously false. Let us state them clearly.

In the first place, to prove the personality of the holy spirit from this passage, it must either be assumed,—

That when three objects are mentioned together in a sentence, and two of them are persons, the third must be a person also (as to the tenableness of this assumption, see 1 Samuel xxv. 32, 33; Acts xx. 32); that is the Father and Son being persons, the holy spirit must be a person also:

Or, it may be assumed,—

That when three persons or objects are thus mentioned together, they must all be of equal dignity (See 1 Timothy v. 21; Revelation i. 4, 5); so that, in the present case, the Father being God, the same character must also belong to the Son and holy spirit.

These are the only grounds on which the deity of the Son and of the holy spirit can be inferred from the passage before us.[8]

Thus, Matt. 28:19 is consistent with the supremacy of the Father, and lends no support for the abstruse claim of a three persons existing in one being.

2 CORINTHIANS 13:14

The second verse thought by some to contain a statement of the doctrine of the Trinity is 2 Corinthians 13:14: "The grace of the Lord Jesus Christ, and the love of God, and the communion of the Holy Ghost, be with you all." This is sometimes referred to as the "apostolic benediction."

A trinity of co-equal persons is inferred on the same grounds as it is from Matthew 28:19, which is that the mention of three subjects in the same verse is thought to allude to the co-equality and "godhood" of the subjects. This verse, contrary to being a favorable argument for the notion of three persons in one God, is directly opposed to it. Here, God is distinguished from the Lord Jesus Christ and the holy ghost, making it clear that Jesus could not be God:

The form of the benediction then, "The grace of the Lord Jesus Christ, and the love of God, and the communion of the Holy Ghost," contains a strong argument *against* the Trinity, instead of being an argument in favor of it. Not only is the subject of the second clause God—"the love of God,"—but

---

8 Norton, 215-218.

the subjects of the first and third clauses are shut out of Deity by the particle and—"the grace of the Lord Jesus Christ, *and* the love of God, *and* the fellowship or communion of the Holy Spirit be with you all." [9]

The second instance in which the doctrine of the Trinity is thought to be clearly expressed in the New Testament occurs again in an accidental kind of way, in the last verse of one of St. Paul's Epistles (2 Cor. 13:14):—"The grace of the Lord Jesus Christ, and the love of God, and the communion of the Holy Ghost be with you all." The words are easily shown to be inconsistent with the doctrine they are supposed to express. For it is plain that the Almighty Being is separated, in the writer's conception, from Jesus Christ and from the Holy Spirit. "The grace of the Lord Jesus Christ, *and* the love of God, *and* the communion of the Holy Spirit:"—three objects of thought, GOD being one of them, distinctly apart from the others. What the Apostle wishes for his Corinthian friends is simply this, that the grace (or favour) of Jesus Christ (their expected Judge) may be with them, and God's love, and a participation in the good gifts and influences, constantly denoted in the New Testament by the phrase Holy Spirit. [10]

"No text of the New Testament has been more frequently cited, perhaps, in proof of the Trinity, than the last verse of Paul's second epistle to the Corinthians. It is a benediction, 'The grace of our Lord Jesus Christ, and the love of God, and the participation of the Holy Spirit, be with you all.' Here, it is said, are the three persons of the Trinity, brought together, made equal, and more than this, made the objects of worship. But all appearance of intimating such a doctrine, is instantly dissipated by a consideration, which seems to have been strangely overlooked. The second person of this Trinity is *God*, the whole Deity, without any distinction of person. 'The love of *God*.' So far then from supporting the doctrine of the Trinity, this passage contains a strong argument against it.

---

9 Burnap, 29.

10 Smith, 90-91.

Divinity is by implication *denied* to Christ, for he is spoken of in connexion with God, but as distinct from him. 'The grace of our Lord Jesus Christ, and the love of God.' There is no intimation that these two persons are one being, or that they are both God, or constitute one God. One is God, in the most unlimited sense, *comprehending* the three persons, if the word God ever can be supposed to do so. The other is the Lord Jesus Christ, connected with God by the particle *and*, proving, if any thing can prove, that the Lord Jesus Christ is out of the Deity, and not in it.

"In the last clause the word 'fellowship' serves to mystify this passage. In common language, this word is nearly synonymous with the word 'companionship,' and would seem to intimate that the Apostle wished the early Christians the companionship of the Holy Spirit. But the English word, which comes nearest to it, is 'participation.' We have fellowship with a person, but participation *in* a thing. It is only by a figure of speech, that we can participate in a person. We participate in a thing without a figure. The meaning, therefore, evidently is, 'May you be partakers of the Holy Spirit.'

"The phrase, 'the Holy spirit,' so far from indicating a person, is in the original in the neuter gender, signifying that it is not a person, but a thing. There are doubts then, suggested by the very language, not only whether the Holy Spirit be a Person of the Trinity, but whether it be a person at all. Those doubts are much strengthened, when we compare such parallel passages as these: 'Ye shall be baptized with the Holy Ghost not many days hence.' The same writer expresses the same meaning in another place; 'I send the promise of my Father upon you—ye shall be endued with *power from on high*.' To be baptized with a person, hardly makes sense. Besides, what is called the 'Holy Ghost,' in one passage, is evidently called 'power from on high' in the other. Power from on high is evidently not a person." [11]

Instead of favoring the doctrine of the Trinity, this pas-

---

[11] George Burnap, *Expository Lectures,* 13-15; quoted in Dana, App. H, 288-289.

sage bears strongly against it. Three objects are distinctly mentioned—God, Christ, and the Spirit. If Christ and the Spirit were persons in the Trinity, the distinct mention of them would be superfluous, they being included in God. But as one of the objects mentioned is called "God," it follows that neither of the other two can be God; for we know that "there is none other God but one." If the three objects were the three persons in the Trinity, why is the name "God" given to one of them only? [12]

When properly understood, 2 Corinthians 13:14 is the essence of the Christian faith. It is in accord with Matthew 28:19. God is our heavenly Father, Jesus is Lord, and holy spirit denotes the internal influences which assist people in living a life connected with God.

1 JOHN 5:7

The third verse that has been thought to prove the doctrine of the Trinity is 1 John 5:7: "There are three that bear record in heaven, the Father, the Word, and the Holy Ghost, and these three are one." This is the easiest one to address since it is a known forgery, and many learned Trinitarians acknowledge its spuriousness. It is easy enough for anyone to discover by comparing the English with the Greek to see that the words "in heaven, the Father, the Word, and the Holy Ghost, and these three are one. And there are three that bear witness in earth" were added to the Bible at a later date. These words are not in any manuscripts of reputation. In the introduction of a letter to a friend which (the letter) was subsequently published as a book, Sir Isaac Newton, in his lengthy study on 1 John 5:7 and another verse, writes:

> SIR,
>
> SINCE the discourses of some late writers have raised in you a curiosity of knowing the truth of that text of Scripture concerning the testimony of the Three in Heaven, 1 John v. 7, I have here sent you an account of what the reading has been in all ages, and by what steps it has been changed, so far as

---

[12] Morgridge, 117.

I can hitherto determine by records. And I have done it the more freely, because to you, who understand the many abuses which they of the Roman Church have put upon the world, it will scarce be ungrateful to be convinced of one more than is commonly believed. For although the more learned and quick-sighted men, as Luther, Erasmus, Bullinger, Grotius, and some others, would not dissemble their knowledge, yet the generality are fond of the place for its making against heresy. But whilst we exclaim against the pious frauds of the Roman Church, and make it a part of our religion to detect and renounce all things of that kind, we must acknowledge it a greater crime in us to favour such practices, than in the Papists we so much blame on that account: for they act according to their religion, but we contrary to ours. In the Eastern nations, and for a long time in the Western, the faith subsisted without this text; and it is rather a danger to religion, than an advantage, to make it now lean upon a bruised reed. There cannot be better service done to the truth, than to purge it of things spurious: and therefore knowing your prudence, and calmness of temper, I am confident I shall not offend you by telling you my mind plainly; especially since it is no article of faith, no point of discipline, nothing but a criticism concerning a text of Scripture which I am going to write about.[13]

In the next fifty-eight pages of his work, Newton proceeds to expose the history of 1 John 5:7, when it was added to the epistle, by whom, and how it gained entrance into later manuscripts, including the King James Version. It is widely recognized that the verse is spurious:

The words are now generally known and acknowledged to be spurious. On this point it is sufficient here to cite the testimony of Dean Alford [a Trinitarian]. He observes that the words *"are omitted by all Greek MSS. (till the sixteenth century); all the Greek Fathers; all the ancient versions; and most of the Latin*

---

13 Sir Isaac Newton, *An Historical Account of Two Notable Corruptions of Scripture* (London: John Green, 1841), 1-2.

Fathers." [14]

The passages usually adduced as the strongest proof of the Trinity, among which we cannot seriously admit the words of John, 1st epistle, 5c. 7v. "There are three" &c., because it is admitted by most competent judges of all religious parties, to form no part of sacred writ. Those who have made this confession, are amongst the most eminent divines who have ever adorned this or any other country, viz. Erasmus, Martin Luther, Bentley, Sir Isaac Newton, Waterland, Adam Clarke, Jortin, Porson, Priestly, and many others. [15]

Unfortunately, there are still some who are unaware that 1 John 5:7 is a forgery and continue to base their belief in the doctrine of the Trinity upon it. For some reason, the forged words have not been removed from later versions of the Bible. Is it inappropriate to wonder about a system of doctrines whose only expressly stated formula is a forgery?

---

[14] Smith, 88.

[15] Thomas, 5.

CHAPTER 4

THE DOCTRINE OF THE DOUBLE NATURE OF CHRIST

One of the primary elements of Trinitarian dogma is that Jesus Christ has two natures, one of God and the other of man. This is a different claim than that of the Trinity, which is that God exists in three persons. The doctrine of the double nature of Christ arose from the circumstances that Jesus is called a man throughout the Bible, but some of his later followers began to think he was also God or a god. In order to reconcile the seemingly irreconcilable views, arguments were developed over the centuries to account for the fact that Jesus is clearly delineated as a man in the biblical and historical texts, which, absent any extrinsic and compelling evidence, would naturally disqualify him from being God.

The special need for this doctrinal development arose because the Bible presents Jesus in a different "class" than the Father. The Father is spoken of as having no limitations. Jesus, being a man, was limited, and there are explicit statements that make his limitations clear. Jesus was ignorant of the day and hour of his return (Mark 13:39). He said his Father was greater than himself (John 14:28). John said that nobody has seen God at any time (John 1:18). Timothy wrote that there is one God, and one mediator between God and men, the man Christ Jesus (I Tim. 2:5). To maintain the belief that Jesus is God, many verses need to be accounted for that so clearly represent Jesus as a man:

> We now proceed to examine another branch of orthodoxy intimately connected with the Trinity, which is the hypostatic union of the second person of the Trinity with the man Christ Jesus. The opponents of anti-Trinitarianism cannot deny that Jesus is frequently spoken of in Scripture as a man, and as dis-

tinct from and inferior to the Being who is usually spoken of under the name of 'God.' But they maintain also that the names and titles, the attributes, the works, and the worship of the Father are also given to the Son. Hence they are led to suppose that he was constituted of a nature both human and divine, which constitution of his person took place at his birth of the Virgin Mary, by his taking the manhood into the Godhead, or by his taking the human nature into union with his Deity.[1]

The reasoning employed in the development of the doctrine is so arbitrary it is as if those who developed it decided to accept it as true without considering what their arguments and conclusions sounded like. Perhaps they were frustrated with such a difficult task as making three persons in one God, making a man into God, and then making a case for this doubled-natured man part of a triune godhead. It requires little scrutiny before the mind recoils at the propositions put forth in support of the doctrine of the two natures in Christ. The claim that Jesus is a man and God is a matter of prejudice, and is manifestly absurd in light of some of the accounts of Jesus's own statements:

> Assuredly, his language, as recorded by St. Mark, must then be understood to admit, nay, with emphasis to declare his ignorance both as man and as God, both in his human and in his divine nature, "of that day and hour." If ignorant in that respect, if ignorant on any one, and but one point, he was not Omniscient. And I cannot help adding, though not discussing that topic now, that if in his divine nature, if as God the Son, he was not Omniscient, then that divine nature was not the highest; then, as God the Son he was not the Supreme; he was God only in an inferior and subordinate sense, or as he himself, on another occasion, expressed it, as being one "to whom the word of God came."
>
> The argument is not weakened by reading "no one" instead of "no man" in the first clause, as the Greek might at least with equal correctness be rendered. For the words "the

---

[1] Hyndman, 33.

Son" are still there; they still stand in full force, used by Christ himself to distinguish himself from the Father, whom he describes as "the ONLY TRUE GOD;" while the expression "no one" is so sweeping of itself as to carry with it all other beings, even if none of them were specified, and unless some were excepted. One glorious exception, as we have seen, is made—"the Father only." The Father alone being Omniscient, is GOD alone and supreme.[2]

It seems it should be unnecessary to make assertions such as God is not a man. But it is necessary to state things as elementary as this when addressing the arguments in favor of the doctrine of two natures in Christ. By his own admission Jesus was ignorant of the day and hour of his return, which would seem to immediately disqualify him from being God. This is not only because of his claim of his own ignorance on the issue, but because he said that only the Father, and therefore not the holy spirit, knew the day and hour of his return. If, as Trinitarians argue, Jesus said this in his capacity as a man, why is the holy spirit, which is, according to Trinitarians, co-equally God, omitted from having knowledge of Jesus's return? If the holy spirit were co-equal with the Father, "he" would have been just as knowledgeable as the Father. But Trinitarian arguments continue unabatedly, trying by any means to save what was absurd from the very beginning. The Father is represented as the only being without any limitations—limitations which Jesus himself admitted to having:

The frequency with which God is called or described as "the Father," is also in this connection to be borne in mind. In the New Testament He is called simply "the Father" in no less than one hundred and twenty-two passages; in nineteen, "God the Father;" in various places, "God our Father," "Our Father," "God, even our Father," "God, even the Father," "Father of Mercies," or merciful Father, "Father of Glory," or glorious Father. He is declared in express terms to be "the God and Father of our Lord Jesus Christ;" while our Lord himself described Him as "your Father which is in heaven," "thy Father," "your Heavenly Father," "your Father;" and after his

---

2 Farley, 12-13.

Resurrection, directed Mary to say to his disciples: "I ascend unto my Father and your Father, to my God and your God." Never in Scripture, not in one solitary instance, is there the phrase God the Son—which is so familiar to our ears that its profanity passes unnoticed.[3]

There are a few verses that are used to support the doctrine of the double nature of Christ. In these, Jesus is thought to be referred to as God, so, taken literally, the inference is made that Jesus must be God as well as a man. One such verse is Hebrews 1:8: "But unto the Son he saith, 'Thy throne, O God, is for ever and ever; a sceptre of righteousness is the sceptre of the kingdom; thou hast loved righteousness and hated iniquity.' " Contrary to the contentions of some Trinitarians, this verse is recognized by other Trinitarians as an incorrect translation, and therefore does not contain the proof that some had hoped. Even if we allow the title *God* to be applied to Christ in this verse, it does not mean that he is the supreme God. The title *God* (or *god*) was applied to people who were obviously not the supreme God. This custom is not practiced in the West, but by looking at a few parts of Scripture we may see how it was applied:

> There is probably no text oftener quoted against us, than the first part of the Epistle to the Hebrews, particularly the eighth verse: "But unto the Son he saith, the throne, O God, is for ever and ever; a sceptre of righteousness is the sceptre of the kingdom; thou hast loved righteousness and hated iniquity." The word God is here applied to Christ, and is understood as proof of his deity. This, however, would be an uncertain proof, for the same word is applied quite frequently in a subordinate sense. It was applied to Moses, who was said to be "a god to Pharaoh." Exod. vii. 1. Those also were called Gods to whom the word of God came. See John x. 35. We must look, therefore, to the connection to see what its meaning is in this case; and we read directly after the words quoted, "Therefore God, even the God, hath anointed thee with the oil of gladness above the fellows." Observe, therefore, which is the point of our argument in this case, that, even when spoken

---

3 Farley, 13-14.

of as God, there is the Supreme God over him, from whom he receives his anointing, and by whom he is raised above his equals. Let me read to you, also, the beginning of that same chapter, that you may see how plainly the dependence of Christ upon the Father is expressed.

"God, who at sundry times and in divers manners spake in time past unto the fathers by the prophets, Hath in these last days spoken unto us by his Son, whom he hath appointed heir of all things, by whom also he made the worlds; Who being the brightness of his glory, and the express image of his person, and upholding all things by the word of his power, when he had by himself purged our sins, sat down on the right hand of the Majesty on high; Being made so much better than the angels, as he hath by inheritance obtained a more excellent name than they. For unto which of the angels said he at any time, Thou art my Son, this day have I begotten thee? And again, I will be to him a Father, and he shall be to me a Son?" We admit that words cannot easily express higher exaltation than this. It was the Apostle's intention to speak in the strongest terms which were consistent with truth, and he has done so. In reading them we perceive that the exaltation of Christ is greater than we can fully comprehend. But at the same time we perceive, with equal plainness, delegated authority and absolute dependence on the Father. On the one hand, we can have no doubt that his highest nature is here spoken of, for there is no passage in which stronger words are used. On the other hand, we read that he did not speak of himself, but that God spoke by him; that in all his highest offices he was the agent of God; working only by God's power; that he obtained a more excellent name than the angels by inheritance, according to the appointment of God; that there was a time when his existence began, as plainly expressed in these words, "*This day* have I begotten thee." In the tenth, eleventh, and twelfth verses, which are a quotation from Psalm cii., the Almighty himself is addressed as the source of all power and might; after which the Apostle returns to his former subject, the dignity of Christ, which he again ascribes to God as the Author and Giver.[4]

This is an important point in the debate regarding the supremacy of the Father. He is always designated as the origin and giver of power and authority. So if Jesus is anywhere called *God* (or *god*), it is to be understood in a subordinate sense. He is one unto whom the word of God came and, just as the prophets and judges before him, is, by idiom, entitled to the title of *God*.

Another verse that some think is proof of Jesus's deity is Philippians 2:6: "Who, being in the form of God, thought it not robbery to be equal to God." If this verse were meant to prove Christ's deity, it would stand as a prime example of verbosity and circumlocution. Thinking that the phrase "thought it not robbery to be equal with God" is equivalent to "is God" is to pervert the sense of the words employed. If Jesus were God, this verse would say something like, "Who, being God, etc." But it is unnecessary to address this verse at length here. The following quote sheds light on the meaning of this verse, and is an interpretation which harmonizes with the whole of Scripture:

> In the sixth verse it is said of Christ, "Who, being in the form of God, thought it not robbery to be equal to God;" of which Calvin says, "The form of God here signifies majesty; I acknowledge, indeed, that Paul does not make mention of Christ's divine essence." To be in the form of God means, to be the image or manifestation of God; which is also the interpretation adopted by Le Clerc and Macknight. The proper meaning of the words, "Thought it not robbery to be equal with God," is that given by Bishop Sherlock, namely, "He was not tenacious of appearing as God; did not eagerly insist to be equal with God." This is the meaning adopted by Coleridge, Professor Stuart, Martin Luther, Melancthon, Archbishop Tillotson, Paley, and many others of the most eminent Trinitarian writers. But the exact meaning of the words is not important to our present argument. Whatever they mean, their limitation is found in the ninth and following verses. "*Wherefore God hath highly exalted him*, and given him a name which

---

4 Eliot, 52-53.

is above every name, that at the name of Jesus every name shall bow, of those in heaven, and those in earth and those under the earth, and that every tongue should confess that Jesus Christ is the Lord, to the glory of God the Father." [5]

To comprehend the breadth of complex and abstruse arguments used to support the Trinitarian system, it is important to understand the doctrine of the double nature of Christ in light of the doctrine of a triune God. The doctrine of the Trinity asserts there are three *persons* in one *nature*, while the doctrine of the double nature reverses the order of this terminology and states that there are two *natures* in one *person*:

> "As before, of the doctrine of the Trinity, so now of the doctrine of the Hypostatic Union, as it is called, I ask for a single hint throughout the New Testament of the inconceivable fact that, in the body of Jesus, resided the mind of God and the mind of man—two natures, the one finite, the other infinite, yet making but one person—a difficulty you will perceive the very opposite of that of the Trinity; for whereas that teaches three persons in one nature, this teaches two natures in one person." [6]

The doctrine of the double nature of Christ creates a distorted view of Jesus. When we try to conceive of a being who is both God and man, we become bewildered, as our notions of what it is to be a man are very different from our notions of what it is to be the almighty God. The two terms have their own unique characteristics and are so different that they cannot rationally be predicated of the same being:

> Now by the *nature* of a thing we mean its *qualities*. To say therefore that Christ possesses both a divine and a human nature, is to say that he possesses both the qualities of God and the qualities of man; that the *same mind* consequently is both created and uncreated, both finite and infinite, both dependent and independent, both changeable and unchange-

---

[5] Eliot, 54-55.

[6] Rev.J.H. Thom, *:Liv. Lect. 7th Unitarian Lec.,* 72; quoted in Farley, 129, footnote.

able, both mortal and immortal, both susceptible of pain and incapable of it, both able to do all things and not able, both acquainted with all things and not acquainted with them. Here is one of the persons of the Trinity united to the person of the man; here there is a person or mind both finite and infinite. Now, to use the words of another in expressing my own sentiments, if it be not certain that such a doctrine as this is false, there is no certainty on any subject. It is in vain to call it a mystery; it is an absurdity—it is an impossibility. According to my ideas of propriety and duty, by assenting to it I should culpably abuse those faculties of understanding which God has given me to distinguish between right and wrong, truth and error.[7]

The doctrine of the double nature of Christ, like that of the Trinity, is a doctrine of inference. Neither doctrine is declared in any verse, nor can they be expressed in the language of Scripture. Just as the language of a triune God is absent from the Bible, the language of a double nature is also absent. The term *double nature* isn't in the Bible just as the term *triune* isn't, so scattered verses are assembled in quasi-syllogistic form, inferences are drawn from newly-created contexts, and it is assumed that Jesus is both a mortal man and the almighty God. The absurdity of this method is manifest in the body of theology that comes from it:

> The Church of England, like the Catholic church, says: "The Son—took man's nature—so that two whole and perfect natures, that is to say, the Godhead and manhood were joined together in one person, never to be divided, whereof is one Christ, very God and very man."
>
> Professor Stewart, speaking of Jesus Christ, says, "He must, as it seems to me, be God omniscient and omnipotent, and still a feeble man and of imperfect knowledge."
>
> Now this doctrine is to be rejected, because, like that of the Trinity, it is essentially incredible. It is not a mystery, but as palpable a contradiction as can be stated. By the *nature* of any person or being, is always meant his essential qualities. If

---

7 Hyndman, 34-35.

Christ possess a Divine and Human nature, he must possess the essential qualities of God and the distinctive qualities of man. But these qualities are totally incompatible with one another. The qualities of God are eternity, independence, immutability, exemption from pain, sorrow, and death, omniscience, omnipotence, and omnipresence. But the qualities of MAN are derived existence, dependence, mutability, susceptibility of pain, sorrow and death, comparative weakness and ignorance, and locomotivity. To assert, therefore, that the same mind possesses both a Human and a Divine nature, is to assert that the same mind is both created and uncreated, both finite and infinite, both dependent and independent, both mutable and immutable, both mortal and immortal, both susceptible of pain and unsusceptible of it, both able to do all things and unable, both acquainted with all things and not acquainted with them, both ignorant of some things and possessed of the most intimate knowledge of them, both in all places and only in one place at the same time. Now if this doctrine is not an absurdity, I know not how to conceive of or describe an absurdity. It is a doctrine "which councils and parliaments may decree, but which miracles cannot prove." It is not pretended that any passage of Scripture expressly asserts the doctrine of the Two Natures. Like that of the Trinity, it is a mere inference from the premises laid down by Trinitarians. I know of no allusion in the Bible to the doctrine of the Two Natures, either with or without modification.[8]

This doctrine makes utter confusion of our understanding of Jesus. There is simply nothing in Scripture that supports the amazing supposition that he is both God and man. Unless one borrows creative ideas from various mythologies, there is nothing anywhere, no analogy, no terminology, no defense of any sort that can be produced to support the idea that anybody could be both God Almighty and a man. The doctrine of the double nature of Christ, like that of the Trinity, turns the Bible into confusion, rendering the clearest verses obscure and clouding what we know to be true about God and man:

---

[8] Morgridge, 69-71.

According to those that maintain the doctrine of the two natures in Christ, Christ speaks of himself, and is spoken of by his Apostles, sometimes as a man, sometimes as God, and sometimes as both God and man. He speaks, and is spoken of, under these different characters indiscriminately, without any explanation, and without its being anywhere declared that he existed in these different conditions of being. He prays to that being whom he himself was. He declares to be ignorant of what (being God) he knew, and unable to perform what (being God) he could perform. He affirms that he could do nothing of himself, or by his own power, though he was omnipotent. He, being God, prays for the glory which he had with God, and declares another is greater than himself (see John xvii; Mark xiii. 32; John v. 30; xiv. 28). In one of the passages QUOTED IN PROOF OF HIS DIVINITY, he is called the image of the invisible God; in another of these passages, he, the God over all, blessed for ever, is said to have been anointed by God with the oil of gladness above his fellows; and in a third of them, it is affirmed that he became obedient to death, even the death of the cross (Colossians i. 15, seqq.; Hebrews i. 8, 9; Philippians ii. 5—8). If my readers are shocked by the combinations which I have brought together, I beg them to do me the justice to believe that my feelings are the same with their own. But these combinations necessarily result from the doctrine which we are considering. Page after page might be filled with inconsistencies as gross and as glaring. The doctrine has turned Scriptures, as far as they relate to this subject, into a book of riddles, and, what is worse, of riddles admitting of no solution. I willingly refrain from the use of stronger language which will occur to many of my readers.[9]

As the very Infinite, his [Jesus's] words can have no sincere meaning,—his suffering must be unreal,—his temptation a dramatic show,—his prayers an insincerity,—his sorrowing affection an assumed disguise,—his example of no application to our mortal state. Analyze your own thought of

---

[9] Norton, 60-61.

him, and you will find it resolves itself very much into what I have said... Forced and strained beyond this simple truth, the doctrine is one reposing on insufficient evidence, and in the highest degree confounding to our reason. He is taken from the sphere of our sympathy, and put in a position merely official towards us. An arbitrary and artificial array of "offices" is assigned him, in place of the free, natural, spontaneous exercise of spiritual power by a gloriously endowed and sincerely faithful soul. The charge of assuming such a character he repels as explicitly as possible, in the words which best express his true spiritual relation to man and God:—"If he called them gods unto whom the word of God came, how say ye of him whom the Father hath sanctified and sent into the world, Thou blasphemest, because I said, I am the Son of God?" His own exposition of his lofty claim, "I and my Father are one," is when he prays for all his disciples throughout the world, "*that they all may be one*; as thou, Father, art in me, and I in thee, that they also may be one in us; that the world may believe that thou hast sent me." [10]

If Jesus could not have failed in his life, there would be no way for us to relate to him. His life would become devoid of meaning because we relate to others based on our experiences. Our experience tells us we can fail. If Jesus were God he could not have failed, and therefore could not be somebody with whom we can relate. The doctrine of the double nature of Christ strips us of a true appreciation of the challenges he faced and the manner in which he handled them.

Biblical research is to be conducted in a manner no different than any other type of investigation—it all involves similar thought processes. While researching something, we of course use our minds to sort out whatever information is presented to us. When examining the notion of a three-in-one God or a double-natured God-man, we are confronted with a new approach, one in which common sense is not required or employed. New words and phrases are invented that are incomprehensible and that find their final resting place in the realm of mystery. I wonder if persons who accept the tenets of

---

[10] Allen, 87-88.

their religion on such grounds would confidently embrace flying in an airplane which was constructed by engineers employing the same methodology as those involved in the establishment of Trinitarian dogma. If the method of constructing the airplane were a mystery to its builders, who in their right mind would get on it? Confidence is based upon the reasonableness of the way in which a final product, whether an airplane or a theological claim, is constructed. An exception to standards of reasonableness must be made by someone who decides to accept Trinitarian dogma. This by itself does not bother me, as we each have our own standards of proof and reasons for what we believe, and why. The problem arises when those ardently defending absurdities pronounce those who do not embrace such methodologies as heretics or some other form of spiritual troublemaker. It is desirable to use the mental faculties we human beings have when interpreting the Bible, which is to be interpreted like other books:

> For the obvious principle that Scripture is to be interpreted like any other book, we have the high orthodox authority of Prof. Stuart, and of other orthodox critics of equal eminence with him. "If there be," he says, "any book on earth that is addressed to the reason and common sense of mankind, the Bible is preëminently that book...... If the Bible is not a Book which is intelligible in the same way as other books are, then it is difficult to see how it is a *revelation* .... the Bible is addressed to our reason and understanding and moral feelings; and consequently we are to interpret it in such a way as we do any other book that is addressed to these same faculties." These principles and the rule they involve, are inevitably violated by this hypothesis. By its admission, the Bible cannot be interpreted like other books. Plain language in other books is taken in its plain significance; but here the plainest becomes a riddle. When our Lord says, "My Father is greater than I," he meant only that his divine nature was greater than his human nature! But who can prove that he so meant? Neither he nor his disciples, give the slightest reason to suppose that he or they meant any thing but what their words obviously mean. Besides, we cannot tell when to apply the hypothesis. We are all in the dark; and the Scripture may be made to mean by it

the most contradictory things. Whatever Christ said or did may thus be done away, and the entire New Testament become a mass of enigma.[11]

If we are to gain anything from Scripture, we must understand words according to their plain meaning. Unless some part of speech requires an unusual interpretation, such as an idiom, we ought to interpret the words according to their normal meanings. But exceptions to this must constantly be made for one to accept Trinitarian doctrines as true. Jesus said such things as "My Father is greater than I." The obvious meaning of this must be circumvented in order to sustain the notion that he is co-equal with God. The notion of a double nature in Christ was invented to do exactly this, which makes it acceptable to cast Jesus's recorded words in an entirely different sense than their obvious import:

> We find no fault with those who are satisfied with this answer, but it does not satisfy us. It does not seem to us the fair interpretation of plain language. For, first, we find no passage in the Bible, and there is none, in which it is taught that our Savior had two natures, one human and one divine; but he is always spoken of as a single being, "the Christ, the Son of the Living God." And secondly we think that when he spoke of himself without qualification, using the personal pronouns, *I,* and *myself,* and *me,* he must have used them in their common meaning, and he was certainly, at the time, so understood. If he had intended to have been understood differently, he would have given some indication of it. As he gave none, we take his words in their plain and obvious meaning. Just as you would understand me, if I were to say, "I do not know such a thing," without qualifying the words, so do we understand him. We dare not understand him otherwise. For would it be right for me to say, "I do not know such a thing," if I really know it? and defend myself by saying, that my body does not know it, but my mind does? or that I know it as a clergyman, but not as a citizen? Such would not be a fair use of language; and if the Scriptures were to be interpreted in such a manner,

---

[11] Farley, 130-131.

there is absolutely no doctrine that could not be proved from it. We understand Jesus simply as he spoke, and therefore, while we pray for the time when "at the name of Jesus every knee should bow, and every tongue confess him to be the Lord," we remember that this must always be done "to the glory of God the Father." [12]

The practices of interpretation that give rise to the doctrine of the double nature of Christ foster the negation of the words of Jesus, rendering them unintelligible. The idea that Christians would accept a mechanism that allows such blatant disregard for Jesus's own words is shocking. The idea that Jesus delivered distinct precepts to his church, and then following generations would work feverishly to alter his words and make them a mysterious hypothesis, is unconscionable. It would be impossible to understand the words of anyone, including Jesus, without a clear idea of who they were, and the doctrine of the double nature prevents anyone from obtaining an understanding of his identity:

No words can be more destitute of meaning, *so far as they are intended to convey a proposition which the mind is capable of admitting,* than such language as we sometimes find used, in which Christ is declared to be at once the Creator of the universe, and a man of sorrows; God omniscient, and a feeble man of imperfect knowledge.[13]

By inventing a theory which makes Jesus to be both God and man, Trinitarians have, perhaps unwittingly, assigned to him a split personality:

A being of complex constitution like man is not a being of a *double nature.* The very term double nature, when one professes to use it in a strict, philosophical sense, implies an absurdity. The nature of a being is ALL which constitutes it what it is; and when one speaks of a double nature, it is the same sort of language as if we were to speak of a double individu-

---

12 Eliot, 50-51.

13 Norton, 58.

ality.[14]

Entertaining the notion that Jesus has a split personality is naturally damaging to one's perception of him, and the doctrine of two natures causes him to be an unknowable creature. If we view him as a man, the biblical records that supposedly speak of him as God will mean nothing to us. If we think of him in his supposed capacity as God, then the records of him as a man will mean nothing to us. The two views are too disparate to combine into a workable idea because it moves it into the realm of fantasy, of mythology. If we endeavor to merge the two views, we must end by saying we do not understand him since there is such a large gap between our conception of what God is and what man is. Happily, nowhere in the biblical accounts do we find Jesus affirming any such thing about himself, it was something attributed to him years after his crucifixion. It is merely the inferences of misguided and prejudiced theologians who impute such contrary characteristics to him:

> And what becomes of this individuality, the personality of Christ, the consistency of his character, and the identity of his consciousness, when in the sacred drama of his Gospel manifestation he is represented as performing in two parts, and without change of fleshy garb or tone or speech lays aside now his Deity and now his humanity in alternate moments and in successive sentences of his discourse? His prayers must be construed as soliloquies: his deeds of power must be referred to himself, and his professions of dependence to one element of that self, speaking of another element in the same self. The incongruity, the incoherence, which the Orthodox doctrine of two natures in Christ either puts into or draws from the Scriptures, is not the least of the confounding conditions of the theory. When an individual speaks of himself to others, they understand him as speaking of all that is embraced under his seeming and his real individuality. Unless he has announced himself as representing two characters, and as free to pass from one impersonation into the other without giving warning of the transition, his two characters

---

14 Norton, 60.

will be regarded as making up one character, and some deeds and utterances which would have been intelligible if assigned to either of his impersonations, become inexplicable if referred to his composite character. Only through the help of an illustration—for which, however, we need not apologize, as the candid will recognize the simple intent of a parallelism at only one point—can we express the real embarrassment which we meet in attempting to deal with the theory of a double nature in Christ. Let it be allowed us, then, to conceive of a man who is concerned in business under two relations,—first as an individual, and second as a member of a firm of three partners. Under each of these he receives and writes letters, meets at his two offices those whom he has dealings, and speaks and acts under the exigencies of his double mercantile connections. As a member of the firm he has visited its place of business, consulted its books, and read letters which have made known to him certain facts of a very serious import and interest to others. He goes to his place for transacting the business which he does on his private account. While there, a friend, who is deeply concerned in the very matters of which he has just come to the knowledge, enters and asks for information about them, addressing him as an individual possessing one mind, one consciousness. He replies that he knows nothing about the matter, keeping in reserve, however, the explanation which he makes to himself, that he means that his private letters are silent on the subject. Does he deal fairly with his questioner, especially if that questioner has appealed to him on the very ground of his well-known extended and various relations to the business affairs of the world, and perhaps on the day previous has heard him speak in that character? Precisely this question would be continually presenting itself to us in embarrassing and painful shapes if we accepted the theory of a double nature in Christ, under which, when questioned as an individual on the ground of all he ever claimed to know and to be, he replied according to his choice of characters for the moment, by a claim founded on his Deity, or a profession of limited knowledge or ignorance justified by his humanity.[15]

The doctrine of the double nature of Christ develops the idea that there are two distinct persons in Christ, each with different cognizant abilities. Ardent Trinitarians refute the claim that they have made two distinct persons out of Jesus, but the language employed produces this undesired consequence. It is argued that he made some of his statements as God and others as a man, which is an hypothesis that shows Trinitarians represent Jesus as two separate persons:

> But, our Trinitarian brethren, believing in the two natures of Christ, a doctrine, the consequences of which it is impossible to conceive anything more fatal to Christianity, deserves our particular attention. Having during the last winter evenings, directed your attention to the doctrine of the two natures of Christ, it will only be necessary for me on the present occasion, to beseech of you to look at the consequences of such an hypothesis. If Christ possessed two perfectly distinct natures—perfect manhood and perfect Deity, then he certainly must have had two distinct minds, and consequently two distinct persons; a being this, which even the most mystery-loving mind cannot acknowledge.[16]

The following quote from a Trinitarian writer is an example of how God is viewed as having a split personality. In it we can see just how acceptable it is to believe, fantasy-like, that God can be construed as constituting multiple personalities:

> The more one studies the work of the Holy Spirit compared to that of God as Jehovah, or as "The Almighty," the more one grows convinced of a divine being that overflows the bounds of single personality.[17]

The doctrine of the double nature of Christ is an extension of this way of thinking about God. But Scripture represents Jesus, in arguably his most important mission, as a man:

---

[15] Ellis, 139-140.

[16] Thomas, 29.

[17] Verkuyl, 83.

The Apostle says, that, since by man came death, by man came also the resurrection of the dead.—1 Cor. xv, 21. This declaration favours not the notion of two natures in our redeemer: it rather seems to exclude the necessity of such an hypothesis.—Heb. x, 10.[18]

It is argued by some who favor the doctrine of two natures in Christ that whatever he did on earth prior to his resurrection he did as man, and after his resurrection he returned to being God. This does not agree with I Timothy 2:5, which says that after Jesus's resurrection he is still a man: "For there is one God, and one mediator between God and men, the man Christ Jesus." Paul's letter to Timothy consistently represents Jesus as a man, regardless of timing.

The idea that Jesus is God is negated by Jesus's own testimony of his reliance upon the Father. What need would there have been for the Father to be instrumental in Jesus's life if Jesus could have done it himself? Every part of Scripture that speaks of God's involvement in Jesus's resurrection would be pretentious if the Father was not really needed:

> For it is apparent that, had he enjoyed such an Independent Divine Nature, he would have *lived necessarily*; and it is highly reasonable to think, that his inferior part would have been raised by his *own* omnipotence (and the fact specially recorded; the very contrary seems to be recorded, *remember that Jesus Christ, of the seed of David, was* raised *from the dead, according to my Gospel.*—2 Tim. ii. 8), without any aid or interference of the Father: the exertion of whose mighty Power (Eph., i. 19, 20), where it was really wanted, would appear nugatory, and unbecoming of the divine wisdom. This must be allowed by those who, to solve the difficulties which Scripture presents against their system; so often insist on the *two* natures *complete* in Christ, the *divine* and *human*. But they do not seem to reflect that, if they were pressed on this article, they would find themselves driven to maintain that Jesus Christ is not *one*, but *two* persons or intelligent agents. This was the doctrine of *Nestorius*, condemned and anathematized

---

[18] Gifford, 189, footnote.

in the Council of Ephesus, at which more than two hundred Bishops assisted.[19]

In a similar line of reasoning, Trinitarians also contend that Jesus said "My Father is greater than I" in his human capacity, though as God he was co-equal with the Father. What Trinitarians are really arguing in this case is that Jesus's statement is not true, which is an outright dismissal of Jesus's own declaration that his Father is supreme, and has the effect of making Jesus a liar. It should also be observed that the holy spirit, which is supposedly co-equal with the Father and therefore entitled to the same degree of reverence, is not even mentioned here. The Father is uniformly described as the supreme God, the only one who is greater than Jesus. With the supremacy of the Father recognized, Jesus's words may be readily understood; without this recognition, Jesus's words would be untrustworthy:

> An objection of a graver character lies against the doctrine of the Two Natures. It implicates the moral character of the Holy Jesus; it impeaches his veracity; and exposes him to the charge of equivocation, duplicity, and falsehood. These are weighty charges; and we cannot endure, for a moment, an hypothesis which throws suspicion of dishonesty upon our blessed Saviour.
>
> Jesus said, "I can of mine own self do nothing." The Trinitarian says, Jesus can of himself do everything that God can do. Jesus said, "My Father is greater than I." The Trinitarian says, Jesus is as great as the Father. To one unacquainted with the use that is made of the doctrine of the Two Natures, these assertions appear to be palpable contradictions. He cannot perceive how the assertions of Jesus, and those of Trinitarians, can both be true. But here comes in the doctrine of the Two Natures to reconcile the apparent contradictions. "Jesus is both God and man," says the Trinitarian. "And though as man, he can do nothing of himself, yet as God, he can do everything. Though as man, he is not his Father's equal, yet as God, he is equal with the Father in substance, and power, and glory." But if he is God, can he say in truth, that he can

---

[19] Gifford, 151.

do nothing of himself? What, can God do nothing of himself! If he is God, can he say in truth, My Father is greater than I? What, is the Father greater than God! For a *man* to assert that he cannot do what he is conscious that he can do, is to say what is not true. For what a man can do, in any way, or by any means, he can certainly do. Suppose a man should be required to subscribe his name to a written instrument; and that he should refuse to do it, saying, "I cannot write. I cannot wield the pen. I never learned to write." Suppose it should be known that this man could write; that an explanation should be demanded; and that he should say, he only meant that he could not write with his left hand, though he could use the pen with his right hand as well as any man. Would not such a man subject himself to the charge of equivocation, duplicity, and falsehood?

Let us suppose that a murder is committed in the city of Boston, at noon, by some person or persons unknown—that suspicion fastens upon an innocent man, who, at the time of the murder, was in New York—and that he is charged with the crime, apprehended, and brought to trial. The prisoner summons in his defence a witness, who saw him in New York, about noon, the same day the murder was committed in Boston. This witness, being under oath, is asked, "Did you see the prisoner in New York on the day?" The witness answers, "I did not." This being the only witness for the defendant, he is convicted, and hanged. After the execution, this witness confesses that he did see the man that was hanged, in New York, on the day and hour specified at the trial. Being required to answer for himself, he says, under oath, that his left eye was defective; only his right eye was sound. And when he testified in court that he did not see the prisoner, he meant that he did not see him with his defective eye; but he saw him distinctly with his sound eye. Now, I ask, would not all *honest* men consider such a witness perjured? The only difference I can see, between the conduct of such a witness, and that which the doctrine of the Two Natures imputes to Jesus, is, that what Jesus said was not said under the solemnity of an oath. Knowledge is the eye of the mind. Jesus is said to have two capacities of knowledge—his divine and his human nature. The one is strong and piercing, knowing all things. The other is weak and defective, being ignorant of many things. As such an one, he says, in regard to the time of a certain event, he does not know the day nor the hour. He makes no exception of one of his capacities of knowledge; but says, absolutely, he does not know the time. No one knows but the Father. Yet the doctrine of the Two Natures supposes that Jesus did know the day and hour; and that when he said he did not know, he spoke only of his capacity of knowledge which is weak and defective.

Another objection to the doctrine of the Two Natures is, that it renders it impossible to understand or believe any thing that Jesus says of himself. The terms *I, me, myself, mine own self,* always denote one person, an individual; they include the whole person, all that constitutes him a person. In this sense they were unquestionably used by Christ. When he said, *I, me, myself,* he could not have meant a part of himself. He could not have meant that part of himself which is infinitely less than another part of himself. If it be admitted that Jesus did not mean himself, his whole self, all that constitutes his proper personality, there is no assertion he ever made but what may be contradicted. One has only to say, "This he did as man, it is not true of him as God, therefore it is not true; and this he did as God, it is not true of him as man, therefore it is not true." In this way, every assertion he ever made of himself, may be contradicted. In this way, we may deny his birth, his crucifixion, his death, and his resurrection, because these were true of him only as man, not as God. If, instead of saying, "My Father is greater than I," he had said, "I am not so great as my Father, I am not equal with the Father, I am not God, I am not equal with God," we have only to say, "This he spoke as man, hence it is not true," in order to set his testimony, concerning himself, aside. Now can a doctrine be admitted which renders his plainest sayings unintelligible, and makes it absolutely impossible for him to deny that he is

God, if he had a mind to do so? [20]

It is thought that elevating him to the status of God bestows greater honor upon him, but in reality it has the opposite effect. His words have become nonsense when explained according to the Trinitarian model. The reasoning employed to overthrow the clear meaning of Jesus's words makes him appear deceitful by those who espouse two natures in Christ:

> Regarding it then as the merest hypothesis, for that is all it is, we object, aside of its superfluity, that its admission makes difficulty where there is none; renders vague or obscure the plainest and most explicit language of Scripture. It demands on its face the surrender of reason, and involves positive absurdity. Divine and human qualities, as the essence of being, cannot co-exist in the same person. God is infinite, man is finite, and no being can be at once and essentially finite and infinite. It estops inquiry by its plea of mystery; and drives us, would we believe it, to the old position of Tertullian: *Credo quia impossibile est,* (I believe because it is impossible).
>
> It destroys Christ's unity, and makes him two distinct and opposite beings. That Christ is both God and man, is a proposition plain enough in its statement; but the two predicates are incompatible. But a graver objection is, that in effect it charges our Lord with duplicity. When he declared on one occasion: "Of that day and hour knoweth no man; no, not the angels which are in heaven, neither the Son, but the Father"—what more precise and significant words could he have used, to show that he laid no claim to omniscience, that attribute essential to Deity, without which no being could be God? If there was any one thing of which our Lord was ignorant, he could not be God. And how should we have understood him, had we been present—how did the Apostles, how did the multitude who were present, understand him at the time? They must have understood him as we do, to have made a positive, express declaration, that "of that day and hour" he had no knowledge; and therefore to suppose that he

---

[20] Morgridge, 71-72, 73-74.

made a mental reservation, as to his divine knowledge, while he declared only his human want of it, is to charge him with duplicity, with double-dealing, with deceit.[21]

When Christ declares, without qualification, that there was a certain day and hour of which he knew nothing, we, who are Unitarians, *believe* him. You, on the contrary, make him prevaricate, and, in one nature, deny what he certainly must have known in the other; and yet these two natures you declare to have been in constant and intimate union. You continually make him contradict himself. This is, in my view, sadly to *dishonor* him.[22]

One of the effects of long-standing doctrines is that their terminologies become so entrenched that it no longer seems strange to hear them. The words and phrases that constitute Trinitarian theology have been heard so frequently that the most absurd, confusing and meaningless terms and phrases go unchallenged. This is a prime example of the adage, "If you say something long enough and loud enough, people will believe it." Jesus, because of his alleged double nature, is represented as knowing what he said he did not know. Whatever the current arguments may be, his hearers at that time did not take years to deliberate on his supposed meaning when he spoke. Those present understood him as he spoke, and it is certain that Jesus was well aware of this:

> It is a law of veracity, laid down in the most common books which treat of moral obligation, that to speak the truth, you must say that which is true in the sense you will be understood by your hearers. To say that, which, without further explanation will mislead your hearers, without giving the explanation, is to equivocate.[23]

No one, surely, will deny that Jesus lived and was known among his contemporaries as a man. As such he was loved, welcomed, followed, entreated; as such he was arrested, tried, accused, and put to death; and even his nearest friends were

---

21 Farley, 129-130.

22 Dana, 97.

23 Burnap, 59-60.

so far from suspecting a superior nature in him, that on his death they fell into complete despair, as if his project of restoring "the kingdom of Israel" had wholly failed. Evidently, then, during his ministry he had displayed only the qualities, attributes, characteristics of a man.[24]

If the Bible had been written to prove the doctrine of two natures in Christ or the doctrine of a triune God, it would have been written entirely differently:

On this hypothesis, what mean all his declarations of dependence on God? "Of mine own self I can do nothing; as I hear I judge; and my judgment is just, *because* I seek not mine own will, but the will of the Father which hath sent me;" just as he had before said: "The Son can do nothing of himself, but what he seeth the Father do."—What mean his expressions of trust in God? To Pilate's haughty menace he replied, "Thou couldest have no power at all against me, except it were given thee from above;" and in that most solemn hour when he was drawing his last breath upon the cross, he said: "Father, into the hands I commend my spirit!" To whom were these words addressed? To whom was he accustomed to pray? To one part of his nature—to himself—to a part of himself? What mockery all this seems! [25]

One seeking comfort from Jesus's example may not find it in the Jesus of Trinitarianism. Trinitarian dogma presents a doctrine that makes it impossible to obtain comfort from his example since, according to their hypotheses, he has become incomprehensible. We cannot identify with a being so utterly foreign to us. For example, if he were God, what sort of example could his prayers to God be?

We object to the doctrine of the Two Natures, because it would, if admitted, deprive us of the comforts and advantages arising from the example of Christ's prayers and sufferings. In commenting on the secret morning prayer of Jesus, (Mark i. 35) Dr. Adam Clark, in his great zeal for the doctrine of

---

24 Allen, 81-82.

25 Farley, 131.

the Two Natures, says—"Not that *he* needed any thing, for in him dwelt all the fullness of the Godhead bodily; but that he might be a pattern to us." If the learned Doctor be correct, Jesus must have asked his heavenly Father for innumerable blessings which he did not need, that he might be a pattern to us. But how can we imitate such a pattern without praying for such things as we do not need? If Jesus is God, he must have prayed to himself. But of what benefit to us can such an example be? What comfort or instruction can be derived from contemplating the prayers of Jesus, if every prayer he offered was addressed to himself, and he was so independent that he needed nothing? "Being in agony he prayed more earnestly: and his sweat was as it were great drops of blood falling down to the ground." Was all this only to set us an example? What sympathy can we feel with the sufferer, if he needed nothing he prayed for? Prayer is an expression of dependence and want. If a person who needs nothing prays, is it not mere pretence?—is it not hypocrisy? [26]

All this has the unfortunate effect of pushing Jesus farther from us, which is distinctly *un*-Christian. If everybody accepted the varied Trinitarian opinions on how to read the Bible and what to find there, Jesus would forever remain an enigma to the entire church. Despite Jesus's efforts to teach in a fairly simple manner, the new readings of these simple texts render his and other sayings obscure:

The doctrine of the Two Natures throws obscurity over the sacred pages, and renders passages which are sufficiently plain, quite unintelligible. Take, for example, Heb. i. 1, 2: "God, who at sundry times and in divers manners spake in times past unto the fathers by the prophets, hath in these last days spoken unto us by his Son, whom he hath appointed heir of all things, by whom also he made the worlds." Admitting that this passage relates to the creation of the natural world, what does the word Son denote according to the doctrine of the Two Natures? Does it denote the divine, or the human nature? Or does it comprehend both natures? Son cannot

---

[26] Morgridge, 78.

mean the divine nature, because God cannot be appointed heir of all things, inasmuch as he is the original proprietor and independent owner of all things. Son cannot mean the human nature, because the worlds were created thousands of years before the human nature existed. Son cannot denote both natures, because that would involve both the difficulties just stated; and render the passage more unintelligible and contradictory than either of the other expositions. Thus, by applying the hypothesis of the Two Natures, this perfectly clear and easy text becomes totally unintelligible.[27]

The language employed in explaining or defining the double nature of Christ entails oddly bifurcated thoughts. For example, the human "nature" of Jesus is said to have died on the cross, while his divine nature lived on elsewhere. At the same time we are told that since sin is "infinite," mankind needed an infinite atonement which only the death of God could satisfy. Now, aside from the idea that God could provide a one-time, permanent substitute of His own choosing to assist man in atoning for sin, just as He did when He instructed Israel to sacrifice a lamb once a year for their sins, the argument that only the human part of Jesus died is itself a denial that God died for us. Here, the doctrine of the double nature of Christ conflicts with other Trinitarian arguments:

A comparable difficulty faces Trinitarians when they assert that only the human part of Jesus died. If Jesus were God, and God is immortal, Jesus could not have died. We wonder how it is possible to maintain that "Jesus" does not represent the whole person. Nothing in the Bible suggests that Jesus is the name of his human nature only. If Jesus is the whole person and Jesus died, he cannot be immortal Deity. It appears that Trinitarians argue that only Deity is sufficient to provide the necessary atonement. But if the divine nature did not die, how on the Trinitarian theory is the atonement secured? [28]

---

[27] Morgridge, 75-76.

[28] Sir Anthony Buzzard and Charles Hunting, *The Doctrine of the Trinity: Christianity's Self-Inflicted Wound* (Restoration Fellowship and Atlanta Bible College, 1994), 132.

Another consequence of the doctrine of the two natures in Christ is that it obviates the need for a mediator between God and man. If Jesus is God, then what, according to 1 Timothy 2:5, would be his function as a mediator?

In regard to the necessity of an infinite mediator, Emlyn says: "I judge, that to assert Jesus Christ to be the Supreme God, *subverts* the Gospel doctrine of his mediation; for if I must have one, who is Supreme God and man, for my mediator with God, then, when I address Jesus Christ as the Supreme God, *where* is the God-man that must be my mediator with him? To say he mediates with *himself*, is the same as to say that I must go to him without a mediator; and turns the whole business of mediation into a metaphor, contrary to the common sense of things, as well as against the Scripture."

Now, I ask, is he mediator in his divine or in his human nature? If in his human, he cannot, *according to your ideas*, know what all God's creatures want and pray for. If he mediates in his divine nature, or in both united, then, as Emlyn says, he mediates with himself. But St. Paul says, 1 Tim. ii. 5, "There is but one God, and one mediator between God and men, *the man* Christ Jesus." [29]

When, in Scripture, *God* is declared to be *the head of Christ*: When our Lord says, *The Son can do nothing of himself: My Father is greater than I,* &c., the meaning is, say the writers, that *the Father* is indeed *superior* with respect to Christ's *human nature*, but not with respect to his *divine*. Now, this amounts to the very same as to say, that *the Father* is *greater* than the *human person* of Christ, but not *greater* than his *divine person*; Which is directly supposing *Christ* to consist of *Two Persons*, the one very *different* from the other.... The scheme of *two natures* in Christ, was adopted pretty early (to support the opinion of his *equality* with the *Father*), but it was sometimes thought to be very weakly applied. *Gregory Nazianzen*, about the latter end of the *Fourth Century*, treats it with great indifference. "To affirm (says he) that the Fa-

---

[29] Dana, 212-213.

ther is greater than Christ, considered in his human nature, is True, indeed, but of no great Moment; For what wonder is it, that God should be *greater* than a *man?*"—*Orat. 36.*

Again, when Christ said expressly, *my Father is greater than I;* did he then allude to his *divine,* or to his *human nature?* If to the first, then he certainly declared the *Father* to be *greater* than himself in the *highest respect:* But if he referred to his *human nature* only, then we must suppose that he affirmed the *Almighty Father,* the all-perfect, unchangeable, and *eternal* GOD *of the universe,* to be *greater* than his *human nature!* Could such a declaration as this be at all necessary? It is utterly incompatible with the wisdom of our Lord, and therefore impossible that he should have intended it. "When any person affirms another to be *greater than himself,* he must of necessity mean, *greater than he himself is in his greatest capacity.*"—Dr. Clarke[30]

The phrase "divine nature" is, in Trinitarian thought, applied exclusively to Christ. It is never applied to the Father or to the holy spirit which, however unwittingly, demonstrates that the three supposed members of the Godhead are different in some way, and if different in any way, then the claim that these three are not distinct beings is not true. When applied to Jesus, Trinitarians use the terms *divine* and *deity* synonymously. The inference is that, since Jesus has divine qualities, he is therefore deity. But the two terms are not synonymous. In 2 Peter 2:14, we are told that Christians are "partakers of the *divine* nature," and it is never argued that we are God. But by applying Trinitarian reasoning to this verse, we may conclude that each Christian is God or part of the godhead, which is absurd. There must be some other explanation as to what it is to be divine:

> St. Paul says to the Corinthians, in the 2nd epistle, 2c. 6-16v., "Ye are the temple of the living God, as God hath said, I will dwell in them and walk in them." Christ tells the Philippians, in 2c. 13v., "That God worketh in them both to will and to do." He tells the Ephesians in 4c. 6v., "There is one God and Father of all, who is in you all." John says, 1 John 4c. 15v.,

---

[30] Gifford, 209, 211, 131-132.

"Whosoever shall confess that Jesus is the *Son of God, God dwelleth in him and he in God.*" St. Peter declares, 2 Pet. 1c. 4v. that "By the precious promises of the Gospel, Christians are made partakers of the *divine nature.*" This is a very strong expression—and when St. Paul says, "That in Christ dwelleth all the fullness of the Godhead," he must have used this language in the sense in which he prayed that the Ephesians might be filled with all the fulness of God,—Ephesians 3c. 19v. and in John 1c. 16v. In both cases the texts show that *divine knowledge,* and not *essence,* is intended. Hence, then, when God is said to dwell in Christ, it evidently means that Christ was inspired by God—filled or actuated by a divine power.[31]

Our effort to obtain greater understanding of spiritual matters is partly what makes Jesus an example to us. He grew in grace and wisdom. He was a man who always walked by inspiration of God and, because of his dedication, we have someone to emulate:

We do think that the doctrine of our Lord's two natures, actually impeaches his veracity. What scope it affords for tampering with his words—for is there be a particular moral precept which may not accord with a man's desire and judgment—can he not escape the applying such an injunction, by saying that it was evidently spoken by our Lord in his human capacity and not in his divine nature. Thanks be to God, Unitarians entertain no such views of their Saviour, but maintain that he always spoke under divine inspiration.[32]

In spite of the acknowledged irrationality of Trinitarian doctrines, efforts to sustain them persist. The most unreasonable means of maintaining Trinitarian dogma are still employed, and with each new development the Trinitarian system produces greater confusion:

Here perhaps the advocates of the contrary opinion will interpose with the same argument which was advanced before; for they are constantly shifting the form of their reasoning,

---

[31] Thomas, 22.

[32] Thomas, 31.

Vertumnus-like, and using the twofold nature of Christ developed in his office of mediator, as a ready subterfuge by which to evade any arguments that may be brought against them. What Scripture says of the Son generally, they apply, as suits their purpose, in a partial and restricted sense; at one time to the Son of God, at another to the Son of Man—now to the Mediator in his divine, now in his human capacity, and now again in his union of both natures.[33]

With so much depending on one's view of God and Jesus, we must understand the simple verses according to their plain meanings. To reason that Jesus actually meant that he was equal with God from statements such as "My Father is greater than I," or that he actually knew the day and hour of his return from his outright denial of it, defies all sensibility:

No resort can here be had, as has been attempted by Trinitarians, to their favorite hypothesis—that merest hypothesis, that shallowest assumption, as I hope hereafter to show—namely, the Double Nature, or, as it is technically and theologically called, the Hypostatic Union; according to which Christ is both God and man. Whenever attempted, the conclusion has been only the more palpably impotent. The obvious difficulty of the text, on the supposition of the truth of the doctrine of the Trinity, cannot be overcome "by supposing that our Lord spake of himself here only as a man." For as the orthodox Macknight says: "The name *Father* following that of *Son*, shows that he spake of himself as the Son of God, and not as the Son of man. Besides, the gradation in the sentence seems to forbid this solution. For the Son being mentioned after the angels, and immediately before the Father, is thereby declared to be more excellent then they, which he is not in respect of his human nature; and therefore he cannot be supposed to speak of himself in that nature." [34]

---

33 John Milton, *Milton on the Son of God and the Holy Spirit* (London: British and Foreign Unitarian Association, 1908), 76-77.

34 Farley, 11-12.

There is no difficulty in saying that Jesus is divine, but this does not equate him with God any more than other things that are spoken of as divine. Others are spoken of as partakers of the divine nature, which is nothing more than saying that some have lived, or endeavored to live, a godly lifestyle:

Another definition of the word *Divinity* is, *state of being divine*, or *godlike*. In this sense of word we speak of the *Divinity* of the Scriptures; meaning that they came from God. According to this interpretation of the phrase, also, we firmly believe in the Divinity of Christ. We believe in the Divinity of his *person* and *nature*; because he is the Son of God. If every son is the image and likeness of his father, and if Jesus is *"God's own Son,"* he must be divine or Godlike. If we believed him not to be divine, we should also believe him not to be the Son of God, but the Son of Joseph, or some other man.

We believe in the Divinity of his *mission*; because God sent him. He said, "I am come in my Father's name.... I proceeded forth and came from God; neither came I of myself, but he sent me."—*John* v. 43, and viii. 42. This is an explicit declaration of the Divinity of his mission. God confirmed the Divinity of Christ's mission by wonders and miracles which he wrought by him; and also by raising him from the dead, and exalting him at his own right hand. Nicodemus testified that no one but a messenger *sent from God* could do the works which Christ did. The miraculous powers he communicated to his Apostles, the fulfillment of his predictions in the destruction of the holy city, the dispersion of the Jews, and the early triumphs of the gospel, completed the evidence of the Divinity of Christ's mission.

We believe in the Divinity of his *office*; because it was established not by human authority, but by the will of heaven. God qualified him for his office, appointed him to it, and sustained him in it. Jesus opened his commission in these words: "The Spirit of the Lord is upon me, because he hath anointed me to preach the gospel to the poor; he hath sent me to heal the broken-hearted, to preach deliverance to the captives, and recovery of sight to the blind, to set at liberty them that are bruised, and to preach the acceptable year of the Lord."—*Luke* iv. 18, 19.

We believe in the Divinity of his *doctrine*; because it did not originate from himself, but came from God. As he came not to do his own will, but the will of God, so he spake not his own words, but the words of God. He said, "My doctrine is not mine, but he that sent me... I have not spoken of myself, but the Father which sent me, he gave me a commandment, what I should say and what I should speak."—*John* vii. 16, and xii. 49. The message Jesus brought was divine. It was the message of God, *who hath spoken unto us in these last days by his Son.—Heb.* i. 2. The revelation *of Jesus Christ* was a revelation *which God gave unto him.—Rev.* i. 1.

We believe in the Divinity of his *works*; because of himself he could do nothing; but it was the Father that performed the works by him. *"The Father that dwelleth in me, he doeth the works."—John* xiv. 10. "Jesus of Nazareth, a man approved of God among you by miracles, and wonders, and signs, *which God did by him."—Acts* ii. 22.

We believe in the Divinity of the *fullness* that was in Christ, and the *blessings he communicated.* For *it pleased the Father that in him should all fullness dwell. In him dwelleth all the fullness of the Godhead bodily.—Col.* i. 19, and ii. 9. As the Son of God he was *full of grace and truth.—John* i. 14. *God giveth not the Spirit by measure unto him.—John* iii. 34.

We believe in the Divinity of his *authority, wisdom, power,* and *glory*; because God gave them to him. He said, *all things* are delivered unto me of my Father.—*Matt.* xi. 27. We believe in the Divinity of *all he was, all he did, and all he suffered,* because *God made him both Lord and Christ, exalted him to be a Prince and Saviour, and ordained him Prophet, Priest, and King;* and all he did, and all he suffered, *was by the grace of God.*[35]

And so it is written in Paul's first letter to the Corinthians (15:28), that according to the biblical prophecies, Jesus will also be subject

---

[35] Morgridge, 21-23.

unto the Father: "And when all things shall be subdued unto him, then shall the Son also himself be subject unto him that put all things under him, that God may be all in all." At all stages of Jesus's life and ministry, according to the many biblical texts, there is one God, the Father, and everyone else, including Jesus, are subordinate to Him.

CHAPTER 5

CORRUPTIVE INFLUENCES IN THE CHURCH

Given the nature and history of man and that we see through a glass darkly (1 Cor. 13:12), our best efforts will contain some measure of error, so it requires a continual effort to rid ourselves of it. Christianity was born into a polytheistic and heathenistic world, and converts were made from among practitioners of paganism. The tendency towards error is still so great that little seems to resemble the first century church, and the removal of one of the most unusual system of errors, Trinitarianism, almost seems a task too great to be realized. The mechanisms are in place, the orthodoxy police have been so energetic in preserving this system, that few challenge the absurdities their forerunners invented. The simplest truth, that *God is one*, has not escaped the powerful sweep of corruption, and is proof that there is no statement so simple that, given enough time and enough councils, cannot be so altered as to become utterly unintelligible:

> To consider the system (if it may be called a system) of Christianity *a priori*, one would think it very little liable to corruption, or abuse. The great outline of it is, that the universal parent of mankind commissioned Jesus Christ, to invite men to the practice of virtue, by the assurance of his mercy to the penitent, and of his purpose to raise to immortal life and happiness all the virtuous and the good, but to inflict an adequate punishment on the wicked. In proof of this he wrought many miracles, and after a public execution he rose again from the dead. He also directed that proselytes to his religion should be admitted by baptism, and that his disciples should eat bread and drink wine in commemoration of his death.

Here is nothing that any person could imagine would lead to much subtle speculation, at least such as could excite animosity. The doctrine itself is so plain, that one would think the learned and the unlearned were upon a level with respect to it. And a person unacquainted with the state of things at the time of its promulgation would look in vain for any probable source of the monstrous corruptions and abuses which crept into the system afterwards. Our Lord, however, and his apostles, foretold that there would be a great departure from the truth, and that something would arise in the church altogether unlike the doctrine which they taught, and even subversive of it.

In reality, however, the causes of the succeeding corruptions did then exist; and accordingly, without anything more than their natural operation, all the abuses rose to their full height; and what is more wonderful still, by the operation of natural causes also, without any miraculous interposition of providence, we see the abuses gradually corrected, and Christianity recovering its primitive beauty and glory.

The causes of corruptions were almost wholly contained in the established opinions of the heathen world, and especially the philosophical part of it; so that when those heathens embraced Christianity they mixed their former tenets and prejudices with it. Also, being disciples of a man who had been crucified as a common malefactor, that Christians in general were sufficiently disposed to adopt any opinion that would most effectually wipe away this reproach.

The opinion of the mental faculties of man belonging to a substance distinct from his body or brain, and of this invisible spiritual part, or soul, being capable of subsisting before and after its union to the body, which had taken the deepest root in all schools of philosophy, was wonderfully calculated to answer this purpose. For by this means Christians were enabled to give to the soul of Christ what rank they pleased in the heavenly regions before his incarnation. On this principle went the Gnostics, deriving their doctrine from the received oriental philosophy. Afterwards the philosophizing Christians went upon another principle, personifying the wisdom, or *logos* of God the Father. But this was mere Platonism, and therefore cannot be said to have been unnatural to their circumstances, though at length they came, in the natural progress of things, to believe that Christ was, in power and glory, equal to the Father himself.

From the same opinion of a soul distinct from the body came the practice of praying, first for the dead, and then to them, with a long train of other absurd opinions, and superstitious practices.[1]

The variety of opinions on many issues within the Christian community is to be expected when so many cultures read and apply what they believe the texts say—this doesn't point to an intrinsic irrationality merely because there are different interpretations. For example, some believe it is proper for infants to be baptized, others believe it is proper for those of a more mature age. Some immerse in water, others sprinkle the water. Some believe it is a requirement for salvation, others that it is merely ceremonial. All of these opinions cannot be correct. Here we have an illustration of the development of differences, but not necessarily a tortuous logic.. When the texts were originally written there was probably one preferred or intended way to carry out baptism, but the issue is now so confused due to the variety of opinions regarding it. Some think baptism isn't in water but serves as a metaphor, and that baptism refers to receiving the gift of holy spirit. Many of these positions make sense, even though they are radically different from one another.

Entropy is a concept that Sir Isaac Newton introduced into physics in the nineteenth century. Known as the second law of thermodynamics, entropy is the theory that things go from a state of higher order to a state of higher disorder. In other words, things fall apart given enough time. An example is shoelaces becoming untied—after tying the laces, forces begin to act upon them, causing them to loosen. Scientists have benefited from approaching their research from the standpoint that things change from their original state. In their investigations they may work "in reverse" by identifying the forces

---

[1] Joseph Priestley, *An History of the Corruptions of Christianity* (c. 1770): quoted in Parke, 48-49.

that acted upon the original condition, and the current object of investigation is commonly in a different state than it was when it started out. The erosion of the methodologies and simple logic required for biblical interpretation seems to have followed this principle, and it is unnecessary.

Creeds are one place we may turn to see how they gradually strayed from what appears in the biblical texts. It was a gradual process, and Trinitarian dogma was a big part of the contentions that arose among those in the early church, as well as among the early church fathers. So, do the words of the creeds indicate a departure by mankind from what is in the Bible? Regarding God being one, not three-in-one, it does, in accordance with the concept of entropy:

> The first creed in which the Trinitarian faith is stated, as now received, is the Athanasian Creed. It was not composed by Athanasius, but by some unknown author in the fifth century. It is such a creed as was needed in the Church, after it had completely abandoned the Unitarian faith; and it is a strong argument in our favor, that no such creed is to be found until the fifth century, a time when corruptions of every sort abounded. You will thus perceive how gradually the transition was made, step by step, and "as the first creed is avowedly the one held by Unitarians, and the last one held by the Trinitarians, the inference is irresistible, that the Church, which was Unitarian in the beginning, gradually became Trinitarian." [2]

The most probable direction of corruptive influences, given what we know of the society in which Jesus lived, is a tendency to want more deities, not fewer. It is probable (biblical arguments aside) that the early church started with one God, the Father, and moved to adopt other gods into their worship and theology:

> Certain it is, that the great body of professing Christians have long ceased to resemble the first believers, in purity and elevation of character; nor can the difference be well accounted for, but by supposing, either that a religion from heaven may become enfeebled by age, and cease to be followed by the

---

[2] Eliot, 90.

effects which it was designed to, and originally actually did, produce; or, that the corruptions of the gospel have materially interfered with its regenerating and sanctifying efficacy. There can be no hesitation in adopting the latter supposition. Even amid the glories of primitive Christianity, the seed of these evils was traced lurking in the churches. It soon sprung up, and when the apostles were removed, had a rapid growth.

Certain indications of danger and apostasy were noticed by the apostles in the primitive church. They were such as might lead from Unitarianism towards Trinitarianism; but could not possibly conduct in the opposite direction. They were, in fact, the causes whose results we see in ecclesiastical history. The principal of these deserves mention. 1. Temporizing with that mythology, in the belief of which the Gentile converts had been educated. "Flee from idolatry—the cup of blessing which we bless, is it not the communion of the blood of Christ? The bread which we break, is it not the communion of the body of Christ? Ye cannot drink the cup of the Lord, and the cup of demons; (the deities of Heathenism;) ye cannot be partakers of the Lord's table, and of the table of demons. To partake of the sacrificial feasts of the popular gods; to confound with these feasts, as to its nature and design, the eucharistic commemoration of Jesus; to transform his supper into a sacrifice, and him into a god; and to elevate him from a god in the Pagan, to God, in the Christian sense of the term; these are gradations of a progress in error, which is very conceivable and probable in itself, and which, by combining Scripture with history, may be discerned with tolerable distinctness. The Gentiles would with difficulty divest themselves of the notion of subordinate deities. They had been accustomed to gods of various powers and provinces; who were corporeal and of human shape; and whom they honoured by feasts on sacrificed animals in their temples. How natural to identify with such ceremonies the Lord's Supper, and to place in such a rank the Founder of their new religion! He who healed the lame and blind, chained the winds and waves, raised the dead, and himself ascended to heaven, would, in their native phraseology, be of course a god. When Paul and

Barnabas wrought a miracle at Lystra, the people said, "The gods are come down to us in the likeness of men." They would have formed a similar opinion of Christ, had they seen of or heard of him; and where apostolic authority did not reach, or as soon as the first race of believers was dead, it would be difficult to oppose the notion.[3]

Departing from the starting point that the Father is God can be accomplished in several ways. It need not be the case that an evil being or an animal is exalted to equality with Him—*any* substitution or false elevation of another will do the trick. Jesus was a most likely candidate for such exaltation since so much attention was upon him and his teachings. There was little possibility during his ministry of confusing him with God because he rebuked those inclined to do so. He was elevated to this status decades after the news about him spread over vast land expanses and over centuries, and it became too difficult to prevent the idolatrous tendencies of the Christian converts.

The tendency of the early church to go from a belief in one God to a belief in more than one is quite likely. It is unlikely that there would be a movement in the early church that would *remove* two gods from a system of beliefs and be left with only one, the Father. This is due to the polytheistic culture into which Christianity was introduced. From what we know, the church started with one God, the Father, and moved, through subtleties and culturally accepted polytheistic influences, towards incorporating more gods into their system of beliefs:

> Priestley observes, "So popular was Unitarianism in this age (the third century), that, according to Epiphanus, when the Unitarians met with any of the plainer Christians, they would say, 'Well, friend, what doctrine shall we hold, shall we acknowledge one God, or three?' " The fierce disputes of the fourth century, when Athanasius and Arius divided the Christian world, were caused, not by the introduction of Arianism, as a novelty, but by a strong public expression of Trinitarian sentiments, which even yet had not arrived at that

---

3 W.J. Fox, *A Course of Lectures Connected With the Corruption, Revival, and Future Influence of Genuine Christianity* (London: G. Smallfield, 1819), 31, 108-109

systematic perfection which they finally attained. Can there be a doubt, then, who were the innovators, or which way the stream was flowing? Every thing indicates a progression, of which the starting point was simple Unitarianism, and the final reach, Athanasian Trinitarianism of the creed.[4]

What is either unknown or overlooked by the proponents of the doctrines contained in the Athanasian Creed, is that it did not eliminate disagreement among Trinitarians regarding Jesus. Trinitarians have always disagreed with one another because some think others say too much, too little, or something they consider deficient in another's opinion of him:

> The Athanasian Creed says we must "neither confound the persons, nor divide the substance:" and one or the other of these two has been done, in every attempt to make a plausible comment on the doctrine. One class of expounders is always accused of destroying the personal identity of Christ, or else of detracting from his true dignity; and the other, of setting up three distinct gods on the throne of the universe,—a notion utterly strange and idolatrous to the general sense of Christendom.[5]

Trinitarian dogma has had the opportunity to proliferate because the Bible has been translated almost exclusively by Trinitarians. Every known alteration of the texts favors the Trinitarian hypothesis—there are no alterations showing God to be only one. All marks are in the opposite direction. This is another of the corruptive influences that has caused the idea of who God is to become confused. It is difficult enough in the present age of universities and mass education to oppose the absurdities of Trinitarian doctrine, even though people today are generally better educated than our predecessors. How difficult it must have been in the early church, in a polytheistic and relatively uneducated world, to oppose the tendency to make gods out of people and things.

Once error is entrenched, it is far more energy-consuming to get

---

[4] Fox, 113.

[5] Allen, 57.

back to the original order than was required to establish it in the first place. Traditional views are difficult to dislodge once people have individually and collectively become comfortable with them. But the early church, despite the commands not to be enticed by (false) philosophies of men, became corrupt by the exact influence about which they were forewarned:

> And, indeed, one should imagine, with regard to the present subject, that those early converts to Christianity, allured by the pleasures of philosophic speculation, or seduced by the force of long custom and example, had declined from their heavenly guide, and unhappily fallen back again, in some measure, into the strong and prevailing tide of polytheism. Thus, as the Grecians had converted the *wisdom* of Jupiter into a Goddess; so they, *personifying the divine attributes*, resolved the wisdom and power of the Supreme Being into a *distinct* deity; and then, by the subtlest refinements, they in vain endeavoured to preserve the divine *Unity*, which Christ and the Prophets had taught the world, and which the airy delusions of a borrowed philosophy had clouded and confounded.[6]

Many Christians since the fourth century have claimed to have discovered doctrines that are admitted by some of their most knowledgeable advocates to be absent from Scripture. It is argued that those who came after Christ by about three hundred years discovered truths about God and Jesus that previous generations did not know. Trinitarian doctrine is said to be a fundamental article of Christian faith, yet it is admitted by learned Trinitarians that it was not known or established until the fourth century. Once the rudimentary belief that *God is one* was changed to *God is three-in-one*, it would not be long before other simple beliefs would become convoluted as well.

It is not difficult to understand that Christianity, having been born into a world of polytheism and other potentially corruptive influences, would itself become corrupted once exposed to them. Now it will take a concerted effort to collectively get back to a simpler understanding of relatively simple texts:

---

[6] Gifford, 68-69.

Where, then, do we stand? We desire, we aim to get back to the original, simple, primitive Christianity*the Christianity of Christ and his Apostles; to recover the faith which was in the beginning, long before the age of Systematic Theology. Systematic Theology*what is it the world over, but the piling up of human opinions? "Jesus," says Hagenbach, "is not the author of a *dogmatic theology*, but the 'author and finisher of our faith'; not the founder of a school, but emphatically the founder of religion and of the Church." Again he says: "The first disciples of the Lord were, like their Master, far from propounding dogmatic systems." (*Hist. of Doctrines*, vol. i. 33, 35). So Neander: "When, in the after course of development, the power of Christ's spirit, which subordinated the human element to itself, no longer predominated, but the human individuality asserted its own importance, then partial systems arose, running counter to each other, which, in one way and another, did great injury to the cause of divine truth." (*Hist. of the Church*, vol. i. 337, 6th Boston Ed.) Our appeal, therefore, is finally and confidently to the Scriptures. We hold no peculiar or distinguishing doctrine which cannot be stated in the express, unaltered, unqualified words of Holy writ; a thing which our Trinitarian brethren cannot do for theirs.[7]

It is apparent, in accordance with entropy, that we really do see through a glass darkly, a statement which, if it were understood, would engender moderation on behalf of those who presume to have the truth, whomever these may be.

EXAMPLES OF WEAK TRINITARIAN ARGUMENTATION

The doctrine of the Trinity has become the cornerstone of many Christians' system of faith and, since it is relied upon, the Bible is interpreted and reinterpreted in light of it. Some Trinitarian explanations will be explored in this section in order to shed light on the process of biblical reinterpretation and the sorts of doctrines and arguments it leads to.

---

7 Farley, 55-56.

If a person wrongly interprets a biblical subject, the more frequently the subject appears in the Bible the greater will be the misunderstanding of not only that topic, but of the Bible as a whole. This is why it is important to use common sense in an effort to get our first principles correct. Since God and Jesus are among the foremost subjects of the New Testament, any foundational misunderstanding regarding them will necessarily result in trickle-down, erroneous re-interpretations of the Bible and become a slippery slope leading to greater ignorance about them.

One argument given for the doctrine of the Trinity is the following: "In the Old Testament, God made an everlasting covenant with Israel to be their God forever (e.g. Exodus 29:45, 46). But since there are two covenants that constitute the Bible, the Old and the New, God had to either kill Himself or all of mankind in order to conceal that he was changing the everlasting covenant. He chose to kill himself by becoming a man and being crucified."

In considering this, it is shocking that anyone could ever think this is a sound argument, and I wish there were no need to address it. But this argument was, as I came to understand by speaking with its proponents, a commonly-accepted argument within their church. I will address this argument at some length in order to illustrate the process one must occasionally go through when challenging Trinitarian dogma.

In the first place, the two types of covenants which they referred to are different. One is specific and one is general, and both are in agreement with each other. The first covenant, or promise, was that God will be a God to Israel. This has not changed, and bears little relation to the two covenants, or testaments, composing the Christian Bible. The promise God made to Israel "to be their God" is still in effect. It is God's promise to Israel and He will uphold it just as He said. Thinking otherwise is to undermine one's confidence in God. Thinking that God would adopt measures to cover up a purported failure of His is immeasurably worse; it represents Him as deceitful. The new covenant is in accordance with God being God to Israel and delivering them from their oppressors, as it is the fulfillment of the Old Testament promises of a Messiah leading people from danger and back to God. This is expressly stated in Luke 1:68-75 (NIV): "Praise be to the Lord, the God of Israel, because he has come and has redeemed his people. He has raised up a horn of salvation for us in the house of his servant David (as he said through his holy prophets of long ago), salvation from our enemies and from the hand of all who hate us—to show mercy to our fathers and to remember his holy covenant, the oath he swore to our father Abraham: to rescue us from the hand of our enemies, and to enable us to serve him without fear in holiness and righteousness before him all our days." We have an explicit statement that God will keep His promise to Israel.

Another problem with the above argument is that, according to its advocates, God actually killed himself in order to hide the fact that He made a covenant (the Old) and then changed it (to a New). It must first be acknowledged that if God attempted to hide something, it would remain hidden. Since those arguing this position had "detected" God's cover-up, it suggests that God is inefficient in carrying out his own plans. Secondly, if God chose to kill Himself to allow for a new covenant, then God must have died. God, according to Trinitarian dogma, is triune. So all three members of this deity must have died, but it is acknowledged that only the Son died while the other "two" remained alive. This reveals a deeper problem with Trinitarian theology: it is argued that God died for our sins; but it is also argued that only a part of the godhead—Jesus—died. This brings us full circle back to the original argument, which is that God had to kill Himself to cover up an error of his. If He actually did kill Himself, all of Himself—Father, Son and Spirit—who was in heaven to raise him/them from the dead? This is emblematic of the inconsistencies of the various dogmas within the Trinitarian system.

Another argument that is not entirely different from the one above, is that, since sin is infinite, redemption could only be accomplished by an infinite sacrifice, thereby requiring God, once again, to kill himself. In this case the same inconsistencies arise as mentioned above, namely, if God is defined as Father, Son and Holy Spirit, and it was only Jesus who died, God (all of him/them) did not die for our sins, hence our salvation has not been secured. The implications of reading into Scripture doctrines that are not there manifest themselves in glaring inconsistencies such as these.

The argument that the doctrine of the Trinity was unknown to the Jews of the Old Testament is frequently given to account for the lack of its development in the Hebrew texts. The most common reason given is that the Jews could not understand it. It is fair to wonder whether it is right for those living after the time of Jesus to assume greater abilities than Solomon, a man who, prior to Jesus, is recorded as having been the wisest man ever to have lived. Where do we find in Scripture that we, simply by virtue of being born after Jesus, are gifted with greater minds than those who lived before him? The problem with this assumption is found in the acceptance of the doctrine itself, but once accepted as true, the Bible must be reinterpreted and explained to account for its absence in so many places. Many Christians are satisfied with the arrogant assessment that they are smarter than the Israelites, the people to whom the Bible says God revealed Himself, the law and the Messiah. These subjects are discussed at length in the Old Testament, so it is wrongheaded to assume that Israel would not be able to understand the doctrine of a triune God had it been true. But it becomes an acceptable defense once it is assumed the doctrine of the Trinity is true. A natural consequence of this is that we may now reinterpret their texts without recourse to the understanding which they would impart to us. Jews have been consistent in telling us there is no teaching in the Hebrew Bible of a triune God. But Trinitarians have a defense that allows them to circumvent this: superior intelligence. In other words, modern Jews do not really know the Hebrew Bible. So not only is error adopted as truth, but arrogance is developed as a consequence of upholding the doctrine of a triune God at all costs.

One fairly common method of explaining the doctrine of the Trinity comes in the form of an analogy. It involves finding things that occur in threes in nature, then analogizing this to the three-in-one concept of God. One such example is that matter exists in three states: liquid, solid, and gas. This, it is argued, is like God; there are three different states, but all are matter. This analogy is sometimes augmented with a reference to water, which can exist in a liquid, a solid or gaseous state. There are various ways of showing these arguments to be inadequate, but the first thing to be recognized is that matter is currently known to exist in at least four states; the three already mentioned and plasma, which is what interstellar space is made of. It is estimated that plasma constitutes more than ninety-nine percent of all matter in the known universe. Whether this percentage is accurate is immaterial to the present discussion. What it shows is that the process of seeking analogies that conform to the Trinitarian conception of God is unbridled advocacy research. But the unintelligibility of the doctrine that God exists in three persons sends people seeking some way to justify it. And if we accept analogies of things in threes as representative of God, what are we to make of things that are not in threes, such as the number of seasons most countries experience, the number of legs on a horse or wings on a bird, the number of directions on a compass, the number of eyes a healthy baby is born with, the number of apostles originally chosen, etc.? The dissection of God into three parts is simply a matter of argumentative prejudice. It assumes a conclusion then seeks evidence to support it. In the case of analogizing God to the states of matter, this not only assumes the conclusion is true, but even if we allow this for a moment, it works contrary to the Trinitarian system since it would prove, if it proved anything, that God exists in three modes, which is modalism, a form of Trinitarianism that is rejected by the majority of Trinitarians. It would be the equivalent of saying that, in the analogy of water, which can only be in one state at a time (i.e. it can exist as water or solid or gas at one time, but not all three simultaneously), God exists at any one moment as either the Son, or the Father, or the Holy Spirit, but not all three at once.

Another example of Trinitarian reinterpretation derives from Mark 10:17-18: "And when he was gone forth into the way, there came one running, and kneeled to him, and asked him, Good Master, what shall I do that I may inherit eternal life? And Jesus said unto him, Why callest thou me good? there is none good but one, that is, God." It appears plain that Jesus corrects this person's use of the word "good" since its usage meant, in this instance, *supremely good*. Jesus corrected him by directing his attention to the fact that God, and not Jesus, is supremely good. The following is explained by a Trinitarian, who, due to his foundational opinions regarding Christ, offers a forced explanation of this text:

> A young ruler, evidently ignorant of the character of Jesus, addressed him by a title, which, under such misapprehension, was improper; a title, too, which the Jewish Rabbis are said to have affected, and which, on that ground also, was likely to call forth our Lord's animadversion; "Why dost thou call

me good, whom thou regardest only as a prophet sent from God, and dost not look upon to be any more than a mere man? Thou shouldest remember that none is perfectly good but one glorious and immutable Being, even the blessed and eternal God." [8]

By considering the whole chapter in which this verse is contained, the person speaking to Jesus clearly regarded him as more than a mere man. The ruler's heart was pure—he went *running* to Jesus and *knelt* at his feet, he observed the law all the days of his life, he had accepted Jesus as the Messiah. His question was pure. He was corrected, though, in applying to Jesus a much *higher* superlative than that which was rightfully his due. This is opposed to Rev. Hill's supposition that a much lower one had been applied. Jesus was actually telling him not to use the adjective *good* lest it be assumed that Jesus possessed the supreme good that belongs only to the Father. Reverend Hill makes the man regard Jesus as a mere man, which cannot be sustained from a fair reading of this record. The man was sincerely inquiring as to what was required for him to obtain eternal life. This is a serious inquiry, and to think that he went in the opposite direction by applying lesser attributes to Jesus is the consequence of reinterpreting the Bible in light of a tortured idea. This bears out Professor Norton's sentiments regarding addressing the doctrine of the Trinity:

But there are other causes which make this an unpleasant subject. It presents human nature in the most humiliating aspect. The absurdities that have been maintained are so gross, the zeal in maintaining them has been so ferocious, there is such an absence of any redeeming quality in the spectacle presented, that it spreads a temporary gloom over our whole view of the character and destiny of man. We seem ourselves to sink in the scale of being, and it demands an effort to recollect the glorious powers with which God has endued our race. While inquiring concerning the truths of religion, we appear to have descended to some obscure region where folly and prejudice are the sole rulers....And is this all that mankind have to hope? Must this dreary prospect for ever lie before

---

[8] Hill, 16-17.

us? We trust not. Still, in the confutation of such doctrines as have been taught, the triumph, if it may be so called, is humbling. It is a triumph over our common nature reduced to imbecility.[9]

Commenting on the intensity and the methods employed in the establishment of Trinitarian dogma, John Wilson writes:

To uphold this doctrine, the stores of erudition, the subtleties of philosophy, the eloquence of the pulpit, and the productions of the press,—not to mention the decrees of synods and of councils, the articles of one church, and the confessions and catechisms of others,—have all been called into requisition. On behalf of this doctrine, in particular, have treatises and comments unnumbered been written and published. For this purpose the Bible has been ransacked, re-ransacked; and its texts—in fractions, in units, and in thousands—have been brought into logical and metaphysic play. The first words in Genesis have been deemed to intimate a plurality of persons in the Godhead; the last in the book of the Apocalypse, the Deity of Christ. Indeed, we might say, almost without a rhetorical figure, that nearly every sentence in the Sacred Records has been adduced, either by itself or in combination with others, to prove, confirm, or defend the dogma of a Triune God.[10]

Such an intense, energy-consuming effort wouldn't be required if the doctrine were biblical. Some ardent Trinitarians would have us renounce reason as "rebellious." We must submit, we are told, to God's revelation of Himself, which requires us to simply accept what He says and not argue with it. Fair enough. If God said it, it would be prudent to embrace it. But there are two problems with this statement. First, we must know what God actually said in order to submit to it, which brings us back to the original issue of God's identity. Second, nowhere in the Bible does it say to renounce reason, but to renounce error. We are to *prove* all things. Where in the Bible do we

---

9 Norton, 33-34.

10 Wilson, 5.

find that our mental capacities are to be suppressed rather than fully engaged? Is it possible to love God with all our heart, soul, *mind* and strength if we renounce our mental faculties?

The claim that we are to suppress our reason is a means of making it more comfortable for people to accept preposterous notions about God. Without the use of reason we are prone to accept any idea thrown our way. And why does the Trinitarian system necessitate the removal of reason from the realm of inquiry? This is an indictment against the whole system itself.

Trinitarian argumentation is replete with *ad hoc* arguments. *Ad hoc* is the term logicians use when referring to an argument that has such serious flaws it is no longer sustainable on reasonable grounds, but its advocates continue to construct arguments to defend it. Instead of admitting an argument is unsound and abandoning it, more arguments continue to pour forth from its advocate, yielding results that progressively become more ridiculous. This is the folly of Trinitarian theologians, who ask us, for example, to stop thinking and accept this incomprehensible doctrine on the grounds that it is a mystery. We are told that the doctrine is undoubtedly true, despite admissions that it is not understood!

The doctrine of the double nature of Christ is an example of ad hoc argumentation. In order to reconcile the belief that Jesus is equal to the Father with the biblical texts that say he is a man, a theory emerged that he is *both* God and man. The refusal to abandon a belief built upon spurious foundations is what we might expect from children, but not from adults who have enjoyed the advantages of education:

> It may appear strange, that, after giving up as weak and irrelevant the strongest and the most pertinent proofs that can be adduced in support of an opinion, good and wise men should still cling to it with a tenacity which cannot be loosened by evidence of a contrary nature; that, after abandoning their best arms as perfectly useless, and their most secure positions as wholly untenable, they should not at last be constrained to yield up the whole matter of debate, with all their instruments of aggression and defence, instead of having recourse, as they do, to ground unfirm as a morass, and to weapons

weak as straw. But this inconsistency is often observable in predilections of various kinds. Every day do we see men, judicious and sensible in other respects, tenaciously holding opinions, which they have been in the habit of cherishing from an early period, not only in religion and theology, but in politics, in literature, in matters of business, and in the common affairs of life, long after they have acknowledged that the main grounds for adherence to them have given way. And thus it seems to be in regard to those who, abandoning proof after proof, text after text,—some of these being passages of Scripture which have been generally adduced as the very bulwarks of the Trinitarian doctrine,—still cling with affection, if not with ardor, to the doctrine itself. To their minds it may be hallowed by the sentiment of filial love, by the reminiscences of youthful piety, by the associations of kindred and of social brotherhood, and by the spiritual nutriment which they have drawn from such portions of truth as have been blended and incorporated with it, but which, by an illusion of the imagination, they suppose to be derived from the doctrine itself. The mere fact, then, of a belief in dogmas whose chief proofs have been conceded to be weak, irrelevant, or nugatory, can afford no reason for supposing that arguments of a more shadowy and obscure nature are sufficient for the truth of the dogmas themselves.[11]

Why is it so difficult for so many to admit the falsity, or at least the strangeness, of the notion of a triune God? What keeps the pursuit for this hypothesis when the doctrines produced generate inconsistencies when compared to obvious biblical statements, and to themselves? Perhaps it is that many Christians today are following the lead of the people who first established the doctrine of the Trinity and who lacked a reasonable methodology in generating their new statements of faith:

But what a dreary and repelling task it is to go over the New Testament, or the whole Bible, to hunt out words, phrases, and sentences that may constructively or inferentially be

---

[11] Wilson, 13-14.

turned to the support of a doctrine which ought to lie patent on the page. It would seem as if Trinitarians had reconciled themselves to the condition, that the only consistent way in which Scripture could convey to us such an enigmatical and puzzling doctrine, was by a method which should engage the most tortuous, adroit, and mazy ingenuity of the human faculties in seeking for results that must partake of the character of the process for reaching them.... Those who have argued for the Trinity, having started with a bias, helped by their ingenuity and guided by their fancy, have, with a vast deal of pains, gone through the whole Bible, trying to see how many intimations of this doctrine they could cull out. There has been an amazing amount of trifling exercised in this direction. Some who have ridiculed or censured the follies of Rabbinical and allegorical interpretation, or the puerilities of the Cabala, have rivaled these follies in their attempts to find hints of the Trinity in sentences whose writers evidently never dreamed of the doctrine.... Sentences are quoted asserting that no man hath seen or can see God, and are compared with other sentences which speak of the manifestations of God to the patriarchs and others; and the conclusion is drawn, that the Jehovah of the Old Testament was the revealing Son, not the Father. Yet even the chain of intended proofs breaks at one link, while another link is in the welding....We have no heart for going through this unnatural, this offensive task of tracing the windings of this textual ingenuity, or of answering its characteristic results. The process has no reasonable basis, no first grounds. It is all a forced work, and fancy will make more or less of it according as it is pursued by those who have more or less of fancy,—fancy, however, of a very inferior sort.[12]

Though all this be so self-evident as to require no explanation—namely, that the Father alone is the self-existent God, and that a being which is not self-existent cannot be God,—it is wonderful with what futile subtleties, or rather with what

---

[12] Ellis, 126, 127, 128.

juggling artifices, certain individuals have endeavoured to elude or obscure the plain meaning of these passages; leaving no stone unturned, recurring to every shift, attempting every means, as if their object were not to preach the pure and unadulterated truth of the gospel to the poor and simple, but rather by dint of vehemence and obstinacy to sustain some absurd paradox from falling, by the treacherous aid of sophisms and verbal distinctions, borrowed from the barbarous ignorance of the schools.[13]

This depicts the current state of Christianity, and it is wholly unnecessary. The statements of Milton are as applicable today as they were in his time. Every absurdity of the Trinitarian system is defended as though it were, or even could have been, revealed by God. It seems reasonable that one would at least consider some other account of God and Jesus other than those its advocates find incomprehensible. This is the normal method of investigation—we try to make sense of things. But for some reason many persist in defending a senseless conception of the Father, perhaps unaware that the lack of a solid foundation of this system has been exposed:

> From what we know, we are led involuntarily to suspect, that the Bible has been corrupted to favor orthodoxy *farther than we know*. It is certainly not a little remarkable, that all the important readings of Scripture, which have been shown to be spurious, have clearly been introduced to favor orthodoxy. And is it altogether unreasonable to *suspect*, that, besides these spurious readings which we have detected, some others of the same kind may have crept into the received text, whose spuriousness, however, we may not at this late day have the means of detecting? We are to remember, that all the documents which we have for forming a pure text, have been from the beginning in the hands of the orthodox; in times too when they are known not to have been very scrupulous as to the means which they employed for advancing their opinions, and when their ability to corrupt the text of Scripture was greater than we can well imagine in the present state

---

[13] Milton, 20.

of things. Our suspicions on this subject may be confirmed still more, by finding that the manuscripts which have come down to us, bear frequent marks of attempted alterations, though with very unequal success. Mark xiii. 32: 'Of that day and that hour knoweth no man, no, not the angels which are in heaven, neither the Son, but the Father.' Those important words, *'neither the Son,'* are omitted in a few manuscripts, and were rejected by some fathers because they were thought to favor the Arians. As we find, therefore, that some vicious readings favoring the Trinity have found their way into a *few* manuscripts, and others again into a *great many*, and others into *almost all*, is it unreasonable to suppose that some few vicious readings favoring the Trinity may have found their way into ALL *the manuscripts now extant*, and of course cannot be detected? It is idle, then, to pretend that the proofs of the Trinity are not shaken by the acknowledged spuriousness of some of the principal texts supporting it; for not only are its authorities diminished, but suspicion is also brought upon those that remain. The proofs of the Trinity are not only shaken, but shaken to the very foundations.[14]

It can be difficult for anyone to reject beliefs adopted earlier in life, especially those that may have been considered life-saving tenets. Exacerbating the pain of separation is that one's social life may be dependent upon maintaining the doctrines they and their group have espoused for years. But standing in the face of adversity is what separates those who wish to see things as they are, not as they are told they are.

---

14 Morgridge, 98-99.

CHAPTER 6

THE HISTORICAL AND TRADITIONAL DEVELOPMENT OF TRINITARIANISM

There has been much controversy regarding whether or not the doctrine of the Trinity was believed in the first century. Trinitarians commonly, though not universally, contend that the doctrine was generally known in the first century. Unitarians believe that the doctrine is unbiblical and that it therefore formed no part of Christian doctrine at any time, including the first century, and that the doctrine was a later intrusion upon the Father's supremacy. Only after the councils of the fourth century was the doctrine promulgated.

The writings of the early church fathers reveal a disparity of thought regarding the development of Trinitarian dogma. The doctrine was stated in different ways (much as it is today), and the earliest speculations of the fathers indicate that there was no clear conception of the doctrine of the Trinity. This disparity of thought makes sense, since Greek philosophy, not the Bible, played a major role in the development of Trinitarian thought. Franks, a Trinitarian, writes:

> No one has exercised more influence on the actual shape taken by the doctrine of the Trinity than Tertullian, except only Origen.... The truth is that Tertullian is in two minds at once, as comes clearly to view in *Adv. Prax.*, 9. On the one hand, he says, 'The Father is the whole substance, but the Son is a derivative and portion of the whole.' Yet the Father is one, and the Son is another; and the Spirit makes a third.
>
> [Origen] differed also from Clement in another way in that he was contemporary with, and was influenced by, a new philosophical movement, which in Clement's time was only just beginning and had not yet attained to clarity. This new phi-

losophy was Neoplatonism. It was, to be sure, only a further development of Greek thought along the lines already struck out in Neopythagoreanism. But in the hands of Plotinus, Origen's contemporary, it became a great coherent system, speculative and scientific at the same time; it was indeed the magnificent bloom on the tree of Greek philosophy.[1]

If Franks is right in his assertion that Origen was the most influential figure in the development of the doctrine of the Trinity, then the doctrines Origen propounded should not be understood as establishing the so-called co-equality of the Son with the Father. Origen believed that Jesus Christ was subordinate to the Father:

> Athanasius in his *De Decretis* (*c.* A.D. 350) has recorded two passages from Origen of a definitely anti-Arian character, and he argues that these represent the considered opinion of 'the laborious man': where he wrote otherwise it was by way of enquiry and discussion only. But this defence of Origen only goes part of the way; for on the other hand, the Emperor Justinian, wishing to prove Origen a heretic, quotes strongly Arianizing passages from the now lost Greek text of *De Principiis*, containing positive doctrinal statements which show how much Rufinus has done in the way of alteration.[2]

So the early church fathers were not in agreement with one another. They expressed the doctrine in vastly different ways, with different conceptions of the members of the supposed godhead. Origen, one of the most influential figures in the early church, embraced the doctrine that the Father was the supreme God, and was perhaps considered an Arian by his contemporaries.

The doctrine of the Trinity has been acknowledged to be absent from Scripture by more than a few Catholic scholars, who generally agree that the genesis of the doctrine was in the fourth century. Some have even argued that the doctrine itself was not revealed until it was revealed to the bishops attending the fourth-century councils. From this we may conclude that the first, second and third-century church-

---

[1] Franks, 72, 80, 83, 86-87.

[2] Franks, 89.

es abided by the simple doctrine that our heavenly Father is the one true God, and that Jesus was a man who was of course subordinate to Him. The creeds of the councils would turn this conception of God into something unrecognizable.

The creeds of the fourth century were markedly different from Scripture, as they used virtually none of the Bible's language. Once this departure occurred and used in creeds, its language was codified and enforced as the rule of faith. Thereafter, anybody differing from the final creedal product was branded heretical and dealt with accordingly. But there is nothing that indicates the those in the church of the first three centuries incorporated the doctrine of the Trinity into their daily lives and worship:

> The modern doctrine of the Trinity is not found in any document or relic belonging to the Church of the first three centuries. Letters, art, usage, theology, worship, creed, hymn, chant, doxology, ascription, commemorative rite, and festive observance, so far as any remains or any record of them are preserved, coming down from early times, are, as regards this doctrine, an absolute blank. They testify, so far as they testify at all, to the supremacy of the Father, the only true God; and to the inferior and derived nature of the Son. There is nowhere among these remains a co-equal Trinity. The cross is there; Christ is there as the Good Shepherd, the Father's hand placing a crown, or victor's wreath, on his head; but no undivided three,—co-equal, infinite, self-existent, and eternal. This was a conception to which the age had not arrived. It was of later origin.[3]

It is easy to see that the doctrine of the Trinity required time for man, upon speculation, to develop. Wainwright, a Trinitarian, writes:

> It is difficult to decide precisely when the doctrine first emerged. If the use of the word "Trinity" is a necessary feature of a statement of the doctrine, then it does not appear to have emerged before Theophilus (second century), who used the

---

3 Alvan Lamson, *The Church of the First Three Centuries* (Boston: Walker, Fuller and Co., 1865), 396.

Greek Triad (triad) to describe Father, Son, and Holy Spirit, or before Tertullian (late second century), who used the Latin trinitas for the same purpose. But in these writers the words Triad and *trinitas* do not have the depth of meaning which they later acquired, and Trinitarian doctrine did not receive its orthodox form until over a century later.[4]

The *Catechism of the Catholic Church* says:

During the first centuries the Church sought to clarify its Trinitarian faith, both to deepen its own understanding of the faith and to defend it against the errors that were deforming it. This clarification was the work of the early councils, aided by the theological work of the Church Fathers and sustained by the Christian people's sense of the faith.[5]

The idea that the church sought to "clarify its Trinitarian faith" reveals several points. It assumes that the early church was Trinitarian to begin with, which is not possible given the way the Bible was written. The church of the first three centuries is generally acknowledged to have abided by what is called the Apostles' Creed which, as we will shortly see, stated that the Father is the one true God. Further, it shows that a movement was in effect to clarify (i.e. develop) its faith, which suggests that those who were inclined to believe that others other than the Father were God were originally not as dogmatic about their faith as Trinitarians would later become. Once formulated, the Trinitarian system would depart from the widely-held belief that the Father alone is God. This leads to the third point, which is that this movement to develop the belief that others are equal to the Father was not a general movement; it was a movement of a select few, the clergy, who decided the matter for everyone else. The "church," in the sense in which it is used by *The Catechism of the Catholic Church*, meant the clergy, not the church-goers. A few hundred bishops, who disagreed vehemently with one another on many things, were forced by Constantine to sign the Nicene Creed or face imprisonment. This movement would shape the faith of future generations.

---

4 Wainwright, 4-5.

5 *The Catechism of the Catholic Church* (New York: Doubleday, 1995), § 250, 74.

Whatever the councils may have decreed, early believers in Jesus considered him to be subordinate to the Father:

> The development of Trinitarian doctrine from the New Testament proceeds hand in hand with the development of Christology, and to a large extent the two doctrines share the same terminology. A high Christology inevitably encouraged a differentiated understanding of Godhead. In the earliest period, Jesus was often considered subordinate to God, but the tendency was more and more to declare him equal with the Father.[6]

This "tendency" was most likely due to the religious climate of the times in which the doctrine of the Trinity emerged. Polytheism was common and thus wasn't frowned upon, and it would not have been difficult to bring up the idea that there was more than one God. The New Catholic Encyclopedia describes its development as follows:

> There is ... recognition on the part of historians of dogma and systematic theologians that when one does speak of an unqualified Trinitarianism, one has moved from the period of Christian origins to, say, the last quadrant of the 4th century. It was only then that what might be called the definitive Trinitarian dogma "one God in three Persons" became thoroughly assimilated into Christian life and thought.... The dogmatic formula "one God in three Persons" ... was the product of three centuries of doctrinal development.[7]

This supports the position that most Christians of the first few centuries believed in the supremacy of the Father. It has always been recognized that the Father is God; what was left to be developed was that others were His equal, and it would take approximately four hundred years from Jesus's and the apostles' deaths to arrive at a statement remotely resembling modern Trinitarianism. The "Apostles' Creed" was the first "Rule of Faith" held by Christians until the fourth century. There is nothing in it that is objectionable to a Unitarian:

---

6 William Gentz, *The Dictionary of the Bible and Religion* (Nashville: Abingdon Press, 1986), "Trinity," 1066.

7 *New Catholic Encyclopedia* (1967), "Trinity, Holy."

When converts were made from among the heathens, another article was necessarily added, expressive of the belief in One God, even the Father. Hence was formed, with some further additions, what is called the Apostles' Creed. It was not written by the Apostles themselves, but it was in general use in the first three centuries, and was regarded as containing the whole apostolical faith. Now we contend that it is nothing more or less than a Unitarian creed. We can adopt it, word for word, without any explanation:—

"I believe in God the Father Almighty, and in Jesus Christ, his only Son, our Lord; who was, by the Holy Spirit, born of the Virgin Mary; under Pontius Pilate he was crucified and buried; the third day he rose from the dead; he ascended into heaven and sitteth on the right hand of the Father; from thence shall he come to judge the quick and the dead. I believe in the Holy Spirit; the holy Church; the forgiveness of sins; the resurrection of the body, and life everlasting."

This is the exact form of the creed which was used in the second, third, and fourth centuries, and it was considered the sufficient rule of faith in the Church until the year 325. I think that it would not have been regarded as sufficient if the Trinitarian belief had generally prevailed. It would not be regarded alone as sufficient in the present day. It would not be considered safe in the Episcopal and Roman Catholic Churches to discard the Nicene and Athanasian Creeds and retain this as the only confession of faith; nor in the Presbyterian Church would it be considered safe to adopt it, instead of the Assembly's Catechism. But it satisfies us, as Unitarians, and if we thought it right to use any confession of faith, other than the New Testament itself, I know of none which we could adopt more heartily than this which is called the Apostles' Creed.[8]

Franks agrees that the rule of faith in the early church was the Apostles' Creed:

The first bulwark against Gnosticism was set up by the recog-

---

[8] Eliot, 88-89.

nition of the baptismal confession as the Rule of Faith. Here it was the confession of the Roman church about A.D. 150 that set the pattern. Its sentences can be recovered from the writings of Justin Martyr, Irenaeus and Tertullian: in substance it differed little from what today is known as the Apostles' Creed. This Creed or Rule of Faith stood as a concise statement of the common belief of all true Christians.[9]

From a simple reading of the Apostles' Creed it is apparent that the early church believed that the Father alone was God. And not only was this rule of faith embraced by Christians prior to the establishment of the Nicene Creed, for some time and in some places the Apostles' Creed was preferred as the rule of faith *after* the Nicene Creed was written:

> This creed became dominant in the West as a result of the Filioque controversy, which centered on an interpolation in the Nicene Creed. The East rejected that interpolation, and the Franks insisted on it. In order to avoid the issue, the popes began using the so-called Apostles' Creed instead of the Nicene.[10]

Even today, Trinitarianism is still in a state of development. As well-reasoned challenges arise against its various doctrines, new theories are invented to account for its inconsistencies and Trinitarianism is thus not the same today as it was in its earlier years of development. As deficiencies in Trinitarian dogma were brought to light, new dogmas were developed to rescue the old ones. These new dogmas fueled the same process, until we arrive at today's system of utterly unrecognizable and contradictory statements. The development of the doctrine has consistently been guided by man's ingenuity. The mechanism of its original establishment was largely the councils of the fourth century and beyond:

> It was in such a state of things, as the fruit of a controversy which rent Christendom in pieces, and much in accor-

---

9 Franks, 62-63.

10 William Gentz, ed., *The Dictionary of Bible and Religion* (Nashville: Abingdon Press, 1986), "Constantine, Emperor," 61.

dance with the prevailing philosophy of the age, that having established the deity of the Son even in the qualified sense we have seen, the next step should be taken towards completing the dogma of the Trinity, namely, the deification of the Holy Ghost. This was done, as has been shown, at the Council of Constantinople, A.D. 381; concerning which says Mosheim: "A hundred and fifty bishops, who were present at this Council, gave the finishing touch to what the Council of Nice had left imperfect; and fixed, in a full and determinate manner, the doctrine of three persons in one God, which is as yet received among the generality of Christians." But Mosheim, as I have had occasion to remark before, is too hasty. "The finishing touch" was much later. This Trinity was a work of time. A doctrine so mysterious, so self-contradictory, not patent on the face of Scripture, was only by degrees forced on the faith of the church. The Nicene Creed stopped with saying: "We believe in the Holy Ghost." The Creed of Constantinople declared: "We believe in the Holy Ghost, the Lord and Giver of Life; who proceedeth from the Father; who, with the Father and Son together is worshipped and glorified; who spake by the prophets." Here distinctly appears the Personality of the Spirit; and its Deity as a joint object of worship. But the Creed says that it "proceedeth from the Father" only; and in less than fifty years "the unity and equality of the persons which necessarily resulted from holding sameness of essence," and which "was not fully acknowledged at once even by the Nicenians, but continued to be more clearly perceived, was at last expressed by Augustine for the first time with decided logical consequence." Augustine died A.D. 430; and in a little more than a century of constant strife thereafter, A.D. 589, the third Council of Toledo added the clause, "and the Son" to the Creed, and anathematized all who disbelieved the doctrine it conveyed. Thenceforth it read—"who proceedeth from the Father and the Son;" an alteration which, says Hagenbach, "afterwards led to the disruption between the eastern and western Churches."

Still the modern doctrine of the Trinity was not complete. But without attempting to follow the growth of it through the various and tedious disputes which from time to time continued to arise, it is enough to say that "the finishing touch" was reserved for the fourth Council of Lateran, so late as A.D. 1215; that Council to which belongs the baleful preëminence of having established the monstrous dogma of Transubstantiation, ordered the extermination of heretics, and by its persecuting edicts, laid the foundation of the Inquisition. By such a Council was the modern doctrine of the Trinity completed, and for the first time by authority proclaimed as the faith of the Church; that doctrine, in the words of Cudworth, of a "Trinity of Persons numerically the same, or having all one and the same singular existent essence; a doctrine which seemeth not to have been owned by any public authority in the Christian church, save that of the Lateran Council only." [11]

Trinitarians of the fourth century had a different conception of the doctrine of the Trinity than Trinitarians have today:

I WISH, however, first to observe, that the ancient opinions concerning the Trinity, before the Council of Nice (A.D. 325), were VERY DIFFERENT from the modern doctrine, and had this great advantage over it, that, when viewed simply in connection with the Unity of God, they were not *essentially* incredible. According to that form of faith which approached nearest to the modern Orthodox doctrine, the Father alone was the Supreme God, and the Son and Spirit were beings deriving their existence from him, and far inferior, to whom the title of God could be properly applied only in an inferior sense.

MANY Trinitarian writers have maintained a modification of the doctrine, in some respects similar to what has just been stated to be its most ancient form. They have considered the Father as the "fountain of divinity," whose existence alone is underived, and having regarded the Son and Spirit as deriving their existence from him and subordinate to him; but, at the same time, as equally possessing all divine attributes. Every

---

[11] Farley, 249-251.

well-informed Trinitarian has at least heard of the Orthodoxy and learning of Bishop Bull. His *Defence of the Nicene Creed* is the standard work as regards the argument in support of the doctrine of the Trinity from Ecclesiastical History. But one whole division of this famous book is employed in maintaining the *subordination* of the Son. "No one can doubt," he says, "that the Fathers who lived before the Nicene Council acknowledged this subordination. It remains to show that the Fathers who wrote after this Council taught the same doctrine" (Bishop Bull, *Defensio Fidel Nicaenae*, § 3—quoted in Norton, 44-45). Having given various quotes from different writers to this effect, he proceeds: "The ancients, as they regarded the Father as the beginning, cause, author, fountain, of the Son, have not feared to call him the one and only God. For thus the Nicene Fathers themselves begin their creed: *We believe in one God, the Father omnipotent;* afterwards subjoining: *and in one [Lord] Jesus Christ.—God of God.* And the great Athanasius himself concedes, that the Father is justly called the only God, because he alone is without origin, and is alone the fountain of divinity" (Ibid., § 6).[12]

To better understand the world into which the doctrine of the Trinity was born, we must recognize that Greece and its philosophers, especially Plato, had an impact on the early church Fathers and the formulation of their beliefs. Pope John Paul II commented on philosophy's impact on the early church:

The Christian tradition before Thomas Aquinas, and therefore also Augustine, was tied to Plato, from whom it nonetheless rightfully wanted to distance itself.[13]

The church of the thirteenth century was still trying to distance itself from Platonism! Even today the church has still not separated itself from the Platonic influence, which is evident from the fact that so many Christians today continue to recite creeds that were devel-

---

12 Norton, 44-45.

13 Pope John Paul II, *Crossing the Threshold of Hope* (New York: Alfred Knopf, Inc., 1994), 28.

oped when the church was actively influenced by Greek philosophy. The Pope's admission may be sufficient justification for rejecting the doctrine of the Trinity, but the fact that the doctrine is not mentioned in Scripture at all makes an easy case for rejecting the entire Trinitarian system:

> We object, finally, to this doctrine, that we know its origins to have been, not in the Scriptures, but outside of them. It was the Greek Philosophy of Alexandria, and not the Hebrew or Christian Theology of Jerusalem, that gave birth to this doctrine. We can trace its fount, its spring, its incomings. There is no historical fact more supported than that of the addiction of the Church Fathers to the study of the Greek Philosophy; they loved it, they fondly pursued it, they were infected by it, their speculations were influenced by it, their Christian faith received intermixture from it. Dr. Caesar Morgan acknowledges this fact most candidly, though he pursues a critical examination of all the passages in Plato which are thought to contain references to an ante-Christian Trinity, for the sake of proving that the Fathers did not get the doctrine from the philosopher. But the argument which he assails does not yield to his assault upon it. We might as well dispute whether an ancient tragedy, whose catastrophe turns on Fate, were of Grecian or Jewish origin, as debate the issue whether a theosophical fiction concerning the Godhead, which involves the most acute subtlety of philosophy, sprang from the Abrahamic faith or from Hellenistic Gnosticism. The history of the doctrine of the Trinity makes to us an evident display of a development, an amplification and steady augmentation, from a germ which was forced into an artificial growth. It was an evolved doctrine which was constantly seeking to define itself, which was never at rest, and which never has been at rest under any of the definitions which it has found for itself. A comparison of the three old creeds, the so-called Apostles', Nicene, and the Athanasian, with a reference to their dates, will unmistakably reveal of what processes and elements the

doctrine of the Trinity is the product.[14]

Theories about God proliferated in the early church, and in the second century a group of philosophers/theologians known as the Apologists became prominent. These men borrowed ideas from the earlier Greek philosophers about various subjects, among which were the concepts of the *logos* and the relationship of the Father to the Son. The Apologists lived after the twelve apostles and before the council of Nicea, and the Apologists' writings undoubtedly influenced those who attended the Nicene Council. Rusch, a Trinitarian, says:

> The Apologists set the future course for Trinitarian theology
> and enabled Christianity to take seriously the presuppositions
> of Greek philosophy.[15]

When Mr. Rusch speaks of Christianity taking Greek philosophy seriously, he can only be referring to the church fathers, not the majority of Christians. Most people in that time were illiterate and uneducated, and therefore unable (and perhaps unwilling) to engage in the subtle speculations required to participate in these philosophical discourses. The early church fathers—who were given this title due to their impact on the church, not the accuracy of their theologies—infused Greek philosophy into their theologies. This was not the philosophers' fault per se; the fault rests with those purportedly representing God while incorporating unbiblical ideologies. Thomas Jefferson, our nation's third president, was decidedly against the doctrine of the Trinity and well aware of Greek philosophy's influence on Christian thought and teachings. Having studied the Bible and Greek philosophy at length, Jefferson concluded:

> The time had come to submit Plato to the test of Reason. "His
> foggy mind is forever presenting the semblances of objects
> which, half seen thro' a mist, can be defined neither in form
> or dimension." This mistiness, which should have consigned
> [Plato] to oblivion, on the contrary—and quite incredibly—
> brought "him immortality of fame and reverence." Plato by
> himself could be simply dismissed. What he had done to

---

14 Ellis, 128-129.

15 William G. Rusch, ed., *The Trinitarian Controversy* (Philadelphia: Fortress Press, 1980), 6.

Christianity, however, with the help of priests, could not.

When the Christian clergy, said Jefferson, discovered that the simple message of Jesus could be understood by everyone, that it was "too plain to need explanation," they got busy building an artificial system, as misty as Plato's that would require constant explanation, cause endless controversy, and—most important of all—give the priests steady employment into perpetuity. A child could understand Jesus. Thousands of ponderous volumes have not yet clarified Plato.[16]

The doctrine of the Trinity was not debated by the church until the councils of the fourth century developed creeds that began to gradually incorporate Trinitarian notions of God. It has been argued that this is because the church of the first three centuries accepted the doctrine without question, which is a preposterous assumption because it does not agree with the opposition it would have faced from Jews:

> We have seen that the doctrine is not contained in the recorded discourses of Christ and his Apostles; neither is it found in the confessions of faith required of the primitive converts—neither is it recognized in the earliest controversies, which agitated the church; no traces of the Trinity are found in ecclesiastical history, until after the Apostolic age. But after Christianity began to be corrupted by the speculations of philosophers, then it became developed, and was the subject of serious contention. The Trinity sprung up subsequently to the times of the Apostles. Mosheim, whose religious bias was in favour of the Trinity, says, "in the year 317, a new contention arose in Egypt, which kindled deplorable divisions in the Christian world." It was the doctrine of three persons in the Godhead, a doctrine which in the three preceding centuries, had happily escaped the vain curiosity of human researches. The Emperor Constantine, not considering the importance of the discussion, addressed a letter to the contending parties, in which he admonished them to end their disputes; but

---

16 Edwin Gaustad, *Sworn on the Altar of God* (Grand Rapids: Wm. B. Eerdman's Pub. Co., 1996), 133.

when the prince saw that his admonitions were without effect, and that the troubles and disputes were daily spreading throughout the empire, he assembled in the year 325, the famous council at Nice, in Bithynia, wherein the deputies of the church were requested to put an end to the controversy. And, in 381, 150 bishops gave the finishing stroke to what the council of Nice had left imperfect, and fixed, in a full and determinate manner, the doctrine of the three persons in one God, which is yet received among Christians as the gospel of Jesus Christ. From this time the Trinity became enrolled amongst the orthodox doctrines, and though Calvin expressed his disapprobation of the word as barbarous, and savouring of heathenism, and Melancthon, bewailed the sanguinary tragedies it would cause to be enacted, the reformation did not destroy its roots, and it is still a upas tree [a tree that produces poison used to make poison arrows] in the garden of theology, withering the tender plants of truth and righteousness.[17]

Advocates of Trinitarianism frequently seem to overlook that so little attention has been given to the belief that the Holy Spirit/holy spirit is God or a god. It is ordinarily assumed that the doctrine of the Trinity has been proven if it can be shown that Jesus is God. This is not true. It must be kept in mind that it is just as important to show the holy spirit is equal with the Father as it is to show the same thing about Jesus. Trinitarians spend very little time on this aspect of their system. The refinement of the (orthodox) doctrine of the holy spirit, like that of the doctrine of the double nature of Christ, took place over a long period of time, which may be seen by comparing the language of the Bible to the language of the creeds:

Look, moreover, at those solemn charges which St. Paul gave to Timothy his "own son in the faith." "I charge thee before God, and the Lord Jesus Christ, and"—(the Holy Ghost? No. But)—"the elect angels." (1 Tim. 5:21). "I give thee charge in the sight of God, who quickeneth all things; and before Christ Jesus, who before Pontius Pilate witnessed a good

---

[17] Thomas, 16-17.

confession that thou keep this commandment without spot, unrebukable, until the appearing of our Lord Jesus Christ; which in His times He shall show who is the Blessed and Only Potentate, the King of Kings, and Lord of Lords; who only hath immortality, dwelling in the light which no man can approach unto; whom no man hath seen nor can see: to whom be honor and power everlasting. Amen." (1 Tim. 6:13-16; vid also, 2 Tim. 4:1). Not only is the same distinction preserved in both passages, on which I have remarked before, between the Father as God, and Christ as Lord; but in the last, the Apostle, as if for the very purpose of keeping before the mind of Timothy the unchallenged and absolute Supremacy of the One God the Father, breaks forth into a glowing and sublime description of Him, and yet makes no reference to or mention of the Holy Spirit. Why did he not, in those introductory salutations above recited, in these charges thus solemnly given, speak of Christ as "God the Son," instead of Lord, if such he knew or believed him to be? Why did he not charge Timothy *before "God the Holy Ghost,"* as well as before the other august names there named, if such he knew or believed the Holy Ghost to be? There can be but one answer. He neither knew nor believed the one or the other.

Finally, the history of this doctrine of the Personality and Deity of the Holy Spirit condemns it. For nearly four centuries it was scarcely dreamed of; it had no place, certainly, in the "Christian consciousness" of the mass of believers. It was a thing of time, and of degrees, because the doctrine of the Trinity of which it is a part, was such. "The desire of bringing the doctrine of the Trinity *to a conclusion*, led *gradually* to more definite views on the personality of the Holy Ghost." So says Hagenbach, writing of what was accomplished during what he styles "The First Period" of the history of the church or from A.D. 80 to A.D. 254. (Hist. of Doctrine, vol. i. 125). Could any language better illustrate the fact, that not upon clear Scripture testimony, but upon the arguments of polemics, and the decrees of councils, this doctrine was built? "The subject of the personality and divinity of the Holy Spirit," says Prof. Norton—and his testimony, after his profound study of the subject is not lightly to be set aside—"was in a very unsettled state before the Council of Constantinople (A.D. 381.)" [18]

The Council of Constantinople, convened fifty-six years after the Council of Nicea, is typically credited with supplying the deficiencies of the Nicene Creed, yet it only mentions the holy spirit, without supplying any statement about it:

> If the doctrine of the Trinity, while in *embryo*, could be the occasion of so much evil, of what inconceivable mischief is it capable, having grown to *maturity*! It had been well for the church, well for the world, if it "had happily escaped the vain curiosity of human researches," not only during "the three preceding centuries," but to the end of time! The same author [Mosheim] speaks more definitely, as to the time when, and the place where, the doctrine of the Trinity was *first* decreed by the Christian church.

> "An hundred and fifty bishops, who were present at this council, [Constantinople, A.D. 381] gave the finishing touch to what the council of Nice had left imperfect, and fixed in a full and determinate manner, the doctrine of *three Persons in one God,* which is as yet received among the generality of Christians." (Mosheim's *Eccl. Hist.,* vol. i. 326.)

The second witness I will summon is DR. MILNER, who, in describing the council of Constantinople, says:—"This council very accurately defined the doctrine of the Trinity, and enlarging a little the Nicene Creed, they delivered it as we now have it in our communion service. The Macedonian heresy which blasphemed the Holy Ghost, gave occasion to a more explicit representation of the *third Person* in the Trinity."

The Nicene Creed was defective in two respects. It recognized neither the *Divinity* of the Holy Ghost, nor the Son's *equality* with the Father. These defects were supplied by the Council of Constantinople. Whether this was enlarging the Nicene Creed *"a little,"* as Dr. Milner calls it, the reader can judge.

---

[18] Farley, 145-147.

Mr. Yates gives the following. "Another learned Reformed and vigorous defender of orthodoxy, who maintains the same opinion, is M. JURIEU. Speaking of the doctrine of the Trinity as believed both by Papists and Calvinists, he says, 'Every one knows that this mystery remained incomplete (*informe*), without its right form or shape, until the council of Nice, nay, until that of Constantinople;' and he asserts, and by proper citations fully proves, that all the ancients of the three first ages believed the Son to have been created by, and inferior to, the Father."—*Vindication, &c.* 278, 279.[19]

The majority of ardent Trinitarians, whose system of faith is relatively static today as compared to the church of the fourth and fifth centuries, seem to think that the doctrine of the Trinity has always existed in its modern form. A simple study of the its development shows that it was in a constant state of change and that it did not become widely accepted until Roman emperors put their stamp of approval on it. The doctrine was then enforced as the rule of faith, it was not accepted by the masses by choice. This is generally not known by Christians today, who perhaps think that the same conditions existed in the early church as exist today. When the history of the church, especially the Unitarian character of the early church, is understood, perhaps more Christians will realize that Unitarianism is not and was not heretical, but was the faith of the early church.

THE PLATONIC ORIGINS OF TRINITARIANISM

The language of the earlier church creeds regarding the doctrine of the Trinity is the language of early Greek philosophy. The philosophy of Plato is generally recognized as having influenced the early church Fathers and the language they used in their creeds. Plato was a student of Socrates, and died roughly 350 years before Jesus was born. Some learned Trinitarians acknowledge that the doctrine of the Trinity has its origins in Platonism:

I will produce a few passages from modern *Trinitarian* writers, to show the near resemblance between the Christian and

---

[19] Morgridge, 163-164.

Platonic Trinity. The very learned Cudworth, in his great work on the Intellectual System, has brought together all that antiquity could furnish to illustrate the doctrine. He institutes a long and minute comparison between the forms in which it was held by the Heathen Platonists, and that which it was held by the Christian Fathers. Toward the conclusion of this, we find the following passages:—

"Thus have we given a true and full account, how, according to Athanasius, the three divine hypostases, though not *monoousious*, but *homoousious* only, are really but one God or Divinity. In all which doctrine of his, there is nothing but what a true and genuine Platonist would readily subscribe to."—Ch. IV. § 36. 620 [Vol. II. 15, Andover edit.]

"As the Platonic Pagans after Christianity did approve of the Christian doctrine concerning the Logos, as that which was exactly agreeable with their own; so did the generality of the Christian Fathers, before and after the Nicene Council, represent the genuine Platonic Trinity as really the same thing with the Christian, or as approaching so near to it, that they differed chiefly in circumstances, or the manner of expression."—Ibid., 621 [al. II. 17.]

Basnage was not disposed to allow such a resemblance between the Christian and Platonic Trinity as that which Cudworth maintains, and has written expressly in refutation of the latter. It is not necessary to enter into this controversy. The sentence with which he concludes his remarks on the subject, is enough for our purpose. "Christianity, in its triumph, has often reflected honor on the Platonists; and as the Christians took some pride in finding the Trinity taught by a philosopher, so the Platonists were proud in their turn to see the Christians adopt their principles."—Histoire des Juifs, Liv. IV. ch. 3, 4.[20]

The idea that most Christians are propounding a doctrine that originated in Greek philosophy will perhaps come as a shock to many. The doctrine has been regarded as the primary doctrine of Christian

---

[20] Norton, 98-100.

faith, with a minority espousing a contrary view—the Unitarian. Although Trinitarians admit that their dogma has been intermixed with Greek philosophy, they never argue that Unitarian dogma suffers from the same intermixture. What Unitarians have been charged with throughout the centuries is not abiding by a post-Nicean view of God, which is true. The charge against Trinitarians, the truth of which has been acknowledged by Trinitarian scholars, is that the doctrine of the Trinity has its genesis in Greek philosophy. Although triune conceptions of deities pre-date the Platonic conception, it is the Greek conception, most notably that of either the Platonists or neo-Platonists, that early Trinitarians adopted as their own:

> There has been no more noted defender of the doctrine in modern times than Bishop Horsley. The following is a quote from his Letters to Dr. Priestley.
>
> "I am very sensible that the Platonizers of the second century were the Orthodox of that age. I have not denied this. On the contrary, I have endeavored to show that their Platonism brings no imputation upon their Orthodoxy. The advocates of the Catholic faith in modern times have been too apt to take alarm at the charge of Platonism. I rejoice and glory in the opprobrium. I not only confess, but I maintain, not a perfect agreement, but such a similitude as speaks a common origin, and affords an argument in confirmation of the Catholic doctrine [of the Trinity], from its conformity to the most ancient and universal traditions."—Letters to Dr. Priestley, Letter 13.
>
> In another place he says: "It must be acknowledged, that the first converts from the Platonic school took advantage of the resemblance between the Evangelic and Platonic doctrine on the subject of the Godhead, to apply the principles of their old philosophy to the explication and confirmation of the articles of their faith. They defended it by arguments drawn from Platonic principles; they even propounded it in Platonic language."—Charge, IV. § 2.[21]

These statements are as condemning of this doctrine as any that

---

[21] Norton, 103.

could be produced. The doctrine pre-dated Christianity and was first developed in an entirely separate medium, Greek philosophy. And a distinction may be drawn between true philosophy, or a love of wisdom, and false philosophy, or deceit. I do not object to the term *philosophy* or the study of it simply because it is called by this name. Fundamentalist Christians are generally alarmed by anything connected to what is called philosophy, but this is unwarranted. Colossians 2:8 says, "Beware lest any man spoil you through philosophy and vain deceit, after the tradition of men, after the rudiments of the world, and not after Christ." Some, perhaps many, have inferred from this that philosophy itself is bad, and therefore shrink from any mention of it. It is not on these grounds that I disapprove of philosophy, as a modern author, himself a Trinitarian, writes:

> It is unfortunate but true that this passage [Col. 2:8] has often been read as intended to steer the Christian believer away from philosophy. What it attempts to warn the Christian against, however, is *false* philosophy.... *philosophy* is etymologically "the love of wisdom"...[22]

A primary objection against incorporating philosophy, particularly Plato's, into Christian thought, is that his ideologies were not rooted in the Bible, and this discussion about the Unitarian-Trinitarian controversy is predicated on the Bible being the common playing field. Any similarity between Plato's conception of God and Scripture would be coincidental. Plato (c. 428-374 B.C.) preceded the church councils by about seven hundred years, so the notion that Christianity influenced him is impossible. Only the opposite may be true, and we know from historical writings that this is the case. The most reasonable assessment of the Platonic influence on the early church is that Plato was a speculator on divine things. He did not have the New Testament available to him since the letters that would later be incorporated into it hadn't yet been written, but future generations, including those of the church councils, borrowed ideas and language from his philosophy. If his ideas agreed with the church it would have been a fascinating coincidence, to say the least.

Nonetheless, and what isn't widely known, is that the church of

---

[22] Thomas Morris, *God and the Philosophers* (New York: Oxford University Press, 1994), 6.

the fourth century was reluctant to receive the doctrine of the Trinity. It was a doctrine that, due to its subtleties, was not even capable of being understood by the masses. The notion of breaking down the individuality of the Father and the Son and blending them into one being made early Christians uncomfortable. Prior to the introduction of the notion of one "substance" or "essence" of the supposed Godhead, the church kept the Father and the Son separate. Virtually all the information we have today shows that they believed that Jesus was subordinate to the Father. Even *after* the doctrine of the "same substance" of the Father and Son was introduced at the Council of Nicea, it was still not widely accepted:

> The defence of the creed of Nicæa, to which Athanasius devoted his life, was made necessary because the solid front at the Council, where all but two bishops signed the creed, broke up at once in the East into the discordant parts that had only been temporarily united by the influence of the Emperor and the desire for peace. There were now three parties. There were the Arians proper, called the Anhomoians since they held that the Logos was unlike the Father. Then there were the few genuine Eastern Nicæans or Homoousians; they... had the support of the West. Finally, there was the great Oriental majority, of which Eusebius of Cæsarea is typical: these were named Homoousians, since they preferred to say that the Logos was of like essence with the Father, rather than that He was of the same essence...The majority held firmly to the three hypostases of Origen, and disliked anything that tended to amalgamate them so as to destroy their individuality.[23]

So the doctrine of the equality of Jesus with the Father was not popular when it was introduced. History is commonly interpreted anachronistically, and since most Christians today profess to be Trinitarian, even if only nominally, many assume this was also the character of the early church. It is apparently inconceivable to those who embrace the doctrine of a triune god that the doctrine has Platonic, rather than Judeo-Christian, origins. The subtle and unbiblical nature of the doctrine required time, as well as ecclesiastical and govern-

---

[23] Franks, 107-108.

mental interference, for it to become popular:

> Finally, this has been *practically* admitted by every Trinitarian that ever attempted to prove the contrary. All have retired from the field without success. Dr. Dwight, already consulted, page 29, has given us the best he could on the subject, but failed to produce a single testimony to the point. The latest able controversy on this subject was between Dr. Priestley and Bishop Horsley, of the last century: the former maintaining that the primitive believers were Unitarians; the latter, the contrary. And though Bishop Horsley was a man of great learning, and fully competent to do justice to his cause, yet the attempt was a total failure. If such men as Dr. Dwight and Bishop Horsley could not prove that the primitive Christians believed in the doctrine of three co-equal and co-eternal Persons in the Godhead, we may rest assured that it never can be proved.

Having shown that the first Christians knew nothing of the doctrine of the Trinity, I will conclude with some extracts from Professor Norton, touching its ORIGIN.

"We can trace the history of this doctrine," says Mr. Norton, "and discover its source; not in the Christian revelation, but in the Platonic philosophy; which was the prevalent philosophy during the first ages after the introduction of Christianity; and of which all the more eminent Christian writers, the Fathers, as they are called, were, in a greater or less degree, disciples. They, as others have often done, blended their philosophy and their religion into one complex and heterogeneous system; and taught the doctrines of the former as those of the latter. In this manner, they introduced errors into the popular faith.

" 'It is an old complaint of learned men,' says Mosheim, 'that the Fathers, or teachers of the ancient church, were too much inclined to the philosophy of Plato, and rashly confounded what was taught by that philosopher with the doctrines of Christ, our Saviour; in consequence of which, the religion of Heaven was greatly corrupted, and the truth much obscured.'

"I might produce more authorities in support of the facts which have been stated. But I conceive it to be unnecessary. The fair inference from these facts, every reader is able to draw for himself. The doctrine of the Trinity is not a doctrine of Christ and his Apostles, but a fiction of the later Platonists, introduced into our religion by the Fathers, who were admirers and disciples of the philosophy taught in this school. The want of all mention of it in the Scriptures is abundantly compensated by the ample space which it occupies in the writings of the heathen Platonists, and of the Platonizing Fathers.

"But what has been stated is not the only evidence which Ecclesiastical History affords against this doctrine. The conclusion to which we have just arrived is confirmed by other facts. But these, however important, I will here but barely mention. They are the facts of *its gradual introduction; of its slow growth to its present form; of the strong opposition which it encountered; and of its tardy reception among the great body of common Christians.*

"Cudworth after remarking 'that not a few of those ancient Fathers, who were therefore reputed Orthodox because they zealously opposed Arianism,' namely, Gregory Nyssen, Cyril of Alexandria, and others, entertained the opinion that the three persons on the Trinity were three distinct individuals, 'like three individual men, Thomas, Peter, and John;' the divine nature being common to the former as the human nature is to the latter; observes that 'some would think that the ancient and genuine Platonic Trinity, taken with all its faults is to be preferred before this Trinity.' He then says; 'But as this Trinity came afterwards to be decried for tritheistic; so in the room thereof, started there up that other Trinity of persons numerically the same, or having all one and the same singular existent essence; a doctrine which seemeth not to have been owned by any public authority in the Christian church, save that of the Lateran council only.'

"This is the present orthodox form of the doctrine of the Trinity. Cudworth refers to the fourth general Lateran council, held in 1215, under Pope Innocent the Third. The same council which, in the depth of the dark ages, established the modern doctrine of the Trinity, established, likewise, that of Transubstantiation; enforced with the utmost rigor the persecution of heretics, whom it ordered to be sought out and exterminated; and prepared the way for the tribunals of the Inquisition." (Statement of Reasons, 51-61.)[24]

If it is true that, as some Trinitarians assert, the doctrine of the Trinity was revealed for the first time to the bishops who attended the council of Nicea, it is futile to argue the doctrine of the Trinity from the Bible. Paul's letter to the Colossian church, which was written long before the council of Nicea, may have been written to prevent the very philosophizing that eventually infected and overpowered the church. Paul was learned and knowledgable about Greek philosophy. In Col. 2:6-8, Paul writes: "As ye have therefore received Christ Jesus the Lord, so walk ye in him: Rooted and built up in him, and established in the faith, as ye have been taught, abounding therein with thanksgiving. Beware lest any man spoil you through philosophy and vain deceit, after the tradition of men, after the rudiments of the world, and not after Christ." Paul instructed the Colossians to stand firm in the faith as they had been taught, and there is no way they could have done this and received the doctrine of the Trinity since it had not yet been taught. Paul told the Colossians how their faith would be spoiled (ruined), if they were to allow it to happen—through *philosophy*. It may have been the intermixture of Greek philosophy with early church teachings to which Paul was alluding:

> But whence came this doctrine of the Trinity, or, in other words, what was its origin? Its origin was clearly Platonic. It was brought into the Christian Church by those of the early Fathers who admired and had adopted the philosophic views of the later Platonists. I say advisedly, the later Platonists; because, in the words of Prof. Norton: "Nothing resembling the doctrine of the Trinity is to be found in the writings of Plato himself. But there is no question that, in different forms, it was a favorite doctrine of the later Platonists, equally of those who were not Christians as of those who were." (Norton, 96) There is an obvious distinction to be borne in mind between

---

[24] Morgridge, 165-168.

what is positively taught by the Athenian Philosopher, and what belongs to the Platonic philosophy as held and expounded by Philo Judeaus, a contemporary of our Lord, who has been styled the Jewish Plato, and by the Fathers, or Christian writers of the first four centuries. The most eminent of these men, especially those of Alexandria, the birthplace of Philo, and the scene of his labors, had in general embraced this philosophy to a greater or less extent; and they carried its modes of conception and reasoning into the faith which they were converted. It was, as Mosheim admits, "the impure source of a great number of errors, and most preposterous opinions;" but of them all, none is more marked than this doctrine of the Trinity, which Mosheim himself accepted. Basnage, in his History of the Jews, remarks, that these Fathers almost made Plato to have been a Christian before Christianity was introduced; in allusion to some of their efforts to show that Plato himself taught the doctrine.[25]

Augustine (354-430 A.D.) is considered to be among the most influential of the early church Fathers. Regarding how he became "enlightened" to the doctrine of the Trinity, he said he was "in the dark with regard to the Trinity until he found the true doctrine concerning the divine word, in a Latin translation of some Platonic writings, which the Providence of God had thrown in his way."[26] Augustine's intermixture of Platonic philosophy with Christian dogma is well documented:

As a Roman he inherited and restated for his own time the political philosophy inaugurated by Plato and adapted to the Latin world by Cicero, and as a Christian he modified that philosophy to suit the requirements of the faith. He thus appears if not as the originator at least as the foremost exponent of a new tradition of political thought characterized by its attempt to fuse or reconcile elements derived from two originally independent and hitherto unrelated sources, the Bible and classical philosophy.... Unlike either Judaism or Islam,

---

[25] Farley, 26-27.

[26] Eliot, 95.

the other two great religions of the Western world, Christianity did not reject philosophy as an alien or merely tolerate it but sought early to enlist its support, making room for philosophy within the walls of Christendom, where it continued to thrive with varying degrees of ecclesiastical approval and supervision.[27]

Since Augustine incorporated Greek philosophy into his theology, the extent to which Christians may rely upon his teachings depends upon the extent to which Plato's teachings coincide with those of the Bible, which, it is not difficult to apprehend, is not great. Augustine's influence on the church is as undeniable as his fusion of philosophy and theology.

It is evident from the following quotes of various early church figures that the doctrine of the Trinity was not a part of the early church. Only after the councils asserted a different statement of faith did it begin to take root:

> TERTULLIAN expressly says, "That God was not always a Father or a Judge; since he could not be a Father before he had a son, nor a judge before there was sin, and there was a time, when both sin, and the Son, which made God to be a Judge and a Father, *were not.*"
>
> ORIGEN, the most learned of the Fathers, wrote about the year 225; he says, "The Father only is 'the Good,' and the Saviour, as he is the image of the invisible God, so is he the image of his goodness." Again he says, "If we know what prayer is, we must not pray to any created being, not to Christ himself, but only to God the Father of all, to whom our Saviour himself prayed." "We are not to pray to a brother, who has the same father with ourselves; Jesus himself saying, that we must pray to the Father, through the Son." Yet this same Origen frequently calls Christ God, although in a subordinate sense. For when accused of believing in two Gods, he explained himself as follows:—"He who is God *of himself* is The God; for which reason he says in his prayer to the Father,

---

27 Ernest Fortin, *History of Political Philosophy* (Chicago and London: University of Chicago Press, Leo Strauss and Joseph, eds., 3rd ed., 1987), "Augustine," 176-177.

that they may know thee the only true God; but whatever is God besides him, (who is so of himself,) being God only by a communication of his divinity, cannot so properly be called The God, but rather A God," or divine.

Such language is very common until the beginning of the fifth century; and whenever Christ is called God before that time, the word is to be understood in the sense in which Origen used it. And LACTANTIUS says, "Christ taught that there is one God, and that he alone ought to be worshipped; neither did he ever call himself God; because he would not have been true to his trust, if, being sent to take away Gods and insert One, he had introduced another besides that one. Because he assumed nothing at all to himself, he received the dignity of perpetual Priest, the honor of the Sovereign King, the power of a Judge, and the name of God."

I shall quote but one other authority, EUSEBIUS, who wrote about the year 320. He says, "There is one God and the only-begotten comes from him." "Christ, being neither the Supreme God, nor an angel, is of a middle nature between them; and being neither the Supreme God, but a Mediator, is in the middle between them, the only-begotten Son of God." "Christ, the only-begotten Son of God, and the first-born of every creature, teaches us to call his Father the true God, and commands us to worship him only." [28]

Once the doctrine of the Trinity was decreed to be the rule of faith, the doctrine of the Father being the one true God gradually eroded. After the doctrine of the Trinity became part of the religion of the times it became hard to challenge, no matter how unbiblical and nonsensical:

It were here pertinent to ask, what authority had these men—for whom no special illumination, not to say inspiration, can with any show of plausibility be pretended, nay, which is never assumed for them—to foist upon the Church this great "mystery," to charge upon the sacred writers this strange concealment? Every man of common sense will answer, none

---

[28] Eliot, 92-93.

whatever. The claim of such authority is preposterous, and not for a moment to be regarded. So far, however, as their admissions go to the point, that Holy Scripture, on its face and in plain language, does not teach the doctrine, the same have been made in every age since down to our own—alike by Romanist and Protestant. Learned men of Romish Communion, though firmly holding to their Trinitarianism, make the same admissions. Sacroboscus, in his "Defence of the Council of Trent," declares that "the Arians appealed to the Scriptures in support of their opinions; and that they were not condemned by the Scriptures, but by Tradition." Alphonso Salmeron says: "Christ did not receive testimony from the Evangelists that he was God."—(Comm. in Ev. Prolog. xxvi. tom. 1, 394). Cardinal Hosius says: "We believe the doctrine of a Triune God, because we have received it by tradition, though not at all mentioned in Scripture." —(Conf. Cath. fid. Christi. cap. 27). And, most distinctly and boldly, Remundus,—(Hist. of Rise and Progress of Heresies, Pt. i. l. 2, cap. 15), addressing the Lutherans and Calvinists, warns them in these words: "You will be obliged to confess, however unwillingly, that if you rely on Scriptures you will be compelled to yield to modern Arians, *no less than the Fathers were to those of ancient times*; unless, like them you appeal to Tradition, and the unanimous consent of the Church. *They* were taught *by Tradition* that there are Three Consubstantial Persons of the same nature and essence which we worship as One God in the fullness of the Trinity; and also, that in Jesus Christ there are Two perfect substances, but only One Person. Tell me, if you listen to the Scriptures, and the express word of God alone, with what arms can you expect to engage with these men? In what way can you extricate yourselves from the *innumerable* arguments which they advance, unless you cling to Tradition, and the consent of the Church, as the only anchor of safety?" In our own day, Mr. Newman, a convert to Rome from the Church of England, in his "Arians of the Fourth Century," —(Page 55.) says: "It may startle those who are but little acquainted with the writings of this day, (fourth century,) yet I believe the most accurate consideration of the subject will lead us to acquiesce in the statement as a general truth, that the doctrines in question (the Trinity, Atonement, etc.) have never been learned merely from Scripture. Surely the Sacred volume was never intended, and was not adapted, to teach our creed. ***From the first, it had been the error of heretics to neglect the information provided for them, and to attempt for themselves a work for which they are unable—the eliciting of a systematic doctrine from the scattered notices of the truth which Scripture contains." [29]

The last sentence above reveals how highly some of the educated persons thought of themselves, and how lowly they regarded those whom they taught. It also gives an indication as to how easy it was to force a doctrine of their choosing on the masses. As mentioned earlier, educational institutions such as universities weren't developed until about the sixteenth century. Most people didn't have access to higher learning; those who did were able to interpret the Scriptures for others. What is also clear from the last sentence above is the dubiousness of the doctrine—it was elicited from "scattered notices (!) of the truth which Scripture contains."

Regarding the early church, there is ample evidence from early writings that its character was Unitarian:

My object this evening is to show the argument for the Unitarian doctrine derived from Ecclesiastical history.

It is a subject to which more importance is attached than it really deserves. For, as we have the Bible in our own hands, we can read the words of Jesus and of his Apostles for ourselves, and these alone are enough to form our faith. They are indeed the only conclusive authority. To Jesus the Holy Spirit was given without measure. Whatever he declared himself to be, therefore, we are bound to believe; neither more nor less. Show us that he laid claim to be the Infinite and Supreme God, and we will so receive him; but as we can find no such words from his lips, but, on the contrary, repeated and distinct declarations of his entire dependence on God the Father, we receive this doctrine, and shall hold to it, let those who are

---

[29] Farley, 34-26.

called the Christian Fathers teach what they may. We do not, therefore, regard the subject of this evening as essential to our general argument. It becomes important chiefly because of the stress laid upon it by others.

By the Roman Catholics, the early traditions of the Christian Church, and the writings of the Christian Fathers are regarded as the bulwarks of their faith. They do not hesitate to admit that the leading doctrines of Christianity cannot be proved by the Bible alone. Let me quote some of their language to this effect.

"Those who bind themselves to Scripture alone, and who do not set up any other rule of law or belief, labor to no purpose, and are conquered by their own weapons, as often as they join battle with such pests [the Unitarians], that conceal and defend themselves likewise with the language of Scripture alone. And we know from history, that this frequently happened to them in the conferences into which they entered with the Photinians and the Arians."—Petavius, De Trin. Lib. III. Cap. xi. 9; Theol. Dog., Vol. II. 301.

"That the Son is of the same essence as the Father, or consubstantial with him, is not manifest in any part of sacred Scripture, either in express words, or by certain and immutable deduction. These and other opinions of the Protestants no one can prove from the Sacred writings, the traditionary word of God being laid aside. This request has often been made, but no one has made it good. Scripture itself would, in many places, have seemed to exhibit the opposite doctrine, unless the Church had taught us otherwise."—Masenius, Apud Sandium, 9-11.

To the same purport I might quote many other Roman Catholic authorities. "It is also a remarkable fact, that the Roman Catholic has often triumphed over his Protestant antagonist by demonstrating that the principle of Protestantism, the right of individuals to interpret Scripture without resting on tradition and the authority of the Church, inevitably leads to Unitarianism."

Protestant believers in the Trinity will not of course go as far as this, but even among them concessions have been made of almost equal importance. Many of their best writers, as Hooker, Bishop Beveridge, Bishop Smallridge, and even Carlile (author of the work "Jesus Christ, the great God our Saviour"), and many others, admit that the doctrine of the Trinity is not "directly and explicitly declared, but a doctrine of inference, which ought not to be placed on an equal footing of equality with a doctrine of direct and explicit revelation."—Carlile, 81, 369. [30]

Regarding the Unitarian-Trinitarian debate, the fact that the printing press was not in widespread use until about the 16th century is no small point. Since people did not have Bibles, there was virtually no way of checking the veracity of the doctrines propounded by the church leaders. Seeking the opinions of those in a position to expound upon theological matters became the mode of learning what to believe about God. Prior to the printing press and the advent of mass learning, biblical texts had been almost exclusively in the hands of theocratic rulers so there was no way to check the veracity, or even the plausibility, of what was being taught. That period is today demarcated as the Dark Ages, which left a legacy from which many have yet to recover.

EARLY COUNCILS AND CREEDS

The two creeds that figure most prominently in the development of Trinitarian dogma are the Nicene and the Athanasian (the Athanasian is also referred to as the Constantinopolitan Creed). The Nicene Creed, written in 325 A.D., is by far the most commonly cited of all the creeds produced in the fourth century, and it is typically believed to be the one that first announced the doctrine of the Trinity. To those familiar with it, it is manifestly not Trinitarian. The Nicene Creed is:

> We believe in One God the Father All-sovereign, maker of all things visible and invisible;
>
> And in one Lord Jesus Christ, the Son of God, begotten of the Father, God of God, Light of Light, true God of true God, begotten not made, of one substance with the Father,

---

[30] Eliot, 83-85.

through whom all things were made, things in heaven and things on the earth; who for us men and for our salvation came down and was made flesh, and became man, suffered, and rose on the third day, ascended into the heavens, is coming to judge the living and the dead.

And in the Holy Spirit.

And those that say 'There was a time when he was not,'

and, 'Before he was begotten he was not,'

and that, "He came into being from what-is-not,'

or those that allege, that the son of God is

'Of another substance or essence,'

or 'created,'

or 'changeable,'

or 'alterable,'

these the Catholic and Apostolic Church anathematizes.[31]

The meeting of the clergy who developed this creed was convened by Emperor Constantine, who had adopted some Christian beliefs, and given up (at least some of) his pagan beliefs. It has been argued that Constantine's conversion to Christianity from Mithraism was complete, but this is not supported by what is known about him after his conversion. That he espoused some Christian beliefs is evident from his writings, but his theology was a mixture of Christian and Mithraic dogma. Constantine's conversion to Christianity was anything but complete:

He retained the traditional Pagan title of Pontifex Maximus, as did his Christian successors of the 4th century, and his coins still bear the figures and the names of the old gods."[32]

The meeting which Constantine convened at Nicea was the single largest meeting of bishops ever convened up to that time. Prior to winning favor with Constantine, religious leaders were not permitted to gather in large numbers, presumably due to the fear they might conspire to overthrow whoever was in power at the time. But Con-

---

31 Philip Schaff, *The Creeds of Christendom* (Grand Rapids, Baker Book House, 1931, reprinted 1996), vol. II, 58-59.

32 *Universal Standard Encyclopedia* (1956), "Constantine, Emperor."

stantine recognized that the contentions arising between the religious leaders within his empire could divide it, and he sought to put an end to the disputes. It was not politically expedient to permit factions to grow due to the possibility of a particular faction becoming so powerful that the emperor's sovereignty would be jeopardized. So the bishops met at Constantine's invitation, but instead of coming together harmoniously on this momentous occasion, they immediately presented accusations against one another to the emperor:

> Constantine being desirous of meeting so great a number of prelates as were assembled at Nice, as well as of promoting peace and unanimity, repaired to that city, after he was informed of their arrival. But as it too frequently happens, many of that sacred order, as if they had met together on their private concerns, and supposing that they had found a favourable opportunity of having their grievances redressed, presented to the emperor written complaints against their brethren. As he was almost continually importuned with memorials of this kind, he deferred the consideration of them all to a certain day.[33]

It apparently became too much for Constantine, as not only were there so many accusations the clergy brought against one another, the offenses they accused each other of were such that they would bring dishonor upon the church:

> He declared that the delinquencies of the prelates ought not to be published, lest they should prove an occasion of offence to the people; and even added, that if he should surprise a bishop in adultery, he would cover him with his imperial mantle, for fear that the example of the crime would be prejudicial to those who might witness it. He then commanded them to desist from their unseemly recriminations, and ordered their memorials to be thrown into the fire.[34]

---

[33] Eusebius Pamphilus, *Ecclesiastical History* (Grand Rapids: Baker Book House, reprinted 1994), publisher's appendix, 14.

[34] Eusebius Pamphilus, *Ecclesiastical History* (Grand Rapids: Baker Book House, reprinted 1994), publisher's appendix, 15.

However unintentionally, Constantine himself had contributed to the climate of the Council of Nicea. Economic conditions, brought about by the emperor during his reign, were so bad that the creeds made at Nicea should not, in our day, be given much weight in a discussion about regarding who God is. Even if we momentarily set aside the questionable character of Constantine, the questionable character of the presiding bishops cannot be so easily dismissed:

> It was also a state of affairs which caused demoralization among rich and poor alike.... The trouble went further than social collapse: it amounted to a general unnerving of the will, a paralysis of character, a failure of strength.
>
> It was hollow mockery, then, that each man was told he could do what his soul desired, and that Constantine and his friends repeatedly called him the 'restorer of freedom.'
>
> What made matters even worse, a good deal worse, was the widespread corruption—the universality of the employment of power, public and private alike, as a source of profit.
>
> Everybody was out for what they could get. Officers treated their soldiers dishonestly, and pay was stolen. There were bribes at church councils, and recurrent charges of handing over money in order to become a priest and gain high church office.[35]

In addition to financial advantages for members of the clergy, Constantine granted them privileges that others did not enjoy. Bishops, for example, did not have to perform such civic duties as going to war. A consequence was non-Christians claiming to be Christians in order to become clergy so they could partake in these privileges. Pagans were claiming to be Christians, and until measures were taken to prevent them from easily becoming members of the Christian clergy, their influence had an impact on the development of Christian doctrine and practice:

> By Constantine, the long tension between "love of honour" and immunity from civic burdens was given a new twist: the Christian clergy were exempted from civic duties. The arbi-

---

[35] Michael Grant, *Constantine the Great* (New York: Macmillan Pub. Co., 1993), 99-100.

tration and judgment of bishops was given a new legal backing: on the likeliest interpretation of a complex law, Constantine allowed the parties in a civil or criminal suit to appeal to a bishop's final "judgement" and "testimony." The bishop's decision was then binding on any other judge... These privileges were a strong inducement to join the Church: in 320 and again in 326 Constantine already had to legislate against pagans who were claiming to be clerics in order to avoid their civic duties.[36]

There is no telling what impact these pagan clerics had on the development of the doctrines contained in the creeds, but the recognition that they were involved in forming the creeds suggests they be disregarded. Pagan doctrines had influenced the church, we do not know the extent of the damage they caused. The unintelligible doctrines announced by this Council, along with the unbiblical terminologies they introduced, are enough to alert us that something of a corrupt nature was present. Since Nicea set a foundation which future councils would build upon, it would result in greater absurdities, culminating in God becoming unknown to the Christian community. This is precisely the impact that Trinitarian dogma has on those embracing a faith that was established, to some degree, by pagans who bought their way into the church.

Grant stresses that Constantine was primarily interested in the unity of his empire. In addition to Constantine's suspect actions, such as ordering the execution of his son Crispus and his second wife, Faustus, in 326 A.D., and arranging to be buried in the Church of the Holy Apostles, "of whom he had not been ashamed to declare himself the Thirteenth,"[37] his desire to remain in power superseded all his other pursuits. Some modern Christians argue that Constantine was primarily interested in establishing the truth about God and other things. He was not. Church unity was his perceived means of keeping the empire in a state of tranquility. He thought it would reduce the development of rival factions that might eventually challenge his sovereignty, and creeds were Constantine's tool for unifying Christians

---

36 Robin Lane Fox, *Pagans and Christians* (New York: Alfred A. Knopf, Inc., 1989), 667.

37 Grant, 214.

within his empire. Since unification was his goal, it is fair to conclude that any creed would have served the purpose. The creed then became a severe restriction on the religious freedom of the people, especially on the clergy who were bound to it. But by both unifying and subordinating the church to his rule, Constantine thought peace would result and his primary interest would have been achieved:

> Mention has already been made of the Christians' admirable social cohesion: theirs was the only organized force in the empire, aside from the army. And its enemies had come to bad ends. Edward Gibbon saw that Constantine realized the utility of Christianity, but believed that this realization was derived from his avarice and ambition. Anyway, the emperor saw that it could, and would, be useful. For he liked the idea of backing Christianity because he wanted to have its effective organization on his side. That is to say, he believed firmly that by doing so he could restore to the Roman state the unity which the persecutions [of Christians] had shown to be so sadly lacking. Indeed, that was his dominant aim, to achieve, through the adherents of this religion, *unity* in the Roman empire—although the 'heresies' disappointed this aim....
>
> For, apart from his deep emotional involvement, the main reason why he had favoured Christianity, as we have seen, was because he believed that it would encourage unity in the empire. This was the dominant theme in Constantine's practical thinking and in his life. Unfortunately, however, the Christian faith failed to achieve that aim, owing to the dissensions between one Christian group and another. Constantine wanted an established church, to which all good Christians would belong; and those who would not belong to it were dismissed as 'heretics'—a term resounding with mutual Christian accusations, and with a long and ominous history ahead of it. Constantine deplored this ridiculous proliferation of dissension, believing that imperial unity required unity of creeds.[38]

Constantine used his imperial power on the bishops who attend-

---

[38] Grant, 150-151, 161-162.

ed the council to agree on a creed since, with a formal declaration of faith, non-conformity would be easy to recognize. The emperor eventually wore down the clergy and a creed was finally consented to, but with the aid of criminal sanctions against those who would not sign it. Without Constantine's pressure it is doubtful that the creed developed at the Council of Nicea would have been ratified because there was little theological agreement among the clergy. But they did agree that it would be expedient to accommodate the emperor's desire to have a formal declaration of faith:

> At the council the emperor himself had spoken, and no one in the emperor's lifetime moved against his creed. In a real sense the council was a product of the emperor. The Council of Nicaea was invited by the emperor. Meetings and doctrinal discussions were in his hands. A new chapter in church and state relations had opened. The differing interpretations of what the council was teaching may have been an advantage initially, for with imperial pressure all but two bishops finally subscribed to the creed.[39]

Rather than establishing freedom of conscience in religious matters, the Nicene Creed restricted it. The first part of Canon XVI of the Creed declares:

> Whoever, not having the fear of God before their eyes, and disregarding the ecclesiastical canon, shall rashly withdraw from the church, whether they be priests or deacons, or in any other ecclesiastical order, such persons ought by no means to be received by any other church, but should be compelled to return to their own parishes; and those who are obstinate, should be deprived of the communion.[40]

The seeds of coercion were planted there, and many Christians today follow Canon XVI, though most are unaware it even exists. After it was codified, people were no longer free to believe what they thought was true. After Nicea, people's consciences were bound to a few statements; they could only wander beyond them at the risk of

---

[39] Rusch, 121.

[40] Eusebius Pamphilus, in the appendix by Rev. Isaac Boyles, 58.

losing their communion with others. Perhaps this is a broader commentary on human nature, but little has changed since Constantine's time, particularly when we observe the means currently employed in forcing people to accept the incomprehensible tenets of the orthodox. Excommunication and banishment from fellowship are still common, as are invectives directed toward those who dare to disagree with the old creeds which were produced under conditions unfavorable for producing something rational.

It is not well known today, since the Nicene Creed is considered by many Christians as having established the doctrine of the Trinity, that not only was there little theological agreement among the clergy during the council, there was not much agreement *after* the council regarding the creed that they had signed. It is generally unknown that the clergy made efforts to repeal the Nicene Creed:

> A number of councils were held that tried to move away from the Nicene Creed by producing moderate formulas, critical of Arianism but omitting the phrase homoousios. When Constantine's son Constantius, who leaned towards Arianism, ruled as sole emperor between the years 350 and 361, obvious efforts were made to undo the decisions of Nicaea.[41]

One of the reasons it is important to understand the controversy surrounding the development of the Nicene Creed is that some in the Christian community today commonly refer to many Christians of the first three centuries as heretics because they did not maintain the doctrine of the Trinity that was developed *later*. This is a misunderstanding of the concept of heresy, since in order to be an heretic one must maintain opinions that are contrary to *prevailing* beliefs, not later beliefs. And since it is frequently admitted that the doctrine of the Trinity was not announced until 325, it could not have been the *prevailing* belief of earlier centuries. It is incorrect to suggest someone is an heretic for not believing in a triune God when the prevailing belief was not that of a three-in-one godhead. When properly applied, the term *heretic* more accurately applies to those who began formulating the doctrines that would lead to the notion that our heavenly Father is not the one true God. Prior to the councils, the prevailing belief

---

[41] Rusch, 21.

was that the Father was supreme and that Jesus was created by Him.

The charge of heresy is frequently meant to discredit anybody who, at *any time in history*, disagreed with what are now the most widely-held beliefs. This charge, of course, is selectively applied by those who presume to possess the truth, and who are unaware that virtually every influential person in the church was, at one time or another, considered heretical:

> Heresy, of course, is a tendentious concept. It is an accusation leveled by one group of believers against another; and it can only exist if the accusers believe in their own dogmatic monopoly of the truth. In Christian history, it only emerges in the second and third centuries as the general consensus solidified. Most of the Church's Fathers were heretical in varying degrees.[42]

Davies then goes on to list the various sects of ancient Rome that were considered heretical as defined by *later* orthodoxy. This method of retro-labeling groups is entirely improper. Something is properly called heretical only if it contradicts the prevailing beliefs of the same period, and this, it must be noted, has no bearing on the veracity of the beliefs. It simply implies that there is a prevailing system of beliefs and, at the same time, a competing system of beliefs to which it is being compared. But history demonstrates that a majority may be wrong as easily as a minority, so the label of heretic is largely meaningless. But the label serves to raise a bias against a person or group. Sebastian Castellio, a sixteenth-century writer, eloquently discussed the impropriety of using the word heretic against those with whom one disagrees:

> In view of the many sins which are laid to us all, the best course, would be for each to look to himself, to exercise care for the correction of his life and not for the condemnation of others. This license of judgment which reigns everywhere today, and fills all with blood, constrains me, most Clement Prince, to do my best to staunch the blood, especially that blood which is so wrongfully shed,—I mean the blood of

---

[42] Norman Davies, *Europe, A History* (New York: Oxford University Press, 1996), 205.

those who are called heretics, which name today has become today so infamous, detestable, and horrible that there is no quicker way to dispose of an enemy than to accuse him of heresy. The mere word stimulates such horror that when it is pronounced men shut their ears to the victim's defense, and furiously persecute not merely the man himself, but also those who dare to open their mouths on his behalf; by which rage it has come to pass that many have been destroyed before their cause was fully understood.

Now I say this not because I favor heretics. I hate heretics. But I speak because I see here two great dangers. And the first is that he be held for a heretic, who is not a heretic. This happened in former times, for Christ and his disciples were put to death as heretics....[43]

The astronomer Galileo was branded an heretic by the church for believing the earth revolves around the sun. Though he was right, he suffered during his lifetime by this charge of heresy; it is extremely effective in swaying people's opinions against a person or a group and their beliefs, and typically without seriously considering what the group actually believes or believed. In a similar fashion, Rosa Parks, a black woman who refused to give up her seat at the front of a bus and take one at the back of the bus, was considered heretical. She went against the majority-held belief, codified and enforced by law, that black folks should be treated differently. Her actions, based on her beliefs, were so heretical that she was arrested, and a great storm of controversy surrounded the whole incident. Few people today, though, would agree that she was wrong in her actions. So the charge of heresy should not be understood as a valid indictment against the veracity of an opinion; it is merely a reflection of the fact that someone disagrees with a widely held belief or practice.

As mentioned earlier, the belief that the Father has equals was not maintained in the church of the first three centuries. The notion of a triune god was later adopted by the Catholic Church, which does not negate the fact that Trinitarian dogma was a alteration of the earlier writings of the epistles and gospels. In fact, from the very beginning,

---

[43] Sebastian Castellio, *Concerning Heretics* (1579): quoted in Parke, 10.

force was applied to the bishops just to get the Nicene Creed signed:

> Although many Arians signed the Creed, their signatures, therefore, were given under pressure, and before long, they understood its wording in senses which suited their own case. At Nicaea, the Emperor himself imposed criminal sentences of exile on the bishops who refused to sign.[44]

What makes this whole scenario even worse is that, even though Constantine oversaw the proceedings at the Nicene Council, he had little knowledge of Scripture:

> Constantine had no great taste for speculation, and not much knowledge of the Bible. But he worked hard to give his simple, emotional, somewhat weird beliefs a scriptural backing, and spent many hours in theological study, especially in his later years. Yet his religion has been called a crude fetishism, and he was said to be at the mercy of any theologian who caught his ear.[45]

Once Athanasius caught his ear, a creed emerged and Constantine announced the following:

> It has ... been decreed, that Arius and his followers be called Porphyrians, so that they may bear the name of him whom they have imitated; and that if any book written by Arius shall be found, it shall be committed to the flames, that no monument of his corrupt doctrine may descend to future ages. He declares that whoever shall be convicted of having any book composed by Arius, instead of burning it, shall suffer death immediately after his apprehension.[46]

This put an end to whatever freedom of religion had been exercised by Christians at that time. But Constantine appeared to have been a bit hasty in his position against Arius and Arianism, because in 327 A.D. the second council of Nicea sided with Arius and in 335 he was re-admitted to the province. Constantine may have been incon-

---

[44] Robin Lane Fox, 656.

[45] Grant, 151.

[46] Eusebius Pamphilus, in the appendix by Rev. Isaac Boyles, 26.

sistent in his theology, but he was consistent in punishing those with whom he disagreed. First Arius was exiled, then, a few years later, it was Athanasius's turn:

> The council [of Nice] condemned Arius, and to this Constantine added his sentence of banishment for Arius as well as for his main supporters. Three years later, however, he began to reverse his policies, partly through the influence of Arian bishop Eusebius of Nicomedia. It was then that he ordered Athanasius and other Nicene leaders into exile.[47]

The second council concurred with the emperor's pro-Arian sentiments and reversed the earlier council's position:

> Unfortunately for the emperor, however, although there had been this large and more or less compulsory measure of general agreement at the First Council of Nicaea, the question of Arianism could by no means be brushed aside in this way. For Arius still had many sympathizers. In 327 the Second Council of Nicaea readmitted him and his chief supporters to Communion, and a Synod that met at Antioch was pro-Arian.[48]

Interestingly, though, ardent defenders of the doctrine of a triune god frequently point to the success of the Nicene Creed in establishing the doctrine, without acknowledging or publicizing that the framers of this creed were themselves exiled. Arius's banishment is the clarion call of many proponents of Trinitarianism; he is commonly spoken of as the heretic against whom the church took swift and certain action. This, of course, implies that Constantine and the clergy never wavered in their beliefs regarding God and Jesus and, for that matter, Arius. This sort of misunderstanding and argumentation is common, as is evident from the following quote of a contemporary defender of Trinitarianism:

> The Watchtower has never failed to echo the old Arian heresy. This was a theory popularized by Arius of Alexandria (in

---

47 William Gentz, ed., *The Dictionary of Bible and Religion* (Nashville: Abingdon Press, 1986), "Constantine, Emperor," 223.

48 Grant, 175.

Egypt) in the fourth century A.D., which taught that Jesus was the first creature, a second and created god, inferior to Jehovah, the Father. It is upon this theological myth, banished from the Church in 326 A.D. with Arius, that Jehovah's Witnesses unsteadily base their whole system.[49]

Martin's argument, though biased and incomplete, is effective. He points out that Arius was banished from the church, but omits pertinent information: Arius was re-admitted to the empire, the majority of synods between the years 325 and 381 A.D. favored Arius, and Athanasius, who was at the center of the debate against Arius, was banished from the empire. This is indicative of a common problem for Unitarians in discussing the historical development of Trinitarian dogma, as Trinitarians are themselves provided only a partial view of the development of their system of beliefs. Not only are verses of Scripture taken out of context, but history is too. So Unitarians are not the only ones who suffer from accounts of the development of Trinitarianism given by some Trinitarian scholars and many of the laity.

The methods employed by Constantine and the clergy of that era in enforcing church dogma by no means passed away with the fall of the Roman Empire. I will here note one example, from the sixteenth century, of the severe methods employed in enforcing church dogma to illustrate how the doctrine of the Trinity has become so widespread since its invention. The cruelty of one who has been heralded as among the greatest and most notable Christians in history will be evident. John Calvin, the reformer, due to his theological disagreements with Michael Servetus, a Unitarian whose views were gaining popularity, "had once boasted that should Servetus ever come to Geneva he would never let him get away alive."[50] In 1553, Calvin's wish came true when he presided over Servetus's execution:

> Calvin was in possession of the secret that Servetus was the writer of this obnoxious book, a copy of it having been forwarded to him by the author. By means of a young man named William Trie, a native of Lyons, then residing at Gene-

---

[49] Martin, 66.

[50] David Parke, *The Epic of Unitarianism* (Boston: Starr King Press, 1963), 7.

va in consequence of having embraced the reformed religion, he procured some sheets of it to be conveyed to France, and put into the hands of the inquisitor at Lyons, with an intimation that the author was in his neighborhood. He afterwards sent several of the letters which, in the course of a confidential correspondence, he had received from Servetus, in order to furnish additional evidence to convict him of heresy and blasphemy. On the ground of these documents Servetus was arrested at Vienne, and committed to prison; whence, however, he soon effected his escape. After his flight he was tried, convicted, and sentenced to the stake; his books were committed to the flames, and himself burnt in effigy.

Servetus escaped early in the month of June 1553. His intention was to proceed to Naples; and with this view, after wandering for some time, he went to Geneva, where he was recognised in the month of August, and at the instigation of Calvin committed to prison. Various attempts have been made by the apologists of the Reformer to remove from him the foul stigma of being the author of his adversary's arrest; but, in truth, Calvin himself never denied or disguised the fact. On the contrary, he expressly avows it in more than one of his printed works, and takes credit to himself for having thus acted towards a man whose principles he held in abhorrence, and whom, on more than one occasion, he thought fit to brand with the opprobrious epithet of DOG.

Servetus, on being taken into custody, was deprived of the property he had about him, which was of considerable amount, and thrown, like a common malefactor, into a damp, squalid, and noisome dungeon. Proceedings were immediately instituted against him for his alleged blasphemies. The accusations were preferred by Nicholas de la Fontaine, a person residing in Calvin's house, either in a menial situation, or for the benefit of his instruction; but the real prosecutor, as was manifested in the course of the trial, was the Reformer himself. Servetus repelled the whole of the charges with great firmness, and openly avowed himself the author of the writings that were stated to contain the heretical opinions for which he was arraigned. His trial proved exceedingly tedious and vexatious, and lasted from the 14th of August to the 26th of October, when, a majority of his judges having decided against him, he was condemned to be burnt to death by a slow fire.

When exhorted on the last morning by Farell, the minister of Neufchatel, and the friend of Calvin, who was appointed to attend him, to return to the doctrine of the Trinity, he calmly requested his monitor to convince him by one plain passage of Scripture, that Christ was called the Son of God before his birth of Mary.

The day following that whereon sentence had been passed upon him he was led to the stake, praying, "O God, save my soul; O thou Son of the Eternal God, have mercy on me." In order to aggravate his sufferings he was surrounded by green faggots, which, after half an hour of excruciating tortures, completed the work of death. In the same fire was burnt, attached to his body, his last book, *Christianismi Restitutio*. Thus perished Servetus at the age of forty four, in a PROTESTANT state, for exercising that right of private judgment in the formation of his religious opinions, which his persecutors had themselves acted upon in dissenting from the Church of Rome![51]

To further the cause of forced agreement regarding the dogma of a triune god, in 1648 British Parliament "voted the death penalty to deniers of the Trinity."[52] With such drastic measures employed to force agreement regarding the doctrine of a triune God, it is no wonder the doctrine has been adopted by so many Christians.

THE NICENE CREED IS NOT TRINITARIAN

Contrary to what is widely believed, the Nicene Creed is not Trinitarian in its formulation, which is evident from the mere mentioning of the Holy Spirit without any sort of doctrinal development regarding

---

[51] Thomas Rees, *The Racovian Catechism* (originally published in Poland in 1604; reprinted in London in 1818), Historical Introduction, xiv-xviii.

[52] Parke, 31.

it in the entire creed:

> The Nicene Creed (325) was the church's official statement to explain the relationship between the first *two* Persons of the Godhead.[53] [emphasis mine]

Organized speculation regarding God and Jesus had begun, and it would be many years before more "advanced" and convoluted thoughts regarding the holy spirit would emerge. Learned Trinitarians acknowledge that the Nicene Creed is not the final development of Trinitarian dogma. Trinitarianism being the product of centuries of development may be attributed to it not being contained in Scripture. If it were, it would not have taken centuries to develop. Regarding the absence of Nicene doctrines in the New Testament, William Rusch, a Trinitarian, writes:

> No doctrine of the Trinity in the Nicene sense is present in the New Testament. However, the threefold pattern is evident throughout, in spite of the fact that there is usually nothing in the context to demand it.[54]

The Nicene Creed was, however, the starting point that would shape future creeds and the definitions assigned to God, Jesus and holy spirit:

> Although the doctrine of the Trinity had a Platonic origin, it is not to be understood that it at once assumed its modern form. It advanced towards that by measured steps. Previous to the Council of Nice, A.D. 325, the nearest approach to the modern doctrine of the Trinity was, that the Father alone was Supreme God, and the Son and Holy Ghost beings created by and subordinate to Him, each called God, but in a lower sense. In the Nicene Creed, so called because *voted in* by the Council above referred to—a mode of rather doubtful propriety for establishing what is Revealed Truth—"the Father" is alone described as "Almighty," and alone in the absolute sense called "One God." But "Jesus Christ" is described as

---

53 William Gentz, ed., *The Dictionary of Bible and Religion* (Nashville: Abingdon Press, 1986), "Monotheism," 705.

54 Rusch, 2.

"One Lord," "the Only-begotten Son of God, Begotten of his Father before all worlds." Could any language more plainly mark derivation? and if in such a case derivation were rightly predicable, it of necessity made the derived being, "the Son," inferior and subordinate to the Being from whom he was derived—"the Father Almighty." "The Holy Ghost" is not even called "God" in any sense. Beyond this the church had not yet gone. The Council of Nice "established as the inviolable doctrine of the Catholic Church, that the Son is of the *same essence* with the Father; but sustains to Him the relation in which that which is begotten stands to that which begets." It decided nothing as respects the nature of the Holy Spirit. It contented itself with simply saying, "and in One Holy Ghost." In this unsettled state the doctrine remained for more than fifty years, as we shall by and by see, before another step towards modern Trinitarianism was taken.[55]

Even though many of the works written in favor of Unitarianism have been destroyed, enough has come down to us that demonstrates the early church embraced the belief that God and Jesus were distinctly different beings, as can be seen from the simple confession of faith contained in the Apostles' Creed. Modern Christians seem to place a great deal of confidence in the faith of the early church, which many wrongly believe was Trinitarian. The following is an example of this sort of sentiment:

As the Godhead of Christ was accepted as a fact, though not understood, so the personality of the Holy Spirit was received by the Apostles and those with them as undeniable; for there was no other way to interpret their experiences. Jesus had promised the Spirit; the Holy Spirit made Himself known to them. With wonderment they received Him; joyfully they proclaimed Him, and heartily they obeyed Him. And all the while they worshipped one God without the slightest sense of contradiction. They knew that they were extending the Kingdom of God in agreement with Christ's command, preaching repentance from sin, forgiveness through Christ, and pow-

---

[55] Farley, 30-31.

er of the Spirit. Out of the Hebrew faith they emerged fulf-ledged Trinitarians.[56]

Dr. Verkuyl's opinion is interesting, to say the least, since the historical records reveal no such thing. Historians generally recognize that the initial intimations of Trinitarian sentiments do not appear until late in the second century. Formal statements of Trinitarian doctrine do not appear until the councils of the fourth century and beyond. So Verkuyl's contentions are merely prejudicial and conjectural. The assertion that the early church was Trinitarian is a popular one because it makes it more comfortable to accept the doctrine of a triune god. The apostles did not emerge from the Hebrew faith as Trinitarians, but maintained their monotheistic foundation derived from the prophets, the law and the writings of the Hebrew Bible. The belief that the Father is the one true God was continued until the fourth century, as a contemporary Trinitarian writes:

> Whatever the uncertainties, however, it is clear that in the church of the early fourth century there was a substantial body of theological opinion which regarded the Son as a creature, produced in time, out of nothing, and distinguished from other creatures only by his existing before the world was made and by his being indwelt by the Logos in a unique way. As far as his nature went, he was utterly different from God.[57]

The Nicene Creed maintains the supremacy of the Father as the one true God, whatever it further qualified of Christ. Jesus was not considered to be equal with God, but this creed set the wheels in motion for the further development of Trinitarian dogma. Later councils would also develop creeds, borrowing the Nicene Creed's unbiblical language and concepts and expanding upon them. Today it is a popular notion that there was unanimous consent among the participants at the Council of Nicea. This perception is not true, however:

> The next is the *Nicene Creed*; which is entitled to no great reverence on account of its original authors. Jortin observes, "the first thing they did was to quarrel, and to express their re-

---

56 Verkuyl, 10-11.

57 Donald McLeod, *The Evangelical Quarterly*, April, 1996.

sentments, and to present accusations to the Emperor against one another.—If such councils made righteous decrees, it must have been by strange good luck." Orthodoxy was now grown bolder; yet the ancient and still popular doctrine of the divine Unity is respected by an introduction similar to that of the Apostles' Creed. "We believe in one God, the Father Almighty, maker of all things visible and invisible." Here we find the Deity of Christ; and yet a subordination to the Father is apparent: he has but a derived Godhead, and is spoken of as suffering. But where is it taught in Scripture that Christ was "God of God; light of light; very God of very God; begotten, not made; of one substance with the Father"? The original [Nicene] creed had simply, "We believe also in the Holy Ghost." The advance of Trinitarianism again appears in the interpolations which the Church has adopted, relative to the third person, who is styled, "The Lord and giver of life; who proceedeth from the Father and Son; who with the Father and Son is worshipped and glorified." These adoptions are compensated, indeed, by the omission of the original conclusion: "The holy, catholic, and apostolic Church anathematizes those who say that there was a time when the Son of God was not, and that before he was begotten he was not, and that he was made out of nothing, or out of another substance or essence, and is created, or changeable, or alterable." [58]

Even though the clergy did not agree with one another regarding doctrine or each other's conduct, they nevertheless signed a document endorsing a uniform statement of belief that would used for everyone else. The phrase "of one substance," which was essential in developing the idea of a three-fold deity, is translated from the Greek word *homoousios*. This word, which has a history of its own, was not universally agreed upon at the time it was introduced. But once Constantine endorsed it, it stuck:

It must be supposed that Constantine himself, who was not very much at home in Greek, did not have a particularly clear idea of what *homoousios* was supposed to mean. But he reck-

---

[58] W.J. Fox, 36-37.

oned that it would serve to obtain more or less general agreement (against Arius), and he was right: less for theological reasons than because hardly anyone had the nerve to contradict him.[59]

Once the Council of Nicea established a rule of faith, it was not long before councils became the common method for the church and politicians to resolve religious and political disputes:

> Councils, or Synods, as the Greek word is, were now the rage. In the fourth century no less than forty-five were held, and the strife of party became as embittered as that of the worst modern political cabal. Constantine seconded the anathema of the Nicene Council; banished Arius into a remote Illyrian province; ordered his writings to be burned, and all who possessed and attempted to conceal, or did not at once produce and cast them into the flames, to death. But in three years afterwards he recalled Arius and his friends, and would probably have loaded him with honors had not the Presbyter suddenly died soon after his return. His son, Constantius, who finally alone held his throne, favored the Arian party. The tables were now turned, but persecution had, alas! only changed hands. "The Christian religion," says a contemporary Roman Historian, and an eye-witness and observer of what was doing, "which, in itself, is plain and simple, Constantius confounded by the dotage of superstition. Instead of reconciling the parties by the weight of his authority, he cherished and propagated, by verbal disputes, the differences which his vain curiosity had excited. The highways were covered with troops of bishops galloping from every side to the assemblies, which they call Synods; and while they labored to reduce the whole sect (of Christians) to their own particular opinions, the public establishment of the posts was almost ruined by their hasty and repeated journeys.[60]

Farley makes the following observation in a footnote on the same

---

[59] Grant, 173.

[60] Farley, 248.

page:

> "Thirteen Councils against Arius, fifteen for him, and seventeen for the Semi-Arians." (Jortin, ii. 210.) The Semi-Arians wished "that the doctrine of Christ's divinity should be settled only in such general expressions as had hitherto satisfied the Christian want, so that, with regard to the difference which divided the two contending parties, nothing was to be defined, and each might be allowed to interpret the language according to its own meaning."—Neander, Hist. of the Church, vol. ii. 373.[61]

If Christians today understood the climate in which the Council of Nicea took place, the character of those who presided over and attended it, as well as the church's reversal of opinions regarding Arianism, they would be better positioned to decide how much confidence to place in that creed. Too many rely upon opinions generated by people who lived seventeen hundred years ago and of whom they are largely ignorant.

THE ATHANASIAN CREED

The other council that features prominently in the Unitarian-Trinitarian saga is the Council of Constantinople, convened in 381 A.D., which developed the Athanasian Creed (see Appendix III). The clergy, 56 years after the Council of Nicea, were still divided as to who God is, who Christ is, and who or what the holy spirit is. The doctrinal development of holy spirit was still in its infancy and is largely absent in the earliest creeds. This absence is reason to reject the later formulations since holy spirit is supposedly co-equal with the other two "members" of the Godhead and is, according to Trinitarians, a fundamental article of faith. The deity of the holy spirit, were it true, would entitle "him" to equal attention in the creeds. That the holy spirit is not so recognized is typical in Trinitarian theology, though. The doctrine of the Trinity is supposed to establish *three* members in the Godhead, yet the doctrine is assumed to be true if only the Son is shown to be equal to the Father. Not only is the establishment of

---

[61] Farley, 248, footnote.

three co-equal persons not accomplished in the Athanasian Creed, there is virtually nothing biblical in it:

> Last comes that tremendous compilation, *the Athanasian Creed*, which is the very sublime of impiety and absurdity: in which contradiction is piled on contradiction, till the sight makes one giddy: where the Infinite Spirit is anatomized, and laid out in distinct persons: where such tricks are played with the Eternal God as jugglers use to make fools laugh: and all is crowned with the declaration that "except every one do keep this faith whole and undefiled, without doubt he shall perish everlastingly."
>
> These three Creeds [the *Apostles'*, *Nicene*, and *Athanasian*] the 8th Article declares, "may be proved by most certain warrants of Holy Scripture"! [62]

Regarding the claim that the doctrine "may be proved by most certain warrants of Holy Scripture," it is still not agreed upon by Trinitarians whether the doctrine of the Trinity, more than 1600 years after the Athanasian Creed was written, is found in the Bible, which would seem to have been ample time to find it there. In recent centuries, the Athanasian Creed has been recognized as unbiblical even by the most orthodox of institutions. The Church of England came close to beginning the process of abandoning it:

> So compelling was the Unitarian position that in 1689 the Commissioners of the Church of England seriously considered omitting the Athanasian Creed from the Book of Common Prayer; it was this creed that the Socinians and Unitarians rejected as contrary to both Scripture and reason.[63]

There must have been compelling reasons for the orthodox clergy to have *seriously* considered deleting this creed from their worship books. If this creed were at least subjected to some form of scrutiny, the result would be that many would see it is both unbiblical and unreasonable. This is what many clergymen fight against today, because creeds help the clergy form a common link to one another

---

[62] W.J. Fox, 37.

[63] Parke, 40.

and has helped to give them their identity. This could just as easily be accomplished by adopting the truth as the common link, though, but would require the arduous task of asking people to change their opinions.

What does one gain by relying upon creeds, and what does one lose? The gain, in the best-case scenario, is a restatement of biblical precepts, which is not really a gain since these may be obtained from studying the Bible itself. The loss is great, because the creeds have strayed from the language of the Bible and anathematized those who do not subscribe to the new ideas. The nonsensical doctrines propounded by creeds, of which the doctrine of the Trinity is chief, blemish the whole character of Christianity:

> Why, then, argue against a doctrine, which among intelligent men has fallen into neglect and disbelief? I answer, that the neglect and disbelief of this doctrine, and of other doctrines of like character, has extended to Christianity itself. It is from the public professions of nations calling themselves Christian, from the churches or sects, and from the writings of those who have been reputed orthodox in their day, that most men derive their notions of Christianity. But the treaties of European nations still begin with a solemn appeal to the "Most Holy Trinity"; the doctrine is still the professed faith of every established church, and, as far as I know, of every sect which makes a creed a bond of communion; and if any one should recur to books, he would find it presented as an all-important distinction of Christianity by far the larger portion of divines. It is, in consequence, viewed by most men, more or less distinctly, as a part of Christianity. In connection with other doctrines, as false and more pernicious, it has been moulded into systems of religious belief, which have been publicly and solemnly substituted in the place of true religion. These systems have counteracted the whole evidence of divine revelation. The proof of the most important fact in the history of mankind, that the truths of religion have not been left to be doubtfully and dimly discerned, but have been made known to us by God himself, has been overborne and rendered ineffectual by the nature of the doctrines ascribed to God. Hence

it is, that in many parts of Europe scarcely an intelligent and well-informed Christian is left. It has seemed as idle to inquire into the evidences of those systems which passed under the name of Christianity, as into the proof of the incarnations of Vishnu, or the divine mission of Mahomet. Nothing of the true character or our religion, nothing attesting its descent from Heaven, was to be discovered amid the corruptions of the prevailing faith. On the contrary, they were so marked with falsehood and fraud, they so clearly discovered the baseness of their earthly origin, that, when imposed upon men as the peculiar doctrines of Christianity, those who regarded them as such were fairly relieved from the necessity of inquiring, whether they had been taught by God. The internal evidence of Christianity was annihilated; and all other evidence is wasted, when applied to prove that such doctrines have been revealed from Heaven.[64]

Zealots are still claiming for them [the creeds] the authority which belongs of right to true religion; and to the inquiry what Christianity is, the public, official answer, as it may be called, is still returned, that it is to be found in the traditionary creed of some established church, or of some prevalent sect; that it is to be identified with the grim decrepitude of some obsolete form of faith. We are referred back to some one of those systems that have dishonored its name, counteracted its influence, perverted its sanctions, inculcated false and inadequate conceptions of the religious character, and formed broods of hypocrites, fanatics, and persecutors; that have been made to minister to the lust of power, malignant passions, and criminal self-indulgence; and that have striven, if I may so speak, to retard the intellectual and moral improvement of men, seeing in it the approach of their own destruction.[65]

A characteristic of the developmental process of creeds is that the members of the church are not consulted by the clergy about the

---

[64] Norton, 5-7.

[65] Norton, 19.

articles of faith that the laity will be expected to abide by. Whatever was first declared to be the rule of faith by the few in authority must be abided by from that point on. An extension of this practice is a *de facto* collusion among leaders of all orthodox churches to exclude from fellowship those who do not accept their definitions of God, and in the case at hand those definitions written over sixteen hundred years ago. What results is either a lack of desire to change the creeds or failure whenever such an attempt is made:

> The sense of the members of the Church of England never was taken on this mass of creeds and articles. They have never been consulted: for, by a dexterous juggle, whenever any thing of this description is the subject, the Church means either the Clergy, or the Bishops, or the Parliament, or the Sovereign, or one, or all of these powers, but never the community. In this case, faith was fixed by the Convocation, passed the Legislature, and was ratified by Queen Elizabeth: they were the Church; and could have given another gospel to the good people of England for all generations.

> This is another extraordinary circumstance in this spiritual usurpation, that it was to extend not only to contemporary subject millions, but to all futurity. The one hundred and seventeen Priests of the Convocation in 1562, are to be, instead of Christ, for ever the spiritual lawgivers of this realm. Though many could not write their own names, and others voted by proxy, yet their opinions are the standard of truth, the perfection of wisdom, and the boundary of improvement.

> No less than eight attempts have been made at a reformation in the Church, since the passing of the Act of Uniformity, and all have totally failed. There seems to be a horror of removing the greatest absurdity, or changing the merest trifle. What must be the ultimate fate of a system which thus obstinately resists the progressive illumination of the human mind, and the desires of its best and wisest votaries? [66]

Another effect of creeds is that once accepted they tend to inhibit private judgment regarding the meaning of the biblical texts. There

---

[66] W.J. Fox, 34-35.

are so many Christians, indeed it appears to be emblematic of the Christian character, who have not availed themselves of the right and responsibility of independent thought. Many churches, acting contrary to the right of private judgment, exclude those who differ with their doctrines. It is this coercion and duress that contributes to the unwillingness of Christians to formulate individual opinions, giving rise to a tell-me-what-to-think mentality:

> It may be said, that when Dissenting Churches exclude a heretic from their communion, they deprive him of no civil rights. True: his civil rights are not at their disposal: they deprive him of all that is in their power, the comforts of Christian society. But has not every society a right to make its own laws? No, not Christian churches: their laws are made for them by their Master; and they cannot legislate without renouncing, virtually, the Christian character. Personal liberty of thought and opinion is essential to a Christian Church.[67]

How will iron sharpen iron if we all think according to one creed or another? Can it be reasonably expected that we would all think alike, with such a diversity of experience, culture, and educational backgrounds? Without the freedom to challenge one another, it is no wonder so little change occurs in the Christian community.

The United States of America was settled in large part due to the founding Fathers' desire for religious liberty. They did not want the Church of England, or any other organization, whether governmental or theological, dictating beliefs to the people. But many have returned to the former ways of enforcing dogmas: abide by the creeds of the early church councils and exclude those who do not agree with them.

John 8:32 says, "And ye shall know the truth, and the truth shall make you free." This is a broad statement that was addressed to people as individuals, for their own well-being. Even if everybody else differed from us on an issue, we would still be responsible for abiding by what our own conscience tells us is right, or at least not assenting that which makes little sense. A modern defender of Christianity

---

[67] W.J. Fox, 54.

writes that "theology teaches that the conscience is supreme." [68] If he is right, then the severe methods employed by many Christians today interfere with the development of the individual's conscience. And since Christians are typically judged by their acceptance of the most popular creed, their acceptance into Christian society almost categorically depends upon receiving it. All this is contrary to freedom of private judgment, yet it is this religious freedom of conscience that is so necessary for the development of Christians as individuals:

> Well might Paley remark of the establishment of creeds and confessions, that "they are at all times attended with serious inconveniences: they check inquiry; they violate liberty; they insnare the consciences of the clergy."
>
> The professed object of these creeds was, *to avoid diversity of opinions!* Suppose it gained: and if the standard thus erected be not the real gospel after all; as, unless the framers were infallible, could not be assumed without presumption; they are then found false witnesses for God; or rather against him, in his revelation; and suborners of false witness from contemporary millions, and successive generations,
>
> If they be the truth, still that truth is held in unrighteousness when not received on proper authority—that of Christ. What is truth without inquiry; without knowledge; without those moral influences which only attend principles when clearly understood and firmly believed? [69]
>
> From the very law of our intellectual constitution, from the nature of the working of our thinking faculty, when our assent is imperatively demanded, we ask why and how, and demand to know the reason. We become captious and cavilling, perhaps, and our mind is not in a condition to receive truth healthily. To demand assent before the proof is the most unfair way of dealing with the mind. Argument is foreclosed. Candor is made no account of, and set aside. If the inducement to feign belief is strong, some will become hypocritical

---

[68] William F. Buckley, Jr., *Happy Days Were Here Again: Reflections of a Libertarian Journalist* (New York: Random House, 1993), 114.

[69] W.J. Fox, 39-40.

and insincere. If the argument is weak, it throws suspicion on the whole class of topics on which it bears. And, more than all, if threats are superadded to the argument,—if terror is brought in to help out a halting demonstration,—if awful penalties are hinted at for unbelief,—if the inquirer is told that just such an answer he must come to, or else his salvation is lost forever,—it cannot be but that the mind is unhinged, and made unfit to reason. Either one yields, in blind and implicit fear, not to persuasion or proof, but to overbearing and despotic dogmatism, and purchases the hope of spiritual safety at the cost of intellectual honor and independence, or else he despises the threat, defied the doom, and turns his back in anger on those who sought to overawe when they could not convince.

Now, in however slight a degree, qualified by never so many circumstances, it cannot be denied that these effects of make-believe, hypocrisy, and unbelief have been found wherever it has been attempted, in whatever way, to enforce a religious creed. I say nothing of the amount of truth or error there may be contained in it. I should dread it as much for my own form of belief as any other. Whatever the nature of the propositions, to present them as a foregone conclusion, to anticipate the proof and demand a previous consent, and to denounce a penalty, however slight, on one's failure to be convinced, must work that harm in some one or more to whom such a process of thought is addressed. Such, to some extent, has been the result in every church that has attempted it.[70]

Part of the original design of Christian society was freedom to contemplate large and small issues, including who God is, what life is about, how to treat others. People may serve as aids to others seeking truth, but are not to prescribe doctrines that must be believed. Since the development of creeds, Christianity bears little resemblance to the free society it was designed to be:

As the corruptions of Christianity have passed in review before us, it cannot but have been noticed how closely they were

---

[70] Allen, 26-28.

connected with ecclesiastical usurpation. There is a natural alliance between error and slavery, truth and liberty. For a time they may be dissociated; but reason and Scripture, history and observation, bear witness that they cannot permanently maintain a separate existence. Freedom of inquiry and profession is the atmosphere in which pure religion breathes, or the soil in which it grows; and which it must find, or make, or itself wither away. Hence the subjects of this Lecture are an appropriate transition from the mischiefs and miseries of the antichristian apostasy, to the gospel in its native simplicity, power and blessedness.

The religious liberty of Christian Churches is external and internal; that which they claim of the civil power, and that which they allow to their own members. The first consists in the absence of all interference from the magistrate; in being subject to neither penalties nor privations, on account of faith or worship: the latter, in the freedom of the individuals composing such churches, to form and avow their own opinions of what Christ taught, without being subject to censure, excommunication, or loss of the advantages of Christian society and friendship. Both are of great importance. The latter, even by sincere and eloquent advocates of the former, had been too often misunderstood, overlooked, or violated. They are alike emanations from the same principle, the right of private judgment; a right which, as it ought not to be controlled by the civil magistrate, so neither should it be yielded by the Christian to the dictate of a priest, or council, or to the decision of the majority of a church: it is personal and inalienable.[71]

The loss of religious liberty and expression can occur through various means. Governmental interference has the greatest impact on freedom of worship, since it can stop the promulgation of religious ideas as well as imprison those who advance unsanctioned views. This deterrent ultimately results in a people largely unable to freely worship and is commonly associated with communist states

---

[71] Allen, 52-53.

or state-sponsored religions. But a subtler form of the deprivation of freedom occurs when a society has freedom from governmental interference, but the people themselves choose to enforce their dogmas by excluding those with theological differences. This is an insidious form of coercion which can be found anywhere dogma is used as a means of testing one's allegiance to an organization. In Christendom today there are those who lead exemplary lives, but who are even denied the title "Christian" because they disagree with a prevailing opinion. Jesus preached freedom, whereas many of his followers in later centuries have infrequently permitted it:

1. The first violation, therefore, of religious liberty, and which leads to all the rest, is that of particular societies infringing on the right of individual members, by defining Christianity. A Christian Church is only a body of *disciples*; all are to obey the Master, but they are not to obey one another. The majority has no more right than the minority to erect a standard of faith. Those who cannot, or will not, worship with them, they have no power to retain; but those who can, or wish to do so, they have no authority to reject. He who believes the divine mission of Christ, and acts accordingly, ought not to be kept out of any church professing to be Christian. This was the case originally, and consequently there were neither sects, nor parties, nor party names. When opinions were made a test, and believers were named from some doctrine or leader, then,

2. Churches lost their liberty—the reign of Sectarianism commenced. Those who agreed as to some disputed tenet, had a stronger affinity with each other, than with the rest of the Christian body: they united for the sake of strength in this internal warfare. Hence, meetings and councils of their pastors and leaders; and at length, authority to enforce the decisions of such meetings upon the whole sect; so that the church which had tyrannized over the individual, was, in turn, tyrannized over by the party. To this succeeds,

3. The successful appeal of some one sect or party to the civil magistrate, who declares that party to be the exclusive possessors of Christianity, bestows upon them wealth and honours, and brands their opponents with disgrace, deprives them of their rights, per-

haps sends them to the dungeon or the scaffold. There was but another step in the ascent, when

4. The Church itself became a temporal power, making monarchs and nations bow to its decrees. This is the mode in which believers lost "the liberty wherewith Christ hath made us free," and just in the inverted order has its restoration proceeded. The Reformation broke off so many limbs from the temporal sovereignty of Rome, but left the magistrates of each country lords of their subjects' consciences, and used their authority to patronize one sect at the expense of all others. The Presbyterians countenanced this usurpation as completely as the Episcopalians. The Assembly's Confession declares, that "the civil magistrate hath authority, and it is his duty to take order, that unity and peace be preserved in the church; that the truth of God be kept pure and entire; that all blasphemies and heresies be suppressed; all corruptions and abuses in worship and discipline prevented or reformed; and all the ordinances of God duly settled, administered and observed. For the better effecting whereof, he hath power to call synods, to be present at them, and to provide that whatsoever is transacted in them, be according to the mind of God." Many of the sects which had not the opportunity of forming this unholy alliance, yet retained a most oppressive despotism over their ministers and churches. These same Presbyterians declare, that "it belongeth to synods and councils ministerially to determine controversies of faith and cases of conscience; to set down rules and directions for the better ordering of the public worship of God and government of his church; to receive complaints in cases of mal-administration, and authority to determine the same." Can anything be more arbitrary and absurd than the following oath, exacted by the heads of the French Protestants, in the year 1620: "I swear and promise before God, and this holy assembly, that I receive, approve and embrace all the doctrine taught and decided by the national Synod of Dort. I swear and promise, that I will persevere in it all my life long, and defend it with all my power, and never depart from it in my sermons, college-lectures, writings, or conversation, or in any other manner, public or private. I declare also and protest, that I reject and condemn the doctrine of the Arminians, &c. So help me God, as I swear all this without equivocation

or mental reservation"? [72]

It is an unwillingness of many to reconsider their doctrines and practices that has resulted in division and stunted growth within the church. "Is Christ divided?" is rhetorically asked in the New Testament. The correct answer should be no, but the actual practice among many is an emphatic yes! Allegiance to particular groups is as prevalent in the Christian community today as it has ever been. The coercion that was once supplied by government is now supplied, in a different form but with a similar conscience-breaking effect, by Christians themselves. Not only do elders within their respective churches maintain the creeds they were sworn to, but the members also take up their swords even though they hadn't taken an oath.

A predisposition towards forced agreement has taken root among many Christian sects, but agreement cannot be forced upon people without a price. Freedom of thought is essential to Christians in our relationships with God and man. Without this freedom it is impossible to love one's neighbor as oneself, since the restrictive influence would preclude an honest and spontaneous manifestation of love. Implicit in this freedom is a responsibility that demands the highest moral character if we are to manifest the kindness and patience that are a large part of the point of the spiritual life, and are consistent with a pursuit of truth:

> You are certainly laboring under a mistake when you assert that Unitarianism "would persuade men to be at peace with themselves, not to flee from wrath." Unitarianism does not persuade men to a *false* peace. It is not an easy, indolent religion. No, no, very far from it. Let any one read Dewey's Sermons on the Law of Retribution, and see whether Unitarianism points out an *easy* road to Heaven. "This is a system," says Dr. Gannett, "which requires of its disciple the greatest measure of goodness that he can render, which prohibits every indulgence contrary to the strictest virtue, and imposes continual effort and conflict. Who that comprehends its requisitions would ever think of pronouncing them light? ....

---

[72] Allen, 59-62.

Unitarianism as we receive it, the patron of a lax morality and a worldly spirit! Verily, it requires a confidence by no means enviable to make such an assertion in the face of everything that has been said by advocate and by opposer."

But, the fact is, I know of no easier mode of arriving at Heaven, than by the Calvinistic scheme, if that scheme be true. To depend for salvation entirely upon the merits of another, who has become our substitute, is a very comfortable thing. But then, under these circumstances, what moral progress can a man be expected to make? I joyfully acknowledge that those who hold this faith do make advances in moral growth and vigor; but I believe they do it in the very teeth of their creed, they do it because both Scripture and common sense teach them that "as a man sows, so shall be also reap." On the other hand, the Unitarian doctrine that men are to be rewarded hereafter according to their works, while it is a doctrine of reason and of revelation, is, from its very nature, a prodigious incentive to constant watchfulness and warfare. All the expressions of the Apostle Paul, in regard to the Christian's life of conflict and danger, Unitarians fully understand, appreciate, *feel*. They well know what he means when he speaks of "striving for the mastery." They can enter into his feelings of joyful exultation when he was able to say, "I have fought the good fight." They believe the Apostle James was correct when he said, that "by works a man is justified, and not by faith only." They attend to the injunction of the Apostle Peter, "Be *diligent* that ye may be found of him in peace, without spot, and blameless." At the same time they believe that their salvation is all of grace, or favor; that it is obtained through the abounding mercy of God, in Christ; who has graciously promised to forgive the sins, and to overlook the shortcomings of those who earnestly repent and endeavor to reform. They believe that the lives which they live in the flesh, they must live by the faith of the Son of God, who loved them, and gave himself for them. They endeavor to follow *him—he* is their example—and thus it is they live by faith *in him*—a faith which will inspire them with zeal and with strength to follow him "fully."

It seems strange to me, that any one can believe that the requisitions of the Unitarian faith are easy; that only those who wish to lead careless lives choose that religion. I solemnly declare to you, that I hesitate now at many things which I formerly deemed matters of trivial importance. My standard of gospel morality is higher, my views are more elevated, my aspirations after moral excellence altogether more ardent than they were before my change of views. I earnestly wish that my standard of duty had been all my life what it is now; it would undoubtedly have saved me a vast amount of sorrow and regret. At the same time I frankly confess, that many things which I once deemed wrong I now think innocent. I have learned, I hope, to discriminate more justly between *essentials* and *non-essentials*; and I am more than ever persuaded that, instead of binding myself by certain outward rules and regulations, the only safe and certain way to live a truly Christian life, is to see faithfully to it that *my heart* is right with God.[73]

---

73 Dana, 238-241.

CHAPTER 7

MYSTERY VERSUS CONTRADICTION

In order to escape the contradictoriness of the doctrine of the Trinity, most of its advocates argue that it is a mystery and must simply be "taken on faith." We are sometimes told that our minds are too small to comprehend it. What many fail to recognize is that mystery is one thing, contradiction is quite another. Trinitarians have been of the opinion that Unitarians will believe something only if we have *complete* knowledge of it. Robert Bowman, a Trinitarian, in making this very point, writes: "Trinitarians are willing to live with a God they cannot fully comprehend." [1] So are Unitarians, and we do every day.

The debate is not whether or not God is fully comprehensible under either system of beliefs. The debate is whether or not Trinitarians have reasonably made the leap from God being *one* to Him being *three-in-one*. The debate is also about whether or not Trinitarians have justifiably made the leap from Jesus being a man to him being *both* man and God. In both cases the use of reason is trivialized in order to enable people to receive both doctrines more comfortably. The trivialization of reason is absolutely essential for the reception of the doctrine of a tri-une god. Many of Trinitarianism's advocates have not spent much time studying their own system of beliefs, and perhaps take the easy route by referring to the age-old claim that it is a mystery. They are probably right in this, insofar as the doctrine is a mystery *to them* because they have not spent much time getting familiar with the doctrine they embrace. But fleeing to the claim of mystery demonstrates the doctrine is one that is not understood. If the doctrine and its development were better understood, fewer would place so much confidence in it. R. S.

---

[1] Bowman, back cover.

Franks, a Trinitarian, writes:

> It is best to recognize that the doctrine of the Trinity has been a matter of debate throughout the Christian centuries and still is so. It is therefore necessary that the issue should be discussed with the best means at our disposal. It is not satisfactory to take refuge in the common notion that it is a mystery. It is the result of a rational and intelligible process, and its value can only be appreciated through a study of this process.[2]

Though I do not believe the doctrine is the product of a rational and intelligible process, if more people would follow Mr. Franks's advice and venture outside the notion that it is a mystery and study the doctrine at some length, many would see the folly involved in the doctrine's development and would perhaps abandon it or, in the least case, be more accepting of those who don't see the logic in it and embrace only the Father as God.

Unitarians believe that the Bible does not teach that God is triune, but have never maintained that God is *completely* knowable. We disagree with those who maintain the Father has equals because we believe that they have introduced unbiblical, absurd and contradictory conceptions about Him into Christianity and unnecessarily complicating it. Trinitarians say the doctrine of the Trinity is a mystery, whereas Unitarians say it is not a mystery, but a confusing compilation of tenets introduced by men into the purity of the Judeo-Christian faith. The argument that Unitarians will believe something only if we know *everything* about it is simply a device used to sidetrack the focus of the debate through personal attacks.

The term *mystery* typically refers to something that is difficult to know or comprehend. Such things as how God created the heavens and the earth, what infants think, or how hummingbirds flap their wings three hundred times per second are examples of mysteries. We find them difficult to comprehend, but we generally believe them to be true. In this class the Trinitarian places the doctrine of the Trinity, which is an inaccurate assessment of the character of the doctrine. It is not something that is merely difficult to comprehend, but is a series of contradictions which make it impossible to comprehend, regard-

---

[2] Franks, 1.

less of how educated about it one becomes.

It is one thing for us not to comprehend something we do not fully understand. Everything falls into this category to some extent because there is always something we will miss. Regarding theological issues, I Cor. 13:9 says "we know in part." This pertains not only to biblical matters, but to all matters—we are human, after all, which bespeaks limitations. However, it is quite another thing for it to be *impossible* to know something to be true. This latter case arises when contradictory assertions are made about the same thing. For example, on the Trinitarian hypothesis God is said to be both three and one, but due to the way in which we use language disqualifies such a statement from being true. Something is either three or one, but not both. Since in Trinitarian theology no reasonable qualifications of the predicates *three* and *one* are offered, the proposition about God being both is rightly rejected.

Another problematic aspect of Trinitarian thought is the contention that Jesus is both *God* and *man*. When we define the terms *God* and *man* it is impossible for both to be predicated of the same being. It is not, therefore, that the doctrine of the Trinity is a mystery that it is to be rejected, but because it is a series of contradictions:

> Mystery and contradiction are very different things. The former is something beyond our sight, or seen imperfectly. The latter is plainly seen to be untrue. It may concern subjects of which we know very little, but of *every* subject we know enough to see that two contradictory statements cannot both be true. We know very little, for example, about electricity; but if any one were to say that it is a self-moving and independent power, and also an agent which never moves except by our will, we should answer, that, although the subject is one enveloped in mystery, the statement concerning it is manifestly false. Applying this to religious things: The union between God and Christ is a subject beyond our perfect comprehension—it is therefore a mystery; but as Christ has declared that he could "do nothing of himself,"—that he "spake not of himself," but only "as the Father gave him commandment,"—we are prepared to see that those who assert that he was equal with the Father, and independent in his authority,

are in error. The subject is mysterious, but the contradiction is plain. So when Christ asserts that he did not know of a certain future event (Mark xiii. 32), the assertion that he was nevertheless Omniscient, is evidently a denial of what he said. The limits of his knowledge we cannot define, but he plainly asserts that some limits do exist, which is a distinct denial of Omniscience.[3]

According to Trinitarian reasoning, it seems that we cannot know anything about God. If this assessment is inaccurate, then it follows that we can know *some things* about Him. This being the case, we must decide what things we can know, and therefore believe, about Him. He is certainly not fully knowable, but we can know Him in part. In other words, God is incomprehensible, but He is not unintelligible:

We grant that God is incomprehensible, in the sense already given. But He is not therefore unintelligible; and this distinction we conceive to be important. We do not pretend to know the whole nature and properties of God, but still we can form some clear ideas of him, and can reason from these ideas as justly from any other. The truth is that we cannot be said to comprehend any being whatever, not the simplest plant or animal. All have hidden properties. Our knowledge of all is limited. But have we therefore no distinct ideas of the objects around us, and is all our reasoning about them unworthy of trust? Because God is infinite, his name is not therefore a mere sound. It is a representative of some distinct conceptions of our Creator; and these conceptions are as sure and important and as proper materials for the reasoning faculty as they would be if our views were indefinitely enlarged. We cannot indeed trace God's goodness and rectitude through the whole field of his operations; but we know the essential nature of these attributes, and therefore can often judge what accords with and opposes them. God's goodness, because infinite, does not cease to be goodness or essentially differ from the same attribute in man; nor does justice change

---

[3] Eliot, 6.

its nature, so that it cannot be understood, because it is seated in an unbounded mind. There have, indeed, been philosophers, "falsely so called," who have argued from the unlimited nature of God that we cannot ascribe to him justice and other moral attributes in any proper or definite sense of those words; and the inference is plain that all religion or worship, wanting an intelligible object, must be a misplaced, wasted offering. This doctrine from the infidel we reject with abhorrence; but something, not very different, too often reaches us from the mistaken Christian who, to save his creed, shrouds the Creator in utter darkness.[4]

It is not trivial that so many have adopted a line of reasoning that makes it acceptable to believe anything simply by labeling it a mystery. By labeling something a mystery, deplorably it becomes something to be believed, or at least somewhat credible, in Christian thought. It also renders it impervious to criticism, since the argument that we do not know everything about God may be trotted out in defense of what has been labeled a mystery. We must recognize, though, that false ideas may be designated as mysteries as easily as true ones. We must therefore decide what things are appropriately designated as mysteries and what things constitute mere contradictions, and therefore cannot be true. Some Trinitarians have recognized the difference between contradiction and mystery, but ignored the difference and continued to believe in the "mysteriousness" of the doctrine. Dr. South, a Trinitarian, writes:

> "For that any one should be both Father and Son to the same person [to David], produce himself, be cause and effect too, and so the copy give birth to the original, seems at first sight so strange and unaccountable, that, were it not to be adored as a mystery, it would be exploded as a contradiction."[5]

Dr. South recognized the contradictory nature of the doctrine of the Trinity, but was unwilling to part with it. I have no problem with

---

4 William Channing, *Unitarian Christianity and Other Essays* (Liberal Arts Press, 1957), 49-50.

5 Dr. Robert South, *Sermons,* vol. iii, 240; quoted in Wilson, 321.

this, as we are all trying to make it through this world in our own way, but Dr. South's fondness of mystery caused him to circumvent the warnings his mind gave him. Unitarians reject the doctrine of the Trinity on the same grounds that Dr. South would have if he had not inclined himself toward mysteriousness in matters of religion:

> We object, in general, to the doctrine of the Trinity, that it is an invention of the human mind, for which the Scriptures afford no warrant; and that its prominent effect is to introduce into the system of truths taught in the Scriptures an extraneous, artificial, and perplexing dogma, wholly inconsistent with, utterly unlike to, the acknowledged and accepted doctrines of Scripture. We do not object, as is often charged upon us, that the doctrine involves a mystery. On the contrary, we object that the doctrine when urged upon us as a mystery misuses and perverts the word *mystery*, and avails itself of the acknowledged and allowed credibility of what the word *mystery* properly signifies, to propose to us something quite unlike a mystery; namely, a statement that is absurd, so far as it is intelligible, and that is inconsistent in the very terms which it brings together for making its proposition. We accept all such religious truths as can fairly be covered by the word *mystery*. We live religiously upon such truths; they are the nutriment of our spirits,—of infinitely larger account to us than anything we can learn or understand. We are made familiar, by every moment's exercise of close thought, with the necessity of accepting mysteries, and we know very well what a sensation and sentiment they send down into the innermost chambers of our being. But we are conscious of feeling quite a different sensation and sentiment when this doctrine of the Trinity is proposed to us under the covert of a mystery. Quite another quality in it than that of its mysterious character at once suggests itself to us. Its utter absurdity, its attempt to say something which it fails to say *intelligibly*, simply because it cannot say it *truly*, is the first painful consciousness attaching to the doctrine. If the doctrine be true, then it is the only doctrine of the Gospel which causes the same sort of puzzling, confounding, bewildering effect on the mind that seeks to

entertain it. It sets us into the frame into which we fall when any one proposes to us an enigma, or a conundrum. It lays at the very threshold of the Christian faith an obstacle at which we stumble. It requires of us a summoning of resources, or a concession, a yielding up, of our natural desire for intelligent apprehension, as if to be addressed by some profound truth, when in fact we are only bewildered. The state of mind into which we should be driven by an attempt to accept the doctrine of the Trinity as fundamental to the Gospel, would be of no service to us in dealing with the real doctrines of the Gospel. The doctrine is not homogeneous with the contents of revelation; it is unevangelical and anti-evangelical in all its characteristic elements. Just where we need the clearest exercise of our thoughts, and wish to accommodate our ideas to our theme, and to engage the orderly action of all our faculties, we are beclouded and staggered, and thrown into a maze. Has not our whole theology been made to suffer, by thus taking its start from a metaphysical subtlety which confuses the mind instead of from one august truth which lifts and solemnizes the spirit?[6]

The designation of the doctrine of the Trinity as a mystery is the only framework, or perhaps escape hatch, from which it may be explained such that people would have some grounds, nebulous as they may be, on which to believe it. It is the only possible mechanism whereby one may be led to accept the doctrine and is a mechanism which, once adopted, opens the floodgates of assault upon reason and what we consider to be true. It is a man-made artifice, one that the biblical texts instruct everyone to avoid since we could not be certain of anything by applying this method. If a longing for mystery is to be satisfied, anything that makes sense would not satisfy it and would be rejected. This approach contradicts the injunction to prove all things:

> But it is "a Mystery," this great doctrine of the Trinity! This is the easy and constant resort of its advocates. From the days of Tertullian, who exclaimed, "Credo quia impossible est"—*I believe because it is impossible*—to our own, it has been their

---

6 Ellis, 118-120.

refuge, nay, even their ground of glorifying.

Here let me remark, that the fact that a doctrine is above the grasp of unaided human reason, is not alone a sufficient argument against its truth. It is not, therefore, merely that the Trinity is mysterious, that Unitarians reject it, but—leaving the purely Scriptural argument out of the question for the moment—because it is self-contradictory, opposed to all right reason, positively absurd. Trinitarians themselves have over and over again admitted this. Bishop Hurd admits that "Reason stands aghast, and Faith herself is half-confounded" at the manner in which, on the Trinitarian scheme, "the grace of God was at length manifested." [7]

Complete confidence in the veracity of the doctrine of the Trinity, based on reason alone, is simply impossible. When something is admitted to be a mystery, by its very nature it produces within us sentiments that make it impossible to have full confidence in it. As one might expect, Trinitarian writings are full of statements that illustrate the lack of confidence many have in this doctrine. Such statements demonstrate that Trinitarianism is not mysterious, but unintelligible. For example, the use of the word persons, which is essential to the development of the doctrine of a triune god, is not at all understood:

> They are not to take shelter under any plea of mystery, where the mystery is of their own making. No word [the word *person*] in our language has a more obvious and simple significance. The late Prof. Stuart of Andover, lamented that it should have ever crept into the symbols of the churches, and preferred "distinctions," much as Dr. Smith did "somethings;" while the late Pres. Dwight of Yale College, says he does not know *what* the word means, but yet thinks it "a convenient term." Convenient! for what? when confessedly it is, in the connection used, so ambiguous as to be utterly unintelligible![8]

Trinitarian dogmas consistently defy comprehension. Incomprehensibility appears to have become the criterion of preference in de-

---

[7] Farley, 24-25.

[8] Farley, 31.

termining the so-called truth of the various elements that comprise this system. It is the criterion of preference because it is voluntary. To Unitarians, then, the doctrine of the Trinity is simply an unnecessary collection of contradictory and senseless statements:

> When I am told that the same being is both God and man, I recognize, I have before said, a very *intelligible*, though a very absurd proposition, that is, I know well all the senses which the words admit. When it is affirmed that "the Father is God, and the Son is God, and the Holy Ghost is God; and yet there are not three Gods, but one God"; no words can more clearly convey any meaning, than those propositions express the meaning, that there are three existences of whom the attributes of God may be predicated, and yet that there is only one existence of whom the attributes of God may be predicated. But this is not an incomprehensible mystery; it is plain nonsense.[9]

Unitarians have been accused of placing reason above revelation. We are charged with setting our minds above what is revealed in Scripture because we do not fully comprehend it. In actuality, the opposite is true. It is the Trinitarian who sets his reason above the Hebrew and Greek texts. The Trinitarian has invented a theology, employs an invented vocabulary, then calls it a mystery because he does not understand his own beliefs! In this very process the Trinitarian sets his own reason above the contents of the Bible.

An obvious hypocrisy has arisen from the Trinitarian claim of mystery. It is argued that, in order to receive the doctrine of the Trinity, one's reason must be suspended. This is because, as Thomas rightly observes, "reason will refuse to lend its testimony to support a contradiction."[10] In an effort to get others to accept the Trinitarian faith, reason is employed to cause others to stop using it:

> Did I say I rejected the doctrine of the Trinity *because* it was incomprehensible? No, dear friend, I have not said so. I have rejected it because I cannot find it in the Bible. If I could

---

9 Norton, 169-170.

10 Thomas, 17.

satisfy myself that it was there, I would instantly receive it, however incomprehensible. The doctrine of the Trinity is, to me, so plainly a contradiction, that I deem it *impossible* it could be found in a revelation from God.

Were I disposed to retort, I might say that those who receive the doctrine of the Trinity are the persons who are depending upon human reason. It appears to me they fall into two strange and opposite errors. They first construct the doctrine upon inference and human reason, and then prostrate reason to receive it.[11]

Recognizing the doctrine of the Trinity as a contradiction leads to the next step in our evaluation of it: it is an absurdity. When a contradiction is developed and believed, and then others are also expected to believe it, the whole process is an absurdity. Absurdities must be rooted up whenever they are discovered, but ardent Trinitarians seem content not following this course of action, but content themselves with preposterous notions of God:

There is reason to believe that three parts of those who profess to hold the Trinity, have scarcely bestowed one half hour's serious thought upon the subject; they content themselves with the reflection that it is a mystery, and therefore not to be explained, and hence they are satisfied with confessing a doctrine with their lips, which is, on their own showing, inexplicable. But how any Christian can believe that doctrine which they cannot understand or explain, we are at a loss to imagine. As it regards the mystery of the Trinity, the last refuge of the Trinitarian, when pressed with the difficulties that attend his doctrine, what is more humiliating to him than to be obliged to fly to mystery, to shelter him from the argument of an opponent. The Trinitarian asserts that the Trinity cannot be explained because it is a mystery; we do not call upon him to explain the doctrine, but merely to state it in terms we can understand; and when he employs language in expressing the doctrine which according to its common interpretation, represents three distinct deities, to use the language of holy writ,

---

¹¹ Dana, 84-85.

and not that of fallible men. If he attaches a peculiar meaning to the word in which he states his doctrine, let him explain this meaning to us, but it is mere evasion to tell us he cannot explain the doctrine because it is a mystery, when we only ask him to explain the expressions in which he clothes the doctrine. When so much difference of opinion prevails among the Trinitarian advocates themselves respecting the Trinity—when it cannot be stated by them in intelligible terms, surely Unitarians are at liberty to doubt the truth of such a doctrine. We should like to know what the unlearned man can make of the Trinity, when one Divine tells him it is the union of *three persons*, in the Godhead—another that it consists of three *differences*, by another of three *subsistencies*—by another of three *distinct cogitations*, and by another of three *somewhats*. When so many opinions are intended among Trinitarians themselves, respecting their own doctrine, surely Unitarians may be permitted to entertain an opinion different from all the rest, which is that the Trinity itself is an error.[12]

It is astounding that so many have predicated their system of beliefs upon mysterious dogma, and then either desire or demand others adopt the same method of formulating their beliefs. Implicit in this approach is that there is not enough written in the biblical texts to formulate a sensible idea about who God is. But it must be said that it is preferable to have a comprehensible system of beliefs rather than an incomprehensible one. As a general rule, comprehensibility should govern our beliefs. The mind cannot rest comfortably having accepted doctrines it cannot understand, and without understanding it is impossible to know whether a doctrine is true. The formal introduction of mystery into the Christian faith undermines the confidence one could have in its various tenets, or the theological system as a whole.

---

[12] Thomas, 13-14.

CHAPTER 8

REASON AND REVELATION

For those who look to the writings of the Hebrew Bible and the New Testament, it is reasonable to assume that there is enough there for us to form an understanding of who God is. It is also reasonable to assume that reason and revelation are entirely compatible with one another. The Bereans demonstrated this compatibility, as mentioned in Acts 17:11: they "searched the scriptures daily whether these things were so." By what faculty other than reason could they have ascertained *whether* these things were so? And it is by this faculty of reason, as opposed to mystery, that Unitarians arrive at the belief that the Father is unrivaled in majesty and dominion. The advocates of Trinitarian dogma ultimately set their ability to reason aside in favor of unintelligible and mysterious sophisms, even though they paradoxically exert great effort reasoning why we should not rely on reason in contemplating who God is.

Reason and revelation are essential if we are to gain an accurate understanding of God. According to the biblical texts, God has been appealing to mankind in order to help us understand Him and His ways. For example, Isaiah 1:18 says: "Come now, and let us reason together, saith the LORD: though your sins be as scarlet, they shall be as white as snow; though they be red like crimson, they shall be as wool." Here we see a snapshot of God's method of helping mankind benefit from a relationship with Him—He reasons with us. If reason were as dangerous as Trinitarians postulate, we might assume that using it less frequently would yield more favorable results. If we stop to think about this approach for a moment, we would easily recognize the confusion that would result from not employing reason:

The outcry against reason, made by many religionists, is not only unwise, but inconsistent with their own practice; nor are there any Christians who adhere more closely to the plain and direct meaning of the Bible than Unitarians. The doctrine of the Trinity is nowhere plainly taught in Scripture, nor can it be stated in Scripture words; it is a *doctrine of inference*, built up by arguments, and depending upon distinctions so nice and difficult that it requires a good deal of metaphysical acuteness to perceive them. A crusade against reason comes with ill grace from those who use it so freely. There is no such doctrine in the Unitarian system, but it would be puerile to deny that reason is used in our religious researches. We become Christians only by its use. There is no other means by which we can guard ourselves from gross superstition. We cannot use it too freely or too much, so long as we use it reverently and with prayer.[1]

Without question, there are many things that are above our ability to fully comprehend, but this does not preclude us from having the means of discriminating between truth and error, sense and nonsense:

This very plain subject has been obscured by a loose and ambiguous use of language. It is said, that we believe truths which we do not comprehend;—that we believe that the grass grows; but do not know how it grows;—that we believe that some things are infinite; but that we do not comprehend infinity;—that we believe that God knows all things; but that we cannot form a conception of omniscience. Let us examine these propositions. *The grass grows:* do we not know what we mean when we use these words? It is as intelligible a proposition as can be stated. We affirm, and we intend nothing more than to affirm, that certain well-known, sensible phenomena take place. It is true that we do not know how it grows, that is to say, we do not know the proximate causes of its growth; and it is equally true, that we affirm nothing about those causes in the proposition stated. Our affirmation does not extend beyond our knowledge. The fact that there are many phenomena of which we cannot assign the causes, does not

---

[1] Eliot, 7-8.

tend to prove that, when we affirm those phenomena exist, we utter incomprehensible propositions.[2]

That God is infinite, and that man often errs, we affirm as strongly as our Calvinistic brethren. We desire to think humbly of ourselves and reverently of our Creator. In the strong language of Scripture, "We now see through a glass darkly." "We cannot by searching find out God unto perfection. Clouds and darkness are round about him. His judgments are a great deep." God is great and good beyond utterance or thought. We have no disposition to idolize our own powers, or to penetrate the secret counsels of the Deity. But, on the other hand, we think it ungrateful to disparage the powers which our Creator has given us, or to question the certainty or importance of the knowledge which He has seen fit to place within our reach. There is an affected humility, we think, as dangerous as pride. We may rate our faculties too meanly or too boastingly. The worst error in religion, after all, is that of the skeptic, who records triumphantly the weaknesses and wanderings of the human intellect and maintains that no trust is due to the decisions of this erring reason. We by no means conceive that man's greatest danger springs from pride of understanding, though we think as badly of this vice as other Christians. The history of the church proves that men may trust their faculties too little as well as too much, and that the timidity which shrinks from investigation has injured the mind, and betrayed the interests of Christianity, as much as irreverent boldness of thought.[3]

One of the reasons some are attracted to Christianity is that its ideas make more sense than what they may have formerly believed. In the process, they employed their mental faculties in their studies, and their mentors obliged them with lines of reasoning meant to make sense. To discontinue this process and give up seeking those things that make sense would be to quit the pursuit of truth. Truth will make sense. For those using the Bible as the standard of truth as

---

2 Norton, 165.

3 Channing, 46-47.

the Bereans did, using reason is the means by which anyone may see what things are true and what things are questionable or wrong. In this way reason and revelation are entirely compatible:

> It is often said that we set Reason in opposition to Revelation, or above it, and that therefore we do not come to Scripture with a teachable spirit. This is not true, nor is anything like it true. We do indeed think that the Unitarian system of Christianity is more rational than what is commonly called Orthodoxy at the present day, and this is one argument for its truth; for, as Reason and Revelation are both of them God's work, there cannot be any real opposition between them.[4]

The charge made by some Trinitarians that Unitarians place reason above revelation is untrue, since we make our appeal to the Bible to find out what is said in its pages. But ardent defenders of the Trinity are not shy in leveling this charge against Unitarians, as a modern Trinitarian writes:

> Unitarianism is a product of the deification of Reason, the rejection of Biblical authority and an indescribably fierce pride in one's ability to save himself from the awful penalty of sin.[5]

Those are strong and sweeping statements. It is one thing for Mr. Martin to disagree with Unitarians, but to charge us with deifying reason is plain foolishness. Unitarian beliefs are explicitly stated in Scripture, whereas his are mere "intimations"[6] and require a great deal *more* reasoning to construct than Unitarian doctrines. In defending their system of beliefs, ardent defenders of Trinitarianism freely employ reason, but denounce Unitarians for using the same faculty. Trinitarians do this simply because reason is the enemy of Trinitarianism:

> In other words, we believe that God never contradicts, in one part of Scripture, what he teaches in another; and never contradicts, in revelation, what he teaches in his works and

---

[4] Eliot, 6-7.

[5] Martin, 506.

[6] *See* page 61 of his book, *Kingdom of the Cults.*

providence....

We do not announce these principles as original or peculiar to ourselves. All Christians occasionally adopt them, not excepting those who most vehemently decry them when they happen to menace some favorite article of their creed. All Christians are compelled to use them in their controversies with infidels. All sects employ them in their warfare with one another. All willingly avail themselves of reason, when it can be pressed into the service of their own party, and only complain of it when its weapons wound themselves.[7]

Trinitarianism is a system that elevates reason, in the guise of mystery, above the simple meaning of many biblical texts and the understanding we gain from our common human experiences. The extent to which inferences, which greatly depend upon reason, are relied upon to support this theology indicates how highly prized reason is by Trinitarians. But once it is shown that reason does not support the absurdities and contradictions that comprise Trinitarian theology, the outcry against reason begins *at that point*. This is merely an evasive tactic employed by those who cannot make sense of their own doctrines. And by not employing reason and sound principles of interpretation, Trinitarians have developed a theology that makes no sense even to themselves! Unitarians endeavor to know God and what we believe about Him through more practical means:

"But is it not presumptuous in man," it is continually said, "to sit in judgment on God?" We answer that to "sit in judgment on God" is an ambiguous and offensive phrase, conveying to common minds the ideas of irreverence, boldness, familiarity. The question would be better stated as this: Is it not presumptuous in man to judge concerning God, and concerning what agrees or disagrees with his attributes? We answer confidently, No; for in many cases we are competent and even bound to judge. And we plead first in our defense the Scriptures. How continually does God in his word appeal to the understanding and moral judgment of man! "O inhabitants of Jerusalem and men of Judah, judge, I pray you, between me and my

---

7 Channing, quoted in Parke, 89.

vineyard. What could have been done more to my vineyard, that I have not done in it?" We observe, in the next place, that all religion supposes and is built on judgments passed by us on God and on his operations. Is it not, for example, our duty and a leading part of piety to praise God? And what is praising a being but to adjudge and ascribe to him just and generous deeds and motives? And of what value is praise except from those who are capable of distinguishing between actions which exalt and actions which degrade the character? Is it presumptuous to call God *excellent*? And what is this but to refer his character to a standard of excellence, to try it by the established principles of rectitude, and to pronounce its conformity to them: that is, to judge of God and his operations?[8]

Trinitarians make an exception for their system of beliefs which would not be granted to others. They have made an exception regarding the reasonableness of their opinions, and only their opinions. Their opinions need not be reasonable at all. They accept their doctrines on the grounds of mysteriousness, but Unitarians, because the doctrines of this theology are comprehended, are denounced. It appears that only Trinitarians are entitled to such an exception. If the Unitarian were to claim this same exception (though wholly unnecessary), I am confident it would not be granted by Trinitarians, who nonetheless grant it to themselves. This exception, which involves the suppression of reason, is permitted to apply to only that system and is necessary only for that system.

John Locke, the much-revered English philosopher, did not embrace the notion of a triune God. In *The Reasonableness of Christianity* (1695), he eloquently expressed the need to use reason in religious matters and the consequences of its suppression:

> Though the works of Nature, in every part of them, sufficiently evidence a Deity; yet the world made so little use of their Reason, that they saw him not, where even by the impressions of himself he was easy to be found. Sense and lust blinded their minds in some, and a careless inadvertency to others, and fearful apprehensions in most (who either believed there

---

were, or could not but suspect there might be, superior un-known Beings) gave them up into the hands of their priests, to fill their heads with false notions of the Deity, and their worship with foolish rites, as they pleased: and what dread or craft once began, devotion soon made sacred, and religion immutable. In this state of darkness and ignorance of the true God, vice and superstition held the world. Nor could any help be had, or hoped for from Reason; which could not be heard, and was judged to have nothing to do in the case: the priests, every where, to secure their Empire, having excluded Reason from having any thing to do in religion. And in the crowd of wrong notions, and invented rites, the world had almost lost the site of the only true God. The rational and thinking part of mankind, 'tis true, when they sought after him, found the one supreme, invisible God: but if they acknowledged and worshipped him, it was only in their own minds. They kept this truth locked up in their own breasts as a secret, nor ever dared venture it amongst the people, much less among the priests, those wary guardians of their own creeds and profit-able inventions. Hence we see that reason, speaking never so clearly to the wise and virtuous, had never authority enough to prevail on the multitude, and to persuade the societies of men, that there was but one God, that alone was to be owned and worshipped. The belief and worship of one God, was the national religion of the Israelites alone: and if we will consider it, it was introduced and supported amongst the people by Revelation. They were in Goshen, and had light, whilst the rest of the world were in almost Egyptian darkness, without God in the world.[9]

Inasmuch as Christians study the Old and New Testaments to find meaning to life, we can have more rational discussions about the texts and what they may mean. But if we are going to use any texts as a basis for discussion, we must first agree to stay within the parame-ters of those texts when contemplating them. As it stands today, there is a great chasm between the emphasis placed on Scripture by Unitar-

---

[9] John Locke, *The Works of John Locke* (London, 1714), II, 540-541; quoted in Parke, 37.

ians and Trinitarians. Disregarding this difference, many Trinitarians boldly pronounce their doctrines to be true to the extent that those who find a different doctrine in their biblical searches may be asked to leave the church. This fosters division, not the love we ought to have for all people:

> Why do we prize our bodily liberty, but that we may exert our bodily powers? But if we were allowed to take only a certain number of steps, and were obliged to take those steps only in a certain direction, would that be liberty? Would it be worthy of the name? True, the limbs may be unfettered, we are at liberty to use them, but how? Exactly according to the dictation of another. Would that be liberty? Would that be freedom? Yet this is all the mental freedom you are willing to concede to me. Use your reason, you virtually tell me; take the Bible, read it for yourself; but if you come to any other conclusion than that which we think to be right you must of course be wrong. You did not search in the right way; you are without the influences of the Holy Spirit; you can only be right when you think *just as we do.*
>
> Yes, my friend, you appear quite willing that I should read the Scriptures for myself, if I will only read them with *your spectacles.* But if I must understand the Bible exactly as you do, why you might as well take the Bible from me. Just give me *your sense of it,* and I need give myself no further trouble about it. Why, my dear Sir, this is Popery in all its length and breadth.
>
> But our Master said, "search the Scriptures, for they are they which testify of me." And those private Christians were commended who searched the Scriptures daily, to see whether those things which they were taught were true. How different is this from your real meaning when you direct us to the Bible. Considering that our religious teachers in these days are not inspired men, as the first teachers of Christianity were, the ground you take is very strange. *You* also say, search the Scriptures; but you say at the same time, beware of your conclusions; let me direct your inquiries, and control your final judgment. You give me leave to search the Scriptures,

provided I find there just what you do; and if I cannot find those things, if I am not so fortunate as to understand with *your understanding*, you insist upon it that I have not searched aright. Is this freedom of inquiry? Is this the right of private judgment for which you, as a Protestant, contend? Is this the liberty you are so kind as to grant me? If it is, I want it not. If I must arrive at your conclusions, why should I take the trouble to search for myself? Why not save myself such an expenditure of time, such an amount of anxiety and fatigue, and such a waste of strength? You have searched the Bible; you are very sure you are right; if I should come to different conclusions, it would be certain I was wrong; therefore my wisest plan would be just to give up the whole business into your hands. But before I could be persuaded to adopt your conclusions, you must, as I have elsewhere said, guaranty that I shall not be called to account for my opinions at the last great day. This I know you cannot do, and therefore I will make the Bible, understood as well as it can be by the reason which God has given me, my *only* standard of faith; I will have no other. Blessed be God for giving us an *infallible* standard. Praise be to his holy name forever! And shall I cast aside this revelation from God himself, and submit to be fettered by articles and creeds, the productions of imperfect creatures like myself? No, my dear Sir, God helping me, I never will. The Bible—the Bible for me. I will bind it to my heart; it shall be my guide through life, and my comfort in death.[10]

Part of the process of contemplation and studying and discussing things related to God and the Bible, we will of course err at times. We will change our minds over time, as well. This is normal. But this is not sufficient reason to abandon the process of reasonably sorting out truth from error. It is through thinking that we may discover our mistakes and become kinder, more loving people, which is among the highest goals one can achieve. The abandonment of reason is not part of the plan:

To confide in God, we must first confide in the faculties by

---

10 Dana, 191-194.

which the proofs of his existence are weighed. A trust in our ability to distinguish between truth and falsehood is implied in every act of belief, for to question this ability would of necessity unsettle all belief. We cannot take a step in reasoning or action without a secret reliance on our own minds. Religion in particular implies that we have understandings endowed and qualified for the highest employments of intellect. In affirming the existence and perfections of God, we suppose and affirm the existence in ourselves of faculties which correspond to these sublime objects and which are fitted to discern them. Religion is a conviction and an act of the human soul, so that in denying confidence to the one, we subvert the truth and claims of the other. Nothing is gained to piety by degrading human nature, for in the competency of this nature to know and judge of God all piety has its foundation. Our proneness to err instructs us, indeed, to use our power with great caution, but not to contemn and neglect them. The occasional abuse of our faculties, be it ever so enormous, does not prove them unfit for their highest end, which is to form clear and consistent views of God. Because our eyes sometimes fail or deceive us, would a wise man pluck them out or cover them with a bandage, and choose to walk and work in the dark? Or, because they cannot distinguish distant objects, can they discern nothing clearly in their proper sphere, and is sight to be pronounced a fallacious guide?[11]

The doctrine of a triune God has been handed down through the ages, and Christians have trusted the so-called orthodox for their beliefs, not what their reason tells them can and cannot be true. But what is it to say that one is orthodox? Does it mean one who is right in his religious opinions? If so, this is certainly presumptuous:

> To continue in the faith, as we have been taught it in the Bible, is one thing, and to continue in the faith as we have been taught by human interpretations, is another. To continue in the faith of the Bible, we must first find out what there is taught. And here, at once, opinions are formed as various as

---

[11] Channing, 47.

the human mind. Dr. Campbell remarks, "As to orthodox, I should be glad to know the meaning of the epithet. Nothing, you say, can be plainer. The orthodox are those, who, in religious matters, entertain right opinions. Be it so. How, then, is it possible I should know who they are that entertain right opinions, before I know what opinions are right? I must therefore unquestionably know orthodoxy, before I can know or judge who are orthodox. Now, to know the truths of religion, which you call orthodox, is the very end of my inquiries: and am I to begin these inquiries on the presumption that without any inquiry I know it already? .... There is nothing about which men have been, and still are, more divided. It has been accounted orthodox divinity in one age, which hath been branded as ridiculous fanaticism in the next. It is at this day deemed the perfection of orthodoxy in one country, which in an adjacent country is looked upon as a damnable heresy. Nay, in the same country, hath not every sect a standard of its own? Accordingly, when any person seriously uses the word, before we can understand his meaning, we must know to what communion he belongs. When that is known, we comprehend him perfectly. By the orthodox he means always those who agree in opinion with him and his party; and by the heterodox, those who differ from him. When one says, then, of any teacher whatever, that all the orthodox acknowledge his orthodoxy, he says neither more nor less than this: 'All who are of the same opinion with him, of which number I am one, believe him to be in the right.' And is this anything more than what may be asserted by some person or other, of every teacher that ever did, or ever will exist? .... To say the truth, we have but too many ecclesiastic terms and phrases which savor grossly of the arts of a crafty priesthood, who meant to keep the world in ignorance, to secure an implicit faith in their own dogmas, and to intimidate men from an impartial inquiry into holy writ."—*Letters on Systematic Theology*, 112–115.[12]

---

[12] Dana, Appendix W, 317-318.

Revelation is information given to our faculty of reason—it seems impossible to properly exalt God without it:

> It is somewhat surprising, that in the present day there should be found any persons bold enough to affirm that Revelation, supersedes the necessity of reason, "that we have nothing to do with the word of God, but to believe and obey it;" surely man without reason, cannot ascertain either the nature or the worth of religion, and it cannot be more absurd to prohibit the use of reason in matters of religion, than it would be to demand of us to shut our eyes to enjoy the light of day and the beauties of creation. Reason is a talent given to us by a merciful Parent, not to be thrown aside as useless, but to be exercised and improved. Away then with the folly of rejecting reason in matters of religion. To offer any argument, that reason should be so rejected, would be to reason *against* the use of reason.
>
> Reason and Revelation being *gifts* of the same infinitely wise God, it is impossible they can clash with each other,—coming from the same eternal source of light, and sent, to promote man's moral perfection, his present and final happiness, each must be of equal value, in the sight of God, and in perfect accordance one with the other. Let us not be deterred from the free exercise of reason on religious subjects, for by this can we hope to carry forward the work of reformation, to remove error and superstition from the earth, and to send abroad the pure and holy light of the Gospel, into every benighted mind.[13]

How can Christians adopt a method which allows us to suppress our reason, when, without the use of reason, we would have no means of *knowing* God? Such an approach, if practiced in all areas of life, would result in chaos and misery. We are accustomed to exercising our mental faculties because we desire to reduce the risk of unwanted outcomes. But the tenets of Trinitarianism are predicated upon mystery, which, for those embracing them, causes uncertainty at every turn. If it would at least be admitted that Trinitarian doctrine should

---

[13] Thomas, 2, 3.

be judged according to the same criteria that we judge other things by, people would have little hesitation in rejecting it:

> You say "you should be lost if your own reason were to be your guide." Your expression is rather indefinite, and it depends upon what your *exact* meaning is, whether or not I can agree with you. If you mean that it would be dangerous—aye, fatal—to depend on reason *alone*, I fully and heartily acquiesce in your declaration. But if you mean that reason is to be laid *entirely* aside, I cannot at all agree with you. Without reason, of what *possible* use would a revelation be? Place the Bible in the hands of an idiot, who never enjoyed the gift of reason—or of a madman, whose reason had been dethroned—and what a mockery you make of their sad misfortunes? You cannot then mean that we are to make *no* use of reason. But if you believe that, with the revelation from our Heavenly Father in our hands, we are to use our utmost efforts to ascertain what it is that God has spoken, why then, as I said before, in this matter we entirely agree. I am as much opposed as you can be to exalting reason above revelation—to deciding what ought and what ought not to be in the Bible; but we must certainly use our highest faculties and our best efforts to ascertain what is there. And if the Scriptures any where *seem* to teach doctrines contrary to those which they have elsewhere plainly taught, we are bound, if possible, to give those seemingly discordant passages a different construction; and if, as may be the case, we cannot find out what they mean, we must imitate the great John Locke, and humbly say so; and we must patiently wait until we enter upon a more perfect state of existence, when all will be explained to us—when all that is dark will be brought to light—when faith will be exchanged for sight.

The Rev. John Wesley, in his controversy with Toplady concerning Election, said, that he would not believe any doctrine which charged God with unrighteousness. No words nor texts of Scripture, he said, would compel him to do it. So I say in regard to the Trinity. No words nor texts of Scripture will compel me to believe that the Bible contradicts itself.

We must keep reason in its right place, but we must not undervalue it. It is dangerous to use it rashly, but it is quite as dangerous not to use it at all. There is danger in everything. The very fact that we possess reason places us in responsible circumstances; and responsibility implies danger. Our reason is the highest gift of God; let us see to it that we neglect not "the gift that is in us." If we make no use of our reason, would not our Heavenly Father justly charge us with the guilt of hiding our talent in the earth? Is it not clear, that as each man, in his individual capacity, is responsible to God, so each individual must sift and determine this matter for himself? At the same time, I heartily respond to your exclamation, "Let him that thinketh he standeth, *take heed* lest he fall!"

Again, you observe, "When I draw instruction from the Bible, I like to take the *whole* of it." My dear Sir, so do I. And this is a great Unitarian principle. They take the whole Bible, and judge of detached passages by its general scope and tenor. In this position, I am glad to be able to inform you, you will find yourself sustained by the whole body of Unitarians. And it is by adhering strictly to this great, this radical principal of all just interpretation, that they arrive at Unitarianism.[14]

The Bible was written to all levels of learners, not just to those with some advanced gift of interpretation. It would be an exclusive book otherwise, preferring certain people over others. The doctrines of Trinitarianism, as opposed to those of the Bible, are incapable of comprehension. There are few who can even recite more than a couple of its tenets, let alone understand them:

The Bible was intended to suit every diversity of intellectual capacity. Its truths were designed to come within the cognizance of the savage as well as of the sage, within the embrace of the uncultivated peasant's understanding as well as the grasp of those who by habits of mental application and the energy of innate powers of intellect are able to understand subjects of depth and difficulty. The principle, you are aware, on which we found the present argument is this, that a doc-

---

14 Dana, 236-237, 238.

trine of so much importance as the Trinity must be stated with great plainness and perspicuity, guarded with great care, and that it must be both with great frequency. The Trinity, then, to say less than could be said, is a most abstruse and incomprehensible tenet. It confessedly baffles research, mocks investigation, and devours human thought. It bids defiance to the most strenuous efforts of the mightiest and most gigantic mind, ranking among the inscrutabilities of the universe, and of the highest class of the wonders of infinitude.[15]

In all pursuits of human inquiry, whether in theology or economics, medicine or physics, simple ideas are preferable to those that are complex and abstruse. In order to communicate ideas they need to be presented simply, which is another way of saying they must be presented in a way in which they may be understood. Any system that produces absurdities or contradictions when driven to its limits must be rejected. Such a system would be detrimental to our well-being. If, for example, I ask a man what day it is, and he replies that it is "Tuesday and Wednesday and Thursday," I recognize this as incapable of being true. In my judgment of things I must reject his assessment of what day it is and move on. I may not know what day it is, but I know his answer cannot be right. If I ask someone to tell me who God is, and he tells me he is God the Father *and* God the Son *and* God the holy spirit, I immediately recognize the absurdity of the response and seek an answer elsewhere. Otherwise I would be prone to the most absurd propositions in all areas of my life. We must not be afraid to reject what we believe is absurd:

> Let us remember, that *God is not the author of confusion, but of peace.* An extravagant and rooted *fondness of mystery*, especially in religious tenets, prevailed anciently in an extraordinary manner, and brought on endless disputations, even amongst the most eminent advocates of Christianity, as is conspicuous enough in their writings; and to this hour it is evident that the same infatuation, in some degree, possesses us; inasmuch that we are often unwilling, or afraid to trust plain sense and reason in our researches into Scripture, notwithstanding we

---

[15] Hyndman, 49-50.

are directed in those very Scriptures to employ our Judgment; *to prove all things, and hold fast that which is good.*—1 Thess. v. 21; see Luke xii. 57; 1 Pet. iii. 15.[16]

All people would do well to embrace a desire to make sense of all things, including Scripture. According to 1 Thes. 5:21 and other verses, we are obligated to have our doctrines make sense before assenting to them. It would certainly be difficult, perhaps impossible, to "be ready always to give an answer to every man that asks you a reason of the hope that is in you" (1 Peter 3:15), if you did not know what those reasons were:

Christianity is eminently simple, intelligible and reasonable. "He that hath ears to hear, let him hear. Yea, and why even of yourselves, judge ye not that which is right? I speak as unto wise men, judge ye what I say." Here let our opponents decide. They have decided. Are they not continually accusing us of leveling every thing to our own comprehension; of spoiling Christianity of its mysteries; of not prostrating the understanding; of demanding explanation where it cannot be given; of being only rational believers? Could such appeals as those quoted, have been ever made by Christ and the apostles, had they taught the paradoxes of modern Orthodoxy?[17]

The following are a few of the phrases that make clear the importance of reason:

- Eph. 1:18—That ye may know the hope of his calling.
- 1 John 5:20—That ye may know him that is true...
- Rom. 1:20—The things of God are known by the things that are clearly seen.
- John 7:24—Look not on the appearance, but judge righteous judgment.
- John 17:3—And this is life eternal, that they might know thee, the only true God, and Jesus Christ whom thou hast sent.

The Bible was written for people to understand. Thinking that it

---

[16] Gifford, xxix-xxx.

[17] W.J. Fox, 105.

is primarily composed of mysteries and riddles that cannot be interpreted reasonably is to defeat the purpose for which it was written:

> "If," says the late Prof. Stuart of Andover, "if there be any book on earth that is addressed to the reason and common sense of mankind, the Bible is preëminently that book. What is the Bible? A revelation from God. A REVELATION! If truly so, then it is designed to be *understood*; for if it be not intelligible, it is surely no *revelation*. It is a revelation through the medium of human language; language such as men employ; such as was framed by them, and is used for their purposes. It is a revelation *by men* (as instruments) and *for men*. It is made *more humano* (after the manner of men) because that on any other ground it might as well not be made at all. If the Bible is not a book which is not intelligible in the same way as other books are, then it is difficult to see how it is a *revelation*. [18]

Since Trinitarian dogma cannot be comprehended by the ablest of scholars, this alone precludes the majority of persons from having an active faith in it. The Bible, on the other hand, is written to those of common understanding. Simple people may understand it, and a primary tenet is that our heavenly Father is the one true God:

> God, out of the infiniteness of his mercy, has dealt with man as a compassionate and tender Father. He gave him Reason, and with it a Law: that could not be otherwise than what Reason should dictate, unless we should think, that a reasonable Creature should have an unreasonable Law. But considering the frailty of man, apt to run into corruption and misery, he promised a Deliverer, whom in his good time he sent; and then declared to all mankind, that whoever would believe in him to be the Saviour promised, and take him now raised from the dead, and constituted the Lord and Judge of all men, to be their king and ruler, should be saved. This is a plain intelligible proposition; and the all-merciful God seems herein to have consulted the poor of this world, and the bulk of mankind. These are articles that the laboring and illiter-

---

[18] Farley, 60-61.

ate man may comprehend. This is a religion suited to vulgar capacities; and the state of mankind in this world, destined to labor and travail. The writers and wranglers in religion fill it with niceties, and dress it up in notions, which they make necessary and fundamental parts of it; as if there were no way into the Church, but through the Academy or Lyceum. The greatest part of mankind have not leisure for learning and logic, and superfine distinctions from the schools. Where the hand is used to the plough and the spade, the head is seldom elevated to sublime notions, or exercised in mysterious reasoning. 'Tis well if men of that rank can comprehend plain propositions, and a short reasoning about things familiar to their minds, and nearly allied to their daily experience. Go beyond this, and you amaze the greatest part of mankind: and may as well talk Arabic to a poor day laborer, as the notions and language that the books and disputes of religion are filled with.... Had God intended that none but the learned scribe, the disputer or wise of this world, should be Christians, or be saved, thus religion should have been prepared for them, filled with speculations and niceties, obscure terms and abstract notions. But men of that expectation, men furnished with such acquisitions, the Apostle tells us, I Cor. i. are rather shut out from the simplicity of the Gospel; to make way for those poor, ignorant, illiterate, who heard and believed promises of a Deliverer, and believed Jesus to be him; who could conceive of a man dead and made alive again, and believe that he should at the end of the world, come again and pass sentence on all men, according to their deeds. That the poor had the Gospel preached to them; Christ makes a mark as well as business of his mission, Mat. xi. 5. And if the poor had the Gospel preached to them, it was, without doubt, such a Gospel as the poor could understand, plain and intelligible: and so it was, as we have seen, in the preachings of Christ and his Apostles.[19]

Trinitarianism is entirely subversive of the idea that the Bible was

---

[19] Locke, *The Works of John Locke* (London, 1714), II, 540-541; quoted in Parke, 38-39.

written for everybody. Trinitarian ideologues have, at times, considered simple people, to whom the Bible was written, to be essentially no different than beasts, presuming that they are incapable of understanding the primary tenets of Scripture. And once the masses became convinced that they could not, or, perhaps, should not, interpret Scripture, they opened themselves up to any absurdity the clergy propounded. As long as Christians are convinced they cannot and should not be able to understand the primary tenets of their faith, a deterioration of intelligent discourse will continue.

CHAPTER 9

RULES OF INTERPRETATION

Without knowing how we have arrived at the doctrines we embrace, we cannot be sure we have done our best to eliminate the possibility of error. Rules of interpretation are necessary to guide us in our efforts to gain the most likely meaning of a verse or section of Scripture. It is not only important for us to arrive at sensible conclusions, but that we arrive at them by following reasonable principles of interpretation. By following such principles, our conclusions may be judged as to whether or not they may be relied upon, further developed, or abandoned. By following rules and investigating Scripture ourselves, we may arrive at a faith that we understand and has a solid foundation. Without following them, we would either infer the most absurd things or might eventually settle for adopting someone else's theology, and not go through the trouble of sorting the issues ourselves. By merely accepting the notion of a triune god without questioning it, Trinitarians have followed the latter course.

Some parts of the Bible were written in highly figurative language, and without understanding how to understand such language we would conclude things that were not meant by the writer. Understanding such things as figures of speech, context, idioms and the language of emotion, helps us better understand the writings. Some verses (e.g. John 1:1) contain inherent difficulties that we may never overcome due to cultural peculiarities and meanings that existed at the time they were written but that don't exist now. The majority of verses, when a literal reading yields no intelligible meaning, can be understood through the observation of a few rules of interpretation.

Another difficulty that needs to be overcome by those seeking to understand Scripture is that we do not have the original manuscripts. We therefore try to get as close to the meaning of the original versions of the gospels and epistles as we can. As difficult a task as this can be, it will serve us to better understand the intent of the author in any particular passage. In some cases we may not be able to trace the intent of the original author:

> Each of the books of the New Testament has had its own textual history and has been preserved with varying degrees of accuracy. Nonetheless, all of the books were altered from the original state due to the process of manual copying decade after decade and century after century.[1]

This is an unfortunate reality facing every Bible student. The texts have been altered, so there must be some way for us to ascertain the probable meaning of particular words or phrases from the texts we have. Our ultimate goal is to find their meaning as the original author intended, and we need to reduce the amount of guesswork. This is the problem with the idea that Trinitarians rely so heavily upon mystery for proof of their system. Any conjecture, no matter how absurd, may be labeled a mystery. If this is an acceptable method of proving a statement, there is no way to eradicate error by proving it false or even absurd. Proof requires standards that are uniformly applied, and mystery as the foundation of a theological system is not a standard at all. When we are unsure of something, it is best to say we are unsure of it rather than label it a mystery and then assent to it.

Because investigative research requires a sound methodology, one of the first things Bible students must do—as much as possible—is divorce themselves from preconceptions. In this way, impartial decisions may be made regarding what to believe and why to believe it. It is through deliberate biblical inquiry and the observation of a few rules of interpretation that a person can be rooted in a sound faith.

Since the time the doctrine of the Trinity was first decreed as the rule of faith, many people have believed the Bible must be interpreted in light of it. But, and this is especially important for the newer Bible student, the Bible is not to be interpreted in light of a particular doctrine, but according to standard rules of interpretation:

---

[1] Phillip Wesley Comfort, ed., *The Origin of the Bible* (Wheaton, IL: Tyndale House Publishers, 1992), 184.

Like a great part of Scripture, the passages adduced in support of the Trinitarian doctrines have been interpreted upon no general principles, or upon none which can be defended. But many persons have been taught from their childhood to associate a false meaning with words and texts of the Bible. This meaning, borrowed from the schools of technical theology, is that which immediately presents itself to their minds, when those words and texts occur. They can hardly avoid considering the expositions so familiar to them, as those alone that could be obvious to an unprejudiced reader. He who would break the associations which they are accustomed, appears to them to be doing violence to the language of Scripture.

Now these prejudices, so far as they are capable of being removed, can be removed only by establishing correct principles of interpretation, applying them to the subject in hand, and pointing out the true or the probable meaning of the more important passages that have been misunderstood.[2]

Principles of interpretation must apply equally to everyone. When we agree on rules of interpretation, we have a basis to decide, on common and presumably reasonable grounds, the exact or probable meaning of particular verses. One of the benefits of rules is that if someone violates one, somebody else can identify the error and attempt to help correct it. But Trinitarians do not abide by consistent rules of interpretation. Trinitarian assessment of accurate theology is based upon reaching the conclusion that God is triune, not whether or not standard principles have been observed. This results in *advocacy research*, and is so labeled because its advocates care only about the conclusion and not the accuracy of the premises or the soundness of the methods involved in reaching that conclusion. Error is therefore rarely corrected because no standards have been established, and therefore none can be violated.

Some common problems with biblical interpretation arise due to the dynamic nature of language. Language is not static, and words acquire new meanings over time. Some cultures define words in many different ways. Eskimos are said to have over thirty-five variations of

---

2 Norton, 136-137.

the word "snow," whereas others may not be able to comprehend any of their meanings since people living on the equator, for example, may never have even heard of snow. Words are relative to a person's culture and environment. When an Ecuadorian says "it's cold," it reflects a different environmental reality than when an Icelandian says the same thing. This illustrates why principles of interpretation are necessary to understand works written by people of a different culture and era. When we read the Bible, which was written by people of a much different culture and era, there will be phrases which, if we do not observe reasonable standards, will be unclear to us:

> It is, then, to the intrinsic ambiguity of language, that the art of interpretation owes its origin. If words and sentences were capable of expressing but a single meaning, no art would be required in their interpretation. It would be, as a late writer, Dr. Thomas Chalmers, thoroughly ignorant of the subject, supposes, a work to be performed merely with the assistance of a lexicon and grammar. The object of the art of interpretation is to enable us to solve the difficulties presented in the intrinsic ambiguity of language. It first teaches us to perceive the different meanings which any sentence may be used to express, as the different words of which it is composed are taken respectively in one sense or another; as it is understood literally, or figuratively; strictly and to the letter, or popularly and in a modified sense; as the language of emotion, or as a calm and unimpassioned expression of thoughts and sentiments; as the language of one age or nation, or that of another; and it then teaches us (which is its ultimate purpose) to distinguish, among *possible* meanings, the *actual* meaning of the sentence, or that meaning which, in the particular case we are considering, was intended by the author. And in what manner does it enable us to do this? Here, again, a full and particular answer to this question is not to be comprised in the compass of a few pages. The general answer is, that it enables us to do this by *directing our attention to all those considerations which render it probable that one meaning was intended by the writer rather than another.*

Some of these considerations are, the character of the

writer, his habits of thinking and feeling, his common style of expression, and that of his age or nation, his settled opinions and belief, the extent of his knowledge, the general state of things during the time in which he lived, the particular local and temporary circumstances present to his mind while writing, the character and condition of those for whom he wrote, the opinions of others to which he had reference, the connection of the sentence, or the train of thought by which it is preceded and followed, and, finally, the manner in which he was understood by those for whom he wrote,—a consideration, the importance of which varies with circumstances. The considerations to be attended to by an interpreter are here reduced to their elements. I cannot dwell long enough upon the subject, to point out all the different forms and combinations in which they may appear. But where the words which compose a sentence are such, that the sentence may be used to express more than one meaning, its true meaning is to be determined SOLELY by a reference to EXTRINSIC CONSIDERATIONS, such as have been stated. In the case supposed (a case of very frequent occurrence), all that we can learn from the mere words of the sentence is the different meanings which the sentence is capable of expressing. It is obvious that the words, considered in themselves, can afford no assistance in determining which of those different meanings was that *intended by the author.* This problem is to be solved solely by a process of reasoning, founded upon such considerations as have been stated.[3]

One of the most fundamental rules of biblical interpretation is that all verses are not to be understood literally:

We may reject the literal meaning of a passage when we cannot pronounce with confidence what is its true meaning. The words of our Saviour just quoted [John 6:53—"Then Jesus said unto them, Verily, verily, I say unto you, Except ye eat of the flesh of the Son of man, and drink his blood, ye have no life in you"], are an example in point. One may be fully justi-

---

[3] Norton, 147-149.

fied in rejecting their literal meaning, who is wholly unable to determine their true meaning. To do this is certainly no easy matter. Similar difficulties, that is, passages about the true meaning of which we can feel no confidence, though we may confidently reject some particular meaning which the words will bear, are to be found in all other ancient writings as well as the Scriptures.

The writers of the New Testament partook of the character of their age and nation. Their circumstances, likewise, were in the highest degree peculiar, and produced corresponding feelings, which we cannot fully apprehend without an effort of thought and imagination. They were Jews, accustomed to strong Oriental modes of speech, and to figurative language of a kind not familiar to us, and the force of which, therefore, we are liable to misapprehend. All these circumstances contributed to produce a style of expression in the New Testament which is not to be judged of by the standards of our own. We may satisfy ourselves that we have ascertained the true meaning of a writer, even when his language varies much from that which the habits of out time might lead us to adopt in conveying the same ideas.[4]

Interpreting words or sentences in light of their context is essential, otherwise Scripture can appear to imply the most absurd things. For example, in Matt. 16:23 (and elsewhere) Jesus said to Peter, "Get thee behind me, Satan." Were we to interpret this literally, it would cause us to perceive Peter quite differently than we commonly do. By keeping the expression in context and understanding it in light of what we know about the culture in which Peter lived, we realize that Jesus meant something entirely different than what a literal reading would yield. Once again, some principle must be employed that serves as an aid in determining when to apply a literal or when to apply a figurative interpretation of a verse. This principle is commonly designated as common sense, and is perhaps the most foundational principle of biblical interpretation—our premises and conclusions must be reasonable. As has been admitted by eminent Trinitarians,

---

[4] Norton, 153, 287.

the doctrine of the Trinity is not rooted in reasonableness, but in it being a mystery. So when Trinitarian conclusions are reached, they are reached in violation of the most fundamental standard of biblical research, which is the standard of reasonableness. This standard is not violated accidentally, but is purposely ignored. If Trinitarians were to adopt a standard of reasonableness they would end up dismantling their own system.

Jesus was called by names and titles that Trinitarians argue could only have been spoken of him if he were God. This is due to incorrect inferences arrived at by not applying reasonable standards of interpretation. A common error involved in the development of Trinitarian theology is that words are interpreted literally when it is improper to do so:

> Supposing the doctrine maintained by Trinitarians to be capable of proof, the state of the case between them and their opponents would be this. They quote certain texts, and explain them in a sense which, as they believe, supports their opinions. We maintain that the words were intended to express a very different meaning. How is this question decided? We do not deny that there are certain expressions in these texts, which, nakedly considered, *will bear* a Trinitarian sense; how is it then to be ascertained, whether this sense or some other was intended by the writer?
>
> In order to answer this question, it is necessary to enter into some explanation of language and the principles of its interpretation. The art of interpretation derives its origin from the *intrinsic ambiguity of language*. What I mean to express by this term is the fact, that a very large portion of sentences, *considered in themselves*, that is, *if regard be had merely to the words of which they are composed*, are capable of expressing not one meaning only, but two or more different meanings; or (to state this fact in other terms) that in very many cases, the same sentence, like the same single word, may be used to express various and often very different senses. Now in a great part of what we find written concerning the interpretation of language, and in a large portion of the specimens of criticism which we meet with, especially upon the Scriptures, this fun-

damental truth, this fact which lies at the very bottom of the art of interpretation, has either been overlooked, or not regarded in its relations and consequences. It may be illustrated by a single example. St. John thus addresses the Christians to whom he was writing, in his First Epistle, ii. 20:—

"You have an anointing from the Holy One, and know all things."

If we consider these words in themselves merely, we shall perceive how uncertain is their signification, and how many different meanings they may be used to express... The term *Holy One*, in such a relation as it holds to the other words in the present sentence, may denote either God, or Christ, or some other being.

You know all things, literally expresses the meaning, *You have the attribute of omniscience.* Beside this meaning it may signify, *You are fully acquainted with all the objects of human knowledge;* or, *You know every truth connected with Christianity;* or, *You have all the knowledge necessary to form your faith and direct your conduct;* or the proposition may require some other limitation; for *all things* is one of those terms, the meaning of which is continually to be restrained and modified by a regard to the subject present to the mind of the writer.

I will mention, and I can barely mention, some of the principal causes of the intrinsic ambiguity of language.

1. Almost every word is used in a variety of senses; and some words in a great variety. Now, as we assign one or another of these senses to different words in a sentence, we change the meaning of the whole sentence.

2. But beside their common significations, words may be used in an undefined number of figurative senses. A large proportion of sentences may, therefore, be understood either figuratively or literally. Considered in themselves, they present no intrinsic character that may enable us to determine whether they are literal or figurative. They may often be understood in more than one literal, and in more than one figurative sense; and a choice is then to be made

among all these different senses.[5]

In ordinary speech we speak in different ways. We speak differently when we are excited than when we are merely making an observation about something. Regarding the writings of the Bible, this same principle is to be observed, especially when an account of an event has been given which involved heightened emotions at the time of the event. Sometimes people are excited and at other times we are impartial:

> In eloquence, in poetry, in popular writing of every sort, and least in the Scriptures, a great part of the language used is the language of emotion or feeling. The strict and literal meaning of this language is, of course, a meaning which the words may be used to express; but this is rarely the true meaning. The language of feeling is very different from that of philosophical accuracy. The mind, when strongly excited, delights in general, unlimited propositions, in hyperboles, in bold figures of every sort, in forcible presentations of thought addressed indirectly to the understanding through the medium of the imagination, and in the utterance of those temporary false judgments which are the natural result, and consequently among the most natural expressions, of strong emotion. Different senses in which such language may be understood often present themselves; and it is sometimes not easy to determine which to adopt.[6]

An example of the language of calm inquiry is 1 Thes. 5:21: "Prove all things; hold fast that which is good." In it we find statements made with little or no emotional attachment. It contains directions for us to follow. The book of Proverbs was largely written in this manner. In contrast to this stands the language of Thomas in John 20:28. His words are recorded upon his finding out that the person standing before him was the risen Lord and Saviour, Jesus Christ himself, in the flesh once again: "And Thomas answered and said unto him, 'My Lord and my God.'" Here we have the words of Thomas, spoken in

---

[5] Norton, 138-140, 141.

[6] Norton, 142.

an excited state, which are frequently relied upon by Trinitarians as proof of Jesus's deity. But is this how we are to read this verse, or any verse for that matter, as merely a dispassionate statement of fact? Of course not. This would reduce the Bible to a series of facts, entirely removing the personal aspects that emotional and colorful language imparts. This would also have the effect of causing the reader to assume that simply because words are contained in the Bible, they are to be taken literally and assumed to be true, no matter who spoke them:

> Supposing that Thomas had believed, and asserted, that his Master was God himself; in what way should this affect our faith? We should still know the fact on which his belief was founded, the fact of the resurrection of his Master, and could draw our own inferences from it, and judge whether his were well founded. Considering into how great an error he had fallen in his previous obstinate incredulity, there would be little reason for relying upon his opinion as infallible in the case supposed. I make these remarks, not from any doubt about the meaning of his words, but, as I have said, for the purpose of pointing out one example of the incomplete and unsatisfactory mode of reasoning, which appears in the use of many quotes from the Old and the New Testaments.

But is it not marvellous that theologians have made of this exclamation a *proof-text*, construing language of the strongest emotion as if it were the language of a creed? A more rational view, however, has been taken of the passage by such commentators as Michaelis, Rosenmüller, Kuinoel, and Lücke,—and, apparently, Neander and Tholuck,—who recognize the invalidity of the Trinitarian argument which has been founded upon it. Meyer, in the first addition of his commentary (1834), remarked, very judiciously, that expressions uttered "in such ecstatic moments" are "entirely misused when applied to the proof of doctrinal propositions." But in his second edition (1852) he does not seem quite willing to give up the passage. He speaks of Thomas as expressing "his faith in the divine nature [or essence, *Wesen*] of his Lord"; and, though he observes that the strong feeling under which the exclamation was uttered renders it less fitted for doctrinal use, he cites as important the remark of Erasmus, that Christ accepted the acknowledgment of Thomas, instead of rebuking him, as he would have done if he had been falsely called God. The obvious reply to this is, that Christ accepted the acknowledgment of Thomas as *he meant it*, not in the irrational sense which modern theologians have put upon the words. And as Greenwood has well remarked:—

"The answer of Jesus himself excludes the supposition that he was addressed as the Supreme God. For he said unto his disciple, 'Thomas, because thou hast seen me, thou hast believed; blessed are they that have not seen, and yet have believed.' Now this must mean, 'Because thou hast seen me here alive, after my crucifixion and burial, thou hast believed that I am raised from the dead; and it is well; but blessed are they who cannot have such evidence of the senses, and yet shall believe in the glorious truth, from your evidence, and that of your brethren.' He could not have meant, that they were blessed who, though they had not seen him, yet had believed that he was God; because there is no connection between the proposition; because the fact of the resurrection of Jesus cannot, to the mind of any one, be of itself proof of his deity; and because no one thinks of requiring to see God, in order to believe that he exists." (*Lives of the Twelve Apostles*, 2nd ed., 139)[7]

John 20:28 will be discussed at greater length later in this work, but the point here is that the language of emotion is rarely used to establish a doctrine. When emotional language is used, the words typically contain different meanings than they would literally convey.

Figures of speech are another departure from literal speech, and which may cause difficulties in understanding Scripture. If a figure of speech is properly understood it will convey a richness that would not have been gained through a literal interpretation. When figures of speech are not interpreted figuratively they usually produce absurdities. For example, in Galatians 2:20, the beginning of the verse

---

[7] Norton, 302-304, inc. footnote.

reads, "For I am crucified with Christ…" Without understanding this phrase figuratively we would be left with the impression that we were literally on the cross with Jesus, which is absurd.

Whenever possible, we should interpret more difficult verses, such as highly figurative ones, in light of simpler, more literal texts. That this is not the method of Trinitarian interpretation is plain from observing how frequently difficult verses have been used as foundational doctrines, when it should be the simple ones that are used as foundational:

MY DEAR SIR:

YOU say I would never have arrived at my present conclusions by reading the Bible alone, and insinuate that I have received my ideas from Unitarian books. You forget my assertion, in a letter to my father, that my mind was satisfied upon the subject before I had read a single Unitarian author, excepting, of course, the writers of the New Testament. As this matter is evidently misunderstood, I will give a particular account of it.

I started then in my investigation, with one idea firmly fixed in my mind—this idea was the *unity* of God, which doctrine is *certainly* revealed in the *Old* Testament. This, then, I considered a *certain truth*, and now my object in examining the New Testament was to learn whether a *Trinity* was there taught. I soon discovered *another* certain truth, namely, that Christ was a distinct being from God; and *another*, namely, that he was called the *Son* of God; and *yet another*, namely, that he was a *human* being. Here, then, were several certain truths, *plainly revealed.*

But I soon arrived at some passages, which *seemed* to assert, inferentially, that Christ was *God.* Here, then, was something at variance with those certain truths contained in the same revelation. Here was a truth, apparently revealed, which contradicted the certain truth of the Unity of God, and those three other certain truths, namely, that Christ was a distinct being from God, and that he was the *Son* of God, and that he was a human being. These truths were contradicted; but still I saw nothing about the *Trinity.*

I noted down these passages, and read on. The rest of the book still recognized, in the *plainest* and *most explicit* manner, all those certain truths of which I have spoken. The whole tenor of the New Testament certainly proved them. Now what was to be done with those texts which *seemed* to contradict them? I reasoned with myself thus; if, in reading any other book, I should come to hints and statements which seemed to contradict the plain assertions, and to differ from the general scope and tenor of the work, I should endeavor to give to those hints and statements an interpretation and a meaning which would harmonize with what was plainly laid down. To do this, it would not be correct nor natural for me to *assume* incredible propositions. This would be no way to harmonize discordant ideas, nor to reconcile contradictions.

But this strange and unnatural plan, it appeared to me, had been pursued with the Bible. That holy book had been treated as we should not think it right to treat any other. The doctrine that Christ possessed two natures, a finite and an infinite one, had been *assumed* to account for those passages where he seemed to be spoken of as God. I say this doctrine had been *assumed*, for it is nowhere *plainly* laid down. This course I could not justify, and what next was to be done?

Was it not *possible* that those perplexing passages might be interpreted in some other way? If they proved what they were said to prove, namely, that Christ was God, they proved that there were, at the same time, one only God, and two Gods; and that the same being had both a finite and an infinite nature. These things were contradictions, and could not be proved in any way; nor did I see anything about the *mystery* of the *Trinity*. These passages then, *must* have some other meaning. I now read the various interpretations of learned men, both Trinitarians and Unitarians, and was soon satisfied that they did not assert the deity of Christ, but that a fair interpretation *could* be given to all of them, which would perfectly harmonize with those plainly revealed truths, of which I have spoken, and which were likewise taught by the whole tenor of the New Testament. These passages then did not teach the deity of Christ. Christ was not God—the Bible was consistent with itself—and the doctrine of the Trinity existed no longer in my mind as an article of faith.[8]

There are verses that are difficult to understand, and in such cases it can be difficult to decide whether to interpret them literally or figuratively. Is there, for example, an idiom contained in the verse with which we are unfamiliar? In such cases all difficulty cannot be expected to be removed, but it might be mitigated enough to help us determine its probable meaning. There are, as mentioned earlier, inherent difficulties in translating figures of speech and other expressions into another language. Even with these difficulties, most expressions can be reduced to their likely meaning without forcing an absurd explanation about them. We must maintain reasonableness in understanding unusual or figurative expressions:

> Christ says, that he who would be his follower must "hate father and mother." The genius of our language hardly admits of so bold a figure, by which, however, nothing more was signified, than that his followers must be prepared to sacrifice their dearest affections for his cause.
>
> Sometimes a verbal rendering gives a sense altogether false: "Now I beseech you, brethren, that ye all speak the same thing." (1 Cor. i. 10) So St. Paul is represented as addressing the Corinthians in the Common Version. But "to speak the same thing" was a phrase used in Greek in a sense unknown in English, to denote "agreeing together"; and the exhortation in fact was that they should "all agree together."—These examples, few as they are, may serve to illustrate the mistakes to which we are exposed from the want of analogy between languages; and to show that the true meaning of a passage may be very different from the sense which, without further inquiry, we should receive from a verbal rendering of it into English. A verbal rendering of an ancient author must be often false, ambiguous, or unintelligible, and when not exposed to graver charges, will commonly fail in preserving the full significance, the spirit and character, of the original.[9]

---

8 Dana, 234-236.

9 Norton, 144, 146-147.

A good example of the difficulties involved in translating idioms of one culture into the language of another that does not have the same idiom, is in John 1:1: "In the beginning was the Word, and the Word was with God, and the Word was God." This verse is commonly cited by Trinitarians as proof that Jesus is God. In verse 14 of the same chapter we read that "the Word was made flesh," which is in some way a reference to Jesus. Thus, by taking a portion of verse one,—"and the word was God"—it is thought that a clear case is made that Jesus, who may be the one referred to as "the Word" in verse 14, is God. Violation upon violation is involved in such an interpretation, which will be discussed later in this book, but simple questions will illustrate the intrinsic difficulties involved in translating concepts into other languages: What is the Word? How do we define it and what does it represent? The uneducated or inexperienced will reply that it is Jesus himself, in essence just another name for him. But this is unsatisfactory because it fails to explain what the term fully signifies. It is at times it may be a reference to Jesus, and at other times a reference to the words of the Bible, since both usages are translated from the same Greek word, *logos*. This subject has been the topic of much debate, but one thing is admitted by Unitarians and Trinitarians alike: the Word (or, *logos*) is a difficult concept for us to assign an exact meaning. For the typical Bible student, one of the reasons for this difficulty is that the New Testament does not shed much light on the term, and the Old Testament was written in a different language than the New, so finding comparative terms may be somewhat difficult. The most reasonable approach is to do what many theologians have done, which is to not assign it a precise meaning. We will see later that those who claim to understand it perfectly and use it in their proofs of the doctrine of the Trinity are mistaken. For even though we may not understand its precise meaning, we can rule out suggestions that are self-contradictory or that disagree with other clear verses in Scripture. We should never assign a meaning to a word or verse merely for the sake of assigning it a meaning. There will always be terms and phrases that we are unsure of, and making absurd suggestions only makes the matter worse. There are reasonable ways of handling verses that are difficult:

We have now examined the most important texts which are

supposed to be at variance with the Unitarian belief. If I have omitted any, they are such, I think, as are sufficiently explained by the connection in which they stand. For we again say, the highest terms of exaltation applied to Christ give us no trouble, so long as the connection shows that he received his exaltation, "because it pleased the Father that in him all fulness should dwell." We may be at a loss to define the degree of his authority, but one such expression as that proves, beyond all doubt, that his authority was not independent or supreme. As to the greater part of these texts, I feel sure that our explanation is good and sufficient. In a few cases only it remains doubtful whether the Unitarian or Trinitarian explanation is the most natural. But even if there were a great many such cases, the weight of evidence which has been adduced from the general testimony of the Bible is enough to decide for us. For my own part, my mind rests upon this subject without any doubt or wavering, for to me the meaning of the Bible seems so plain, that if there were fifty texts which I could not perfectly understand, although I should feel the difficulty, they would not shake my faith.[10]

This brings to light another aspect of Trinitarian argumentation that is as presumptuous as it is unreasonable. If a verse is assigned a meaning by a Trinitarian, and if I, as a Unitarian, abstain from assigning a meaning to it because I am unsatisfied with *any* explanation as to its meaning, it is not infrequently assumed by the Trinitarian that, by default, his explanation is the correct one. For a Unitarian this is an exercise in futility. It is as if no verse can be admitted to be too difficult to be understood, despite the foreign character of the original Hebrew and Greek texts and the inherent differences between languages. When one assigns a meaning to a verse before identifying the character of the verse, whether figurative or literal, he cannot be reasonably assured he has ascertained the true meaning of it. It is preferable to withhold judgment regarding difficult verses. For this reason all of the interpretations of John 1:1 and similarly difficult texts may be wrong. That is what it is to be a *difficult* text. We simply cannot be

---

[10] Eliot, 81-82.

sure what its exact meaning is.

As has been noted, there are a few verses that, taken by themselves, seem to contain a Trinitarian sense. When a verse is separated from all others, one may infer a meaning that is not contained in the context of the verse. Interpretations that yield Trinitarian conclusions typically, and perhaps always, involve separating verses from their contexts. What commonly follows after a verse has been taken out of context and assigned a Trinitarian meaning, is that it is then assumed that this is the only possible meaning that could be assigned to it, and that all other interpretations must therefore be wrong:

> We do not deny that there are expressions in some of these passages, which, the words alone being considered, will bear a Trinitarian sense. How is it to be ascertained whether this sense, or some other, was intended by the writer?
>
> Now this is a question which, as we have shown, is to be determined solely by extrinsic considerations; and all those considerations that have been brought into view in the former part of this discussion bear directly upon the point at issue. My purpose has been to prove that the Trinitarian doctrines were not taught by Christ and his Apostles. If this has been proved, it has been proved that they were not taught by them in any particular passage. All the considerations that have been brought forward apply directly to the interpretation of any words that may be adduced; and if these considerations are decisive, then it is certain that the Trinitarian exposition of every passage of the New Testament must be false. Their force can be avoided but in one way; not by proving, positively, that certain words will bear a Trinitarian meaning,—that is conceded; but by proving, negatively, that it is impossible these words should be used in any other than a Trinitarian meaning,—that they admit of but one sense, which, under all circumstances, they must be intended to express. But this no man of common understanding will maintain. If, then, there be not some gross error in the preceding reasonings, the controversy respecting the Trinitarian exposition of those passages is decided. Whatever may be their true sense, the Trinitarian exposition must be false.

But I will now recur to the essential character of the Trinitarian doctrines, for the purpose of showing, that, though there are words in the New Testament which, abstractly considered, will bear some one or other Trinitarian sense, yet that this sense can be ascribed to them only in violation of a fundamental principle of interpretation.[11]

In Trinitarian exegesis, literal meanings of verses are frequently assigned to figurative verses, and vice-versa. As a rule, literal interpretations are preferable to figurative ones, except where a literal meaning yields a contradiction or nonsense:

A thorough investigation supposes, in the third place, that we arrive at a true or just interpretation of the sacred text. Such an interpretation must greatly depend upon the solution of the questions, whether the words of the writer are to be taken in a literal or in a figurative sense. Undoubtedly the literal sense is in all cases to be preferred, except it violate common sense; or on its face is self-contradictory or absurd; or contradict other and plain statements or declarations of Scripture*since Scripture must be consistent and harmonious with itself. Again; obscure passages are to be explained by those which are more perspicuous, clear and explicit; so that, wherever possible, Scripture may explain itself or be its own interpreter. Still again; the great principle in this connection, the one always to be borne in mind is, that the Bible is to be interpreted as all ancient books are; that no superstitious feeling of its peculiar sanctity is to disturb or embarrass that natural course of investigation into its contents or its significance, which we should pursue in the study of any other ancient record which has come down to us. Occasional expressions are to be explained by the general, pervading sense or tenor of the book. Strict regard, as far as possible, is to be had to the time, place, circumstances of the writer, to the manners and customs of the age and country. Rhetorical, figurative, allegorical expressions or allusions, are to be specially noted, and their plain import and meaning unfolded

---

[11] Norton, 154-155.

and made clear. For example, our Lord declares of the bread at the Last Supper, "This is my body"*of the Wine, "This is my blood." Deny the principles above stated, insist on the literal meaning of Scripture being in all cases accepted, and how impregnable becomes the position of the Roman Catholic Church, including as it does to this hour the largest part of Christendom, when it plants itself on the precise words of Christ, and then demands assent to its astounding dogma of Transubstantiation![12]

We must be willing to abide by rules of interpretation in our attempts to understand the figurative language applied to Christ. The doctrine of the double nature of Christ, however, was not developed according to any such rules:

> It appears that the doctrine of Christ's two natures was assumed, in order to reconcile the apparently discordant language used in Scripture, respecting our Lord. That Jesus Christ was in all respects a *human being*, Trinitarians find too plainly to be doubted, but perceiving epithets and expressions applied to him which they consider can only properly apply to God, they immediately assume that Christ was God as well as a man; that he possessed two natures, the one divine, the other human. But surely this is an unfair rule of interpreting the Scriptures. That because they appear to teach two doctrines inconsistent with each other, *both* should be admitted, instead of one being made to conform to the other. If a writer makes two assertions which apparently contradict each other, which cannot both be literally interpreted, *common* sense tells us we must receive one of the assertions either in a figurative or different sense to the other. Now apply this mode of reasoning to the doctrine under consideration. If Christ is declared in Scripture to be a man, and also has expressions applied to him therein, which seem to belong to a superior nature, as he was well known to exist in his human nature—it follows of course, that the expressions which seem to denote his possession of a divine nature, must be figura-

---

tively received; for to suppose two natures so different, not to say opposed, as are the divine and the human, to subsist together, in one person, is to suppose a manifest inconsistency. Surely those who argue the deity of Christ from the exalted epithets and expressions which are used respecting him in the Scriptures, are unacquainted with the character of the Eastern style of writing. Eastern phraseology must not be interpreted by the rules which govern the languages of colder climates. The inhabitants of the East and West, do not differ more in their *character*, *habits*, and *costume*, than in their languages. There is a simplicity and soberness pervading the language of the North of Europe, unknown to that of the inhabitants of the East. We know very well, that Eastern rulers who exercise despotic sway, are addressed by epithets which really sound to an European's ear, blasphemous. Remember, the Bible is Eastern, it relates to Eastern countries, to Eastern people and manners, and in the Bible we consequently find that frequent use of metaphor, and that extravagance of expression, for which the Eastern language is so remarkable. Hence we find kings and even judges styled Gods, Exodus 22c. 28v. "Thou shall not revile the Gods or the Rulers." Exodus 21c. 6v. "His master shall bring his servant to the Gods," *i.e.* to the judges. God said to Moses, "see I have made thee a God to Pharaoh." Exodus 7c. 1v. "Thou shalt be to him instead of God." Exodus 4c. 16v. David's reproof of the judges is remarkable in Psalm, 82c. 1 to 6v. "God standeth in the congregation of the mighty, he judgeth among the Gods, I have said ye are Gods, and all of you are children of the most high." [13]

There is a simple rule of interpretation that will assist us in understanding the Eastern character of the Bible. This rule enables us to make sense of the few references in Scripture in which a person, whether Christ, a king or a judge, is referred to as God (or god). The principle, if given a formal name, is the Principle of Agency. It refers to one acting on behalf of another, essentially as an agent:

If you will keep this rule of interpretation in your mind,

---

[13] Thomas, 24-25.

namely, that the same language will often be applied directly to the principal and also to the agent, because whatever the agent does the principal may be said to do, it will remove much of the obscurity of the sacred writings.[14]

The main point of the Jewish law of agency is expressed in the dictum "A person's agent is regarded as the person himself" (*Ned.* 72b; *Kidd.* 41b). Therefore any act committed by a duly appointed agent is regarded as having been fully committed by the principal.[15]

Insisting on a literal application of the title *God* that might be applied to Jesus on two or three occasions, is improper. Not recognizing that Jesus, as God's representative, may be called *God* in a subordinate sense, according to the principle of agency, has forced Trinitarians to spend so much effort in reconciling the many verses in which Jesus is qualified as a man. And since others were called *God* in the Bible, it is obvious that this term must be further qualified. This term is covered at length in a later chapter, but it is enough to state here that a literal rendering of the term *God* as applied to Christ violates the vast majority of other texts, and violates common sense.

Another difficulty with biblical interpretation is that the original manuscripts were without punctuation. The later addition of punctuation was made to facilitate biblical study, but it introduced into the text markings that set words apart, by periods and commas, that would have otherwise not been separated. This helped those who were accustomed to separated words, but also introduced the translator's personal biases into the text:

> Let me in passing make another remark on what should always be borne in mind in reading and studying the Scripture, whether in the original or the vernacular. The punctuation, the divisions into chapters and verses, are all modern, and of course without authority. The most ancient MSS. are with a few exceptions without any points. The points at present in the New Testament are coeval with the invention of print-

---

ing; and in the early printed editions varied in their placing with almost every fresh issue. The division into chapters still in use, was the work of Cardinal Hugo, who introduced it into the edition of the Bible which he published in the thirteenth century. That into verses is still more modern; and is traced to Robert Stephens, who introduced it into his edition of 1551. The titles of chapters and running inscriptions at the top of the pages in our English Bibles are the work of King James translators, and have nothing corresponding in the original Scriptures. Therefore, when we find printed over the first chapter of St. John's Gospel, in many editions, the words, "The Divinity and Preëxistence of Jesus Christ," we should remember that they are merely the words of the translators or editors, and no legitimate part of the Scripture; they are wholly without authority, and may be rejected by every reader. The Bible, indeed, when professedly "without note or comment," should be printed without these titles and inscriptions, since they virtually are notes or comments, and often mislead the uninstructed, who mistake them as parts of the original book.[16]

These are just some of the principles of interpretation that are violated when assigning Trinitarian meanings to verses. When reasonable principles of interpretation are observed, there is no valid basis from which to infer the doctrine of a triune God.

---

[16] Farley, 63-64.

CHAPTER 10

CONTINUITY OF BELIEF IN ONE GOD

A continuity of belief in our heavenly Father being the one true God was established by the writers of the Old Testament and maintained by those of the New. To the Christians of the early church, the large part of whom at first were Jews, the Father was the only God. This did not change until the councils of the fourth century and beyond declared that the Father had equals. This change caused division in the Christian world, but was eventually declared to be the rule of faith by force of both the Roman government and the Catholic Church. Prior to this, nobody was considered equal with the Father, neither could any be without negating what was established by Moses and the other writers of the Hebrew Bible. It was through a strong influence of Greek thought that new conceptions of God entered the church. Both Testaments are consistent in establishing the Father as unrivaled in majesty and dominion:

> We find that the Gentile converts to Christianity brought with them into the new religion certain ideas of their philosophy, and elaborated from them much of the system of modern orthodoxy. Among these men, we can easily see when and where the doctrine of the Trinity began to be, and how it gradually assumed its now prevailing form (see a clear and concise historical account in Réville's *Histoire du Dogme de la Divinité de Jesus Christ*, English translation, 1870: compare also Donaldson's *Christian Literature*, Book ii.). But this is not to be seen within the pages of Scripture. Here, we have One God at the beginning, and One God at the end, without any limitation or qualification whatever. As, for example, we read in the words of Moses, "Hear, O Israel, Jehovah our God, Jehovah is one."

Christ takes up the same strain, and when he was asked by the scribe what was the first commandment of all, Jesus, we are told, answered him in the same ancient words, "The first of all the commandments is, Hear, O Israel, the Lord our God is one Lord; and thou shalt love the Lord the God with all the heart, and with all the soul, and with all the mind, and with all the strength: this is the first commandment." (Deut. vi. 4; Mark xii. 29, 30) The Apostle Paul re-echoes this declaration: "To us," he says, "there is one God, the Father, of whom are all things, and we in him." (1 Cor. viii. 6; comp. Ephes. iv. 5, 6)

Where, then, does it appear that Jews or Christians were ever taught a different doctrine respecting God from that of the great founders respectively of Judaism and Christianity?—where does this clearly and explicitly appear?—until indeed, as before observed, we come far down into the post-apostolic times, when there is no doubt whatever either as to the fact of a new doctrine having been introduced, or as to the source from whence it was immediately derived? [1]

Before our Trinitarian brethren pronounce Unitarianism a false and dangerous doctrine, let them seriously consider the following facts: that in the old Testament, there are about 2000 passages in which the Unity of God is either positively expressed or implied. In the New Testament, the Father is styled *one*, or *only God*, seventeen times; he is also styled God *absolutely*, by way of eminence or supremacy, 320 times. The highest epithets or attributes are applied to him 105 times, and there are no less than 90 passages which shew that all prayers and praises ought to be offered to him; and there are no less than 300 passages wherein the Son is represented as subordinate to the Father, deriving his being from him, receiving from him his divine power, and acting in all things, agreeably to the will of God. Surely amidst all this evidence in favour of God's Unity and of his supremacy to the Saviour, Unitarians are justified in maintaining that altho' "there be

---

[1] Smith, 84-85.

that are called Gods, whether in Heaven or in earth, (as there be gods many and Lords many) yet to *us*, there is but one God, the Father, of whom are all things, and we in him, and one Lord Jesus Christ by whom are all things and we by him." 1 Cor. 8c. 5 and 6v.[2]

The *one* only God who was acknowledged and adored by Moses and the Prophets, must be, identically, also, the *only true* GOD of the Christians, namely *the God and Father of our Lord Jesus Christ.*—See Acts. iii, 13; 2 Tim. i, 3. There is not the least *vestige*, in the Old Testament, of the Jews having worshipped a *Trinity of Persons* in the divine substance; there can be no possible Change in a being absolutely *immutable*. Neither can it be said with any colour from the Scriptures, nor with any semblance of reason, that GOD (or the object of adoration) was revealed to Moses and the Prophets, *imperfectly* or *incompletely*. What appearance of verity is there, that the *Almighty* on that awful occasion (as on many other occasions), when He proclaimed the true *object* of divine worship (Exod. xx), and spake of Himself as a *single Being or Person*, and LORD *of All* (xix, 5), did thereby conceal from his faithful servants the essential knowledge of his intimate union with *two other* Divine Persons, *equal* with *Himself* in *perfection*, *dominion*, and *power*; and, consequently, *equally* entitled to the highest worship, and the *marked attention* of all mankind *in all ages?*—Surely the spirit of that man must be waxed gross, that doth not tremble at the ideas which even the mention of such opinions unavoidably suggests.[3]

One might wonder how Moses, Solomon and the other God-loving Jews in the time of Moses and the prophets would react upon being raised from the dead, only to discover that God is an entirely different being than the one they worshipped, composed not of a single being as they'd supposed, but of three-in-one, something which they were neither taught nor confessed. Would they not feel some discontentment knowing that if God really were three-in-one, they

---

2 Thomas, 17.

3 Gifford, 195-196.

were deprived of the ostensible benefits of worshipping two more "persons"?

The Old Testament is clear that God is only one "person" (as opposed to three). This is not only admitted by most learned Christians, among them many Trinitarians, it is taught by Jews, both modern and ancient, as the most fundamental tenet of Judaism. The monotheistic character of these texts is unquestionable, and contain statements that were to apply to all future generations as the stamp of God's immutable character:

> Judaism was Unitarian in its institutions. There was no revelation of a Trinity to the patriarchs who succeeded Abraham. Adoration is offered to, promises are made by, the same individual Jehovah. One after another is celebrated for treading in his steps. His posterity are enslaved in Egypt; the time of their deliverance arrives; Moses is commissioned to effect it. "Thou shalt say unto you the children of Israel, the Lord God of your fathers, the God of Abraham, the God of Isaac, and the God of Jacob, hath sent me unto you. This is my name for ever, and this is my memorial unto all generations." We are not then left to infer, from its not being recorded, that in the intermediate time no revelation of some other person or persons in the Godhead had been made: it is here directly negatived, not only for the past but for futurity. The laws afterwards given are such as from this we might expect. So far as they relate to worship, their great object is to inculcate that there is but one person to whom it is due. "I am the Lord your God, that brought thee up out of the land of Egypt. Thou shalt worship no other God, for the Lord whose name is jealous, is a jealous God. Hear, O Israel, the Lord our God is one Lord." The worship instituted on Mount Sinai was, like that of the patriarchs, the worship of one God. It is not addressed to a Trinity; but effectually and absolutely excludes that, and every other notion of a divine plurality.[4]

Deuteronomy 6:4 was not issued for the mere purpose of giving a doctrinal assignment to Israel, though it was its foundation,

---

[4] W.J. Fox, 96-97.

which made it unique in a polytheistic world. It was given so that they would be united in worshipping God and protected by Him so that their promised Messiah would be born and deliver Israel from its enemies, as well as effect world peace. The Messiah would thus have an opportunity to complete his mission by fulfilling the prophecies regarding him:

> Judaism was Unitarian in its administration. The laws of Moses were not designed, like Christianity, to work their way among other nations, and become universal. Their design was, to preserve in Judea a certain degree of religious knowledge till the Messiah came. For this, the laws were aided by inspired men, raised up from time to time to restore and preserve their purity. Till within three hundred years, perhaps less, before Christ, there was a succession of prophets. The doctrines inculcated by these men are not unimportant in the present controversy. They were the guardians and expounders of the law of Moses. If that law was erroneously supposed to teach the proper unity of God, they would have exposed the error. If the Trinity was there obscurely taught, and had been overlooked, they would have brought it to light; if the Jews, in Moses's time, were not fit for the reception of that mystery, and were gradually prepared for it, they would have made the revelation. Have they exposed such a revelation? Have they offered such an interpretation? Have they unfolded such a discovery? Nothing like it. Elijah by a miracle rescued the people from the worship of Baal; and they exclaimed, "The Lord, *he* is God!" Was this miracle wrought to turn them from idolatry, one fatal error, to Unitarianism, another fatal error? And was a prophet satisfied with such a triumph? The Psalmist interprets providential judgments to be for this purpose: "That men may know that thou, whose name alone is Jehovah, art the Most High over all the earth." Ps. lxxxiii. 18. Isaiah introduces the Deity asserting, "I am Jehovah, that is my name, and my glory I will not give to another." Isaiah xlii. 8. Zechariah, in the next text, predicts the universal prevalence of this doctrine, "The Lord, whose name is one, shall be king in all the earth."

Take Judaism in its origin, text or commentary; the patriarch with whom it commenced; the code in which it was embodied; the prophets by whom it was administered; and it is clear that a plurality of divine persons was no part of it, was excluded from it, was inconsistent with it, and could only be established upon its destruction.

The results of this system appear in the Jews, who conceive the reception of the doctrine of the Trinity to be equivalent to denying those of Moses.[5]

The texts assert that maintaining the truth of one God was essential to Israel's survival. This was especially important in the heathenistic and polytheistic world in which they lived. The distinguishing feature of their religion was the worship of one God, whose name, they were informed, is *Jehovah*.[6]

When Moses was appointed the leader of Israel, he found his people buried in gross superstition and idolatry. He led them forth from Egypt in the name of the great I AM, the Jehovah, The God of Abraham, Isaac, and Jacob. He instructed them in the history of past times, and for this purpose the book of Genesis was written: to show that the God in whose name he spoke was the same God by whom the heavens and the earth were created, by whom the wickedness of men had in times past been punished, by whom a part of the human race had been saved from the general destruction, by whom their ancestors, Abraham and his children, had been greatly blessed, in that land of promise to which he was now about to lead them, and establish them there as a great people. When he brought them to the foot of Mount Sinai in the wilderness, after they had been rescued by the strong hand and outstretched arm of the Almighty, in the midst of the fire and the smoke this eternal truth was spoken: "Hear, O Israel, Jehovah the God is one Jehovah." I use the word Jehovah, instead of Lord, because, as you know, wherever the latter is printed in capitals in the Old Testament the original Hebrew is Jehovah.

---

5 W.J. Fox, 97-99.

6 The more accurate pronunciation is most likely *Yahweh*.

Now this word is derived from HAYAH, to be, and means self-existence; so the meaning is, "Hear, O Israel, the self-existent one, the God, is the only self-existent."

That was the great central doctrine of the Jewish religion. They received it slowly and unwillingly; it was too grand for their degraded minds, and they returned again and again to the idolatries of the heathen. For a thousand years, their history is a succession of defeats and victories. So long as they held fast to their national belief in Jehovah as the only God, they were superior to all their enemies, but whenever they were corrupted by idolatrous practices they were shorn of their strength and brought low. Thus it continued through the time of the Judges and of the Kings during which prophets were sent to them from time to time to reiterate the one great truth, on the preservation of which their existence as a nation depended. They declared it in the most emphatic language; they enforced it by threats of the most terrible punishment if it was forsaken, and by the most glorious promises if it was faithfully adhered to.

There would be no end to the task if I were to attempt to give quotations in proof of this. Let me offer, however, a few as a sample: Deut. xxxii. 39, "See now that I, even I, am He, and there is no God with me! I kill and I make alive." Isaiah xliv. 8, "Thus saith Jehovah: Beside me there is no God; I know not any." Isaiah xlv. 5, and elsewhere, "I am Jehovah, and there is none else. To whom then will ye liken God, or what likeness will ye compare unto him; to whom then will ye liken me, or shall I be equal" saith the Holy One; for I am God, and there is none else, I am God, and there is none like me." If it were needful, we might bring several hundred instances as strong and conclusive as these; but those who are familiar with the great labor of all the prophets, from Moses till the time of captivity, was to teach the Unity of God and the purity of his worship. It is all a commentary upon the words spoken upon Mount Sinai, "Jehovah, the God, is one Jehovah."

But their instructions were almost in vain. The people were still corrupted, again and again, by the nations around, until the judgments of God came upon them with more dreadful calamities. They were completely subdued and carried into captivity by the Assyrians and Chaldeans. There, in the land of strangers, when their harps were hung upon the willow, and they remembered with sadness the desolation of the temple of God, the eternal truth of God's Unity was indelibly impressed upon the heart of the Jewish people; it was burnt in by sorrow, never again to be erased. When a small remnant returned to Palestine, it was the worshippers of one God, and to them the prophet Zechariah spoke, when prophesying of the Messiah's time, in the words of our text, "Jehovah shall be king over all the earth; in that day there shall be One Jehovah, and his name One." The nation had yet many calamities to endure, many vicissitudes of fortune; but among them all they never departed again from the lesson which had been so severely learned.

Such is a general view of the Old Testament, which is, I think, decisive of the question before us. If it had been intended by those who spoke under the inspiration of God, to convey some peculiar idea of unity, different from that which the word ordinarily conveys, as, for example, a Trinity in Unity instead of absolute unity, would it not have been somewhere distinctly expressed? Would the chosen people of God, whose special mission was to teach the truth concerning God's nature, have been left in ignorance of so great a doctrine as this? Would it not rather have modified all the instructions of the prophets, and appeared in all their teaching? But what hint do we find of such a thing? From Genesis to Malachi, where do we find a single expression which would convey to an unprejudiced mind such an idea? [7]

It requires a prejudiced mind to find the dogma of a triune god in the Old Testament, and the working of this prejudice is virtually everywhere in Christendom. Once Christians viewed their religion as separate from Judaism, rather than based upon it and a continuation of it, it would be only a matter of time before the Hebrew

---

[7] Eliot, 12-15.

understanding of God would be presumed to be inadequate. What is worse, the doctrines given to the Jews by God are not only viewed as incomplete, but the Jews themselves are viewed, through revisionist and separatist lenses, as inadequate to understand the Scriptures *delivered to them*! If Christians were mindful that Christianity is not founded upon a separate set of principles from those delivered to Israel, the monotheistic tenets would still be abided by today. When Jews pronounce Christianity to be contrary to Judaism, even idolatrous, they have not made a judgment precipitously or prejudicially. It is as though God is constantly witnessing in such testimonies for Christians to return to the first principle of true religion, which is that there is one God, our heavenly Father.

It was essential for Israel to maintain the simple truth that God is one—this is evident from God's declaration of this central truth through the Prophets and then through Jesus, a Jew. The reception of the doctrine of the Trinity depends upon a number of assumptions, not the least of which is that the Jews were ill-equipped to understand religious principles—even their own. Various conjectures have been made by Christian revisionists as to why the Jews would not have been able to understand the doctrine of a triune god. Implicit in these conjectures is that the early church did not believe in a three-in-one concept of God since the first Christians were Jews:

> The only times in which the ancient Hebrews and their Kings prospered, and obtained even a series of *miracles* in their favour, were, when they adhered (as they had been instructed) to the LORD *God alone*; to only *one* object of divine worship. Indeed their happiness and safety depended upon the close observance of the fundamental precept, to which all the others were subordinate. It is impossible to read the Old Testament without perceiving this. In that sacred depository it is completely evident throughout, that Moses and the prophets, who acted immediately under a *divine revelation*, acknowledged but one God, but *one divine person* or intelligent agent, and worshipped *no other*. If, therefore, the *present* doctrine of *three divine persons* of the Godhead, *each* of them objects of religious worship, be true: It will follow, that the *worship* so jealously and rigorously insisted on by Moses and

the Prophets, must have been, in the very foundation, *imperfect* or *defective*. But it appears very harsh, if not impious to conceive this. They were *taught of God*. It cannot then be presumptuous, we hope, to believe that the God of light and truth would assuredly have informed the Prophets, if there were any other *whatsoever* to be acknowledged as God *besides Himself*; because any *error* or *defect* in that most *essential* point would, in fact, have been as great *then* as at this day. The New Testament is a declaration of *a new and more glorious covenant* with man, by Jesus Christ; but not of any new or different objects of worship. *It is written*, saith that Great Messenger, *Thou shalt worship the Lord the God*, and HIM ONLY *shalt thou serve.*—Matt. iv, 10; Luke iv. 10. Our Saviour, most certainly, here refers to the strict commands on this head, which are recorded so frequently in the Old Testament. The revelations from God can in no wise be discordant, especially with respect to the object of religious adoration. If there were *three different persons* in the Godhead, EQUAL and ETERNAL, it is hardly possible to conceive that two of them should have been wholly unnoticed when the OBJECT of divine worship was so professedly and openly *declared* by the Prophets, on numberless occasion, and in the most solemn manner. Would the *second* and *third* Persons of the (supposed) Trinity, have been then neglected or passed over? There can be little or no doubt but that *They* also would have had *their* rights as *clearly* asserted and proclaimed;—in every period, *in the times of the Prophets* as well as now, might *discriminate* them in their *worship*; administer the honours *ever* justly due to *each of them*; and implore *their respective* blessings and protection.[8]

The old Apology of the Fathers, viz. that "the Ancient Hebrews were not taught the doctrine of the *Trinity*, (by Moses, &c.) lest it should lead them into *Polytheism*, will hardly be advanced by the Orthodox of this day; unless they can prove that all such danger is now removed.[9]

---

[8] Gifford, 36-38.

[9] Gifford, 38, footnote.

There is no difference that exists today, as compared to conditions in the early church, which would prevent one from being led into polytheism upon accepting the doctrine of the Trinity. It is the nature of the doctrine that causes one to become polytheistic, not the nature of the society into which it is born.

The Old Testament was written to familiarize mankind with our Creator—His essence, His being and His attributes are spoken of there. The New Testament built upon this foundation and could not alter it without nullifying it. It was so basic that amending it would mean that the first account of Him was incorrect. For many hundreds of years, Christians have labored to show how the Old Testament can be read to give a Trinitarian sense to it. With all this effort, though, it is still widely acknowledged that the Old Testament does not contain the doctrine. So we have another contradiction among Trinitarian theologians: many acknowledge the doctrine's absence from the Old Testament, yet verses are offered from the Old Testament by others who claim it is clearly there. Revisionist attempts persist, but to the extent they succeed they subvert the doctrine of one God:

> "In the first place, then," he [Prof. Sparks] says, "it will not be denied that the great design of the revelations, contained in the Old Testament, was to acquaint the Jews with *the true nature of God;* nor will it be denied, that from all these revelations, they had no conceptions of any other mode of existence, than that of his simple unity. It was perpetually enforced upon them, as a fundamental truth, that 'the Lord their God was *one*.'" No history, either sacred or profane, acquaints us with a single fact, from which it can be inferred, that the Jews had any knowledge of a three-fold nature in the Deity. On the contrary, all history is against such an inference; and the demonstrable certainty, that these people, for whose light and improvement the Old Testament was expressly designed, never had the remotest suspicion of such a doctrine being contained in their sacred books, is the clearest possible evidence, that it is not plainly taught there, whatever may now be deduced from types, and shadows, and dark sayings, and

Hebrew idioms, and double meanings.[10]

In the Old Testament, the term *God* refers to the one who created the heavens and the earth and we find no divisibility within Him spoken of there. Many Christians now believe that the term *God* has a new meaning: it now means there are three beings in one. This cannot be true, since there is no express change in the meaning of the term when it was used in the New Testament. The term is consistently used to denote one indivisible being, who is our heavenly Father. If, as Trinitarians suggest, a change had been made in how the term was applied, there would have been an unmistakable notice given given the magnitude of the impact such a change would entail. Since there is no such notice, then the one God revealed in the Old Testament is the same one God of the New. There is therefore a continuity of belief in the one God, Jehovah (or, Yahweh), throughout the entire Bible:

> I do not know of any other arguments now used, to prove that a plurality of persons is hinted at in the Old Testament. One thing, very important, is certain, that, if any such hints were conveyed, the Jews never understood them. The presumption is, that they knew their own language, and it is certain they understood that the Unity of God was taught by their Scriptures in the most absolute and unqualified manner. Such was their interpretation of Moses and the Prophets at the time when Christ came. In all Palestine there probably could not have been found a single man or woman, who supposed that there was any distinction of persons, such as is now taught, in the Unity of God.
>
> If, therefore, such a doctrine is contained in the New Testament, it must have been completely a new revelation to the Jews; and not only new, but also strange. At first sight it must have appeared to them then, as it does now, subversive of their ancient doctrine. It would have been necessary, therefore, for the Saviour and his Apostles to state it very plainly, and to prove its consistency with the law of Moses. If we find no such statement, we may conclude there was no such doctrine. Silence, under such circumstances, would be a full

---

[10] Dana, 172-173.

consent to the Old Jewish belief in the Unity of God.[11]

In his discourses, Jesus himself demonstrated that the term *God* was applied uniformly by both the unbelieving Jews and the believing Jews. This means that the supposed difference in usage after Pentecost did not produce the change Trinitarians argue for. Pentecost is central to a common argument Trinitarians make, which is that a spiritual illumination took place in the Jews upon receiving holy spirit on the day of Pentecost. If there were a change in the concept of God for those who received holy spirit, the term *God* would have meant something different to those Jews who had received it versus those who had not. But Jesus used it in the same sense to both the believing and unbelieving Jews alike, without any sense that it meant something different to each group:

> Jesus himself bore witness to the correctness of the Jews, as to this point, in his conversation with the woman of Samaria: "Ye worship ye know not what; but we know what we worship, for salvation is of the Jews." John iv. 22.
>
> By similar assertions of the Divine Unity. "Thou believest that there is one God; thou doest well." James ii. 19. "God is one." Gal. iii. 20.
>
> Christianity takes from Judaism not merely the truth of this doctrine, but its importance also; and as we have already seen, associates it with whatever is most interesting in religion and morality. With Christ, as with Moses, it is "the first of all the commandments:" with Christ, as with Moses, it is the foundation of devotion to God and benevolence to man. With the advance of the divine communications its rank is not degraded. No brighter or nobler truth appears to obscure its lustre.[12]

That there was no questioning by the Jews of a new concept of God clearly indicates that there was no change. The Jews were the guardians of the truth given to them by God. They protected it. Anyone presenting a new concept would have been challenged relent-

---

[11] Eliot, 17-18.

[12] W.J. Fox, 101-103.

lessly. The intensity with which some of the Jews opposed Jesus and his apostles was constant, and occasionally it was petty. If Jesus had presented a different concept regarding who the God of Israel was, he would have been questioned about it at length, especially since many of them opposed his claim that he was the Messiah and resented his effort to persuade other Jews to follow him:

> Christianity, it must be remembered, was planted and grew up amidst sharp-sighted enemies, who overlooked no objectionable part of the system, and who must have fastened with great earnestness on a doctrine involving such apparent contradictions as the Trinity. We cannot conceive an opinion against which the Jews, who prided themselves on their adherence to God's unity, would have raised an equal clamour. Now, how happens it, that in the apostolic writings, which relate so much to objections against Christianity and to the controversies which grew out of this religion, not *one word* is said, implying that objections were brought against the Gospel from the doctrine of the Trinity; not one word is uttered in its defence and explanation; not a word to rescue it from reproach and mistake? This argument has almost the force of demonstration. We are persuaded, that had three divine persons been announced by the first preachers of Christianity, all equal, and all infinite, one of whom was the very Jesus who had lately died on the cross, this peculiarity of Christianity would have almost absorbed every other, and the great labour of the apostles would have been to repel the continual assaults which it would have awakened. But the fact is, that not a whisper of objection to Christianity, on that account, reaches our ears from the apostolic age. In the epistles we see not a trace of controversy called forth by the Trinity.[13]

It is astonishing that anyone reading just the Bible would assert that it was written to establish the idea that the Father has equals. If the doctrine of the Trinity were true, the writers of both Testaments went to great lengths to avoid revealing their thoughts and feelings on the subject. If, for example, the apostles thought they were convers-

---

13 Hyndman, 54-55.

ing with God when they were conversing with Jesus, they purposely withheld their thoughts on this point since there is so little that even remotely approaches Trinitarian suppositions in their writings. Believing that they would have withheld this is foolish, as it would have been the single greatest influence in all of their writings:

The doctrine is proved to be false, because *it is evident from the Scriptures that none of those effects were produced which would necessarily have resulted from its first annunciation by Christ, and its subsequent communication by his Apostles.* The disciples of our Saviour must, at some period, have considered him merely as a man. Such he was, to all appearance, and such, therefore, they must have believed him to be. Before he commenced his ministry, his relations and fellow-townsmen certainly regarded him as nothing more than a man. "Is not this the carpenter, the son of Mary, and brother of James and Joses and Judas and Simon? And are not his sisters with us?" (Mark vi. 3;—I have retained the words "brother" and "sisters," used in the Common Version, not thinking it important, in the connection in which the passage is quoted, to make any change in this rendering; but the relationship intended I believe to be that of cousins.) At some particular period, the communication must have been made by our Saviour to his disciples, that he was not a mere man, but that he was, properly speaking, and in the highest sense, God himself. The doctrines with which we are contending, and other doctrines of a similar character, have so obscured and confused the whole of Christianity, that even its historical facts appear to be regarded by many scarcely in the light of real occurrences. But we *may* carry ourselves back in imagination to the time when Christ was on earth, and place ourselves in the situation of the first believers. Let us, then, reflect for a moment on what would be the state of our own feelings, if some one with whom we had associated as a man were to declare to us that he was really God himself. If his character and works had been such as to command any attention to such an assertion, still through what an agony of incredulity, and doubt, and amazement, and consternation must the mind pass, before it could settle down into a conviction of the truth of his declaration! And when convinced of its truth, with what unspeakable astonishment should we be overwhelmed! With what extreme awe, and entire prostration of every faculty, should we approach and contemplate such a being! If indeed man, in his present tenement of clay, could endure such intercourse with his Maker. With what a strong and unrelaxing grip would the idea seize upon our minds! How continually would it be expressed in the most forcible language, whenever we had occasion to speak of him! What a deep and indelible coloring would it give to every thought and sentiment in the remotest degree connected with an agent so mysterious and so awesome! But we perceive nothing of this state of mind in the disciples of our Saviour; but much that gives evidence of a very different state of mind. One may read over the first three Evangelists, and it must be by a more than ordinary exercise of ingenuity, if he discover what may pass for an argument that either the writers, or the numerous individuals of whom they speak, regarded our Saviour as their Maker and God; or that he ever assumed that character. Can we believe, that, if such a most extraordinary annunciation as has been supposed had ever actually been made by him, no particular record of its circumstances, and immediate effects, would have been preserved?—that the Evangelists in their accounts of their Master would have omitted the most remarkable event in his history and their own?—and that three of them at least (for so much must be conceded) would have made no direct mention of by far the most astonishing fact in relation to his character? Read over the accounts of the conduct and conversation of his disciples with their Master, and put it to your own feelings whether they ever thought that they were conversing with their God. Read over these accounts attentively, and ask yourself if this supposition does not appear to you one of the most incongruous that ever entered the human mind.[14]

The Jews assuredly would have questioned Jesus about any new

---

[14] Norton, 74-77.

concept of God, and these questions would undoubtedly have been recorded *somewhere* in the Bible:

> The unbelieving Jews, in the time of the Apostles, opposed Christianity with the utmost bitterness and passion. They sought on every side for objections to it. There was much in its character to which the believing Jews could be reconciled. The Epistles are full of statements, explanations, and controversy relating to questions having their origin in Jewish prejudices and passions. With regard, however, to this doctrine, which, if it had ever been taught, the believing Jews must have received with the utmost difficulty, and to which the unbelieving Jews would have manifested the most determined opposition,—with regard to this doctrine, there is no trace of any controversy. It appears, then, that while other questions of far less difficulty (for instance, the circumcision of the Gentile converts) were subjects of such doubt and controversy that even the authority of the Apostles was barely sufficient to establish the truth, this doctrine, so extraordinary, so obnoxious, and so hard to be understood, was introduced in silence, and received without hesitation, dislike, opposition, or misapprehension.

What was the business of the Apostles but to teach and explain, to enforce and defend, the fundamental doctrines of Christianity? I say to defend these doctrines; for he who reads the Epistles with any attention, will not think that the mere authority of an Apostle was decisive in bearing down at once all error, doubt, and opposition among believers. Even if this had been the case, their converts must still have been furnished with some answer to those objections with which the unbelieving Jews would have assailed a doctrine so apparently incredible, and so abhorrent to their feelings. From the very nature of the human mind, if the minds of the Apostles at all resembled those of other men, the fact that their Master was the Almighty, clothed in flesh, must have appeared continually in their writings, in direct assertions, in allusions, in the strongest possible expressions of feeling, in a thousand different forms. The intrinsic difficulty of the doctrine in question is so great. and such was the ignorance of the first converts, and their narrowness of conception, that the Apostles must have continually recurred to it, for the purpose of explaining it, and guarding it against misapprehension.[15]

Jesus prayed to one whom, by his own and frequent admissions, was greater than himself. The apostles, learning from his example, did the same, and by so doing kept intact the doctrine that God is one. The apostles, remember, were themselves Jews, and carried pre-conceptions about God into their relationship with Jesus that Jesus did not change. The Hebrew concept of God was maintained by the apostles in accordance with what they had learned from Moses, and they continued to employ the same monotheistic language of their pre-Messianic education and experience:

> The Saviour's testimony is therefore the same with that of Moses. But although this is admitted by many Trinitarians, it is said that the revelation of the new doctrine was reserved until after the descent of the Holy Spirit at the day of Pentecost. Let us look then at the preaching of the Apostles at that time, and subsequently. We find it to be exactly the same; the same language is used concerning God, without any hint that it is to be taken in a peculiar sense. These are their words: "The God of Abraham, and of Isaac, and of Jacob, the God of our fathers, hath glorified his son Jesus, whom God hath raised from the dead." And again: "This Jesus hath God raised up. Therefore, being by the right hand of God exalted, and having received of the Father the promise of the Holy Spirit, he hath shed forth this, which ye now see and hear." This language is repeated in the first six or seven chapters of the Book of Acts, over and over again; and God is always spoken of without any qualifying word, as the only Supreme Being, by whom Christ was sent, raised up, and glorified. Does this look like the revelation of a new doctrine?
>
> The same God whom the Apostle elsewhere calls "the King eternal, immortal, invisible, the only wise God, who is the blessed and only Potentate, the King of kings, the Lord of

---

15 Norton, 80-82.

lords, who only hath immortality, dwelling in the light which no man can approach unto, whom no man hath seen nor can see, to whom be honor and power everlasting." (1 Tim. vi. 15.) All these are words of the New Testament. I ask you again, Could they be made more explicit? If I, as a Unitarian minister, were to task myself in finding words to express the perfect unity and absolute supremacy of God the Father, could any words be more conclusive than these? [16]

One need only consider some verses from both Testaments to recognize a common meaning of the term *God:*

It is, therefore, exceedingly wonderful how such opinions should ever have maintained any hold in the minds of serious and intelligent men. If we collect again (and it cannot be done too often on this occasion) a few of the plain and emphatical expressions of the Old Testament, and likewise some of the New, their united force may, possibly, demonstrate the difficulty and danger that we throw ourselves into, when we depart, in any manner, from our obedience to such solemn injunctions; in which, it is evident, no more than *One Divine Person* is intended. *I am the* LORD *your God.—There is none like* ME.—*Thou shalt worship no other God.—The* LORD *your God is God of gods, and Lord of lords.—He is the praise, and He is the God.—Thou shalt fear the* LORD *the God, Him shalt thou serve, and to Him shalt thou cleave, and swear by His name. He that sacrificeth unto any God, save unto the Lord* ONLY, *he shall be utterly destroyed.—And if ye will not for all this hearken unto Me, but walk contrary unto Me; Then I will walk contrary unto you also in fury; and I, even I, will chastise you seven times for your sins.* Again: *I will forewarn you whom you shall fear: Fear* HIM *who, after He hath killed, hath power to cast you into hell; yea, I say unto You, Fear* HIM.—*For my Father is greater than I.—My Father is greater than All.—Why callest thou me good? none is good, save One, that is God.—And thou shalt love the* LORD *the God with all the heart, and with all the soul, and with all the mind. This is the first and great commandment.—When*

---

[16] Eliot, 19-20, 21.

thou prayest, enter into the closet, and when thou hast shut the door, pray TO THE FATHER *who is in secret, and the Father who seeth in secret shall reward thee openly.—The hour cometh, and now is, when the true worshippers shall worship* THE FATHER *in spirit and in truth: for the Father seeketh such to worship* HIM.

Here is a minute assemblage of the declarations and precepts of GOD, of Moses, and of Christ. They are in exact harmony, and as perfectly clear as harmonious: but it appears altogether impossible that they should ever be properly reconciled with the Athanasian doctrine: the very attempt to do it, leads us into dangerous perversions, and fills us with the most distressing perplexity. It would be well, therefore, if men whose minds are illumined with true wisdom, and who, on mature reflection, feel no danger in the received doctrine, when it is fairly discussed before the impartial tribunal of Scripture and sound reason;—it would be perfectly congenial with Christian charity, if they would with temper and perspicuity reconcile, if it be possible, the hitherto insuperable difficulties found in *that* doctrine, which have, for ages, shaken the tranquillity and the belief of multitudes (and from which the Unitarian faith is, at least comparatively, free);—that the spirits of those who are anxious to hold the truth in righteousness may be in peace.[17]

In a conversation with some Pharisees, Jesus referred the creation of man to someone other than himself. Then, in the same conversation, he speaks of God in reference to a present event, marriage. The language he used makes it impossible to conclude that he meant anyone other than the Father in both instances. Mark 10:6 (NIV) says: "But at the beginning of creation God 'made them male and female.'" Then three verses later he said, "Therefore what God has joined together, let man not separate." He who was God "at the beginning" is shown by Jesus to be the same God that Jesus referred to when he was here on earth. Jesus was, after all, talking to Jews who were operating under a strictly monotheistic understanding of God, and he used language that was perfectly agreeable to their understanding of

---

[17] Gifford, 196-198.

who God was (is).

Another comparison on this subject can be made using one text from the Old Testament and one from the New. The latter text gives the words of our Lord Jesus Christ who was quoting Moses, these passages of Scripture demonstrate that the concept of one God was not changed to a three-in-one concept:

Deuteronomy 6:4—Hear, O Israel, the Lord our God, the Lord is one.

Mark 12:29—And Jesus answered him, The first of all the commandments is, Hear, O Israel, the Lord our God, the Lord is one.

Here we have the same terminology regarding God. The speaker of the second verse is Jesus, pointing to the identical usage and application of the concept of God by those living before and after him.

CHAPTER 11

JESUS

The idea that Jesus is a man is a common theme throughout the biblical texts. By applying reasonable standards of interpretation, the idea that Jesus is equal with the Father is easily seen to be false. In trying to establish the doctrine of the double nature of Christ and of three persons in one God, Trinitarians typically focus on establishing Jesus's title, which they say is God, and Unitarians focus on that being untrue, that Jesus is now confused with the God whom he prayed to. So Christians are in a dog-fight, rarely venturing outside the parameters which Trinitarian dogma has set and limiting the discussion to the narrow focus of whether the notion of a triune god is right or wrong. Many other aspects of life spoken of in the Bible and life are lost sight of in this, as so many minds are anchored to seek proof of one position or another. Delicate and intricate subjects, such as kindness, proper mindsets, how the Christian texts do or don't agree with the Hebrew texts, are lost sight of in order to win the larger battle that was set in motion in the fourth century.

But here we are, sorting through the history and arguments. Harking back to an earlier point in this book, in the debates it is easy to lose sight of the lack of representation of the holy spirit's lack of representation in the theological development of Trinitarian thought. The issue focuses primarily on who Jesus is or isn't, on whether God could have divisibility within his nature, and so on. As will be discussed later, it is relevant at this juncture to point out the lack of argumentation involving Jesus's dependency upon the holy spirit who, it is posited by Trinitarians, is equal with the Father. With that said, Jesus's subordination to the Father is evident throughout the texts:

He is also "the Son of God"; a phrase elsewhere bestowed upon prophets and righteous men, but here [Matt. 16:16] used with particular solemnity,—"the Son of the living God,"—and with peculiar meaning; the same as when he is called "the beloved Son," or "the only begotten Son of his Father." Such words, I think, announce peculiar exaltation,—peculiar nearness to God. I doubt if we can at present understand their full meaning. To me, when taken in connection with other expressions used by our Saviour concerning himself, they convey an idea of mystery, of union with God inexplicably close; a mystery into which we can but imperfectly penetrate, because it is but imperfectly revealed. But at the same time, while the expression conveys the idea of unknown exaltation, it distinctly implies derivation and dependence. If words mean any thing,—if we are to use them according to their intelligible meaning,—the Son owes his existence to the Father, and cannot therefore be self-existent. The very idea of sonship is of derivation, and is therefore inconsistent with the doctrine both of identity and of equality. If words mean any thing, he who is the Son of the living or supreme God cannot be himself the supreme God, but must be derived from him, and dependent on him.[1]

Many of the descriptions of Jesus directly imply the Father's supremacy over him. For example, the word *son* indicates a subordinate relationship to the Father. No elaboration is required to clarify its meaning. If Jesus is equal to the Father in any way, it is by virtue of what the Father has bestowed upon him. *Son* demonstrates that the Father is the originator of what Jesus has and that Jesus is the recipient of what the Father has given him. But the Trinitarian hypothesis of the double nature of Christ was developed to circumvent the obvious import of this term and others of a similar simple nature. We are so familiar with the term *son*, just as we are with the term *father*, that when we are told that God is a father to Jesus, and Jesus is a son to the Father, these become relatable according to their common usage. The doctrine of Jesus's co-equality with the Father and of his alleged double nature makes mass confusion of such simple terms, and clouds

---

[1] Eliot, 39-40.

the understanding of Jesus's relationship with God throughout the texts:

> In his state of exaltation, after he had left the earth, God is still the acknowledged source of his power; while the very fact that he is or could be "exalted," implies his subordination and inferiority to the Being who did or could exalt him. After his Resurrection, and when about to ascend, to "leave the world and go to the Father," giving his parting commission to the Apostles, he said: "All power is given unto me in heaven and in earth." (Matt. 28:18) He did not even then say, when his personal mission on earth in the flesh was "finished"*as though he were about to resume a place, an authority, a power which he had once abandoned*"All power in heaven and in earth is mine again;" or, "All power in heaven and in earth, which of course I could not possess in that human nature which I now lay aside, but in my Divine Nature ever held and still hold;" but he said: "All power in heaven and in earth" in the exalted state to which the Father now raises me, "is given unto me." This is the obvious significance of his words, and amply borne out by other passages. "I appoint unto you," he said to the disciples at the Last Supper, "a kingdom, as my Father hath appointed unto me." (Luke 22:29) At the effusion of the Spirit on the day of Pentecost, Peter's words were: "This Jesus hath God raised up, whereof we are witnesses. Therefore, being by the right hand of God exalted, and having received of the Father the promise of the Holy Ghost, he hath shed forth this which ye now see and hear.... Therefore, let all the house of Israel know assuredly, that God hath made that same Jesus whom ye have crucified, both Lord and Christ." (Acts 2:32, 33, 36) So St. Paul: "God hath highly exalted him (Jesus) and given him a name which is above every name. That at the name of Jesus every knee should bow, of things in heaven, and things in earth, and things under the earth. And that every tongue should confess that Jesus Christ is Lord, to the glory of God the Father." (Philip. 2:9-11) What could be plainer, than that in his exaltation all his power is the gift of

God, and held in subordination to the glory of the Father? [2]

Jesus is spoken of and represented as being subordinate to the Father in all contexts, whether in prophecies of the future age or in records of past events. He is always and without elaboration placed in a position of reliance upon the Father, to the extent that whatever he taught was the teaching of the Father. This bespeaks intimacy and dependence, not equality:

> The precepts of Jesus inculcate the same important doctrine. He said to the Tempter in the wilderness, "It is written, Thou shalt worship the LORD [Jehovah] the God, and HIM ONLY shalt thou serve." The word here rendered *serve*, always denotes *religious* service. It is used, I think, in the New Testament 21 times, but *not once in reference to Jesus Christ*. Is not this as *decisive* as it is remarkable? Jesus said to the woman of Samaria, "The hour cometh and now is, when the *true worshipers shall worship the* FATHER *in spirit and in truth: for the* FATHER *seeketh such to worship him."* If Jesus had said the true worshippers shall worship God in spirit and in truth, the Trinitarian might infer that he meant the *Triune* God—Father, Son, and Spirit. I cannot conceive how it is possible for Trinitarians, who professedly worship two other objects besides the Father, to claim the character of *"the true worshipers:"* since they have no written authority, but "the tradition of the elders," to urge against this plain decision of Jesus Christ.
>
> In compliance with the request of his disciples to teach them to pray, Jesus said unto them, "When ye pray, say, OUR FATHER which art in heaven. Hallowed be the name."—*Luke* xi. 2. So in *Mat.* vi. 9. *"After this manner*, therefore, pray ye: OUR FATHER which art in heaven." If Jesus had intended to teach his disciples to pray to the *Triune* God of human creeds, is it not morally certain, to say the least, that he would have directed them to use the general appellation GOD? Had he done so, the idea of a Trinity would not have been so certainly precluded. But by teaching them to pray to one person *only*, the FATHER. to whom he himself prayed, to whom their

---

[2] Farley, 81-82.

fathers prayed, and whom he declares to be the **ONLY** TRUE GOD, he has entirely precluded even the possibility of such an inference. And is it not more than probable that it was one design of our Saviour in being thus explicit in regard to the object of prayer, to leave no room for such an inference?

Had our Saviour, in prophetic vision, surveyed the age in which we live, and had it been his intention to give instructions relative to the object of prayer in such a manner as to leave no pretext to infer the doctrine of a Trinity of persons in God, I cannot conceive how he could have employed better phraseology, or chosen more appropriate words.[3]

There are certain qualities of God that are generally attributed to Him, and are thought to apply to Him only. Among these are omniscience, omnipotence, self-existence and infinite goodness. Each of these was addressed by Jesus and he expressly denied *all* of them. Had he denied only one it would have been reason enough to show the notion that he is equal with God to be wrong. That he denied them all makes it incontrovertible.

Omniscience is generally understood as "having complete and perfect knowledge of all things."[4] This is an attribute that we assign to God, as most assume it is inherent in God's being. If we are correct in this assumption, then Jesus cannot be equal with God since he expressly denied having this quality. He always referred to the one above him as his source of knowledge. Jesus *learned* what he knew, hence he was not omniscient:

> Omniscience. This is the attribute by which he who possesses it knows all things. An omniscient being needs not to be instructed. Thus it is written of the Almighty, Isaiah xl. 13, "Who hath directed the spirit of the Lord, or, being his counsellor, hath taught him? With whom took he counsel, and who instructed him, and taught him in the path of judgment, and taught him knowledge?" Compare these words with the words of the Saviour, John vii. 16, "My doctrine is not mine,

---

[3] Morgridge, 42-43.

[4] Terry Miethe, *The Compact Dictionary of Doctrinal Words* (Minneapolis: Bethany House Publishers, 1988), "Omniscience."

but his that sent me"; and xiv. 24, "The word which ye hear is not mine, but the Father's who sent me." And again, viii. 28, "As my Father hath taught me, I speak these things." And even more strongly, xii. 49, "I have not spoken of myself, but the Father who sent me, he gave me a commandment, what I should say and what I should speak. Whatsoever I speak, therefore, even as the Father said unto me, so I speak." All this is an expression of imparted knowledge, which, however great it may be, must always be less than omniscience. And accordingly we find, Matthew xxiv. 36, and Mark xiii. 32, when asked concerning a future event, Jesus answered, "Of that day and hour knoweth no man; no, not the angels in heaven, neither the Son, but the Father." In Matthew it says, "but my Father only." We cannot escape from these words if we would. We place implicit reliance upon whatever Christ taught. We believe that God spake through him; and upon his own authority we say, that omniscience is the attribute of the Father only.[5]

We, therefore, do not perceive how such an opinion can be supported without great confusion; nor indeed without expunging very many passages from the New Testament. For example: If our Lord had really *known* the day of Judgment, by any innate perfection, or absolute and complete union of divine prescience, would he then have denied that knowledge directly and indefinitely (Matt. xxiv, 36; Mark xiii, 32), without the least caution to his hearers concerning his *omniscient* nature? Who will venture to charge him with such duplicity? He might have concealed his knowledge without denying it; by signifying that it would be highly improper (as is most likely) to reveal the particular day of judgment. But he say positively, that *he did not know it, but his Father only.*—Matt. xxiv. 36.[6]

Omnipotence is commonly understood as the quality of being all-powerful. There is nothing God cannot do except, perhaps, for

---

[5] Eliot, 49-50.

[6] Gifford, 129-131.

the limitations He has voluntarily placed on Himself.[7] The power to create the heavens and the earth is a prime example of the exercise of His omnipotence. This power was and is resident in God alone:

> Omnipotence. Jesus distinctly and repeatedly declares that he is not in possession of this attribute. He uniformly speaks of his power as being given by the Father and exercised under his direction. But the idea of omnipotence is inconsistent with that of derived power and delegated authority. Omnipotence cannot be given by one to another. In such a case he who gives must be greater than he who receives. Therefore, when the Saviour says, Matt. xxviii. 18, "All power is given to me by the Father," the word *given* necessarily limits the word *all*. The text is sometimes quoted to prove omnipotence, but we think it proves just the contrary. Again he says, John v. 19, "The Son can do nothing of himself"; and again, verse 30, "I can of mine own self do nothing." And still more pointedly, when he was asked for a certain distinction by James and John, he answered, Matt. xx. 23, "To sit on my right hand and on my left is not mine to give; but it shall be given to them for whom it is prepared of my Father." In his last conversation with his disciples he says, "If ye loved me, ye would rejoice, because I said, I go unto the Father; for my Father is greater than I." (John xiv. 28) These declarations are distinct and unqualified. We are therefore ready to receive Christ in the highest exaltation which the Scripture accords to him. But we feel at the same time compelled to believe his own words. These are the best authority. They do not teach us that he is Almighty, but that he is dependent in all things upon the Father.[8]

Self-existence is the attribute in which one has no need of anything or anybody else for their existence. Such a being necessarily always existed, and the reaches of logic suggest there would have been nobody to bring such a being into existence. God alone is capable of such existence. If it can be shown that a person is in need of assistance of *any* kind, he is not self-existent and therefore not God:

---

[7] E.g. He cannot lie—Titus 1:2.

[8] Eliot, 48-49.

Of Self-existence. This attribute implies absolute independence; an existence to which no other being is necessary; self-derived and self-sustained. But Christ himself declares a hundred times that he came not of himself, but that the Father sent him; see John viii. 42, "Neither came I of myself, but he sent me." He declared that he was indebted to the Father for the support of his existence; John vi. 57, "As the living Father hath sent me, and *I live by* the Father"; and again, John v. 26, "As the Father hath life in himself, *so hath he given* to the Son to have life in himself. I can of mine own self do nothing; as I hear I judge, and my judgment is just, because I seek not mine own will, but the will of the Father who sent me." He says also, John x. 18, "No man taketh my life from me, but I lay it down of myself; I have power [the literal meaning is *authority*] to lay it down, and I have authority to take it again; *this commandment have I received* of my Father." Which also agrees with 2 Cor. xiii. 4, "Though he was crucified through weakness, yet he liveth by the power of God." Here is a distinct and full denial of underived and independent existence. Upon the authority of Christ himself, therefore, we say that he was not the Self-existent God.[9]

The apostles undertook the responsibility of sharing the things that Jesus had taught them, so it makes sense to consult the texts they are recorded as having said about Jesus:

One of the most important books in the New Testament, in a doctrinal point of view, is the Acts of the Apostles. It contains their first preaching after they had been fully instructed in their work. Whatever they knew of Jesus or believed concerning him will undoubtedly be found there. They were impelled at the same time by strong affection for their master, by a deep sense of their former unfaithfulness to him, and by the direct command of God, to declare the whole truth. Now what is the substance of their preaching? Read the first ten chapters of that book and determine. I think that you will agree with me that it is a series of Unitarian discourses. There

---

[9] Eliot, 47–48.

is not an expression, not a single word that I cannot use, or that I am not accustomed to use as a Unitarian believer. They indeed declare that Christ is a Prince and a Saviour, that he is both Lord and Christ; but how is it that he obtained this authority? Let them answer in their own words: "Therefore let all the house of Israel know assuredly that *God hath made* that same Jesus whom ye have crucified both Lord and Christ." Acts ii. 36. "Then Peter and the other Apostles answered and said, We ought to obey God rather than men. The God of our fathers raised up Jesus, whom ye slew and hanged on a tree. *Him hath God exalted* with his own right hand, to be a Prince and a Saviour, to give repentance to Israel and forgiveness of sins." Acts v. 29. This is the utmost of their preaching; further than this they never go; and thus far we as Unitarians go with them.[10]

If Jesus were God himself, it is strange, to put it mildly, that he would be declared to be a mediator between God and man, since He would not be *between* God and man. In 1 Timothy 2:5 we are told that even in his exalted state he is a man in the position of a mediator: "For there is one God, and one mediator between God and men, the man Christ Jesus." If Jesus were God, the office of mediator would be a reduction in responsibility and stature. It would effectively be a demotion, since being a mediator signifies something other than what it is to be God:

I Tim. ii. 5, 'there is one God, and one mediator between God and men, the man Christ Jesus.' Here the mediator, though not purely human, is purposely named man, by the title derived from his inferior nature, lest he should be thought equal to the Father, or the same God, the argument distinctly and expressly referring to one God. Besides, it cannot be explained how anyone can be a mediator to himself on his own behalf; according to Gal. iii. 20, 'a mediator is not a mediator of one, but God is one.' How then can God be a mediator of God? Not to mention that he himself uniformly testifies of himself, John viii. 28, 'I do nothing of myself,' and v. 42, 'nei-

---

[10] Eliot, 55.

ther came I of myself.' Undoubtedly therefore he does not act as a mediator to himself; nor return as a mediator to himself. Rom. v. 10, 'we were reconciled to God by the death of his Son.' To whatever God we were reconciled, if he be one God, he cannot be the God by whom we are reconciled, inasmuch as that God is another person; for if he be one and the same, he must be a mediator between himself and us, and reconcile us to himself by himself; which is an insurmountable difficulty.[11]

---

[11] Milton, 19-20.

CHAPTER 12

THE LOGOS

The concept of *the word*, translated from the Greek term *logos*, as it applies to Jesus in John 1:1 and 1:14, is not easily understood, which has been admitted by theologians of all stripes. But Trinitarians have urged that these two verses, when taken out of context and interpreted in connection with each other, contain proof that Jesus is God. One of the realities about the subject of the *logos* is that it is not as clear as some claim it is, as there is no exact word corresponding to it in English. John 1:1 and 14 both contain the word *logos* and, taken out of context and put side by side, are:

1:1 In the beginning was the word,
   and the word was with God,
   and the word was God.

1:14 And the word was made flesh,
   and dwelt among us...

It is assumed from these verses, since Jesus was a man and dwelt among us, that he is the word. It is then inferred, since the third phrase of verse one says that the word was God, that Jesus is God. This inferential process involves a quasi-syllogism, whereby parts of separate verses are laid out next to each other, inferences are drawn from the newly contrived context, and conclusions are drawn. Not only is this process improper, but the whole doctrine of the *logos* is laden with difficulties that make it virtually impossible in our era to determine its precise meaning.

Attempts to illuminate the meaning of the *word* are conjectures, since the term has no equivalent in the English language. In Trinitarian theology, though, the term has been associated with Jesus, frequently limited as a reference only to him. Thus, the term *word* and the name Jesus are improperly used as synonyms for each other. That this is improper we shall see, but first I will show with what futility some have labored to construct a theology based upon the assumption that the *logos* refers only to Jesus.

The methodology employed in interpreting these two texts in a Trinitarian sense is improper because only a partial verse is used in combination with another partial verse, and a term within these two partial verses is given a particular meaning when we do not know what its meaning is. One only needs to substitute a different term, any term, for the term *word* in order to see the faultiness of the Trinitarian interpretation. I will employ, for the purpose of illustration, the rearrangement of the original order of the verses, and take them out of context according to the Trinitarian methodology. I will at the same time substitute the word *wisdom* for the word *word*, which yields:

v. 1   In the beginning was wisdom,
And wisdom was with God,
And wisdom was God.

v. 14   And wisdom was made flesh,
and dwelt among us...

By this process one could infer that Jesus is God. In verse 14 we read that wisdom was made flesh and dwelt among us, which would, once again, appear to be a reference to Jesus. So the name Jesus would serve as a replacement for the word *wisdom* wherever it appears. Looking back at verse one it occurs three times, so we substitute for it three times; when we arrive at the last phrase of verse one, by substitution we produce, "And wisdom (Jesus) was God." The book is then closed, the deductive work appearing to be done satisfactorily, all possibility of error confidently removed. A simple response that demonstrates the incompleteness of this line of reasoning is in the form of a question: What does it mean that wisdom was made flesh? Does it mean that God's entire wisdom, or some part of it, was invested in a man who lived among us? Is this the complete explanation or is there more to it? These questions reveal the incompleteness of the Trinitarian method of investigation into what the *word* represents, because a substitution is made without knowledge of what the term actually means.

Most Trinitarian expositors do not have even an approximate meaning of the *word* as it is used in this context, but some are nevertheless bold in assigning a meaning to it. This involves a violation of a simple rule of biblical interpretation: if we are to substitute words for one another, we must first know what each of the terms means *before* transpositioning them. A ready indication that this transposition is likely to produce error to some extent is that not only is the *word* said to be God, but in the second phrase it is said to be *with* God. This is clearly a difficult topic, and we will not obtain an understanding of the *word* based on a simple, literal reading. If we are to substitute words for each other, we must first know if the substitution is proper, and for this we need to know what the separate terms mean. In the present example, what does it mean that Jesus is the *word*? Is he, in an *unlimited* sense, the *whole word*, or are there limitations implied? Finding out what the *word* is is the first issue to be resolved, and if not resolved to a significant degree of certainty we must refrain from substituting other words or names for it.

Another issue to be resolved is whether the *word* is a person or a thing. In parts of the Bible it is clearly used as a thing, as when the Bible is referred to as "the word (*logos*) of God." It appears from John 1:1 that it is also a thing and not a proper person, since we are told that the "word was with God." What exactly was with God, then? The best answer is that we simply do not know.

Substitution can be used to show the absurdities that arise from the process of substitution when we do not know what the terms actually mean.

John 1:1
Substitution of terms,

    A. Where the term *word*, which is assumed to refer to Jesus only, and hence is the Trinitarian equivalent of "God the Son," and the term *God* is the Trinitarian equivalent of "God the Father, God the Son, and God the Holy Spirit":

<u>King James Version</u>	<u>Trinitarian Equivalent</u>
In the beginning was the word,	In the beginning was God the Son,
and the word was with God,	and God the Son was with God the Father, God the
Son, and God	
	the Holy Spirit,
and the word was God.	and God the Son was God the Father, God the Son
and God the	Holy Spirit.

John 1:1
Substitution of terms,

B. Where the term *word* is the Trinitarian equivalent of "God the Son," and the term "God" is the Trinitarian equivalent of "God the Father":

<u>King James Version</u>	<u>Trinitarian Equivalent</u>
In the beginning was the word,	In the beginning was God the Son,
and the word was with God, Father,	and God the Son was with God the
and the word was God.	and God the Son was God the
Father.	

Neither A. nor B. can be true, because A. yields the following:

1. God the Son was with God the Father, God the Son, and God the Holy Spirit, which is absurd.
2. God the Son was God the Father, God the Son, and God the Holy Spirit, which is also absurd;

and B. yields:

1. God the Son was God the Father, which contradicts the doctrine that there are three *separate* persons in the godhead. According to this formulation, Jesus is the Father, which is another absurdity.

Such examples demonstrate a larger problem with Trinitarian dogma: there is no definition, no delimiting factors, and therefore no concept of what it is when we refer to God. Anything may be postulated about God since neither common sense nor rules of interpretation are applied. Because of this, the various Trinitarian explanations of the *logos* simply do not make sense:

[John 1:1] is an obscure and difficult passage of Scripture. But its obscurity arises, chiefly, from our failing to consider the object which the Apostles had in view, and the circumstances under which he wrote. Upon these it chiefly depends on what meaning shall be given to the word Logos, and therefore to the whole passage in question. It is commonly supposed that his object was to declare that Jesus Christ was God, the second person of The Trinity. The Logos is taken as another term for Christ, as if the Apostle had said, "In the beginning was Jesus Christ, and Jesus Christ was with God, and Jesus Christ was God."

This explanation is thought by those who receive it to remove all difficulty, and to make the whole passage plain. But it is only because they are accustomed to it, and do not perceive the force of the words used. In fact it expresses a direct contradiction, which cannot itself be explained, except by saying that the terms used have no distinct or intelligible meaning. When we say that James is *with* John, we cannot take a plainer way of saying that James and John are two separate beings. To say that James is *with* John and that James *is* John, is a contradiction in terms. Why does the same not hold true of God and of Christ? If by the Logos we understand a personal existence distinct from God, we may say that the Logos was with God, but not at the same time that the Logos was God. To say one is to deny the other. We shall not, therefore, escape the difficulty of the passage by adopting the

Trinitarian theory. We may not be quite satisfied with our own explanation, but we cannot receive an explanation which so evidently contradicts itself.[1]

The most reasonable understanding of the logos is to understand it as a thing rather than a person. We have seen what nonsense a literal rendering vis-à-vis the substitution of terms in the gospel of John yields. The recourse we have is to consider it as a concept, like love or wisdom. Not that logos means these things, but love is a concept, and 1 John 4:8 says that "God is love," though love is not a proper person. Love is an attribute of God, part of His very essence, and we might gain some understanding by viewing the logos as an attribute of God.

It is not uncommon for things of God to be represented as being *with* Him. Things, such as wisdom, take on a richer identity when spoken of as being with Him, but do not represent real persons any more than the logos does:

> It is an assumption that by "word" John meant a second uncreated personal being alongside the One God. John elsewhere recognizes that the Father is the "only true God" and "the one who alone is God." Many have recognized an obvious connection between the "word" and what is said of wisdom in the Hebrew Bible. In Proverbs "Wisdom" is personified and is said to be "with" God—8:30. John says that the "word" was "with [pros] God." In the Old Testament a vision, word or purpose is said to be "with" the person who receives it or possesses it. The "word" has a quasi-existence of its own: "The word of the Lord is with him," "the prophet....has a dream with him." It was in the heart of David (literally, "with him") to build a temple. Wisdom is "with God."—II Kings 3:12; Jer. 23:28; 1 Kings 8:17; II Chron. 6:7; Job 12:13, 16. The latter is a striking parallel to John's opening sentence. In the New Testament something impersonal can be "with" a person, as, for example, where Paul hopes that "the truth of the Gospel might remain with [*pros*] you," present to the mind.—Gal. 2:5. At the opening of John's first epistle, which may provide just the commentary we need on John 1:1, he

---

[1] Eliot, 71.

writes that "eternal life was with [*pros*] God."—1:2. On the basis of these parallels it is impossible to say with certainty that the "word" in John 1:1-2 must mean a second member of the Trinity, that is, the Son of God pre-existing.[2]

The logos is therefore not to be understood as a real person:

The conclusion which seems to emerge from our analysis thus far is that it is only with verse 14 ["the word became flesh"] that we can begin to speak of the personal Logos. The poem uses rather impersonal language (became flesh), but no Christian would fail to recognize here a reference to Jesus—the word became not flesh in general but Jesus Christ. *Prior to verse 14* we are in the same realm as pre-Christian talk of Wisdom and Logos, the same language and ideas that we find in Philo, where as we have seen, we are dealing with *personifications rather than persons*, personified actions of God rather than an individual divine being as such. The point is obscured by the fact that we have to translate the masculine Logos as "he" throughout the poem. But if we translated Logos as "God's utterance" instead, it would become clearer that the poem *did not necessarily intend the Logos of vv. 1-13 to be thought of as a personal divine being*. In other words, the revolutionary significance of v. 14 may well be that it marks not only the transition in the thought of the poem from pre-existence to incarnation, but also the transition from *impersonal personification to actual person*.[3]

In Jewish theology, it is common to speak of something as pre-existing if it originated in the plans (or mind) of God. Trusting that God will complete His plans enables us to speak figuratively of future events as having already happened. This may explain the phrase in the first part of John 1:1, "In the beginning was the word":

It is no wonder therefore that some scholars should be impressed with its relation to the Old Testament and Rabbinic Judaism, and that the hypostatized Logos or Word in Jn. i. 1

---

2 Buzzard and Hunting, 130.

3 James Dunn, *Christology in the Making* (Philadelphia: Westminster Press, 1980), 243.

should be explained by them through reference to Isa. lv. 11, Ps. xxx. 6 and cxlvii. 15, 18, 19, along with the Wisdom figure and Rabbinic ideas about the pre-existence of the Torah (the Mosaic law).[4]

According to Franks, the Torah (Old Testament) pre-existed its actual existence, and he likens this to the pre-existence of the logos. Both were in the plans of God that would eventually be manifested. Franks then goes on to give the most likely translation of the whole verse:

This is, however, only one evidence that the personal language of Jn. i. 1 can not be pressed. Another is the remarkable parallel with Wisd. viii. 3, where Wisdom (in ix. 1 equated with Word) is said to live with God and be loved by God, and in ix. 4 to sit by Him on His throne. Finally, the text Jn. i. 1 itself is sufficient evidence when read in the original, which may be translated: 'In the beginning was the Logos, and the Logos was with God, and the Logos was Divine.' The above translation accurately reproduces the distinction between *ho Theos* (with the article), which means 'God', and *Theos* (without the article), which means 'Divine'.[5]

The logos, then, represents that which is divine, and many things fall into this category. Things from God or connected with Him are divine. God's plans, collectively and separately, are divine. Those who are instrumental in carrying out the plans of God are divine. Places are divine. Miracles are divine. How, then, do we shed more light on this elusive concept of the logos? We may start by testing suggestions and comparing them to other biblical texts to judge whether a suggestion can be sustained with any degree of reasonableness. From this approach, what is likely is that the logos is most likely not a proper person, but a concept.

As a matter of cultural and literary significance, which naturally made its way into how the letters that would eventually be canonized into the New Testament were written, the logos was a concept of

---

4 Franks, 54-55.

5 Franks, 51.

Greek philosophy. Its origin has been traced to the Greek philosophers, and its meaning can therefore be conjectured. But there are difficulties inherent in understanding concepts that were developed in previous millennia, just as there are difficulties translating concepts from one language to another. Compounding the difficulty in translating one language to another is when the language being translated is ancient:

According to this [Platonic] philosophy, there existed an archetypal world of IDEAS, formed by God, the perfect model of the sensible universe; corresponding, so far as what is divine may be compared with what is human, to the plan of a building or city which an architect forms in his own mind before commencing its erection. The faculty by which God disposed and arranged the world of Ideas was his Logos, Reason, or Intellect. This world, according to another, was identified with the Logos. The Platonic philosophy further taught, that the Ideas of God were not merely the archetypes, but, in scholastic language, the essential forms, of all created things. In this philosophy, matter in *its primary state,* primitive matter, if I may so speak, was regarded merely as the substratum of attributes, being in itself devoid of all. Attributes, it was conceived, were impressed upon it by the Ideas of God, which Philo often speaks of under the figure of seals. These Ideas, indeed, constituted those attributes, becoming connected with primitive matter in an incomprehensible manner, and thus giving form and being to all things sensible. But the seat of these Ideas, these formative principles, being the Logos or Intellect of God,—or, according to the other representation mentioned, these Ideas constituting the Logos,—the Logos was, in consequence, represented as the great agent in creation. This doctrine being settled, the meaning of the term gradually extended itself by a natural process, and came at last to comprehend *all the attributes of God manifested in the creation and government of the universe.* These attributes, abstractly from God himself, were made an object of thought under the name of the Logos. The Logos thus conceived of was necessarily personified or spoken of figuratively as a person. In our own language, in describing its agency,—agency in its nature personal and to be ultimately referred to God,—we might indeed avoid attaching a personal character to the Logos considered abstractly from God, by the use of the neuter pronoun it. Thus we might say, All things were made by it. But the Greek language afforded no such resource, the relative pronoun in concord with Logos being necessarily masculine. Thus the Logos or Intellect of God came to be, figuratively or literally, conceived of as an intermediate being between God and his creatures, the great agent in the creation and government of the universe.[6]

Let us look, next, at the literal meaning of the Greek word Logos. There is no word in English which exactly answers to it. In Latin, it was sometimes translated *ratio*, or reason, sometimes *verbum*, a word, or *sermo*, a discourse. The connection alone must determine, in each case, which of these meanings should be used. In the present case, if we translate it by *ratio*, reason, it would mean the Divine Mind or the Wisdom of God. Tertullian, one of the Christian Fathers, whose authority as a learned man is very high, understood it in this way (Tertullian, advers. Praxeam, Cap. 5). The same meaning was adopted by Le Clerc and by Dr. Wall, both of them Trinitarians, and no Greek scholar will deny that such a translation of the word Logos is strictly correct. If we prefer it, therefore, or if we think that this meaning suits the connection we are at liberty to adopt it. We have no objection, however, to the translation which is given in the English Bible, if it is rightly considered; for by the Word of God we can understand nothing else but God's power and wisdom, and it is but another expression for the Divine Mind, the Spirit of God, or God Himself. So when we read in the book of Psalms, that "by the Word of Jehovah the heavens were made, and all the host of them by the breath of his mouth," it is only another mode of saying that these things were done by the power and wisdom of God, or by God himself. It is precisely this which the Apos-

---

6 Norton, 308-309.

tle John asserts in the first verses of his Gospel; namely, the Word of God, considered as creating and upholding, is only another expression for God himself.[7]

Some have suggested that the term logos refers to God's power:

It is, then, of the attributes of God as displayed in the creation and government of the world, that St. John speaks under the name of "the Logos." To this name we have none equivalent in English, for we have not the conception which it was intended to express. In rendering the first eighteen verses of St. John's Gospel, I shall adopt the term "Power of God." It is, perhaps, as nearly equivalent as any that we can conveniently use. But in order to enter into the meaning of the passage, we must associate with this term, not the meaning alone which the English words might suggest according to their common use, but the whole notion of the Logos as present to the mind of the Apostle.

Adopting this term, we may say that the Power of God, personified, is the subject of the introductory verses of his Gospel. It is first said to be God, and afterwards in its relation to God in Jesus through whom it was manifested. Viewed in the former relation, what may be said of the Power of God is true of God; the terms become identical in their purport. Viewed in the latter relation, whatever is true of the Power of God is true of Christ, considered as the minister of God. His words were the words of God, his miracles were performed by the power of God. In the use of such figurative language, the leading term seldom preserves throughout the same determinate significance; its meaning varies, assuming a new aspect according to the relations in which it is presented. Thus, an attribute may be spoken of as personified, then simply as an attribute, and then, again, as identified with the subject in which it resides, or the agent through whom it is manifested. In regard to the personification of the Logos by St. John, which is a principal source of embarrassment to a modern reader, it was, as I have said, inseparable from the terms in

---

7 Eliot, 72-73.

which the conception was expressed, the actions ascribed to the Logos being of a personal character, and the use of the neuter pronoun being precluded by the syntax of the Greek language. St. John, then, says:—

"In the beginning was the Power of God, and the Power of God was with God, and the Power of God was God...." [8]

Norton, then, viewed the logos as representing the power of God, which may be exercised by God and hence spoken of as separate from him. When properly understood, it represents God Himself, insofar as whatever God did or created through His own power is to be attributed to Him.

It becomes clear from reading Norton and Eliot that the Trinitarian interpretation of the logos is too simplistic, given the difficult nature of the concept. There are other plausible interpretations as to what logos means or refers to, all of which are preferable to the unintelligible Trinitarian interpretation:

It pleased the Almighty, that his wisdom, power, and benevolence, should shine conspicuously and fully, or competently, in Christ his sacred Messenger; who, *faithful* (Heb. iii, 2) *to him that appointed him*, declares accordingly, *the Father that dwelleth in me, He doeth the works* (John xiv, 10); and again, My doctrine is not mine, but his that sent me.—John vii, 16. *For I have not spoken of myself, but the Father which sent me, he gave me a commandment, what I should say and what I should speak,*—John xii, 49. Now, it must appear highly unnecessary and discordant, that a Being ever possessing (according to the current opinion) *supreme perfection*, and *commands* concerning *what he should say and what he should speak.* Christ not only received them from God, but also always most willingly obeyed them. *As the Father gave me commandment, even so I do.*—John xiv, 31.

These very plain declarations of our Lord, that his Power, and his Wisdom also, were derived from the *Father*, will assist us in comprehending what is advanced in the famous passage, which introduces with great dignity, the writings of

---

the Apostle who records these declarations. By the *Logos*, or *the Word*, in the beginning of St. John's Gospel, the Divine *Wisdom* or *Reason* seems to be meant (so it is pretty generally now understood); namely, *the Wisdom of God, manifested to the World by His anointed Messenger, the Christ or Messiah, and residing in him for that purpose.* Such a large unprecedented degree of the Father's *Wisdom* (and Power) was imparted to Christ, as enabled him to fulfill all the momentous purposes of his mission. This Divine *Wisdom*, or *Reason*, we think, has much the same signification here, as the more usual *comprehensive* phrase, *Spirit of God*, the *Spirit of Wisdom and Understanding*, and of *Might or Power* (Isa. xi, 2), of which, Christ is said, in the other Evangelists, to have been full. St. John, therefore, most probably meant the *Divine Reason*, by which God had planned the universe around us. What He planned by His *Reason* or *Wisdom*, He *himself* created by His *Great Power.*—Jer. xxvii, 5.[9]

It is more than interesting that the apostle John is the only one who refers to Jesus as the logos. If, as Trinitarians postulate, the logos means that Jesus is God himself, why did the other New Testament writers not employ it in their accounts of Jesus and what Jesus taught? Perhaps this is because, a term has been selected because it can be, when taken out of context and improperly interpreted, used to support the Trinitarian hypothesis. But by comparing the different ways in which Paul and John speak of Jesus we may get better insight into the concept of the logos as it was used in the apostles' time. Paul and John each use different terminologies with essentially the same meaning, and neither suggest that Jesus is God:

As we have said, no writer of the New Testament except John calls Christ "the Word of God." Other writers use the term "image." This seems to be a favorite term with Paul. Paul never applies the term "Word" to Christ. He never calls Jesus "the Logos," but he calls Him "the Ïkon," the image of God. His thought, however, is the same. John uses a term which addresses the ear; Paul, one that speaks to the eye. As Dorner

---

[9] Gifford, 161-163, inc. footnote.

says: "The word 'Logos' is absent in Paul; he uses 'Ikon' (image). But what a word is to the ear, namely, a revelation of what is within, an 'Ikon' is to the eye; and thus in the expressions there is only a translation, as it were, of the same fact from one sense to another" That is, what John means by "the Word," Paul means by "the image." A word is a sound picture addressed to the ear; an image is a light picture addressed to the eye. They signify therefore the same thing, that is, the representation of the thought or idea for which they stand.

Hence when Paul calls Christ "the image of the invisible God" (Colossians i. 15), he means precisely what John does when he calls Him "the Word of God." He means that Christ was the positive, objectified likeness of God, His perfect representative among men. He does not mean that Christ was God,—for the image of anything cannot be the thing itself,—but he means that He was a perfect picture of God, representing in an actual human life and character the thoughts, feelings, and purposes of God. Paul seems to take his figure from God's creating man in his own image, while John goes farther back and takes His from God's creating the world by His word. As God created man in his own image by nature, so Paul assures us that Christ was in all respects the very image of His Father.

The author of Hebrews (who probably was not Paul) expresses the same idea in a still different term: he calls Christ "The brightness of" God's "glory and the express image of His person" (i. 3); or as the New Version translates: "The effulgence of His glory and the very image of His substance." Here Christ is called "the image of God;" but the word is not "Ikon," but "Karakter," a much stronger and more expressive word. It is the word from which we derive the term "character." It means "an engraved image," one wrought into or cut out of, as sculpture in marble. Hence Christ is the engraved, developed, sculptured image of God. His character is in the very image of the Divine character. His glory is a reflection of the infinite glory, and His character is the very likeness,—cut, as it were, with an engraver's chisel,—of the real soul and substance of God,—that is, the very heart of the Infinite is revealed in Jesus Christ. Here again is a very strong confirmation of the doctrine we are unfolding: that Christ is not God, but the true Son of God, the living representative, the exact likeness, of the Most High.[10]

There are various explanations given for the difficult parts of the beginning of John's gospel, and since Trinitarian explanations make little sense our searches must take us elsewhere. There are various explanations offered—both Unitarian and Trinitarian—such as those above, but one is still free to reject all of these if they do not seem to be sound. Two principles must always be observed: Whatever meaning we assign to a word or verse, it should not contradict other parts of Scripture, and it must make sense. If either of these is violated, we must not settle there but continue our search for a better meaning. One other principle is worth keeping in mind—if we know the purpose for which a writer has written, everything within the writing must agree with it and be interpreted in light of it. John gives us his purpose for writing his gospel in chapter 20, verse 31: "And these were written that ye might believe that Jesus is the Christ, the Son of God." Since it is in the prologue of John's gospel that Trinitarians argue that Jesus is God, it is fair to advert to the very same author's words and compare what is said within that same writing. John stated his purpose for writing his gospel in a concise summation, in much simpler and more familiar language than in the prologue, so we must explain his other verses in light of this. He told us that he wrote so that we might believe that Jesus is the Son of God, which is very different than what Trinitarian dogma claims about him.

---

[10] Crane, 58-61.

CHAPTER 13

HOLY SPIRIT

The subject of holy spirit in Trinitarian theology is the most under-developed regarding the three supposed persons in the Godhead. The bulk of Trinitarian dogma rests on showing that Jesus is equal with the Father, and if this is done to some degree of satisfaction it is assumed that the doctrine of the Trinity is proven. This is a false assumption:

> The most important step in their argument is to prove the Deity of Christ, that is, his equality or identity with the Father, and it might naturally be expected that this would form the next subject for our inquiry. Such is the usual course; but I have two reasons for departing from it by taking the doctrine of the Holy Spirit first. In the first place, I think that sufficient prominence is not given to this doctrine in the Trinitarian controversy. It is too often taken for granted, or accepted with almost no proof. Trinitarians, if they can satisfy themselves of the Deity of Christ, consider that their whole work is done. Very few are aware upon what slender proof the separate personality of the Holy Spirit rests. Very few are aware of what is the fact, that this doctrine was not even asserted in the Christian Church, nor made a part of the creed, until the end of the fourth century, by the Council of Constantinople.[1]
>
> The weakest point of all the arguments in support or defence of Trinitarianism, is that which attempts to prove from Scripture the separate personality of the Holy Spirit. Yet weak as this point in such arguments always is, laboring at the very start, made essential by an indirect instead of a direct and inde-

---

[1] Eliot, 27-28.

pendent necessity, and requiring a most tortuous and unsatisfactory dealing with the phraseology of Scripture, it is the very point on which Orthodox divines spend the least of their strength, as if conscious of this weakness. The personality of the Spirit is expected to come in by indulgent construction after the divisibility of the Godhead has been affirmed for the sake of sharing its attributes between Christ and the Father. So obvious is it to all minds not prejudiced by a dogma, that the term Holy Spirit, wherever it is used in the Bible, may always have its whole meaning recognized when it is regarded as expressing the agency or influence of God's Spiritual operations. We might as well attempt to claim a distinct personality for the Wisdom of God, or the Power of God, or the Fear of God, or the Love of God, as to claim it for the Spirit of God.[2]

For the doctrine of the Trinity to be established, it is just as necessary to prove that the holy spirit is God as it is to prove it about Jesus. And the so-called proofs for the deity of the holy spirit make an easy case for the rejection of the Trinitarian system because they are so glaringly wrong.

The Greek phrase transliterated *pneuma hagion* has been variously translated (note the differences in capitalization as well as word choice) as "holy Spirit," "Holy Spirit" and "Holy Ghost." The translators of the King James Version translate the phrase as "Holy Ghost" in all but four instances, whereas the New International Version translates it predominantly as "Holy Spirit." Due to the theological biases of the translators, the majority of whom are or were Trinitarian, both phrases are capitalized since the translators believed that the Holy Spirit is a third member of the Godhead. As we shall see, the phrase is more appropriately left uncapitalized since it denotes an object and not a person. The translators were fairly inconsistent in translating the word *pneuma* (spirit), as they sometimes capitalized it and sometimes left it in the lower case. There appears to have been some confusion among the translators regarding when or why to capitalize the phrase. Therefore the fact that the words "Holy Spirit" are capitalized should not cause the Bible student to infer anything other

---

[2] Ellis, 116-117.

than that the translators themselves were not sure what *pneuma hagion* is. The phrase "holy spirit" most likely refers to the exercise of God's power, his operational presence, which has been given, in some measure, to man, which is evident from the abundant contexts in which it appears.

The subject of holy spirit is one of the least understood in Christendom. What it denotes and what its function was in the lives of Moses and others, as well as how it is manifested in current times, has not been explored at length by most Christians, whether Unitarian, Trinitarian, or any other denomination. But because the doctrine of the Trinity is assumed to be true, many assign it the status of personhood without investigating the rationale for this idea. Throughout the Bible, holy spirit most frequently denotes an object, not a person:

> Jesus represents the Father as the only agent in all that was miraculous in his ministry. Much more frequent mention, however, is made of the Holy Spirit toward the latter part of his ministry than in the former, and through the Acts and Epistles, than in any other part of the Bible. This arises from the different manner in which the Gospel was set up in the world from the law. The Mosaic dispensation came with outward demonstration. External miracles, but slightly connected with persons, accompanied the Israelites for forty years, and demonstrated to them the divine origin of their law.
>
> The Gospel, on the other hand, came not with observation or outward show. It was borne witness to by God, by the miraculous powers conferred on individuals. In the words of the Evangelist, "And they went forth, and preached every where, the Lord working with them, and confirming the word with signs following."
>
> The whole evidence, on which the establishment of Christianity depended, was miraculous powers conferred on individuals. They were so operated upon by divine power, that from timid, obscure, and uneducated men, they became bold, eloquent and unembarrassed; they had a collectedness and a wisdom on sudden emergencies, to which, in their former lives, they had been strangers. They possessed, likewise, miraculous knowledge and power, could speak languages with

which they were before unacquainted. They possessed the power of communicating these divine gifts to their converts, by the imposition of their hands and prayer. The possession of these gifts not only demonstrated to the world the verity of their commission, but likewise was a source of the greatest comfort and encouragement to themselves, as it made them confident in their cause, and certain of the presence and favor of God. These powers continued with the apostles during their lives. From this circumstance it is, that the Holy Spirit is so frequently mentioned in the apostolic writings, in the Acts, and in the Epistles.[3]

The holy spirit was called the comforter because, in part, it provided the apostles with comfort that they had made a good decision to follow Jesus, a man who showed them a new way of kindness, patience, love, strength, joy, proper judgment, and other aspects of a spiritual and holy life. This is a big point of the Torah in its teachings about God, and given that first followers of Jesus were Jews, the Hebrew texts were what they knew and would have been relevant to their lives. For instance, Jeremiah 9:24 says: "But let him that glorieth glory in this, that he understandeth and knoweth me, that I am the LORD which exercise lovingkindness, judgment, and righteousness, in the earth: for in these things I delight, saith the LORD." In the New Testament, similar statements are made about the spiritual and holy life. In Galatians 5:22-23, we read: "But the fruit of the spirit is love, joy, peace, long-suffering, gentleness, goodness, faith, meekness, temperance: against such there is no law." It was this internal quality of seeking the good aspects of our being, of our humanity, that was to govern the lives of all people, whether Jew or Gentile convert, and still applies today.

But to return. The holy spirit is sometimes personified and assigned masculine pronouns. It is partly because of this personification that some Christians believe it is a real person. But the translators, whose theological dispositions have been predominantly Trinitarian,

---

[3] Burnap, 83-84.

in some places inserted the neuter pronoun *it* when referring to the holy spirit, which is rarely, if ever, done when reference is made to a person. It is acceptable to refer to an object as a person, which is simple personification, but it is not acceptable to refer to an actual person as *it*. The failure to recognize this has caused innumerable errors in understanding holy spirit. Jesus personified it to comfort those whom he was about to leave:

> And here comes in the great and sole argument on which the personality of the Holy Spirit is founded. Jesus personified it in his conversation with his disciples in his last interview with them, when he promised them divine aid. "I will pray the Father, and he shall send you another comforter," or more literally, "teacher, that he may abide with you forever, even the Spirit of truth." Here it is asked, if the Spirit were not a person, why should Christ in this place have personified it? We reply that this form of speech arose out of the circumstances of the case. He was comforting them in the prospect of leaving them. "You will not be forsaken, for my place as your teacher and comforter will be filled by ample communications of immediate inspiration. You shall not be without a teacher and comforter, for the divine communications of knowledge and power, which God shall give you, to enable you to carry on the work of preaching and establishing the Gospel, shall guide you into all the truth."
>
> Now this conversation is the only unequivocal instance throughout the Bible of personification of the Holy Spirit. To my mind it is infinitely more probable to suppose that what is in reality a thing, and is so represented in a vast majority of cases, should be occasionally personified, than that a person should be almost universally represented as a thing, and in a few instances only spoken of as it really is, as a Person. Exceptions prove a rule, not disprove it. If you consider this as proving the personality of the Spirit, then you make a solitary exception the rule, and a vast majority of cases, more than fifty to one, the exceptions. On the same principle you might make the Grace of God a person. For Paul says that he has done certain things, "yet not I but the Grace of God was in

me." So has he personified Sin and Death. But it is answered that the general tenor of Scripture represents grace as the favor or assistance of God, and not a person. So we answer that the Scriptures generally represent the Holy Spirit as the essence, power, or influence of God, and not a person.[4]

A further complication arises when we consider how the words *pneuma* and *hagion* have been inconsistently translated in different translations. As previously mentioned, at times they are translated as holy Spirit, at others as Holy Ghost, and others as Holy Spirit. The word *pneuma* (without *hagion*) has been inconsistently translated, as it is sometimes capitalized and sometimes not. For example, Rev. 3:1 says: "And unto the angel of the church in Sardis write: These things saith he that hath the seven Spirits of God..." Here, the word *pneuma* (spirit) was capitalized. What was the basis for translating it this way? Why was the upper case preferred, and what are we supposed to gain from this versus a lower-case translation? This is part of the confusion. The translators have assigned different senses to the words, producing some difficulty in understanding the concept of holy spirit. The New International Version did not use the upper case in their translation of *pneuma* in Rev. 3:1. What was the translators' basis for putting the word in the upper case in the King James Version and not in the New International Version? This demonstrates that there has been little consistency in translating these two words, which underscores a general lack of understanding of what holy spirit is.

Another potentially confusing factor in understanding what holy spirit is is that at times the phrase "Holy Spirit" (upper case) might refer to God, our heavenly Father, as another title for Him. We read in Isaiah 53:10 and elsewhere that "God is holy," and in Isaiah 31:3 and elsewhere that "God is spirit." By conjoining the two attributes, then capitalizing them according to common practice when referring to God, the phrase "Holy Spirit" emerges and may occasionally refer to the Father. In the majority of cases in the New Testament, though, the phrase refers to the influences which holy spirit produces in the lives of those who are "partakers of the divine nature" (2 Peter 1:4), a phrase which is recorded elsewhere as "partakers of His [the Father's]

---

4 Burnap, 86-87.

holiness" (Heb. 12:10):

> There are three principal uses of the term Holy Spirit when applied to God in the Scripture which we must examine. 1. Sometimes it means God himself; 2. Sometimes the power, or some other attribute, of God; and 3. Sometimes (which is the most common use) the various influences which proceed from God.
>
> First: It is sometimes used as another expression for God himself, just as the Spirit of man is sometimes used for the man himself. Of this we have an instance in 1 Cor. ii. 11, "For what man knoweth the things of a man, save the spirit of man which is in him? even so the things of God knoweth no man, but the Spirit of God." [To which I add the observation that in this verse the Greek word *pneuma* was translated twice, once in the upper case and once in the lower. We can only guess why there was a difference. —D. Snedeker] As we should not think of saying that the Spirit of man is here any thing but the man himself, so the Spirit of God is God himself.
>
> The second use of the term "Spirit of God" is to express God's power, or some other attribute. When the Saviour said, Matt. xii. 28, "If I by the Spirit of God cast out devils," he meant by the power of God; as we find in the corresponding passage by another Evangelist, Luke xi. 20, "If I by the *finger* of God cast out devils"; in both cases meaning exactly the same. So in Luke i. 35, "The Holy Spirit shall come upon thee, and the power of the Highest shall overshadow thee," the exercise of the Divine power is intended.
>
> Such modes of expression are quite common in the Bible. They are intended simply to express the exertion of God's power. Whatever God himself does, he is said to do by his Spirit, or by his word, or by his hand, or by the breath of his mouth; all of which means substantially the same thing.
>
> There are two instances in which the descent of the Holy Spirit was accompanied by a physical demonstration. Both of them are referred to as a proof of the personality of the Spirit of God, separate from the Father. They are undoubtedly the

strongest instances to that effect which can be alleged. The first of them is at the baptism of Jesus, and the second at the day of Pentecost. In the former, it is said that "the Spirit of God descended like a dove, lighting upon Jesus, and a voice came from heaven saying, 'This is my beloved Son, in whom I am well pleased.' " It was an outward token of God's approbation; the visible appointment of Christ as the Messiah. It was to this that the Apostle referred when he said, speaking of this very incident, "That God anointed Jesus of Nazareth with the Holy Ghost and with power." Acts x. 38. Observe that expression, which is used as descriptive of Christ's baptism: "That God *anointed* him with the Holy Spirit." Is it not perfectly inapplicable to the idea of separate personality?

The other instance is at the day of Pentecost, of which we find similar language used. The event is described by Peter as the pouring out of God's Spirit, and he declares that "Jesus, being by the right hand of God exalted, and having received of the Father the promise of the Holy Spirit, has *shed forth* that which was seen and heard." And he exhorts his hearers to "receive the gift of the Holy Spirit, the promise of which had been made to them." You will observe how strongly all this language confirms the view which we take of the doctrine, and how difficult to be reconciled to any other.[5]

One question reasonably interposed at this juncture is, when you think of God, do you think of the holy spirit, or do you think of the Father? The answer to this is revealing. The doctrine of the Trinity, if it had the effects on people's minds that a true and well-understood doctrine would, would result in an equal distribution between thoughts of God, Jesus and the holy spirit when answering this question. That this is not the case shows that people in reality consider the Father to be the one true God, regardless of the arguments that have been produced to show they believe in a three-in-one God:

Now I would appeal to all who hear me, if when they turn inwardly to their own minds, they find among those ideas which they have formed from the Word of God, the same

---

5 Eliot, 30, 31, 33-34.

clear conception of personality when they think of the Holy Spirit, which they have when they think of God or Jesus? Is there not something extremely vague in your ideas? When you think of the Deity, do your thoughts as often fix themselves on the Holy Spirit, as on the Father? What can be the cause of this, but that the Scriptures, from which you derive your ideas of the Divine Nature, express on every page in bold relief the personality of the Father, while they leave that of the Holy Spirit, in dim obscurity.[6]

The holy spirit, which is spoken of as the comforter, does not have proper personality, which is evident from the impersonal pronouns assigned to it:

"The Comforter" is in Greek a masculine noun, and should have masculine pronouns. But "the Comforter" is "the Holy Spirit;" and "Spirit" is a neuter noun, and should have neuter pronouns. This rule is strictly adhered to in the original; but not in our version, where in one of these extracts the neuter noun "Spirit," is followed by the personal instead of neuter pronouns. In the Rev. L. A. Sawyer's new Translation—heralded by so many orthodox trumpets—this error is corrected; and there the passage thus reads as it ought—"the Spirit of truth, which the world cannot receive, because it beholds *it* not, nor knows *it*; but you know *it*, because *it* continues with you and shall be in you." It is plain, then, that the use of the personal pronouns does not here prove personality in the subject to which they are applied; for the synonym here used for *"the Comforter,"* which, being masculine, has the masculine pronouns, is "the Holy Spirit;" which, though neuter, has in our version the masculine pronouns.

Still more; if the use of pronouns is to determine this question, then the Greek original viewed as a whole, conclusively decides against the alleged personality of the Holy Spirit. The words Holy Ghost, Holy Spirit, (both, in Greek, the same phrases,) the Spirit, the Spirit of truth, occur more than a hundred times in Scripture; always in the neuter gen-

---

6 Burnap, 73-74.

der, of course; always, of course, with corresponding neuter articles, adjectives, participles, pronouns; not once, therefore, is the Holy Ghost spoken of in all these times as a *person* but a *thing*. In this discourse of our Lord occurs the only exception; and this, where he gives the Holy Spirit the new title of "the Comforter," using a Greek noun of the masculine gender, and so of necessity or design, or both, so far personifying it. Yes, this is a solitary exception; it stands alone; and may have been as already said, a mere matter of necessity by reason of the Greek syntax. Taking it, however, in its strongest aspect, as a designed personification, it is only of figurative significance and certainly proves no personality. The single exception cannot destroy, but rather, proves the rule. The single passage, or class of passages, where the figurative expression was used on a single occasion, cannot control the more than a hundred literal and plain ones.[7]

As figures of speech go, personification is used so frequently in Scripture it seems that few things escape its application:

The principal argument for the separate personality of the Spirit is found in the four passages which I have read to you this evening from John xiv., xv., and xvi., in which the divine influences promised by Christ to his disciples are personified under the name of the Comforter. I think that if it can be shown that this personification does not, according to common Scripture usage, imply literal personality, very little argument will be left.

What is the Scripture usage in this respect? A brief examination will show us that no mode of expression is more common than that which inanimate objects and qualities are spoken of as if they were living beings, having personal properties and performing personal actions. Thus, the sea and the mountains are represented as having ears; a song, a stone, an altar, water, blood, the rust of gold and silver, are spoken of as witnesses. The sword and arm of Jehovah are addressed as individuals, capable of being roused from sleep. The ear, the

---

7 Farley, 137-138.

eye, the foot, the law, righteousness, and the blood of sprinkling, are exhibited as speakers; and destruction and death, as saying that they had heard with their ears. In the language of Holy Writ, the sun rejoiceth and knoweth his going down; the deep lifts up his hands, and utters his voice; the mountains skip like rams, the little hills like lambs; wisdom and understanding cry aloud, and put forth their voice; the heart and the flesh of the prophet cry out for the living God. The Scripture is a seer and preacher; the word of Jesus is a judge; nature, the heavens, the earth, are teachers. God's testimonies are counsellors, his rod and staff are comforters; the light and the truth, and the commandments of God, are leaders or guides. Sin is described as a master, and death as a king and an enemy. Flesh and the mind are treated of as having a will; fear and anger, mercy, light, and truth, the word and commandments of God, are exhibited as messengers. Charity is represented as in possession of all the graces and virtues of the Christian character.

Such is the usage in Scripture. It is so common that I may almost call it universal. Some of the instances to which I have now referred are also much stronger as personifications than that in which the Holy Spirit is personified as the Comforter. For instance, if you will read the thirteenth chapter of the First Epistle to the Corinthians, you will find that charity is spoken of as a living person, who "suffereth long and is kind, who envieth not, who seeketh not her own, is not easily provoked, thinketh no evil, rejoiceth not in iniquity, but rejoiceth in the truth, beareth all things, hopeth all things, endureth all things." I refer you also particularly to the ninth chapter of the book of Proverbs.

It is evident, therefore, that personification is a very common figure of speech in the Scripture, and we are perfectly justified in this mode of interpreting those passages in which the influences of the Holy Spirit are called a Comforter. We can fully account for the language, without the necessity of supposing literal personality; and we are confirmed in this view, because we find that the Apostles regarded the "shedding abroad" of the divine influences at the day of Pentecost as a fulfillment of the Saviour's promise. (Acts ii. 33.) These influences were to them "the Comforter," which brought all things to their remembrance, and qualified them to be the ministers of Christ.[8]

But lest any mistake should arise from the use of the masculine word rendered 'Comforter,' by supposing it to be a real person, Jesus fully explains himself on the first mention of the Spirit under that character. "I will pray the Father and he will give you another Comforter, that he may abide with you for ever:" and then he adds, "even the Spirit of truth; which the world cannot receive, because it seeth it not, neither knoweth it: but ye know it; for it dwelleth with you, and shall be in you."—*John* xiv. 17. Thus Jesus explains the personal word παράκλητος (comforter) by the impersonal word πνεῦμα (Spirit,) and by the following pronouns *all of the neuter gender;* which he would not have done had he believed in the personality of the Spirit. The fulfillment of this promise is a complete confirmation of the argument. Jesus said to his disciples, "These thing have I spoken unto you in proverbs:" that is, in figurative or metaphorical language; "but the time cometh when I shall no more speak unto you in proverbs." Hence after his resurrection, and the consequent fulfillment of the promise to send the Spirit, we find the figurative language entirely laid aside; and the Spirit is spoken of plainly, and without metaphor throughout the New Testament. The promise was fulfilled on the day of Pentecost, not by the mission of a *person* among them, but by such an effusion of the Spirit as invested them with miraculous powers. As the word πνεῦμα (Spirit) means *wind,* or *air in motion,* the promise was fulfilled accordingly, thus:—"Suddenly there came a sound from heaven, as of a rushing, mighty wind; and it sat upon each of them. And they were filled with the Holy Ghost, and began to speak with other tongues, as the Spirit gave them utterance"—*Acts* ii. 2-4. Here was a literal fulfillment of the promise to send them another Comforter, even the Spirit of

---

[8] Eliot, 35-37.

truth, which should be in them and abide with them forever.[9]

It cannot be overstated that the phrase *pneuma hagion* is assigned impersonal pronouns because it is a neuter phrase, which indicates a thing, not a person:

> The Greek word πνεῦμα, which is translated 'Spirit,' and 'Ghost' in the New Testament, and the pronouns standing for it, are of the neuter gender; and consequently *impersonal*. A neuter noun is not used to express the proper name of a person; nor is a neuter pronoun used instead of a personal pronoun. It would not be proper to say, "There is one God, and none other but *it*." "God *itself*, even our Father." "Christ loved the church, and gave *itself* for it." Sometimes the pronouns are translated correctly, and rendered *it, its, itself*. "The Spirit *itself* beareth witness with our Spirit." "The Spirit itself maketh intercession for us." Had the Translators *always* done so, instead of giving us 'he,' 'his,' 'him,' they would have been correct, and would have appeared consistent. In John xiv. 17, the pronoun is four times mistranslated. It should have been, "Even the Spirit of Truth; which the world cannot receive, because it seeth *it* not, neither knoweth *it*: but ye know *it*; for *it* dwelleth with you and shall be in you." In the Greek the pronoun is αὐτό, neuter gender.
>
> The Spirit of truth is contrasted with the Spirit of error; 1 John iv. 6. If the Spirit of Truth, which the Translators have *incorrectly* personified in John xiv. 17, be a *person*, then it is a *person* in 1 John iv. 6. But if the Spirit of truth be a person, the Spirit of error, with which it is contrasted, is a person also. The word 'Spirit' in both passages means the influence under which persons act.
>
> Had the translators been consistent with themselves, and rendered the impersonal neuter pronouns correctly, 'it,' 'its,' 'itself,' instead of 'he,' 'his,' 'him,' in all places, as they have in some, the appearance of the personality of the Spirit would have been almost entirely removed from the New Testament. But they were Trinitarians, who believed that God and his

---

9 Morgridge, 153-154.

Spirit were two distinct persons; consequently they gave us the personal pronouns instead of the impersonal as in the Greek.[10]

When studying Trinitarian dogma, a peculiarity may be perceived: the terms "Father" and "Son" are relational terms, whereas "holy spirit" is a descriptive phrase. Had we not become so familiar with holy spirit being considered as a person by Trinitarians, the very fact that it is a descriptive phrase would have been significant enough to indicate that it is the name of an object, not a person:

Next consider the very name by which it is called, *the* Holy Spirit. Is this the name of a person or of a thing? It is in the original language of the New Testament in the neuter gender, and the pronoun which refers to it is IT. Would this be the case were it a person? It is without a proper name. What being, what person is there throughout the universe, without a proper name to distinguish him from every other individual? "Jehovah," said God, "that is my name." Jesus was the proper name of the Saviour. The Holy Spirit is not a proper name. Proper names, names of individuals, do not admit the article before them, unless to distinguish them from others of the same name or kind. Spirit is a general term, applicable to many separate existences, applicable to men, to angels, or devils, as well as to states and dispositions of the mind. Holy is an epithet apparently to distinguish it from other Spirits that are unholy. Now does not this very language imply that there is no person intended by this expression? Besides, it is quite as often called "the Spirit *of* God." And whenever this is the case, the very words show that there is no personality intended, separate from God the Father.[11]

Throughout the Bible, *spirit* is analogized to objects, which would not be appropriate if it were a person:

The breath of God and the Spirit of God are synonymous. "By the blast of God they perish, and by the *breath* of his

---

[10] Morgridge, 148-150.

[11] Burnap, 74.

nostrils are they consumed."—*Job* iv. 9. "By the word of the Lord were the heavens made; and all the host of them by the *breath* of his mouth."—*Ps.* xxxiii. 6. "And Jesus breathed on his disciples and said, Receive ye the Holy Ghost."—*John* xx. 22. "And then shall that wicked be revealed whom the Lord shall consume by the Spirit of his mouth."—2 *Thess.* ii. 8. "The Lord breathed into his nostrils the breath of life; and man became a living soul."—*Gen.* ii. 7. "Thou takest away their breath and they die. Thou sendest forth the *Spirit* and they are created."—*Ps.* civ. 29, 30. Jesus illustrates the regenerating influences of the Spirit by the effects which the wind produces: *John* iii. 8. "While the Spirit of God is in my nostrils, my lips shall not speak wickedness."—*Job* xxvii. 3. Here the Spirit of God means the *air*, which by the agency and blessing of God, Job breathed through his nostrils.

Hence it appears that under the idea of breath, wind, and air, we obtain the most correct apprehension of the nature and operation of the Spirit of God of which we are capable. But no ideas are more incompatible with proper personality. It is absurd to speak of a self-existent and almighty person as the *breath* of another person. Spirit is essential to personality. If the Spirit of God the Father be a distinct *person*, that person must have a Spirit peculiar to himself, and distinct from the Spirit of the Father. If God be three equal persons, the third person can no more be the Spirit of the first, than the first can be the Spirit of the third. The Spirit of God can have no connection with personality, only as it is the Spirit, or power, or sufficiency, or fullness, or something else, of a real person.[12]

The Spirit of God is synonymous with the hand, and the finger of God. "The *Spirit* of the Lord lifted me up, and took me away.... but the *hand* of the Lord was strong upon me."—*Ezek.* iii. 14. "By his *Spirit* he hath garnished the heavens; his *hand* hath formed the crooked serpent."—*Job* xxvi. 13. "When I consider the heavens, the work of the *fingers*."—*Ps.* viii. 3. "But if I cast out devils by the *Spirit* of God, then the kingdom of God is come unto you,"—*Matt.* xii. 28.

---

12 Morgridge, 149-150.

"But if I with the *finger* of God cast out devils, no doubt the kingdom of God is come upon you."—*Luke* xi. 20.

But what can be more disrespectful and absurd than to call a self-existent and almighty person the *hand* and the *finger* of another co-equal person? As the hand and finger of a person are mere instruments and subordinate to his will, so the Spirit of God is represented as subordinate to his will. As what is done by the *hand* of a man is done by the *man*, so what is done by the *Spirit* of God is done by *God*. If the *Spirit* of God is the third person in the Trinity, then the *finger* of God is the very same blessed person.

To fortify his disciples against the terrors of persecution, Jesus said to them, "But when they deliver you up, take no thought how or what ye shall speak; for it shall be given you in that same hour what you shall speak: for it is not ye that speak, but the Spirit of your Father which speaketh in you."—*Matt.* x. 19, 20. "For it is not ye that speak, but the Holy Ghost."—*Mark* xiii. 11. "For the Holy Ghost shall teach you in the same hour what ye ought to say."—*Luke* xii. 12. "For I will give you a mouth, and wisdom, which all your adversaries shall not be able to gainsay or resist."—xxi. 15. By comparing these passages it appears that the Spirit of the Father is synonymous with the Holy Ghost; that the speaking of the Spirit, and the teaching of the Holy Ghost, was the same thing as Christ giving them a mouth and wisdom; and that the meaning of the promise was, that on such occasions they should have all necessary supernatural assistance.

Isa. i. 14. "Your new moons and your appointed feasts my soul hateth." Isa. xlii. 1. "Mine elect, in whom my *soul* delighteth." Heb. x. 38. "If any man draw back, my soul shall have no pleasure in him." Here is as much evidence that the soul of God is another person, as we have that the Spirit of God is another person.

Job xxvii. 3, 4. "All the while my breath is in me, and the *Spirit of God* is in my nostrils; My lips shall not speak wickedness, nor my tongue utter deceit."

Would the Trinitarian have us believe that the third person in the Trinity was, in some mysterious manner, in the nostrils of Job? [13]

And holy spirit is analogized to water, which is also an object:

> The Holy Spirit, with which the Apostles were baptized on the day of Pentecost, was analogous to the water with which the disciples of John were baptized. 'John truly baptized WITH *water*, but ye shall be baptized WITH *the Holy Ghost.*' The *Spirit*, with which the Apostles were baptized, answers to the *water* with which John baptized. But this analogy is totally inconsistent with, and subversive of, the personality of the Spirit. For as the water, in John's baptism, was not a person, or agent, so neither was the Holy Ghost a person or agent in the baptism at Pentecost. Water is often used as a metaphorical representation of the Holy Spirit. Hence baptizing with the Holy Spirit is in perfect accordance with that metaphor. Though baptizing with the Holy Spirit is mentioned frequently in the New Testament, yet the Spirit is never represented as an agent in that ordinance. It is uniformly spoken of as that *with* which the subjects were baptized, as water is that *with* which the subjects were baptized. Personality has no more connection with the Spirit than with the water. [14]

Personification is so common that few things connected with the Father escape this figure of speech. Some things are personified more than others. Things that are commonly personified are things most closely associated with God and godliness, such as love in 1 Cor. 13, wisdom throughout the Old Testament and holy spirit throughout the New. The concept of holy spirit was no exception to the common practice of personification:

> The Holy Ghost is personified—what then? Personification is a figure of speech; and by it any thing may be made to appear, so far as language is concerned, a person. We constantly use it, in familiar, as well as in solemn discourse. The Holy Ghost is personified, and that is all; being only personified, it is not a Person, any more than is "the Law"—Rom 3:19—which is

---

13 Morgridge, 150-151.

14 Morgridge, 154-155.

said to be *speaking*; or "the Scripture" (the Old Testament)—Gal. 3:8—which is represented as *foreseeing* and *preaching*; or Sin,—Rom. 7:11—which is described as *deceiving* and *slaying*; or Charity,—1 Cor. 13—because so beautifully personified by St. Paul. Remarkable instances of the personification of Wisdom were cited in the last Lecture, from the Proverbs and the Apocryphal Books of the Old Testament. Is Wisdom, therefore, or the Law, or Scripture, or Sin, or Charity, each a Person? And if the Holy Spirit be personified as the Comforter, as teaching, speaking, testifying, reproving, why any more should it be regarded as a distinct Divine Person—or still more, as God from all eternity? [15]

The belief that holy spirit is another God or is equal with the Father is simply a matter of prejudice. No person picking up the Bible without this preconceived notion would adopt such a belief. The Jews were monotheists, so it follows that the Jewish writers of the New Testament would continue their belief in one God. John, who is regarded as the most learned of the gospel writers, would not, without a specific discourse which such a change would have required, have introduced *another* concept of God. It is now alleged that he introduced, or at least articulated a belief in, two other gods, one of which is said to be the holy spirit. This perception of the character of John's writings is incorrect:

It is very observable that St. John, the most lofty and *figurative* writer of all the Evangelists, is (speaking under correction) the only one of them who *seems*, in a few passages, directly to *personify* the Holy Ghost; or to make it an agent *distinct* from God. (See John xiv, 16, 17, 26; xvi, 7, 13.) But, when all reasonable allowances are made for his exalted style, he cannot, without great affectation, be supposed to contradict himself on so important a matter:—for (besides his own intimations of what is to be understood by the Holy Spirit (1 John ii, 20, 27), his declarations that *all power* is derived alone from God the Father, are, perhaps, as explicit as any throughout the whole Bible. A remark lately made by a learned writer (see

---

[15] Farley, 141.

Mr. Lindsey's *Catechist*, 104, 105), will help us to judge of the Oriental Idioms contained in the sacred writings. He very justly reminds us that *wisdom* is made a *being* in the viii of *Proverbs*, and that *charity* is directly *personified* by St. Paul, in 1 Cor. xiii, as is also the *wisdom* of God (Luke xi, 49); but no one can possibly understand such language in a *literal* sense; unless, as the same writer observes, it be from a predetermination to support a favourite hypothesis.

We humbly apprehend that it is in the like animated manner with the last mentioned instances, that St. John, in recording the sublime discourses of Christ, has *personified* the Divine *Assistance* of God: for it appears highly injurious to suppose that this Apostle, who was himself a Jew, would superinduce another God, in express contradiction to his own writings (John 17:3), to the declarations of his beloved Master, of Moses, and all the Prophets.[16]

Worship is necessarily implicated in the discussion of who God is. Whatever one's perception of God will reflect in worship. If God is perceived as a Trinity, then one will address him/them as such. If one believes the Father is the one true God, then only the Father will be addressed as God in prayer. One would reasonably expect the belief that the holy spirit, being one of three persons in the godhead to be worshipped, would find its way into practices of worship. Of significance is that the Bible contains no examples of anyone worshipping the holy spirit, including Jesus, all of whose prayers were addressed to the Father. He never taught or practiced praying to the holy spirit:

After all this entire negation of any worship to the Holy Spirit, is it not absolutely amazing that a community of Christians, who profess to derive their religion from the Bible, can be heard to pray in such language as this, "O! God, the Holy Ghost have mercy on us"? Point, if you can, to a single passage of Scripture, in which such a petition can find the least shadow of a precedent or a justification. Here, then, is a new object of worship, unknown as such to patriarchs and prophets, to Christ and his apostles. Consider well, when you hear

---

16 Gifford, 75-78.

this petition, the commandment, "Thou shalt worship the Lord the God, and him only shalt thou serve." Examine your Bibles, and see if you can find any model of prayer, which contains such an expression as this; "O! holy blessed and glorious Trinity, three Persons in one God, have mercy on us." [17]

The holy spirit is distinguished from God in 2 Cor. 5:5 (NIV): "Now it is God who has made us for this very purpose and has given us the Spirit as a deposit, guaranteeing what is to come." Here, the "spirit" is referred to as a deposit, which is entirely inconsistent with how we would speak of it if it were God. When holy spirit is understood to be an object, it is agreeable with the development of the subject in the whole Bible.

One more example to consider is 2 Cor. 6:6: "By pureness, by knowledge, by longsuffering, by the Holy Spirit, by love unfeigned." Is there any basis for assuming that Paul departed from his train of thought here by first mentioning three *objects* (pureness, knowledge, longsuffering), then inserting a person (Holy Spirit) into a series of objects, and then complete the thought by ending it with another object (love unfeigned)? Paul develops his thoughts in such a way that precludes one from reasonably concluding that the holy spirit is being spoken of as a person. Had Holy Spirit not been capitalized in this instance, the representation of objects would have been consistent throughout the verse and would have reduced confusion. But the translators' biases got in the way, making it a tendentious rendering.

We are told, though, that the Holy Spirit can be "blasphemed against," which, it is frequently argued, is language that could be used only in reference to God. In Matt. 12:31-32, we read: "Wherefore I say unto you, all manner of sin and blasphemy shall be forgiven unto men: but the blasphemy against the Holy Ghost shall not be forgiven unto men. And whosoever speaketh a word against the Son of man, it shall be forgiven him: but whosoever speaketh against the Holy Ghost, it shall not be forgiven him, neither in this world, neither in the world to come." It is only by inference that one could arrive at the conclusion that the Holy Ghost is God because it may be blasphemed against. That blaspheming against the Holy Ghost does not

---

[17] Burnap, 79.

necessarily imply the thing blasphemed against is a person, as Robert Bowman, an ardent defender of the doctrine of the Trinity, writes:

> There are two things here of note. The first is that the Holy Spirit can be blasphemed. This does not by itself prove that the Holy Spirit is a person or that he is God, since, for example, "the word of God" can be blasphemed (Titus 2:5). However, the fact that this is the worst sort of blasphemy that can be committed suggests strongly that the Holy Spirit is God himself.[18]

The author above recognized that there are things other than persons that can be blasphemed (or spoken) against. In light of this, the most reasonable course to follow would be to first discover what the phrase means rather than to assume it is a reference to God to the exclusion of all other possible explanations.

Blaspheming against the holy spirit seems to be nothing more than speaking evil against the doing of good by people, sometimes referred to as fruits of the spirit (love, kindness, patience, good judgment, etc.). There were those impugning Jesus's character, which was meant to deride the good works he was doing:

> Our Saviour tells the Scribes (Matt. xii. 31, 32), that *blasphemy against the Holy Spirit shall not be forgiven, neither in this world, neither in the world to come.* Now those men, filled with malice, were denying and blaspheming the holy Ghost, at the very time he said these words (which indeed occasioned them), for they, with great dissimulation, affirmed that our Lord had a *Devil*, that he was confederate with *Beelzebub*, when he was *casting out demons* by the immediate cooperation of the holy spirit, or *power of God* (allusively *finger of God.*—Luke xi. 20. Aaron is said to work a miracle by the same means—Exodus viii. 17, 19). *But if I cast out devils by the Spirit of God, then the Kingdom of God is come unto you.* This verse has reference to the severe denunciation above, and plainly declares, that the Holy Spirit is no other than *the Spirit of our God*; that it is precisely so meant in the Scriptures;

---

18 Bowman, 118.

and the context shews also, that those people, the Scribes and Pharisees, were sinning against the strongest reprehensions of their own *consciences*; for they could not, as our Saviour observes, possibly *believe*, "that *Satan was casting out Satan* and thereby *destroying his own Kingdom*." They contumaciously resisted and gave the lie, therefore, on a great and affecting occasion, to their own *inward* feelings and conviction: and moreover *uttered* a most impious insinuation (Mark iii, 30—that "Jesus hath an unclean Spirit"), which, in the Gospel language, was *blasphemy against the Holy Ghost*, the all-quickening Spirit or energy of the Supreme Being! which, while it manifested by a gracious *miracle*, that the *Divine Power* was eminently present with our Saviour, did not fail to enable him to detect their inmost thoughts, and to expose immediately their malicious hypocrisy and falsehood. Hence, and from the texts below, it will appear, that the terms *Holy Ghost*, or *Holy Spirit, Power of God, Divine presence*, &c. are *identical*, and *referable* to God *alone*. It is easy to discern from the warmth with which Christ declared the dreadful consequences of blaspheming the Spirit or Power by which he acted (and from the distinctions which he makes, Matt. xii. 31, 32), that he considered it, in effect, as the blaspheming of *God himself*. [19]

Since holy spirit is not a person, then it follows that worshipping it violates the commands that supreme homage is to be given to the Father. Jesus, by example, showed us that the Father is the one true God:

Jesus directs us to worship the Father (e.g. John 4:23, 24; Matt. 6:9.), and his own example is uniformly consistent with that direction (e.g. Matt. 11:25; John 17.) He instructs us to ask the Father for the GIFT of the Spirit (Luke 11:11.) How carefully do he and his Apostles distinguish the Spirit as "the Spirit of GOD"! (Matt. 12:28; Rom. 8:9, 14; 1 Cor. 2:11.) "The Spirit" is never joined with "the Father" and "Son" in the very places where it were most natural to expect it would

---

[19] Gifford, 57-60.

be, if it were intended we should understand or interpret it according to the Trinitarian theology. For example, our Lord, in solemn prayer to the Father, says: "This is Life Eternal, to know Thee, the only true God, and Jesus Christ whom Thou hast sent." (John 17:3.) I lay stress on these words. Can it be supposed that he did not know whom he thus addressed? Not a word is said of, no allusion is made to, the Spirit. Throughout the prayer, full and prolonged as it is, this holds true. Remark, then, that he, the SON, that same Jesus of whom he himself speaks as—not God—not "God the Son"—but the CHRIST, "sent" of the Father, addresses that FATHER as the ONLY TRUE GOD. I feel that I might well content myself with this, so emphatic, so explicit the language; so memorable the occasion when it was used, when, if ever, he would speak as the case demanded; when he would declare who was the ONLY TRUE GOD; and as is the fact did declare that THE FATHER was HE.[20]

We may adduce that the holy spirit is not as Trinitarians argue, based on its absence in those parts of Scripture where it would be entirely appropriate for it to appear. This is especially so since "God our Father" and the "Lord Jesus Christ" are both mentioned in the following verses, and the holy spirit is not. This is agreeable to the idea that the holy spirit is reference to a thing and not a person. Perhaps the most profound instances of its absence are in the salutations of the epistles. If the holy spirit were a separate part of the godhead, it would be mentioned somewhere, in some connection, in the following verses. What we observe is a consistent separation between the Father, who alone is called God, and Jesus, who is called Lord, and no mention of the holy spirit:

- Romans 1:7—To all that be in Rome, beloved of God, called saints: Grace to you and peace from God our Father, and the Lord Jesus Christ.
- 1 Corinthians 1:3—Grace unto you, and peace, from God our Father, and the Lord Jesus Christ.

---

20 Farley, 142-143.

- 2 Corinthians 1:2—Grace to you and peace from God our Father, and the Lord Jesus Christ.
- Galatians 1:3—Grace to you and peace from God the Father, and our Lord Jesus Christ.
- Ephesians 1:2, 3—Grace to you, and peace, from God our Father, and the Lord Jesus Christ. Blessed be the God and Father of our Lord Jesus Christ, who hath blessed us with all spiritual blessings in the heavenlies in Christ.
- Philippians 1:2—Grace unto you, and peace, from God our Father, and the Lord Jesus Christ.
- Colossians 1:2—To the saints and faithful brethren in Christ which are at Colosse: Grace unto you, and peace, from God our Father, and the Lord Jesus Christ.
- 1 Thessalonians 1:1—Paul and Sylvanus, and Timotheus, unto the church of the Thessalonians in God the Father and the Lord Jesus Christ: Grace unto you, and peace, from God our Father, and the Lord Jesus Christ.
- 2 Thessalonians 1:2—Grace unto you, and peace, from God our Father and the Lord Jesus Christ.
- 1 Timothy 1:2—Unto Timothy, my own son in the faith: Grace, mercy, and peace, from God our Father and Jesus Christ our Lord.
- 2 Timothy 1:2—To Timothy, my dearly beloved son: Grace, mercy, and peace, from God the Father and Christ Jesus our Lord.
- Titus 1:4—To Titus, mine own son after the common faith: Grace, mercy, and peace, from God the Father and the Lord Jesus Christ our Saviour.
- James 1:1—James, a servant of God and of the Lord Jesus Christ, to the twelve tribes which are scattered abroad, greeting.
- 2 Peter 1:1, 2—Simon Peter, a servant and an apostle of Jesus Christ, to them that have obtained like precious faith with us through the righteousness of God and our Saviour Jesus Christ: Grace and peace be multiplied unto you through the knowledge of God, and of Jesus our Lord.
- 1 John 1:3, 4—That which we have seen declare we unto you, that ye also may have fellowship with us: and truly our fellowship is with the Father and with his Son Jesus Christ. And these things write we unto you, that your joy may be full.
- 2 John 1:3—Grace be with you, mercy, and peace, from God the

Father, and from the Lord Jesus Christ, the Son of the Father, in truth and love.

- Jude 1—Jude, the servant of Jesus Christ, and brother of James, to them that are sanctified by God the Father, and preserved in Jesus Christ, and called.

Another thing to be observed in these salutations is the order in which the names appear. Not only is the holy spirit missing, but the order of the two persons mentioned in the salutations is always the same: God first, then Jesus. This agrees with the supreme homage to be given to the Father. If the Trinitarian theory were true, we are at liberty to inquire why the holy spirit is so noticeably absent from these verses, and why the Father, without exception, is placed before the Son. If Jesus were equal with the Father, it is fair to assume that his name would be placed at least occasionally before the Father's. The deity of the holy spirit is manifestly negated by its absence from not only the salutations above, but from its absence in other parts of Scripture where it would be natural to appear were it equal with the Father:

> If there are three equal persons in the Godhead, their mutual love and affection must be equal. Much is said in the Scriptures of the mutual love of the Father and Son. But there is no intimation that either the Father or the Son loves the Spirit; or that the Spirit loves either the Father or the Son. If they be equal persons, their claims upon our love, service and gratitude, must be equal. But we are not required, in the Scriptures, to love, serve, or honor the Spirit. If they be equal, their love to us must be equal. But no Scripture asserts that the Spirit loves us; while expressions of the Father's love and of Christ's love are very numerous. John speaks of the throne of God and the Lamb; and Christ speaks of his Father's throne, and his own; but we have no intimation that there is a throne for the Spirit. St. Paul asserts that in the end of the world, the Son will deliver up the kingdom to God, even the *Father*; but why not the *Spirit*, as well as to the Father, if they be equal persons in the Godhead? Is the Spirit to have no share in the glory of redemption? Where the Spirit is personified, he is represented as subordinate to the will of another. He is *sent*.

He speaks only what he *hears*. But if he obeys he is entitled to a reward. The Son is exalted, crowned and rewarded for his services; but there is no intimation of any reward for the Spirit. All this seems sufficiently decisive against the Spirit's personality and equality with the Father.[21]

Our argument is now closed. Let us sum it up, and consider it in the aggregate. We have said that the Holy Spirit is not a Person of the Trinity, or a person at all, because, in the first place, it is represented in Scripture as sustaining the same relation to God that the Spirit of man does to man. In the second place, I appealed to the personal experience and consciousness of all to say, if there were in their minds the same ground and material for the personality of the Holy Spirit, which there is for that of the Father and of Christ? Thirdly, we inferred it was not a person, from its want of a proper name, the name by which it is designated being the name of a thing, not of a person, being in the neuter gender with neuter adjectives and pronouns to agree with it. Fourthly, it was never recognized nor worshipped by the Jews as a Person. The same general language respecting its office and operations is current and common in the Old Testament, and yet no one appears to have considered it a Person, or other than the power or energy of God. Fifthly, and what seemed to us demonstration, there is no instance in the Bible, from the beginning to the end, of an act of worship being paid to the Holy Ghost.... In the seventh place, we brought forward many instances, in which Spirit of God is evidently used for his power or essence, considered in action, and in all cases spoken of as *his* Spirit, in such a manner as is totally inconsistent with all idea of independent existence or action....

If, when there is in the Scriptures such a mass of evidence against the personality and Deity of the Holy Spirit, any continue to regard it as a Person, and worship it as such, all we can say is, they do so not only without one example in Scripture, without any authority whatever, except tradition, but

---

[21] Morgridge, 156-157.

against a mass of evidence which, were it possible to abstract the subject from religious prejudices, would be absolutely irresistible.[22]

One verse of note makes it clear that the apostles did not teach that the holy spirit is God. Acts 19:1-5 (NIV): "While Apollos was at Corinth, Paul took the road through the interior and arrived at Ephesus. There he found some disciples and asked them, 'Did you receive the Holy Spirit when you believed?' They answered, 'No, we have not even heard that there is a Holy Spirit.' So Paul asked, 'Then what baptism did you receive?' 'John's baptism,' they replied. Paul said, 'John's baptism was a baptism of repentance. He told the people to believe in the one coming after him, that is, in Jesus.' On hearing this, they were baptized into the name of the Lord Jesus."

So, could it be that *after* the baptism performed by John (v. 3), they had not even heard that there was a holy spirit? Here are two daggers in the heart of Trinitarian dogma. Not only had the recent converts not even heard of the holy spirit, they had not heard of it *after* their baptism, which flies in the face of the supposed Baptismal Formula inferred from Matt. 28:19. The record of John's baptism was that they were baptized into the name of Jesus only, which would lead them to continue to do good works and lead holy, spiritual lives.

---

22 Burnap, 88-90.

CHAPTER 14

NAMES AND TITLES

The names and titles of the Father demonstrate that He is the supreme God over all of creation, including Jesus. And when God assigned names to people, their names demonstrated their active inclusion in a plan which God intended to carry out. The given names commonly included a reference to the Father, and were not limited to people—places were also assigned names in the same way. The name "Jerusalem," for example, means "God is our peace." Jerusalem was and is intended as a place where everyone would dwell in peace. John's vision of a new Jerusalem descending out of heaven is consistent with the idea that God's peace will ultimately reign in that city (*see* Rev. 21:2). Since God made a place which will be peaceful, our affections are directed to the provider, God, more than to the provision. As we have seen, this is how Jesus approached everything, inasmuch as he always directed man's primary affections to worship the one who is above him—God.

Jesus was given names and titles that are *representative* of some quality of God or of a plan of His. Trinitarians contend that these names and titles imply that Jesus is equal with the Father, rather than His representative. As we shall see, inferring that Jesus is God because his name literally means "God is our salvation" would be no different than concluding that Jerusalem is the God of peace. God implemented a nomenclature that recognized Him as the originator, or chief architect, of those plans which are spoken of in Scripture. When the tenor of Scripture is taken into consideration, it is clear that Jesus was the Father's representative, and as His representative was not His equal.

Since Trinitarian dogma is based on a collection of inferences, we may isolate the inferences and see if they are reasonable. Trinitarians place great emphasis on inferences drawn from names and titles given to Jesus; names which, it is said, could only be spoken of him if he were

God. In respect to this line of reasoning we will examine only those arguments that are attempts to show Jesus to be equal with God. So much emphasis is placed in Trinitarian theology on proving Jesus to be equal with God that there is little need to belabor the issue by examining the relatively few arguments that are given in favor of the holy spirit being God.

THE NAME JESUS

As previously discussed, "Jesus," in Hebrew, means "God is our salvation." When the name is interpreted literally and applied narrowly, some believe it shows Jesus to be God in the capacity of a savior. That this is not the case is easily seen from other instances in which names with similar meanings were given to people or places. The name "Jerusalem" literally means "God is our peace," but nobody infers from this that Jerusalem is God. The principle of agency is applicable in instances in which people and places are given names that incorporate a reference to God, or, in some cases, in which the person is actually called God. Agency is the Hebrew concept of representation:

> The main point of the Jewish law of agency is expressed in the dictum, 'A person's agent is regarded as the person himself.' Therefore any act committed by a duly appointed agent is considered as having been committed by the principal.[1]

The judges of Israel, who were called gods[2] by virtue of their work being in accordance with God's purposes and sense of justice. They became judges, according to the texts, by God's appointment, and in recognition of the origin of their authority were given a similar title as God, with the lower case *g* in *god* designating the lower sense in which it was to be understood. That much was obvious. Nobody in their right mind would have confused a judge with God. Regarding the name Jesus and in accordance with the texts about him, he was given a name that recognized a part of God's plan he represented, so is called "savior."

---

[1] *Encyclopedia of Jewish Religion* (New York: Adama Books, Werblowsky and Wigoder, eds., 1991), "Agency."

[2] Exodus 22:28: Thou shalt not revile the gods, nor curse the ruler of the people.

The absurdity of the claim that names literally identify a person can be seen when considering that Peter himself was called "Satan" by Jesus: "But he (Jesus) turned, and said unto Peter, Get thee behind me Satan: thou art an offence unto me: for thou savourest not the things that be of God, but those that be of men" (Matt. 16:23). Jesus, by employing the strongest terms available to him, called Peter, a man who supported and promoted Jesus as the messiah, got Peter's attention by calling him the harshest name available. Peter was interested in human comforts, particularly his own, wishing Jesus would not depart but stay and restore the Kingdom to Israel immediately. This temporary name for Peter is not to be understood literally or even as a formal name for him. The principle of agency dissolves the difficulty in such instances.

THE NAME IMMANUEL (or, EMMANUEL)

In Matthew 1:23, we are told that Jesus's name shall be "Emmanuel": "Behold, a young woman shall be with child, and shall bring forth a son, and they shall call his name Emmanuel, which being interpreted is, God with us." Some Trinitarians have argued that this implies that Jesus is literally God with us, which is as erroneous as believing that Jerusalem is literally the God of peace. Wainwright, himself a Trinitarian, recognizes this:

> [Matt. 1:23] can be translated in two ways:
> And they shall call his name Immanuel; which is, being interpreted, God with us.
> And they shall call his name Immanuel; which is, being interpreted, God is with us....
> The translation "God with us" implies that Jesus is God. The translation "God is with us", however, may mean no more that the coming of Jesus is an instance of God's activity among men. Because of its ambiguity this passage cannot be used as evidence that Jesus was called God.[3]

Agreeing with the second interpretation given by Wainwright above ("God is with us"), *Webster's New World Bible Dictionary* says:

---

[3] Wainwright, 72.

Immanuel, a name meaning "God (is) with us," given by Isaiah to the child to be born to a young woman as a sign from God to Ahaz that he would be successful against the enemies of Israel because God was with the Israelites (Isa. 7:14). The passage in Isaiah has traditionally been taken to be a prophecy of the coming of the Messiah; the Gospel of Matthew interprets the passage as referring to the virgin birth of Jesus (Matt. 1:23). "Immanuel" is interpreted by Christians to mean that God is with man in the person of Jesus Christ.[4]

Though the title "Immanuel" is interpreted by some to mean God literally was Jesus, this is simply a matter of bias. There is nothing in the text that suggests that this literal interpretation is the correct one to the exclusion of all others. Since God was "with the Israelites" because a child would be born to a young woman, and this would be a sign to Ahaz that God really was with the Israelites, the same principle just as readily applies to Jesus:

The first is Isaiah 7:14, cited and applied to Christ in St. Matthew's Gospel, 1:23: "Behold, a virgin shall conceive, and bear a son, and shall call his name Immanuel, which (Immanuel) being interpreted is, God with us." The whole force of the argument for our Lord's Supreme Deity, drawn or attempted to be drawn from this passage, consists in the significance of a Hebrew name, and its being applied in Matthew to Christ. But it was a common Hebrew custom to give names to children, significant or commemorative of Providential or Divine favors expected, or conferred at the time. For one example of this, you have the case of Hagar's child, whom Abram was directed by the angel to call Ishmael, which signifies, God shall hear, or God hath heard. Gen. 16:11. Admitting that the passage in Isaiah was strictly prophetic of our Lord, even Bishop Lowth says that in its "historical" or primary sense it referred to a child then, that is, in the prophet's time, to be born; and that before he should reach the age of knowing to refuse the evil and choose the good, that is, within a few years, (compare 8:4,) the enemies of Judah should be destroyed. (Lowth's Is.

---

4 *Webster's New World Dictionary* (New York: Simon and Schuster, Inc., 1986), "Immanuel."

vol. ii. 85.) Hence that child was to be called "God with us;" God then manifesting Himself remarkably for the rescue of His people. Take, then, "the higher secondary sense" in which it is applied in Matthew to Christ, and the same meaning results. At his Advent, God was in him about to bestow the choicest spiritual blessings on mankind, to work a far higher deliverance than that of Judah. In this sense, most gratefully do all Christian Unitarians believe, that Jesus is IMMANUEL, GOD WITH US.

But, further to show the utter futility of any attempt to prove the Supreme Deity of Christ from the application of this name to him, think of the consequences to which such a mode of reasoning must lead. The argument proves, if it prove any thing, altogether too much. If the name Immanuel applied to Christ prove him to be verily God, what shall we say of the name "Abiel," which is, being interpreted, "God my Father;" or "Eli," "My God;" or "Elihu," "My God Himself;" or "Elijah," "God the Lord, or Jehovah God;" or "Ithiel," "God with me"? Well might the late Prof. [Moses] Stuart admit that*"To maintain, as some have done, that the name 'Immanuel' proves the doctrine in question, (Christ's Divine nature,) is a fallacious argument. Is not Jerusalem called 'Jehovah our righteousness'? And is Jerusalem divine because such a name is given to it? (Letters to Channing, Miscel. 148.)[5]

It is sometimes asserted that the name Immanuel—"God is with us"—given to Jesus proves that he is God. If that were so, then the child born soon after the prediction given by Isaiah in the days of Ahaz would also have been God. The name, however, does not tell us that Jesus is God, but that in his life God had intervened to save his people. The parents who in Old Testament times called their son Ithiel (Prov. 30:1)—"God is with me"—did not believe their offspring to be deity. Names of this type indicate the divine event associated with the life of the individual so named. God, the Father of Jesus, was certainly with Israel as He worked through His

---

[5] Farley, 108-109.

unique Son. In the life of Jesus, the Son of God, God had visited His people.[6]

Another indication that Jesus was not literally God with us is that he was not called Immanuel anywhere in the New Testament. Just as with the so-called Baptismal Formula, which itself was not carried out, Jesus was not called Immanuel by his followers. If this name were as decisive as some insist, we would expect the name Immanuel or the title *God* to have been given to Jesus virtually everywhere he was addressed or alluded to in the Bible. That he was not called by this name is proof that no one took the name literally.

A fundamental distinction will perhaps increase our appreciation of the concept of agency. The originator of a plan is the person *from* (Greek, *hypo*) whom a thing is given. The agent is the mediator, or the person *through* (Greek, *dia*) whom the thing is given. God is the originator of all good things and Jesus is now the mediator through whom these things are distributed. The distinction between *dia* and *hypo* is:

> The preposition *dia*, here translated by, and which occurs nearly three hundred times in the New Testament, universally signifies instrumental agency in distinction from *hypo*, which almost universally implies primary original operation and causation. Those who wish fully to understand the subject, can find no difficulty in ascertaining the correctness of this remark. And, on this ground, what can be plainer than that Jesus is not possessed of almighty power; that, supposing him to have pre-existed, he was but the agent of God in the production of the world; a being, therefore, both distinct from him, and inferior to him.[7]

Even in his greatest capacity, Jesus is still an agent of God. While here on earth he was His representative, and now, according to Ephesians 1:20, being seated at "the right hand of the Father," he still is His representative. Jesus will be seated at the right hand of the Father, until that day "when he shall have delivered up the kingdom to God,

---

6 Buzzard and Hunting, 132.

7 Hyndman, 125-126.

even the Father; when he shall have put down all rule and all authority and power. And when all things shall be subdued unto him, then shall the Son also himself be subject unto him that put all things under him, that God may be all in all" (1 Cor. 15:24, 28).

THE NAME ELOHIM AND OTHER PLURAL WORD ENDINGS

In the Hebrew Bible, *Elohim* is typically translated into English as "God," though a more literal translation is "gods" since it has a plural word ending. For reference, *cherub* is one angel, *cherubim* means two or more. Some think the plural ending of this word *Elohim* is proof of multiple persons in God, with the number of persons being fixed, by other inferences, at three. This is not the correct, and certainly not the only, understanding of the title *Elohim.*

It is common to speak of those in authority in the plural. This figure of speech is known as a plurality of majesty, and is given as a title of respect for one who is sovereign. It is a common Hebrew idiom that, when properly understood, underscores the Father's unrivaled majesty:

> Mr. Christie, in his discourses on the Unity of God, says, "that in all languages there are words of a plural termination, that have a singular signification, and that this is an idiom of the Hebrew language, and is acknowledged to be so by some of the best Trinitarian critics themselves."
>
> Wilson, in his Hebrew Grammar, 270, says, "Words, that express dominion, dignity, majesty, are commonly put in the plural."
>
> Thus it is evident to the mere English scholar, that the Hebrew names for God, which have plural terminations, may, according to a common rule of syntax, be used as singular, to denote but one.[8]

The frequency with which words with plural endings refer to only one person or thing negates conceiving of God as a plurality of persons:

---

8 Morgridge, 103.

We must also refer to two arguments, which, although they are abandoned by the most learned Orthodox critics, are still insisted upon by many persons. The first is, that the Hebrew word "Eloheem," translated God, is in the plural number, indicating, as is supposed, a plurality of persons in the Godhead. Our answer to this is the same which is given by John Calvin and Professor Stuart, whose orthodoxy will not be questioned, and is in these words: "For the sake of emphasis, the Hebrews commonly employed most of the words which signify Lord, God, &c., in the plural form, but with the sense of the singular." In proof of which, I refer to Exodus vii. 1, where the word *god* is applied to Moses, "And the Lord said unto Moses, See, I have made the a god to Pharaoh." The Hebrew is here in the plural, and, literally translated, would be *gods*. A similar passage occurs in 1 Sam. xxviii. 13, where the word *gods*, in the plural number, is applied to Samuel. In fact, this plural form to nouns of a singular number is a common idiom in the Hebrew language where intensity of meaning is expressed. The names of many of the heathen idols, as of Baal, of Dagon, of Ashtoreth, Beelzebub, and even of the golden calf made by Aaron, Ex. xxxii. 4, are all in the plural number. So in Gen. xxiv. 9, where it is said the servant put his hand on the thigh of Abraham his master, the word master is in the Hebrew plural, that is, *masters*. The same mode of expression occurs in other places, of Potiphar, of Pharaoh, and of Joseph, all of whom are spoken of in the plural number, as a token of unusual respect. I have before me no less than fifty instances, in which words having a singular meaning are in the plural form, according to the Hebrew usage. As in Prov. i. 20, "Wisdom crieth without; she uttereth her voice in the street"; the Hebrew word for wisdom is in the plural. In the same manner, I can give you instances in which the words salvation, love, truth, desolation, death, pride, and many others, are in the plural form in the Hebrew, though translated in the singular. These considerations are enough to show that the use of the word Eloheem is, according to Professor Stuart's explanation, nothing but a Hebrew idiom, upon which no doctrine of a plurality of persons can be built.[9]

The *Encyclopedia of Religion and Ethics* (1913) says:

"It is exegesis of a mischievous sort that would find the doctrine of the Trinity in the plural form *Elohim*."

There are various terms translated as *God* in Scripture, and each has unique connotations. *Elohim* is generally thought to be expressive of God's majesty and power:

Of the two principal terms, ELOHIM and JEHOVAH, by which the Hebrew writers denote the Supreme Being, the former was the older, as it was also the more general in meaning and application. By its etymology, the word Elohim was expressive of power; as though God were thought of as pre-eminently the Mighty One; much, indeed, as we now employ the term Almighty.[10]

If the plural ending indicated a plurality of persons in God, this, if anything, would teach a plurality of Gods, which would be polytheism:

If the word *Aleim, Adonim,* &c. necessarily implies plurality at all, it denotes a plurality of Gods. It is impossible to translate the word *Aleim* so as to favor the Trinitarian hypothesis. It must be rendered either God, or Gods. If it be rendered God, the idea of a plurality does not appear; if it be rendered Gods, we have a plurality of Gods, which no Christian will admit. Dr. Wardlaw, pressed with this difficulty, has translated Deut. vi. 4, "Hear, O Israel, JEHOVAH, OUR GODS (ALEIM) IS ONE JEHOVAH." (Wardlaw, Andover ed. 1815; 11.) Mr. Robbins thinks the plural termination implies a plurality of persons. After giving a few examples, such as "Remember the Creators," he says, "These texts of Scripture seem to establish the fact that there is a plurality of persons in God, though they do not fix the number." (Robbins on the Trinity, 31.)

If the word *Aleim* necessarily implies plurality, how is it

---

[9] Eliot, 15-16.

[10] Smith, 69.

that the Jews have never understood it in that sense, when applied to God? That they have not so understood it, is certain from the fact, that, in the Septuagint, they have always translated it in the singular number.[11]

Most Jews understand the word *Elohim* to be singular, implying only one being. In some cases, the word *Elohim* is applied to things! Many Christians today interpret the Hebrew Bible vastly differently than the Jews do, which, to say the least, is presumptuous. It was written to a particular people who understood its primary tenets and passed these tenets on through the centuries. Those who convert to a belief in Jesus as the messiah would still do well to build upon the monotheistic foundation revealed by God to the Jews rather than reinterpret what was first revealed to them:

> The Jews have never been Trinitarians. The very people by whom, and for whom, the Scriptures of the Old Testament were written, in their own language, and from whom we have derived all our knowledge of that language, have always maintained the doctrine of the Unity of God, in opposition to a plurality. Is it possible that they could have remained ignorant, to this day, of the true meaning of a most important word in their native tongue; a word connected with every part of their religion? If we suppose the Jews to have been thus ignorant, is it possible that Jesus Christ and the Apostles should not have corrected their error, if indeed it was an error? Yet they have always translated the *Aleim, Adonim,* &c. when they denote God, by a word absolutely of the singular number.[12]

The term *Elohim* is also given to inanimate objects, such as idols, which by itself should arrest the attention of anyone trying to prove a plurality of persons in God:

> *Aleim* is not only used to denote one single person, but is frequently applied to an *idol.* Let the reader critically examine Exodus xxxii. 3, 4, 7, 8, 31, and he will find *Aleim,* when used

---

11 Morgridge, 101-102.

12 Morgridge, 102.

to denote the golden calf that Aaron made, rendered Gods, though neither Moses the writer, nor the translators, had the least suspicion that there was a plurality of persons in that dumb idol.

By consulting Judges viii. 33, and xvi. 23, 24, it will appear that the plural *Aleim* is no less than five times used to denote one single idol, which was never thought to possess a plurality of persons; and that it is translated *god*, not *gods*, as in the case of the golden calf. 1 Kings, xi. 33: Ashtoreth, the goddess of the Zidonians, Chemosh, the god of the Moabites, and Milcom, the god of the children of Ammon, are designated by the plural word *Aleim*, though each of these idols was but one person. If other examples are necessary, the reader may consult Num. xxv. 1-5; Deut. iv. 7; 1 Sam. iv. 5-8; 1 Kings, xi. 5; 2 Kings, i. 2, xix. 37. [13]

There are some Trinitarians who have recognized that a plurality of persons in God cannot be argued from the word *Elohim*, but many still believe plurality is implied. Therefore this subject warrants more explanation than would otherwise be necessary.

Elohim is not the only plural word that Trinitarians use as proof of their doctrines. Plural pronouns, such as *us* in Genesis 1:26 and in a few other verses, have been given great weight by those who believe they find an expression of a triune God in plural pronouns. But it is easy to see that plural word endings and plural pronouns are the same type of expression, sometimes called a "plurality of excellence":

The other argument to which I refer is of a similar sort. It is founded upon the words, Gen. 1:26, "Let us make man in our image, after our likeness," which we also regard as an idiomatic mode of expression, commonly called the plural of excellence or of dignity.... We might quote other passages showing the same use of the plural, but it is not needful, as the argument is abandoned by a large part of Trinitarian writers. Martin Luther, Grotius, Bishop Patrick, Dr. South, Dr. Samuel Johnson, Archbishop Whately, are all good Orthodox

---

[13] Morgridge, 104-105.

authorities, and all of them agree with us on this point.[14]

Just as the term *Elohim* is assigned to single persons and objects, the pronouns *we* and *us* are applied to single persons, usually sovereigns:

The following examples from the Scriptures further illustrate this universal custom.

Rehoboam, king of Israel, uses the pronoun *we* when speaking of himself, thus, "What counsel give ye, that *we* may answer this people, who have spoken to *me*."—1 *Kings*, xii. 9. See also 2 *Chron*. x. 6—9.

Artaxerxes, king of Persia, uses the pronoun *us* when speaking of himself, thus "The letter which ye sent unto *us*, hath been plainly read before *me*."—*Ezra*, iv. 18.

Zedekiah, king of Judah, speaks of himself in the same manner, thus, "As the Lord liveth, that made *us* this soul, I will not put thee to death."—*Jer*. xxxviii. 16.

Who would infer from this manner of speaking. that in each of these kings there was a plurality of persons? Nor is this manner peculiar to kings. Christ uses the words *we* and *our*, when speaking of himself, this, "Verily, verily; I say unto you *we* speak that *we* do know, and testify that *we* have seen; and ye receive not *our* witness: If I have told you earthly things, and ye believed not, how shall ye believe, if *I* tell you heavenly things?"—*John* iii. 11, 12.

St. Paul, in describing his situation and feelings, uses the pronouns *we, our, us*, almost as frequently as *I, my, me*. And where is the writer, or the public speaker, who does not employ the same style? Are we to believe that every preacher and every orator of the present day, who says *we, our, us*, when he means no one but himself, employs a phraseology indicative of a plurality of persons in himself? If not, why should we believe God to be a plurality of persons, because in three or four instances he has spoken in this manner? [15]

Let us pass now to examine some of the arguments by

---

[14] Eliot, 17.

[15] Morgridge, 107-108.

which it is attempted to maintain the doctrine. We are referred to the use of the plural pronouns in the Old Testament, where God speaks of Himself, and of the plural form of the Hebrew proper names of the Deity. In the first case, only three instances occur in the whole of the Old Testament. "And God said, Let *us* make man in our image, after our likeness." (Gen. 1:26.) "And the Lord said, Go to, let *us* go down." (Id. 11:7.) "Also I heard the voice of the Lord, saying, Whom shall I send, and who will go for *us?*" (Isa. 6:8.) Now it is an obvious answer to any argument drawn from such citations, that if these *three* seem to indicate a plurality of persons in the Godhead, the supposition is utterly rebutted by the fact, that the singular pronoun is used thousands on thousands of times, implying that God is but one Person. Besides, it is a common idiom in all languages, and in every age, for persons in authority to speak of themselves in the plural; as, for example, "We, Victoria, by the Grace of God, Queen," etc. Nothing is more common in the Old Testament. In Ezra, Artaxerxes, king of Persia, begins his royal reply, "The letter which you sent unto *us*"—and proceeds, as if to show the idleness of the argument under consideration—"hath been plainly read before *me*." (4:18.) That this idiom is only a common one, and by no means indicative of any plurality of persons in the being using it, is proved conclusively in that the same Lord or Jehovah who in the second of the two passages cited from Genesis says, "Let *us* go down," says in another, with a precisely similar purpose, *"I* will go down." (18, 21.) In the second case, the plural forms of Hebrew names of God, the simple explanation is found in what the best Hebrew Grammars say. Wilson, in his (P. 270), says: "Words that express dominion, dignity, majesty, are commonly put in the plural." And Prof. Stuart, in his (P. 326), says even more distinctly: "For the sake of emphasis, the Hebrews commonly employed most of the words which signify Lord, God, etc., in the plural form, but with the sense of the singular. This is called the *pluralis excellentiæ*." Learned Trinitarians, Romanists, as Bishop Tostat, Cardinal Cajetan, Bellarmine—Protestant, as Calvin, Grotius, South, Campbell, Michaelis, Rosenmüller, with a host of others, among whom are the best critics and lexicographers, alike recognize the rule of the Hebrew syntax. Trinitarians being our authority, the point is too plain to be longer dwelt upon. Not even a plurality of persons in the Godhead, much less any definite plurality such as a trinity, can be with any propriety argued from the plural form of Hebrew words.[16]

One might wonder why plural pronouns are so rarely applied to God. Since they express majesty, excellence and dominion, it might be inferred that they were not applied more frequently to Him in order to prevent the very polytheistic opinions that have proliferated:

> "If therefore we consider," says Mr. Yates, "how common throughout the world has been the use of plural pronouns to express the dignity and authority of the speaker, and that in the Scriptures this phraseology is employed by a Prophet, an Apostle, or a Prince, we cannot be surprised, that in three instances the King of Kings should employ the same majestic language. The wonder is, that the examples are so rare. Perhaps this form of expression was in general studiously avoided, in order to preserve the great doctrine of the Unity of God in one person, from the possibility of misapprehension." [17]

It is so common to represent a ruler in the plural that it goes virtually unnoticed. On the other hand, a group of persons representing themselves in the singular is entirely improper:

> A plurality of persons, when speaking of themselves, never say *I, my, me, mine, myself.* There is no rule, or custom, known among men, to justify such a style. Yet God always speaks of himself in the use of the singular pronouns, except in three or four cases. This proves, beyond all debate, that God is but one individual person. One person can say *we, our, us;* but a plurality of persons cannot say *I, my, me, mine, myself.* [18]

---

16 Farley, 41-42.

17 Morgridge, 108.

18 Morgridge, 108-109.

THE REPETITION OF PHRASES

Once the idea of a triune god became more popular, it was only a matter of time before proof for it would be sought in the subtlest nuances of Scripture. Plural word endings were one place to look, the repetition of phrases was another. Isaiah 6:3 and Revelation 4:8 contain a similar repetition of phrases. Isaiah 6:3 says: "And one cried to another, and said, Holy, holy, holy, is the Lord of hosts; the whole earth is full of his glory"; and Revelation 4:8 says: "And the four beasts had each of them six wings about him; and they were full of eyes within: and they rest not day and not, saying Holy, holy, holy, Lord God Almighty, which is, which was, and is to come." In these verses the word *holy* was simply repeated to intensify the sense of God's holiness:

> Hebrew is deficient in adjectives....Adjectives that do exist in Hebrew have no comparative or superlative forms....The idea "very deep" is literally "deep, deep" (Eccl. 7:24); the "best song" is literally "song of songs" (compare "king of kings"); "holiest" is literally "holy, holy, holy" (Isa. 6:3).[19]

In spite of this, repetition of phrases continues to be used to support a plurality of persons in God. This is a classic example of reinterpreting the Bible in light of a pre-established system of beliefs. Another example in which the repetition of words occurs is Jeremiah 22:29: "O earth, earth, earth, hear the word of the Lord"—are there three earths? Ezekiel 21:27 says: "I will overturn, overturn, overturn, it..." Clearly this figure of speech is useful is an intensifying expression, common in all languages, and meant to draw our attention to a given thing, and not prove such an abstruse notion as multiple people existing in one being.

---

[19] Larry Walker, "Biblical Languages," in *The Origin of the Bible;* Philip Wesley Comfort, ed. (Wheaton, IL: Tyndale House Publishers, 1992), 217.

THE TERM GOD

In English versions of the Hebrew Bible, the word "God" is primarily translated from two Hebrew words, *Elohim* and *Jehovah*. In the New Testament, the word "God" is translated from the Greek word (transliterated as) *Theos*. Many Trinitarians believe that the title "God," in the three or four cases in which it is thought to be applied to Jesus, is applied to Jesus in the highest sense, thus deriving his supposed equality with the Father. With this line of reasoning Trinitarians either ignore or fail to apply the common principle that words and titles are used in higher and lower senses. When the same title is applied to both Jesus and God, it is necessarily used in a lower sense in its application to Jesus. Once again, it must be understood that representation is implied, not equality.

A modern analogy of a title that has a higher and lower sense is the title "boss." Within a large corporation one may have many bosses, some are higher in authority than others. The supreme boss within a company might be the owner or the chairman. He delegates authority to others, who by virtue of their derived authority are also called boss. There are typically many levels of management, each manager, or boss, with his or her own degree of authority and responsibility. A lower-level employee will have an immediate boss as well as higher-level, more remote bosses. The higher-level bosses typically have authority over the lower-level bosses.

This same principle applies to the term "God." There were many gods in the Greco-Roman world at the time, which even Paul stated in 1 Corinthians 8:5: "For though there be those that are called gods, whether in heaven or in earth (as there be gods many, and lords many…)." In many contemporary societies, it is uncommon to think of the terms "God" or "god" used in different sense; when we talk of God, we usually use in one sense—the highest. But this wasn't so in the polytheistic world into which Paul and the apostles were born and lived. In Greek mythology, Zeus was a supreme being (God), the god of the sky who sends thunder bolts and lightning. Zeus was the Greek version of Jupiter, the Roman god. In both Greece and Rome there were many gods, and this is what Paul was saying in 1 Cor. 8:5. But he went on to repeat part of what was in the Torah, which is that "to us there is but one God, the Father…" Judaism was the only religion that posited one God who is to be worshipped, and Paul was reiterating this. In the continuation of the same verse, 1 Cor. 8:5, Paul goes on to say, "…but to us there is one God, the Father, and one Lord, Jesus Christ." This is the fuller picture of the meaning of there being one God among many. In this same verse Paul distinguishes Jesus from God, which would eliminate the confusion about the Father's supremacy for those who claim to be monotheists. In the world in which Paul lived and wrote, there were greater and lesser deities, and there were men who were considered to be gods, but in a much lower sense than the gods who occupied the heavenly realms. To Paul, as well as to anyone reading his words, when the term "god" is applied to anyone other than the Father it is to be understood in a lower sense. Trinitarians, however, have interpreted the title "God," in the few cases it is thought to be applied to Jesus, in its highest sense. This results, among other things, in more than one almighty God which, by definition, is impossible.

In one such instance, John 20:28, Thomas is recorded as having said to Jesus, "My Lord and my God." This is one of the verses offered in support of the doctrine of Jesus's supreme divinity. Most Trinitarians believe Thomas applied the word "God" in the highest sense in which it can be applied, which, as we have seen, is not the way in which that word or title was used within that culture. An early Baptist catechism explains the various senses in which the title "God" is applied:

> " 'Qu. *What are we then to believe of Christ Jesus? It is commonly said we allow him to be no more than a mere man, such as ourselves.*
>
> Ans. But this is untrue. For we confess Jesus Christ *was in the beginning* of the world, *with God and was God.* And after his Resurrection, he was made and appointed *Lord* and *God over all, the Father only excepted, who put all things under him.*
>
> Qu. *Whence came this Calumny?*
>
> Ans. Why hence; we say, though Jesus Christ was God above all other Beings but the Father, he was not the Most High God: but the Father only was greater than Christ, and his God and Head.
>
> Qu. *You seem to make two Gods, but the Scripture declares*

there are no more Gods than one?

Ans. The Scripture uses the word *God* in two different significations, *first*, to denote *the Supreme* or *Most High*, who is so called by Way of Eminence. And in this sense the Scriptures use the Word, when they assert *there is but one God:* There being but one supreme God, and no more. But at other Times, the Word God denotes any Person of Power and Authority; and so Angels, Magistrates, and Prophets, whom God invests with Authority and Power by his Commission, are called Gods, and in this sense, *there are Lords many and Gods many.'* "[20]

Accordingly, Jesus may be called "god," but only in the proper sense of the word:

That the Blessed Jesus has the Title of God ascribed sometimes to him in the holy Scriptures, is not denied by Arians or Socinians; but it remains to be examined in what sense that character, as given to him, is intended. Nor is this an unreasonable or needless inquiry, since it is beyond all reasonable denial, that the title of God is given in very different senses in the Scripture.

1. Sometimes it signifies the most High, Perfect and Infinite Being, who is of Himself alone, and owes neither his being nor authority, nor any thing to another: and this is what is most commonly intended, when we speak of God in ordinary discourse, and in prayer and praise; we mean it of God in the most eminent sense.

2. At other times it has a lower sense, and is made the character of persons who are invested with subordinate authority and power from that Supreme Being. Thus angels are styled Gods, Psal. 8. 5. Thou hast made him a little lower than the Gods, as 'tis in the margin: So Magistrates are Gods, Exod. 22. 28. Psal. 82. 1. John 10. 34, 35. And sometimes in the singular number, one person is styled God, as Moses is twice so called, a God to Aaron, and afterwards a God to Pharaoh: and thus the Devil is called

---

[20] Early Baptist Catechism, quoted in Dana, 275-276.

the God of this world, i.e. the Prince and mighty Ruler of it; tho by unjust usurpation, and God's permission. Now as he who alone is God, in the former sense, is infinitely above all these; so we find him distinguish'd from all others who are called God, by this character, viz. a God of Gods, or the Chief of all Gods, with whom none of those Gods may be compared. So Philo describes him, to be not only the God of Men, but the God of Gods also. This is the highest and most glorious epithet given him in the Old Testament, when it is designed to make a most magnificent mention of his peerless greatness and glory....

Now the question to be resolved is, in which of these two senses Christ is said to be God in the holy Scriptures? The bare character of God determines nothing in this case, because it belongs both to the supreme and to subordinate Beings in power and authority: but the question is, Whether Jesus Christ be the God of Gods, or above all Gods?

He is indeed the Lord of Lords; but that notes an inferior character, compared with that of God of Gods, as appears by I Cor. 8. 5, tho it be included in the Superior; so that he who is above all Gods, is also over all Lords, but not contrariwise. In short, has Jesus Christ any God over him, who has greater authority, and greater ability than himself, or not? This will decide the matter: for if he have a God above him, then he is not the absolutely supreme God, tho in relation to created beings, he may be a God (or Ruler) over all.

Nor can we more clearly demonstrate this point, than by showing, First, That Jesus expressly speaks of another God than himself. Secondly, That he owns this God to be above or over himself. Thirdly, That he wants (i.e. lacks) those super-eminent and infinite perfections, which belong only to the Lord God of Gods.[21]

Many Christians have not understood that beings other than the Father may be designated as God or god, bearing in mind that upper

---

[21] Thomas Emlyn, *An Humble Inquiry Into the Scripture Account of Christ* (Boston, 1702), quoted in Parke, 41-42.

and lower cases are a later development of the alphabet system, which makes it convenient to use the same word but with a different sense intended. Scripture is replete with examples of others who are called "god" or "God":

> There would have been no occasion for the supporters of these opinions to have offered such violence to reason, nay even to so much plain Scriptural evidence, if they had duly considered God's own words addressed to kings and princes, Psalm lxxxii. 6, 'I have said, Ye are Gods, and all of you are children of the most High'; to those of Christ himself, John x. 35, 'if he called them gods, unto whom the word of God came, and the Scripture cannot be broken—'; to those of St. Paul, 1 Cor. viii. 5, 6, 'for though there be that are called gods, whether in heaven or earth (for there be gods many and lords many,) but to us there is but one God, the Father, of whom are all things,' etc.; or lastly of II Peter i. 4, 'that by these ye might be partakers of the divine nature,' which implies much more than the title of gods in the sense in which that title is applied to kings; though no one would conclude from this expression that the saints were co-essential with God.... It must be observed in the first place, that the name of God is not infrequently ascribed, by the will and concession of God the Father, even to angels and men,—how much more then to the only begotten Son, the image of the Father. To angels, Psalm xcvii. 7, 9, 'worship him all ye gods... thou art high above all the earth; thou art exalted far above all gods,' compared with Heb. i. 6. See also Psalm viii. 5. To judges, Exod. xxii. 28, 'thou shalt not revile the gods, nor curse the ruler of the people.' See also, in the Hebrew, Exod. xxi. 6, xxii. 8, 9; Psalm lxxxii. 1, 6, 'he judgeth among the gods.' 'I have said, Ye are gods, and all of you are children of the most High.' To the whole house of David, or to all the Saints. Zech. xii. 8, 'the house of David shall be as God, as the angel of the Lord before them.' [22]

If Thomas meant to call Jesus "God" in the highest sense of the

---

[22] Milton, 12-13, 41-42.

word, why did he employ the term "Lord" at all? This would be a title that would diminish his perception of Jesus, since, according to common usage and especially within the realm of Trinitarian thought, the title "God" is the highest term that may be applied to an individual. By adding the lesser title "Lord," Thomas would be diminishing his perception of Jesus, which would be unnatural if he really thought Jesus were his God. If Thomas thought Jesus were God, an oddity in his expression arises due to the order in which the terms appear; He said "Lord" first, then "God," which would be strange if he really believed he was talking with God. This illustrates another problem with the Trinitarian interpretation of "God" when it appears to be applied to Jesus: Jesus is never plainly called God. Other words which refer to Jesus as less than God are present in every context in which he is thought to be called God. Mitigating words such as "Lord," "logos," "Son," etc., are applied to Jesus in every context in which Trinitarians assert that he is called God. Would this have been a sensible way to make a point, by putting *subordinate* terminologies in contexts that are supposed to establish Jesus's *equality* with the Father? Jesus could have simply been called God, just as the Father is in hundreds of places. There is no way one can prove from Thomas's words that he thought Jesus was the supreme God. Only in a lower sense can Jesus be considered as God or a god:

> That Christ is a God in a just sense, in the sense in which he himself (John 10:35) explained of others*as one "to whom the word of God came"*is beyond question. In this sense, Angels*Moses*Samuel*the Kings and Judges of Israel, are called gods. Seventeen passages at least of this character are to be found in the Old Testament. (E.g. Ps. 8:5; Judges 13:22; Exod. 7:1; 1 Samuel 28:13, 14; Ps. 82:1, 6; Exod. 15:11, etc.) The question, therefore, is not whether Christ is ever called in Scripture, or even whether he be, a God; but in what sense? And then, I repeat, on his own express authority in the text just cited from St. John's Gospel, he is a God as being preëminently one "to whom the word of God came." This was his vindication of himself when charged by the cavilling Jews around him with blasphemy, because he had, as they alleged*"being a man, made himself God." In no other sense

was he a God. This, we affirm, is the obvious sense. Not that he was the Supreme God, the one Living and True God, the God over all; because Scripture forbids such a belief.[23]

The titles "God" and "god" are applied to various people in Scripture because they represent God. This form of expression is not commonly used in modern times so, due to unfamiliarity with the idiom, when somebody is referred to as "God" in Scripture it is commonly mistaken as a reference to the supreme God. This is evident in the following statement from a learned Trinitarian who expresses his astonishment at Jesus's reaction to the charge that he had "called God his Father, thereby making himself equal with God":

> It is, however, remarkable that Jesus meets the Jewish accusation by appealing to Ps. lxxxii. 6, where those who represent God are called gods (Jn. x. 34-36).[24]

It would not be remarkable if it was understood that Jesus was repelling the charge that he was making himself equal with the Father, and was establishing his relationship to the Father as that of a son and representative. In the face of Jesus's own testimony it is difficult to sustain the notion that anybody is equal with the Father:

> The name of God is ascribed to judges, because they occupy the place of God to a certain degree in the administration of judgment. The Son, who was entitled to the name of God both in the capacity of a messenger and of a judge, and indeed in virtue of a much better right, did not think it foreign to his character, when the Jews accused him of blasphemy because he made himself God, to allege in his own defence the very reason which has been advanced. John x. 34-36, 'Jesus answered them, Is it not written in your law, I said, Ye are gods? If he called them gods unto whom the word of God came, and the Scripture cannot be broken; say ye of him whom the Father hath sanctified and sent into the world, Thou blasphemest; because I said, I am the Son of God?'—especially when God himself had called the judges children of

---

23 Farley, 73-74.

24 Franks, 53.

the Most High, as has been stated before. Hence 1 Cor. viii 5, 6. 'for though there be that are called gods, whether in heaven or in earth, (as there be gods many, and lords many,) but to us there is but one God, the Father, of whom are all things, and we in him; and one Lord Jesus Christ, by whom are all things, and we by him.[25]

In practical, non-academic terms and thought, when we stop to think of our conception of God, it is difficult to conceive of a person who does not think of the Father alone. Despite the arguments put forth for the triune nature of God, the mind must perceive that the Father is the only one who is unequivocally God—there must be reservations in believing two others to also be God. Claiming that others are God negates the Father being the supreme God since, by definition, there cannot be more than one *supreme* God. According to the Trinitarian conception of God, the Father has been dethroned and dishonored:

Again: the Father is God. Nothing can be added to his infinity or perfections to complete our idea of God. Confused as men's minds have been by the doctrine we are opposing, there is no one who would not shrink from expressly asserting anything to be wanting to constitute the Father God, in the most absolute and comprehensive sense of the term. His conceptions must be miserably perplexed and perverted, who thinks it possible to use language on this subject too strong or too unlimited. In the Father is all that we can conceive of as constituting the One and Only God. What, however, can any one mean by this proposition, who understands and assents to the perfectly intelligible and indisputable propositions just stated? Is the meaning, that Christ as well as the Father—or, if the Father be God, we must say, as well as God—is the One and Only God? Is it that we are in error about the unity of God, and that Christ is another God? No one will assent to either of these senses of the proposition. Does it imply, then, that neither the Father nor the Son is the One and Only God, but that together with another, the Holy Spirit, they consti-

---

25 Milton, 46-47.

tute this mysterious Being? This seems at first view more conformed to the doctrine to be maintained; but it must be observed, that he who adopts this sense asserts, not that Christ is God, but that he is not God; and asserts at the same time that the Father is not God.

Once more: if Christ be God, and if there be but one God, then all that is true of God is true of Christ, considered as God; and, on the other hand, all that is true of the Son is true of God. This being so, open the Bible, and where the name of God occurs, substitute that of the Son; and where the name of the Son occurs, that of God. "The Son sent his beloved Son"; "Father, the hour is come; glorify *the Son* that *the Son* also may glorify thee." I will not, for the sake of confuting any error, put a change on this most solemn and affecting passage. I have felt throughout the painful incongruity of introducing conceptions that ought to be accompanied with very different feelings and associations into such a discussion, and I am not disposed to pursue the mode just suggested of exemplifying the nature of the errors against which I am contending. But one who had never seen the New Testament before would need but to read a page of it to satisfy himself that "the Son of God" and "God" are not convertible terms, but mean something very different.[26]

In the Bible, "God" refers to the Father in thousands of cases, but to others in only a handful, which is a circumstance that changes the direction of the argument—it would be unreasonable to make a case for the few overthrowing the obvious import of the many. A doctrine that stresses the equality of three persons in God, were it true, would have each of the three referred to as "God" in equal proportion in Scripture, or at least within some reasonably corresponding range. This uneven representation of the Father as God is entirely consistent with His supremacy:

But a Trinitarian may answer me, that the word "God" in the New Testament almost always denotes either the Trinity or the Father; and that he does not suppose it to be applied

---

[26] Norton, 86-88.

to the Son in more than about a dozen instances. One would think that this state of the case must, at the first view of it, startle a defender of the doctrine that Christ is God. It is strange that one equal to the Father in every divine perfection should so rarely be denoted by that name to which he is equally entitled.[27]

In the Trinitarian system there has been a failure to delineate the term "God," which allows for the most absurd statements to be made about Him. Jesus, it is said, is God. But God, according to this system, is "God the Father, God the Son, and God the Holy Spirit." So we have an expression that narrows down, by equation, to this: "God the Son equals God the Father, God the Son, and God the Holy Spirit." In each place where the term "God" appears, it is acceptable, according to Trinitarian ideology, to insert the phrase "God the Father, God the Son, and God the Holy Spirit." This process could be performed ad infinitum, resulting in an infinite regression. And there is no mechanism in Trinitarian theology to stop this. Trinitarians are manifestly confused in their understanding of what it is for one to be called God. According to Trinitarians, Jesus is God. If God is a trinity, is Jesus therefore a Trinity?

> Let us assume that the title "Son of God," applied to Christ, denotes, in some sense or other, proper essential divinity. But the Son is but *one* of *three* who constitute God. You may substitute after the numerals the word *person*, or *distinction*, or any other; it will not affect the argument. God is a being; and when you have named Christ or the Son, you have not, according to the doctrine of the Trinity, named all which constitutes this being. The Trinitarian asserts that God exists in three persons; or, to take the wholly unimportant modification of the doctrine that some writers have attempted to introduce, that "God is three in a certain respect." But Christ, it is also affirmed, is God, the Son is God. Does he, then, exist in three persons? Is he three in a certain respect? Unquestionably not. The word "God" is used in two senses. In one case, as applied to the Supreme Being, properly, in the only

27 Norton, 88-89.

sense which a Christian can recognize as the literal sense of the term; in the other case, as applied to Christ, though professedly in the same, yet clearly and necessarily in a different signification, no one can tell what.[28]

If, as Trinitarians assert, "Son of God" is synonymous with "God the Son," then anyone who carries the title "Son of God" would also be interpreted by a Bible student as "God the Son." It must be that the phrase "Son of God" is used in a different way than Trinitarians suppose. When it is understood as signifying authority derived from the Father, there is no difficulty understanding it:

The advocates of the doctrine of the proper Deity of our Lord, often insist that the title, "Son of God," proves it. The title, *Son of God,* is given to Christ some fifty times, and *the Son,* some forty times, in the New Testament. How strange that either should be thought to prove so stupendous a doctrine, as that he is the Supreme God! The term Son, certainly in every other case that can be named, implies distinction from, subordination to, another, a Parent; why not here? Is it urged that, at any rate, it shows his Divine nature? In general terms that may be granted; but not that he is the same person or being*not surely the Supreme God. Angels, Israelites, Solomon, Christians, repeatedly are all called sons of God in the Old and New Testaments. (Job 1:6; 38:7; Hosea 1:10; 2 Sam. 7:14; Rom. 8:14, etc.) Applied to Christ, it is an eminently glorious title, expressive of God's special love, approval, etc., and of his own intimate connection with God*yet not less of his personal dependence and consequent subordination and inferiority. Sixty-six times God is expressly called *his* Father; repeatedly, *his* God; interchangeably and equally, "*his* God and our God, *his* Father and our Father." Even after his Resurrection, he said to Mary: "Go to my brethren, and say unto them, I ascend unto my Father and your Father; and to my God and your God." What must she, what must they, have understood by such a plain and distinct declaration? What reason did he ever afterwards, did he ever before, give them

---

28 Norton, 86.

for interpreting it otherwise than according to its simple, obvious meaning? [29]

If the argument is advanced that Christ is God because there are things said of him that could only be said of God, the argument is false if these same things are said of someone else. Just as "God" is used in various senses in Scripture, other phrases are used in superior and subordinate senses. When adjectives or titles are applied to God, our heavenly Father, we understand them in their superior sense. When applied to Jesus and others we understand them in a subordinate sense. Frequently, the principle of agency is to be understood when a name, title, or attribute of God is given to a person or place:

An argument is drawn for the Supreme Divinity of Christ, from the fact that similar language is sometimes applied to him and to God. The answer in all such cases is, that in its application to God we understand it in its highest sense; but to Christ only in that sense which belongs to him as the Son of God. Thus it is said, "I am Jehovah, and beside me there is no Saviour." Yet Christ is called our Saviour. Jehovah is called the redeemer of Israel, and Christ is also called a Redeemer. Such language gives us no trouble. In the highest sense, all salvation, all help, all guidance, and all support come from God. He alone is the author and giver of every good gift, and thus, in the ascription of praise, we say, "To the only wise God, our Saviour." But Jesus is also in a true and real sense our Saviour, our guide, our supporter, our Redeemer. Not by his independent power, indeed, but because, Acts v. 31, "God hath exalted him with his right hand to be a Prince and a Saviour, to give repentance to Israel, and forgiveness of sins." In the same manner, many things are said to be done by God which are also said to be done by Christ; as, that God will judge the world, and also that Christ is the judge of all. But this is explained when we are taught, Acts. xxii. 31, "That God will judge the world in righteousness by that man whom he hath ordained"; and so in all other instances of the same sort. Christ acts as the agent, the representative, the messen-

---

[29] Farley, 87-88.

ger of God, but we ascribe the work to him, always remembering, however, that he does not speak of himself. John vii. 16, 18. To the same effect I will quote the following very clear language of Professor Stuart: "Nothing can be more erroneous in most cases, than to draw the conclusion that, because the Scripture asserts some particular thing to have been done by God, therefore he did it immediately, and no instruments were employed by him. In interpreting the principles of human laws, we say, 'He who does any thing by another does it himself.' Does not common sense approve of this, as applied to the language of Scripture? Nothing can be more evident than that the sacred writers have expressed themselves in a manner which recognizes this principle." [30]

THE TERM LORD

One of the terms that is applied to both God and Jesus is "Lord," and some infer from this that Jesus is God. This is an improper inference since the term "Lord" simply refers to one who is in a position of authority. The degree of authority varies with circumstances, and the word is used in a similar sense in which we employ the word "boss" today. Acts 2:36 says how Jesus became Lord: "Therefore, let all the house of Israel know assuredly, that God hath made that same Jesus, whom ye have crucified, both Lord and Christ." The authority that Jesus ever had was derived, which was bestowed upon him by one clearly greater than himself—the Father.

Many others are called "Lord" throughout the Bible, but the argument is never advanced that these are co-equal with the Father. Examples of others called "Lord" are: Saul, 1 Sam. 22:12; David, 1 Kings 1:13, 17; angels, Zech. 4:4, 5, 13; Eli, 1 Sam. 1:15; Moses, Numbers 11:28, 12:11; kings, Jer. 38:9, 1 Kings 1:17.

---

[30] Eliot, 64-65.

THE TERM SAVIOUR (and SAVIOR)

The term "Saviour" is applied to Jesus and the Father, and from this it is inferred by some that Jesus is God. This is primarily adduced from Isaiah 43:11, which says, in reference to the Father: "I am the Lord, and beside me there is no Saviour" (*see also* Luke 1:47). But Jesus is called "Saviour" in Luke 2:11 and elsewhere, so the inference is drawn that he must be God. If this were so, this would prove that Jesus *is* the Father since, according to a narrow understanding of Isa. 43:11, there is only *one* saviour. This would also negate our heavenly Father's role of saviour since Jesus would be the only one who is considered to be a saviour. This is something few Trinitarians will admit since it would make Jesus either more important than the Father or make him to be the Father. The latter is what some Trinitarians believe, and their theology is rejected by many other Trinitarians because it fails to make three distinct persons in the Godhead.

As with all titles, "Saviour" is used in different senses:

I have endeavored to show, that whenever a Trinitarian meaning is given to any passage, it is given in violation of a fundamental rule of interpretation. But there are *passages adduced, in the senses assigned to which, not merely this rule is violated, but the most obvious and indisputable characteristics of language are disregarded, and the reasoning proceeds upon the assumption that they do not exist.* Thus, for example, it is said in Isaiah (xliii. 11), according to the Common Version: "I, even I, am the Lord, and beside me there is no saviour." But Christ, it is argued, is our Saviour; and, as it is proved by this passage that there can be no saviour but God, it follows that Christ is God. The reasoning proceeds upon the assumption that the same word is always used in the same sense, with the same reference, and in the whole extent of its signification; and the monstrous conclusions that would result from applying this argument to other individuals beside Christ, to whom the name "Saviour" is or may be given, are put out of sight. (See 2 Kings xiii. 5; Nehemiah ix. 27; Isaiah xix. 20; Obadiah 21.)[31]

---

[31] Norton, 304-305.

Considering Jesus to be an agent in the Father's plan of salvation, rather than the original cause of it, does not diminish who he is. Jesus must be honored as he is, which entails remembering that our heavenly Father is the one we are to have supreme respect for:

Deeply affected as we must, and ever ought to be, at the remembrance of those unspeakable sufferings, and warmed with ardent love for *that good shepherd who laid down his life for us;* still it may be proper to remind ourselves often, that the glory of our salvation is *ultimately* due to *God;* for had not his tender mercies to his creatures prevailed, Jesus Christ had never been sent on earth. It was the *divine will of the Almighty* that he should appear to instruct and save sinful men; *That in the ages to come he might shew the exceeding riches of his grace, in his kindness towards us through Christ Jesus.*—Eph. ii, 7. *Who was sent to deliver us from the power of darkness, that we might serve the living and true God; and to make us meet to be partakers of the inheritance of the Saints in light.*—St. Paul. Yet, *beyond all doubt,* the most unshaken reverence, united with fervent love and gratitude to this great and ready messenger, should be ever preserved; and a firm faith in him and his heavenly doctrines; which, with a steady practice of them, is all he has desired or commanded.[32]

THE TERM JUDGE

The title of "judge" is applied to our heavenly Father since He is the supreme judge of man's heart and behavior. But the Bible says that Jesus is also a judge, and some argue from this that he must therefore be God. It requires very little to see the capacity in which God and Jesus are judges, and the relation in which they stand to each other. Romans 2:16 says: "In the day when God shall judge the secrets of men by Jesus Christ according to my gospel." And 1 Tim. 2:5 says that "God will judge man through a mediator, the man Christ Jesus." But some contend that in order for Jesus to be able to "judge the secrets of men," he must be omniscient and therefore must be God,

---

[32] Gifford, 148-149.

which is an incorrect inference:

I may here take notice, however, of the argument founded by Trinitarians upon the conceptions of the Apostles respecting the judgment of mankind by Christ. It has been contended by them, that what the Apostles expected is still future; that Christ is hereafter to judge all men in person; that, in order to do this, he must be acquainted with every thought and action of every individual; that such knowledge supposes omniscience; that omniscience is the attribute of God alone; and that Christ, therefore, is God. Without examining any of the other steps in this argument, one need only remark upon the very limited notion which it implies of omniscience on the one hand, and of the power of God on the other. The knowledge of all thoughts and deeds which have taken place in this world from its creation would be, compared with OMNISCIENCE, less than the acquaintance that a child may have with its nursery, compared with the apprehensions of an archangel. Would it, then, be an act transcending the power of God to communicate that knowledge? Could he not give to one man a perfect acquaintance with one other? And if this be possible, is his power still so bounded, that he could not give to one who had been a man, a perfect knowledge of the thoughts and deeds of all *other men who have lived?*

In urging such obvious arguments as these, there is a humiliating consciousness of the weakness of the cause we are opposing. One may feel as if he were wasting reasoning upon a subject unworthy of it; as if his remarks implied a want of common intelligence in his readers; as if he were exposed to the same ridicule, as he who should gravely and earnestly labor the proof of an undeniable proposition. But the same is the case with all direct reasoning against the doctrine of the Trinity; and one can reconcile himself to the discussion of it only by considering, not what that doctrine is in itself, but how widely and how long it has prevailed, how obstinately it is still professed, and the manifold mischiefs which have flowed and are still flowing from it.[33]

Many others are called "judge," but these are not offered as co-equals with God. Among these are saints, 1 Cor. 6:2, 3; the governor of Israel, Acts 24:10; a man, Luke 18:2.

THE TERM "KING"

In 2 Timothy 6:15 and Rev. 17:14, Jesus is called the "King of kings," a designation that has been taken by some as elevating him to the status of God since it appears to place him above all other kings. This inference is problematic primarily for two reasons. The first is that if it were literally and unqualifiedly true, it would elevate Jesus to a status *above* the Father since the Father is also called King. The second is that it fails to take into account that the term "King" is applied in various senses. Others are called "King" in Scripture, and no one argues that this makes them equal with the Father.

Some Trinitarians have acknowledged that the title "King of kings" is not a title that may be used to support the deity of Jesus:

> "A great lord is termed *Lord of lords,* because he possesses authority over many other Lords. The title King of kings is used of him who rules over a number of kings; and was formerly employed of the sovereigns of Persia, Assyria, Babylon, and Egypt."—DRUSIUS.
>
> "*King of kings,* or God's vicegerent over the whole earth; a title belonging to him alone whom God hath anointed *his king,* Ps. ii. 2, 6."—PYLE. (Similarly interpreted by Grotius and the Assembly's Annotator.)
>
> "On account of his exaltation to heaven, at the right hand of God the Father, Jesus is called the King of kings and Lord of Lords.—LIMBORCH: *Theol. Christ.* lib. ii. cap. 2, § 16. (To the same purport, Archbishop SECKER, Lect. vii. vol. i. 102, 103.)
>
> "Even as man, Christ is the King of kings, and the Lord of lords."—CALMET on chap. xix. 16.
>
> "*King of kings,* according to the style of the oriental lan-

---

[33] Norton, 284-286.

guages, answers to great, as if it was *the great king,* which was the style of the Greeks when they spoke of the Persian monarchy. But such reduplications were not so proper to the oriental style, but that, to show the excellency of any thing, the Greeks and Romans used them too; of which many instances might be given out of the best author."—DAUBUZ on chap. xix. 16.[34]

THE TERM CREATOR

It is part of the thinking of some that, since Jesus and the Father are each referred to as a "creator," Jesus is therefore equal with the Father. This is typically adduced from Genesis 1:1 and Colossians 1:16. Gen. 1:1 says: "God, in the beginning, created the heavens and the earth." Colossians 1:16 says: "For by him [Jesus] were all things created, that are in heaven, and that are in earth, visible and invisible, whether thrones, or dominions, or principalities, or powers; all things were created by him, and for him." From a cursory reading of these two texts, Trinitarians generally infer that Jesus is responsible for the creation of the physical and spiritual realms, leading to the conclusion that he must therefore be God. As is common, this conclusion is based on an incorrect inference, since the two verses are referring to two different creations, one before the fall of man and the other after it.

The creation spoken of in Genesis 1:1 is the creation of the physical universe (i.e. the heavens and the earth), which is evident from the objects mentioned as having been created. In Colossians 1:16 what is being spoken of are non-physical things, which are commonly referred to as "spiritual." Norton gives the following explanation:

> The language from the Epistle to the Colossians, in which Christ is said to have created all things, is to be explained in a corresponding manner. He created all things in the new dispensation, in the kingdom of Heaven. It has been understood as declaring, that the *natural creation* was the work of Christ. But it is obvious, at first sight, that the words used are not

---

[34] Dana, Appendix F, 287.

such as properly designate the objects of the *natural world*; and not such, therefore, as we should expect to be employed, if these were intended. In speaking of the natural creation, the same Apostle refers it to God in different terms,—to "the living God who made heaven and earth, and the sea, and all things that are in them." (Acts xiv. 15.) [35]

THE PHRASE ALPHA AND OMEGA

Some emphasis has been placed on the phrase "Alpha and Omega" in support of the idea that Jesus is God. The phrase "Alpha and Omega" is applied to the Father, and for the sake of discussion I will grant here that the phrase is applied to Jesus, and most significantly in the book of Revelation, which is by no means certain. Some Trinitarians consider Rev. 1:11 to be spurious, while others partly build their theology upon it, which makes it less likely that a sound theology will come from arguments stemming from it.

Revelation 1:8, 11 says, "I am Alpha and Omega, the beginning and the ending, saith the Lord, which is, and which was, and which is to come, the Almighty…Saying I am Alpha and Omega, the first and the last: and, What thou seest, write in a book…" The phrase "Alpha and Omega" in verse eight is a reference to the Father, which is apparent from verse four, where He is distinguished from Jesus who is mentioned in verse five. Also, the New International Version has the phrase "Lord God," which is in the Greek texts, but the King James Version does not include the word "God," which has caused some confusion regarding who is spoken of in the context.

As with so many other titles and descriptions, "Alpha and Omega," if it was originally meant by John to apply to Jesus, is applied to him in a subordinate sense:

> Instead of [*ho kurios*] "the Lord, [*kurios he theos*] "the Lord God," is adopted by all the modern critical editors who have been mentioned in this note, and even by Bloomfield, who also remarks, "By most recent commentators these words are understood of God *the Father*."

---

[35] Norton, 291-292.

These expressions have been variously interpreted; by some, as denoting eternity, or unchangeableness;—but "the beginning and the end" can hardly mean "without beginning or without end";—by others, as signifying completeness, or perfection. Here, and in ch. xxi. 6, where they are also applied to God, they seem rather used to denote the certain accomplishment of his purposes; that what he has begun he will carry on to its consummation. Thus Hengstenberg remarks: "The emphasis is to be laid upon the Omega. It is as much as: I am Alpha, therefore also the omega. The beginning is surety for the end."—(*The Revelation of St. John, Expounded*, &c., Vol. I. 107, Amer. ed. of the Engl. translation.)

The words in question may be understood in a similar manner when applied to Christ, as in ch, xxii. 13; comp. i. 17, ii. 8. Thus Erasmus remarks in his note on John viii. 25, as cited by Wilson in his Concessions of Trinitarians: "Christ is called *the beginning and the end*, because he is the beginning and the consummation of the Church, which was founded by his first, and will be completed by his second appearance."—(Opp. Tom. VI. col. 376, E.) So one of the Latin Fathers, Fulgentius, says, though he gives other meanings to the words: "*Principium* Christus, quia ipse inchoavit perficienda; *finis* Christus, quia ipse perficit inchoata"; that is, "Christ is *the beginning*, because he himself commenced the work to be accomplished; Christ is *the end*, because he accomplished the work begun."—(Ad Transimundum, Lib. II. c. 5; in Migne's Patrol. Tom. LXV. vol. 250, C.) It is, perhaps, in a somewhat similar sense that he is called by the author of the Epistle to the Hebrews "the Author and Finisher of the faith." [36]

The variety of explanations such as those above illustrates the need to know what the term *Alpha* means and what *Omega* means, and what they mean when brought together into one phrase. Whatever the phrase means, though, it most likely refers to the Father wherever it is used:

Rev. i. viii. "I am Alpha and Omega, the beginning and the

---

[36] Norton, 479-480.

ending, saith the Lord, which is and which was, and which is to come, the Almighty." As St. John attributes the words to the Lord God Almighty, they prove nothing concerning Christ.

"Professor Stuart appears to have felt the force of this reasoning, from the pains he has taken in his letters to Mr. Channing to inculcate the principle, that we are to believe a doctrine as much, provided only one text remains to support it, as if we could see it running through the whole Gospel. And we admit, that this is true, provided the doctrine is *really* contained in that one text, and that a *genuine* one. Still we cannot but think, that a prudent man, if he has ever been led to put great stress upon the testimony of one or two passages of Scripture, and afterwards found that testimony to be false, will be cautious how far he confides in the testimony of one or two single passages again. Dr. Doddridge is known to have depended much on the expression in Rev. i. 11, 'I am Alpha and Omega, the first and the last,' as applied to Christ; admitting that if this text were not in Scripture, he could well conceive of a man's rejecting the Trinity. Now it has been shown by Griesbach, that this text does *not* belong to Scripture, but is to be thrown out as spurious. We mention this fact to show how very dangerous it is to depend much on a single text, especially in a subject like the Trinity, in favor of which it is acknowledged that so many texts have been grossly corrupted.[37]

If it is true (which we consider by no means certain) that it is Jesus who says, Rev. i. 11, "I am Alpha and Omega," its explanation is difficult; for we can scarcely understand how such words are applicable to any but the Almighty. But the difficulty is at once increased and removed, when we find the words used by one who commanded John not to worship him: "See thou do it not; for I am the fellow-servant; worship God"; for it was the same person who used these words who said directly after, "I am Alpha and Omega; the beginning

---

[37] Morgridge, 139, 98.

and the end; the first and the last." Rev. xxii. 8, 13. I can understand such language only by supposing that Jesus and also the angel were speaking in the name of God. In the same manner Moses says, Deut. xxix. 2, 6, "I have led you forty years in the wilderness;.... . that ye may know that I am the Lord your God." See also Deut xi. 13—15. In both of these passages Moses used language, which, if it had been used by Christ, would be stronger in proving his Deity than any now quoted for that purpose. We should not, therefore, attach so great importance to isolated and obscure texts. I am persuaded that it is better to look to the plainer books of Scripture for our chief instruction.[38]

Rev. i. 17, 18. "I am the first and the last; I am he that liveth and was dead." As he who is "the first and the last" was once dead, it cannot [refer to] God who "alone hath immortality." The meaning is, that the Christian dispensation, over which Christ has been ordained of God to preside, was begun and will be completed by him, who is the *author* and *finisher* of our faith. The same remarks are applicable to Rev. xxii. 13, where Christ says, "I am Alpha and Omega, the beginning and the end, the first and the last." When John fell down to worship him, (verse 8) he forbade him, saying, "See thou do it not; for I am the fellow-servant, and of the brethren the prophets, and of them which keep the sayings of this book: worship God." Verse 9. [39]

It is important to inquire about who it is being spoken of in Rev. 21:6-7 and 22:13. It is in no way clear that any of the phrases "Alpha and Omega" are applied to Jesus. In Rev. 1:8 it is applied to the Father; Rev. 1:11 is spurious, so it cannot be used to prove anything. The words in 21:6-7 are a reference to the Father, since verse 7 says, "I will be his God, and he shall be my son."

The idea that these words were first given to Jesus by the Father, and then to John by Jesus is supported by Rev. 1:1: "The revelation of Jesus Christ, which God gave unto him, to show unto his servants

---

[38] Eliot, 70.

[39] Morgridge, 139-140.

things which must shortly come to pass; and he sent and signified it by his angel unto his servant John." In harmony with Rev. 1:1 is Rev. 22:8, where we are informed that it was an angel who spoke to John. Jesus is said to have spoken these things to John through the mediation of an angel. The words, then, in 21:7, "I will be their God," would, according to the Trinitarian method of interpretation, which is to understand the words spoken to John as having originated with the immediate speaker, be referred to the angel, thereby making the angel to be God! If, however, we allow for instrumental agency, or mediation, then words spoken by one person may be referred to a more remote speaker. In this case the more remote speaker is the Father, which is laid out in Rev. 1:1. If we accept the Trinitarian method, we would be left to conclude that it was the angel who is God, since it was the angel who was the immediate speaker, not Jesus. This confusion is eliminated when we understand that a mediatorial process is employed in the book of Revelation. The chain of information leads back to God, so it is He who is spoken of as being *their God* and the *Alpha and Omega*.

THE TERM 'WORSHIP' AS APPLIED TO GOD AND JESUS

The word "worship" means "to pay homage to." The Father is to be worshipped in the supreme sense, insofar as mankind has been instructed in the Hebrew texts not to worship any other God (or gods) but Him. But some Trinitarians point out that in Matthew 28:9 Christ was worshipped: "And as they went to tell his disciples, behold, Jesus met them, saying, All hail. And they came and held him by the feet, and worshipped him." Some Trinitarians infer from this that Jesus is co-equal with the Father.

This inference is incorrect on two grounds. The first is that worship is given to persons in different degrees. Supreme worship is reserved for the Father, but worship of a lesser sort may be given to others. Worship was given to King David in 1 Chron. 29:20: "And David said to all the congregation, Now bless the LORD your God. And all the congregation blessed the LORD God of their fathers, and bowed down their heads, and worshipped the LORD and the king." It is permissible to pay homage to Jesus not as God almighty, but as Lord:

Henceforth it shall be with less and less of reason furnished by us, that our opponents shall say, "You do not make enough of Christ." Having distinguished him from God, we feel all the more our need of him to guide us to God, to manifest God to us. We recognize in our own deepest wants the craving to which he ministers. We know and own that, in a Gospel which comes by Christ, Christ must be the foremost object, and that every sentiment engaged by that Gospel must yield some tribute of heart and soul to him.[40]

In this sentiment the Father is honored in reverence of Jesus as Lord "to the glory of God the Father" (Phil. 2:11).

---

[40] Ellis, 152.

CHAPTER 15

TIMELY STATEMENTS

The following statements about Jesus, made at noteworthy moments, were not recorded to declare or even allude to his supposed equality with the Father. They consistently demonstrate the simple truth of Jesus's relationship to God as that of a son, as well as his relationship to the church as that of Lord. The closeness of the people to Jesus who made the following testimonies should not be overlooked. They knew him, they lived with him, they conversed with him and were instructed by him, and readily understood the Father to be the one true God. If Jesus were God, we would expect the following verses, especially given the timing of the statements, to say something that in some way agrees with the Trinitarian hypothesis. But we find that the supremacy of the Father is consistently maintained by virtue of Jesus being called "son of God":

- God's first vocal announcement regarding Jesus: "And there came a voice from heaven, saying, Thou art my beloved son, in whom I am well pleased."—Mark 1:11.
- Satan's words when tempting Jesus: "And when the tempter came to him, he said, If thou be the Son of God, command that these stones be made bread."—Matt. 4:3.
- Paul's first witness after regaining his sight: "And when he had received meat, he was strengthened. Then was Saul certain days with the disciples which were at Damascus. And straightway he preached Christ in the synagogues, that he is the Son of God."—Acts 9:19-20.
- Jesus's last prayer while here on earth: "And this is life eternal, that they might know thee, the only true God, and Jesus Christ, whom thou hast sent."—John 17:3.

"The beloved Apostle John has recorded at length a most remarkable prayer, offered by our Lord when he was about to leave the world. If he would ever have spoken simply, unequivocally, according to his convictions, nay, his knowledge, it must have been at that solemn hour, in the most solemn act. Hear him, then, addressing the FATHER: "This is Life Eternal, that they might know THEE, the ONLY TRUE GOD—and Jesus Christ whom Thou hast sent." Could any language be more explicit than this?" [1]

- Jesus's words after his resurrection, which he spoke to his own mother: "Jesus said unto her, Touch me not; for I am not yet ascended to my Father: but go to my brethren, and say unto them, I ascend unto my Father and your Father; and my God and your God."—John 20:17.
- The centurion, at the crucifixion of Jesus: "Now when the centurion, and they that were with him, watching Jesus, saw the earthquake, and those things that were done, they feared greatly, saying, Truly this was the Son of God."—Matt. 27:54.
- Peter's response to Jesus's question: "And Simon Peter answered and said, Thou art the Christ, the Son of the living God."—Matt. 16:16-17.
- Mark, at the beginning of his Gospel: "The beginning of the gospel of Jesus Christ, the Son of God."—1:1.
- John's testimony after Jesus was baptized and the holy spirit descended upon him: "And I saw, and bare record that this is the Son of God."—John 1:34.
- The summation of John's Gospel: "But these are written, that ye might believe that Jesus is the Christ, the Son of God; and that believing, ye might have life through his name."—John 20:31.
- At the trial of Jesus he was not accused of claiming to be God. Though this is not a verse, its omission speaks loudly:

    Christ, speaking of his sheep, said, "My Father, which gave them me, is greater than all; and none is able to pluck them out of my Father's hand. I and my Father are one. Then

---

[1] Farley, 11.

the Jews took up stones again to stone him. Jesus answered them, Many good works have I showed you from my Father; for which of these works do ye stone me? The Jews answered him saying, For a good work we stone thee not, but for blasphemy, and because thou, being a man, makest thyself God."—*John* x. 29-33. As this is the only instance recorded in the Bible in which Jesus was accused of making himself God, his answer must be important and decisive. "Jesus answered them, Is it not written in your law, I said, ye are Gods? If he called them Gods unto whom the word of God came, and the Scripture cannot be broken; say ye of him whom the Father hath sanctified and sent into the world, Thou blasphemest; because I said, I am the Son of God?"—Verse 34-36.

In this refutation Jesus denies *being* God; denies *calling* himself God; and repels the accusation of blasphemy even on the supposition that he *had* called himself God. He denies being God, by asserting that he was sanctified and sent into the world by his Father. God could not be *sanctified*, nor *sent*; neither has he any *Father*. He denies calling himself God, by asserting that he had only called himself the *Son* of God. A father and son are two distinct beings; nor is there any term that more strongly marks *derived* existence, than the term *son*. Besides, Jesus founds the propriety of calling himself the Son of God, not on any thing peculiar in his nature, or any supposed resemblance or likeness to his Father, but simply on the ground of his being *sanctified*, and *sent* by the Father. He repels the charge of blasphemy, by appealing to the well known scripture usage, by which they are called Gods unto whom the word of God came. So that if he had called himself God (which he had not done) it would have implied, according to his own explanation, nothing more than that he was a divine messenger—one to whom the word of God came. That this is the sense in which the Jews understood the answer of Jesus is evident from the fact that they never after accused him of making himself God, though urged to do so by considerations as powerful as can well be conceived. When he was arraigned before their Council, and the accusation was blasphemy, they made great efforts to support the charge. They could not obtain the necessary evidence. After they had suborned witnesses, all they could prove by them was, that he had said he could raise up the Temple in three days. Now if Jesus had ever made himself God, or intimated any desire to be considered as God, it is incredible that they should not have urged it against him at a time like this. This would have been the very evidence they felt themselves so much in need of. When they were ready to seize on every circumstance, however trifling; and were driven to extremities, to obtain witnesses to support the charge of blasphemy, it is incredible, I say, that they should not have availed themselves of such an advantage. It is as certain, then, that Jesus never made himself God, as it is that the Jews did not urge it against him at his trial.[2]

- Jesus, at that most solemn moment, on the cross: "And at about the ninth hour Jesus cried with a loud voice, saying, Eli, Eli, lama sabachthani? that is, My God, my God, why hast thou forsaken me?"—Matt. 27:46, Mark 15:34.
- A devil spirit about to be cast out by Jesus: "And cried with a loud voice, and said, What have I to do with thee, Jesus, Son of the most high God? I adjure thee by God, that thou torment me not."—Mark 5:7.

These verses might be added to with ease, but they make the point. All of those testifying about Jesus, including Jesus himself, were consistent in maintaining that he is not equal with the Father, and they knew him well.

---

[2] Morgridge, 44-45.

CHAPTER 16

VERSES COMMONLY USED TO SUPPORT TRINITARIAN DOGMA

Many verses thought by Trinitarians either to prove or allude to the idea that others are equal with the Father will be examined in this chapter. Most of these verses relate to the attempted establishment of the deity of Jesus, while few, as is common in Trinitarian theology, are brought forward in support of the deity of the holy spirit.

As a product of Trinitarianism's sixteen hundred years of development, few verses have escaped a Trinitarian tainting by those who ardently believe the doctrine. Verses that explicitly state that our heavenly Father has no equals have been used to argue that others are equal with Him. Words that have simple meanings are changed into words that have no identifiable meanings. Contexts are ignored, part of one verse is taken out of context and set next to part of another verse that was likewise wrenched from its context. This is how the doctrine of the Trinity has been established, and how it is defended. Yet with all the ostensible certainty its advocates have in the veracity of this system, they still relegate it to the category of *mystery*, the very term undermining the confidence they have in their doctrines:

> To state, however, Trinitarianism in its most general form, and with an accuracy sufficient for our present purpose, it is the doctrine which teaches that in the one God there are three co-essential, co-equal, and co-eternal persons, the second of whom became, in the fullness of time, the Messiah. To uphold this doctrine, the stores of erudition, the subtleties of philosophy, the eloquence of the pulpit, and the productions of the press,—not to mention the decrees and of synods and of councils, the articles of one church, and the confessions and

catechisms of others,—have all been called into requisition. On behalf of this doctrine, in particular, have treatises and comments unnumbered been written and published. For this purpose the Bible has been opened, ransacked, and re-ransacked; and its texts—in fractions, in units, and in thousands—have been brought into logical and metaphysic play. The first words of Genesis have been deemed to intimate a plurality of persons in the Godhead; the last of the book of the Apocalypse, the Deity of Jesus Christ. Indeed, we might say, without a rhetorical figure, that nearly every sentence in the Sacred Records has been adduced, either by itself or in combination with others, to prove, confirm, or defend the dogma of a Triune God.

Happily for the consistency of God's ways, or for the faith of his human family, the doctrine of a Triune God is not only abhorrent to the principles of our nature, but it is not a doctrine of revelation. It is not expressly disclosed in the Bible, if, indeed, it can be proved at all from the records by any just principles of interpretation. Some Roman Catholics say that it cannot be demonstrated from Scripture, but must be received on the authority of the church; and many orthodox Protestants grant, that, so far from being clearly revealed, it can only be inferred from the comparison of one passage with another. It is reasoned out of Sacred Scripture. But reason recoils at the doctrine, and Scripture does not reveal it.[1]

HEBREW-BIBLE VERSES

Genesis 1:26—"And God said, Let us make man in our image, after our likeness..."

See Chapter 14, sub-chapter titled "The Name 'Elohim' and Other Plural Word Endings" regarding the use of plural pronouns referring God.

Genesis 11:7—"Go to, let us go down, and there confound their

---

[1] Wilson, 5, 20.

language, that they may not understand one another's speech."

See Chapter 14, sub-chapter titled "The Name 'Elohim' and Other Plural Word Endings" regarding the use of plural pronouns referring God.

Deuteronomy 6:4—"Hear, O Israel, the Lord the God is one Lord."

See Chapter 14, sub-chapter titled "The Name 'Elohim' and Other Plural Word Endings" regarding the use of plural pronouns referring God.

Isaiah 9:6—"For unto us a child is born, unto us a son is given: and the government shall be upon his shoulder: and his name shall be called Wonderful, Counsellor, The mighty God, The everlasting Father, The Prince of Peace."

This is perhaps the most frequently cited verse from the Old Testament in support of the doctrine of the Trinity. However, it has been translated differently by both Trinitarians and Unitarians alike, and these translations make it clear that it was never intended to show Jesus to be equal with the Father. Biblical scholars from both sides of the debate agree that it may not even be a reference to Jesus, but to a person who was to be born within several years of the time the prophecy was given. First, though, it should be noticed that the Trinitarian method of ascertaining proof for their doctrine is based on a partial phrase taken from the whole of this verse.

The phrase "The mighty God" is interpreted literally by those who believe it is a reference to Jesus. But if we assume this verse has been translated properly and is a reference to Jesus, it generates doctrines that Trinitarians cannot admit. For example, if we interpret other phrases within this verse in the same way Trinitarians interpret the phrase "The Mighty God," it would also prove that Jesus is "the everlasting Father." Since this would destroy the idea that there are three persons in the Godhead, a literal reading, which for some initially seemed to support the Trinitarian hypothesis, plainly contradicts it.

As mentioned, this verse was most likely not a prophecy about Jesus, but to someone to be born soon after the prophecy was given. In addition, Isaiah 9:6 is translated differently by biblical scholars, among whom are highly regarded Trinitarians:

"His name shall be called Wonderful, Counsellor, the Mighty God, the Everlasting Father." Of course this could not mean Jesus,—for the name given is the Father, not the Son, and the best critics are agreed in applying these titles of honor to the triumphant reign of the pious and prosperous Hezekiah; and it was not till comparatively late, that it was even suggested that they might be said of Christ. It is plain to see, by the connection, that they were spoken of a temporal and warlike prince, not of a spiritual teacher.[2]

We are generally directed by our Trinitarian brethren, to the 9th of Isaiah and 6th verse, as positive proof of Christ's deity. "Unto us a child is born, unto us a son is given: and the government shall be upon his shoulder: and his name shall be called *Wonderful, Counsellor*, the *Mighty God*, the *Everlasting Father*," &c. The latter part of this passage, will admit of the following translation. His name, observe this refers to his title, not to his essence, shall be *Wonderful, Counsellor*, the Strong, the Mighty, the Father of the age, the Prince of Peace. Now it is more than doubtful whether this refers to our Saviour at all, but to the times in which the prophecy was delivered. We will give a few reasons for thinking so of this passage. The context plainly shews that the passage predicts the birth of *Hezekiah* the *Son of Ahaz*, who was to establish the kingdom of Judah, the destruction of which was threatened by the kings of Syria and Israel. This will be plainly seen by reference to the 7th of Isaiah. This prophecy may be applied to Christ, though it is worthy of notice, that it has not, that we are aware of, been referred to as applicable to Christ in any part of the New Testament. Now supposing the common translation correct, the application of such lofty epithets to a distinguished personage is quite in unison with the figurative character of the oriental style of writing. And this explanation of the 9th applies as well to the 7th of Isaiah. Indeed it might easily be shewn, if time permitted, that according to the use

---

[2] Allen, 76.

of the very same words, and upon the testimony of learned Trinitarians, as well as Unitarians, that those lofty expressions do not refer to his nature and essence, but to his office, on the admission that the prophecy refers to Christ. But the verse admitted as a prophecy referring to Christ, means that Christ besides being Wonderful, Counsellor, Prince of Peace, was also to be a ruler or potentate, and the author or founder of an everlasting dispensation. And if this be the right interpretation of the passage, then the deity of Christ receives not the shadow of support from it. "Behold a virgin shall conceive and bear a son, and shall call his name *Immanuel.*" Isaiah 7c. This also is a prophecy respecting the birth of Hezekiah. *The virgin*, or so it ought to rendered, not *a* virgin, is the city of Jerusalem, and not *Mary* the mother of our Saviour; that city, as every reader of the Bible knows, is frequently styled by the prophets, "The *virgin*, the *daughter of Zion.*"—Isaiah 23c. 12, 19, 21 v. Jeremiah 14c 17v. Then the city of Jerusalem it is declared, shall produce a son, *i.e.* Hezekiah, who shall deliver the city from the hands of the *Israelitish and Syrian Kings.* Those who demur at this interpretation, and still assert that the 7th of Isaiah refers to the Saviour, are at liberty so to do, but ere they apply this prophecy to Jesus Christ, they have a right to meet and explain the following difficulty. What sign or consolation could it have been to Ahaz, terrified as we may easily imagine he was at the approach of two powerful enemies, and the anticipated loss of his throne and life, to be told that a virgin, or as some will have it *Mary*, should bear and conceive a son 700 years after his death, to restore to him a lost kingdom? As it respects the title Immanuel, *i.e.* God with us, its application to Hezekiah is in the hyperbolic style of the East.[3]

Isa. ix. 6: Of which we remark, first, that the words were originally spoken, not of Christ, but of King Hezekiah. The distinguished Hugo Grotius, and Samuel White, fellow of Trinity College, Cambridge, both of them Trinitarians, take

---

[3] Thomas, 25-27.

this view of it. The words of the latter are as follows: "The government shall be upon his shoulders; that is, that he, King Hezekiah, shall reign in the throne of David, as the metaphor signifies, and as the prophet more fully explains himself in the following verse; which cannot be literally true of our Saviour, whose kingdom was not of this world, as David's was; but in a *second* and *sublimer* sense the expression denotes that power which God devolved on his Son, of governing his spiritual kingdom, the Church." Now we argue that, whatever the names may indicate, if in their primary application they were given to King Hezekiah, they cannot in their secondary application to Christ prove his Supreme Divinity. In the phrase "the mighty God," the word translated "God" means, literally, strong. And we may therefore read "mighty Potentate," if we prefer. The definite article also is wanting in the Hebrew, so that it would be, A mighty God or Potentate. This is the translation which Martin Luther gave, and he declares that the epithet "belongs not to the person of Christ, but to his work and office." Rosenmüller, one of the most learned and Orthodox commentators, says: "It is evident that AEL denotes strong, powerful, and is used in Ezekiel xxxi. 11 of King Nebuchadnezzar, who is called AEL Goyim, 'the mighty one of the heathen,' or, if AEL means God, 'the God of the heathen.'"

The phrase "the everlasting Father" can scarcely be applied to Christ in a literal sense, according to the Trinitarian system; for this would confound the distinction between the Father and the Son. Accordingly we find that Calvin and Grotius translate the words "the Father of the age," or dispensation. Bishop Lowth, Carlile (in his work "Jesus Christ the Great our Saviour"), and Dr. Adam Clarke translate it, "Father of the everlasting age," and in the same manner a great many other Orthodox writers. Such a rendering we are willing to accept, together with the meaning which Calvin gave to the words, namely, "He who is always producing new offspring in the Church." But we prefer the explanation of Dr. Wells, of the Church of England, who says that, when Christ is called the everlasting Father, it means that he is the "author of our eternal salvation, and the Father or head of the world to come, that is, of the Gospel state." I will also add the testimony of Luther, who says that the title Everlasting Father denotes not a person, but his work, and that the Hebrew particle translated "everlasting" does not properly signify eternal, but of indefinite continuance.[4]

Admitting this passage to be a prophetic description of Christ, it is obvious that the argument from it for his Supreme Deity mainly rests on the two titles*"the Mighty God" and "the Everlasting Father." That he is "Wonderful," that he is a "Counsellor"*nay, a "Wonderful Counsellor"*as Castalio, Doederlein, Gataker, and other Trinitarians read the two words, in connection, and have high Rabbinical authority therefore*that he is "The Prince of Peace," preëminently, gloriously, no believer in Christ doubts for a moment. But what is the force of the other two phrases, or how are they applicable to him?

As to the first, Aquila the Jew, the Seventy, (The Septuagint, or Seventy, is the translation into Greek of the Hebrew Bible; executed, probably, by or under the direction of the Jewish Sanhedrim at Alexandria, which, in the second century before Christ, had become the residence of great numbers of that people. The Sanhedrim consisted of seventy or seventy-two members; hence the name of the Translation.) Theodotian, and Symmachus, in their ancient Greek versions of the Old Testament, and the last of them not more recent than the year 200 of our era, all omit the Hebrew word (Al) rendered in our version *God*, and read "Wonderful, Counsellor, Mighty." Le Clerc, a profound Biblical Trinitarian Scholar and critic, translates the passage*"Wonderful, Divine (Al) Counsellor, Mighty." Grotius, certainly no less distinguished, also a Trinitarian*"Consulter of the Mighty God," i.e. one who, in all things, asked counsel of God. Gesenius renders the phrase, "Mighty Hero." (In his *Jesaia*, h. I.; as cited by Gibbs in his Hebrew Lex., under "Al;" Andover ed. 1824.)

---

[4] Eliot, 61-63.

No higher Hebraic authority can be quoted than Gesenius. In Ezekiel 31:11 our own translators have rendered the identical Hebrew phrase into the English "Mighty One." Prof. Noyes, of Harvard University, renders the phrase in his Translations of the Prophets, volumes which should be in the hands of every reader of the Old Testament, "Mighty Potentate," and in this substantially agrees with Luther and De Wette, and as above with Gesenius.

Here, surely, is ample authority, even the highest Trinitarian authority, for understanding the phrase in its application to Christ, in a sense far lower than that of a declaration of his Supreme Deity. Besides, Christ and his Apostles were familiar with the Jewish Scriptures, which constituted, indeed, the chief literature of the nation. They constantly quoted, and sought and used illustrations from them. Is it credible that if he or they ever supposed or understood, or much more knew, that Isaiah had in this passage foreshadowed or declared his Supreme Deity, they never should have cited or referred to the passage?

As to the second phrase*"Everlasting Father," Bishop Lowth renders it in his translation*"Father of the Everlasting Age" or dispensation, that is, the Gospel; as Bishop Jewel, in Queen Elizabeth's time says: "Esay saith that Christ should be 'Pater futuri seculi'; that is, the Father of the world to come; which is, the time of the Gospel." With this agrees Grotius; while Dr. Adam Clarke renders it exactly like Lowth. The Seventy translate it "Messenger of the Great Counsel" or design, and Le Clerc, "Perpetual Father;" because, he remarks, "Christ is perpetual or everlasting Father of all who shall believe in his religion." Prof. Noyes retains the rendering of our Received Version, in his note explaining the words to mean, very much like Le Clerc, "perpetual guardian and friend of his people." Any one of these various interpretations of the phrase, obviously preserves the Sovereignty and Supremacy of God, and subordinates our Lord to Him.

The entire passage, then, may thus be rendered, on the best critical authority*"Wonderful, Divine Counsellor,

Mighty; Father of the Everlasting Age; Prince of Peace." [5]

Isa. ix. 6. "For unto us a child is born, unto us a son is given; and the government shall be upon his shoulder; and his name shall be called Wonderful, Counselor, The Mighty God, The Everlasting Father, The Prince of Peace."

This passage, I believe, is never quoted, or particularly alluded to, by any writer in the New Testament. Yet because the terms 'Mighty God,' and 'Everlasting Father,' are found in it, those who build their faith on the mere sound of words regard it as a decisive proof that Christ is God. The learned Grotius, and some other eminent critics, have understood this passage as referring to Hezekiah the son of Ahaz. But it is generally regarded, and I think justly, as a prediction of the birth of our Savior. The style of the writer is that of royalty; and the establishment of Christianity is described as the setting up of a kingdom.

If this translation is correct, the term 'God' is applied to Christ in the sense described on the preceding page. All that is here affirmed is predicted on one that was a *child born* and a *son given*. But God was never a *child*, nor a *son*; neither was he ever *born* or *given to us*. No one could give him to us; for he belonged to no one. But all this is true of Jesus. He was a child born, and a son given to us.

Can any one believe that the prophet would assert that at some future period God's *name* shall be *called* God? Or that the time will come when the government shall be upon God's shoulder? His name was always God; and the government was always on his shoulder, until his Son came; then *he* bore the burthen of government. God made him King; and set him on his holy hill of Zion.

The word 'name' is pleonastic, and may be omitted. In the original there is nothing answering to the article 'the,' which may also be omitted.

The original word in the Hebrew, which is here rendered God, does not necessarily denote the Supreme Being. The

---

[5] Farley, 68-71.

same word (El) is frequently in the Scriptures applied to mere men, and is variously rendered by our translators.

Ex. xv. 15. "There the dukes of Edom shall be amazed; the *Mighty Men* of Moab shall take hold of them."

2 Kings xxiv. 15. "And he carried away Jehoiachin to Babylon and *the mighty* of the land."

Ezek. xxxi. 11. "I have therefore delivered him into the hand of the *mighty one* of the heathen."

By a comparison of these passages, with the one in Isaiah, it will appear that the same Hebrew words which are translated 'Mighty God,' are also rendered 'Mighty men,' 'the Mighty,' and 'Mighty one.' But as their application to a mere man does not prove him to be God, so neither can their application to Christ prove him to be God. Had the terms in the text last cited been translated as they are in the one under consideration, Nebuchadnezzar would be styled the '*Mighty God* of the nations.' But who would infer from it that he was the Supreme Being? Other similar examples might be adduced. Martin Luther, and many other eminent Hebrew scholars, render the term 'hero,' or 'potentate,' instead of 'God.'

Another title given to our Saviour in the text is 'everlasting Father;' which implies that he will be the perpetual father or friend of his people; as a public benefactor, who has conferred great favors upon the land of his nativity, is called the father of his country. The term '*everlasting*,' relates to the future, not to the past. Christ according to this promise will be the perpetual father of his people.

The following is a translation extensively approved by Trinitarians.

"For unto us a child is born;

Unto us a son is given;

And the government shall be upon his shoulder;

And he shall be called Wonderful,

Counsellor, Mighty Potentate,

Everlasting Father, Prince of Peace." [6]

Jeremiah 23:5-6—"Behold, the days come, saith the LORD, that I will raise unto David a righteous Branch, and a King shall reign and prosper, and shall execute judgment and justice in the earth. In his days Judah shall be saved, and Israel shall dwell safely: and this is his name whereby he shall be called, THE LORD OUR RIGHTEOUS-NESS."

In this verse the word LORD is translated from the Hebrew word Jehovah (or, YHWH), and some interpret this as meaning that Jesus is *Jehovah our righteousness*, rather than Jesus representing Jehovah, our heavenly Father. If the Trinitarian interpretation were right, this would contradict Trinitarian theology, since it breaks down the notion that there are three *separate* persons in the Godhead. Trinitarian dogma rests upon the assumption that Jesus is equal with Jehovah, not that he is Jehovah.

Assuming that this verse refers to Jesus, about which Trinitarian scholars are not in universal agreement, giving someone a name that contains a reference to God is a common form of nomenclature used to assign names to those chosen by God to be a part of His plans. It may also be used to denote those who abided by the Torah and were thus held in high regard by their fellow Jews. It is a form that is illustrative of God's providence as He works within individuals to bring about some desired result, which embodies the Hebrew principle of agency:

> One more passage has been often cited by our Trinitarian brethren, and which I would briefly notice. It occurs in Jeremiah 23:5, 6: "Behold the days come, saith Jehovah, that I will raise unto David a righteous branch, and a king shall reign and prosper, and shall execute judgment and justice in the earth. In his days Judah shall be saved, and Israel shall dwell safely; and this is his name whereby he shall be called, Jehovah our Righteousness." Allowing, for the sake of argument, that this text refers to Christ, which is by no means clear*for Grotius thinks it rather refers to King Zerubbabel and the

---

6 Morgridge, 120-122.

release of the Jews from the Babylonish Captivity*then the exposition of Prof. Noyes, in the note to his translation of the passage well expresses the prophet's meaning. "This symbolical name" ("Jehovah our Righteousness," or, as Dr. Noyes renders it, "Jehovah-is-our-salvation") "was to be given to the glorious king, the Messiah here predicted, to denote that Jehovah would bring salvation to his people by his means, or to denote what is said in the two preceding lines, that 'in his days Judah should be saved, and Israel dwell securely.'" (Noyes's Prophets, vol. ii. 273. Dr. Noyes adds in his note: "In regard to the rendering *salvation*, it is a secondary signification of the original term, which, denoting *righteousness*, was used to denote the *favor* of God consequent upon it, and hence, *deliverance, blessings, salvation*. See Gesenius's Lex. That the substantive verb (is) should be supplied, is evident from the application of the name to the city of Jerusalem in ch. 33:16, and from the application of similar names to various persons in the Old Testament; for instance, *Elijah*. It is not at all probable that he was called *My God the Lord*, or *My God, Jehovah*, but Jehovah *is* my God. So the common version correctly renders Ezek. 48:35, 'The Lord is there.') Dr. Ad. Clarke says: "I believe Jesus to be Jehovah; but I doubt whether this text calls him so. No doctrine so vitally important should be rested on an interpretation so dubious and unsupported by the text." (Clarke's Commentary, h. 1. note.) Dr. Blayney, in his note on the passage, having rendered it*"And this is his name which Jehovah shall call, Our Righteousness,"*says: "A phrase exactly the same as 'and Jehovah shall call him so'; which .... . implies that God will make him such as he called him, that is, 'our righteousness,' or the author and means of our salvation and acceptance.... . I doubt not but some persons will be offended with me for depriving them, by this translation, of a favorite argument for proving the Divinity (Deity) of our Saviour from the Old Testament. But I cannot help it. I have done it with no ill design, but purely because I think, and am morally certain, that the text, as it stands, will not properly admit of any other construction. The LXX. have so translated it before me, in an age when there could not possibly be any bias of prejudice either for or against the before-mentioned doctrine; a doctrine *which draws its decisive proofs from the New Testament only.*" (Blayney's Jerem. h. 1. note.)[7]

We next refer to Jer. xxiii. 6, in which Christ is called "Jehovah our righteousness"; but it so happens that in chapter xxxiii. 16 of the same prophet, exactly the same name is applied to the city of Jerusalem. "In those days shall Judah be saved and Jerusalem dwell safely, and this is the name wherewith she shall be called,—Jehovah our righteousness." So that we have no difficulty in either case. Le Clerc explains the passage for us as follows: "The Messiah is said to be called Jehovah our righteousness to denote that in his days, and by his means, God would, in a remarkable manner, exhibit proofs of his own justice by punishing the wicked and defending the righteous; so in chapter xxxiii. 16, Jerusalem is designated by the same title, meaning that God would cause righteousness to flourish in that city, namely, in the Christian Church." [8]

It cannot be hence proved that the name Jehovah [or, Yahweh] is attributed to Christ: for these words ought to be applied to Israel, who is spoken of immediately before, in the very same verse, "In his days Judah shall be saved, and Israel shall dwell safely." This may easily be made to appear from what the same prophet states, chap. xxxiii. 15, 16, "In those days, and at that time, will I cause the branch of righteousness to grow up unto David; and he shall execute judgment and righteousness in the land. And in those days shall Judah be saved, and Jerusalem shall dwell safely; and this is the name wherewith SHE shall be called—the Lord (Jehovah) our righteousness." For, as commentators have observed, the pronoun (SHE) is in the Hebrew feminine, which must necessarily refer to Jerusalem, answering to Israel, in the passage before quoted (xxiii. 6). Hence it appears that in the place last mentioned the words "he shall be called" are spoken of Israel.—But though we were even to grant, that the name

---

7 Farley, 71-73.

8 Eliot, 63.

Jehovah might here be referred to Christ, yet it appears, from other considerations, that it could not be asserted that Christ was God: for otherwise it would follow that Jerusalem also was God. For it must be understood that the whole clause "the Lord our righteousness" (JEHOVAH-TZIDKENU) is as it were converted into one name, and moreover given to a thing which is not God. In the same manner, the mountain whereon Abraham was about to offer up his son is called, Gen. xxii. 14, "The Lord will see" or be seen, JEHOVAH-JIREH.... Whether therefore the words are to be understood of Christ, or of Israel, the meaning of them is, that the one Lord our God would then justify us: which, with respect to the Israelites, was accomplished by him, when Christ appeared.[9]

Since there are relatively few verses in the Hebrew Bible which Trinitarians use in an attempt to show that others are equal with the Father, I will now consider those in the New Testament.

NEW-TESTAMENT VERSES

Matthew 1:23—"Behold, a virgin shall be with child, and shall bring forth a son, and they shall call his name Emmanuel, which being interpreted is, God with us."

See Chapter 14, sub-chapter titled 'The Name "Immanuel" (or, "Emmanuel")'

Matthew 9:8—"But when the multitudes saw it, they marvelled, and glorified God, which had given such power unto men." Some have inferred from this that God performed the miraculous acts *directly* and was hence glorified by the multitude, and since Jesus was the one who performed the acts, he is, by inference, God. This is not a correct inference because, as has been discussed, things are not always done directly by the principal, but are frequently performed by an agent, and hence *indirectly* performed by the principal *through* the appointed agent. But this issue is more readily resolved because, within the same verse, Jesus is spoken of as a man who had been given power by

---

9 *The Racovian Catechism*, 76-78.

God. Some things are obvious.

But to further pursue the Trinitarian interpretation, in the case of people glorifying God when Jesus performed a miraculous act, they understood that the Father was the source of his power. Jesus was acting at God's behest since he only did things that pleased the Father (John 8:29). This is established by the last clause of Matt. 9:8, which tells us that "they glorified God, who had *given such power* unto men":

> A Spirit every where present at the same time cannot liter-ally leave one place and come to another. But in the highly figurative language of Scripture, Jehovah is said to come to a people whenever his authorized messenger appears. When Jesus restored a young man to life, in the city of Nain, "there came fear on all: and they glorified God, saying, that a great prophet is risen up among us; and, *That God hath visited his people."* Luke vii. 16. God visited his people, that is, came to them, by sending them, "a great prophet." God is said to visit his people when he sends them any peculiar blessing. It is said of Naomi, (Ruth i. 6,) "Then she arose with her daughters-in-law, that she might return from the country of Moab: for she had heard in the country of Moab how that the LORD *had visited his people in giving them bread."* [10]

It is appropriate to give the highest glory and honor to our heav-enly Father since, according to the texts, He is the originator of the power that anybody had. According to Matt. 28:18, Jesus received his power from the Father, so when he performed a miracle the people were thankful to him, but they always knew to give the highest honor to the Father. To them this was simple:

> Thus on the miraculous healing of the sick of the palsy by *Christ* (Matt. ix, 8), *When the multitude saw it, they marvelled, and glorified* GOD *who had given such power unto men.* In con-sequence of his raising the only Son of a widow from the dead (Luke, vii, 16), *There came a fear on all: and they glorified* GOD, *saying, that a great prophet is risen up among us: and that*

---

[10] Morgridge, 135-136.

God hath visited his people; i.e. *visited* them by his great prophet; and by the *signal* power which he communicated to that illustrious representative.—See John ix, 17, 33. Again: on the cure of a child by the same compassionate delegate (Luke ix, 43), the people *were all amazed at the mighty power of* GOD. And when the blind man received his sight near Jericho, *he followed* Jesus, *glorifying* GOD. *And all the people, when they saw it gave praise unto* GOD.—Ibid. xviii, 43. This appears to have been the general sense of all those who on the spot beheld these miracles. *Insomuch that the multitude wondered when they saw the dumb to speak, the maimed to be whole, the lame to walk, and the blind to see: and they glorified the* GOD *of Israel.*—Matt. xv, 31.

Our Saviour, on occasion of these miracles, is sometimes said to have been *worshipped*: at other times suppliants are said to have *fallen at his feet* (Mark v, 22; vii, 25), an eastern custom of shewing very great respect.—See 1 Kings xviii, 7.

The attributing these miracles ultimately to the *Almighty,* was a construction not confined to the crowds that frequently surrounded our Lord merely from curiosity. St. Luke informs us (xix, 37), that, on the remarkable occasion when our Saviour, followed by a vast concourse of the people, made his triumphant entry into Jerusalem; it was then that his numerous *proselytes* united in giving an open and a glorious testimony of *their* conviction from *whom* all those instances of Divine Power had proceeded. For, *at the descent of the Mount of Olives,* on their approach to the city, inspirited by the presence of their Great Master, *the whole multitude of the disciples began to rejoice and praise* GOD *with a loud voice, for all the mighty works that they had seen.* Now that they were not mistaken in thus referring these mighty acts to the *Deity,* and not to any other being; Christ himself, and the apostles also, have fully confirmed.[11]

Matthew 28:19—"Go ye therefore, and teach all nations, baptizing

---

[11] Gifford, 85-88.

them in the name of the Father, and of the Son, and of the Holy Ghost."

See Chapter 3, specifically topics associated with the "Baptismal Formula."

Matthew 28:20—"Teaching them to observe whatsoever I have commanded you: and, lo, I am with you always, even unto the end of the world." Some have argued that the only way Jesus could have fulfilled his promise of being with them "always" was by being omnipresent, and therefore, by inference, he would have to be God. But the promise to be with them always could have been fulfilled without requiring that Jesus be omnipresent:

> There are a great many ways in which this promise we have been considering, and that other promise, "Lo, I am with you always," can be fulfilled, without supposing Christ to be an omnipresent being. If we *abide* in him, and his words *abide* in us, *is he not with us always?* Do we not say of the good man who hath left the legacy of his pure spirit behind him, "He being dead, yet speaketh?" Is not, in a sense, the spirit of WASHINGTON with us still? And is it not our earnest hope and prayer that his spirit may burn and glow in the hearts of his countrymen, even to the end of the world? If then Christ *"is the true vine, and we are the branches"*—if, as the branch cannot bear fruit of itself, except it abide in the vine, so no more can we, except we abide in Christ, is he not always with those *thus united to him?* Are not his *commands* always with us? And here let me pause, and entreat you to ponder with me those significant words, in his last address to his disciples before his crucifixion, "This is my commandment, *that ye love one another."*
>
> But further, are not Christ's *promises* always with us? Is not his wonderful *example* always before us? Who is the Christian's companion but him whom he has chosen as his guide to Heaven? Is he not "the good Shepherd," and do not his sheep *hear his voice*, and follow him as they will not follow

a stranger? [12]

The expression "I am with you always" is therefore to be understood in a spiritual, not physical, sense, which (the physical sense) is what the Trinitarian interpretation depends upon.

Luke 1:47—"And my spirit hath rejoiced in God my Saviour."

See Chapter 14, sub-chapter titled 'The Term "Saviour"' regarding the term "Saviour" in its application to God and others.

Luke 8:38-39—"Now the man out of whom the devils were departed besought him that he might be with him: but Jesus sent him away, saying, Return to thine own house, and shew how great things God hath done unto thee. And he went his way, and published throughout the whole city how great things Jesus had done unto him."

See the explanation given for Matthew 9:8 in this section.

Luke 9:43—"And they were all amazed at the mighty power of God. But while they wondered every one at all the things which Jesus did, he said unto his disciples."

See the explanation given for Matthew 9:8 in this section.

Luke 12:10—"And whosoever shall speak a word against the Son of man, it shall be forgiven him: but unto him that blasphemeth against the Holy Ghost, it shall not be forgiven."

See Chapter 13, specifically words associated with "blaspheme against."

Luke 23:40-41—"But the other answering rebuked him, saying, Dost not thou fear God, seeing thou art in the same condemnation? And we indeed justly; for we receive the due reward for our deeds: but this man hath done nothing amiss." Some contend that the expression "Dost not thou fear God?" is a reference by the malefactor to Jesus. This is an incorrect interpretation since the malefactor qualified his thoughts by stating that he and the other malefactor were receiving the proper punishment for their deeds, but that this *man*, Jesus,

---

[12] Dana, 215.

had done nothing wrong. Jesus, a man, is distinguished from God in this very same verse.

John 1:1, 14—"In the beginning was the Word, and the Word was with God, and the Word was God.... And the Word was made flesh, and dwelt among us, (and we beheld his glory, the glory as of the only begotten of the Father,) full of grace and truth."

See Chapter 12 regarding the concept of the *logos*. *See* also Appendix IV regarding the phrase "In the beginning."

John 1:3—"All things were made by him; and without him was not any thing made that was made."

This is a more involved verse than is commonly recognized, not only due to the introduction of the concept of the logos here, but also due to the way in which masculine pronouns have been assigned rather than the neuter pronoun "it," the way in which the word "God" or "god" has been translated (rather than the word "divine), the way in which the word "with" has been understood, and so on. But for the sake of discussion, we will look at the common Trinitarian interpretation, which is based on a simple, and biased reading of the text. Some interpret the phrase "all things were made by him" as a reference to the physical realm, meaning that Jesus created the physical universe, which is inferred from a similarity between the language in John 1:3 and Colossians 1:16. Colossians 1:16 says: "For by him were all things created, that are in heaven, and that are in earth, visible and invisible, whether they be thrones, or dominions, or principalities, or powers: all things were created by him, and for him."

If the two verses are parallel, then the phrase "all things" in John 1:3 is explained in connection with the specific things mentioned in Colossians 1:16. In Colossians 1:16, the things regarding Jesus and his ministry are non-physical things. They are life and light, thrones, dominions, principalities and powers. The Trinitarian inference that John 1:3 refers to the creation of the physical universe is suspect, as the phrase "all things" is to be interpreted in a qualified sense, which may be seen by comparing this same phrase to other parts of Scripture in which it appears. For example, in 1 John 2:20, Christians are said to know "all things," which is not categorically true, but restricted to a knowledge of a specific subject determined by the context:

The words admit of two interpretations:—First, that the human race were renovated, reformed, restored, and as it were new made, by Christ; because he had conveyed eternal life to them while they were in a lost condition, and obnoxious to eternal death; and had imparted to them the most efficient motives to return to God whom they had forsaken. In reference to this John reproves the world, because that after Christ had delivered it from destruction, and had illumined it with the light of the gospel, it did not acknowledge him, but had spurned and rejected him. For it is agreeable to the Hebrew language, that in such forms of speech the words "to make" and "to create" should have the same meaning as to make anew, and recreate; because that language is destitute of what are called compound verbs. The second interpretation is, that the future world, which we expect, is, as to us, made by Christ; as it is also called future in respect to us, though now present to Christ and the angels.[13]

Jesus, then, according to the New Testament texts, brought about a new circumstance in which spiritual completeness is available.

John 1:15—"John bare witness of him, and cried, saying, This was he of whom I spake, He that cometh after me is preferred before me: for he was before me."

The prologue of John's gospel, which refers to the first eighteen verses, is very unique, so unique that it has been given its designation. It involves very different language and concepts not used by the other writers, so developing a Christology or theology upon this section is risky, to say the least. The language employed is unfamiliar to most people, the concepts introduced are similarly difficult to comprehend and don't comport with ordinary human experience, so extra care must be taken in endeavoring to derive meaning from this section. This includes not detaching single verses in the same way one might the book of Proverbs, which frequently are parcels of wisdom handed out and applicable in their own right and need little contextual or

---

¹³ *The Racovian Catechism*, 90-91.

narrative development.

But to examine a Trinitarian claim about this verse, the phrase "for he was before me" is not necessarily a reference to time, as some contend to support the idea that Jesus pre-existed his birth on earth. The word "before" has more than one connotation. John 1:15 refers not to time, but to the importance of the Jesus's mission as compared to the importance of John's mission. John admitted that he was not worthy of untying Jesus's shoes, which made clear the relative importance of his own ministry to that of Jesus's. There was a need for John to tell the people to switch their attention to Jesus, since prior to Jesus's arrival the people had been following John.

John 2:19—"Jesus answered and said unto him, Destroy this temple and in three days I will raise it up."

This verse and John 10:18 are the only instances in the Bible where the resurrection of Jesus is not referred to the Father, but to Jesus. This stands in contrast to the many times the Father is spoken of as having raised Jesus from the dead. But since God and Jesus are spoken of in a similar manner, some improperly infer that Jesus must also be God. The verses that speak of Jesus's resurrection *after* it occurred are consistent in stating that it was the Father who was responsible for raising Jesus from the dead. The one or two verses in which Jesus said he would raise himself from the dead must therefore be explained in light of the many verses that tell us who, *in hindsight*, raised him up:

> Acts v. 30-33, 'the God of our fathers raised up Jesus ... him hath God exalted with his right hand to be a Prince and a Saviour, for to give repentance to Israel, and forgiveness of sins.' Gal. i. I, 'by Jesus Christ, and God the Father, who raised him from the dead.' Rom. x. 9, 'if thou shalt believe in thine heart that God hath raised him from the dead, thou shalt be saved.' I Cor. vi. 14, 'God hath both raised up the Lord, and will also raise us up by his own power.' I Thess, i. 10, 'to wait for his Son from heaven, whom he raised from the dead.' Heb. x. 5, 'sacrifice and offering thou wouldest not, but a body hast thou prepared me.' I Peter i. 21, 'who by him do believe in God that raised him from the dead.' So many

are the texts wherein the Son is said to be raised up by the Father alone, which ought to have greater weight than the single passage in St. John ii. 19, 'destroy this temple and in three days I will raise it up'—where he spake briefly and enigmatically, without explaining his meaning to enemies who were unworthy of a fuller answer, on which account he thought it unnecessary to mention the power of the Father.[14]

Jesus's declaration in this verse is in agreement with the Father being the one who raised him from the dead. It was Jesus who was responsible for being in a position where he could be raised from the dead by God, since he could have decided to not go through with the plan. He is recorded in various texts as having prayed to God that, if there was any other way things could be accomplished than him being crucified, he'd prefer that way. In the end he said, "not my will, but yours be done." It was up to Jesus to fulfill his part, which would result in the Father fulfilling His.

John 5:18-19—"Therefore the Jews sought the more to kill him, because he not only had broken the sabbath, but said also that God was his Father, making himself equal with God."

Some argue that the phrase "making himself equal with God" means that Jesus was equal with God in every way. This is based on the incorrect assumption that the word "equal" is used in an unlimited sense. The Trinitarian interpretation is easily seen to be incorrect, since Jesus claimed that God was his Father, and because of this his equality *in some respect* could be established. It should also be noticed that it was not Jesus who claimed equality with the Father, but the people who sought to entrap him. Jesus did not think equality with God "was something to be grasped" (Phil 2:6). The apostle John agreed with this: "And these are written that ye might believe that Jesus is the Christ, the Son of God" (John 20:31). This was the purpose of John's gospel, so concluding that John wrote to show that Jesus is completely equal with the Father, is wrong.

It is also apparent that the Jews did not think that Jesus was claim-

---

14 Milton, 36-37.

ing to be God since they did not accuse him of this at his trial. The most they accused him of was that he claimed to be the "King of the Jews,"[15] which was written in Greek, Latin and Hebrew and placed above his head while he was on the cross. Those who succeeded in crucifying him had given great attention to who Jesus said he was, and they did not accuse him of claiming to be God.

John 6:62—"What and if ye should see the Son of man ascend up where he was before?"

Some have thought that the phrase "up where he was before" is a reference to Jesus's existence prior to his birth, which is not a correct understanding. The whole purpose of Jesus's obedience to the Father and his subsequent crucifixion was that he would be raised from the dead. Jesus's question to his disciples was essentially this: "How will you respond if you see me get up from the dead, appearing to you alive just as I was before my crucifixion?" The Trinitarian interpretation ignores the point of Jesus's resurrection, which is that he would be raised from the dead and therefore be alive again.

John 6:64—"But there are some of you that believe not. For Jesus knew from the beginning who they were that believed not, and who should betray him."

This has been interpreted by some as proof that Jesus existed from the beginning of time. But the "beginning" refers to a specific time period, and it must be determined which time period it refers to. In John 6:64, the "beginning" may refer to the beginning of Jesus's adulthood, which, according to Jewish tradition, is age thirteen. Or it may refer to the beginning of his ministry, which was when he was thirty. Or it may refer to the beginning of some other time period, such as the day of Pentecost, Jesus's baptism, etc. So the question must be answered, in the beginning of what timeframe? John 6:64 probably refers to the beginning of the apostles' ministries. Jesus knew from the beginning of their appointments who would betray him. He knew,

---

15 Matt. 27:37, Mark 15:26, Luke 23:38, John 19:19

for example, that Peter would betray him by denying him three times, and that Judas would betray him with a kiss. Jesus knew upon their selection as apostles who would do such things. Whatever timeframe it refers to, it is inappropriate to automatically assume that a word such as "beginning" refers to the beginning of time.

John 8:58—"Jesus said unto them, Verily, verily, I say unto you, before Abraham was, I am."

This is perhaps the most frequently cited verse in support of the belief that Jesus pre-existed his birth, and is also used by some to show that Jesus is God, since the phrase *I AM* is used in Exodus 3:14 in reference to the Father.[16] Some have insisted that the phrase used by Jesus in John's gospel is correlated to that used by God in Exodus. But the expression *I AM*, like the expression *logos*, is one that is not so easily understood. But we may readily rule out the Trinitarian interpretation:

> Then as to the declaration of our Lord, recorded in the Gospel of St. John: (John 8:58.) "Before Abraham was, I am." Why, it may be asked in the outset, why, except for a purpose, have our translators departed here from their usual mode of rendering the exact Greek word so often used by our Lord? Here it reads, "I am"—literally, and without supplement; in other places, "I am *he*"? (Vid. in this same chapter, vv. 24, 28; also, John 4:26; 13:19. Compare also Matt. 24:5; Mark 13:6, and Luke 21:8; also, John 3:28 and Acts 13:25.) Why not here as there—"I am *he*"—the Messiah purposed in the counsels of God long before Abraham had being? This is the interpretation of Grotius, and I believe the true one. Trinitarians are accustomed to insist that our Lord meant to declare that he was the "I AM" of the Old Dispensation, who revealed Himself to Moses by the name or appellation, "I am that I am;" but Dr. J. Pye Smith tells us (Scripture Test. vol. 2 161,) that "the words" there "are in the future tense, 'I will be that which I will be,' Exod. 3:14; and most probably it was not

---

16 Exodus 3:14—"And God said unto Moses, I AM THAT I AM: and he said, Thus shalt thou say unto the children of Israel, I AM hath sent me unto you."

intended as a name, but as a declaration of a certain fulfill-ment of all the promises of God." While Mr. Carlile of the Scotch Kirk says: ("Jesus Christ the Great God our Saviour." 174.) "I do not mean to rest any argument on the expression *I am*, taken by itself. It occurs repeatedly in this chapter, and is translated *I am he*."

If then the use of the word was no assumption, as of in-herent right by our Lord, of the alleged name or appellation of Jehovah, the rendering of the Common Version is mean-ingless. What our Lord meant was, that before Abraham was born, God had purposed that he should be the Messiah. So to speak, in allusion to the Divine purposes, was familiar to the Jews. In Jeremiah, (Jer. 1.) God says to the prophet: "Be-fore I formed thee in the womb I knew thee; before thou camest forth at birth I sanctified thee; and I ordained thee a prophet unto the nations." Repeatedly in this very chapter he had used the same phrase, "I am;" and as repeatedly our translators render it, as essential to the sense, "I am he," that is, the Messiah, for whom the Jews had been long looking. That was what they, he had said must believe, or "die in their sins;" that was, as he had just before told them, what they would "know" when they had "lifted him up;" and that was what he now declared himself to have been in the omniscient councils of God, long before the era of the great Patriarch. (verses 24, 28, 58)[17]

I WILL now consider the import of the phrase *"I am,"* as presented in the extract which forms the subject of the foregoing letter. You remark that, "considering Christ's audi-ence, and their familiarity with the phrase, and the sense they invariably attached to it, you can never doubt he designed to declare himself Jehovah, when he said, before 'Abraham was, I am.'" It is contended by many learned men that the Greek phrase here translated, "I am," is invariably used to mean, I am *he*, that is, the Messiah. Twice before, in this chapter, the same Greek phrase is introduced, and in both instances it is

---

[17] Farley, 105-107.

rendered by the translators of our common version, "I am *he*;" it occurs in the twenty-fourth and twenty-eighth verses. Why King James's translators saw fit to render this verse differently from the others, it is impossible with certainty to decide, though the reason may be very easily conjectured. It certainly would not have injured the sense of the verse to add, as they had done in the two former verses, the pronoun he, and it would have prevented much controversy. To show that in the 28th verse Christ was speaking of himself as *the Messiah*, and *not* as God, he says, "then shall ye know that I am he, *and that I do nothing of myself.*" The same expression may also be found in John 4:26; 13:19; 18:5, 6, 8, and in every instance it is translated, "I am he."

In Exodus 3:14, the term "I AM," is used as a *proper name*, and applied by Jehovah to himself; "thus shalt thou say to the children of Israel, I AM hath sent me unto you." The sentence is perfect and complete. Whereas, if, in the verse under consideration, the phrase is to be understood *in the same sense— as a proper name*, the sentence is an incomplete and unmeaning one. Read it thus, understanding "I am" as a proper name, and you will discover this, for the proper noun is entirely without its corresponding verb. But read it with the pronoun he understood, and it is a complete sentence; though the use of the present tense in connection with the past strikes the ear of a grammarian singularly and unpleasantly. The biblical critic Wakefield says, "the peculiar use of the present tense in the usage of Scriptural expressions is to imply determination and certainty; as if he had said, 'my mission was settled and certain before the birth of Abraham.'"[18]

The Trinitarian argument rests upon the circumstance of Jesus having used a phrase that, when translated into English from Greek, resembles a phrase that God used when translated into English from Hebrew. It is difficult to say whether these phrases are identical, similar or merely coincidental in that they are translated from their respective languages into English as the same phrase. In any case, they

---

[18] Dana, 169-170.

cannot be used to prove such an enigmatic and abstruse notion of three persons in one being.

John 10:18—"No man taketh it from me, but I lay it down of myself. I have power to lay it down, and I have power to take it again. This commandment have I received of my Father."

See the explanation of John 2:19 in this chapter.

John 10:30—"I and my Father are one."

A most astonishing argument for our heavenly Father having equals is drawn from this verse. The argument is essentially that this verse should be interpreted as "I and my Father are one essence" (or "one being"). There is no need to resort to such a bizarre interpretation, since two or more people may be *one* in a variety of ways, each of which is more sensible than the preposterous conclusion that they are one essence, especially since nobody could possibly know what that expression means. Others think it means that God and Jesus are one person. If this interpretation were true, it would break down the notion that there are three separate persons in the godhead, since God and Jesus would thus only be one, and hence negate the most fundamental aspect of Trinitarianism.

Trinitarians commonly make the mistake of assuming that the interpretation they assign to a verse is the only possible one, to the exclusion of all other interpretations. Without question, though, there are always far more reasonable interpretations for verses than those for which the orthodox have assigned a meaning. Regarding John 10:30, there are reasonable explanations as to what the term *one* refers to, which makes it wholly unnecessary to resort to the incomprehensible notion that God and Jesus are the same person:

> The first is John x. 30, 'I and my Father are one'—that is, one in essence, as it is commonly interpreted. But God forbid that we should decide rashly on any point relative to the Deity. Two things may be called "one" in more than one way. Scripture saith, and the Son saith, *I and my Father are one*—I bow to their authority. Certain commentators conjecture that they are one in essence—I reject what is merely man's invention.

For the Son has not left us to conjecture in what manner he is one with the Father (whatever member of the Church may have first arrogated to himself the merit of the discovery), but explains the doctrine himself most fully, so far as we are concerned to know it. The Father and the Son are one, not indeed in essence, for he had himself said the contrary in the preceding verse, 'my Father, which gave them me, is greater than all' (see also xiv. 28, 'my Father is greater than I'), and in the following verses he distinctly denies that he made himself God in saying, 'I and my Father are one'; he insists that he had only said as follows, which implies far less, x. 36, 'say ye of him whom the Father hath sanctified, and sent into the world, Thou blasphemest; because I said, I am the Son of God?'[19]

The first proof, and one perhaps among those most frequently cited from the New Testament Scriptures, of the proper and Supreme Deity of our Saviour, is his own declaration: "I and my Father are one." (John 10:30.) But how did he explain this declaration himself? Did he permit such an interpretation of his words by those whom he addressed, as is alleged? On the utterance of these words the Jews, who, I grant, seem to have understood him as meaning in the most literal sense that he was God, prepared at once to stone him as a blasphemer; and no wonder. But did our Lord admit the charge? Mark the words with which he checked their mistaken purpose: "Is it not written in your law," (a common way among the Jews of designating their Scripture,) "'I said, ye are Gods?' If he called them Gods, unto whom the word of God came," (i.e. who were the authorized, specially commissioned, inspired messengers of God's will, e.g. Moses, the Judges, Angels, etc., as we have before seen)*"and the Scripture cannot be broken; say ye of him, whom the Father hath sanctified, and sent into the world, Thou blasphemest! because I said"*what? that I am GOD, your Jehovah? By no means; but "because I said I am the Son of God? If I do not

---

[19] Milton, 21.

the works of my Father, believe me not. But if I do, though ye believe not me, believe the works; that ye may know, and believe, that the Father is in me, and I in him." (John 10: 30-38)

All, then, that he admitted was, that he had declared himself to be "the Son of God;" this being, as he must have meant, equivalent to his first declaration: "I and my Father are one." The oneness with the Father which he claimed to possess, was not, then, a oneness of essence, but a oneness of purpose, consent, will, affection; such a oneness as might be supposed to exist between an affectionate and good parent and a dutiful, loving, devoted child; such a oneness, indeed, as in his remarkable prayer before the crucifixion, attesting again its subsistence between his Father and himself, he prays may also subsist among his chosen disciples, nay, among "them who should believe on him through their word" or preaching; "that they all," he says, "may be one; as Thou, Father, art in me, and I in Thee, that they also may be one in us." (John 17.) St. Paul spoke of Apollos and himself as One, in the same sense (1 Cor. 3:6, 8); such phraseology is very common in Scripture.[20]

In reviewing this subject it appears that the Jews had no just cause to accuse Jesus of making himself God. He had said, *I and my Father are one.* He did not say one nature, one essence, one being, or one God. A Father and Son are two distinct beings. Christ is assuring his disciples of their safety. He calls them his sheep; and says, *neither shall any man pluck them out of my hand.* As additional security he adds, *My Father who gave them me is greater than all,* and no man is able to pluck them out of my Father's hand. He here declares the Father to be greater than all, consequently, greater than himself. If the sheep had not belonged to the Father before they belonged to Christ, the Father could not have given them to him. If the Father were not greater than the Son, his care of the sheep would have added nothing to their safety. *I and my Father are one,* means one in the business of watching over

---

[20] Farley, 85-87.

and protecting the sheep. Paul and Apollos *are one*. The husband and wife *are one*. All Christians *are one*. Jesus prayed that all his disciples might be one in the same sense that he and his Father are one. "That they may be one, *even as we are one*."—*John* xvii. 22.

The same unfairness, on the part of the Jews, appears in the fifth chapter, where they accused Jesus of making himself *equal with God*, only for saying that God was his Father. A charge which Jesus immediately refuted by saying, *Verily, verily, I say unto you, the Son can do nothing of himself*. If Jesus were God's equal he could do every thing himself. [21]

The following are other examples where people are said to be one:

- John 17:11—"And now I am no more in the world, but these are in the world, and I come to thee. Holy Father, keep through thine own name those whom thou hast given me, that they may be one, as we are."
- 1 Cor. 3:6-8—"I have planted, Apollos watered; but God gave the increase. So then neither is he that planteth any thing, neither he that watereth; but God that giveth the increase. Now he that planteth and he that watereth are one: and every man shall receive his own reward according to his own labour."
- Acts 4:32—"And the multitude of them that believed were of one heart and of one soul: neither said any of them that ought of the things which he possessed was his own; but they had all things common."

John 10:33—"The Jews answered him, saying, For a good work we stone thee not; but for blasphemy; and because that thou, being a man, makest thyself God."

This verse is cited frequently in support of the notion that Jesus, a man, claimed to be God (or divine). But in the verses that follow, Jesus manifestly repels the charge that he made himself God. He responded to his accusers by saying, "Is it not written in your law, I said, Ye are gods?" Then, in verse 36, he said, "Say ye of him whom the Father hath sanctified, and sent into the world, thou blasphemest,

---

[21] Morgridge, 48-49.

because I said, I am the Son of God?" Jesus made it clear that he was not God, but the Son of God, and that, even if he were to be called "God," it would be according to the same principle that permitted the judges of Israel to be addressed by this title.

John 12:44-45—"Jesus cried and said, He that believeth on me, believeth not on me, but on him that sent me.

This verse has been used by some to support the theory that Jesus is God. The statement, however, would be an imprecise and verbose way of saying that Jesus is God. If proof of Jesus's deity were to be asserted by John here, why did he not just come right out and say it? Why resort to so many words that would have led many to misunderstand his meaning? If this were interpreted literally, it would mean that nobody who believes in Jesus really believes in him, which may be seen from the expression, "He that believeth on me, believeth not on me." But there is little need to examine the various nonsensical Trinitarian interpretations, since the verse simply means that whoever believes in Jesus believes that God is his Father, and that God sent Jesus to accomplish his redemptive mission.

John 14:7+9—"If ye had known me, ye should have known my Father also: and from henceforth ye know him, and have seen him.... Jesus saith unto him, Have I been so long time with you, and yet hast thou not known me, Philip? he that hath seen me hath seen the Father: and how sayest thou, Shew us the Father?"

Some have argued that these two verses imply that Jesus is the Father. But this destroys the notion that there are three separate persons in the godhead, which contradicts Trinitarian dogma. In arriving at a Trinitarian interpretation, though, Trinitarians employ a most unnatural and literal reading of these verses. If we were to apply this method of interpretation everywhere this sort of expression occurs, it would teach us that we are Jesus. For example, Matthew 10:40 says, "He that receiveth you receiveth me, and he that receiveth me receiveth him that sent me." According to the Trinitarian method, we would be free to adopt the belief that we are Jesus. But phrases such as these simply mean that since Jesus and the Father have the same purpose, those who accept Jesus become one in purpose with them since Jesus always does the Father's will. It must always be remembered that, according to John 1:18, "no man has seen God at any time," so the expression "he that hath seen me hath seen the Father" must be figurative:

> John xiv. 9, "He that hath seen me hath seen the Father, and how sayest thou then, Show us the Father?" The meaning of these words is sufficiently explained by the connection in which they stand, If you will read the fourteenth chapter through, they will give you no trouble. Christ made a clear revelation of God, and therefore made known of the Father as much as it is possible for us at present to know. So the words are explained by Dr. William Sherlock. "He that hath seen me hath seen the Father, that is, in plain words, the will of God was fully declared to the world by Christ. Thus God was in Christ." [22]

John 14:17—"Even the Spirit of truth; whom the world cannot receive, because it seeth him not, neither knoweth him: but ye know him; for he dwelleth with you, and shall be in you."

The personification of the "Spirit of truth" in this verse, coupled with the capitalization of the word "Spirit," has (understandably) misled some to conclude that the "Spirit of truth" is an actual person which, to say the least, would be an unusual name for a person. But the issue is settled by the fact that the Greek contains neuter pronouns, and the translators substituted masculine pronouns in their place. The verse should read, "Even the spirit of truth, which the world cannot receive, because it seeth it not, neither knows it: but ye know it, for it dwelleth with you and shall be in you."

John 14:26—"But the Comforter, which is the Holy Ghost, whom the Father will send in my name, he shall teach you all things, and bring all things to your remembrance, whatsoever I have said unto you."

---

[22] Eliot, 80.

See Chapter 13 for an explanation of "holy spirit."

John 16:13-14—"Howbeit when he, the Spirit of truth, is come, he will guide you into all truth: for he shall not speak of himself; but whatsoever he shall hear, that shall he speak: and he will shew you things to come."

See Chapter 13 for an explanation of "holy spirit."

John 17:5—"And now, O Father, glorify thou me with thine own self with the glory which I had with thee before the world was."

This is believed by some to prove the existence of Jesus prior to his birth on earth. An argument for his pre-existence is derived from a literal interpretation of the phrase, "which I had with thee before the world was." A cursory reading seems to suggest that Jesus was with the Father before the world existed. This, however, is not the proper understanding of the phrase.

The meaning of the phrase, "which I had with thee," in John 17:5, is to be understood in reference to the Hebrew prophecies that speak of the rewards for Jesus's complete obedience to the Father. In this sense, as a promise, the glory that Jesus referred to was "with God" and, as such, had not yet been manifested because it was in the form of a promise. It would not be manifested until a man remained sinless, was crucified and raised from the dead. Only when Jesus was raised from the dead, which would only have occurred if he remained obedient to the Father, would the promise of glory (i.e. eternal life) be manifested unto him.

Only a sinless man would be given this glory. Some think that the phrase "I had" is to be understood literally and therefore, in order for Jesus to have had anything before his birth, he had to have had literal existence. But Jesus's statement, since he both knew and trusted God's promises, was essentially this: "And now Father, glorify me with the glory that was promised to me through the prophecies that were prepared by you before the world was." The key phrase in John 17:5 is *with thee*. The glory was *with God*, and would be given to the one who was sinless unto death. In this same light, Christians have glory that was promised to us before the world began. 1 Cor. 2:7 says, "But we speak the wisdom of God in a mystery, even the hidden wisdom, which God ordained before the world unto our glory." God prepared things before the world began, and God prepared things for the Messiah, including his reward, before the world began. Jesus was reminding God that, since he was about to die, he had a reward coming to him. Not that God needed a reminder, but it was common then to remind God of things He had promised. If ever there were a time a person felt they needed to remind God of anything, it would be before his undeserved death.

Once the argument is advanced that Jesus pre-existed his birth on earth, the next step in the Trinitarian argument from John 17:5 is to prove that he is equal with the Father. The argument proceeds as follows: Isa. 42:8 says, "I am the LORD: that is my name: and my glory will I not give to another, neither my praise to graven images." John 17:5 says that Jesus had glory, and Isa. 42:8 says that God would not give his glory to another. The inference follows that Jesus must therefore be God. This inference is based upon the incorrect assumption that glory is used only in a supreme sense, which is the sense in which it is applied to God. This inference is easily seen to be incorrect since, in John 17:22, for example, Christians are said to have glory: "And the glory which thou gavest me I have given them; that they may be one, even as we are one." Whatever glory Jesus had was given to him by the Father, and Jesus, in turn, gave it to the members of his church.

John 20:28—"And Thomas answered and said unto him, My Lord and my God."

This is one of the cornerstone verses for the belief that Jesus is God. This belief is based on a literal interpretation of Thomas's usage of the word "God" in this verse, and that he used it in a supreme sense. As we have seen, the term "God" was used in higher and lower senses in Greco-Roman societies, and was applied to those who represent God in some way. It is left for us to decide whether Thomas thought that Jesus was the supreme God, or whether he considered Jesus to be a representative of God. There is little difficulty in seeing that he meant the term in a representative way (which assumes Thomas directed the term "God" to Jesus, as opposed to looking up to heaven and applying it to the Father Himself, which [the latter] is an argument I do not think is correct). Assuming Thomas directed these words to Jesus in John 20:28, he used the word "God" in a lesser sense.

A possible interpretation of Thomas's meaning of the word "God" is the equivalent of the word "judge." When we consider the emotion of Thomas and the equality of terms he would have employed in his excited state, he would not have employed terms of such different magnitudes. If Thomas thought Jesus was God, he could have exclaimed *My God!* That would have said it all. Any other term, including "Lord," would serve to decrease the intensity of his excitement. The terms "Lord" and "God" as used by Thomas may have meant that he recognized Jesus as his Lord currently and his judge in the future at the "great day of judgment." It may have also been an idiom in which two expressions are used to convey one thing, which in this instance would be along the lines of "my divine Lord," with the word "divine" being used in the cultural, and therefore lower, sense of the word "divine." The appellation "God" may have been used by Thomas in the sense of a judge, as one unto whom the word of God came:

> Much reliance is placed on the exclamation of Thomas, John xx. 28, "And Thomas answered and said unto him, My Lord and my God." I am not sure what explanation of these words is the true one. They were not spoken as a confession of faith, as the words of Peter were, when asked by Christ, "Whom do ye say that I am?" but they were spoken by the most skeptical of all the Apostles, under the influence of the most profound astonishment. But I am quite sure that they are not a declaration that Christ is the Supreme God, for this simple reason: that, even if such a doctrine be true, neither Thomas nor the twelve had any knowledge of it at the time. "It may be justly doubted," says Dr. Bloomfield, Bishop of London, "whether the so lately incredulous, because prejudiced and unenlightened disciple, had then, or at any time before the illumination of the Holy Spirit at Pentecost, any complete notion of the divine nature of Jesus as forming part of the Godhead." Indeed, it can be clearly proved, and is admitted by a great many Trinitarian writers, that the Apostles had no conception of Christ's deity when Thomas spoke. I therefore adopt

the opinion of the celebrated Kuinoel, whose commentary on the Scriptures is a standard work in Orthodox universities, and who says, that, of the words addressed to Jesus, "Thomas used the word God in the sense in which it is applied to kings and judges (who are considered representatives of Deity) and preeminently to the Messiah." [23]

We are referred to the words of Thomas, after the Resurrection, who, on being convinced of that stupendous fact by our Lord's offering him the very evidence he demanded, exclaimed: "My Lord and my God!" (John 20:28.) But if Thomas did thus really acknowledge his Master to be God, I should still insist that it was only in the sense of one "to whom the word of God came." Thomas, as a devout Jew, well knew that "no man hath seen God at any time;" his Master he had seen frequently, times without number. Our Lord had said to the woman of Samaria, "God is a Spirit;" and in perfect correspondence with that declaration, when he perceived the fright into which his disciples were thrown at his first appearance among them when "gathered together," he said: "A spirit hath not flesh and bones, as ye see me have." (Luke 24:39.) Surely it is nothing but absurd to suppose that Thomas believed the being before him, who gave to him sensible demonstration that he had "flesh and bones," was the *Invisible* God, as the sacred writers so often style the Almighty. (Col. 1:15; 1 Tim. 1:17; Heb. 11:27.) Under the circumstances, the words seem to me only a perfectly natural expression of sudden and intense surprise and astonishment—the language of strong emotion on the part of Thomas. Of what was the disciple incredulous? Simply of the fact of his Lord's being alive again, the fact of his Resurrection.

At what was he surprised? That there was given him the identical evidence, without which he had declared he would not believe that the others had "seen the Lord"—that he was alive again—that he had come forth from the dead. "A spirit"—an apparition—a phantasm that "had not flesh and

---

[23] Eliot, 78-79.

bones"—they might have seen; but not Jesus, their beloved Master; not him, again in the flesh. That was the point to be proved, and nothing else, nothing more.

Nothing as to his nature, rank in creation, or indeed, what or who he was. But simply and only the actuality of the Lord's Resurrection, his personal identity with the crucified and buried Christ. What wonder at the astonishment or even awe which filled Thomas, when the proof he needed and asked was vouchsafed, and he felt that his revered, beloved, divine Master, stood before him! What wonder that he, an Oriental—"according to the invariable habit of the Jews, Arabs, and almost all other Asiatic nations, who, when struck with wonder, often make exclamations in the name of the Deity" (Ram Mohun Roy's Final Appeal, 232)—thus surprised and struck with this marvelous, this astounding fact, should have exclaimed in the fulness of his emotion, "My Lord and my God!" The language of mere confession—when he would have said, '*thou art* my God"—was too cold for the state of mind in which Thomas was. Our Lord understood that state of mind in his incredulous follower, and his response to the exclamation shows it: "Because thou hast *seen*"—because thou hast seen that it is a being having flesh and bones—"thou hast believed" that it is really me, risen from the dead, and not a mere apparition; "blessed are they that have not seen and yet believed!" [24]

The following interpretation of John 20:28 is given by J. D. Michaelis, a Trinitarian, who argued that the term "God" used by Thomas is a generic term that may be applied to anybody who has been raised from the dead:

"My Lord! and my God!" This has generally been considered an exclamation, and the words seem to admit it; but to me the sense appears to be, "Yes! he is truly my Lord and my God." The exclamation is a recognition of Jesus. I will not go so far as to conclude from these words, that he actually recognized, at the time, the divine nature of Christ, of which we

---

[24] Farley, 88-90.

have no trace amongst the apostles, previous to the effusion of the Holy Ghost; at least, it was not the common doctrine of the Jewish theology. But he rather names him in a figurative sense—as one risen from the dead—*his god*, whom he will always honor and adore. [25]

William Hawkins, a Trinitarian, writes:

It would be ridiculous to suppose that the apostles could believe their Master to be the Son of God in the highest [the Trinitarian] sense, ... when "they all forsook him and fled." [26]

Joseph Allen, a Unitarian, comments:

John xx. 28, where Thomas, in his excitement and surprise at recognizing Jesus, says, "My Lord and my God,"—as if a man in that state of mind, who the minute before had declared his entire unbelief of Jesus's resurrection, could be the chief witness to the most momentous truth of the Gospel! Some suppose it is an ejaculation addressed to God, as if calling him to witness his new faith; others that the word is addressed to Jesus in the qualified sense in which it is used in my text, "He called them gods unto whom the word of God came." Either way, it is of too trifling value as evidence to create a doubt or justify a controversy.[27]

Morgridge says:

This exclamation, considered by itself, without relation to the connection and circumstances, would prove nothing but the surprise of Thomas. Considered in reference to the subject with which it is connected, it proves that Thomas believed that Christ was risen from the dead. His calling Christ his Lord and his God, does not necessarily imply anything more than his belief in the divinity of Christ's mission—that he was one *to whom the word of God came*. No epithets are here em-

---

[25] J. D. Michaelis, *The Burial and Resurrection of Jesus Christ*, 272-273; quoted in Wilson, 428.

[26] William Hawkins, *Discourses on Scripture Mysteries*, 63-64; quoted in Wilson, 353.

[27] Allen, 77-78.

ployed, and no circumstances appear, to show that Thomas used the term 'God' in its highest sense, as denoting the Supreme Being. But the contrary, I think, appears evident. Most certainly he did not believe the self-existent God was dead.[28]

According to the Trinitarian interpretation of John 20:28, Thomas introduced a whole new theology in that moment of excitement, and then never referred to it again. Trinitarians rely so heavily upon this verse that they ignore the relevancy of the other testimonies that Thomas and others gave about Jesus. If Thomas or any of the other apostles thought Jesus was their God, they would have frequently spoken of him accordingly. The term "God" was not applied to Jesus by any of the other apostles, yet Thomas's words that were exclaimed in a moment of excitement are given preeminence. The lack of supporting testimony by the other apostles demonstrates the inappropriateness of assuming Thomas used the word "God" in its highest sense:

> AN argument has been founded by Trinitarians upon the exclamation of the Apostle Thomas, when convinced of the truth of his Master's resurrection: "And Thomas said to Jesus, My Master! and my God!" Both titles, I believe, were applied by him to Jesus. But the name "God" was employed by him, not as the proper name of the Deity, but as an appellative, according to a common use of it in his day. I have already had occasion to remark upon the different significancy of the term ""God" in ancient and in modern times, a difference important to be well understood in order to ascertain the meaning of ancient authors.
>
> Supposing that Thomas *had* believed, and asserted, that his Master was God himself; in what way should this affect our faith? We should still know the fact on which his belief was founded, the fact of the resurrection of his Master, and could draw our own inferences from it, and judge whether his were well founded. Considering into how great an error he had fallen in his previous obstinate incredulity, there would be little reason for relying upon his opinion as infallible in the case supposed. I make these remarks, not from any doubt

---

28 Morgridge, 125.

about the meaning of his words, but, as I have said, for the purpose of pointing out one example of that incomplete and unsatisfactory mode of reasoning, which appears in the use of many quotations from the Old and New Testament.[29]

Acts 7:45—"Which also our fathers that came after brought in with Jesus into the possession of the Gentiles, whom God drave out before the face of our fathers, unto the days of David."

This verse has caused some to conclude that Jesus was alive in the days leading up to the time of David. This is easily cleared up, since in the King James Version the name "Jesus" should have been translated "Joshua." The New International Version translators translated it as follows: "Having received the tabernacle, our fathers under Joshua brought it with them when they took the land from the nations God drove out before them. It remained in the land until the time of David..."

Acts 7:59—"And they stoned Stephen, calling upon God, and saying, Lord Jesus, receive my spirit."

The King James translators inserted the word "God" in this verse, making it appear that Stephen referred to Jesus as God. The New International Version translators recognized that the word "God" is not in earlier manuscripts, and did not include it in their translation. It thus reads: "While they were stoning him, Stephen prayed, 'Lord Jesus, receive my spirit.'" Stephen was apparently speaking to Jesus with the recognition that Jesus has been appointed by the Father to execute judgment, and was requesting Jesus to accept him into the Kingdom:

> There are two texts in which it is supposed that direct prayer is offered to Christ. The first is Acts vii. 59, at the martyrdom of Stephen: "And the stoned Stephen, calling upon God, and saying, Lord Jesus, receive my spirit!" By turning to your Bibles, you will see that the word *God* is in italics, from which we know that it is not in the original, but supplied by the

---

29 Norton, 299-300, 302-304.

translators. We may read, therefore, calling upon *Christ*, or simply "calling out." [30]

There is nothing in the Greek corresponding to the word 'God.'

At this closing period of his life, the dying martyr had a vision of his Saviour. (verse 56.) He invoked Jesus, not as God, but as *the Son of man standing on the right hand of God.*" Believing on him as the resurrection and the life, and seeing him miraculously present, as if to encourage him at this awful moment, by revealing to him the glory of God, it was very natural, and no doubt proper, for the expiring saint to request Jesus to receive his spirit. His peculiar situation and circumstances seem to have authorized and prompted his supplication. A case so singular can furnish no example to those who are not in a similar situation, and to whom no such appearance is presented. We are not commanded to imitate Stephen, but Jesus; who, when he was dying, commended his spirit into the hands of the Father. [31]

Acts 20:28—"Take heed therefore unto yourselves, and to all the flock, over the which the Holy Ghost hath made you overseers, to feed the church of God, which he hath purchased with his own blood."

Some interpret this verse literally and argue that God purchased the church of God with His own *physical* blood. This cannot be the correct interpretation, since, according to John 4:24, "God is spirit" and does not have blood. Many scholars believe that the word "God" in this verse should have been translated "Lord":

In the Acts we read "the church of God which he hath purchased by his own blood." I might remark upon the strangeness of such language, having no parallel to it throughout the Scriptures, and at first sight, and even the more we reflect on and analyze it, shocking to every unsophisticated mind. The "blood" of God! But we need not spend much time about

---

30 Eliot, 67.

31 Morgridge, 131, 63.

it, for Griesbach, after a most careful examination of manu-scripts, Wetstein, Le Clerc, and Grotius, all read "church of the Lord." Adam Clark, in his notes on the passage, though admitting this reading to have "the greater evidence," thinks it necessary to add, "We must maintain that, had not this Lord been God, his blood could have been no purchase for the souls of a lost world;" so according to him, it might as well read, after all, as in our English version. But Kuinoel, Bishop Middleton, Dr. J. Smith, Bishop Marsh, and Olshau-sen, (whose great Commentary has been recently translated by Dr. Kenrick, of Rochester University,) are explicit in favor of Griesbach's reading; "which," says Olshausen, "*all* recent critics recognize as the right one." (Kenrick's Olshausen, vol. iii. 384.) Prof. Stuart, and Dr. Barnes of Philadelphia, are of the same mind; and nothing more need be said of a text, which is thus relieved of all difficulty, and furnishes not a shadow of support to the doctrine I am controverting.[32]

It should be, "church of the Lord," or "master." The phrase "blood of God" is abhorrent to Christian feeling, and was not used till the ninth century, the darkest of the Dark Ages.[33]

The third of these favorite Trinitarian proof-texts is Acts xx. 28. The question raised by variations in manuscripts, and other sources of critical information, is whether we should read "the Church of God" or "the Church of the Lord." Our aim here is not to present the merits on either side of the results which criticism reaches on these texts, but simply to show that the passages which Trinitarians would be most like-ly to quote are the very ones which are most embarrassed or dubious in their authority or their signification. Profes-sor Samuel Davidson, an Orthodox critic whose conclusions are among the most recent ones which have been offered to scholars, after a most candid arbitration between the disputed words in the Greek which give the two renderings, decides strongly in favor of "the Church of the Lord." (Treatise on

---

[32] Farley, 94-95.

[33] Allen, 76.

Biblical Criticism, Vol. II. 441-448.)[34]

Wainwright, a Trinitarian, writes:

In any case, this verse cannot be used as certain evidence that Jesus was called God.[35]

Even if we were to accept the word "God" in any sense, it would still be figurative:

The true reading of this passage is the "blood of the Lord"; but I do not care to insist upon this. The expression is of course to be understood figuratively. No one will contend that it was literally the blood of God. It can mean nothing else than that God purchased the Church with the blood of his own Son Jesus Christ, which, on account of his intimate union with the Father, may be figuratively called God's own blood. This is the meaning which is adopted by the celebrated Baxter, author of the Saints' Rest.[36]

And Milton says:

Nor is the passage in Acts xx. 28 more decisive—'the Church of God, which he hath purchased with his own blood'; that is, with his own Son, as it is elsewhere expressed, for God properly speaking has no blood; and no usage is more common than the substitution of the figurative term blood for offspring. But the Syriac version reads, not 'the Church of God,' but 'the Church of Christ'; and in our own recent translation it is, 'the Church of the Lord.' [37]

Romans 9:5—"Whose are the fathers, and of whom as concerning the flesh Christ came, who is over all, God blessed for ever. Amen."

Some Trinitarians believe this verse establishes that Jesus is "God blessed for ever." That this is not the correct reading of this verse,

---

34 Ellis, 126.

35 Wainwright, 74.

36 Eliot, 80.

37 Milton, 51.

Franks, a Trinitarian scholar, writes:

> It should be added that Rom. ix. 5 cannot be adduced to prove that Paul ever thought of Christ as God. The state of the case is shown in the R. V. margin.... In correspondence with his doctrine of the Sonship of Christ Paul continually speaks of God as the Father. But though he speaks of Christ as God's 'own Son' (Rom. viii. 3), while we are sons by adoption (Rom. viii. 13), yet he never leaves the ground of Jewish monotheism. It has been pointed out that Rom. ix. 5 cannot be brought in to question this statement. On the contrary, God is spoken of by the Apostle as not only the Father, but also the God of our Lord Jesus Christ (II Cor. i. 3; Eph. i. 17).[38]

The original writings of the prophets and apostles were not punctuated. Even though the King James translators may have inserted the punctuation in such a way they thought best represented the sense of the original, translations reflect the theological biases of the translators. In this case it is easy to see that the translators were not in agreement about how this verse should be translated:

> All that gives to this passage the appearance of an argument for the Deity of Christ, is the punctuation. But this is of no authority. It was not done by the pen of inspiration. It is well known that the ancient manuscripts were written without points. The punctuation as in the Common Version, has been introduced by later transcribers and by editors. The proper method of ascertaining the true import of an ambiguous passage, is to come to the examination of it in its original form, as delivered to us by the inspired writer; and not in the artificial form given to it by uninspired men. Any scholar who will read the Greek text of this passage, without the points, will readily perceive that it may be translated at least three or four different ways; and each in perfect accordance with the rules of Greek syntax. Hence it is clearly certain that its true meaning cannot be ascertained by the rules of grammar, but

---

[38] Franks, 34, 36.

must be determined by other considerations.

Mr. Locke renders it thus: "Of whom Christ came, who is over all, God be blessed for ever." This construction differs from that of the Common Version in nothing but the supply of the substantive verb, which in the Greek is omitted, according to the idiom of that language. From the 4th to the 8th verse inclusive, of the chapter containing this text, the verb is wanting at least six times. See also Rom. viii. 33, 34. 1 Cor. i. 26. 2 Cor. v. 6. Eph. iv. 4. Col. ii. 17. In these passages the verb is in *italics* in the Common Version, which denotes that it is wanting in the Greek. Nothing is more common in the Hebraistic Greek in which the New Testament is written, than the ellipsis of the substantive verb.

In the Improved Version this text is thus rendered: "Of whom by natural descent, Christ came, God, who is over all, be blessed for ever."

Now if either of the above mentioned constructions is admissible according to the rules of grammar, (and this no scholar will deny) the passage furnishes no proof that Christ is God.

For referring the latter clause to God the Father, the following considerations are submitted.

1. "God over all," and "God blessed for ever," are both the appropriate and peculiar designations of God the Father. (See Rom. i. 25; 2 Cor. xi. 31.; Eph. i. 3, iv. 6; 1 Tim. i. 11, vi. 15.) Neither of them is once given to Christ in the Bible. Now it is quite incredible that St. Paul should thus abruptly, and without note, comment, or explanation, couple together and apply to Christ two well-known appellations of God the Father; and still no use be made of the doctrine.

2. A difficult or ambiguous text is to be explained according to the known sentiments of the writer. Now as we have no evidence that St. Paul believed Christ to be "God over all blessed for ever," we ought to refer the phrase, as he has in other places, to God the Father.

3. By referring the latter clause of the verse to God the Fa-

ther, it expresses an important fact which the Apostle could not have overlooked in describing the prerogatives of the Jews—that God had, in a peculiar manner, presided over all their interests and concerns.

4. Such ascriptions of praise to God are of very frequent occurrence, not only in the Scriptures but in other Jewish writings; and, as in the passage under consideration, in most cases we find the ellipsis of the substantive verb.

5. For referring the latter clause to God the Father, we have the authority of learned authors in general who are not Trinitarians, and also of many of the most eminent critics of unsuspected orthodoxy; among whom are Erasmus, Bucer, and Le Clerk.[39]

If the Trinitarian interpretation of this verse were correct, it is remarkable that no use of it was made by the apostles anywhere else in their writings. It is reasonable to conclude that since no use of it was made elsewhere, it was not intended. As previously mentioned, there are various translations given for this verse. Some show it to be a reference to the Father and not to Christ:

> In the Epistle to the Romans, we read: "Christ... who is over all, God blessed forever. Amen." But look at the passage. He is recounting the distinctive and glorious privileges of the Jews; and, in the third verse, so profound is his interest and anxiety for their salvation, that he almost wishes himself "accursed," or, as the margin reads, "separated from" Christ, for their sake. What is his object? To vindicate the call of the Gentiles into, and the rejection of the Jews as such, from the Christian Church. Throughout the Epistle he seeks to meet and neutralize Jewish prejudices, and the opposition of his "brethren," his "Kinsmen according to the flesh," to the new faith. Would he have been so infatuated as the Trinitarian construction of this text would make him? When he knew how tenaciously, not to say bigotedly, the nation clung to the Unity of God, would he, having in mind the obvious purpose stated above,

---

[39] Morgridge, 127-129.

have riveted at the start of their prejudices, and confirmed all their opposition, by asserting that that Jesus whom they had crucified as a malefactor, was nevertheless that God Himself? Besides, how abruptly, without cause or connection, is such a tremendous statement as is supposed, here introduced! No use appears for it, or is made of it by St. Paul. Nowhere else does he, or any of the sacred writers, call Christ "God over all, blessed forever." Directly the contrary, as we have already seen, and shall see again. Remember, moreover, that the punctuation of the text is a modern and purely arbitrary matter. Every scholar knows that it must depend on what the reader understands this or indeed any passage to mean; for the Apostolic autographs were probably without any punctuation, as are the most ancient manuscripts. Accordingly, we find critics and versions differ, and often widely, in their pointing of this and of other texts. Lachmann, Tischendorf, Ruckert, and a host of the ablest critics, put a period after the word *flesh* and read: "Of whom Christ came, according to the flesh. He, who is above all God, be blessed forever!" Erasmus, without positively adopting it, declares that this punctuation "is perfectly suitable to the purport of the discourse." It is also remarkable, that though the ancient Greek manuscripts are in general without punctuation marks, the celebrated Codex Ephraemi, one of the most authoritative among them, has actually, as above, a period after the word "flesh." With this construction, the clause under consideration becomes a Doxology, or ascription of praise to God for the coming of His Christ or Messiah, in the prophetic line of "the covenants .... the promises .... the fathers;" His preëminent gift. As such, it must be presumed, according to the uniform style and custom of St. Paul, (Vid. Rom. 1:25; 2 Cor. 1:3; id. 11:31; Eph. 1:3.) to have been addressed to the Father as "God above all," and not to Christ.[40]

The learned Dr. Clark admits this passage may be thus rendered: "God who is over all, be blessed for ever." Cooke

---

[40] Farley, 95-97.

reads it thus: "Christ is come who is over all, God be blessed for ever, Amen." It is worthy of observation that some of our received translations omit the verb *to be*, while others have the verb printed in italics. It is well known that the *verb* is frequently *omitted* in the *Greek*, and supplied in the English translation. The Apostle's language appears to be that of a pious exclamation, blessing God for the power and authority he had bestowed on Christ. A similar exclamation is to be found in Romans 1c. 25v., "Who served the creature more than the creator, who is blessed for ever:" and in 2 Cor. 11c. 31v., "The God and Father of our Lord Jesus Christ, who is blessed for evermore, knoweth that I lie not." And we think, were Christians seriously to consider these words of the Apostles, "Christ came who is over all, God be blessed for ever;" they would hesitate before they asserted that the Apostle intended to teach that Jesus Christ was the eternal God. Is it credible that St. Paul meant to say, that a being who was of Jewish descent was the supreme God? "Whose are the Father's, and of whom as concerning the flesh Christ came;" can this be the eternal God? Can a long line of Jewish genealogy end in the birth of the Almighty Sovereign of the universe? [41]

A Trinitarian interpretation of Romans 9:5 requires that the verse be set apart from the rest of context, and further requires that one depart from common sense. When trying to understand parts of Scripture, when no use is made elsewhere of an interpretation, especially when the possible interpretation leans to one extreme or another, the possible interpretation must yield to the idea that there is a better interpretation to be found. Regarding the Trinitarian interpretation of Romans 9:5, this principle forces us to conclude that the Trinitarian interpretation is improper, especially in light of the overwhelming effects such a doctrine would create:

The first which I shall mention belongs likewise to the head of mistranslations. It is Romans ix. 5, thus rendered in the Common Version: "Whose are the fathers, and of whom as concerning the flesh Christ came, who is over all, God blessed

---

[41] Thomas, 34-35.

for ever."

It must, one would think, strike a Trinitarian, who maintains the correctness of this construction and rendering, as a very extraordinary fact, that the title of "God over all blessed for ever," which is nowhere else given to Christ, should be introduced thus incidentally and abruptly, without explanation or comment, and without any use being made of the doctrine. The supposed fact appears still more extraordinary and unaccountable, when we recollect that one main purpose of the Epistle to the Romans was to meet the prejudices and errors of the unbelieving Jews respecting Christianity; and that the doctrine which the Apostle is imagined to have asserted so briefly and explicitly, and then to have left without attempting to clear it from a single objection, must have been in the highest degree obnoxious to them; and one, therefore, which, in consistency with the design of the Epistle, required the fullest illustration and defence. In the second century, Justin Martyr, though far indeed from affirming that Christ was "God over all," maintained that he was "another god," the Logos of the Supreme. In the Dialogue which he represents himself as having held with an unbelieving Jew, Trypho, in defence of Christianity, he brings forward views and arguments similar to those in the Epistle to the Romans; but in addition to these we find a new topic, the deity of Christ, occupying a great part of the discussion. If the doctrine had been maintained by St. Paul, as it was by Justin, one would think that, in answering the objections of the Jews, it would have been as necessary for the Apostle, as for Justin, to explain and defend it. The sentiments of the Jews concerning it, which undoubtedly would have been as strong in the time of St. Paul as they were a century later, appear from the words which Justin ascribes to Trypho: "You undertake to prove an incredible and almost impossible thing,—that a god submitted to be born and become a man."—(Dial. cum Tryph., 283, ed. Thirlb. [c. 68 292, D. ed. Morel.]) "As for what you say, that this Christ existed as a god before time was, and afterwards becoming a man, submitted to be born, and that he was born out of the common course of nature, it seems to me not only paradoxical, but foolish."—(Ibid., 233. [al. c. 48. 267, B.]) "All we [Jews]," says Trypho in another place, "expect that the Messiah will be a man born of human parents."—(Ibid., 235. [al. c. 49. 268, A.])

But it is to be observed that some of the earlier Fathers, especially the Greek Fathers, expressly denied that Christ is "the God over all." This title was applied to him by the Sabellians, and was considered as a distinguishing mark of their heresy. There is no one of the Fathers more eminent than Origen. "Supposing," says Origen in his work against Celsus, "that some among the multitude of believers, likely as they are to have differences of opinion, rashly suppose that the Saviour is the God over all; yet we do not, for we believe him when he said, 'The Father is greater than I.'"—(Origen. cont. Cels., Lib. VIII. § 14. Opp. I. 752.) Even after the Nicene Council, Eusebius, in writing against Marcellus, says: "As Marcellus thinks, He who was born of the holy virgin, and clothed in flesh, who dwelt among men, and suffered what had been foretold, and died for our sins, was the very God over all; for daring to say which, the church of God numbered Sabellius among atheists and blasphemers."—(Euseb. Eccles. Theol., Lib. II. c. 4.)[42]

1 Corinthians 10:4—"And did all drink the same spiritual drink: for they drank of that spiritual Rock that followed them: and that Rock was Christ."

Some Trinitarians believe from this verse that Jesus physically followed the Israelites around, traveling with them, perhaps some distance behind them and keeping his eye on them. But the word "followed" does not necessarily imply that one is in the physical presence of others, it also refers to time and that one event will come *after* another. It is in this sense that Jesus's second coming *followed* (or, will follow) his first coming. Regarding 1 Cor. 10:4, it is in this sense that Jesus followed the Israelites—he would come later, which we know

---

42 Norton, 203-205, 212-213.

from Hebrews 11:39: "And these all, having obtained a good report through faith, received not the promise."

The "spiritual Rock," which is a reference to the Messiah, may refer to one of three stages of the development of faith in the Messiah. The first stage was when he was a promise, which came through prophesy. Trusting in this promise was a requirement for the people of Israel to gain favor with God, as Galatians 3:16-18 (NIV) says:

> "The promises were spoken to Abraham and to his seed. The Scripture does not say "and to seeds," meaning many people, but "and to your seed," meaning one person, who is Christ. What I mean is this: The law, introduced 430 years later, does not set aside the covenant previously established by God and thus do away with the promise. For if the inheritance depends on the law, then it no longer depends on a promise; but God in his grace gave it to Abraham through a promise."

The "promise" spoken of in Gal. 3:18 refers to the promised Messiah, and the Jews, though they did not live to see the fulfillment of the promise, trusted that the Messiah would *eventually* come. Trinitarians argue from 1 Cor. 10:4 that Jesus was with the Israelites *following* them. How could Jesus be rightly spoken of as a promise if he was already present with them?

1 Corinthians 10:9—"Neither let us tempt Christ, as some of them also tempted, and were destroyed of serpents."

The translators of the King James Version have the word "Christ" instead of "Lord." The New International Version translators corrected this and have: "We should not test the Lord, as some of them did—and were killed by snakes." The word "Lord" is a reference to the Father, not to Christ.

> St. Paul has been supposed to countenance Justin's opinion, 1 Cor. x, 9. *Neither let us tempt* Christ, *as some of them* (the Israelites) *also tempted, and were destroyed of serpents.* But, most probably, it should be, *neither let us tempt* GOD, or *the* LORD (and not *Christ*, as in some of our copies). The Apostle manifestly refers to Numb. xxi, 5, 6 (See also Psalm lxxviii, 17, 18). It is said, by *Epiphanius*, that the passage in *St. Paul* was corrupted, at a very early period, by *Marcion*, who

inserted *Christ* instead of *the* LORD.[43]

Here, for [the] Χριστόν, "Christ," or "the Anointed One," the reading [the] Κύριον, "the Lord," is adopted by Lachmann, Meyer, and Alford, as also by Wetstein, Archbishop Newcome, Rückett, Norton, and others. Griesbach (in his manual edition) and Knapp mark it as of equal authority with Χριστόν. Compare Griesbach's Symbolæ Criticæ, II. 114.)

"As some of them also tempted," "also," is admitted by Lachmann, Tischendorf, Meyer, and Alford, is marked by Griesbach as probably spurious, and bracketed by Vater.

Archbishop Newcome observes, "If we read Χριστόν, the sense is, 'Nor let us tempt, try, prove, provoke Christ now, as some of them did God at that time.'" The passage is thus understood by many Trinitarian commentators; but others, supplying the word "him" instead of "God" after "tempted," suppose that Paul represents Christ as the being described in Numbers xxi. 5, 6, as tempted by the Israelites in the wilderness.[44]

2 Corinthians 5:19—"To wit, that God was in Christ, reconciling the world unto himself, not imputing their trespasses unto them; and hath committed unto us the ministry of reconciliation."

The phrase "God was in Christ" has been used by Trinitarians as a catch-phrase supporting the contention that God physically manifested Himself in the person, or physical body, of Christ. But, as is fairly common in Trinitarian explanations, this reduces a spiritual connection to a physical one. A better explanation of this verse is that God was spiritually in Christ, that God was always on Jesus's mind, as Christ only did the Father's will. This is all that is required to understand this verse. A similar expression regarding Christ dwelling in Christians is in Colossians 1:27: "To whom God would make known what is the riches of the glory of this mystery among the Gentiles; which is Christ in you, the hope of glory." The meaning is that, be-

---

43 Gifford, 39, footnote.

44 Norton, 473-474.

cause we now serve the Lord Jesus Christ and follow his example, we are figuratively (or, perhaps more accurately, spiritually) said to have "Christ in us." In this way we are Christ-like, and in this way Jesus is God-like.

2 Corinthians 12:19—"Again, think ye that we excuse ourselves unto you? we speak before God in Christ: but we do all things, dearly beloved, for your edifying."

The phrase "God in Christ" is explained in the explanation given for 2 Cor. 5:19 above.

2 Corinthians 13:14—"The grace of the Lord Jesus Christ, and the love of God, and the communion of the Holy Ghost, be with you all. Amen."

See Chapter 3, subheading titled "2 Corinthians 13:14" for an explanation of this verse.

Ephesians 4:30—"And grieve not the holy Spirit of God, whereby ye are sealed unto the day of redemption."

See Chapter 13 for an explanation of "holy spirit."

Philippians 2:6—"Who, being in the form of God, thought it not robbery to be equal with God."

An argument for Jesus's deity is founded upon the belief that the expression "Jesus was in the form of God" means the same as the expression "Jesus was God." Another argument for his deity is derived from the statement, "Jesus thought it not robbery to be equal with God," which, it is argued, is the same as saying that "Jesus is equal with God." Both arguments are incorrect, and learned Trinitarians have admitted that this verse does not represent Jesus as equal with the Father, but as His humble servant:

> The next, Phil. ii. 6, 7, even as it is translated in our common version, so far from presenting any difficulty to my mind, is, in my view, a strong Unitarian text. *"Who, being in the form of God"*—that is, the brightness of the Father's glory and the

express image of his person—made so by Him who also created man in his own image—*"thought it not robbery to be equal with God."* He came as the messenger of God to man, as God's vicegerent on earth, and in that sense it was not robbery to proclaim himself equal with God, and to demand equal obedience from mankind. He who refuses to obey Christ, refuses obedience to the Father, for the Father spake to the world through him. If we read on, we shall see how it was that he demanded that men should honor him even as they honored the Father. "God," says the Apostle, "hath highly exalted him, and given him a name, that at the name JESUS every knee should bow, and every tongue confess that he is Lord, *to the glory of God* THE FATHER." The whole passage, it seems to me, *even when read as it is in our English Bibles,* is a clear and satisfactory explanation of the grounds on which our Master thought it not robbery to be equal with God; and seems intended to fill our minds with the most exalted ideas of the dignity and authority of the "one Mediator between God and man, the man Christ Jesus." But you are undoubtedly aware that many Trinitarians have contended for a different translation of the passage.

"Above all, it is worthy of remark, that, as humility and obedience are here the subject of discourse, we ought to understand what St. Paul says, *of Christ's humanity*; for his divine nature, being the same as that of the Father, is not susceptible of humility and obedience. These are excellencies, not of the Creator, but of a created being.—LE CLERC: *Le Nouv. Test.*

"*Though he was in a divine form.*—LUTHER.

"*The form of God* here signifies majesty.... I acknowledge, indeed, that Paul does not make mention of Christ's divine essence.—CALVIN.[45]

Franks, the Trinitarian scholar, writes:

In Phil. ii. 5-11 subordinationism is manifest in that Christ is thought of as not originally equal to God, and even the con-

---

[45] Dana, 283, 284, 16-17.

fession of Him as universal Lord is to the glory of the Father.[46]

Few Trinitarians today would agree with Franks's assessment of this verse. The verse simply declares that the Father's glory was (partially) demonstrated and revealed by Jesus. The Father's supremacy is maintained by the context:

> Again we are referred to the following passage in proof of the proper Deity of our Lord. "Who, being in the form of God, thought it not robbery to be equal with God." Assuredly the Trinitarian exposition of this text, is a mere *reductio ad absurdum* of the Apostle's argument, since it makes him say that Christ, being God, thought it not robbery to be equal with himself! It would indeed be absurd to say that of any thinking being.
>
> Prof. Stuart—"He regarded not the being equal with God as a thing to be eagerly coveted." The last named critic says: "Our common version .... seems to render nugatory, or at least irrelevant, a part of the Apostle's reasoning in the passage. He is enforcing the principle of Christian humility upon the Philippians.... But how was it any proof or example of humility, that *he did not think it robbery to be equal with God*"?—(Ans. to Channing, 84)[47]
>
> To this class belongs Philippians ii. 5, seqq. Here the Common Version makes the Apostle say of Christ, that he "thought it not robbery to be equal with God." This has been considered a decisive argument that Christ is God; though it is an absurdity to say of any being, that he "thought it not robbery to be equal with himself."
>
> Christ was "in the form of God," or "the image of God," or "as God"; he was "like God," or he was "equal with God" (the latter words being correctly understood); because he was a minister in the hands of God, wholly under his direction; because his words were the words of God, his miracles, the works of the Father who sent him, and his authority as a teacher and legislator, that of the Almighty, not human, but

---

divine. Yet notwithstanding that he bore the high character of God's messenger and representative to men, with all the powers connected with it, he was not eager to display that character, or exercise those powers, for the sake of any personal advantage, or of assuming any rank or splendor corresponding to his pre-eminence over all other men.[48]

Last of all, and certainly most difficult, if we wish to know the precise shade of meaning implied, is the passage (Phil. ii. 6) which says of Jesus, that, "being in the form of God, he thought it not robbery to be equal with God." It is in the course of an exhortation to Christian humility. We are to be like Christ in this respect. What! in aspiring to absolute equality with God? Certainly not; but just the opposite,—for the word itself means just as well, that he "did not make it his ambition" to be equal with God,—i.e. to claim divine honor, such as was given to Greek heroes and Roman emperors. Paul was writing to *Greeks* under the *Roman* rule; and it is thus that he contrasts the impious ambition of their pretended gods and heroes with the simple majesty of Jesus, who, "god-like" as he was, ("in the form of God,") never aspired to that sort of worship from his followers which their superstitious devotees claimed for them.[49]

Colossians 1:15-19—"Who is the image of the invisible God, the firstborn of every creature: For by him were all things created, that are in heaven, and that are in earth, visible and invisible, whether they be thrones, or dominions, or principalities, or powers: all things were created by him, and for him: And he is before all things, and by him all things consist. And he is the head of the body, the church: who is the beginning, the firstborn from the dead; that in all things he might have the preeminence. For it pleased the Father that in him should all fullness dwell."

Some Christians believe the phrase, "the image of the invisible

---

48 Norton, 191, 193.

49 Allen, 78.

God," indicates that Jesus is God. If this interpretation were correct, these words would be as indirect and potentially misleading as they could possibly be. If Paul meant to say that Jesus is God, why did he not just come out and plainly say it? He had the vocabulary available to him. Why talk of an *image of* God, rather than saying directly that he is God? This illustrates the futility of every Trinitarian interpretation of verses thought to provide evidence for the notion that Jesus is God. Jesus is nowhere in Scripture unequivocally called God. There are always other words in each context that indicate something other than his alleged deity was meant. The Father is plainly called God in hundreds of places, without any other words that might lead to questioning who He is. In the comparatively few cases Trinitarians think the term refers to Jesus, the term never stands alone in reference to him. True to form, Jesus is not called "God" in Col. 1:15-19, but "the head of the Church and the firstborn from the dead":

> The apostle speaks here of Christ as an intermediate or secondary cause, the verb "to create" is used in Scripture not only with reference to the old, but also to the new creation. Of this you have an instance, Ephes. ii. 10, "For we are his workmanship, CREATED in Christ Jesus unto good works:" and a little further on (ver. 15) "to make" or "create" in himself of twain one new man." So likewise James i. 18, which is commonly understood to refer to the new creation, "Of his own will begat he us with the word of truth, that we should be a kind of first fruits of his creatures." Moreover, that the expressions, "all things in heaven and earth," are not here used for all objects whatever, appears not only from the words of Paul further on, (ver. 20,) where he states that "God by him (Christ) reconciled all things unto himself, whether they be things in earth or things in heaven;" but also from this very passage itself; wherein the apostle does not say that heaven and earth were created, but only those things which are in heaven and earth.
>
> That this passage of the epistle to the Colossians ought to be interpreted of the new creation, may be proved by the three following arguments:—First, a reason is here assigned why Christ is called "the first born of every creature." Now,

since the first born is of the number of those of whom he is called the first born; and as Christ cannot, in reference to the old creation, be understood to be the first among created beings, many generations having intervened between Adam and him; it follows, that he must be so designated in reference to the new creation, which commenced from him;—and to this creation the reason of this designation is accommodated.

Secondly, What are here stated to be created by Christ are not heaven and earth and all things which they contain, conformably to the language used elsewhere, when the old creation is spoken of,—but only rational natures; as being alone susceptible of a new creation.

Thirdly, The very enumeration of the things created by him sufficiently shows that the new creation is here spoken of. For with respect to "things in heaven," the angels are indeed said to have been created by him, but under the names of "thrones, and dominions, and principalities, and powers;" which are not names of simple existences, but of dignities with which the Lord honours them; just as we say that a king, a prince, or a consul, has been created, not when he is born, but when he is so designated.[50]

It should be borne in mind that the Apostle was writing this Epistle to the Colossians, to assure them of the fact that they were under *a new dispensation introduced by Christ*, who had full power and authority for this end. He was opposing, on the one hand, the Judaizing teachers, who were endeavoring to impose upon the Christian Church the ritual law;—and, on the other hand, the philosophizing converts from heathenism, who were aiming to incorporate with the new religion the subtleties of their old philosophy. Paul is writing to remind them of the fact that the simple religion introduced by Jesus Christ was the true faith—that which they had been *taught*—and in which they were to continue. Now let us examine the 16th and 17th verses, with this idea—namely, that he was writing about Christ's *new dispen-*

---

50 *The Racovian Catechism*, 91-93, including footnote.

sation—strongly impressed upon our minds.

You will observe that he does not say that by him were heaven and earth created, but only "*all things* which are in heaven and in earth." Now, if the expression "all things" can be proved to refer to the *new spiritual creation* Christ came to effect, your argument, which makes it prove his divinity only on the supposition that it refers to the *natural* creation, falls entirely to the ground. The effects produced by the Gospel, the new and radically different state of things which had followed and were still to follow its introduction—are very often spoken of under the figure of *a creation*. Turn to Ephesians ii. 10, and you will find that believers are spoken of as *created* in or through Christ Jesus, *unto good works*. In remarking upon this verse, Priestley says, "We see here in what sense Paul sometimes uses the term creation; viz. as denoting the renovation of the world by the Gospel; and when we elsewhere in the Epistles read of the creation of all things by Jesus Christ, the meaning is defined and explained by such passages as these."

Again, see Eph. i. 10, "That in the dispensation of the fulness of times he might gather together in one *all things in Christ*, which are in Heaven, and which are on earth." Here we have the very same expression "all things," certainly applied to spiritual existence alone.

Since writing the above, I have met with some remarks of Professor Norton upon the passage we are considering; perhaps they will interest you, and serve to strengthen my position. "In this passage," he says, "there are some expressions which require explanation. God, says St. Paul, 'has transferred us from the empire of darkness into the kingdom of his beloved Son.' To this metaphor much of the following language corresponds. It was this kingdom which had been newly *created*, that is, had been newly *formed*: for it is thus that the word rendered *created* is to be understood. We find it, and its correlatives, repeatedly used in a similar sense by St. Paul, namely, to denote the moral renovation of men by Christianity. Thus he says:—

'If any man be in Christ, he is a new creature. *The old*

things have passed away, behold, all things have become new.' 2
Cor. v. 17.

'For in Christ Jesus neither is circumcision anything, nor
uncircumcision, but a new creature.' Gal. vi. 15.

'For we are God's workmanship, created through Christ
Jesus unto good works.' Ephes. ii. 10.

'Put on the new man, who is created in the likeness of
God, with the righteousness and holiness of the true faith.'
Ephes. iv. 24.

The language from the Epistle to the Colossians, in which
Christ is said to have created all things, is to be explained in
a corresponding manner. He created all things *in the new dispensation*, in the kingdom of Heaven. It has been understood
as declaring, that the *natural creation* was the work of Christ.
But it is obvious at first sight, that the words used are not
such as properly designate the objects of the *natural world*;
and not such, therefore, as we should expect to be employed,
if these were intended. In speaking of the natural creation,
the same Apostle refers it to God in different terms—to `the
living God, who made Heaven and earth, and the sea, and all
things that are in them.' Acts, xiv. 15." [51]

Genesis 1:27 says that man was created in *the image of* God. This is a
reference to man's holy character until Adam and Eve changed that. It
was not until another sinless man, Jesus, lived that anyone is spoken
of as being *the image of* God, and is an expression that refers to those
who have God's holy character.

Colossians 2:2—"That their hearts might be comforted, being knit
together in love, and unto all riches of the full assurance of understanding, to the acknowledgment of the mystery of God, and of the
Father, and of Christ.

What some think gives this verse an appearance of a Trinitarian
construction is that there are three subjects mentioned in it: God, the
Father, and Christ. Aside from the poor reasoning involved in arriv-

---

[51] Dana, 222-224, including footnote.

ing at that conclusion, the words "of the Father" in the King James Version are not in most Greek manuscripts. The New International Version says: "My purpose is that they may be encouraged in heart and united in love, so that they may have the full riches of complete understanding, in order that they may know the mystery of God, namely, Christ, in whom are hidden all the treasures of wisdom and knowledge." It is also relevant that this verse says that in Christ are "hidden all the treasures of wisdom and knowledge," which would be superfluous had Jesus been God. Also, "hiding" them in Jesus would also be strange if Jesus were God and had always been in possession of all wisdom and knowledge.

Colossians 2:9—"For in him dwelleth all the fulness of the Godhead bodily."

Some think this verse implies that Jesus has all the attributes of God, which would be a silly construction, since it would be the equivalent of saying "in God dwells all the fulness of God." In similar language, Col. 2:9 contains a sort of expression that is in 2 Pet. 1:4, in which Christians are said to be "partakers of the divine nature." Christians may partake of the divine nature, however we may define this, and when Jesus is considered, he partook more fully by virtue of his obedience to God and, as some believe, observance of the law. **1 Timothy 1:1-2**—"Paul, an apostle of Jesus Christ by the commandment of God our Saviour, and Lord Jesus Christ, our hope."

An argument is sometimes advanced that since God is called "Saviour" in this verse, and since Jesus is also called "Saviour" in other parts of Scripture, that Jesus is therefore God. Without addressing this argument at length here, it is easy to see that God and Jesus are distinguished from one another in this verse. God is called "our Saviour" and Jesus is called "our Lord."

1 Timothy 3:16—"And without controversy great is the mystery of godliness: God was manifest in the flesh, justified in the spirit, seen of angels, preached unto the Gentiles, believed on in the world, received up into glory."

This is one the most frequently cited verses to prove the doctrine of the double nature of Christ (which, it should be kept in mind, is different than the doctrine of a triune God). Many modern scholars agree that the word "God" in this verse is a corruption of the original text:

> "God was manifest in the flesh,"—a phrase easily explained by what I have just said of the Word, as the declaration or manifestation of God; but the true text is "he who," or "which." [52]

The text should read, "And without controversy great is the mystery of godliness: he who [or, as some manuscripts read, which] was manifest in the flesh, justified in the spirit, seen of angels..."

1 Timothy 6:15-16—"Which in his times he shall shew, who is the blessed and only potentate, the King of kings, and Lord of lords; Who only hath immortality, dwelling in the light which no man can approach unto; whom no man hath seen, nor can see: to whom be honour and power everlasting. Amen."

Some argue that the word "who" in this verse refers to Jesus, and since, according to this interpretation, it says that he is "the only potentate," he must therefore be God. The word "who," though, is not a reference to Jesus, but to the Father, who Jesus shall show is the blessed and only potentate. If the punctuation reflected the true meaning of the verse, it would read: "Which, in his times, he shall shew who is the blessed and only potentate..." Once Jesus "shows" this in the time he has to do it, then shall "the Son also himself be subject unto him that put all things under him, that God may be all in all" (1 Cor. 15:28).

Titus 2:13—"Looking for that blessed hope, and the glorious appearing of the great God and our Saviour Jesus Christ."

Some have argued that the terms "God" and "Saviour" in this verse both pertain to Jesus, and the crux of the argument is whether the term "God" applies to Jesus or whether it applies to the Father.

---

52 Allen, 76-77.

Most Trinitarians, including the New International Version translators, believe there is only one person, Jesus, represented in this verse. Those who believe in the supremacy of the Father believe there are two: the Father, who is called "God," and Jesus, who is called "our Saviour." In contrast to those who believe that the term God refers to Jesus, Franks, a Trinitarian, says:

> Whether Christ is actually called God in Titus ii. 13 is a matter of dispute.[53]

An accurate interpretation of this verse must be determined by considering other verses that shed additional light on whether the term "God" refers to Jesus Christ or whether it refers to the Father. Granville Sharp, who had a rule of biblical interpretation named after him (the "Granville Sharp rule"), believed the term "God" refers to Jesus. Part of his contention was that, in Titus 2:13, the word and links the term God to Jesus Christ, and is therefore not to be understood as referring to another being—in this case, our heavenly Father. The purpose for Granville Sharp's study was that it was not clear whether the word "and" implied one person or two, and he wanted to clear up the difficulty. But it is difficult for a person to separate himself from his own theological biases, so the arguments regarding the word "and" will not by themselves determine whether God and Jesus are co-equal. The truth about God and Jesus will decide whether or not these arguments are correct. If Jesus is not God, then Sharp's argument that the term "God" refers to Jesus is necessarily wrong.

The whole issue about who the term "God" refers to must be decided by other verses. This is true of any word, phrase, verse or context that is ambiguous, difficult or potentially confusing. The basic rule in such cases is that other, simple verses clarify the difficult ones. We are left, then, to see whether the Granville Sharp "rule" is correctly applied to this verse, or whether Mr. Sharp has assumed the conclusion and then made a rule to support it.

THE GRANVILLE SHARP RULE

According to Granville Sharp, the entire phrase "the great God and

---

[53] Franks, 57.

our Saviour" applies to Jesus, making Jesus both our savior and God. This has not been the universal opinion of Trinitarian scholars, who have recognized that there are two persons referred to in verses which contain this phrase and others similar to it:

> Some Trinitarians have quoted in proof of the deity of Christ a few passages in which they suppose the title "God our Saviour" to be applied to him. The following are all the passages of the New Testament in which this expression occurs: 1 Timothy i. 1; ii. 3; Titus i. 3; ii. 10; iii. 4; and Jude 25. See also Luke i. 47; 1 Timothy iv. 10.

> In some of these texts, as 1 Timothy i. 1, Titus iii. 4-6, the being who is called "God our Saviour" is expressly distinguished from Christ; and one need only compare the others [e.g. Titus 2:13] with these, and with their context, to perceive that it is not only without evidence, but against all evidence, that any of them are referred to Christ. A large majority of Trinitarian commentators recognize this fact.

> In Jude 25 the best ancient manuscripts and versions, and other authorities for settling the text, read, "To the ONLY God our Saviour, THROUGH JESUS CHRIST OUR LORD, be glory," &c. This reading is adopted by Griesbach, Knapp, Schott, Tittman, Vater, Scholz, Lachmann, Hahn, Tischendorf, Theile, and nearly all modern critics. There can be no reasonable doubt of its genuineness.

> We may here notice also 2 Peter i. 1 and Titus ii. 13, in which it has been maintained, on the ground of the omission of the Greek article, that Christ is called "our God and Saviour," and "our great God and Saviour." As to the argument founded on the omission of the article, it is not necessary to add anything to what has already been said. But it is urged by Professor Stuart and others, in respect to Titus ii. 13, that the "appearing" of God the Father is never foretold in the New Testament, and therefore that "the great God" here spoken of must be Christ. The answer to this is, that, according to the literal and correct translation of the original, it is not "the *appearing*," but "the appearing *of the glory,* ἐπιφανείαν τῆς δόξης, of the great God and of our Saviour Jesus Christ," of which

the Apostle speaks; and that our Saviour did expressly declare that he should come "in the glory of his Father." See Matthew xvi. 27; Mark viii. 38; Luke ix. 26; and compare 1 Timothy vi. 14-16. Professor Stuart admits that "the whole argument,....so far as the *article* is concerned, falls to the ground." (Biblical Repository for April 1834, 323.) The title "the great God" in this passage is referred to the Father by Erasmus, Grotius, Le Clerc, Wetstein, Doddridge, Macknight, Abp. Newcome, Rosenemüller, Heinrichs, Schott, Winer, Neander (Planting and Training, I. 509, note, Boehn's ed.), De Wette, Meyer (on Romans ix. 5), Huther, Coynbeare and Howson, and others.[54]

It is important to observe in interpreting Titus 2:13 that nowhere in the Bible is Jesus unequivocally called the supreme God. There are always inferences involved in the attempts to prove that he is, which creates room for personal biases to affect the interpretations. In verses that are assigned a Trinitarian character, there is always some inherent difficulty in the verse itself that is exploited in order to develop the doctrine that the Father has equals. It is also significant that no verse in the whole Bible refers to Jesus as "the great God Jesus Christ." This wording would have cleared up the difficulty, or at least made it possible to take the notion of a dual nature of Christ more seriously. But it is too clear that Scripture consistently preserves a clear line of separation between God and Jesus. But the verses that may be ambiguous or difficult to understand are the ones Trinitarians migrate to because there is more room there to force a Trinitarian sense upon the texts:

> The argument for the deity of Christ founded upon the omission of the Greek article was revived and brought into notice in the last century by Granville Sharp, Esq. He applied it to eight texts which will be hereafter mentioned. The last words of Ephesians v. 5 may afford an example of the construction on which the argument is founded:
>
> ἐν τῇ βασιλείᾳ τοῦ Χριστοῦ καὶ θεοῦ.
>
> From the article being inserted before Χριστοῦ and omitted before θεοῦ, Mr. Sharp infers that both names relate to

---

54 Norton, 305-306, footnote.

the same person, and renders, "in the kingdom of Christ our God." Conformably to the manner in which he understands it, it might be rendered, "in the kingdom of him who is Christ and God." The proper translation I suppose to be that of the Common Version, "in the kingdom of Christ and of God," or "in the kingdom of the Messiah and of God."

The argument of Sharp is defended by Bishop Middleton in his Doctrine of the Greek Article. By attending to the rule laid down by him, with its limitations and exceptions, we shall be able to judge of its applicability to the passage in question. His rule is this:—

"When two or more attributives, joined by a copulative or copulatives, are assumed of [relate to] the same person or thing, before the first attributive the article is inserted, before the remaining one it is omitted." (pp. 79, 80.)

By attributives, he understands adjectives, participles, and nouns which are significant of character, relation, and dignity.

The limitations and exceptions to the rule stated by him are as follows:—

I. There is no similar rule respecting "names of substances *considered as substances.*" Thus we may say ὁ λίθος καὶ χρυσός, without repeating the article before χρυσός, though we speak of two different substances. The reason of this limitation of the rule is stated to be that "distinct real essences cannot be conceived to belong to the same thing"; or, in other words, that the same thing cannot be supposed to be two different substances.—In this case, then, it appears that the article is not repeated, be*cause its repetition is not necessary to prevent ambiguity.* This is the true principle which accounts for all the limitations and exceptions to the rule that are stated by Bishop Middleton and others. It is mentioned thus early, that the principle may be kept in mind; and its truth may be re-marked in the other cases of limitation or of exception to be quoted.

II. No similar rule applies to proper names. "The reason," says Middleton, "is evident at once; for it is impossible that *John* and *Thomas,* the names of two distinct persons, should be predicated of an individual." (p. 86.) This remark is not to the purpose; for the same individual may have two names. The true reason for this limitation is, that proper names, when those of the same individual, are not connected by a copulative or copulatives, and therefore that, when they are thus connected, no ambiguity arises from the omission of the article.

Having thus laid down the rule, with its limitations and exceptions, Bishop Middleton applies it to some of the passages in the New Testament adduced by Mr. Sharp in proof of the divinity of Christ. These were Acts xx. 28; Ephes. v. 5; 2 Thess. i. 12; 1 Tim. v. 21; 2 Tim. iv. 1; Titus ii. 13; 2 Peter i. 1; Jude 4. In four of these eight texts, the reading adopted to bring them within the rule is probably spurious, as may be seen by referring to Griesbach; and they are in consequence either given up, or not strongly insisted upon, by Middleton. In one of the remaining, 2 Thess. i. 12, Middleton is "disposed to think that it affords no certain evidence in favor of Mr. Sharp." The three remaining texts are those on which he principally relies.

It appears by comparing the rule with its exceptions and limitations, that it in fact amounts to nothing more than this: that when substantives, adjectives, or participles are connected together by a copulative or copulatives, if the first have the article, it is to be *omitted* before those which follow, when they relate to the same person or thing; and is to be *inserted*, when they relate to different persons or things, EXCEPT when this fact is sufficiently determined by some other circumstance. The same rule exists respecting the use of the definite article in English.

The principle of exception just stated is evidently that which runs through all the limitations and exceptions which Middleton has laid down and exemplified, and is in itself perfectly reasonable. When, from any other circumstance, it may be clearly understood that different persons or things are spoken of, then the insertion or omission of the article is a matter of indifference.

But if this be true, no argument for the deity of Christ can be drawn from the texts adduced. With regard to this doctrine, the main question is, whether it were taught by Christ and his Apostles, and received by their immediate disciples. Unitarians maintain that it was not; and consequently maintain that no thought of it was ever entertained by the Apostles and first believers. But if this supposition be correct, the insertion of the article in these texts was wholly unnecessary. No ambiguity could result from its omission. The imagination had not entered the minds of men, that God and Christ were the same person.[55]

It is attempted to be shown on two grounds that the epithet "the great God" in this passage ought to be referred to Christ. First, because the rule already referred to, respecting the construction of two or more substantives, with only a single article prefixed, requires it to be so applied;—and secondly, because it is the coming of the Son, and not the Father, that we are looking for. The former of these reasons has already been obviated, in the answer to the preceding question. To the latter it is replied, that Paul does not write (as in the English translation) "looking for the appearing of the great God," but "looking for the appearing of the glory of the great God (ἐπιφανείαν τῆς δόξης τοῦ μεγάλου θεοῦ). Now that it may be truly said, that the glory of God will appear when Christ shall come to judgment, is evident from the declaration of our Lord, that "he shall come in glory," that is, in the glory of God his Father. There is, however, no impropriety in saying that God the Father will come, or rather will appear, when the Son shall come to judge the world. For will not Christ, in judging the world, sustain and represent the person of God the Father, as the sovereign from whom he will have derived his judicial office? [56]

Hebrews 1:2—"Hath in these last days spoken unto us by his Son, whom he hath appointed heir of all things, by whom also he made the worlds."

---

55 Norton, 199-200, 201-202.

56 *The Racovian Catechism*, 81-82.

An argument for Jesus being God is based upon the assumption that Jesus made the physical universe (i.e. the worlds). Hebrews 1:2 is sometimes thought to be a reference to Genesis 1:1, where it says God made the heavens and the earth. This connection is incorrect, however, because the word "worlds" in Heb. 1:2 is translated from the Greek word transliterated *aiones*, which is more properly translated "ages." This is a word designating a period of time and is not a reference to the physical world:

> The Greek word αἰών was used to denote a space of time of considerable length, leaving its precise limits undefined. Hence it denotes, secondarily, the state of things existing during such a period. In this sense it often occurs in the New Testament. We use the age in a like signification, employing it to denote the men of a particular period, considered in reference to their circumstances and character, as when we speak of the "manners of an age," "the learning of an age," &c. So, likewise, the word *time* is used, though, by an idiom of our language, rather in the plural than the singular, as in the phrase, "the times of the Messiah." Shakespeare, however, says in the singular, "the time is out of joint," (Hamlet, Act I. Sc. V.), meaning, "the present state of things is in disorder."
>
> In the passage under consideration, αἰῶνές, "ages," most probably, I think, denotes the "different states of things which, in successive periods, would result from Christianity." .... Thus, then, I would render and explain the meaning of the writer to the Hebrews in the first five verses of this Epistle:—
>
> "God, who at different times and in different ways formerly spoke to our fathers by the Prophets, has at last spoken to us by his Son, whom he has appointed heir of all, through whom also he has given form to the ages, who being a reflection of his glory, and an image of his perfections, and ruling all things with authority from him, after having cleansed us from our sins by himself alone, has sat down at the right hand of the Majesty on high; being as much greater than the angels, as the title which he has obtained is preeminent above theirs. For to which of the angels did God ever say, "Thou art my Son, this day have I made thee so?" And again, "I will be

to him a Father, and he shall be to me a Son?"[57]

Trinitarian interpretations commonly reduce verses that refer to that which is spiritual to that which is physical, and the Trinitarian interpretation of Hebrews 1:2 is no exception. The Trinitarian interpretation makes it appear that Jesus was responsible for the creation of the *physical* universe, which, even if we were to allow for this, where, then, would the Father figure in its creation? A Trinitarian interpretation of Hebrews 1:2 negates the Father's representation in Genesis 1:1, which illustrates the danger of adopting Trinitarian dogma. The Father is pushed aside whenever Jesus is viewed as God.

Contrary to what many Trinitarians argue is the import of the letter to the Hebrews, its emphasis is the humanity of Jesus, as a modern Trinitarian writes:

> The great importance of the Epistle to the Hebrews lies in the fact that it represents a recognition already awakening in the early Church, that Christianity implies a metaphysic, while nevertheless its central theme is of One who is truly man.[58]

Hebrews 1:8—"But unto the Son he saith, the throne, O God, is for ever and ever: a sceptre of righteousness is the sceptre of the kingdom."

Trinitarians have interpreted the apparent application of the title "God" to Jesus as proof that he is co-equal and co-eternal with God. The translation of Hebrews 1:8 in the King James Version, however, is arguably not the best one, and is partly responsible for the belief that Jesus is God. The following explanations clear up the difficulty:

> In the next verse it follows, 'thou hast loved righteousness,' etc. 'therefore God, even the God, hath anointed thee with the oil of gladness above the fellows,' where almost every word indicates the sense in which Christ is here termed God; and the words of Jehovah put into the mouth of the bridal virgins, Psalm xlv., might have been more properly quoted by

---

[57] Norton, 194-196.

[58] Franks, 49.

this writer for any other purpose than to prove that the Son is co-equal with the Father, since they are originally applied to Solomon, to whom, as appropriately to Christ, the title of God might have been given on account of his kingly power, conformably to the language of Scripture.[59]

THERE remain some other passages of the New Testament Scripture to be examined before leaving the topic of the Inferiority and Subordination of our Lord Jesus Christ. In the Epistle to the Hebrews we read, "But unto the Son he saith, the throne, O God, is for ever and ever;" and therefore it is alleged that this proves the proper Deity of the Son. One would think it were only necessary to read the context to see that it proves no such thing, but only that the Son is addressed as God in the lower sense in which they were so addressed "to whom the word of God came." Mark the language. "Thy throne, O God, is for ever and ever .... Thou hast loved righteousness and hated iniquity; *therefore* GOD, even *the* GOD, hath anointed thee with the oil of gladness *above the fellows*." Whatever rank or office the title *God*, in the first instance, implied, it was plainly subordinate to that of the Supreme. He to whom it is applied has himself a Superior, nay, a GOD—which could not be said of the Supreme; is rewarded for his fidelity, his love of righteousness—being "*therefore* anointed," etc.—(but who could "reward" the Supreme?); has "fellows," equals—which it were simply absurd to predicate of the Supreme. The passage is a quotation from one of the Messianic Psalms, or those which the Jews believed to be prophetic of their king Messiah; (Ps. 45:6, 7) and nothing is more beyond dispute than that the Jews expected in their Messiah, although a King, a mighty leader, deliverer, conqueror; still, only "a man born of human parents;" (Vid. Just. Martyr's "Dial. cum Trypho," 235, *et alibi*, cited by Prof. Norton. "Reasons," etc. 204—5.) with which ideas, assuredly, the entire passage is simply consistent.[60]

---

[59] Milton, 50.

[60] Farley, 100-101.

The passage has been translated by some very learned divines, "God is the throne," which would convey the idea of God being the support and stability of Christ's throne, in the same figurative manner in which God is called the shield, the buckler, the hiding place, and the portion of his people. Most certainly the one translation is as warrantable as the other, but it signifies little in the argument which we adopt. Supposing, therefore, the common translation to be correct, what does this passage prove? Nothing more than it proved with respect to Solomon; for to him the words were originally addressed, of which anyone who reads the passage throughout will be convinced. It is a quotation from Psalm xlv. and can apply to no other than Solomon; so that, if it prove the Deity of Jesus, it also proves that of Solomon. To those who recollect that the title 'God' is, in the Old Testament, a common designation of persons of power, eminence, and dignity, and that Christ claimed the application of the title to himself, only in this sense, it will appear not in the least surprising, that Jesus should be here denominated. And that the name is given him only in its common inferior sense in this place, is as evident as that it is given in its supreme sense to him who anointed Jesus. For as the God who anointed him is supreme, Jesus who was anointed cannot be so also, there being confessedly but one Supreme.[61]

Heb. i. 8, which is quoted literally from the Greek Alexandrian translation of the Old Testament (Psalm xlv. 6), and which the best Hebrew scholar in the world translates, "Thy throne is of God for ever," i.e. established by God. It was first addressed to Solomon, on his marriage with the princess of Egypt.[62]

The following are the remarks of Trinitarian writers concerning the passage, "Thy throne, O God, &c." as it occurs in the Psalms, and in the Epistle to the Hebrews. They are taken from a remarkable volume entitled, "The Concessions

---

61 Hyndman, 140-141.

62 Allen, 77.

of Trinitarians;" from which volume I have elsewhere quoted largely. Of the verse, as it occurs in the 45th Psalm, the following interpretations are given:

"Thy throne may God establish forever."—Dr. Geddes.

"Thy throne, O divine Prince! is forever and ever."—Mudge.

"Thy throne, O Solomon! by the blessing of God, is to last for many generations."—Dr. Wells.

Calmet says, the Hebrew word, here translated God, "designates the rank of a judge and sovereign; as if the Psalmist in connecting it with that of the throne of the Messiah, meant to say, that Jesus should be appointed by his Father the judge of the living and the dead, possess the throne of David, his ancestor, and reign over the true Israel .... . during all eternity." Limborch says, the title God, "is attributed to Solomon, by reason of his regal dignity, which was supreme in Israel, and in the same sense as kings and magistrates are called *gods* and *children of the Most High*. Ps. lxxxii. 6. But in a more sublime sense it is spoken of Christ, the antitype of Solomon, on account of his kingly dignity, by which he had all power in heaven and in earth, all things being subject unto him, except He alone who put all things under him."

The remarks which follow are upon the same text as it occurs in the Epistle to the Hebrews. *Griesbach*, "God (is) the throne forever and ever." A writer in the Biblical Repository for Jan. 1839, says, "Here the Son is addressed by the title *God*; but the context shows it is an official title, which designates him as a king; he has a kingdom, a throne, a sceptre; and in verse 9, he is compared with other kings, who are called his fellows; *but God can have no fellows*. As the Son, therefore, he is classed *with the kings of the earth;* and his superiority over them consists in this, that he is anointed with the oil of gladness above them, inasmuch as their thrones are temporary, but his shall be everlasting." See *Concessions of Trinitarians*, 166, 167, 529, 530.[63]

---

[63] Dana, 279-280.

Heb. i. 8, 9. "But unto the Son, he saith, the throne, O God, is forever and ever; a sceptre of righteousness is the sceptre of the kingdom; thou hast loved righteousness and hated iniquity; therefore God, even the God, hath anointed thee with the oil of gladness above the fellows."

"It has ever been the opinion ," says Dr. Adam Clark, "of the most sound divines, that these words, which are extracted from the 45th Psalm, are addressed by God the Father unto God the Son." God the Father may call his Son 'God,' as he calls himself 'Lord;' but I seriously question whether "the most sound divines" approve of expounding this passage so as to represent the Father as *addressing* the Son, in the words, "O God." Who says that GOD THE FATHER addressed these words to the Son? The Psalmist does not say so; neither does the writer of this Epistle. The word "he saith," in the 8th verse, are a mere supply by the English translators. If they meant the Psalmist, by the pronoun "he," they were correct; but if they meant God the Father, they have certainly misrepresented the Psalmist, who was himself the person that addressed the Son, saying to him, "O God," &c. It is evident that the Son is called God according to the inferior sense of the term. None but the ignorant, or the impious or the inconsiderate, will assert that the all-perfect Jehovah can be exalted and rewarded for his services; or that he can have a God who hath anointed him with the oil of gladness above his fellows; that is, he was anointed prophet, priest, and king. "None was ever constituted *prophet*, *priest*, and *king*," says Dr. Clark, "but Himself; some were kings only, prophets only, and priests only; or kings and prophets; but none had ever the *three offices* in his own person, but Jesus Christ." [64]

It is most likely that the correct sense of this verse is, "God is the throne for ever and ever," since the Trinitarian translation is entirely out of place in context. In verse one, it is clear that the Father is spoken of as having spoken unto the fathers: "God, who at sundry times..." The narrative is continued in verse two, where God is said

---

[64] Morgridge, 126-127.

to speak to the apostles and others through the Son: "Hath in these last days spoken unto us through his Son." In verse six God instructs His angels to worship (i.e. adore and support) His Son: "And let all the angels of God worship him." In the eighth verse the narrative continues in the same manner by referring supreme authority to the Father: "But unto the Son he saith, God is the throne for ever and ever." Verse nine maintains the narrative by indicating that the God of Jesus has anointed him: "therefore God, even the God, hath anointed thee with the oil of gladness." If we adopt the Trinitarian translation of Heb. 1:8, we are left to account for a sudden departure in verse eight from the narrative development, then returning in verse nine to the focus being the Father's supremacy once again.

Hebrews 1:10—"And, Thou, Lord, in the beginning hast laid the foundation of the earth; and the heavens are the works of thine hands."

The term "Lord" in this verse is a reference to the Father, not to Jesus as some believe. By following the narrative development from verse one of the same chapter, the Father is being spoken of as the creator and director of the heavenly realm, harkening back to Genesis 1:1.

Hebrews 4:8—"For if Jesus had given them rest, then would he not afterward have spoken of another day."

The name translated "Jesus" in the King James Version should have been translated "Joshua." The New International Version translates it as follows: "For if Joshua had given them rest, God would not have spoken later about another day."

Hebrews 7:3—"Without father, without mother, without descent, having neither beginning of days, nor end of life; but made like unto the Son of God; abideth a priest continually."

Some Trinitarians infer that only God is without father or mother, or without beginning of days, so, since this verse is a reference to Jesus, he must be God. This verse, whatever intrinsic difficulties it may contain, cannot be used to support the Trinitarian hypothesis since it would contradict the hundreds of other verses in which Jesus is said to have a father—God. It also contradicts the almost universally-accepted belief that Mary was his mother. The Trinitarian interpretation involves taking this verse out of context and interpreting it literally, and also contradicts a statement made in this very same verse, which is that Jesus is the *Son of* God, a clear reference to one greater that himself:

> Nor does the type of Melchisedec, on which so much reliance is placed, involve any difficulty. Heb. vii. 3, 'without father, without mother, without beginning of days, nor end of life; but made like unto the Son of God.' For inasmuch as the Son was without any earthly father, he is in one sense said to have had no beginning of days; but it no more appears that he had no beginning of days from all eternity, than that he had no father, or was not a Son.[65]

Hebrews 11:26—"Esteeming the reproach of Christ greater riches than the treasures in Egypt; for he had respect unto the recompense of the reward."

An argument has been made from this verse that Moses esteemed being "reproached" by Christ, and that Christ had to be present with Moses to reproach him. This is not the correct understanding of this verse. It means that Moses was looking forward to the reward of Christ's coming. As a devout Jew and a leader of the Israelites, he awaited the Messiah's arrival. The New International Version translates it as follows: "He regarded disgrace for the sake of Christ as of greater value than the treasures of Egypt, because he was looking ahead to his reward." Moses considered the arrival of the Messiah to be his reward, though it did not happen in his lifetime.

2 Peter 1:1—"Simon Peter, a servant and an apostle of Jesus Christ, to them that have obtained like precious faith with us through the righteousness of God and our Saviour Jesus Christ."

---

[65] Milton, 81.

See the explanation of Titus 2:13 in this chapter.
1 John 3:16—"Hereby perceive we the love of God, because he laid down his life for us: and we ought to lay down our lives for the brethren."

The King James translators forced their theology into this text by inserting the words "of God" into it, which are not in the original Greek manuscripts. Without the addition, the verse would have been a clear reference to Jesus, and we can only guess what the motive behind the addition was:

> There is another text in this Epistle: "Hereby perceive we the *love of God*, because he laid down his life for us." It is enough to say of this that the words "of God"—italicized, remember, by our own translators as not in the Greek, are absolutely rejected by Wetstein, Griesbach, Mill, Bengel, and a host of other distinguished critics. The reference is unquestionably to Christ.[66]
>
> Another passage which is also produced is I John iii. 16, 'hereby perceive we the love of God, because he laid down his life for us.' Here, however, the Syriac version reads *illius* instead of *Dei*, and it remains to be seen whether other manuscripts do the same. The pronoun *he* seems not to be referred to God, but to the Son of God, as may be concluded from a comparison of the former chapters of this epistle, and the first, second, fifth, and eighth verses of the chapter before us, as well as from Rom. v. 8, 'God commendeth his love toward us, in that, while we were yet sinners, Christ died for us.' 'The love of God,' therefore, is the love of the Father, whereby he so loved the world, that 'he purchased it with his own blood,' Acts xx. 28, and for it 'laid down his life,' that is, the life of his only begotten Son, as it may be explained from John iii. 16, and by analogy from many other passages. Nor is it extraordinary that by the phrase, 'his life,' should be understood the life of his beloved Son, since we are ourselves in the habit of calling any much-loved friend by the title of life, or part of

---

[66] Farley, 105.

our life, as a term of endearment in familiar discourse.[67]

1 John 5:7—"For there are three that bear record in heaven, the Father, the Word, and the Holy Ghost: and these three are one."
See Chapter 3 for an explanation of this text.

1 John 5:20—"And we know that the Son of God is come, and hath given us an understanding, that we may know him that is true, and we are in him that is true, even in his Son Jesus Christ. This is the true God, and eternal life."

The issue in this verse is whether the phrase, "This is the true God," refers to the immediate antecedent, Jesus, or whether it refers to a remote antecedent, which is the Father. References to both immediate and remote antecedents are common in in the Bible and in all literature, so we must determine which antecedent is intended. The following explanations remove the difficulty:

> "This is the true God, and eternal life,"—which may or may not refer to Christ, just as we choose, not being in the same sentence where his name is mentioned.[68]
>
> The word *even* you will find in italics, and may therefore omit it and read, "We are in Him that is true, in his Son Jesus Christ." Of which expression Calvin says, that "the Apostle intends to express the means of our union with God, as if he had said, that we are in God by Christ." Erasmus, Archbishop Tillotson, Adam Clarke, and others, interpret it in the same way. Dr. Bloomfield even more plainly: "We are in union with the true God by means of his Son Jesus Christ." The words, "this is the true God," may grammatically refer either to Christ, or to "Him that is true." We refer it, of course, to God the Father, who is the chief subject of discourse. In which construction we have the authority of Erasmus, Grotius, Rosenmüller, and others. The language of Grotius is as follows:—

---

[67] Milton, 56-57.
[68] Allen, 77.

"This is the true God; namely, he and none else whom Jesus hath declared to be the object of worship. The pronoun *outos*, this, not infrequently relates to a remote antecedent; as in Acts vii. 19; x. 6. 'And eternal life'; this is said by metonymy. The Apostle means that God is the primary and chief author of eternal life. So also Christ is called Life, John xi. 25; xiv. 6, because, next to God the Father, he is the cause of eternal life." [69]

There is nothing in the Greek corresponding to the word 'even' which is improperly inserted in the Common Version. The preposition ἐν should be rendered 'through,' as it is in Rom. vi. 23, and in many other passages. The clause thus corrected would read—"we are in him that is true, through his Son Jesus Christ."

"According to the Trinitarian exposition of these words, the true God is the Son of God, and the two persons, who are so clearly distinguished by St. John, are one being." To justify their exposition they maintain that "the pronoun 'this' ought to be referred to the nearest antecedent, which is Jesus Christ"—making Jesus Christ to be the true God. According to this rule of interpretation Jesus Christ may be proved to be *a deceiver and an antichrist.* For John says, "Many deceivers are entered into the world, who confess not that Jesus Christ is come in the flesh. This is a deceiver and an antichrist." *2 John i, 7th verse.* The pronoun is not always to be referred to the nearest antecedent. Other examples of its referring to the more remote antecedent may be seen in Acts, iv. 11, and vii. 19.[70]

The appearance of a Trinitarian meaning is the result of a false translation, particularly of the improper insertion of the word "even." The passage may be thus rendered. Its sense may be made clearer by going back a little, and beginning at verse 18.

"We know that whoever is born of God avoids sin; the

---

[69] Eliot, 77-78.

[70] Morgridge, 131.

child of God guards himself, and the Wicked One cannot touch him. We are assured that we are of God, and that the whole world is subject to the Wicked One. And we are assured that the Son of God has come, and has given us understanding to know Him who is True. And we are with Him who is True through his Son Jesus Christ. He is the True God, and eternal life. Children, keep yourselves from idols."

The meaning is, that He with whom Christians are, He who is True, is the True God, and the giver of eternal life. In the former part of the passage St. John expressed the Jewish conception of the personality and power of Satan. To him, the Wicked One, he regarded the heathen world as subject; while believers were through Christ with Him who is true, the True God. They were, therefore, to keep themselves from idols.[71]

That 1 John v, 20, has been selected by some to shew, that *Jesus Christ* is there said to be *the true God*; notwithstanding the same Jesus Christ solemnly declares (John vxiii, 3), that *the* FATHER *is the Only true God*. The words in 1 John v, 20, *this is the true God*, must therefore, *necessarily* refer to *the Father* (as many have observed):—For, if the *son* be *the true God*, then who is *the Father*? How many *True Gods* have we? [72]

Revelation 1:8, 11—"I am Alpha and Omega, the beginning and the ending, saith the Lord, which is, and which was, and which is to come, the Almighty. (11:) Saying, I am Alpha and Omega, the first and the last: and, What thou seest, write in a book...)"

See Chapter 14, sub-chapter titled "Alpha and Omega."

Revelation 3:14—"And unto the angel of the church of the Laodiceans write; These things saith the Amen, the faithful and true witness, the beginning of the creation of God."

It has been argued from this that Jesus was the first "thing" that

---

[71] Norton, 196-198.

[72] Gifford, 180, footnote.

God created, and therefore must have existed before he was born. This is inferred from the phrase, "the *beginning* of the creation of God." Even if this were so, then it would establish that Jesus had a beginning and that he was created by God, which is Arianism. But the issue is resolved by looking at the Greek text, in which the word "beginning" in the King James Version is translated as "chief."[73] The New International Version translators translated it as "ruler." These two translations have Jesus as the *ruler* or *chief* of God's creation, by virtue of having been made both Lord and Christ (Acts 2:36).

Revelation 4:8—"And the four beasts had each of them six wings about him; and they were full of eyes within: and they rest not day and not, saying Holy, holy, holy, Lord God Almighty, which is, which was, and is to come."

The expression "holy, holy, holy" is thought by some to be a reference to a triune God. That this is not a correct inference, see Chapter 14, subheading titled "Repetition of Phrases" for an explanation of the various repetition of phrases in the Bible.

Revelation 21:6-7—"And he said unto me, It is done. I am Alpha and Omega, the beginning and the end. I will give unto him that is athirst of the fountain of the water of life freely. (v. 7) He that overcometh shall inherit all things; and I will be his God, and he shall be my son."
See Chapter 14, sub-chapter titled "Alpha and Omega."
Revelation 22:13—"I am Alpha and Omega, the beginning and the end, the first and the last."
See Chapter 14, sub-chapter titled "Alpha and Omega."

---

73 *The Zondervan Parallel New Testament in Greek and English* (Grand Rapids, MI: Zondervan Publishing House, 1975).

CHAPTER 17

CONCLUDING THOUGHTS

When I first began my search to see whether the Trinitarian account was better than the Unitarian, or if there was some other way of looking at the various schools of thought, at first glance it seemed there were a few verses that might suggest that our heavenly Father has equals. But since it also seemed that making others equal with the Father is forbidden, there needed to be unequivocal evidence for it in Scripture. I also wasn't willing to jettison my ability to reason, to make sense of things, and that throwing away my ability to think made me defenseless against *anything* someone might offer on any topic. The practice of "taking it on faith" is unacceptable to me, since I might just as easily believe any other view on the same grounds. Since the extra-biblical arguments in favor of a triune conception of God were not something I could understand, and since the verses used to support the notion that the Father has equals admitted of more reasonable interpretations, it was fairly easy to reject the Trinitarian system. It wasn't compelling enough for me to change who God is and the way God is represented in the Bible. In one sense, we either have true monotheism or we don't, and the subterfuge on which the notion of a triune God and a dual nature in Christ just didn't work for me. Altering the idea of the Father's supremacy based on incomprehensible arguments and bad and obviously biased interpretations is not how I was trained to process arguments and their premises.

After studying arguments from both sides, I discovered that the few verses that initially gave me some difficulty were satisfactorily and reasonably explained without resorting to the imaginative and incomprehensible supposition that God is three-in-one, or that Jesus is both God and a man. There is nothing I have studied or experienced in life that leads me to conclude that God is other than one "person," and that

He calls Himself our heavenly Father. The Father is always represented as God, and without qualification. The verses which are brought forward as proof of a triune deity are very badly interpreted, and in some cases are reasonable interpretations predicated upon forgeries and bad translations.

At the point of this writing, there are less than a handful of verses that are difficult for me to understand, but these verses give everybody difficulty (e.g. John 1:1). As a matter of conscience there was no way that I could abandon the thousands of verses that make a clear line of separation between God and Jesus. These verses harmoniously represent the Father as having no equals. The texts and my spiritual grounding appeared to me to hang on this fundamental precept delivered to Israel by Moses and the prophets, and then re-confirmed by Jesus and the apostles. I hold fast to the clear meaning of the many verses that declare the Father to be the one true God, and that Jesus is subordinate:

> Unitarians, therefore, are concerned to hold and to vindicate the sole unity, the undivided sovereignty, of God. If any spiritual penalty is to be visited upon us here or hereafter for our opinion or our teaching on this point, we must submit to bear it. We do and shall plead, however, that some one emphatic sentence—one at least—ought to have been recorded from the Saviour in assertion of his underived Deity, equal in the positiveness of its statement to that of a hundred sentences in which he affirms his subordination to God.[1]

As Christians, we must endeavor to better ourselves as individuals, which includes incorporating reasonable ideas into our theologies, and then purify ourselves as members of a community which purports to represent our heavenly Father. We should attempt to remove error wherever it exists:

> I have explained both what a Unitarian *is*, and What Unitarians *worship*. I venture here to make an addition to these explanations, and to give my own opinion as to what Unitarians should *desire*, and *aim at*, as a great end of their denom-

---

[1] Ellis, 134.

inational existence. It is not, primarily, to make themselves a numerous and powerful sect, with a carefully defined system of doctrine, negative or positive;—of which, indeed, there is very little danger at present. It is, rather, *first*, that they should faithfully help to free the common Christianity, held by themselves as well as by the orthodox churches, from the corruptions of one kind and another which, in the course of ages, have grown up around it and upon it, and the removal of which was by no means completed by the Reformers of the sixteenth century.[2]

Who, then, is Christ? I will not dogmatize. This is not a question on which that would become me or any man. God has been pleased to keep some mystery around it. If it be not so, what can we make of our Lord's positive declaration recorded in Luke, and Matthew, "No man" (or, more conformably with our English idiom, *no one*) "knoweth *who* the Son *is*, but the Father"? (Matt. 11:27; Luke 10:22.) Surely there is that belonging to Christ, if words have any meaning, which no one but the Father knows.

Admit, then, that there is a degree of mystery surrounding this question, making it, perhaps, one of the things which, like "the times and the seasons" of which after his resurrection our Lord spoke, "the Father hath put in His own power," and therefore "not for us to know" till He shall give us more light; what then? Other points, points of the highest practical moment and profoundest interest, are made perfectly plain, and stand out on the sacred page beyond all doubt or dispute by any who rest on the authority of Holy Writ. On that authority I profess to stand. On that authority I plant myself in this entire argument. I make no pretensions to being wise above what is there written. And, therefore, according to that Book which is to Protestants the common standard of revealed truth, I am ready and glad of the opportunity to make full and distinct confession of what I understand and preach as the Unitarian Faith.

---

[2] Smith, vi.

I believe that Jesus is the SON of God; not merely *a* son of God, as we all may be through that "glorious freedom" which is secured to us through the Gospel; not a son of God, as all intelligent beings are, according to our Lord's great revelation of the Fatherhood of the Supreme; but *the* Son of God in a high, special, peculiar, unrivaled sense; a title by which he is designated as holding a singular and most intimate relationship to the Father. This is elsewhere expressed by the phrases, "the only-begotten Son who is in the bosom of the Father;" "my beloved Son;" "the Son of God with power;" "him whom the Father hath sanctified and sent into the world." (John 7:26. The Greek adverb here rendered "very," in our Common Version, occurs previously in the same verse, and is there rendered "indeed;" and again in v. 40 of the same chapter, and is there rendered "of a truth." A good rendering would be by our English adverbs, *truly, really.* Griesbach, and after him Alford, rejects the adverb where it occurs the second time in v. 26. Then the passage would read, "Do the rulers *really* know that this is the Christ"?)

I believe him the one MEDIATOR; according to the words of St. Paul, who declares that "there is One God," also "One Mediator between God and man, the man Christ Jesus." (John 20:31.) I thank God that there is. I bless God that He has provided for me—frail, weak, imperfect, tempted, erring, sinner as I am—this gracious channel of communication between Him and my soul. I confess, humbly yet joyfully confess the need. I know myself too well to deny it.

I believe him to be our SAVIOUR—our compassionate, self-sacrificing, loving, all-sufficient Saviour. My soul gladly responds to that declaration of the same Apostle, "This is a faithful saying, and worthy of all acceptation, that Christ Jesus came into the world to save sinners:" (1 Tim 1:15.) and to that of the Apostle Peter: "Neither is there salvation in any other; for there is none other name under heaven given among men whereby we must be saved." (Acts 4:12.) "Him," whom "God hath thus exalted to be a Prince and a Saviour, to give repentance and forgiveness of sins," (Id. 5:31.) I confess and rejoice in, as "His unspeakable Gift." (2 Cor. 9:15.)

Finally, I believe in Jesus as the INCARNATE WORD—"the Word made flesh." (John 1:14) In Jesus was the Divine Word or *Logos*; which qualified him for his great mission; which constituted him the most illustrious Representative and Manifestation of God—in the glowing language of the Epistle to the Hebrews, "the brightness of God's glory, the express image of His person;" (Heb. 1:3) which made his words the words of God, his works the works of God; which inspired him with superhuman wisdom, clothed him with superhuman powers, took him utterly out of the category of ordinary humanity, placed him far above all previous Prophets and Messengers from God, and gave him rank second only to the Supreme in His moral universe. I gratefully acknowledge and bow to his Authority. In my profoundest religious consciousness, I regard his words as of the same binding force as though they were uttered evidently and audibly to me from the opened heavens by the Almighty Himself.[3]

Does it make sense to receive doctrines that are so strange and corrupt as to be utterly unintelligible, and the only way they can be received is as incomprehensible mysteries?

What, then, is to be done to give new power to the great principles of religion? What is to be done to vindicate its true influence to Christianity? We must vindicate its true character. It must be presented to men such as it is. The false doctrines connected with it, in direct opposition to the truths which it teaches, must be swept away. It is not enough that those who defend them should be disregarded or confuted. They must be so confuted as to be silenced. Those who would procure for Christianity its due supremacy in the hearts of men should feel that their first object is to so operate upon the convictions and sentiments of men, that the public sanction which has been given to gross misrepresentations of it shall be as publicly withdrawn. In promoting the influence of Christianity, the main duty of an enlightened Christian at the present day is to labor that it may be better understood.

---

[3] Farley, 118-123.

Truth and Reason, though they work slowly, work surely. An abuse or an error, after having been a thousand times confuted or exposed, at last totters and falls, abandoned by its defenders.[4]

Whatever the consequences may be, we can try to have our heavenly Father and Jesus known as they are represented in the writings of the Bible. I hope the time has arrived that people will read it with the gift of reason that we human beings are capable of possessing, and make the case that there really is only one God, the Father:

We might name many others, in Germany, in France, and in England, who bore a like testimony; for from that time to this our faith has never been without its martyrs and faithful confessors. Nor have we any reason to be ashamed of those who have borne our name. They have been comparatively few, for the doctrine has been unpopular and opposed by all the strength of the Christian world. But although until modern times they were few in number, they have been great in intellect, profound in learning, and eminent in piety. John Milton, England's great poet; Sir Isaac Newton, her greatest philosopher; John Locke, her profoundest metaphysician; Nathaniel Lardner, author of the most learned work on Christian evidences ever written,—were all of them close students of the Scripture, and all of them believers in the Divine Unity as we receive it. Even Dr. Isaac Watts, whose hymns are the music of every church, became in the last years of his life a Unitarian. If great names could support a cause, these would do it. We might add to them many others of the living and the dead, equally good. But we do not rely on such arguments. We appeal to the Sacred Scriptures alone, to the glorious company of the Apostles and to Christ their living head. Yet surely we may be pardoned, when we hear our Church vilified and ourselves excluded from the Christian communion, if we remind our opponents that so many of the names of which Christendom is most proud are found in the Unitarian ranks.

---

4 Norton, 20, 21.

In the present day, we have every reason to be satisfied with the progress of our faith. It is extending itself far more rapidly than most persons are aware; not only by the growth of Unitarian societies, so called, but by the diffusion of Unitarian ideas everywhere. So far as they are true, we hope that they will continue to prevail more and more. If they are untrue, if they are a perversion of God's word, we hope that they may soon pass away. If we hold error, we do so ignorantly, for we honestly believe that we hold the truth as it is in Jesus.

I will therefore close this sermon in the words, almost the dying words, of Dr. Watts, in his solemn address to the Deity. As sincere inquirers after Scriptural truth, we may adopt them as our own.

"Dear and blessed God! hadst thou been pleased, in any one plain Scripture, to have informed me which of the different opinions about the Holy Trinity, among the contending parties of Christians, had been true, thou knowest with how much zeal, satisfaction, and joy, my unbiased heart would have opened itself to receive and embrace the divine discovery. Hadst thou told me plainly, in any single text, that the Father, Son, and Holy Spirit are three real distinct persons in the Divine nature, I had never suffered myself to be bewildered in so many doubts, nor embarrassed with so many strong fears of assenting to the mere inventions of men, instead of Divine doctrine; but I should have humbly and immediately accepted the words, so far as it was possible for me to understand them, as the only rule of my faith. Or hadst thou been pleased so to express and include this proposition in the several scattered parts of the book, from whence my reason and conscience might with ease find out and with certainty infer this doctrine, I should have joyfully employed all my reasoning powers, with their utmost skill and activity, to have found out this inference, and ingrafted it into my soul."

"Thou hast taught me, Holy Father, by the prophets, that the way of holiness in the times of the Gospel, or under the kingdom of the Messiah, shall be a highway, a plain and easy path; so that the wayfaring man, or the stranger, 'though a fool, shall not err therein.' And thou hast called the poor and the ignorant, the mean and the foolish things of this world, to the knowledge of thyself and the Son, and taught them to receive and partake of the salvation which thou hast provided. But how can such weak creatures ever take in so strange, so difficult, and so abstruse a doctrine as this, in the explication and defence whereof multitudes of men, even men of learning and piety, have lost themselves in infinite subtleties of dispute, and endless mazes of darkness? And can this strange and perplexing notion of three real persons going to make up one true God be so necessary and so important a part of that Christian doctrine, which, in the Old Testament and the New, is represented as so plain and so easy, even to the meanest understandings?"

Such were the last thoughts of a pious and learned man, after more than twenty years of examination of the Scriptures. They are full of instruction to us, and well calculated to confirm us in our present belief. If such a man as Dr. Watts was forced out of Trinitarianism by prayerful and conscientious study of the Bible, we, as Unitarians, have reason to thank God and take courage.[5]

No matter our theology, holding our opinions with kindness and consideration is the preferred approach, not because it proves a point or positions any of us better to have our opinions embraced, but because it is a better way to live and produces greater clarity of thought. God holds his own position in the universe, I hold mine. The fruits of the spiritual life are consistent in both the Hebrew Bible and the Christian New Testament, among which are love, joy, peace, kindness, gentleness, and patience. This is the preeminent demarcation of a spiritually minded person, no matter his or her theological views. As for the Unitarian-Trinitarian debate, I will close the body of this work with the simple words of Thomas Emlyn:

I know Jesus loves nothing but Truth in his cause, and will never be offended, I hope, with any who stand by his own words, viz. The Father is greater than I. I think it a dangerous thing to say God is not greater than he, or is not the Head of

---

Christ; for, to whom will ye equal me, saith the Holy One? I am persuaded 'tis Truth I plead, and that supports me.[6]

---

[6] Emlyn, *Humble Inquiry* (1702), quoted in Parke, 44.

Appendix I—Mary Dana's First Letter

LETTER I.

January 19th, 1845.

MY KIND AND VENERATED PARENTS:

IT has become my solemn duty to make you an announcement, which, I fear, will fill your hearts with sorrow. Would to God, that I could save you from the pain, which, from my knowledge of your views and feelings, I am sure awaits you; but I believe, as God is my Judge, that *truth* is dearer to me than life itself, and I dare no longer disavow the sentiments, which, after thorough, and honest, and prayerful deliberation, I have at length adopted.

I will keep you no longer in suspense, but will proceed to declare, that I do not now believe that my blessed Lord and Saviour Jesus Christ is the Supreme God. I believe that there is but one God, the Father, of whom are all things, and one Lord Jesus Christ, by whom are all things. I believe that "all power" was given unto him in Heaven and on earth; that he was the Messiah predicted by the Old Testament writers, who, in the fullness of time, came into the world with a commission from God, and full power and authority to do the work which God had given him to do. In other words, after long and earnest deliberation, much diligent study of the Holy Scriptures, and fervent prayer to God for the assistance of his spirit, I conscientiously and firmly reject the doctrine of the Trinity.

This doctrine was part of my education. I received it, as many others do, without thorough investigation, though, I must confess, it has often perplexed me beyond measure. Still I held it, as it seems to me all must do, as a strange mystery, which I must not attempt to comprehend; not considering, that a mystery does not necessarily suppose an incomprehensibility; and losing sight of the danger of admitting, what now appears to me to be an impossibility. It is impossible for me, and I now perceive that it has always been impossible to make one of three, or three of one,—one perfect and infinite being equal to three perfect and infinite beings. There may be gifted minds capable of comprehending this doctrine, but such is not mine. It is plain to me now, that I have all my life been worshipping three distinct beings; never having been able, with the most strenuous efforts, to combine the three in my own mind so as to form a simple idea. But now I bow to the divine authority, when I hear Jehovah saying, "Hear, O Israel, the Lord the God is *one* Lord."

But to return. So anxious have I been for clearer views on this point, that I have eagerly read everything upon the Trinitarian side of the question which came my way; yet always without the satisfaction so desirable to an honest and inquisitive mind, and always with the same melancholy feeling, that it was *a strange mystery*; though still I felt *bound* to receive it.

And now I will relate to you the process through which my mind has passed. For many years, I have not been able to believe, that faith in the Trinity was *necessary* to salvation, because I saw a great many exemplary Christians who did not hold the doctrine, but who nevertheless believed that Jesus was "the Christ," and "the Son of God;" and because the Apostle John has said, that whosoever believeth that Jesus is the Christ is born of God, and that whosoever shall confess that Jesus is the Son of God, God dwelleth in him, and he in God.

I have often been startled, by hearing passages of Scripture wrested from what appeared to me to be their legitimate meaning, and forced to an agreement with some favorite hypothesis. Not long ago, in a bible class which I attended, the first part of the gospel by John was examined, and then many doubts found their way into my mind, but not with so much force, or in so tangible a form, as they have recently assumed. But, had I ever been disposed to give the subject a thorough examination, I have never had access to the arguments in favor of Unitarianism, nor have I ever in my life before read upon that side of the question.

Not very long ago, while conversing with a much loved friend, (you will know to whom I allude,) I found that my impressions with regard to Unitarians and to their system were extremely erroneous; and I expressed a wish to know a little more about their faith and practice. Was this desire wrong? Was it not in accordance with that Christian charity, which "hopeth all things," and "thinketh no evil?"

And here let me exonerate from blame the two individuals from whom, entirely at my own request, I have procured the information which I wanted. In both instances, they expressed a hesitation in complying with my request, fearing to be considered obtrusive, if not by myself, at least by my friends. I cannot but believe, that this feeling arose from a confidence in the strength of their position, and a foresight of the consequences which have actually ensued.

Now what was I to do? Shut my eyes resolutely, and blindly cherish the faith in which I had been educated, or sift the matter for myself? What kind of faith is that, which fears to stand the test of impartial inquiry? Would not an ingenuous mind lose all confidence in itself, and its received opinions, while there remained a consciousness of this fear and dread of investigation? Was it not my sacred duty to "prove all things," and "hold fast" only to that which I have found to be good?

Under these circumstances I *insisted* upon having access to some writings on the subject, and such as I wished were accordingly granted me. Now I know too well the candor and nobleness of my dear parents to fear that they will impute blame where none is deserved, unless indeed they carry the doctrine of *imputation* further than I think they do. Yet, in the first overflow of feeling, they may not view the matter as temperately and fairly as they will do hereafter, and this is why I enlarge upon the point.

Now suppose that a Unitarian of my age and mental capacities—one, in fact, situated just as I am—should come to you, and ask you what the Trinitarian faith really was; would you withhold from such a person the means of information? I am very sure you would not. Be generous then, and if there be any blame in the matter, let it rest upon the guilty, and not upon the innocent,—and then it certainly will fall upon no human agent, but upon a *system* which will not bear investigation.

Perhaps you will say, "Why did you not bring your doubts to us? Perhaps we could have solved them." For an opposite course I had several reasons. First, I knew perfectly well what your views were, and I had access to Trinitarian systems of divinity, which were considered standard works; secondly, I wished to examine the subject with an unbiased, unfettered mind; in short, to forget everything but the truth itself; and thirdly, I did not wish to give my friends unnecessary pain.

When the subject first presented itself fully and distinctly before my mind, in connection with a desire and a determination to give it a complete investigation, I felt an instinctive fear, almost a *horror*, at my presumption. I took Dr. Dwight's sermons on the divinity of Christ, and tried to be convinced that I had all my life been in the right—I read them over and over again—I had anxious days and sleepless nights; and even in my dreams my visions were of three distinct Gods, entangled together in dreadful and inextricable confusion. Thus I was driven to the examination of the subject with a power which I could not withstand.

My chief source of information has been the New Testament, and especially the gospel by John. I endeavored to read with an unprejudiced mind, and a teachable spirit, and to explain passages of *doubtful import* by those which could admit of *no possible mistake*. While thus reading, the doctrines of the absolute unity of God, and of the *derived* power and authority of his Son, shone forth from every page of the blessed volume with a brightness and a clearness perfectly convincing to my wondering mind. I could no longer resist the mass of evidence which seemed fully to establish the superiority of the Father to the Son. I found that Christ always spoke of himself as inferior to his Father, of his power and authority as derived from his Father,—and it seemed to me that, if the case were otherwise, (with humility let me say it,) our blessed Lord had studiously endeavored to mislead us.

I also found that the vast number of texts which directly and explicitly asserted Christ's inferiority, could only be set aside by an *assumption* of the doctrine of two natures in Christ Jesus; and even on this assumption, such words could not have been used without apparent equivocation. On the other hand, the small number of texts which are brought forward as evidence of the deity of our Lord, *can* be explained without doing such violence to our reason, as the doctrine of the two complete natures in one person—one infinite and the other finite—always must.

It seemed strange to me, that our compassionate Heavenly Father, who so well knew the weakness of human nature, should require us to receive a doctrine, *violating the common laws of that very reason which he has given us,* without such an explicit statement of it, and such an authoritative command for its reception, as would leave no possible chance for human reason to gainsay or resist it. But I could find no such statement, and no such command in the Bible. Now, I had always read the Scriptures with this doctrine pervading my mind, and *thus preoccupied*, every passage of holy writ was made, if possible, to harmonize with my opinions.

I now found that our blessed Lord had given us a very different clue to the right understanding of the Scriptures when he declared, that *all power* was *given* to him in Heaven and on earth. With this, his own declaration, constantly in view, I found that I could understand many things which were dark before; that I had, in fact, got possession of the most prominent idea,—the current doctrine of the New Testament. This declaration of our Saviour is, to me, a most satisfactory comment on those passages brought forward in support of the deity of the Son of God. Now what are inferences, and what are metaphysical arguments to the unequivocal and oft repeated declarations of Christ himself, and of his apostles? With these for my guide, the Bible becomes plain. And I remember that many of the passages relied upon by the Trinitarians, under the auspices of that pedantic bigot, James I., I feel that the

Trinitarian side of the question has had every possible advantage, and am perfectly satisfied with the views which I have adopted.

And now, when I sit down seriously to compare the system of doctrines with which I have so long been fettered, with those under the influence of which my freed spirit now joyfully springs to meet its benevolent Creator, I cannot but exclaim, "thanks be to God, who hath given me the victory, through my Lord Jesus Christ!" My *mind* is disenthralled, disenchanted, awakened as from a deathlike stupor,—all mists are cleared away,—and this feeling of light, and life, and liberty, arises from a delightful consciousness that I have learned to give the Scriptures a rational and simple interpretation, and that, on the most important of all subjects, I have learned to think for myself.

My views of the Lord and Master are dearer to me than ever before, because they are more definite. He is still my Saviour, and the Saviour of the world—the instrument chosen by his Father through whom to bestow his unmerited mercy; a willing instrument, for he delighted to do his Father's will; an all-sufficient instrument, for *all power* was given unto him. I believe that a living faith that will lead us to imitate him, is the only ground of our Salvation; but, while I fully believe in the divinity of his character and of his mission, I do not believe he was the Supreme God himself. I believe in the efficacy of his death,—the most striking circumstance of his history,—*for it was the seal of a new and better covenant,*—an evidence of his divine commission, and of his devotion to his Father's will; without which he would not have given us such an assurance of the glorious certainty of a resurrection, by being himself the first-born from the dead; without which his work would have been incomplete, and much less calculated to affect our hearts, to bring us to repentance, to lead us to God, and to save our souls.

You cannot suppose, my beloved Parents, that I have embraced these opinions hastily or carelessly. It is painful to expose oneself to the charge of fickleness, and it is very painful to separate oneself from those who are near and dear; but

God is to be my Judge; to Him alone I must answer for my opinions; to my own master I must stand or fall; and I dare not disavow what, upon mature deliberation, I believe to be the truth. I love you, God knows how well! But I love the *truth* better; and your blessed Saviour and mine has said, "He that loveth father and mother more than me, is not worthy of me." If I then embrace in my heart the doctrine which appears to me to be taught by Christ himself, must I not avow it?

With an anxious mind, an honest, tender conscience, and a prayerful spirit, I have searched the New Testament, and the result is what I have told you. My mind is open to conviction, though I do not believe that any views can be presented with which I am not already familiar. Mourn not over me, my beloved Parents, as over one lost to you forever. If you think me in error, rest assured it is not a fatal one. I am firmly convinced that no doctrine can be *necessary to salvation* which is not so plainly revealed that the *conscientious* inquirer after truth cannot possibly *mistake* it. "Believe on the Lord Jesus Christ, and thou shalt be saved," "He that believeth that Jesus is the Christ is born of God,"—about these plain statements there can be no mistake. Here is a glorious platform on which sincere Christians of every name can meet, and exchange the right hand of fellowship, exclaiming in sweet accord, "thanks be to God for his unspeakable gift!"

That our Heavenly Father may enable us all the more perfectly to know him, the *only* true God, and Jesus Christ, whom he has sent; that we may increase in faith, and love, and good works; and especially that I may show in all my future life, that there is indeed the same mind in me which was also in Christ Jesus, is the earnest prayer of your affectionate daughter.

To all which I heartily subscribe, and I therefore claim the name of Christian.[1]

---

[1] Mary Dana, *Letters Addressed to Relatives and Friends* (Boston: James Munroe and Co., 1845), Letter 1.

Appendix II—Creeds

CREEDS.

Remarks on Creeds.

MY aversion to human creeds as bonds of Christian union, as conditions of Christian fellowship, as means of fastening chains on men's minds, constantly gains strength.

My first objection to them is, that they separate us from Jesus Christ. To whom am I to go for my knowledge of the Christian religion, but to the Great Teacher, to the Son of God, to Him in whom the fulness of the Divinity dwelt? This is my great privilege as a Christian, that I may sit at the feet, not of a human, but divine Master, that I may repair to Him in whom truth lived and spoke without a mixture of error; who was eminently the Wisdom of God and the light of the world. And shall man dare to interpose between me and my heavenly Guide and Saviour, and prescribe to me the articles of my Christian faith? What is the state of mind in which I shall best learn the truth? It is that in which I forsake all other teachers for Christ, in which my mind is brought nearest to him; it is that in which I lay myself open most entirely to the impressions of his mind. Let me go to Jesus with a human voice sounding in my ears, and telling me what I must hear from the Great Teacher, and how can I listen to him in singleness of heart? All Protestant sects, indeed, tell the learner to listen to Jesus Christ; but most of them shout around him their own articles so vehemently and imperiously, that the voice of the heavenly Master is wellnigh drowned. He is told to listen to Christ, but told that he will be damned if he receives any lessons but such are taught in the creed. He is told that Christ's word alone is infallible, but that unless it is received as interpreted by fallible men, he will be excluded from the communion of Christians. This is what shocks me in the creed-maker. He interposes himself between me and my Saviour. He dares not trust me alone with Jesus. He dares not leave me to the word of God. This I cannot endure. The nearest possible communication with the mind of Christ is my great privilege as a Christian. I must learn Christ's truth from Christ himself, as he speaks in the records of his life, and in the men whom he trained up, and supernaturally prepared to be his witnesses to the world. On what ground, I ask, do the creed-makers demand assent to their articles as the condition of church-membership or salvation? "Show me your proofs," I say to them, "of Christ speaking in you. Work some miracle. Utter some prophecy. Show me something divine in you, which other men do not possess. Is it possible that you are unaided men like myself, having no more right to interpret the New Testament than myself, and that you exalt your interpretations as infallible standards of truth, and the necessary conditions of salvation? Stand out of my path. I wish to go to the Master. Have you words of greater power than his? Can you speak to the human conscience or heart in a mightier voice than he? What is it which emboldens you to tell me what I must learn of Christ or be lost?"

I cannot but look on human creeds with feelings approaching contempt. When I bring them into contrast with the New Testament, into what insignificance do they sink! What are they? Skeletons, freezing abstractions, metaphysical expressions of unintelligible dogmas; and these I am to regard as the expositions of the fresh, living, infinite truth which came from Jesus! I might with equal propriety be required to hear and receive the lispings of infancy as the expressions of wisdom. Creeds are to the Scriptures what rushlights are to the sun. The creed-maker defines Jesus in half a dozen lines, perhaps in metaphysical terms, and calls me to assent to this account of my Saviour. I learn less of Christ, by this process, than I should learn of the sun, by being told that this glorious luminary is a circle about a foot in diameter. There is but one way of knowing Christ. We must place ourselves near him, see him, hear him, follow him from his cross to the heavens, sympathize with him and obey him, and thus catch clear and bright glimpses of his divine glory.

Christian truth is infinite. Who can think of shutting it up in a few lines of an abstract creed? You might as well compress the boundless atmosphere, the fire, the all-pervading light, the free winds of the universe, into separate parcels, and weigh and label them, as break up Christianity into a few propositions. Christianity is freer, more illimitable, than the light or the winds. It is too mighty to be bound down by men's hands. It is a spirit, rather than a rigid doctrine,—the spirit of boundless love. The infinite cannot be defined and measured out like a human manufacture. It cannot be reduced to a system. It cannot be comprehended in a set of precise ideas. It is to be felt rather than described. The spiritual impressions which a true Christian receives from the character and teachings of Christ, and in which the chief efficacy of the religion lies, can be but poorly brought out in words. Words are but brief, rude hints of a Christian's mind. Its thoughts and feelings overflow them. To those who feel as he does, he can make himself known; for such can understand the tones of the heart; but he can no more lay down his religion in a series of abstract propositions, than he can make known by a few vague terms the expressive features and inmost soul of a much-loved friend. It has been the fault of all sects, that they have been too anxious to define their religion. They have labored to circumscribe the infinite. Christianity, as it exists in the mind of the true disciple, is not made up of fragments, of separate ideas, which he can express in detached propositions. It is a vast and ever-unfolding whole, pervaded by one spirit, each precept a doctrine deriving its vitality from its union with all. When I see this generous, heavenly doctrine compressed and cramped in human creeds, I feel as I should were I to see screws and chains applied to the countenance and limbs of a noble fellow-creature, deforming and destroying one of the most beautiful works of God. From the infinity of Christian truth, of which I have spoken, it follows that our views of it must always be very imperfect, and ought to be continually enlarged. The wisest theologians are children who have caught but faint glimpses of the religion; who have taken but their first lessons; and whose business it is "to grow in the knowledge of Jesus Christ." Need I say how hostile to this growth is a fixed creed, beyond which we must never wander? Such a religion as Christ's demands the highest possible activity and freedom of the soul. Every new gleam of light should be welcomed with joy. Every hint should be followed out with eagerness. Every whisper of the divine voice in the souls should be heard. The love of Christian truth should be so intense, as to make us willing to part with all other things for a better comprehension of it. Who does not see that human creeds, setting bounds to thought, and telling us where all inquiry must stop, tend to repress this holy zeal, to shut our eyes on new illumination, to hem us within the beaten paths of man's construction, to arrest that perpetual progress which is the life and glory of an immortal mind?

It is another and great objection to creeds, that, wherever they acquire authority, they interfere with that simplicity and godly sincerity on which the efficacy of religious teaching very much depends. That a minister should speak with power, it is important that he should speak from his own soul, and not studiously conform himself to modes of speaking which others have adopted. It is important that he should give out the truth in the very form in which it presents itself to his mind, in the very words which offer themselves spontaneously as the clothing of his thoughts. To express our own minds frankly, directly, fearlessly, is the way to reach other minds. Now it is the effect of creeds to check this free utterance of thought. The minister must seek words which will not clash with the consecrated articles of his church. If new ideas spring up in his mind, not altogether consonant with what the creedmonger has established, he must cover them with misty language. If he happen to doubt the standard of his church, he must strain its phraseology, must force it beyond its obvious import, that he may give his assent to it without departures from truth. All these processes must have a blighting effect on the mind and heart. They impair self-respect. They cloud the intellectual eye. They accustom men to tamper with truth. In proportion as a man dilutes his thought, and suppresses his conviction, to save his orthodoxy from suspicion; in proportion as he borrows his words from others, instead of speaking in his own tongue; in that as he distorts language from its common use, that he may stand well with his party; in that proportion he clouds and degrades his intellect, as well as undermines the manliness and integrity of his character. How deeply do I commiserate the minister, who, in the warmth and freshness of youth, is visited with glimpses of higher truth than is embodied in the creed, but who dares not be just to himself, and is made to echo what is not the simple, natural expression of his own mind! Better for a minister to preach in barns or the open air, where he may speak the truth from the fulness of his soul, than to lift up in cathedrals, amidst pomp and wealth, a voice which is not true to his inward thoughts. If they who wear the chains of creeds once knew the happiness of breathing the air of freedom, and of moving with an unencumbered spirit, no wealth or power in the world's gift would bribe them to part with their spiritual liberty.

Another sad effect of creeds is, that they favor unbelief. It is not the object of a creed to express the simple truths of our religion, though in these its efficiency chiefly lies, but to embody and decree those mysteries about which Christians have been contending. I use the word "mysteries," not in the Scriptural, but popular sense, as meaning doctrines which give a shock to the reason and seem to contradict some acknowledged truth. Such mysteries are the staples of creeds. The celestial virtues of Christ's character,—these are not inserted into articles of faith. On the contrary, doctrines which from their darkness or unintelligibleness have provoked controversy, and which owe their importance very much to the circumstance of having been fought for or fought against for ages,—these are thrown by the creedmakers into the foremost ranks of the religion, and made its especial representatives. Christianity as set forth in creeds is a propounder of dark sayings, of riddles, of knotty propositions, of apparent contradictions. Who, on reading these standards, would catch a glimpse of the simple, pure, benevolent, practical character of Christianity? And what is the result? Christianity, becoming identified, by means of creeds, with so many dark doctrines, is looked on by many as a subject for theologians to quarrel about, but too thorny or perplexed for common minds, while it is spurned by many more as an insult on human reason, as a triumph of fanaticism over common sense. It is a little remarkable that most creeds, whilst they abound in mysteries of human creation, have renounced the great mystery of religion. There is in religion a great mystery. I refer to the doctrine of Free-will or moral liberty. How to reconcile this with God's foreknowledge and human dependence, is a question which has perplexed the greatest minds. It is probable that much of the obscurity arises from our applying to God the same kind of foreknowledge as men possess by their acquaintance with causes, and from our supposing the Supreme Being to bear the same relation to time as man. It is probable that juster views on these subjects will relieve the freedom of the will from some of its difficulties. Still, the difficulties attending it are great. It is a mystery, in the popular sense of the word. Now is it not strange that theologians, who have made and swallowed so many other mysteries, have generally rejected this, and rejected it on the ground of objections less formidable than those which may be urged against their own inventions? A large part of the Protestant world have sacrificed man's freedom of will to God's foreknowledge and sovereignty, thus virtually subverting all religion, all duty, all responsibility. They have made man a machine, and destroyed the great distinction between him and the brute. There seems a fatality attending creeds. After burdening Christianity with mysteries of which it is as innocent as the unborn child, they have generally renounced the real mystery of religion, of human nature. They have subverted the foundation of moral government, by taking from man the only capacity which makes him responsible, and in this way have fixed the commands and threatenings of God the character of a cruel despotism. What a lesson against man's attempting to impose his wisdom on his fellow-creatures as the truth of God!

INTOLERANCE AND EXCLUSION.

IT is truly astonishing that Christians are not more impressed with the unbecoming spirit, the arrogant style, of those who deny the Christian character to professed and exemplary followers of Jesus Christ, because they differ in opinion on some of the most subtile and difficult subjects of theology. A stranger, at hearing the language of these denouncers, would conclude, without a doubt, that they were clothed with infallibility, and were appointed to sit in judgment on their brethren. But for myself, I know not a shadow of pretence for the language of superiority assumed by our adversaries. Are they exempted from the common frailty of our nature? Has God given them superior intelligence? Were they educated under circumstances more favorable to improvement than those whom they condemn? Have they brought to the Scriptures more serious, anxious, and unwearied attention? Or do their lives express a deeper reverence for God and for his Son? No. They are fallible, imperfect men, possessing no higher means and no stronger motives for studying the word of God, than their Unitarian brethren. And yet their language to them is virtually this:—"We pronounce you to be in error, and in most dangerous error. We know that we are right, and that you are wrong, in regard to the fundamental doctrines of the Gospel. You are unworthy the Christian name, and unfit to sit with us at the table of Christ. We offer you the truth, and you reject it at the peril of your souls." Such is the language of humble Christians to men, who in capacity and apparent piety are not inferior to themselves. This language has spread from the leaders through a considerable part of the community. Men, in those walks of life which leave them without leisure or opportunities for improvement, are heard to decide on the most intricate points, and to pass sentence on men whose lives have been devoted to the study of the Scriptures. The female, forgetting the tenderness of her sex, and the limited advantages which her education affords for a critical study of the Scriptures, inveighs with bitterness against the damnable errors of such men as Newton, Locke, Clarke, and Price! The young, too, forget the modesty which belongs to their age, and hurl condemnation on the head which has grown gray in the service of God and mankind. Need I ask whether this spirit of denunciation for supposed error becomes the humble and fallible disciples of Jesus Christ?

In vindication of this system of exclusion and denunciation, it is often urged, that the "honor of religion," the "purity of the church," and the "cause of truth," forbid those who hold the true Gospel to maintain fellowship with those who support corrupt and injurious opinions. Without stopping to notice the modesty of those who claim an exclusive knowledge of the true Gospel, I would answer, that the "honor of religion" can never suffer by admitting to Christian fellowship men of irreproachable lives, whilst it has suffered most severely from that narrow and uncharitable spirit, which has excluded such men for imagined errors. I answer again, that "the cause of truth" can never suffer by admitting to Christian fellowship men who honestly profess to make the Scriptures their rule of faith and practice, whilst it has suffered most severely by substituting for this standard conformity to human creeds and formularies. It is truly wonderful, if excommunication for supposed error be the method of purifying the church, that the church has been so long and so woefully corrupted. Whatever may have been the deficiencies of Christians in other respects, they have certainly discovered no criminal reluctance in applying this instrument of purification. Could the thunders and lightnings of excommunication have corrected the atmosphere of the church, not one pestilential vapor would have loaded it for ages. The air of paradise would not have been more pure, more refreshing. But what does history tell us? It tells us, that the spirit of exclusion and denunciation has contributed more than all other causes to the corruption of the church, to the diffusion of error; and has rendered the records of the Christian community as black, as bloody, as revolting to humanity, as the records of empires founded on conquest and guilt.

But it is said, Did not the Apostle denounce the erroneous, and pronounce a curse on the "abettors of another gospel"? This is the stronghold of the friends of denunciation. But let us never forget, that the Apostles were inspired men, capable of marking out with unerring certainty those who substituted "another gospel" for the true. Show us their successors, and we will cheerfully obey them. It is also important to recollect the character of those men, against whom the Apostolic anathema was directed. They were men who knew distinctly what the Apostles taught, and yet opposed it; and who endeavoured to sow division, and to gain followers, in the churches which the Apostles had planted. These men, resisting the known instructions of the authorized and inspired teachers of the Gospel, and discovering a factious, selfish, mercenary spirit, were justly excluded, as unworthy the Christian name. But what in common with these men have the Christians whom it is the custom of the "Orthodox" to denounce? Do these oppose what they know to be the doctrine of Christ and his Apostles? Do they not revere Jesus and his inspired messengers? Do they not dissent from their brethren, simply because they believe that their brethren dissent from their Lord?—Let us not forget that the contest at the present day is not between the Apostles themselves and men who oppose their known instructions, but between uninspired Christians, who equally receive the Apostles as authorized teachers of the Gospel, and who only differ in judgment as to the interpretations of their writings. How unjust, then, is it for any class of Christians to confound their opponents with the factious and unprincipled sectarians of the primitive age! Mistake in judgment is the heaviest charge which one denomination has a right to urge against another; and do we find that the Apostles ever denounced mistake as "awful and fatal hostility" to the Gospel,—that they pronounced anathemas on men who wished to obey, but who misapprehended their doctrines? The Apostles well remembered, that none ever mistook more widely than themselves. They remembered, too, the lenity of their Lord towards their errors, and this lenity they cherished and labored to diffuse.

But it is asked, Have not Christians a right to bear "solemn testimony" against opinions which are "utterly subversive of the Gospel, and most dangerous to men's eternal interests"? To this I answer, that the opinions of men, who discover equal intelligence and piety with ourselves, are entitled to respectful consideration. If after inquiry they seem erroneous and injurious, we are authorized and bound, according to our ability, to expose, by fair and serious argument, their nature and tendency. But I maintain, that we have no right as individuals, or in an associated capacity, to bear our "solemn testimony" against these opinions by menacing with ruin the Christian who listens to them, or by branding them with the most terrifying epithets, for the purpose of preventing candid inquiry into their truth. This is the fashionable mode of "bearing testimony," and it is a weapon which will always be most successful in the hands of the proud, the positive, and overbearing, who are most impatient of contradiction, and have least regard to the rights of their brethren.

But whatever may be the right of Christians as to bearing testimony against opinions which they deem injurious, I deny that they have any right to pass a condemning sentence, on account of these opinions, on the characters of men whose general deportment is conformed to the Gospel of Christ. Both Scripture and reason unite in teaching that the best and only standard of character is the life; and he who overlooks the testimony of a Christian life, and grounds a sentence of condemnation on opinions, about which he as well as his brother may err, violates most flagrantly the duty of just and candid judgment, and opposes the peaceful and charitable spirit of the Gospel. Jesus Christ says:—"By their fruits shall ye know them." "Not every one that saith to me, Lord, Lord, shall enter into the kingdom of heaven, but he who doeth the will of my Father which is in heaven." "Ye are my friends, if ye do whatsoever I command you." "He that heareth and doeth these my sayings," i.e. the precepts of the Sermon on the Mount, "I will liken him to a man who built his house upon a rock." It would be easy to multiply similar passages.

The whole Scriptures teach us that and he only is a Christian, whose life is governed by the precepts of the Gospel, and that by this standard, alone the profession of this religion should be tried. We do not deny that our brethren have a right to form a judgment as to our Christian character. But we insist that we have a right to be judged by the fairest, the most approved, and the most settled rules by which character can be tried; and when these are overlooked, and the most uncertain standard is applied, we are injured; and an assault on character, which rests on this ground, deserves no better name than defamation and persecution.

I know that this suggestion of persecution will be indignantly repelled by those who deal most largely in denunciation. But persecution is a wrong or injury inflicted for opinions; and surely assaults on character fall under this definition. Some persons seem to think that persecution consists in pursuing error with fire and sword; and that therefore it has ceased to exist, except in distempered imaginations, because no class of Christians among us is armed with those terrible weapons. But no. The form is changed, but the spirit lives. Persecution has given up its halter and fagot, but it breathes venom from its lips, and secretly blasts what it cannot openly destroy. For example a Liberal minister, however circumspect in his walk, however irreproachable in all his relations, no sooner avows his honest convictions on some of the most difficult subjects, than his name becomes a byword. A thousand suspicions are infused into his hearers; and it is insinuated, that he is a minister of Satan, in "the guise of an angel of light." At a little distance from his home, calumny assumes a bolder tone. He is pronounced an infidel, and it is gravely asked whether he believes in a God.

At a greater distance, his morals are assailed. He is a man of the world, "leading souls to hell," to gratify the most selfish passions. But notwithstanding all this, he must not say a word about persecution, for reports like these rack no limbs; they do not even injure a hair of his head; and how then is he persecuted?—Now, for myself, I am as willing that my adversary should take my purse or my life, as that he should rob me of my reputation, rob me of the affection of my friends, and of my means of doing good. "He who takes from me my good name" takes the best possession of which human power can deprive me. It is true, that a Christian's reputation is comparatively a light object; and so is his property, so is his life; all are light things to him whose hope is full of immortality.

But, of all worldly blessings, an honest reputation is to many of us the most precious; and he who robs us of it is the most injurious of mankind, and among the worst of persecutors. Let not the friends of denunciation attempt to escape this charge, by pleading their sense of duty, and their sincere desire to promote the cause of truth. St. Dominic was equally sincere when he built the Inquisition; and I doubt not that many torturers of Christians have fortified their reluctant minds, at the moment of applying the rack and the burning-iron, by the sincere conviction, that the cause of truth required the sacrifice of its foes. I beg that these remarks may not be applied indiscriminately to the party called "Orthodox," among whom are multitudes whose humility and charity would revolt from making themselves the standards of Christian piety, and from assailing the Christian character of their brethren.

Many other considerations may be added to those which have been already urged, against the system of excluding from Christian fellowship men of upright lives, on account of their opinions. It necessarily generates perpetual discord in the church. Men differ in opinions as much as in features. No two minds are perfectly accordant. The shades of belief are infinitely diversified. Amidst this immense variety of sentiment, every man is right in his own eyes. Every man discovers errors in the creed of his brother. Every man is prone to magnify the importance of his own peculiarities, and to discover danger in the peculiarities of others. This is human nature. Every man is partial to his own opinions, because they are his own, and his self-will and pride are wounded by contradiction. Now what must we expect, when beings so erring, so divided in sentiment, and so apt to be unjust to the views of others, assert the right of excluding one another from the Christian church on account of imagined error? As the Scriptures confine this right to no individual and to no body of Christians, it belongs alike to all; and what must we expect, when Christians of all capacities and dispositions, the ignorant, prejudiced, and self-conceited, imagine it their duty to prescribe opinions to Christendom, and to open or to shut the door of the church according to the decision which their neighbors may form on some of the most perplexing points of theology? This question, unhappily, has received answer upon answer in ecclesiastical history. We there see Christians denouncing and excommunicating one another for supposed error, until every denomination has been pronounced accursed by some of the Christian world; so that, were the curses of men to prevail, not one human being would enter heaven. To me it appears, that to plead for the right of excluding men of blameless lives, on account of their opinions, is to sound the peal of perpetual and universal war....

Another argument against this practice of denouncing the supposed errors of sincere professors of Christianity is this. It exalts to supremacy in the church men who have the least claim to influence. Humble, meek, and affectionate Christians are least disposed to make creeds for their brethren, and to denounce those who differ from them. On the contrary, the impetuous, proud, and enthusiastic men who cannot or will not weigh the arguments of opponents are always most positive and most unsparing in denunciation. These take the lead in a system of exclusion. They have no false modesty, no false charity, to shackle their zeal in framing fundamentals for their brethren, and in punishing the obstinate in error. The consequence is, that creeds are formed which exclude from Christ's church some of his truest followers, which outrage reason as well as revelation, and which subsequent ages are obliged to mutilate and explain away, lest the whole religion be rejected by men of reflection. Such has been the history of the church. It is strange that we do not learn from the past. What man, who feels his own fallibility, who sees the errors into which the positive and "orthodox" of former times have been betrayed, and who considers his own utter inability to decide on the degree of truth which every mind, of every capacity, must receive in order to salvation, will not tremble at the responsibility of prescribing to his brethren, in his own words, the views they must maintain on the most perplexing subjects of religion? Humility will always leave this work to others. Another important consideration is, that this system of excluding men of apparent sincerity, for their opinions, entirely subverts free inquiry into the Scriptures. When once a particular system is surrounded by this bulwark, when once its defenders have brought the majority to believe that the rejection of it is a mark of depravity and perdition, what but the name of liberty is left to Christians? The obstacles to inquiry are as real, and may be as powerful, as in the neighbourhood of the Inquisition. The multitude dare not think, and the thinking dare not speak. The right of private judgment may thus, in a Protestant country, be reduced to a nullity. It is true that men are sent to the Scriptures; but they are told before they go, that they will be driven from the church on earth and in heaven, unless they find in the Scriptures the doctrines which are embodied in the popular creed. They are told, indeed, to inquire for themselves; but they are also told at what points inquiry must arrive; and the sentence of exclusion hangs over them, if they happen to stray, with some of the best and wisest men, into forbidden paths. Now this "Protestant liberty" is, in one respect, more irritating than Papal bondage. It mocks as well as enslaves us. It talks to us courteously as friends and brethren, whilst it rivets our chains. It invites and even charges us to look with our own eyes, but with the same breath warns us against seeing any thing which Orthodox eyes have not seen before us. Is this a state of things favorable to serious inquiry into the truths of the Gospel? yet how long has the church been groaning under this cruel yoak! [1]

---

[1] This writing was part of a collection of older works of various authors which were contained in one volume. Due to the condition of the volume, neither the author nor the date was discernible, but I believe the author of this writing to be Channing and the date to be around 1850.

Appendix III—The Athansian Creed

1. Whosoev er will be saved: before all things it is necessary that he hold the Catholic Faith:
2. Which Faith except every one do keep whole and undefiled: without doubt he shall perish everlastingly.
3. And the Catholic Faith is this: That we worship one God in Trinity, and Trinity in Unity;
4. Neither confounding the Persons: nor dividing the Substance [Essence].
5. For there is one Person of the Father: another of the Son: and another of the Holy Ghost.
6. But the Godhead of the Father, of the Son, and of the Holy Ghost, is all one: the Glory equal, the Majesty coeternal.
7. Such as the Father is: such is the Son: and such is the Holy Ghost.
8. The Father uncreate [uncreated]: the Son uncreate [uncreated]: and the Holy Ghost uncreate [uncreated].
9. The Father incomprehensible [unlimited]: the Son incomprehensible [unlimited]: and the Holy Ghost incomprehensible [unlimited].
10. The Father eternal: the Son eternal: and the Holy Ghost eternal.
11. And yet they are not three eternals: but one eternal.
12. As also there are not three uncreated: nor three incomprehensibles [infinites], but one uncreated: and one incomprehensible [infinite].
13. So likewise the Father is Almighty: the Son Almighty: and the Holy Ghost Almighty.
14. And yet they are not three Almighties: but one Almighty.
15. So the Father is God: the Son is God: and the Holy Ghost is God.
16. And yet they are not three Gods: but one God.
17. So likewise the Father is Lord: the Son Lord: and the Holy Ghost Lord.

18. And yet not three Lords: but one Lord.

19. For like as we are compelled by the Christian verity: to acknowledge every Person by himself to be God and Lord:

20. So are we forbidden by the Catholic Religion: to say, There be [are three Gods, or three Lords.

21. The Father is made of none: neither created, nor begotten.

22. The Son is of the Father alone: not made, nor created: but begotten.

23. The Holy Ghost is of the Father and of the Son: neither made, nor created, nor begotten: but proceeding.

24. So there is one Father, not three Fathers: one Son, not three Sons: one Holy Ghost, not three Holy Ghosts.

25. And in this Trinity none is afore, or after another: none is greater, or less than another [there is nothing before, or after: nothing greater or less].

26. But the whole three Persons are coeternal, and coequal.

27. So that in all things, as aforesaid: the Unity in Trinity, and the Trinity in Unity, is to be worshipped.

28. He therefore that will be saved, must [let him] thus think of the Trinity.

29. Furthermore it is necessary to everlasting salvation: that he also believe rightly [faithfully] the Incarnation of our Lord Jesus Christ.

30. For the right Faith is, that we believe and confess: that our Lord Jesus Christ, the Son of God, is God and man;

31. God, of the Substance [Essence] of the Father; begotten before the worlds: and Man, of the Substance [Essence] of his Mother, born in the world.

32. Perfect God: and perfect Man, of a reasonable soul and human flesh subsisting.

33. Equal to the Father, as touching his Godhead: and inferior to the Father as touching his Manhood.

34. Who although he be [is] God and Man; yet he is not two, but one Christ.

35. One; not by conversion of the Godhead into flesh: but by taking [assumption] of the Manhood into God.

36. One altogether; not by confusion of Substance [Essence]: but by unity of Person.

37. For as the reasonable soul and flesh is one man: so God and Man
    is one Christ;
38. Who suffered for our salvation: descended into hell [Hades, spir-
    it-world]: rose again the third day from the dead.
39. He ascended into heaven, he sitteth on the right hand of Father
    God [God the Father] Almighty.
40. From whence [thence] he shall come to judge the quick and the
    dead.
41. At whose coming all men shall rise again with their bodies;
42. 4nd shall give account for their own works.
43. And they that have done good shall go into life everlasting: and
    they that have done evil, into everlasting fire.
44. This is the Catholic Faith: which except a man believe faithfully
    [truly and firmly], he can not be saved.[1]

---

[1] Schaff, Philip. *The Creeds of Christendom* (Grand Rapids: Baker Book House, 1931, reprinted 1996), "The Athanasian Creed," 66-70.

Appendix IV—The Phrase 'In the Beginning' in John 1:1

Regarding the phrase 'In the beginning' in John 1:1, the authors of the *Racovian Catechism* contend that it refers to the beginning of Jesus's ministry, as opposed to the belief that it refers to the beginning of creation. Their argument is as follows:

> What are the passages of Scripture from which they endeavour to prove that Christ has existed from all eternity?
>
> They are of two classes: the first comprehends those from which they conclude simply that he has existed from all eternity; and the second, those from which they infer that he has been begotten from everlasting of the essence of the Father.
>
> What are the texts comprehended in the first class?
>
> They are those in which it is declared concerning Christ (John i. 1) that he was in the beginning: (chap. iii. 13) that he was in heaven; and (vii. 58) that he was before Abraham.
>
> What do you say of the first of these testimonies?
>
> In the cited passage (John i. 1) wherein the Word is said to have been in the beginning, there is no reference to an antecedent eternity, without commencement; because mention is made here of a BEGINNING, which is opposed to that of eternity. But the word BEGINNING, used absolutely, is to be understood of the subject matter under consideration. Thus Daniel viii. 1, "In the third year of the reign of King Belshazzar a vision appeared unto me, even unto me Daniel, after that which appeared to me AT THE FIRST." John xv. 27, "And ye also shall bear witness, because ye have been with me FROM THE BEGINNING." John xvi. 4, "These things have I said not unto you AT THE BEGINNING because I was with you." And Acts xi. 15, "And

as I began to speak the Holy Spirit fell on them, as on us AT THE BEGINNING." As then the matter of which John is treating is the Gospel, nothing else ought to be understood here besides the beginning of the Gospel; a matter clearly known to the Christians whom he addressed, namely, the advent and preaching of John the Baptist, according to the testimony of all the evangelists, each of whom begins his history with the coming and preaching of the Baptist. Mark indeed (chap. i. 1,) expressly states that this was the beginning of the Gospel. In like manner John himself employs the word beginning, placed thus absolutely, in the introduction to his First Epistle, at which beginning he states himself to have been present; and besides this, he uses the same term (λόγος) Word, as if he meant to be his own interpreter. For there is no reason why Jesus, whom, in his Gospel, John designates by the absolute term (λόγος) Word, should not be here styled (ὁ λόγος τῆς ζωῆς) "the Word of life," because, as we learn from what follows, he conveyed to us the tidings of eternal life, which, until that time, had been buried in the counsels of the Father.

In a footnote on the same page, the following comments are given:

I have stated in a preceding note what many of the ancients understood by ὁ λόγος, or the Word. Grotius comments in nearly the same manner on this place, the Introduction to John's Gospel, and confirms his interpretation under John xvii. 5; and I John i. 1. Socinus himself, with many others, contends that the first verse of John's First Epistle (which seems to correspond with the beginning of his Gospel) does not relate to the person of the Son of God. They who maintain that by λόγος, with the article prefixed, the Son of God is always designated, are greatly mistaken; so much so, that the contrary, rather, may be asserted. See only in the same Evangelist, John ii. 22, iv. 37, 41, 50; v. 24; vi. 60; vii. 36; viii. 31, 37, 43, 51, 52, 55; xiv. 24; xv. 3, 20; xvii. 6, 14, 20; xviii. 32; xix. 8; xxi. 23; and I John ii. 5, 7, etc. In all these instances ὁ λόγος, is clearly distinguished from the Son of God.

Jesus Christ, the Son of God, may, nevertheless, be correctly denominated ὁ λόγος, on account of the Word of Life dwelling in him, in relation to his office. Moses is, by Philo Judaeus, called νοὺς, that is, the purest mind, and Aaron is denominated by him ὁ λόγος αυτοῦ, or his word. *Lib. de nom. mut.* And he expresses himself in a similar manner elsewhere, *Lib. quod det. pot. insid. soleat.* Indeed, he calls Moses the PRINCE or CHIEF OF THE ANGELS, and THE MOST ANCIENT WORD. For he writes, that he who says, I will stand in the midst between you and the Lord (who was Moses, as evidently appears from Deut. v. 5) was, ὁ ἀρχάγγελος καὶ πρεσβύτατος λόγος. *Lib. quis rer. div. haeres sit.* With equal propriety, then, similar language might be used respecting the Messiah.

Besides what is stated above, the paraphrase of Schlichtingius on the beginning of John's Gospel, which is comprised in his Annotations on I Peter i. 20, deserves to be consulted; as also Brennius's notes on the same passage. It ought, moreover, to be considered, whether Luke, in the opening of his Gospel (chap. i. 2), when he says that the apostles were from the beginning eye witnesses and ministers τοῦ λογοῦ, of the word, did not mean to express the same thing as John stated at the commencement of his Gospel, and of his First Epistle? B. Wissowatius.[1]

---

[1] The Racovian Catechism (originally published in Poland in 1604; reprinted in London in 1818.

Bibliography

Allen, Joseph. *Ten Discourseskj on Orthodoxy* (Boston: Wm. Crosby and H. Nichols, 1849).

Berry, Harold J. *The Truth Twisters* (Lincoln, NE: Back to the Bible, 1992).

Bowman, Robert. *Why You Should Believe in the Trinity* (Grand Rapids, MI: Baker Books, 1989).

Buckley, William F. Jr. *Happy Days Were Here Again: Reflections of a Libertarian Journalist* (New York: Random House, 1993).

Burnap, George. *Lectures on the Doctrines of Christianity* (Boston and Cambridge: James Munroe and Co., 1848).

Buzzard, Sir Anthony, and Charles Hunting. *The Doctrine of the Trinity: Christianity's Self-Inflicted Wound* (Atlanta: Restoration Fellowship and Atlanta Bible College, 1994).

Chadwick, Owen. *A History of Christianity* (New York: St. Martin's Press, 1995).

Channing, William. Unitarian Christianity and Other Essays (Liberal Arts Press, 1957).

Comfort, Philip Wesley, ed. *The Origin of the Bible* (Wheaton, IL: Tyndale House Publishers, 1992).

Crane, Rev. Stephen. *Jesus the Christ* (Boston: Universalist Publishing House,1889).

Davies, Norman. *Europe: A History* (New York: Oxford University Press, 1996).

Dana, Mary. *Letters Addressed to Relatives and Friends* (Boston: James

Munroe and Co., 1845).

Dunn, James. *Christology in the Making* (Grand Rapids: Wm. B. Eerdman's Pub. Co., 1996).

Eliot, William G. *Discourses on the Doctrines of Christianity* (Boston: American Unitarian Association, 1877).

Ellis, George E. *A Half-Century of the Unitarian Controversy* (Boston: Crosby, Nichols, and Co., 1857).

Emlyn, Thomas. *An Humble Inquiry into the Scripture Account of Christ* (1702).

Farley, Dr. Frederick. *Unitarianism Defined: The Scripture Doctrine of the Father, Son, and Holy Ghost* (Boston: American Unitarian Association, 1873).

Fox, Robin Lane. *Pagans and Christians* (New York: Alfred A. Knopf, Inc., 1989).

Fox, W. J. *A Course of Lectures on Subjects Connected with the Corruption, Revival, and Future Influence of Genuine Christianity* (London: G. Smallfield, Pub., 1819).

Franks, Dr. R. S. *The Doctrine of the Trinity* (London: Gerald Duckworth and Co. Ltd., 1953).

Gaustad, Edwin. *Sworn on the Altar of God* (Grand Rapids: Wm. B. Eerdman's Pub. Co., 1996).

Gifford, James. *An Elucidation of the Unity of God, Deduced from Scripture and Reason* (London: 5th ed., 1815).

Grant, Michael. *Constantine the Great* (New York: Macmillan Pub. Co., 1993).

Greunler, Royce Gordon. *The Trinity in the Gospel of John* (Grand Rapids, MI: Baker Book House, 1986)

Guthrie, Shirley. *Christian Doctrine: Teachings of the Christian Church* (Atlanta: John Knox Press, 1968).

Hill, Rev. Thomas. *The Doctrine of the Trinity Vindicated* (London: F. C. and J. Rivington, 1820).

Hyndman, J. S. *Lectures on the Principles of Unitarianism* (Alnwick: 1824).

Kot, Stanislas. *Socinianism in Poland* (Warsaw: 1932; translated into English in 1957 by Earl Wilbur and published in Boston by Starr King Press).

Lamson, Alvan. *The Church of the First Three Centuries* (Boston: Walker Fuller and Co., 1865).

Locke, John. *The Reasonableness of Christianity* (1695)

Locke, John. *The Works of John Locke* (London: 1714)

Martin, Walter. *The Kingdom of the Cults* (Minneapolis: Bethany House Publishers, 1985).

Miethe, Terry. *The Compact Dictionary of Doctrinal Words* (Minneapolis: Bethany House Publishers, 1988).

Milton, John. *Milton on The Son of God and The Holy Spirit* (London: British and Foreign Unitarian Association, 1908).

Morgridge, Charles. *The True Believers Defence Against Charges Preferred by Trinitarians* (Boston: Benjamin Greene, 1837).

Morris, Thomas. *God and the Philosophers* (New York: Oxford University Press, 1994).

Newton, Sir Isaac. *An Historical Account of Two Notable Corruptions of Scripture* (London: John Green, 1841).

Norton, Andrews. *A Statement of Reasons for Not Believing the Doctrines of Trinitarians* (Boston: American Unitarian Association, 10th ed., 1877).

Pamphilus, Eusebius. *Ecclesiastical History* (Baker Book House, reprinted 1994).

Parke, David. *The Epic of Unitarianism* (Boston: Starr King Press, 1963).

Passantino, Bob and Gretchen. *Witch Hunt* (Nashville, TN: Thomas Nelson, Inc., 1990).

Pope John Paul II. *Crossing the Threshold of Hope* (New York: Alfred

Knopf, Inc., 1994)

Priestley, Joseph. *An History of the Corruptions of Christianity* (c. 1770).

Rees, Thomas. *The Historical Introduction to The Racovian Catechism* (Poland, 1604; reprinted in London in 1818), composed by several authors.

Rusch, William G., ed. *The Trinitarian Controversy* (Philadelphia: Fortress Press, 1980).

Schaff, Philip. *The Creeds of Christendom* (Grand Rapids: Baker Book House, 1931, reprinted 1996).

Scott, John Anthony. *Living Documents in American History* (New York: Washington Square Press, 1963).

Smith, Dr. G. Vance. *The Bible and Popular Theology* (London: Longmans, Green, Reader, and Dyer, 1871).

Thomas, T. F. *Familiar Lectures on the Doctrine of the Trinity*, and Other Subjects (Ipswich: R. Root, 1838).

Urban, Linwood. *A Short History of Christian Thought* (New York: Oxford University Press, 1995).

Verkuyl, Dr. Gerrit. *Reclaim Those Unitarian Wastes* (Grand Rapids, MI: Zondervan Publishing House, 1935).

Vos Savant, Marilyn. *The Power of Logical Thinking* (New York: St. Martin's Press, 1996).

Wainwright, Arthur. *The Trinity in the New Testament* (London: S.P.C.K., 1962).

Wilson, John. *Unitarian Principles Confirmed by Trinitarian Testimonies* (Boston: American Unitarian Association, 8th ed., 1872).

REFERENCE WORKS

The Oxford Companion to the Bible, Bruce Metzger and Michael Coogan, eds. (New York: Oxford University Press, 1993).

The Catechism of the Catholic Church (New York: Doubleday, 1995).

New Bible Dictionary (Illinois: Tyndale House Publishers, 2nd ed., 1982).

The Dictionary of Bible and Religion, William Gentz, ed. (Nashville: Abingdon Press, 1986).

Encyclopedia of Religion and Ethics (1913).

Universal Standard Encyclopedia (1956).

Encyclopedia of Jewish Religion (New York: Adama Books, Werblowsky and Wigoder, eds., 1991).

History of Political Philosophy, Leo Strauss and Joseph Cropsey, eds. (Chicago

and London: University of Chicago Press, 3rd ed., 1987).

The Zondervan Parallel New Testament in Greek and English (Grand Rapids, MI: Zondervan Publishing House, 1975).

Name Index